Adobe® Photoshop® CS

fast&easy®

Adobe® Photoshop® CS
fast&easy®

Eric Grebler

Premier Press

Publisher: Stacy L. Hiquet

Senior Marketing Manager: Sarah O'Donnell

Marketing Manager: Heather Hurley

Associate Marketing Manager: Kristin Eisenzopf

Manager of Editorial Services: Heather Talbot

Senior Acquisitions Editor: Kevin Harreld

Project Editor: Argosy Publishing

Technical Reviewer: Lisa Bucki

Retail Market Coordinator: Sarah Dubois

Copy Editor: Amy Lepore

Interior Layout: Argosy Publishing

Cover Designer: Mike Tanamachi

Indexer: Larry Sweazy

Proofreader: Heather Moehn

ISBN: 1-59200-345-1

Library of Congress Catalog Card Number: 2003115739

Printed in the United States of America

04 05 06 07 08 BH 10 9 8 7 6 5 4 3 2 1

Premier Press, a division of Course Technology
25 Thomson Place
Boston, MA 02210

Acknowledgments

Putting together a book like this is truly a group effort and thanks must be extended to the entire Premier Press team. In particluar I would like to point out the efforts of Amy Lepore for making up for my lack of spelling and grammar skills and Lisa Bucki for technically editing the book. Thanks also go to Sally Boylan, Stacy Hiquet, and Kevin Harreld for help in bringing this book together.

Who I am today is a result of the upbringing by my parents, Ricky and Victor, and the relationships with my brothers, Oren, Leor, and Ron. I thank them for the giant contribution they have made to my life. Thanks also to my wife Kara for her constant love and devotion and to the rest of my friends and family for the wonderful dynamic they add.

About the Author

Eric Grebler is an IT professional, author, and certified trainer who has demystified the world of computers for thousands of people. Originally from Ottawa, he currently resides in Toronto, Canada. Eric has developed curriculum and resource material on a wide range of technical topics, including desktop publishing, audio sequencing, graphics, XML, and operating systems.

When he's not writing books, Eric moonlights as a general contractor whose attention to detail is matched by no other. His natural talent for carpentry first appeared when he started making stereo boxes, and it continues to this day as he specializes in curved walls, warped wood, and uneven drywall. Eric takes great pride in rarely having used any of his father's best wood.

Contents at a Glance

Contents

Introduction

This *Fast & Easy* book from Premier Press will help you understand, use, and explore the world of Adobe Photoshop CS. Photoshop is the industry standard when it comes to digital imaging, and this latest version, called CS (*Creative Suite*), continues the tradition of providing powerful image-manipulation tools. In this latest version, many changes have been made to simplify the user experience, to increase the functionality of different tools, brushes, and effects, and to make publishing to the Web as easy as possible.

Being a suite means that there is more than one program in the box. In addition to Photoshop, the other main program in the suite is ImageReady. ImageReady primarily is designed to help get images ready for the Internet and is not covered in this book.

Obviously, no book can teach you everything there is to know about one topic. The goal of this book is to give you a solid introduction to the world of Photoshop and to teach you how to use most of the different tools it has to offer. Along the way, you'll learn a variety of tips for creating your work faster and some creative tricks to make your artwork stand out.

The battles between good vs. evil, wrong vs. right, Coke vs. Pepsi, and Big Mac vs. Whopper are rivaled only by the age-old debate of PC vs. Mac. To avoid getting in the middle of the conflict, Adobe Photoshop CS rides the fence by being available on both platforms. The program works almost identically on both operating systems, with the exception of keyboard shortcuts. Throughout this book, whenever a keyboard shortcut is mentioned, both the PC and the Mac version of the shortcut is mentioned.

Who Should Read This Book?

If you are ready to explore the world of photo editing and digital art, this book is for you. Whether you are a seasoned veteran of Photoshop or just getting started, this book can be of benefit to you. New users can take advantage of the step-by-step, illustrated instructions of common tasks, while veteran users can use the book as a reference for new tools as well as old ones you might have forgotten.

Some Helpful Hints

In addition to the step-by-step instructions, you'll notice that there are three other elements designed to help you:

TIP

Tips provide quick ways or shortcuts to perform certain tasks.

NOTE

Notes provide additional information or background on a particular topic.

CAUTION

Cautions warn you about a particular step or function that might have some detrimental consequences.

PART I

Getting Started with the Basics

1

Touring the Work Area

Imagine going on a long road trip to a place you've never been before without bothering to bring along a map. In no time, you'd be lost, confused, frustrated, or even angry. The same could be true the first time you use Photoshop. It's a very powerful application for creating, correcting, and enhancing image files, but at the same time, it can be very confusing if you don't know your way around. This first chapter acts as your roadmap by leading you through the basics of navigating the Photoshop work area. You'll learn how to:

- Start and exit Photoshop
- Use the toolbox
- Work with a palette or context menu
- View and hide screen elements

Starting Photoshop

As with other applications, you must start Photoshop to be able to work with its tools and create a new image. Use the following steps to start Photoshop:

1. **Click** on **Start** at the left end of the Windows Taskbar. The Start menu will appear. If you are using Mac OS, find the Photoshop icon and double-click on it to launch the program. You can then skip to Step 4.

2. **Move** the **mouse pointer** to All Programs (or **Programs** for Windows versions prior to XP). The Programs menu will appear.

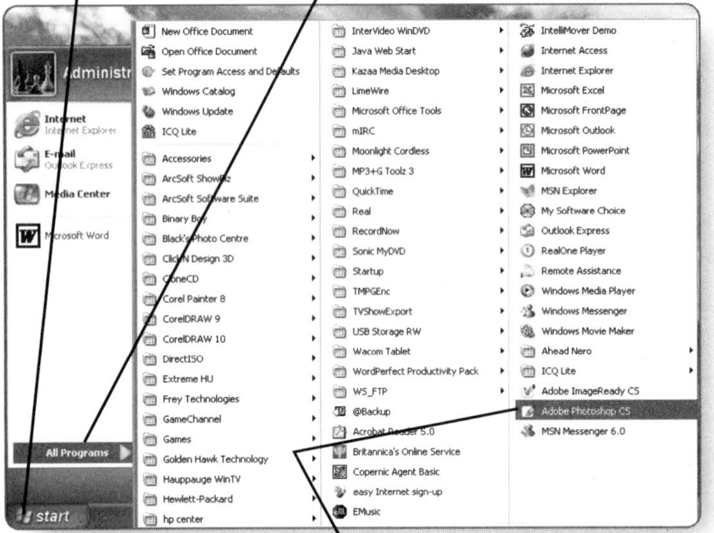

TIP

After you click on Start, you can point to a menu choice with a right-pointing triangle beside it by moving the mouse pointer over it. Pointing will highlight that menu choice and open a submenu. When you see the name of the program you want to start, click on the program name.

3. **Click** on **Adobe Photoshop CS**. The new Photoshop CS Welcome Screen will appear. The Weclome Screen will be covered in detail in Chapter 22, "Getting Help".

4. **Click** on **Close**. The Welcome Screen will close, and the Photoshop CS application window will appear, and you can begin using the program.

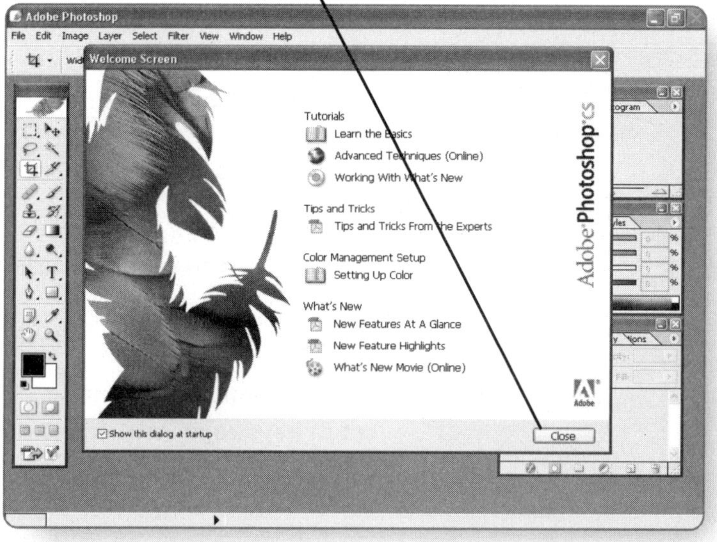

Accessing Photoshop Tools

The work area in Photoshop includes a menu bar like other Windows applications, as well as a few windows that organize the tools you use to do your work. Although later chapters will cover these tools in greater detail, familiarize yourself now with menus and tools and how to use them.

Using Menus

The menus in Photoshop work the same as in most other applications.

1. **Click** on a **menu name**. The menu will open.

2. **Click** on a **command**. The result will differ depending on the nature of the command on which you clicked:

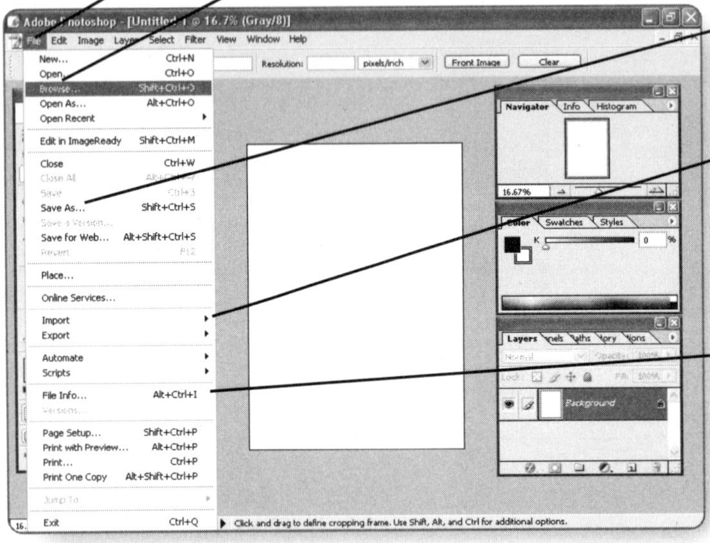

- If the command name is followed by an ellipsis (...), a dialog box will open.
- If the command name has a triangle beside it, a submenu will appear. You can then click on a command in the submenu.
- If the command name has a set of keystroke instructions beside it, this keystroke combination can be used to execute the command at any time.

> **NOTE**
>
> You can't use the various Photoshop tools until you create or open a new file. Chapter 2, "Working with Image Files," explains how to create new files in Photoshop. The illustrations here include a blank file strictly as an example.

Using Dialog Boxes

Dialog boxes are mini windows that allow you to provide Photoshop with information for a particular task.

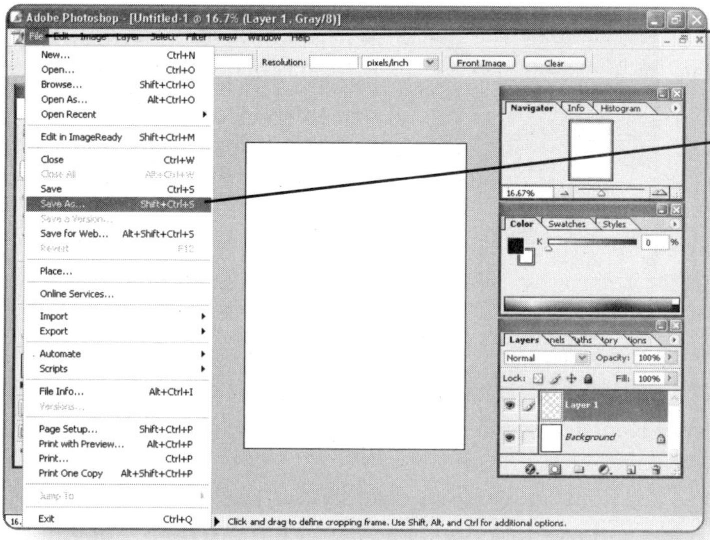

1. **Click** on a **menu name**. The menu will open.

2. **Click** on a **command** that has three dots beside it. A dialog box will open.

3. **Make** selections in the dialog box. Typical dialog box choices include the following:

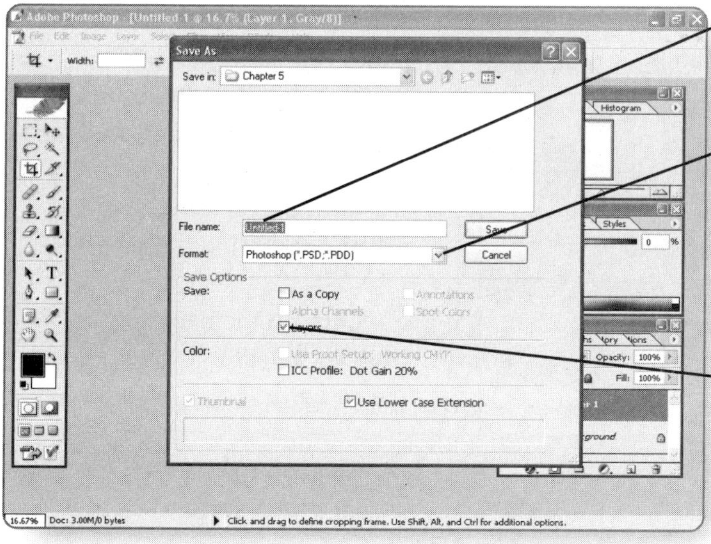

- **Text box.** Drag over a text box entry to select it and then type a new entry.
- **Drop-down list box.** Click on the down arrow or scroll arrow to open a drop-down list or to scroll through a list's choices. Then click on the list item you want.
- **Check box.** Click on a check box to select (check) or deselect (uncheck) it.

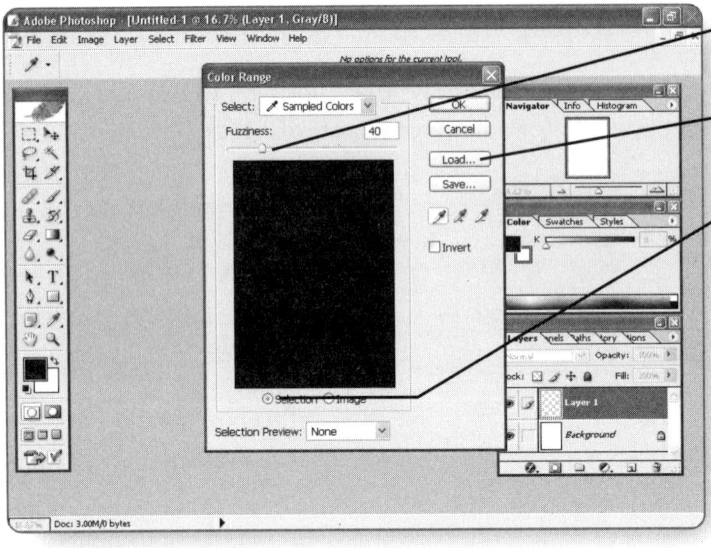

- **Slider.** Drag a slider to choose another setting.
- **Command button.** Click on a command button to choose it.
- **Option button.** Click on an option button to choose it and deselect other option buttons in the group.

Palettes

Palettes are floating windows that can be opened and closed as needed and repositioned anywhere on the screen. They provide additional tools and settings for your projects.

Selecting Palettes

A list of palettes can be found under the Windows menu. Palettes that are already open have a check mark beside them.

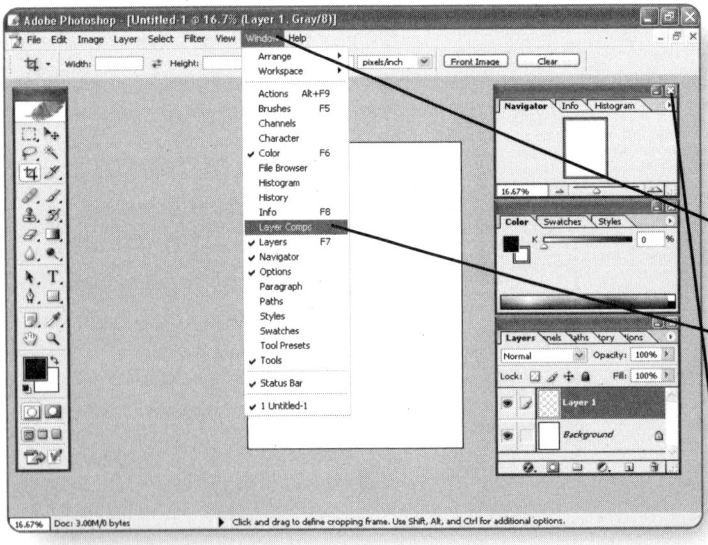

1. **Click** on **Window**. A menu will appear listing the palettes.
2. **Click** on the name of the **desired palette**. It will open on the screen.
3. **Click** on the **x** in the top right corner of a palette to close it.

Moving Palettes

If you have a number of palettes open on your page, you may want to move them to avoid potential clutter on your screen.

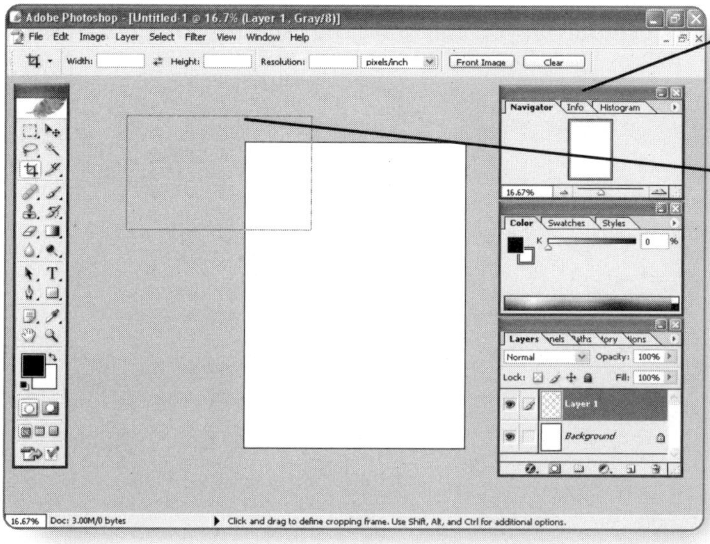

1. **Position** your **mouse pointer** over the **title bar** of the palette you would like to move.

2. **Drag** the **palette** to the desired new location. As you drag, an outline of the palette will appear to indicate its location.

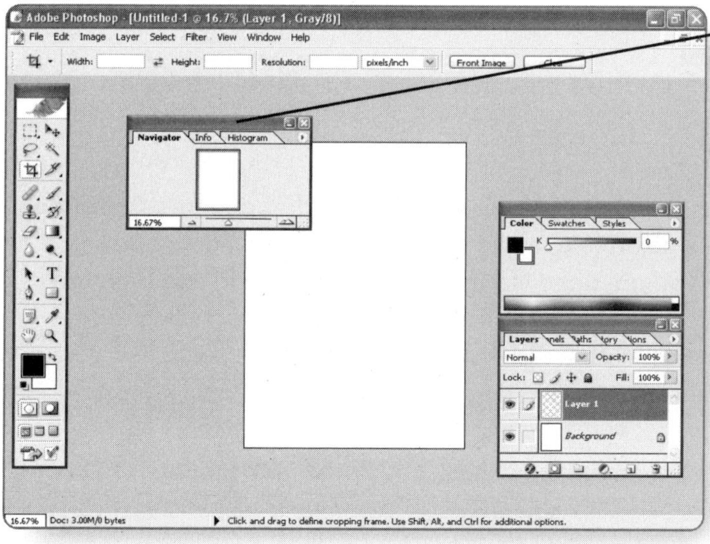

3. **Release** the **mouse button**. The palette will be in its new location.

Resetting Palettes

So you've gone and made a mess of things. Palettes are strewn all over the place, and some have inadvertently been deleted. There's no need to panic, however, because with a few clicks of the mouse button you can reset the palettes to their default look.

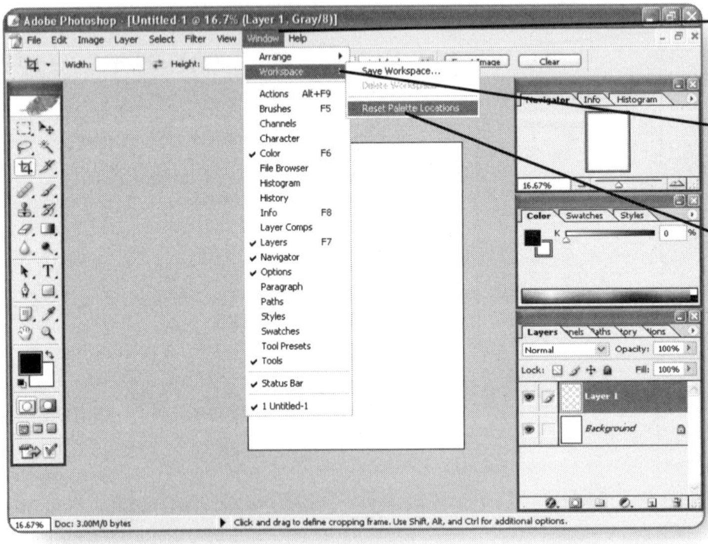

1. **Click** on **Window**. The Window menu will appear.

2. **Click** on **Workspace**. A submenu will appear.

3. **Click** on **Reset Palette Locations**. The pallets will be repositioned to their original locations.

Using Palettes

Rather than having several dozen different palettes, Photoshop groups palettes to make them easier to use. For example, when you open the Navigator palette, the Info and Histogram palettes will also be available. You not only can select from different palettes within a palette window, you can also access a variety of menus and tools.

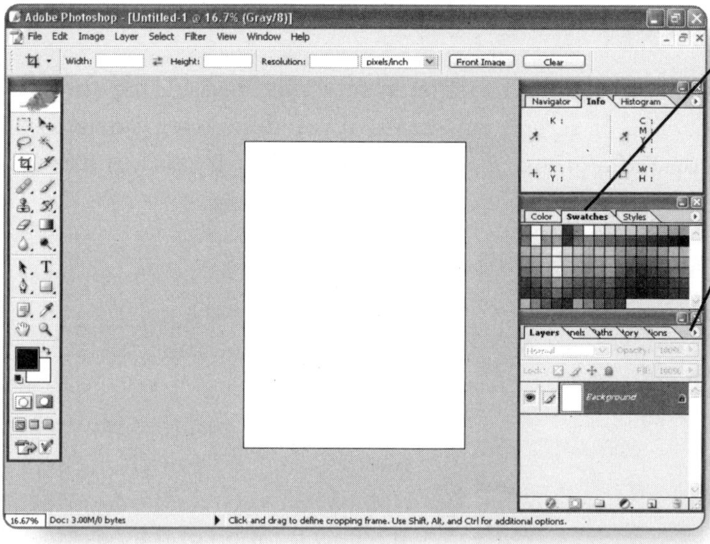

1. Click on the **tab** of the palette you would like to open. The palette will appear in front of all others in that group.

2. Click on the Display palette menu button in the top right corner of the palette. A menu will appear with different options.

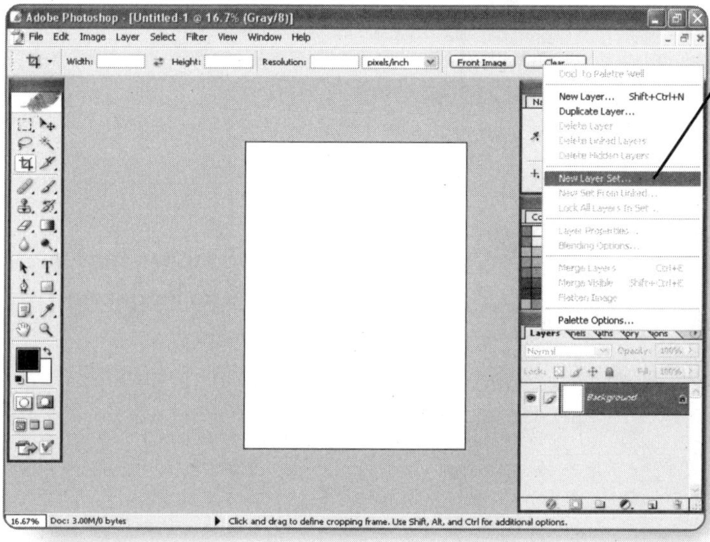

3. Click on the **desired option**. The command will be executed.

Ungrouping Palettes

Palettes are grouped together in small windows for the sake of saving valuable screen real estate. If you don't want a palette to be part of a group of palettes, you can simply click and drag it out of the group to have it appear on its own.

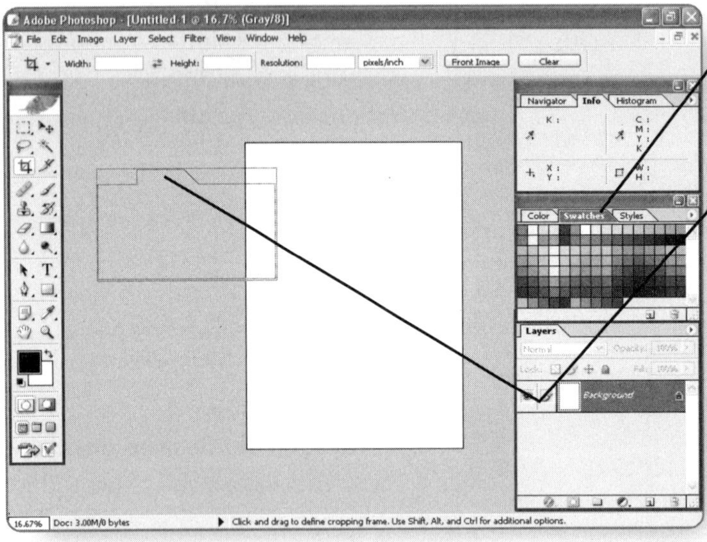

1. Position your **mouse pointer** over the **tab** of the palette you would like to ungroup.

2. Click and **drag** that **tab** to a new location. As you drag, an outline will appear showing you the new location of the palette.

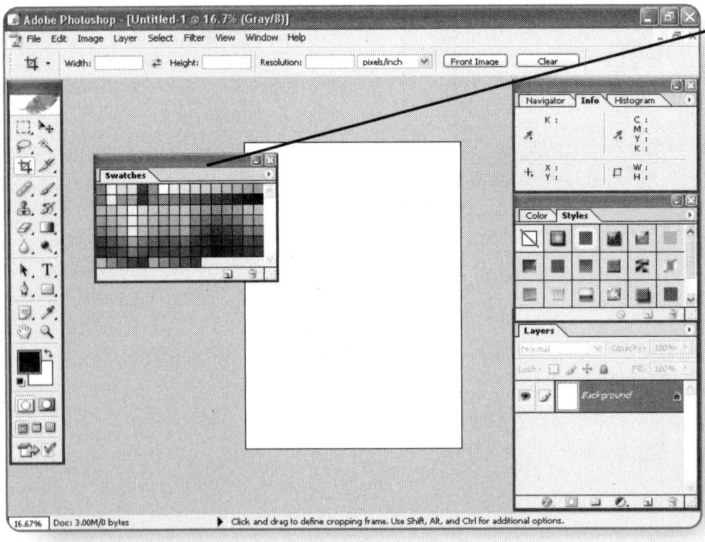

3. Release the **mouse** button. The palette will no longer be part of that group.

The Toolbox

The toolbox provides a central location for the equipment needed to get most of your work done in Photoshop. The toolbox contains many of the tools you will be using while editing your image files.

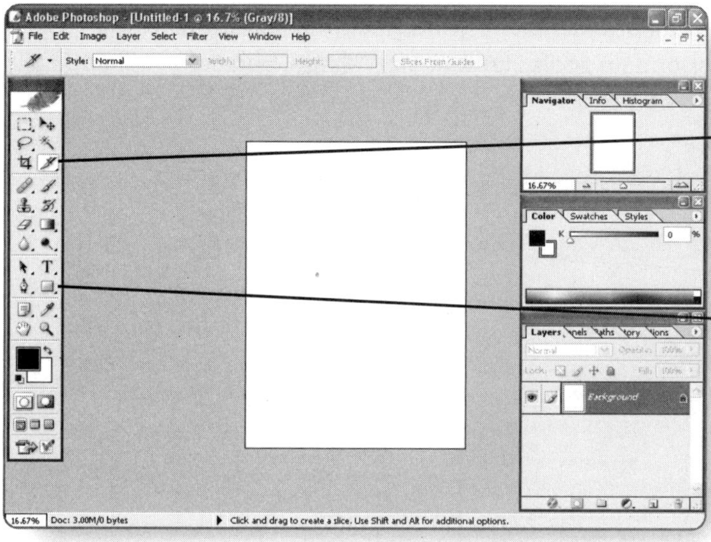

1. **Click** on a **toolbox button**. The button will appear highlighted to indicate that it is selected.

2. **Click** and **hold** on any **button** with a triangle on it. The triangle indicates that there are more tools in that location than can currently be seen. A list of tools will appear.

3. **Click** on the **desired tool**. It will be selected.

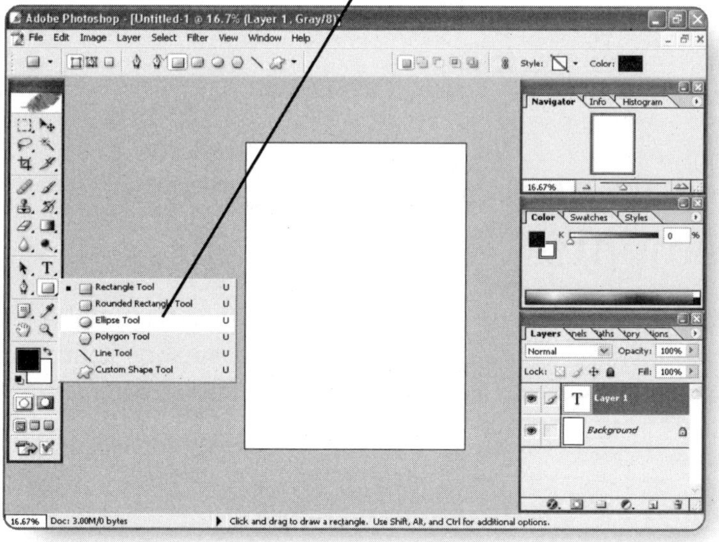

NOTE

If you have certain toolbox tools selected when you right-click on the image, a pop-up palette of settings for the tool appears instead. You'll learn more about using a palette like this in Chapter 3, "Adding Content with Tools."

The Options Bar

Rather than having to search around for different tools, the context-sensitive Options bar allows you to select corresponding elements to the particular tool you have selected. For example, if you select the Text tool, corresponding tools like font size, shape, and color will appear in the Options bar.

1. **Click** on a **tool** in the toolbox. It will be selected.

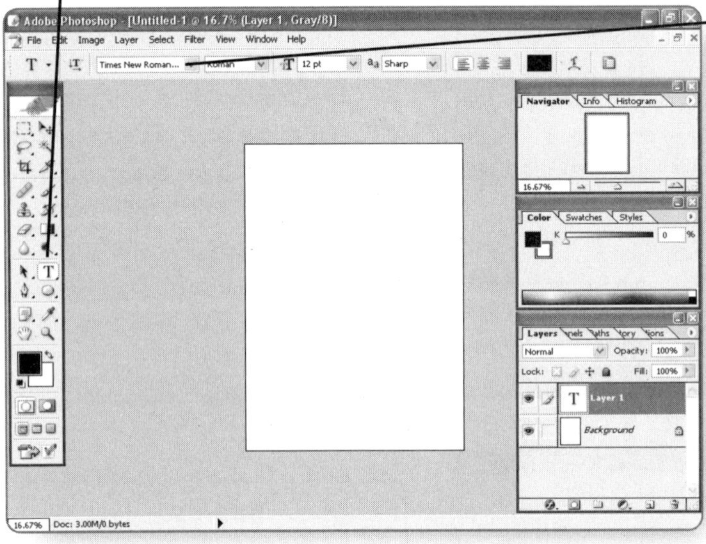

2. **Review** the **options** in the Options bar. They will change to correspond with the tool you have selected.

Hiding and Showing Screen Elements

Most of the elements on your screen can be found under the Window menu. Using that menu, not only can you open and close palettes, you can also show and hide other screen elements including toolbars.

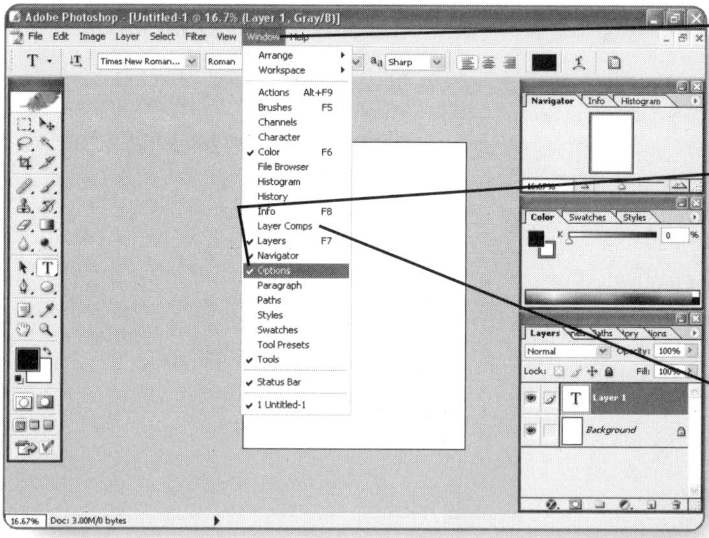

1. **Click** on **Window**. A menu will appear listing the screen elements.
2. **Click** on the **desired palette** or **toolbar**. It will open on the screen. Elements with a check mark beside them are already open.
3. **Repeat Steps 1** and **2** to remove a screen element.

Keyboard Shortcuts

Keyboard shortcuts are commands you can execute from your keyboard rather than having to use menus or dialog boxes. Photoshop has assigned a variety of keyboard shortcuts to various tasks within the program. New to Photoshop CS is the capability to customize any and all of these keyboard shortcuts.

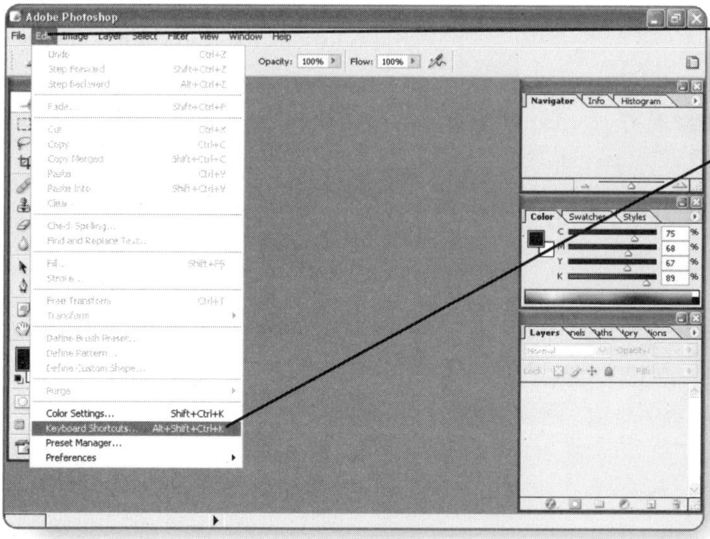

1. **Click** on **Edit**. The Edit menu will appear.
2. **Click** on **Keyboard Shortcuts**. A dialog box will open, allowing you to customize your keyboard shortcuts.

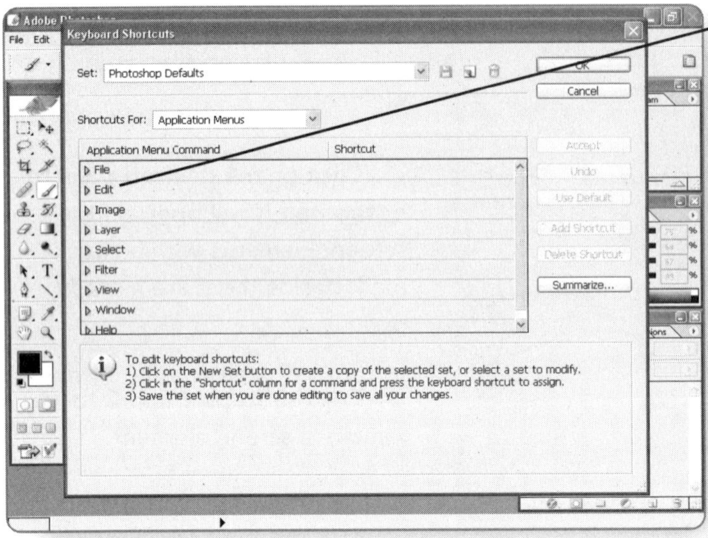

3. **Click** on the **group** that contains the command you would like to modify. A list of the commands that fall within that group will appear.

4. **Click** on the **desired command**. It will be selected, and the keyboard shortcut for that command will appear highlighted.

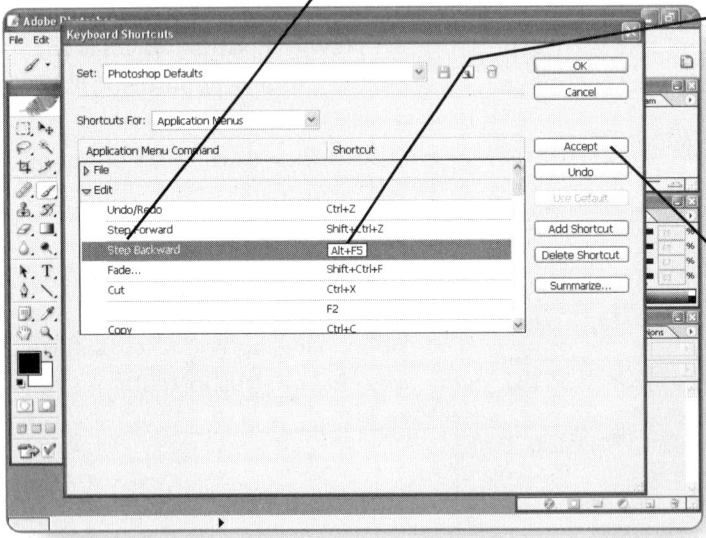

5. **Type** a **new keyboard shortcut**. For example, if you want the new shortcut to be Alt+5, hold down the Alt key and the 5 key at the same time. The new shortcut will appear.

6. **Click** on **Accept**. The keyboard shortcut for that command will be selected.

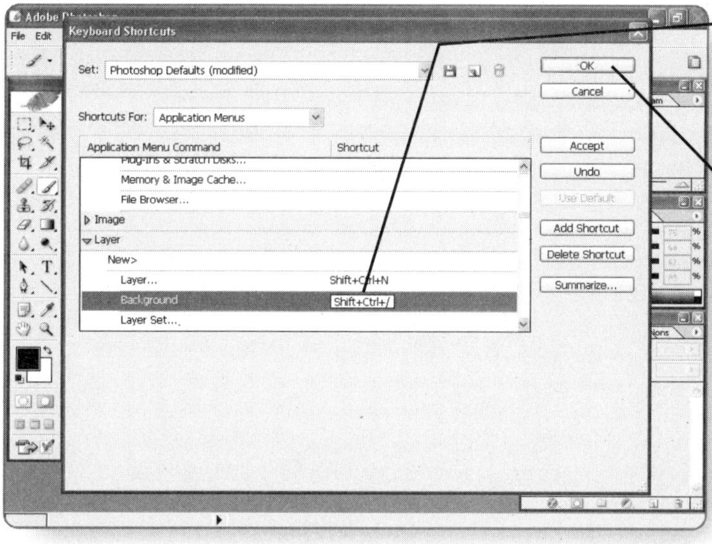

7. Repeat Steps 3 to **6** for any other commands to which you would like to assign new keyboard shortcuts.

8. Click on **OK**. Your changes will be accepted.

Exiting Photoshop

When you finish working in Photoshop or want to shut down your system altogether, you need to exit the Photoshop program. It takes just a few brief steps, as detailed here.

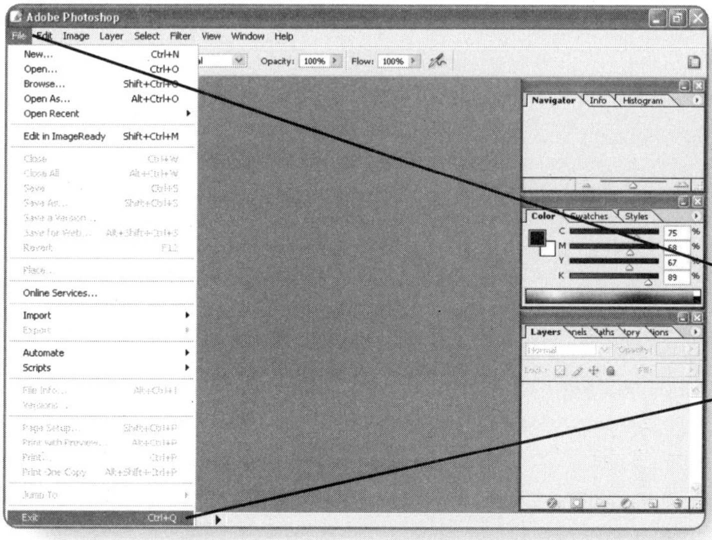

1. Save the currently open **file**. Photoshop will preserve the latest changes to the file. The "Saving a File" section in Chapter 2 will explain how to save a file.

2. Click on **File**. The File menu will open.

3. Click on **Exit**. The Photoshop application window will close.

2

Working with Image Files

Everything that you do in Photoshop is done to an image file. You can either use an existing image file or create one from scratch. Photoshop gives you a variety of methods to open, create, or import images so that they can be further manipulated. In this chapter, you'll learn how to:

- Create a new image file
- Open a file
- Import a scanner or digital camera image
- Add file info
- Save and close a file
- Use the enhanced File Browser
- Save your workspace

Creating a New File

In some cases, you may want to start the creative process with a blank canvas—a new, blank image file. Photoshop doesn't open a blank file by default when you start the program, so you must do it manually. When you create a new file in Photoshop, you can specify the file size, whether it includes a background color, and more.

1. **Click** on **File**. The File menu will appear.

2. **Click** on **New**. The New dialog box will open.

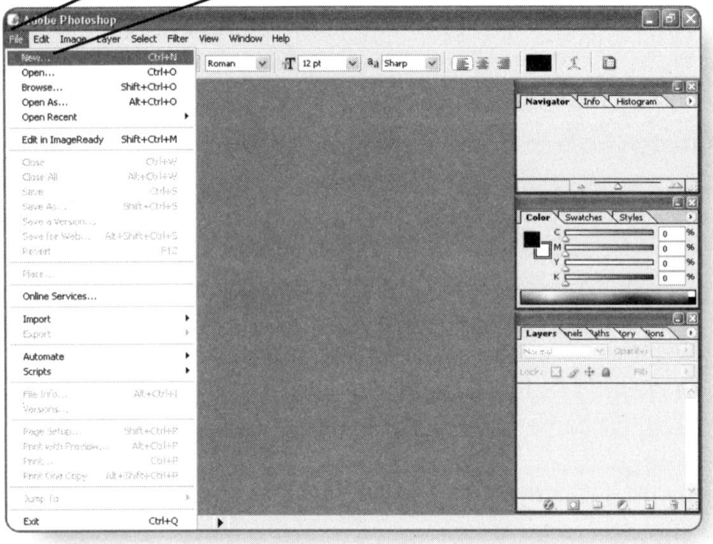

3. **Type** a **name** for your file in the Name text box.

4. **Set** the **image settings** in the Preset box as follows:

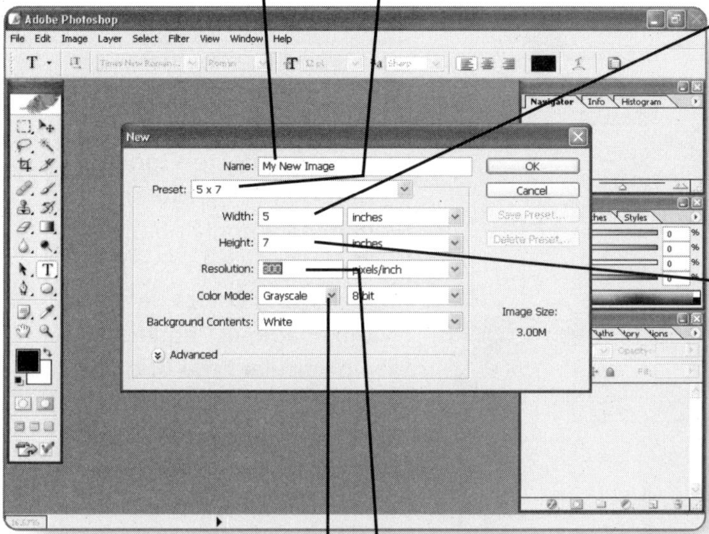

- Double-click on the Width text box contents and type a new image width value. If necessary, click on the down arrow for the unit list and then select another measurement unit.
- Double-click on the Height text box contents and type a new image height value. If necessary, click on the down arrow for the unit list and select another measurement unit.
- Double-click on the Resolution text box contents and type a new resolution value. If necessary, click on the down arrow for the unit list and select another resolution unit.
- Click on the down arrow for the Color Mode list and then click on the color mode to use.

TIP

Rather than specifying image dimensions, you can opt to choose a predefined image size from the Preset drop-down list.

5. **Click** on the down arrow beside the **Background Contents box option**. A list of options will appear.

6. Click on the desired option. The options work as follows:

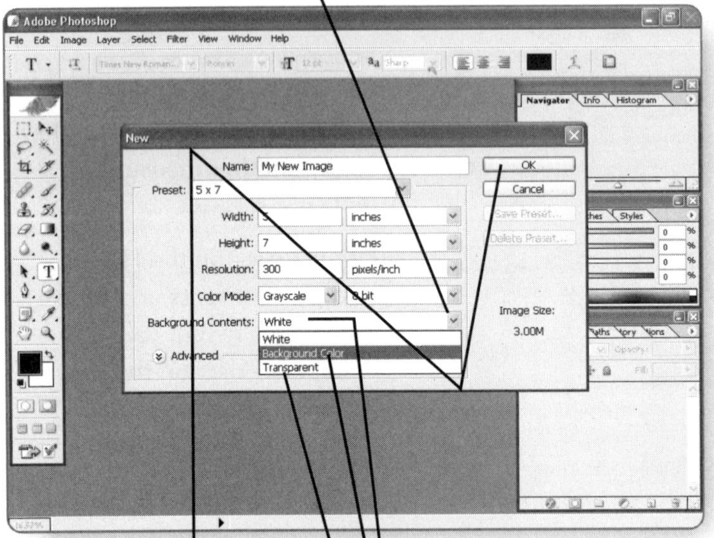

NOTE

Resolution refers to the number of pixels (dots) printed per measurement unit (commonly per inch). The color mode controls how many colors define the image, as required by a particular type of display and output. See Chapter 15, "Understanding Colors and Channels," to learn more about color modes.

- **White.** Fills the image with a default white background.
- **Background Color.** Fills the image with the background color currently selected in the Photoshop toolbox.
- **Transparent.** Gives the image a transparent background so that, when you use the image in a document or Web page, the page background and page elements can show through the image file.

7. **Click** on **OK**. The New dialog box will close, and the new image file will open onscreen.

Opening an Existing File

If you've already saved an image file, you can reopen it at any time to make changes and improvements. You can open not only images that have been created in Photoshop, but almost any other type of image file.

1. Click on **File**. The File menu will appear.

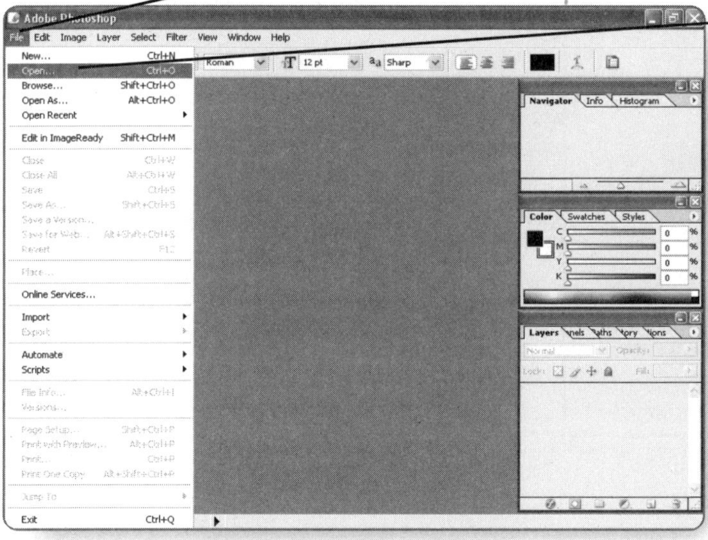

2. Click on **Open**. The Open dialog box will open.

TIP

To open a file you've used recently, click on the File menu, drag the mouse pointer down to the Open Recent command, and then click on the name of the file you want to open in the submenu that appears.

3. **Navigate** to the **file location**. The desired file will be displayed in the file list. You may need to do one or more of the following to locate the file:

- Click on the down arrow to the right of the Look In list, then click on the icon for the disk that holds the file.

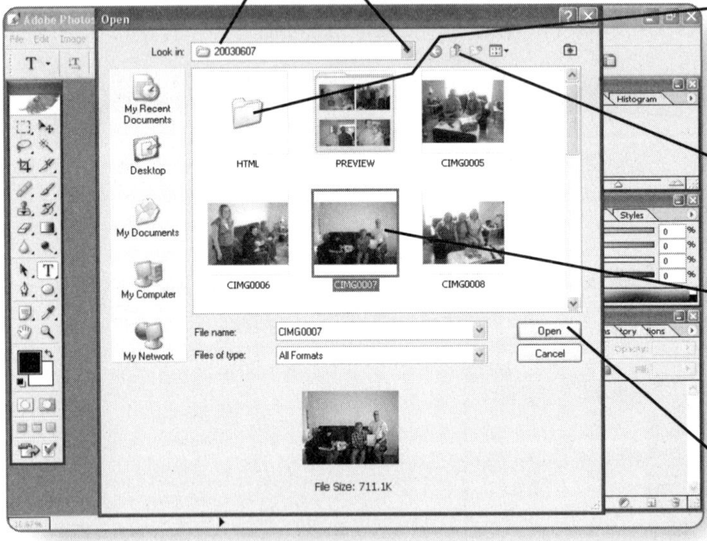

- Double-click on folder icons in the list to navigate to the folder that holds the file to open.
- Click on Up One Level to return to a folder that's one level higher.

4. **Click** on the **file** you want to open. A preview of the file will appear at the bottom of the Open dialog box.

5. **Click** on **Open**. The file will appear onscreen.

Opening and Accessing Multiple Files

You can have a variety of images open at any given time in Photoshop. You can open additional files all at once or one by one. Once you have multiple images open, you can toggle between them during the editing process.

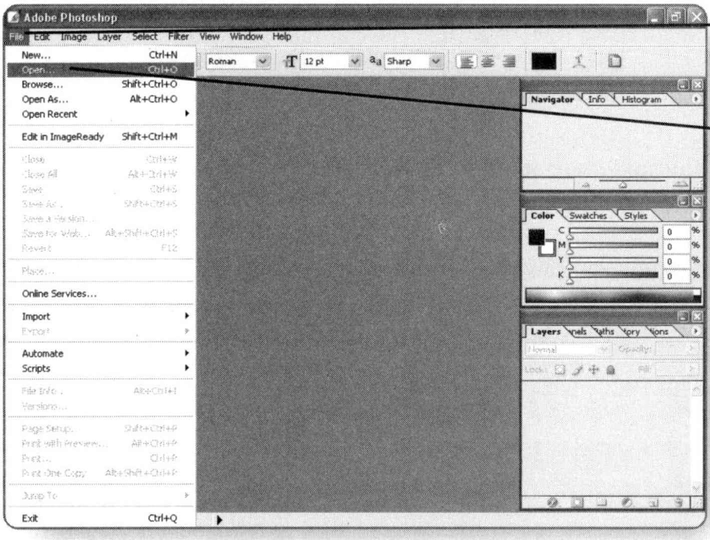

1. **Click** on **File**. The File menu will appear.

2. **Click** on **Open**. The Open dialog box will open.

3. **Click** on one of the **files** you would like to open. It will be highlighted.

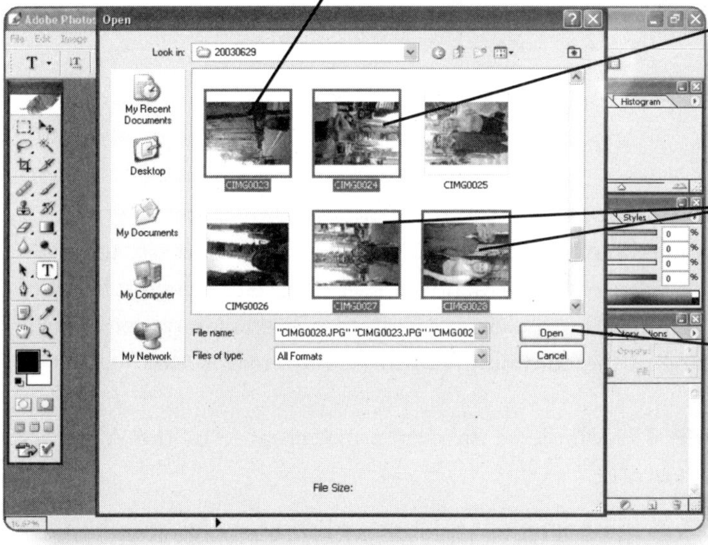

4. **Hold** down the **Ctrl** key (**Command** key for Mac OS) and **click** another file you would like to open.

5. **Repeat** step **4** until you have selected all of the files you would like to open.

6. **Click** on **Open**. All of the files you selected will now open in Photoshop.

Accessing Files

To toggle back and forth between your open images, you can use the Window command in Photoshop. Although you can have multiple images open at any time, you can only work on them one at a time.

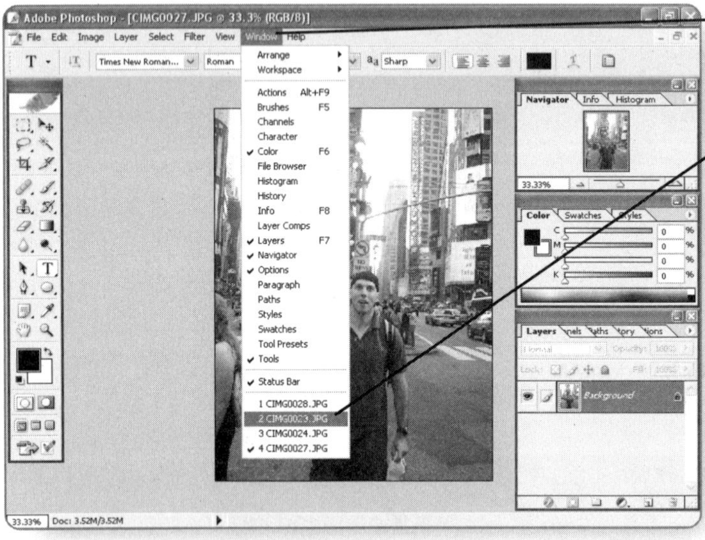

1. **Click** on **Window**. The Window menu will appear.

2. **Click** on the **file name** for the file to display. The file's window moves to the top of other open files and becomes the active image so that you can work with the file.

Using File Formats in Photoshop

Photoshop supports more than a dozen different file formats by default, so chances are you can open an image created in another program by selecting the appropriate file type from the Files of type drop-down list in the Open dialog box. Here are some of the common file formats you might use:

- **.BMP.** The Windows Bitmap format created by the Windows Paint applet.
- **.GIF.** A compact file format often used for Web graphics.
- **.PDF.** The Adobe Acrobat file transfer format. Photoshop CS now supports password protection for .PDF files, so you may be prompted to enter a password when you open a .PDF file.

- **.JPG or JPEG.** Another file format often used for Web graphics.
- **.PCX.** An alternate to the Windows Bitmap format that was originally popularized via the PC Paintbrush program.
- **Photo CD.** A format originally developed by Kodak.
- **PICT.** A Macintosh graphics format.
- **.TIF or TIFF.** A common format for scanned images.
- **.PNG.** Another format for Web graphics.

Importing an Image

You may want to use Photoshop to improve images you generate from another source, such as a scanner or digital camera. Assuming you've installed the Windows software driver that came with the scanner or camera, Photoshop should be able to recognize the device and import images directly from it.

Grabbing a Scanner Image

Impressive scanners costing $300 or less have become widely available. You can use Photoshop to scan hard-copy photos and other graphics for modifications and editing. When you're ready to scan an image, turn on the scanner and position the image on the scanner bed before continuing with the following steps. If you're not sure how to position it correctly, consult the scanner's user manual.

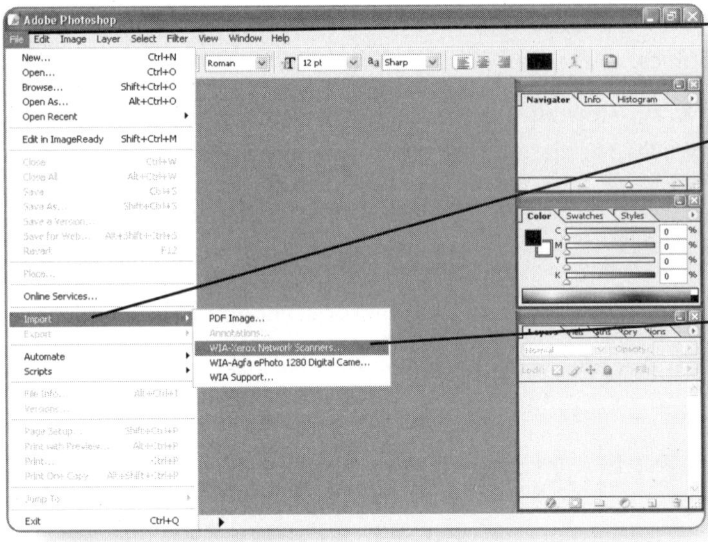

1. Click on **File**. The File menu will appear.

2. Drag the **mouse pointer** down to the Import command. (That is, point to the command.) A submenu will appear.

3. Click on the **name** of your scanner in the submenu. The scanner software (TWAIN or WIA [*Windows Image Acquisition*] software) for your scanner will load.

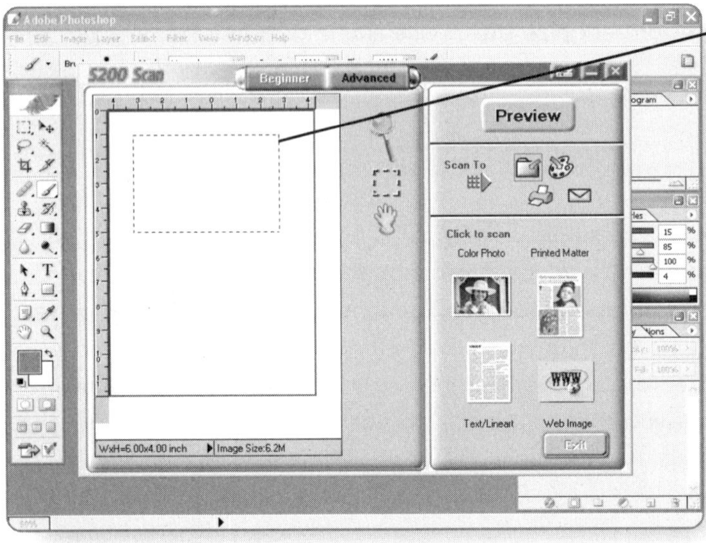

4. Follow the **on-screen instructions** for your scanner. Depending on the type of scanner you have installed, different on-screen options will appear for scanning your image. Once you have finished scanning the image, it will appear in Photoshop and be ready for editing.

Grabbing a Digital Camera Image

My mother recently got a digital camera and can use it like a pro. The reason I mention this is that, if she can work with her digital camera and edit the images in Photoshop, just about anyone else can as well. Digital cameras skip the film and hard-copy stage, storing images digitally directly within the camera. To work with the images, you need to install the camera software, connect the camera to your system via the applicable cable, and place the camera in its playback mode. From there, you use the following procedure to copy images from the camera into Photoshop.

> **NOTE**
>
> Some cameras do not enable you to import images directly into Photoshop. In such cases, an icon for a removable disk representing the camera's removable media appears in the My Computer window, and you can copy the images from that "disk" to the system's hard disk to work with the images.

1. **Click** on **File**. The File menu will appear.

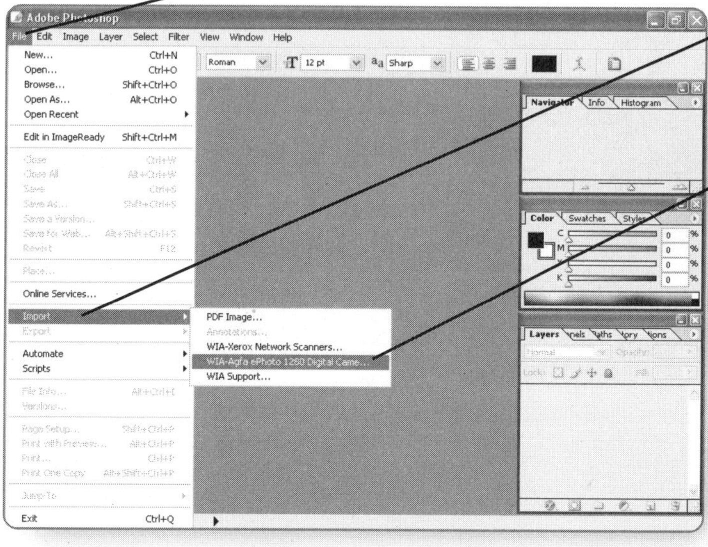

2. **Drag** the **mouse pointer** down to the Import command. A submenu will appear.

3. **Click** on the **name** of your digital camera in the submenu. The software (TWAIN or WIA software) for your camera will load.

4. **Follow** the **on-screen instructions** for your digital camera. Depending on the type of camera, different on-screen

options will appear for scanning your image. Once you have finished scanning the image, it will appear in Photoshop and be ready for editing.

Adding Information

The name of the file alone does not have to be the only way it is identified. You can save special information with an image file to give it a caption, describe its origin, identify who created or shot it, and so on. The information follows professional image identification standards, but even home users may find this information useful in building a digital "photo album."

Embedding Information in the File

Use the following process to store file info for the current file:

1. **Click** on **File**. The File menu will appear.

2. **Click** on **File Info**. The File Info dialog box will open.

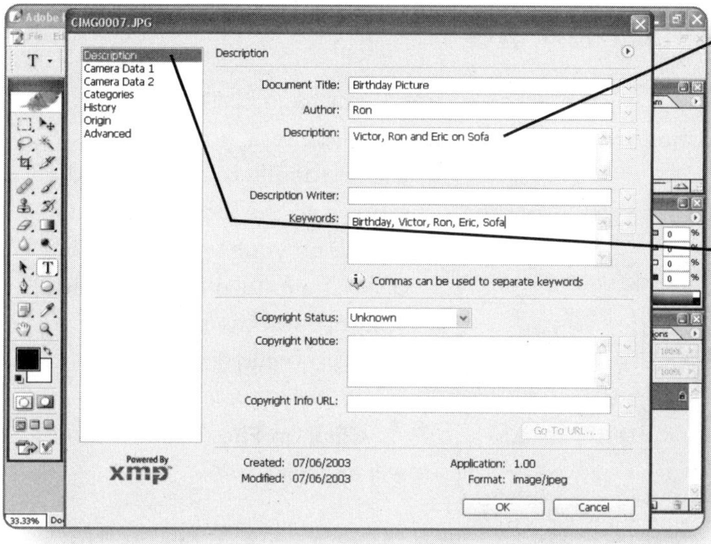

3. Type entries as desired in the text boxes. Of course, you don't have to use all the entries. You can opt to use only those that are relevant to you.

4. Click on a different **category**. A new list of boxes will appear.

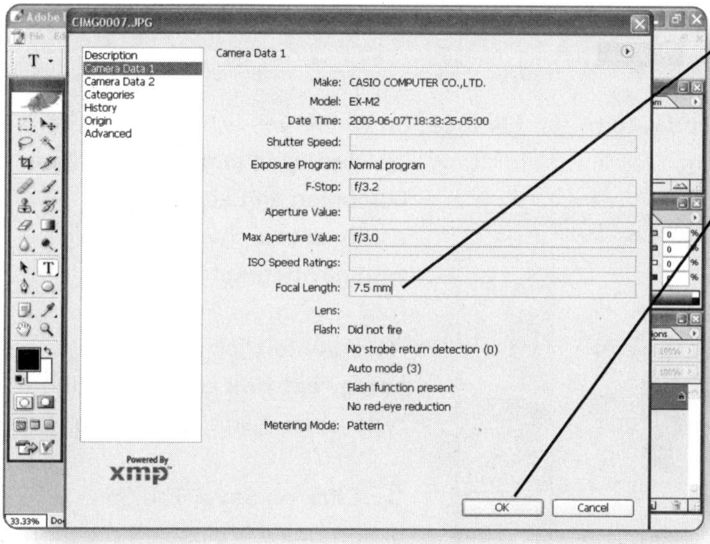

5. Repeat steps **3** and **4** to enter information for other categories of file info.

6. Click on **OK**. The File Info dialog box closes, adding the information to the file.

Saving a File

If you've just created an image file or have just imported it into Photoshop from a scanner or digital camera, you need to save the image file to name it and store it to the location of your choice on your system's hard disk. The following steps lead you through the process for saving the current file:

1. **Click** on **File**. The File menu will appear.

2. **Click** on **Save As**. The Save As dialog box will open.

3. **Navigate** to the **file location** where you want to save the file. The files in that folder will be displayed in the file list. (See "Opening an Existing File" earlier in this chapter for help with navigating folders.)

4. **Double-click** on the **File name text box entry** and then type a new name for the file.

5. **Click** on **Save**. The Save As dialog box will close. Photoshop saves the file and leaves it open onscreen for further work.

NOTE

If you make changes to the file, be sure to click on File and then click on Save to save your changes. The Save As dialog box will not appear for subsequent saves unless you click Save As rather than Save on the File menu.

Saving to Another Format

By default, Photoshop saves new images in its Photoshop (.PSD or .PDD) format. However, you may need to save an image in another format. For example, you might want to save the file in the Windows Bitmap (.BMP) or Paint (.PCX) format to use the file in a word processor document. Photoshop enables you to save images in more than a dozen formats.

Using Save As

Use the following process to save the current file to one of the available graphics formats. (The Adobe .PDF format will be covered in the next section.)

1. **Click** on **File**. The File menu will appear.

2. **Click** on **Save As**. The Save As dialog box will open.

3. Navigate to the **location** where you want to save the file. The files in that folder will be displayed in the file list.

4. Double-click on the **File name text box entry**. The name will be selected.

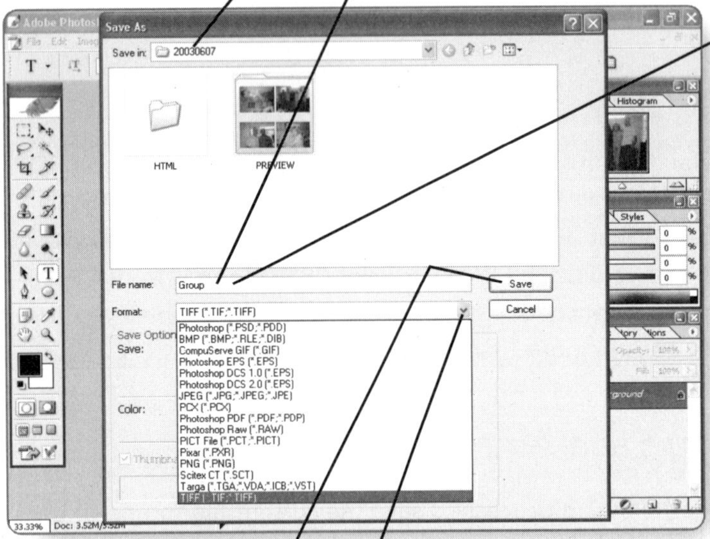

5. Type an **alternate name**, if needed, for the converted file. The new name will be displayed.

> ### TIP
> To save a copy of the current file (in the same file format) rather than the original, click on the As a Copy check box to place a check in it. Then skip to step 7.

6. Click on the **down arrow** for the Format list, then click on the format to use for the converted file in the list. The list will close, and the format will be selected.

7. Click on **Save**. The Save As dialog box will close.

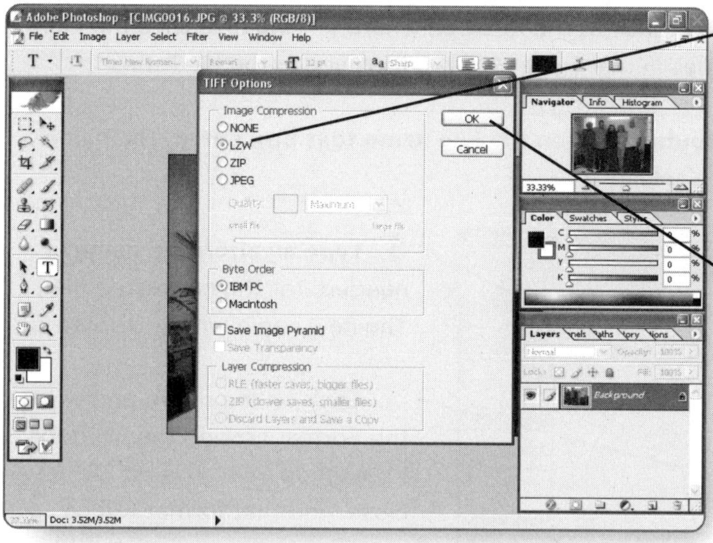

8. **Set** needed **options** if an Options dialog box appears. An Options dialog box appears only for certain types of conversions, and the options vary depending on the conversion format.

9. **Click** on **OK**. Photoshop converts and saves the file, closing the original file. The converted file remains open in Photoshop for further work.

Saving a Password-Protected .PDF File

PDF (*Portable Document Format*) is one of the most convenient ways to send files to other people electronically. You can password protect your PDF file to prevent others from making changes to the file or from doing certain other things with the file.

1. **Click** on **File**. The File menu will appear.

2. **Click** on **Save As**. The Save As dialog box will open.

3. **Navigate** to the **location** where you want to save the file. The files in that folder will be displayed in the file list.

4. **Double-click** on the **File name text box entry**. The name will be selected.

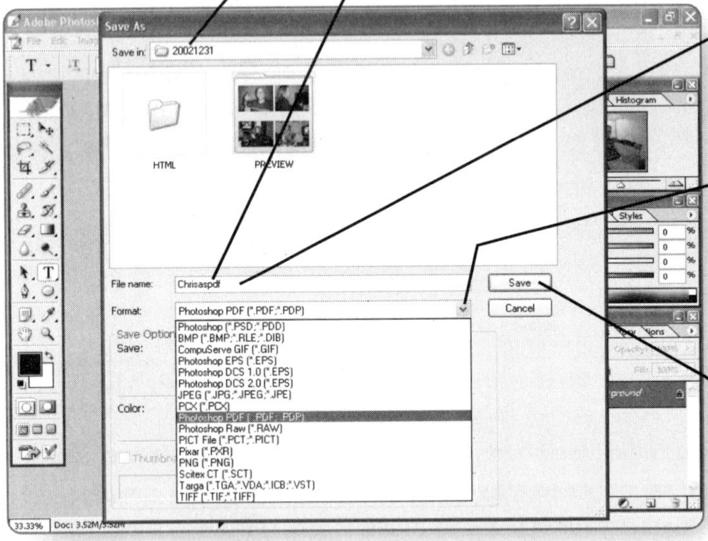

5. **Type** an **alternate name**, if needed, for the converted file. The new name will be displayed.

6. **Click** on the **down arrow** for the Format list and then click on Photoshop PDF. The list will close, and that format will be specified for the converted file.

7. **Click** on **Save**. The Save As dialog box will close, and the PDF Options dialog box will open.

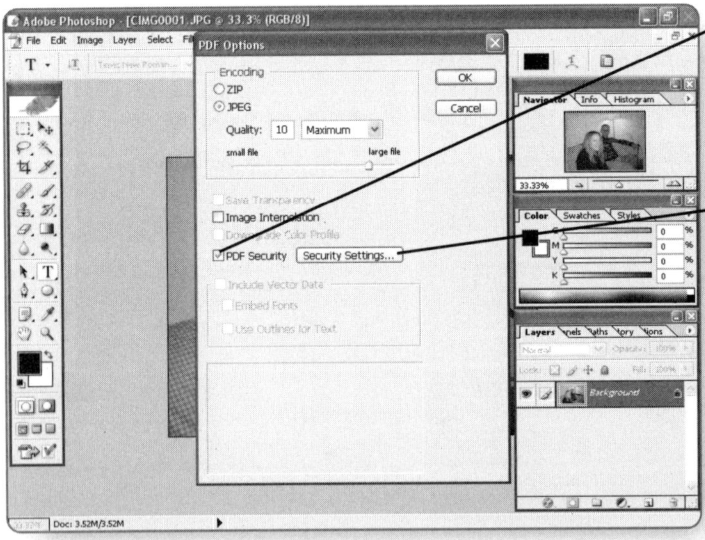

8. **Click** on the **PDF Security** check box. It will be checked, and the Security Settings button will become active.

9. **Click** on **Security Settings**. The PDF Security dialog box will open.

10. Click on the **Password Required to Open Document** check box. It will be checked, and the Document Open Password text box will become active.

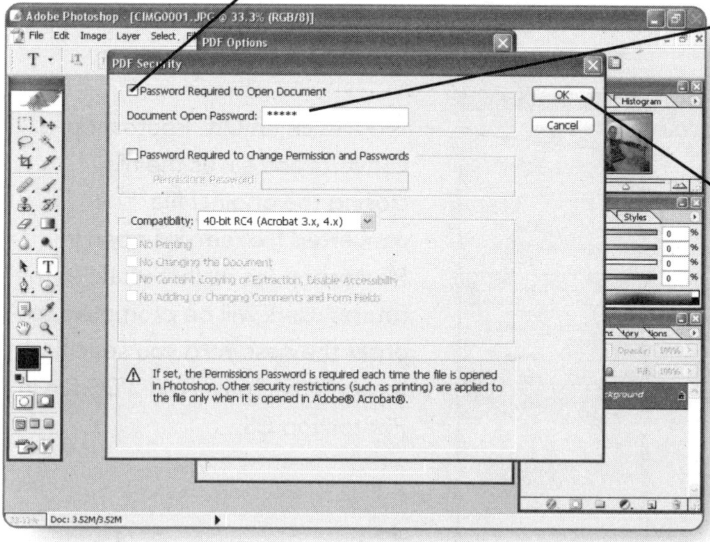

11. Type a **password** in the Document Open Password text box. An asterisk will appear for each character you type.

12. Click on **OK**. The Confirm Password dialog box will open.

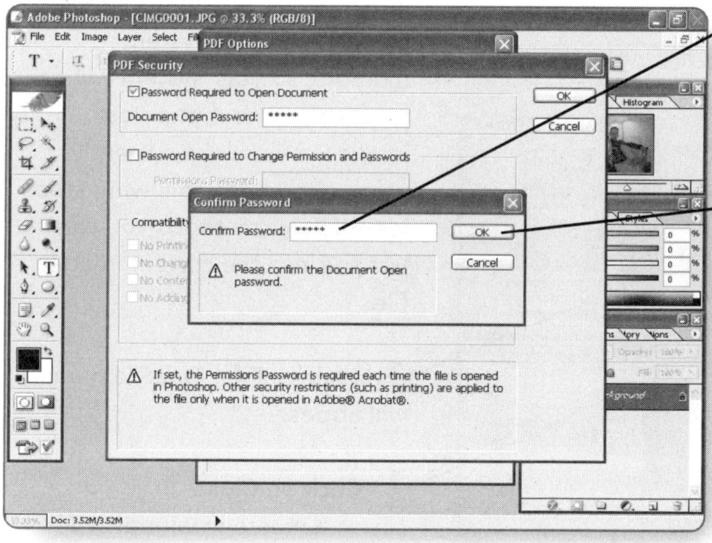

13. Type the **password** again in the Confirm Password text box. An asterisk will appear for each character you type.

14. Click on **OK**. The Confirm Password and PDF Security dialog boxes will close.

> **TIP**
>
> At this point, you could click on the Security Settings button in the PDF Options dialog box to reopen the PDF Security dialog box and specify additional security settings.

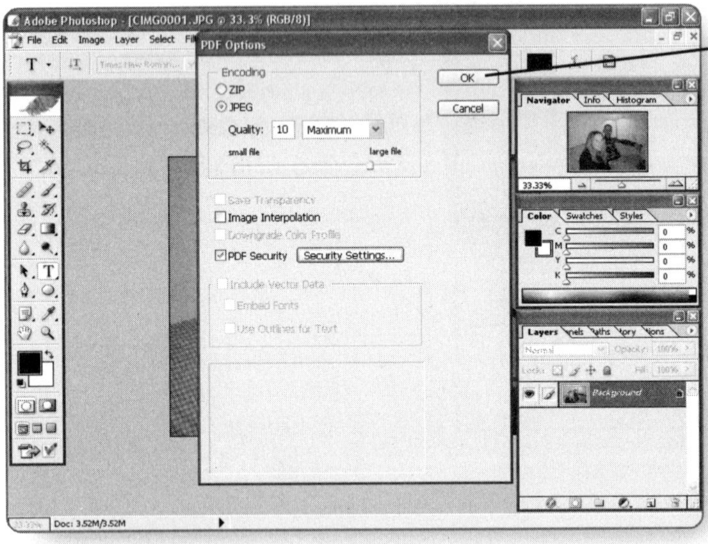

15. Click on **OK**. Photoshop converts and saves the file, closing the original file. The converted file remains open in Photoshop for further work. In the future, users will be prompted to enter the password you specified to open the converted .PDF file in Photoshop CS.

Closing a File

Although you can have multiple images open, image files tend to consume a lot of system memory, so your system will perform better if you close images you are not currently using. Again, the following steps identify two methods you can use to close the current image file.

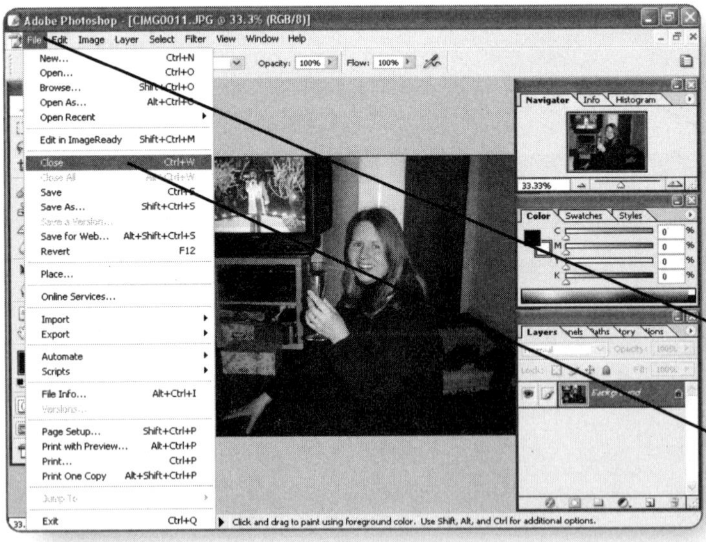

1. Click on **File**. The File menu will appear.

2. Click on **Close**. In some cases, a message window will open.

NOTE

If you added a new text layer, a dialog box may first prompt you to commit (finish) the layer. Click on Commit to do so.

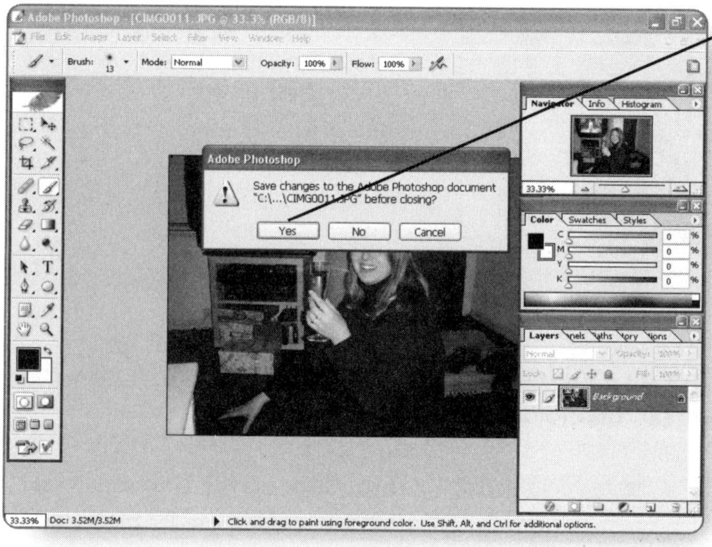

3a. **Click** on **Yes** if you see a message window prompting you to save the file. Photoshop will finish saving it, and the file will close.

OR

3b. **Click** on **Close** for the window of the image file to close. If prompted, save your changes as described in step 3a. Photoshop closes the image window.

The File Browser

Photoshop CS includes an enhanced feature called the File Browser. The File Browser acts as a separate program running from within Photoshop. With it, you can manage all of your image files, including naming files, organizing them, deleting them, and renaming and then performing edits without having to open an image.

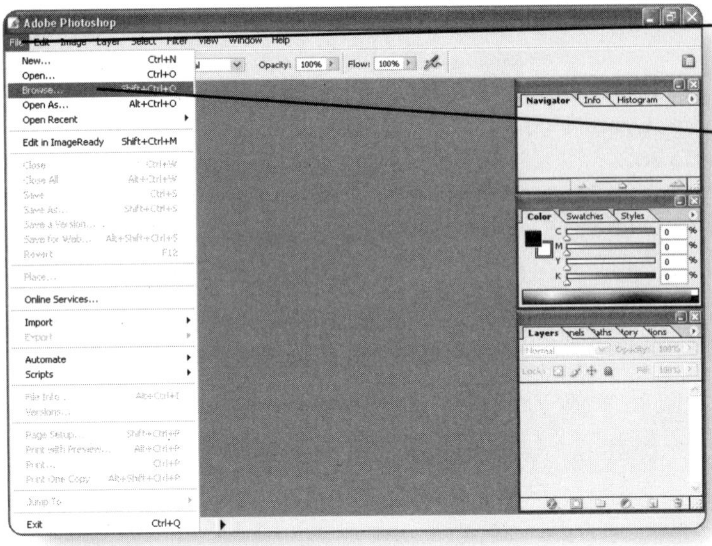

1. Click on **File**. The File menu will appear.

2. Click on **Browse**. The File Browser window will open.

3. Click on a **folder** in the upper-left pane of the window. The contents of that folder will appear.

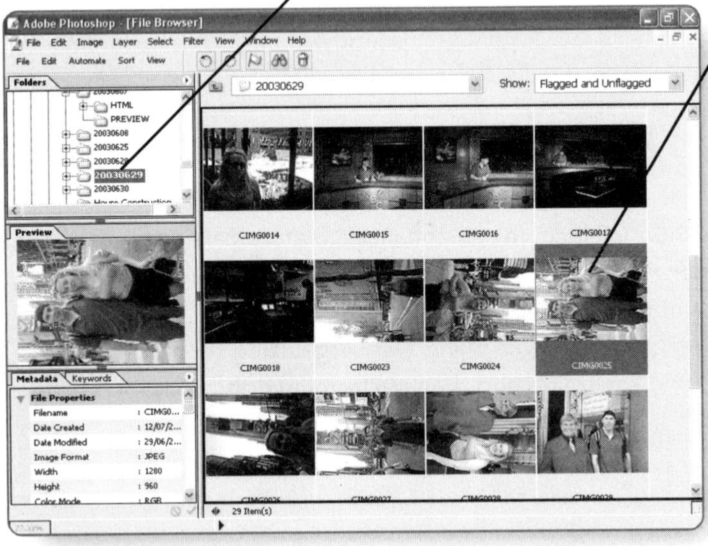

4a. Click on the **thumbnail** for the desired image. Its metadata will appear in the lower-left pane of the File Browser for you to review as needed.

OR

4b. Double-click on the **desired image**. It will open immediately in Photoshop.

Editing Files

Using the File Browser window, you can quickly do minor editing of your image files. One of the editing options includes rotating files. This is perfect for manipulating pictures that were taken in landscape mode, but that you would like to appear in portrait mode or vice versa.

1. **Click** on the **name** of a file. A box will appear around the name of the file, and it will be highlighted.

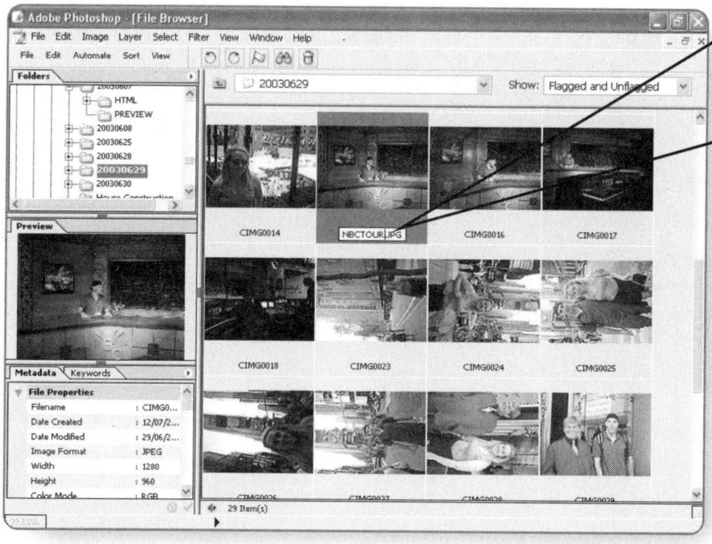

2. **Type** a **new name** for your file. It will appear as you type.

3. **Press Enter**. The file will have a new name.

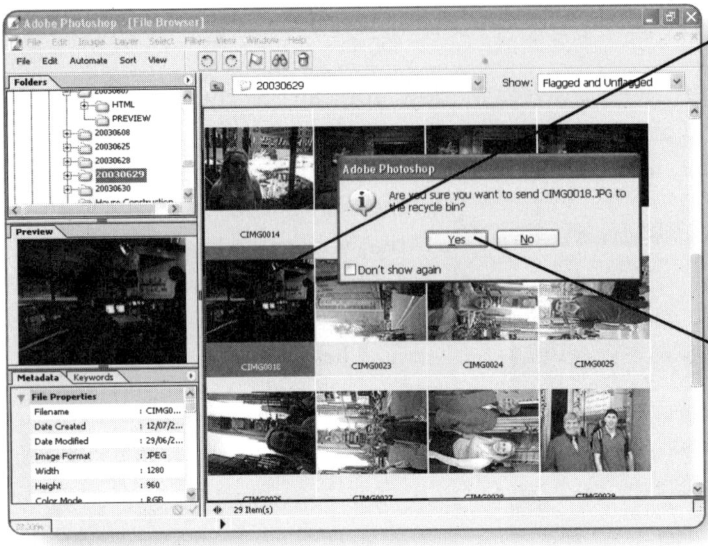

4. Click on a **file**. It will appear highlighted.

5. Press Delete on your keyboard. A dialog box will appear, confirming that you want to send the file to the system's Recycle Bin.

6. Click on **Yes**. The file will be sent to the Recycle Bin.

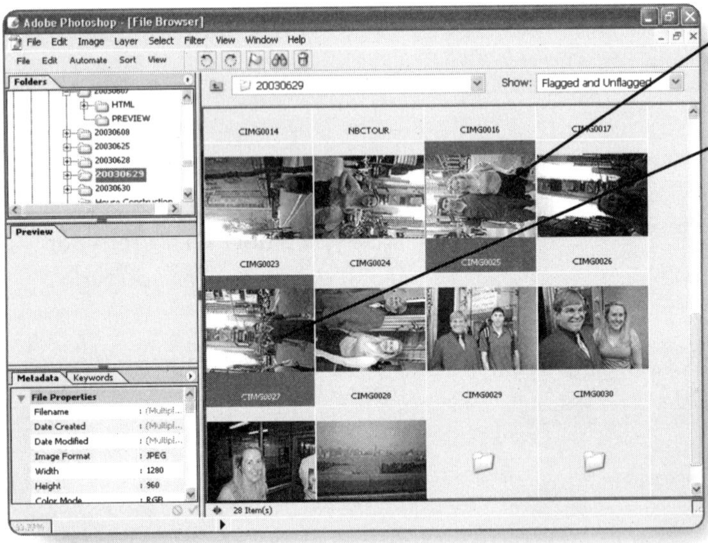

7. Click on a **file** to select it. It will appear highlighted.

8. Hold down the **Ctrl** key (**Command** key Mac OS) and **click** on any other files you would like to select at the same time.

9. **Click** on one of the **Rotate buttons** to rotate the files you have selected. They can be rotated clockwise or counterclockwise by 90 degrees.

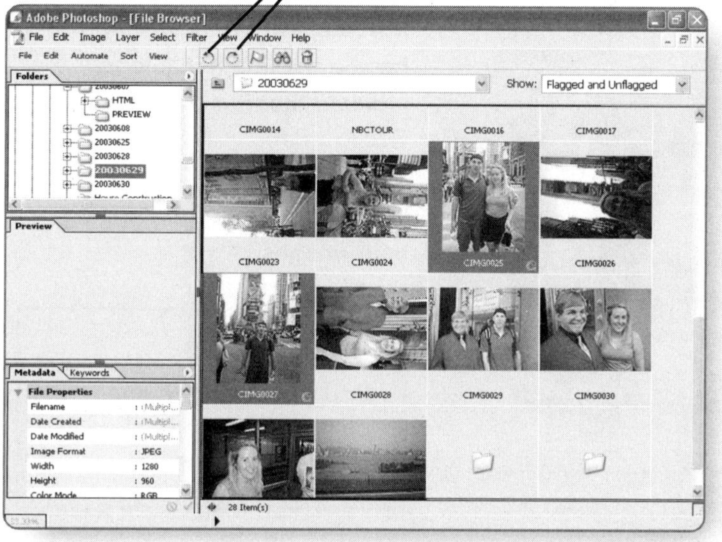

Managing Files

Once you get the hang of your digital camera, your image collection can easily become quite large. The File Browser is a great tool for helping you manage your collection of images. With it, you can mark certain images, add keywords to images, and search for particular files.

Flagging and Accessing Images

The File Browser allows you to mark certain images so that they can be quickly accessed. Imagine flipping through a photo album and placing sticky notes on the pages of the images you would like to go back to. That's pretty much how the Markers in the File Browser work. You simply select the images you would like to mark, and then you can choose how you would like to view those images.

1. Click on an **image** you would like to flag. The image will be highlighted.

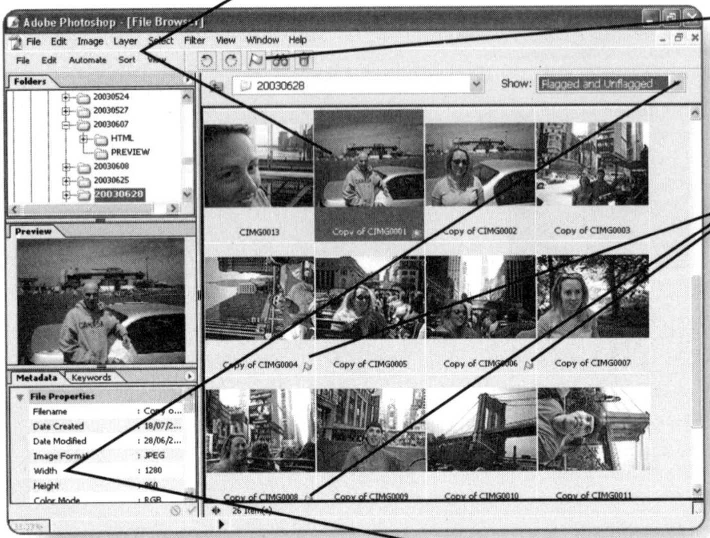

2. Click on the **Flag File button**. A little flag will appear beside the image name to indicate that it is flagged.

3. Repeat steps **1** and **2** until you have completed flagging your images.

> **TIP**
>
> You can deflag an image by selecting it and clicking on the Flag button.

4. Click on the Show drop-down list **arrow** in the top-right corner. A list of viewing options will appear.

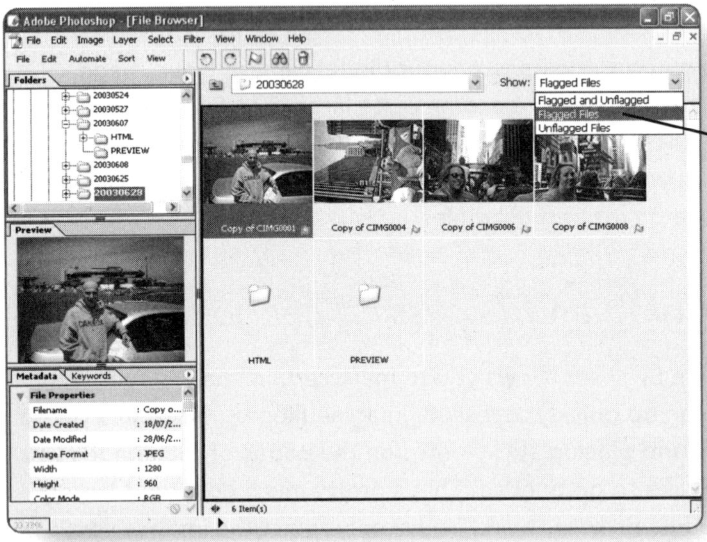

5. Click on the **desired option**. You can choose to view all of the flagged images, all of the unflagged images, or simply all of the images.

Searching Files

The File Browser has a built-in search engine that will allow you to find specific photos based on the criteria you set.

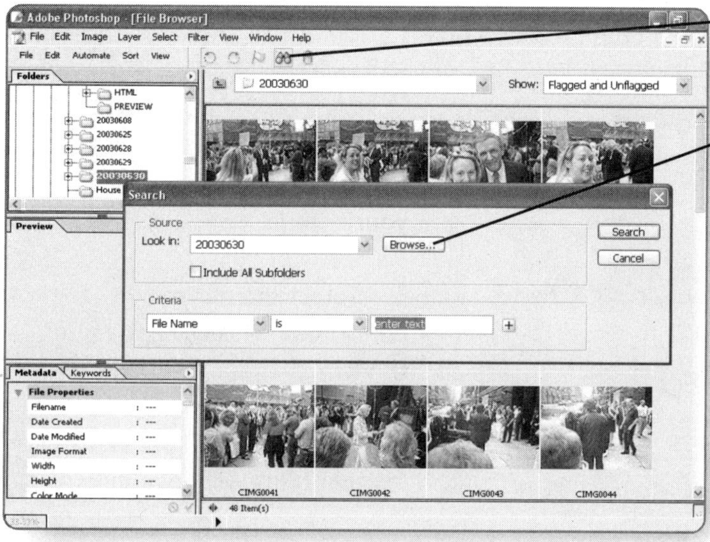

1. **Click** on the **Search** button. The Search dialog box will open.

2. **Click** on the **Browse** button. A Browse for Folder dialog box will open in which you can select where you would like to conduct the search.

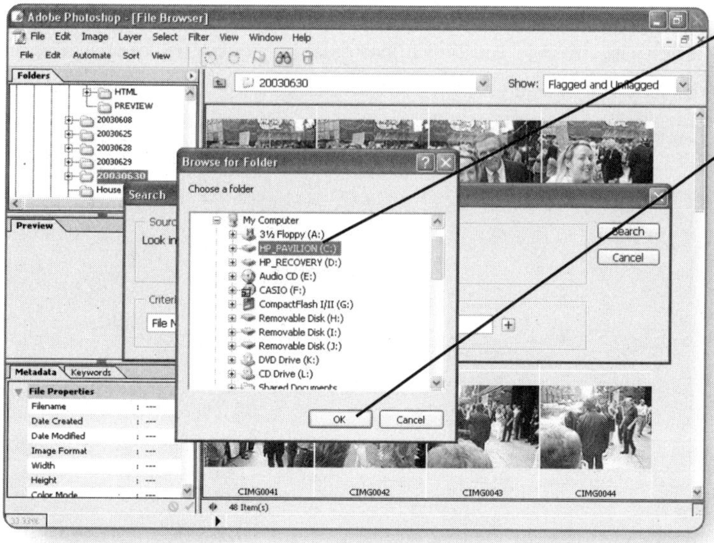

3. **Click** on the desired **drive** or **folder**. It will be selected.

4. **Click** on **OK**. The dialog box will close, and you will now be able to set the criteria for your search.

5. **Click** on the **down arrow** beside the first box in the Criteria area. A list of different criteria will appear.

6. **Click** on the desired **criteria**. It will be selected. Depending on the criteria you select, different parameter options will be available in the next two boxes.

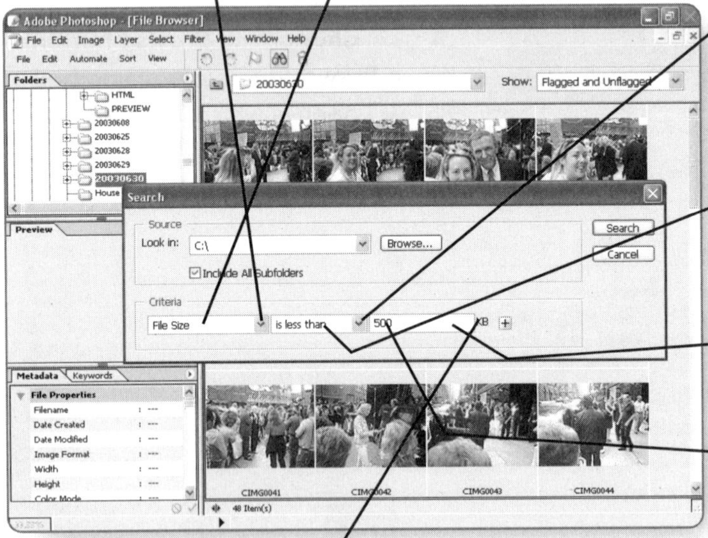

7. **Click** on the **down arrow** beside the next box. This will allow you to set the conditions of your criteria.

8. **Select** the desired **conditions**. This will appear in the box.

9. **Double-click** in the **last box**. The contents will be highlighted.

10. **Type** the **data criteria** for your search. It will appear as you type.

11. **Click** on the **+**. This will allow you to enter another line of criteria for your search.

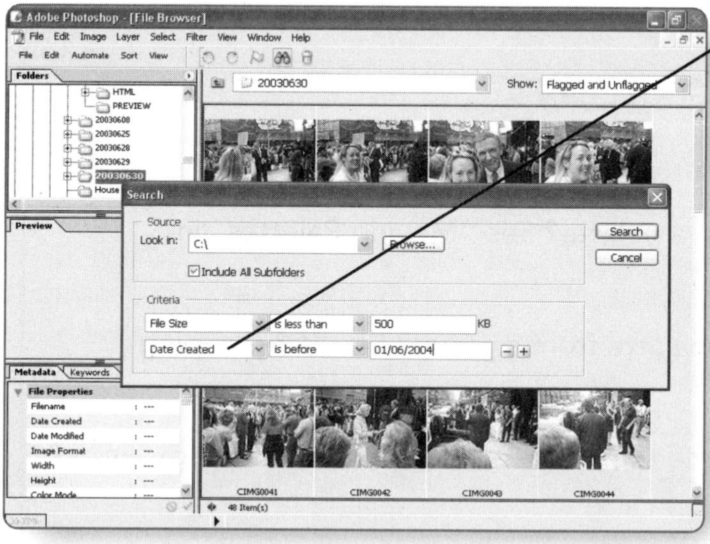

12. **Repeat** steps **5** to **11** for the next line of criteria.

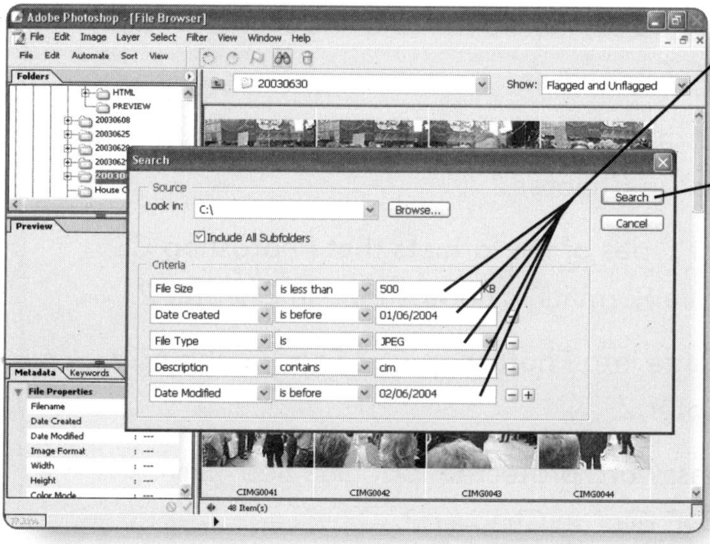

13. **Repeat** step **12** until you are finished adding lines of criteria for your search.

14. **Click** on **Search**. The images that match the criteria you have set will appear in the File Browser.

Part I Review Questions

1. How do you open a palette? See "Selecting Palettes" in Chapter 1.
2. How can you reposition a palette? See "Moving Palettes" in Chapter 1.
3. How do you remove a palette from a group? See "Ungrouping Palettes" in Chapter 1.
4. How do you reveal all the tools in one location? See "Toolbox" in Chapter 1.
5. How do you create a keyboard shortcut? See "Keyboard Shortcuts" in Chapter 1.
6. What are the steps required to make a new blank document? See "Creating a New File" in Chapter 2.
7. How do you open more than one file at a time? See "Opening and Accessing Multiple Files" in Chapter 2.
8. What are three different types of file formats that Photoshop CS supports? See "Using File Formats in Photoshop" in Chapter 2.
9. How do you scan an image into Photoshop CS? See "Grabbing a Scanner Image" in Chapter 2.
10. How do you create a password protected .pdf file? See "Saving a Password-Protected .PDF File" in Chapter 2.

PART II

Making Basic Edits

3

Adding Content with Tools

When most people think of Photoshop, they think of it as a photo-editing application. Although it is very strong in that department, it also has a full range of tools to help you add content to a blank image or to an image you've created or opened from another source. Painting and drawing with your computer may take some practice, but like any other skill, the results are worth the effort. In this chapter, you'll learn how to:

- Select colors for painting
- Paint with the painting tools
- Draw with the drawing tools
- Add and improve text
- Create your own brushes

Choosing Colors

Color can bring your images and creations to life, and Photoshop gives you abundant options when it comes to selecting colors. Typically, you will be setting two types of colors, one for the foreground and one for the background. Photoshop generally uses the selected foreground color when you draw lines and the background color for gradient fills and erased areas. The Foreground Color, Background Color box near the bottom of the toolbox shows the currently selected foreground and background colors. The following steps detail the numerous methods you can use to select a new foreground or background color. You should first ensure that the color palette is open before you attempt to change colors.

1. **Click** on **Window**. The Window menu will appear.

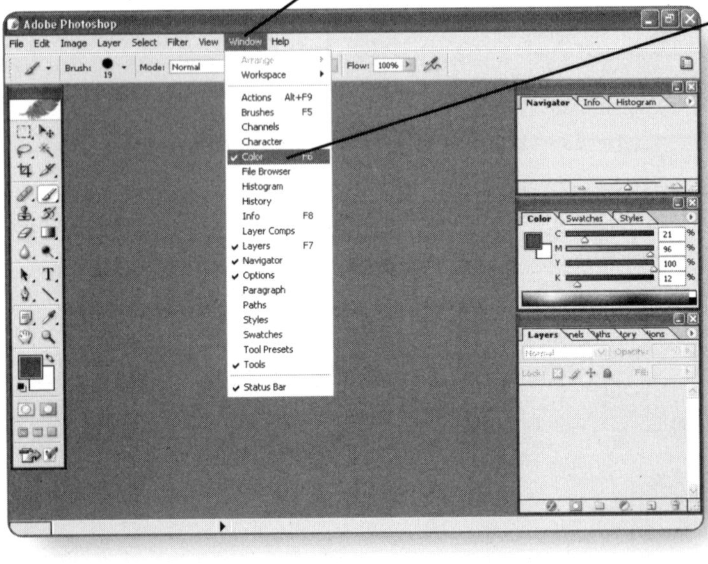

2. **Click** on **Color** if it is not already selected. The color palette will appear.

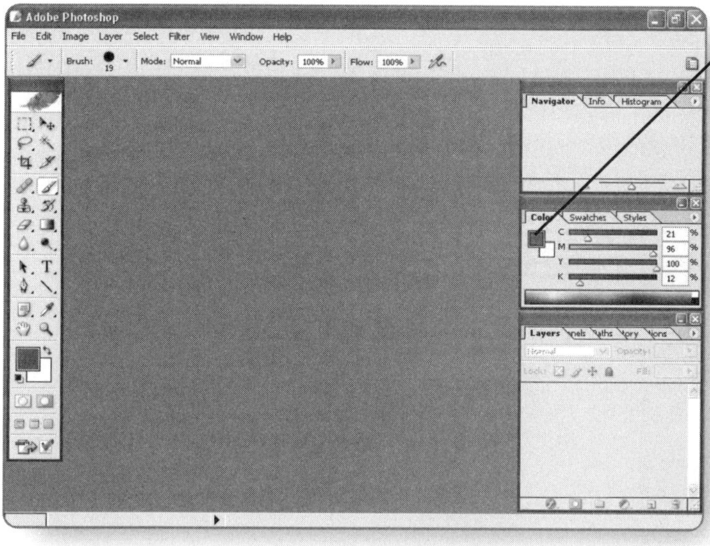

3. Double-click on the Set **Foreground color box**. A Color Picker dialog box will open in which you can select a foreground color.

4. Click on a **hue level**. You can click anywhere along the hue line. Alternatively, you can enter a value for the hue in the hue box.

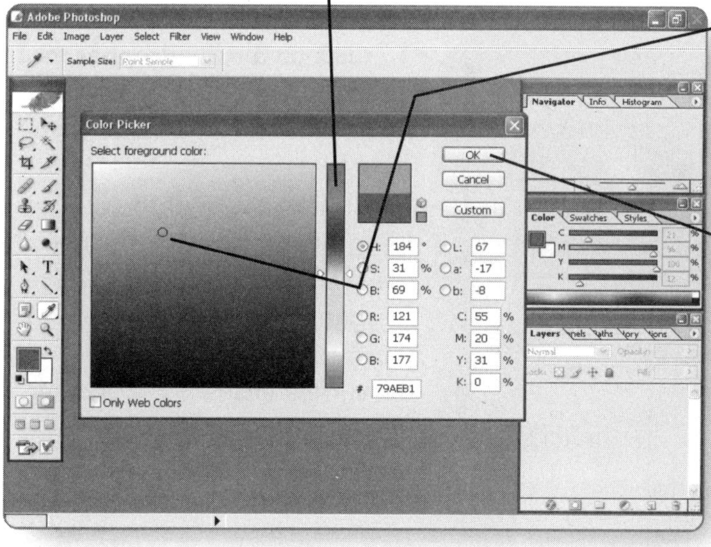

5. Click anywhere in the Select foreground color area to choose a saturation and brightness level. The color will be selected when you click.

6. Click on OK. The foreground color will be set.

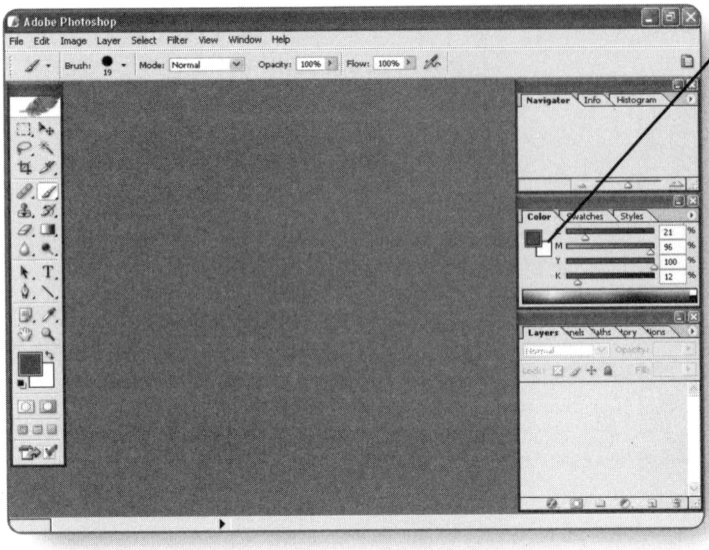

7. **Repeat** steps **3** through **6** for the background color. In Step 3, double click the Set background color box rather than the foreground color box.

Choosing Colors from Images

Rather than selecting a color from a color palette, you can choose specific colors from within your images. The Eyedropper tool enables you to pick a color from your image that can then be used when painting.

1. **Click** on the **Eyedropper tool** in the toolbox. The Eyedropper tool will become the active tool.

2. **Click** on the desired **foreground color**. The color you clicked on will become the active foreground color. You can use those colors to paint and draw in the current image file or another file.

3. **Hold** the **Alt key** and then click to select the desired background color.

Working with Painting Tools

You can bring out your inner Rembrandt with the painting tools you are provided with in Photoshop. You can choose to either paint an image from scratch or paint onto an existing image file.

> **NOTE**
>
> Photoshop places painted information on the background layer by default. You can separate painted information by placing it on different layers in the file; this enables you to move and work with the painted information independent of other information in the image. See Chapter 8, "Working with Layers," to learn how to place content on different layers in an image.

Painting with the Paintbrush

The Brush tool enables you to use the mouse to create freehand strokes with any of a number of brush shapes. Photoshop CS includes a large variety of different brushes for you to choose from. These brushes include both traditional strokes and some more unique brushes including star-, grass-, and leaf-shaped brushes.

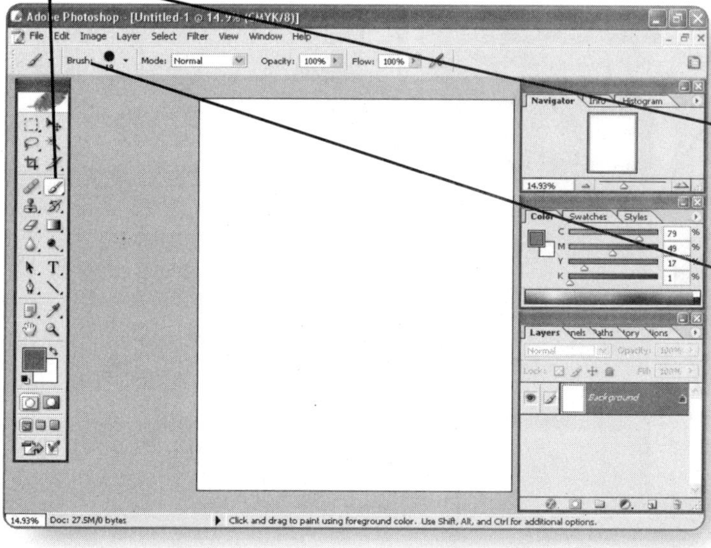

1. **Click** on the **Brush tool** in the toolbox. It will become the active tool.

2. **Click** on the **Brush Preset picker button** in the options bar. A list of different brush options will appear.

3. **Click** on the **scroll buttons** to browse the different brushes.

4. **Click** on the desired **brush**. It will be selected.

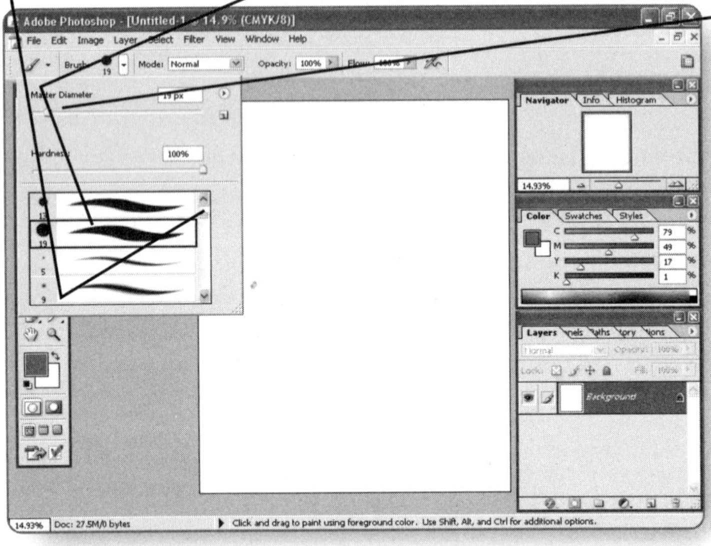

5. **Press** and **hold** the **mouse button** and then **drag** the **slider** to adjust the size of the brush.

6. **Select** the **foreground color** using the method of your choice. The color you select will become active for the paintbrush.

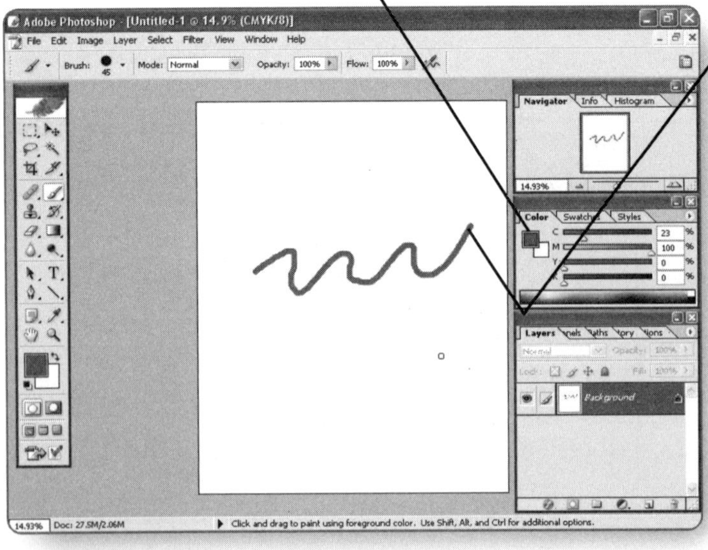

7. **Drag** on the picture in the work area. As you drag, your brush stroke will appear.

> **TIP**
>
> If you paint or draw on the image and make a mistake, immediately press Ctrl+Z or choose the Undo (tool) command on the Edit menu to undo the mistake.

Painting with the Pencil

Technically speaking, the Pencil tool functions as a drawing tool in Photoshop, recoloring pixels as you drag along with the tool. The following example illustrates how to use the Pencil tool:

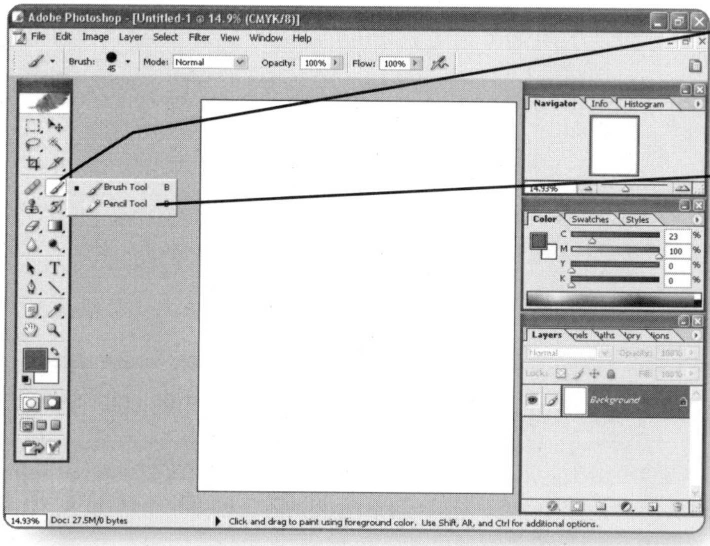

1. **Press** and **hold** the **mouse button** over the **Brush tool** in the toolbox. A list of tools will appear.

2. **Click** on the **Pencil tool**. The Pencil tool will become the active tool.

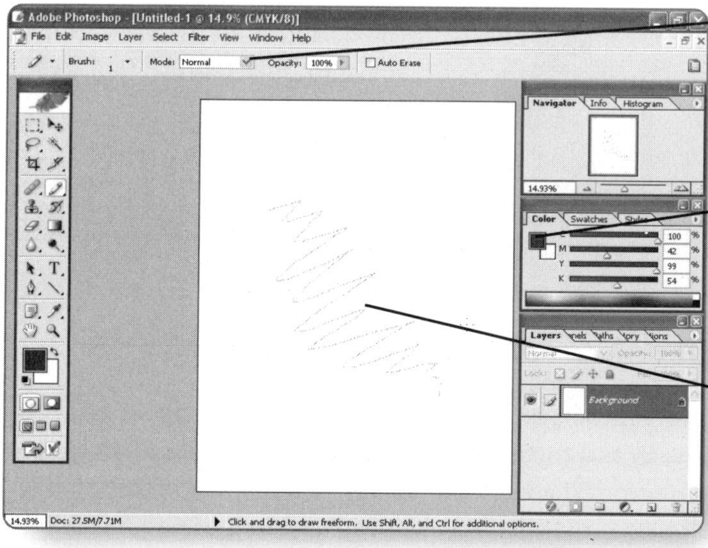

3. **Choose** the desired **settings** in the options bar. Your selections will become the active settings for the tool.

4. **Select** the **foreground color** using the method of your choice. The color you select will become active for the Pencil tool.

5. **Drag** on the picture in the work area. As you drag, your brush stroke will appear.

Painting with the Airbrush

We've all been to a county fair or amusement park where there was a carnie airbrushing t-shirts with people's names or caricatures. Your dreams of being a carnie can now come true because there is an Airbrush tool in Photoshop that mimics real-life airbrushing.

1. **Click** on the **Brush tool** in the toolbox. It will become the active tool.

2. **Choose** a **brush** and other desired **settings** in the options bar. Your selections will become the active settings for the tool.

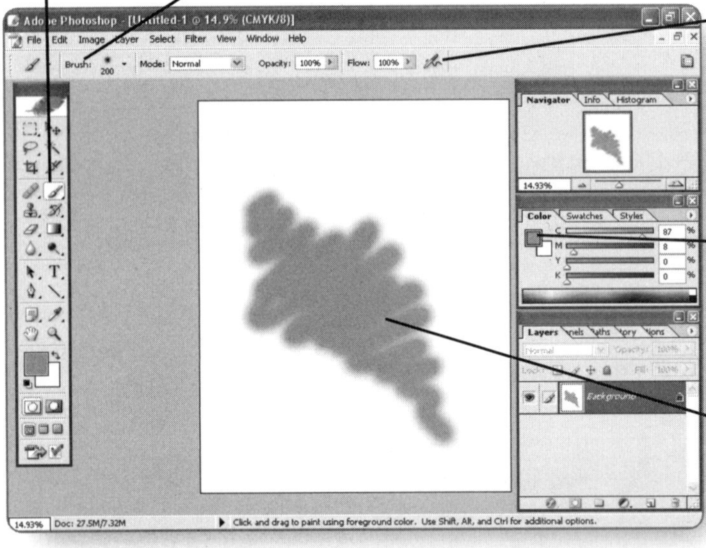

3. **Click** on the **Set to Enable Airbrush Capabilities** button on the options bar. The button will appear pressed, and the airbrush will become active.

4. **Select** the **foreground color** using the method of your choice. The color you select will become active for the Airbrush tool.

5. **Drag** in the work area. As you drag, your brush stroke will appear.

Working with Drawing Tools

The drawing tools enable you to create regular shapes in an image such as a rectangle, rounded rectangle, ellipse, polygon, line, or custom shape. When you draw a shape, Photoshop by default places the shape on its own layer in the image, so refer to Chapter 8 if you have a question about working with layers.

> **NOTE**
>
> The Pen tool is for creating paths, not drawing lines. Chapter 10, "Using Paths," explains how to work with paths.

Drawing a Line

As you might expect, you use the Line tool to draw lines. The following steps explain how to use this tool:

1. **Press** and **hold** the **mouse button** over the Rectangle tool in the toolbox. A list of tools will appear.

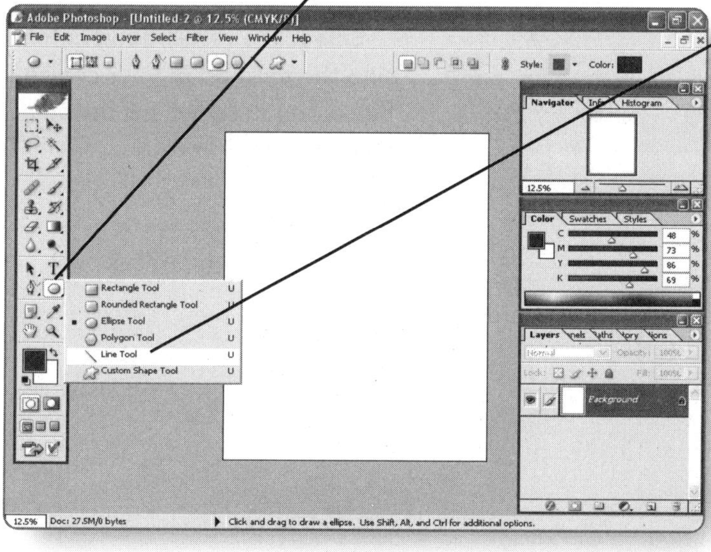

2. **Click** on the **Line tool**. The Line tool will become the active tool.

3. Choose the desired **settings** in the options bar. Your selections will become the active settings for the tool.

> **TIP**
>
> Click on the Fill Pixels button on the options bar if you want to place the drawing on the background layer rather than on a new layer in your image. Otherwise, leave the Shape Layers button selected. If you instead click on the Paths button, Photoshop will create a path and not a line. (You can find these buttons together in a group near the left end of the options bar.) Chapter 10 explains what paths are and how to use them.

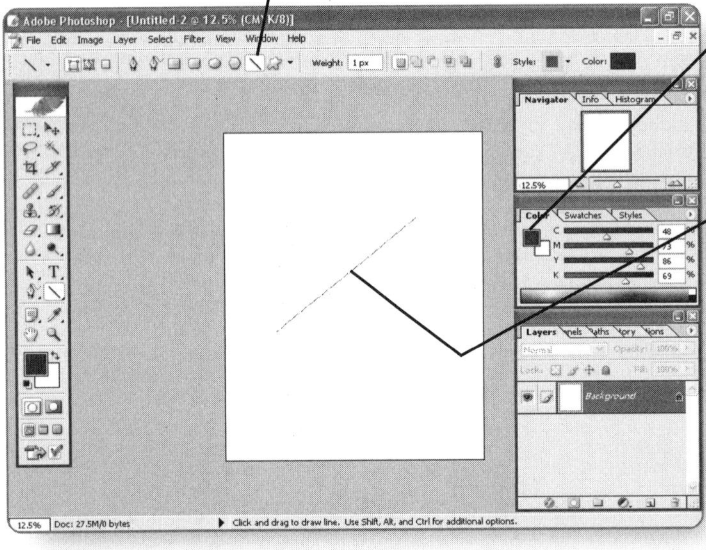

4. Select the **foreground color** using the method of your choice. The color you select will become active for the Line tool.

5. Drag in the work area. As you drag, your line will appear.

Drawing a Rectangle, Oval, or Other Shape

As you may have noticed from the preceding set of steps, the Shape tools are grouped with the Line tool on the Photoshop toolbox. The following set of steps demonstrates how to use one of the Shape tools. (They all basically work in the same way.)

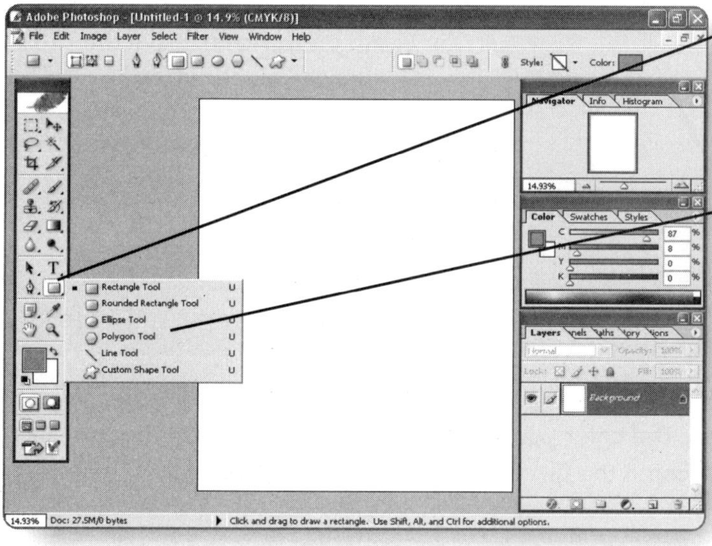

1. **Press** and **hold** the **mouse button** over the Rectangle tool in the toolbox. A list of tools will appear.

2. **Click** on the desired **Shape tool** in the submenu. The selected tool becomes the active tool.

3. **Choose** the desired **settings** in the options bar. Your selections will become the active settings for the tool.

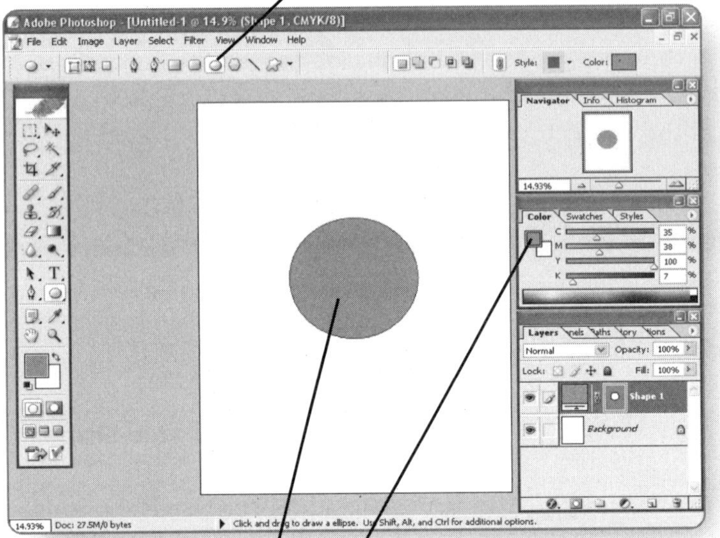

> **NOTE**
>
> If you choose the Custom Shape tool, be sure to use the Shape drop-down list on the options bar to specify which kind of shape to draw. Again, leave the Shape Layers button selected unless you want to add the shape to the current layer (whether it's the background layer or another layer).

4. **Select** the **foreground color** using the method of your choice. The color you select will become active for the tool and will become the fill color for the drawn object.

5. **Drag** in the work area. As you drag, your shape will appear.

Transforming Objects

Once you have created your shapes you can manipulate them into other forms by using one of the Transform Path settings. You'll learn more about Paths in Chapter 10. These transformations aren't limited to just basic shapes as they can be used to manipulate lines, text, and other objects.

Scaling Objects

You can quickly change the size of the shapes that you have created by using the scaling option.

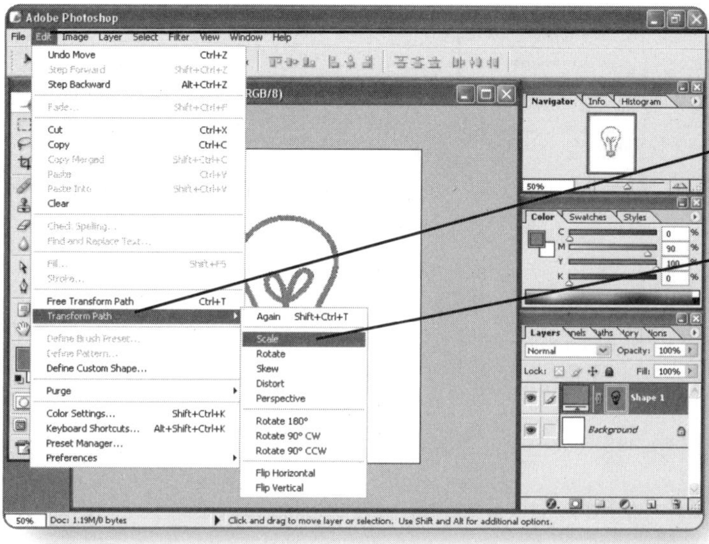

1. **Click** on **Edit**. The Edit menu will appear.
2. **Click** on **Transform Path**. A submenu of options will appear.
3. **Click Scale**. A series of handles will appear around your object.

If an option in the Transform Path menu appears gray, then it is not available for that particular object.

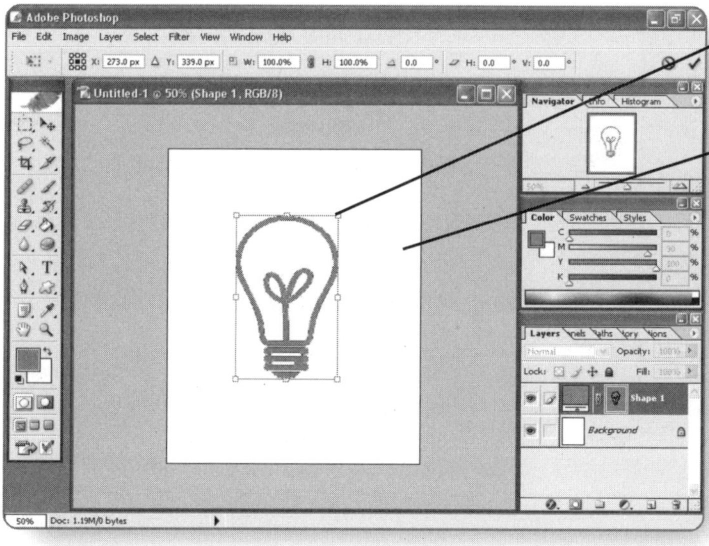

4. **Position** your **mouse pointer** over one of the handles.
5. **Click** and **drag** to change the size of your shape. As you drag, the shape will change size.

6. **Click** on the **Commit** button to finalize the transformation.

Rotating Objects

1. **Click** on **Edit**. The Edit menu will appear.

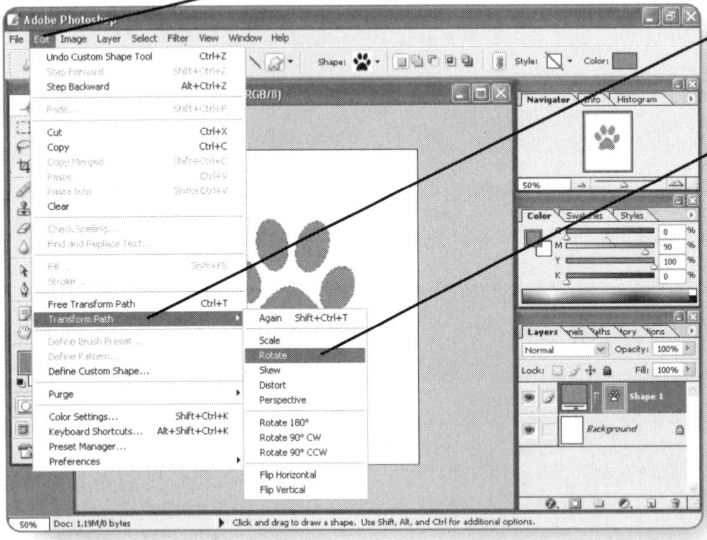

2. **Click** on **Transform Path**. A submenu of options will appear.

3. **Click** **Rotate**. A series of handles will appear around your object.

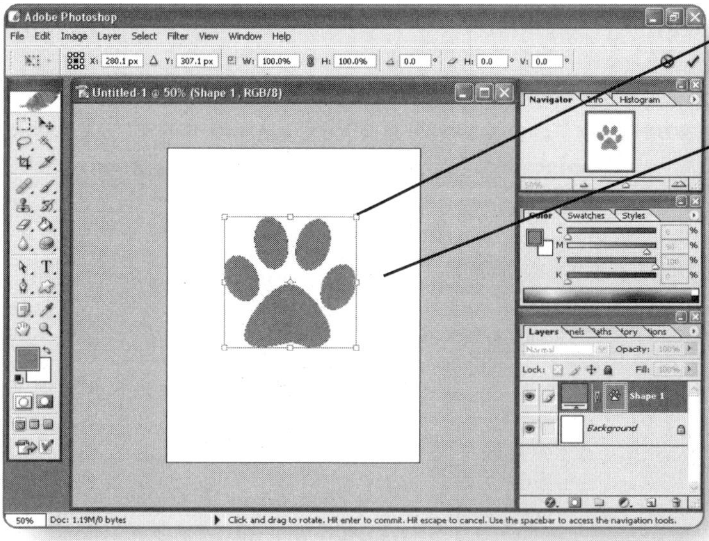

4. **Position** your **mouse pointer** over one of the handles.

5. **Click** and **drag** to rotate your shape. As you drag, the shape will be rotated.

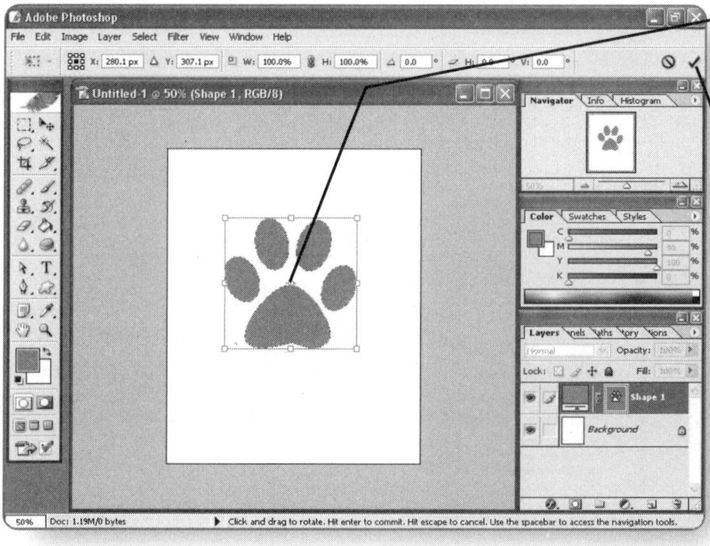

6. **Drag** the **center of rotation icon** in the middle of the shape to change the center of rotation and repeat rotation as required.

7. **Click** on the **Commit** button to finalize the transformation.

Skewing Objects

You're probably familiar with the concept of italizing text. When you apply italics to text, it slants the text forward, which is a form of skewing. You can skew any of your objects in Photoshop CS in any direction.

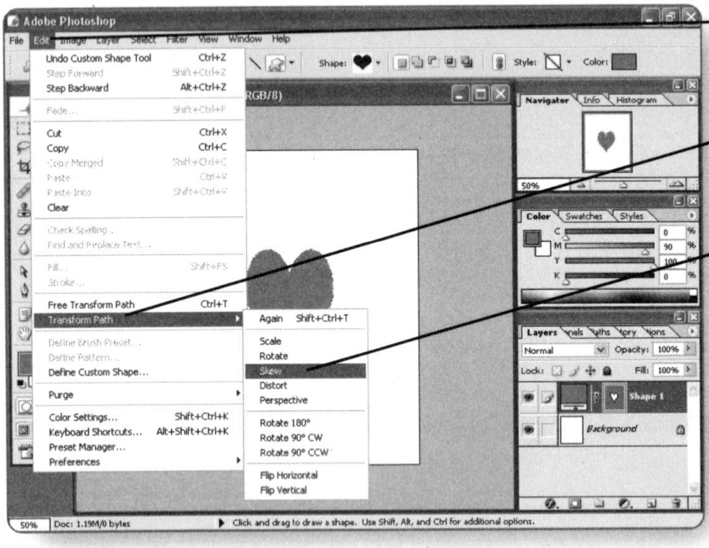

1. **Click** on **Edit**. The Edit menu will appear.

2. **Click** on **Transform Path**. A submenu of options will appear.

3. **Click Skew**. A series of handles will appear around your object.

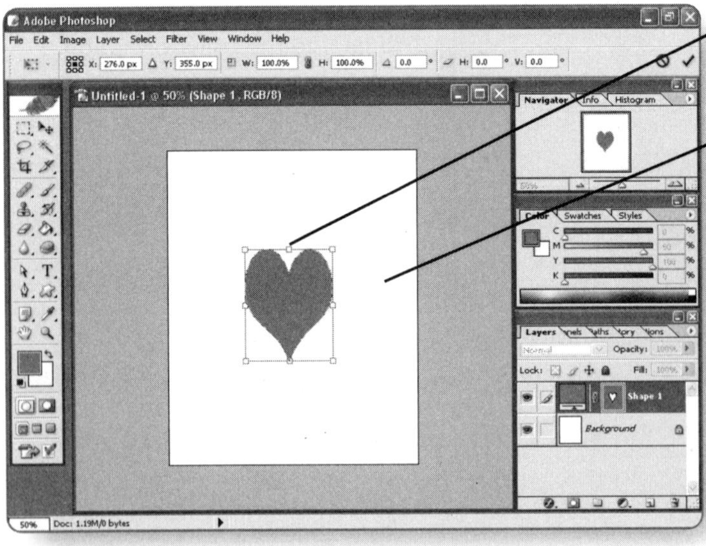

4. **Position** your **mouse pointer** over one of the handles.

5. **Click** and **drag** to skew your shape. As you drag, the shape will be skewed.

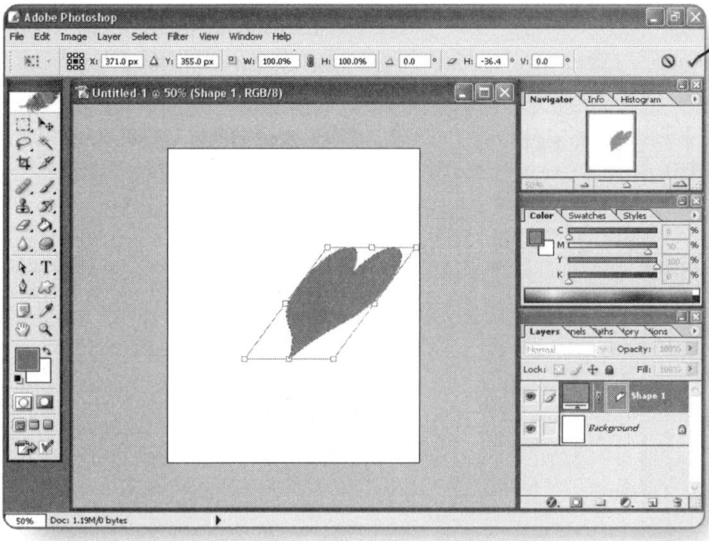

6. **Click** on the **Commit** button to finalize the transformation.

Distorting Objects

The Distort feature allows you to change the dimension of the shape you are manipulating. By dragging on the handles you can change the length and position of each side of your shape.

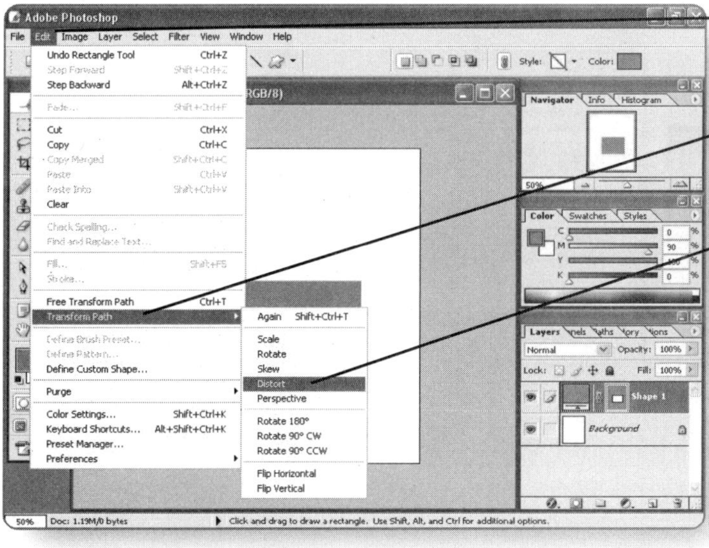

1. **Click** on **Edit**. The Edit menu will appear.

2. **Click** on **Transform Path**. A submenu of options will appear.

3. **Click Distort**. A series of handles will appear around your object.

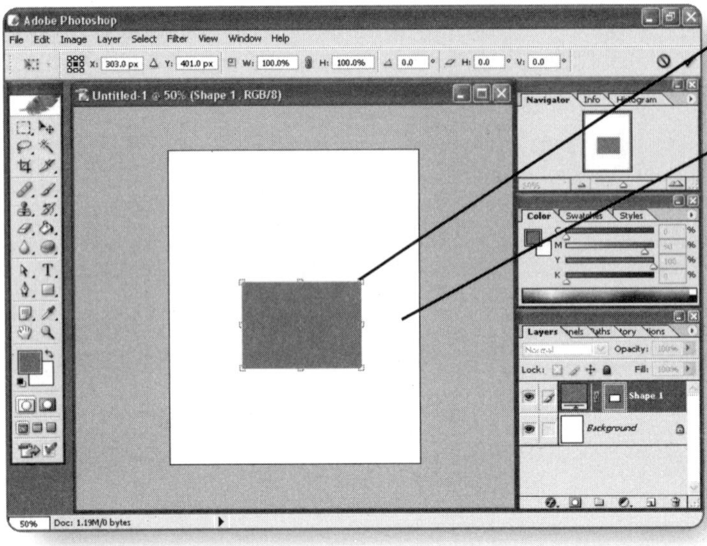

4. **Position** your **mouse pointer** over one of the handles.

5. **Click** and **drag** to distort your shape. As you drag, the shape will be distorted.

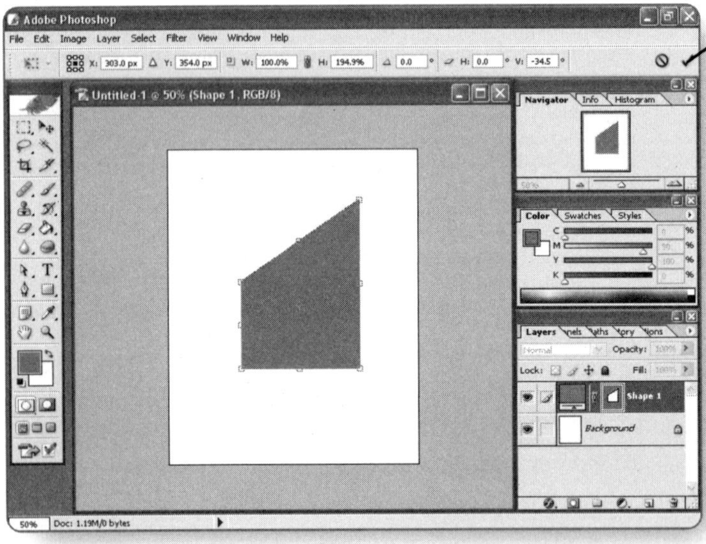

6. **Click** on the **Commit** button to finalize the transformation.

Adding Perspective

You can add perspective to your objects to give them the illusion of three dimensions.

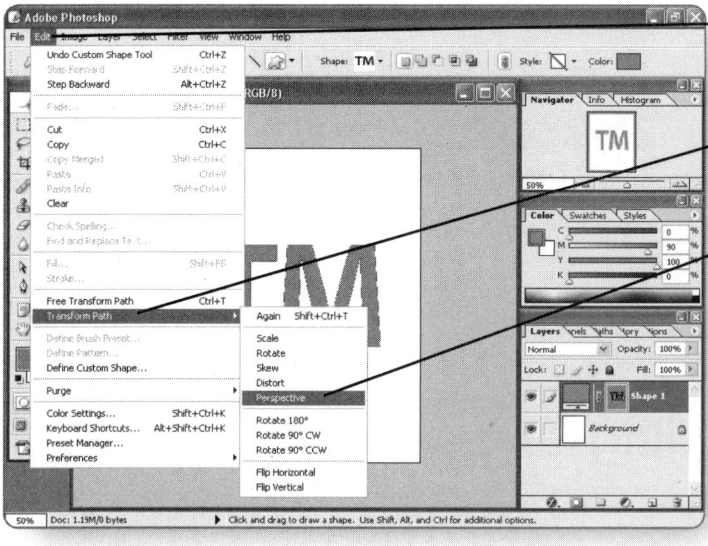

1. Click on **Edit**. The Edit menu will appear.

2. Click on **Transform Path**. A submenu of options will appear.

3. Click Perspective. A series of handles will appear around your object.

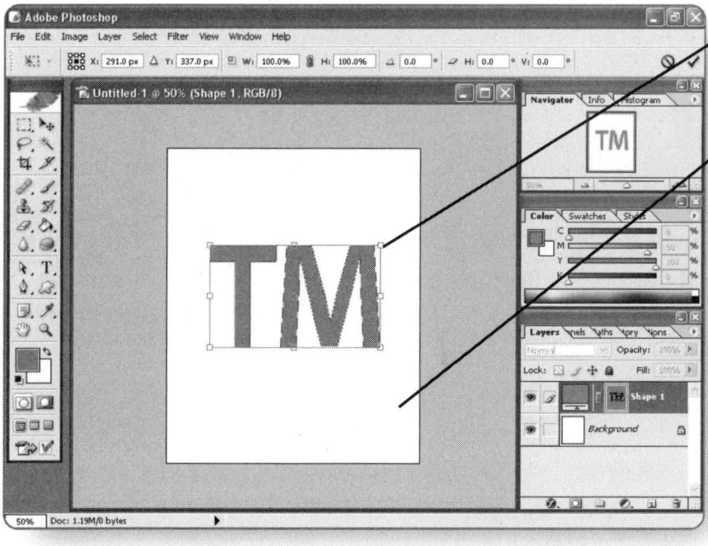

4. Position your **mouse pointer** over one of the handles.

5. Click and **drag** to ad perspective your object. As you drag, the object will change.

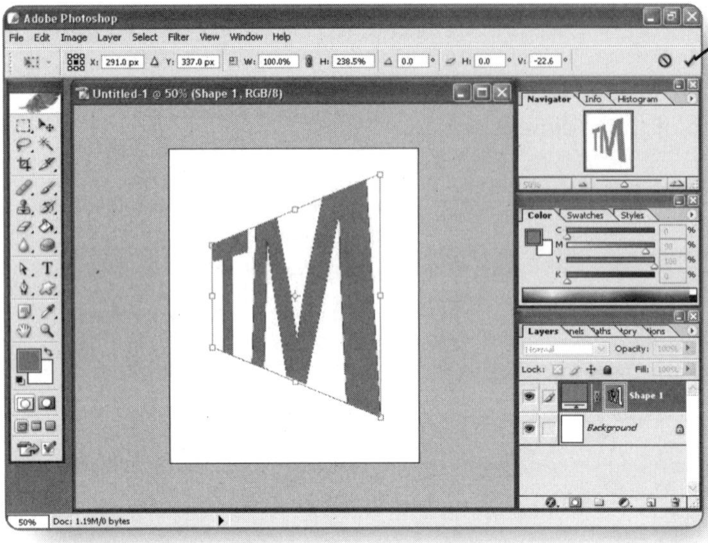

6. **Click** on the **Commit** button to finalize the transformation.

Adding Text

Photoshop CS has enhanced the way in which you work with text, including adding a new editable text on a path feature that allows your text to follow a path as you type. All text that you create appears on a new layer in the image. Photoshop CS offers a variety of tools, such as a spell checker and a find-and-replace feature, to enable you to fine-tune the text in your image.

Creating the Text Layer

Whenever you apply text, it is created on its own separate text layer. By using the options bar, you have a number of choices to customize the text for fun and interesting text treatments in an image.

1. Click on the **Horizontal Type** (or **Vertical Type**) **tool** in the toolbox. It will become the active tool.

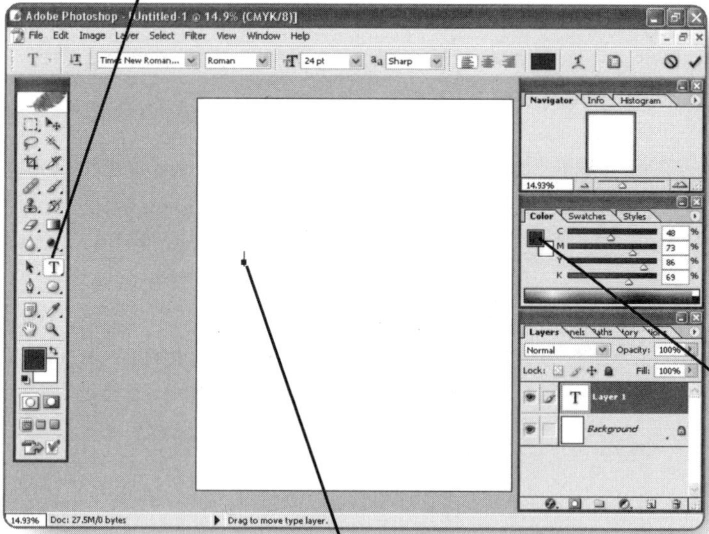

NOTE

To switch between horizontal and vertical type, press and hold the mouse button over the currently selected Type tool and then click on the desired option.

2. Select the desired **foreground color** using the method of your choice. The color you select will become active for the tool and will become the fill color for the text.

3. Click once on the page. An insertion point will appear where you can begin to type.

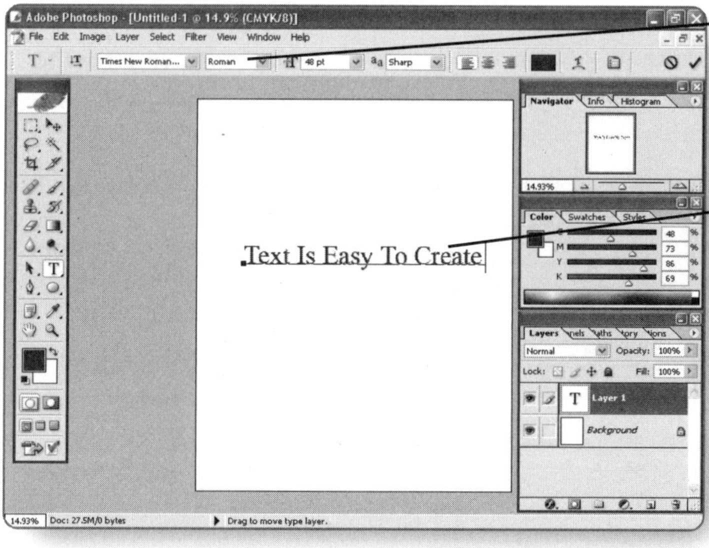

4. Choose the desired **settings** in the options bar. Your selections will become the active settings for the tool.

5. Type the desired **text**. Your text will appear in the text box.

Warping Text

Photoshop CS comes with a variety of warp options for distorting the look of your text. After you've created your text, manipulating it with a warp is simply a matter of selecting the type of warp you'd like to apply.

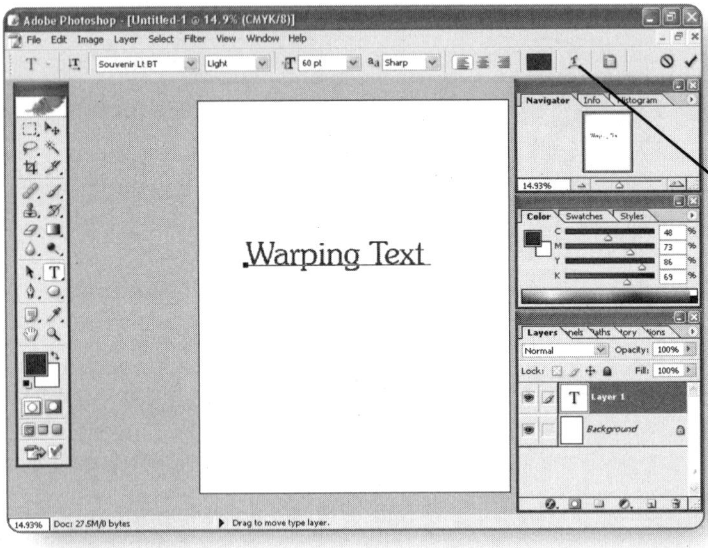

Ensure that you have the text layer selected and the text tool enabled before proceeding with the steps to warp the text.

1. **Click** on the **Create warped text** button. A Warp Text dialog box will open.

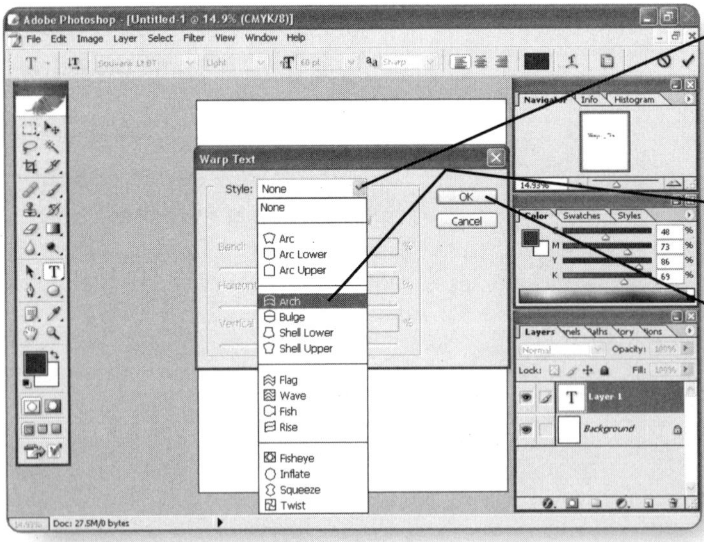

2. **Click** on the **down arrow** to open the Style drop-down list that contains different warp options.

3. **Click** on the desired **option**. It will be selected.

4. **Click** on **OK**. The warp will be applied to your text.

TIP

Once you have warped a piece of text, you are not stuck with that distortion. You can always go back and apply a different warp to the text. You start by selecting the desired text layer, then select any Type tool to bring up the options bar which contains the Warp options that can be reapplied.

Fit Text to Path

One of the enhanced features in Photoshop CS is the capability to create editable text on a path. To do this, you must first create a path. Paths will be covered in detail in Chapter 10, but for now, we will use a simple path for this example.

1. **Click** on the **Pen tool**. It will be selected.

2. **Click** on the **Paths button** in the options bar. It will be activated.

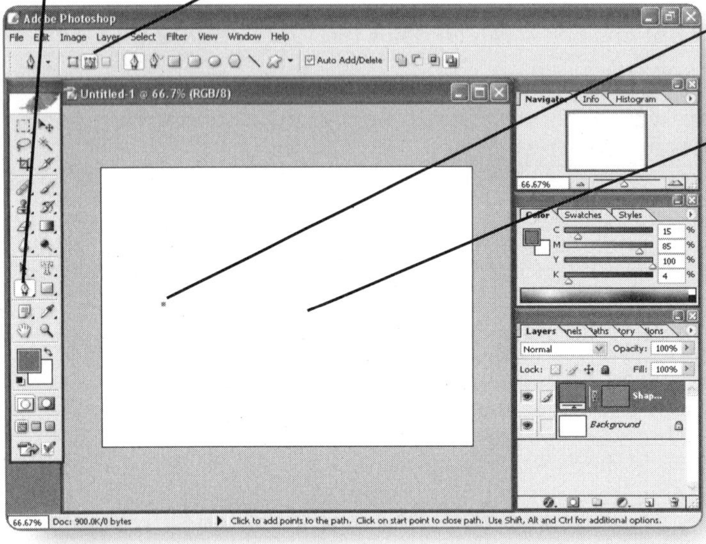

3. **Click once** on the page. A dot will appear.

4. **Position** the **mouse pointer** to the **right** of the dot you have created.

5. **Drag** downward. A path will appear.

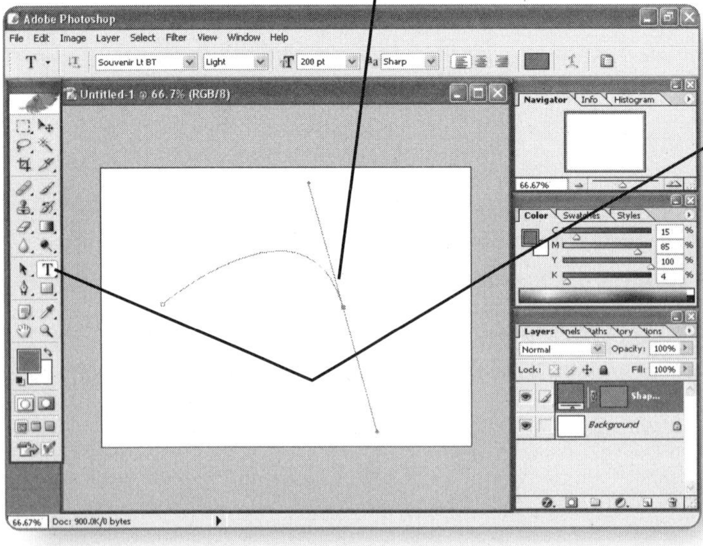

6. **Release** the **mouse button**. A path will now be created.

7. **Click** on the **Horizontal Type** (or **Vertical Type**) **tool** in the toolbox. It will become the active tool.

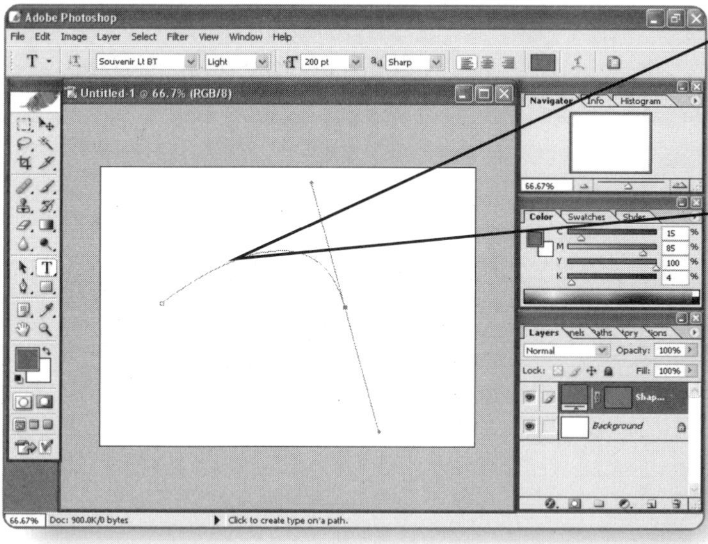

8. **Position** the **mouse pointer** over the **path**. The cursor will have a little line through it when it is over a path.

9. **Click once**. You can now begin typing on the path.

10. **Type** the desired **text**. As you type, the text will appear along the path.

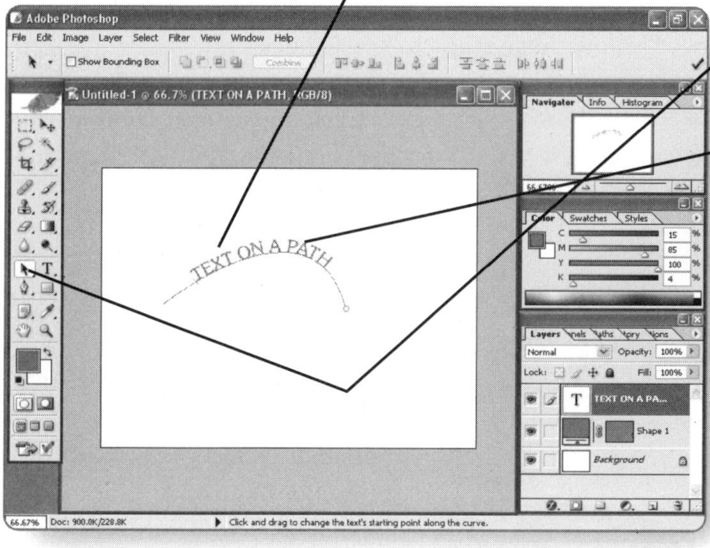

11. **Click** the **Path Selection tool**. It will be activated.

12. **Position** the **mouse pointer** directly over the text on the path.

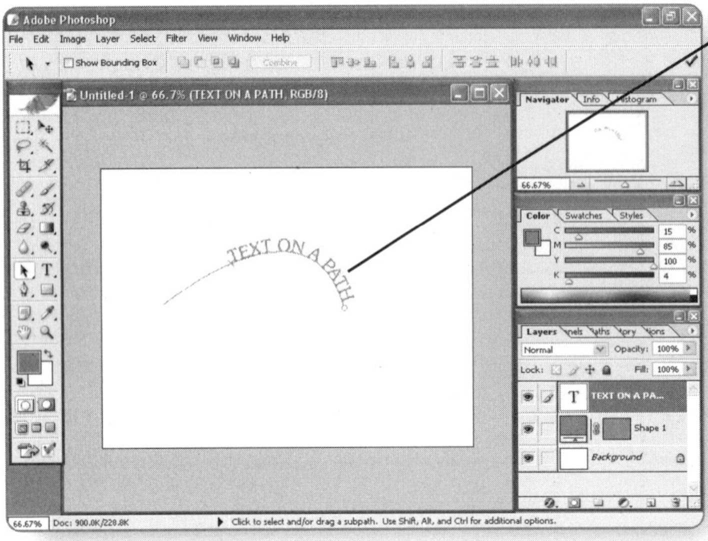

13. Drag to the **left** or **right** to reposition the text along the path.

Spell-Checking Text

You'll be investing a lot of time to add professional polish to the images you create and edit in Photoshop. To ensure that you put your best foot forward in your work, you can spell-check the text you've included in the image to ensure its accuracy. Follow these steps to spell-check text.

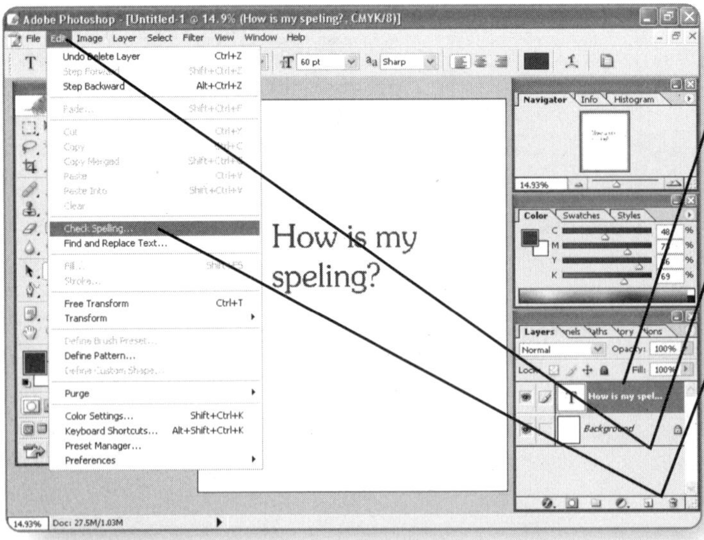

1. **Click** on the **text layer** in the Layers palette. It will become the active layer.
2. **Click** on **Edit**. The Edit menu will appear.
3. **Click** on **Check Spelling**. The Check Spelling dialog box will open and display the first word not found in the spell checker's dictionary.

4a. Click on the **replacement** to use in the Suggestions list. The replacement word will be selected.

4b. Click on **Change**. The spell checker will replace the word in the image file.

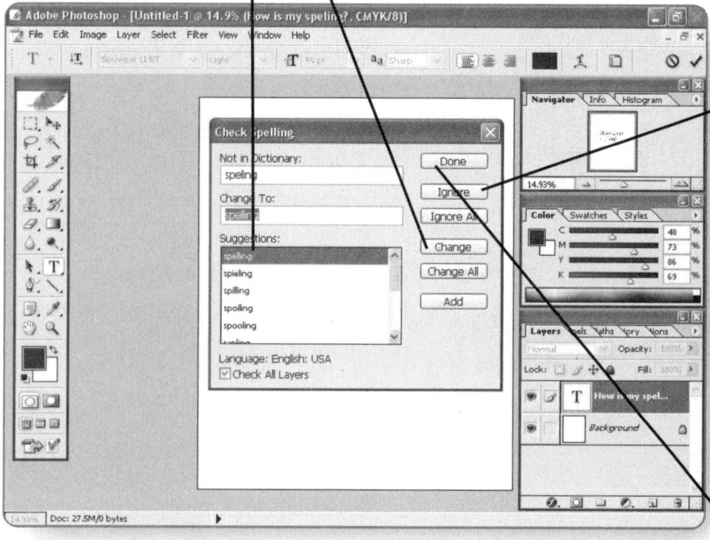

OR

4c. Click on **Ignore**. The spell checker will skip the word without replacing it.

5. Repeat step **4** as necessary. The spell-checking will continue until the spell checker finds no additional unrecognized words, at which point it will display a message telling you that the spell check is complete.

6. Click on **Done**. The Check Spelling dialog box will close.

Creating or Displaying a Brush

Photoshop CS enables you to create your own custom brushes, giving you maximum creative power for editing and developing image files. This section looks at how to create your own brushes and how to use the new Brushes palette to find and work with available brushes.

Sampling a New Brush

The fastest way to create a new brush is to base it on a shape available in your image. To sample a brush, you have to select a portion of the image on a layer. Chapter 5, "Selecting Image

Content," will explain in detail how to make selections. You can refer to that chapter if you need help with step 1 here. The following steps show you how to create your own brush in Photoshop:

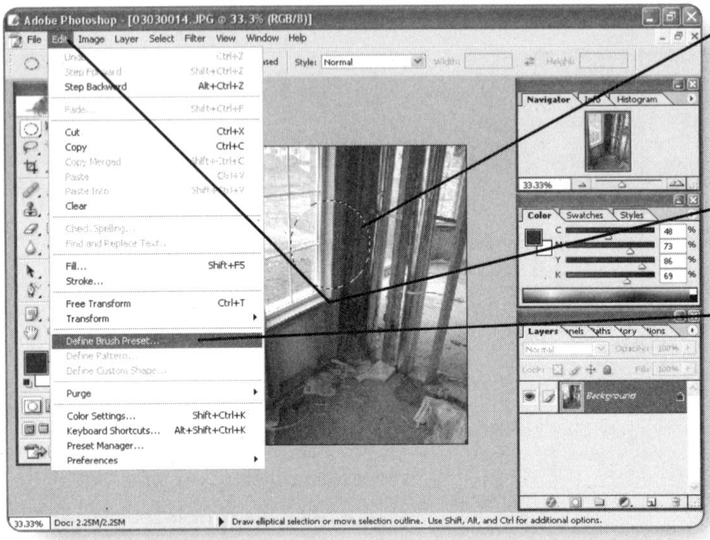

1. **Select** the **image content** to save as a new brush shape. The selection marquee will appear in the image.

2. **Click** on **Edit**. The Edit menu will appear.

3. **Click** on **Define Brush Preset**. The Brush Name dialog box will open.

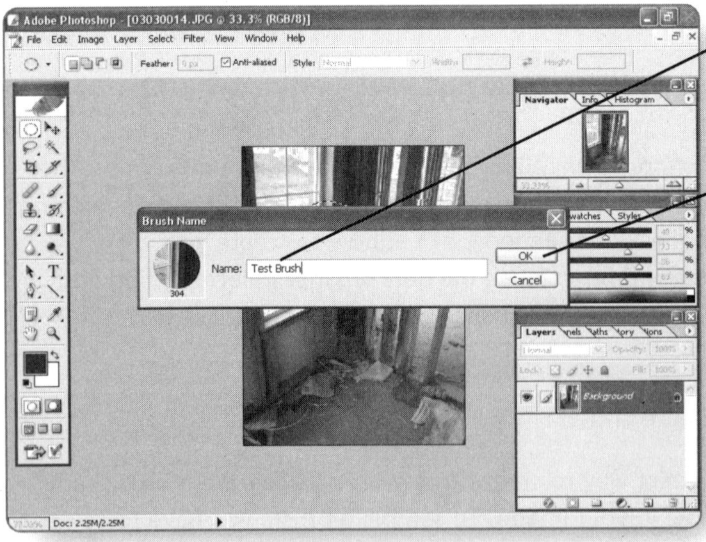

4. **Type** a **brush name**. The name will appear in the Name text box.

5. **Click** on **OK**. The brush will be created and will be included in the Brush drop-down list on the options bar choices for painting tools.

Opening the Brushes Palette

Photoshop CS offers a Brushes palette that you can use to work with available brushes, including custom brushes you've created. The easiest way to access the Brushes palette is from the options bar when you have the Brush tool selected.

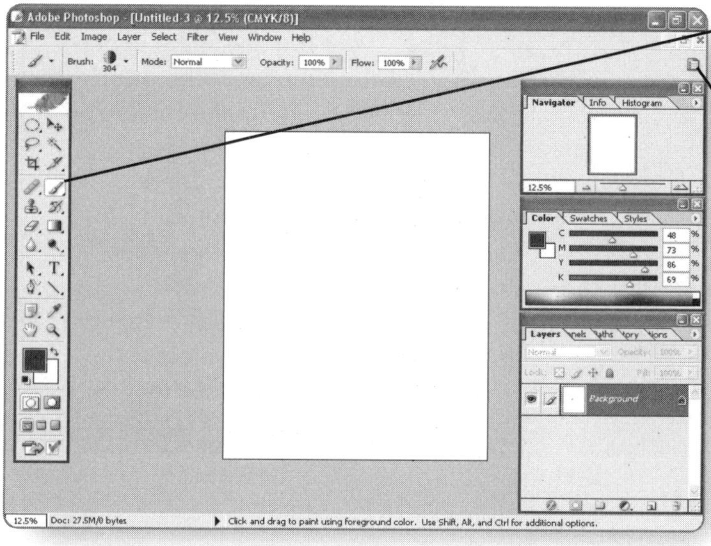

1. **Click** on the **Brush tool**. It will be selected.

2. **Click** on **Toggle the Brush Palette** button in the options bar.

Deleting a Brush

You might create a brush and find that it doesn't offer the effect you had hoped for. In such an instance, you can delete the brush so that it no longer takes up space among the brush choices. Follow these steps to use the Brushes palette to delete a brush.

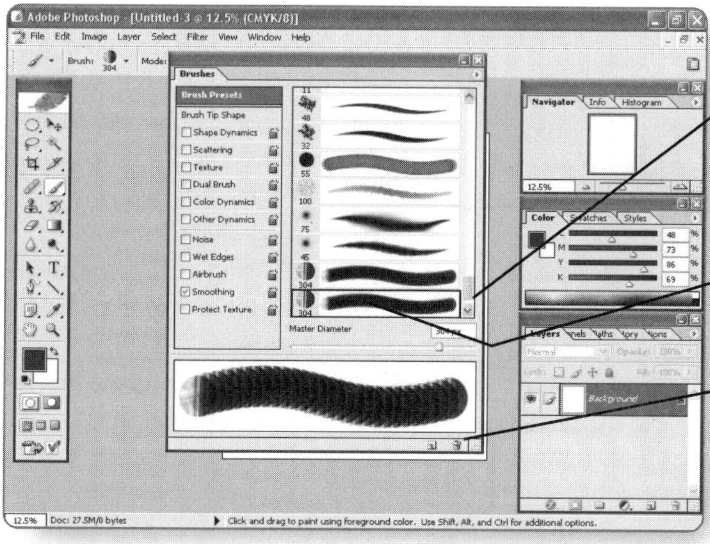

1. **Scroll down** to view additional brushes, if necessary. You will see the brush to delete among the choices.

2. **Click** on the **brush** to delete. It will be selected.

3. **Click** on the **Delete Brush** button in the lower-right corner of the Brushes palette. A message will appear to prompt you to confirm the deletion.

4. Click on **OK**. The brush will be deleted.

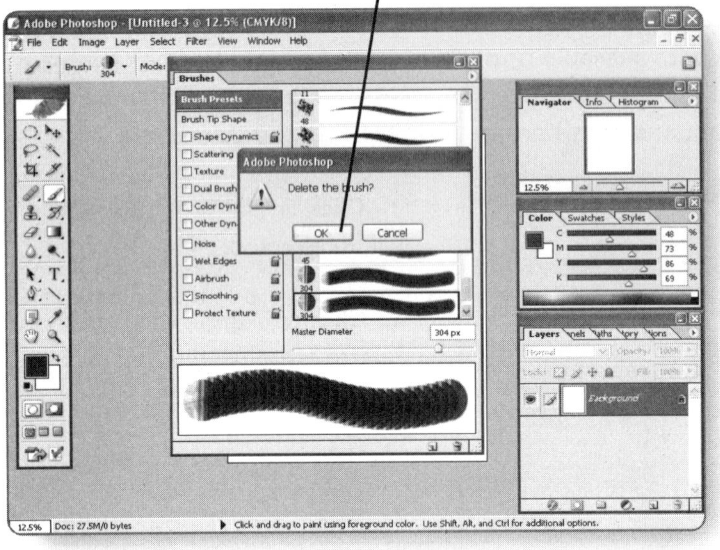

TIP

As with other palettes, the Brushes palette features a menu you can display if you click on the button with the right triangle in the upper-right corner of the palette. You can use the choices on the menu that appears to create, rename, and otherwise work with brushes. The menu also offers a variety of additional brush collections that you can select and display in Photoshop.

Using a Custom Brush

Using a custom brush shape is just like using any other brush shape provided with Photoshop. This final set of steps shows a sample custom brush, not to teach you again how to select a brush, but to show you how cool a custom brush can be and to get you excited about the possibilities in your own work. The following steps show an example of using a custom brush based on the shape of a daffodil.

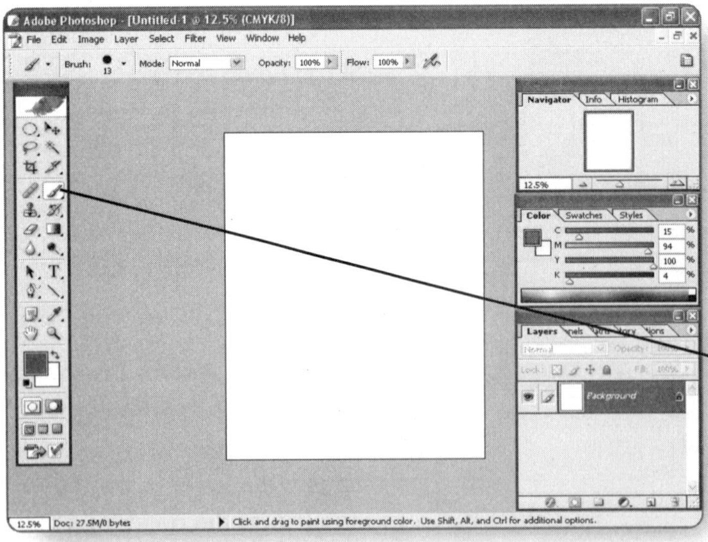

1. Click on the **Brush tool** in the toolbox. It will become the active tool.

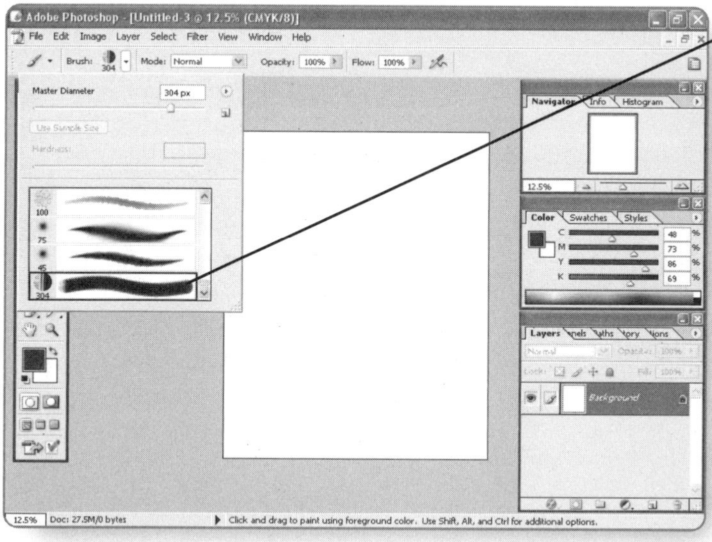

2. **Open** the **Brush** Preset Picker **drop-down list** on the options bar, click on the custom brush to use, and then close the drop-down list. The custom brush you selected will become the active brush shape.

TIP

Custom brushes typically appear at the bottom of the list of brush choices.

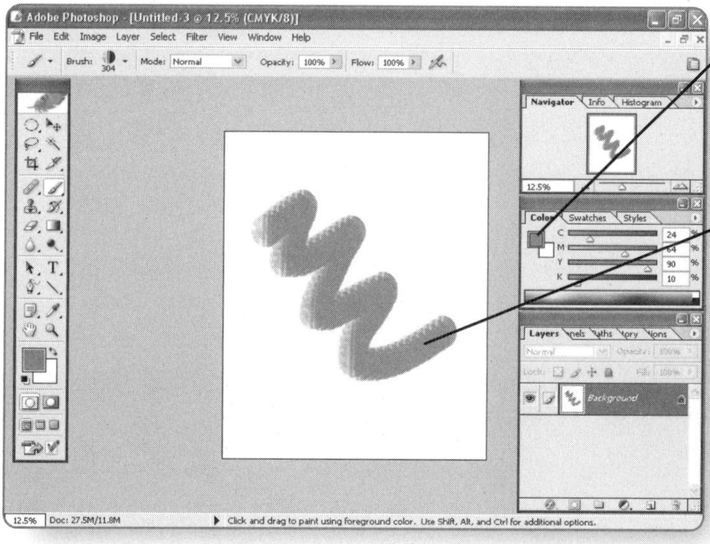

3. **Select** the **foreground color** using the method of your choice. The color you select will become active for the paintbrush.

4. **Drag** in the work area. A paint stroke in the shape of the brush will appear.

4

Zooming and Panning

As you're working with your image, you may need to zoom in to make minute changes, zoom out to see how your image looks overall, and otherwise move around to ensure that you're working with just the image area you need. Photoshop offers a number of techniques you can use to change your view of the image. In this chapter, you'll learn how to:

- Zoom in and out of an image
- View the actual pixel size or print size
- Fit the image to the screen
- Scroll with the scroll bar
- Move around with the Hand tool and Navigator

Using the Zoom Tool

You may have worked with a zoom tool in another program, clicking on a file to zoom in and then clicking again to zoom back out. Photoshop's Zoom tool offers the same behavior plus some additional features to help you quickly display an image in the view that works best. Note that zooming merely adjusts the size of the image file onscreen so that you can work more effectively. Zooming does not adjust the dimensions of the file itself and therefore does not affect the size at which the file prints.

Zooming In and Out

The most common zoom operations are to zoom in (to get a closer view of the image) and to zoom out (to get a farther, more overall view of the image). The steps here illustrate these common uses for the Zoom tool:

1. **Click** on the **Zoom tool** in the Photoshop toolbox. The mouse pointer will change to a magnifying glass, and the options bar will show the options for the Zoom tool.

2. **Click** on the **image**, near the spot you want to magnify. Each time you click with the default zoom pointer (a magnifying glass with a plus sign in it), Photoshop will zoom in on the image by one zoom increment.

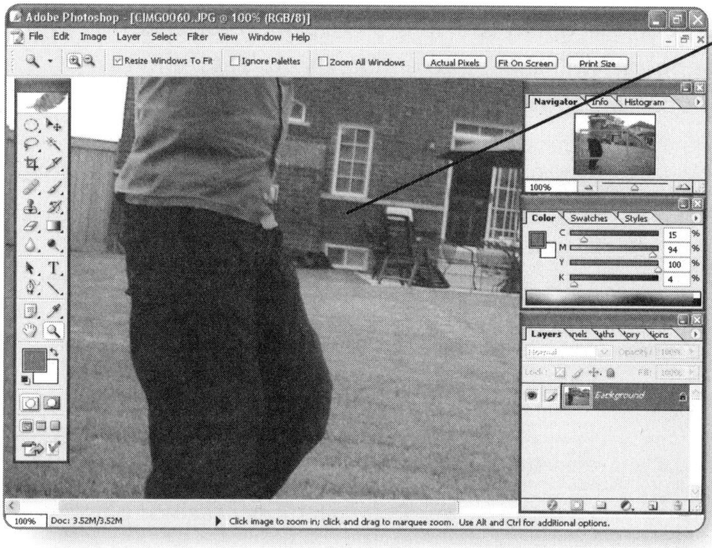

3. **Press** and **hold** the **Alt key** and then **click** on the **image**. Photoshop will zoom out by one zoom increment each time you Alt+click with the mouse pointer for zooming out (a magnifying glass with a minus sign).

> **NOTE**
>
> The remainder of this book will use the phrase Alt+click to indicate when you should press and hold the Alt key while clicking on a screen item.

Zooming to Print and Pixel Size

You also can use the Zoom tool to zoom the image to one of two predetermined sizes: its pixel size (100%) or the actual print size (if you've used the Page Setup commands to change the size for the printout). You'll learn about these two zoom types next.

1. **Click** on the **Zoom tool** in the Photoshop toolbox. The mouse pointer will change to a magnifying glass, and the options bar will show the options for the Zoom tool.

2. **Click** on **Resize Windows To Fit** on the options bar. A check will appear in the box. When checked, Resize Windows To Fit will change the window size to accommodate the zoomed image. Also, leave Ignore Palettes unchecked. (It should be unchecked by default.) Ignore Palettes turns off color palette features that may change the image's appearance as you zoom.

TIP

Double-clicking on the Zoom tool in the toolbox zooms to 100% size.

3. **Click** on **Print Size button** on the options bar. Photoshop will zoom the image to the actual size it will be when printed.

Fitting the Image to the Screen

To take advantage of all the workspace available in Photoshop, you can zoom the image to the screen size using the Zoom tool, as explained here.

1. **Click** on the **Zoom tool** in the Photoshop toolbox. The mouse pointer will change to a magnifying glass, and the options bar will show the options for the Zoom tool.

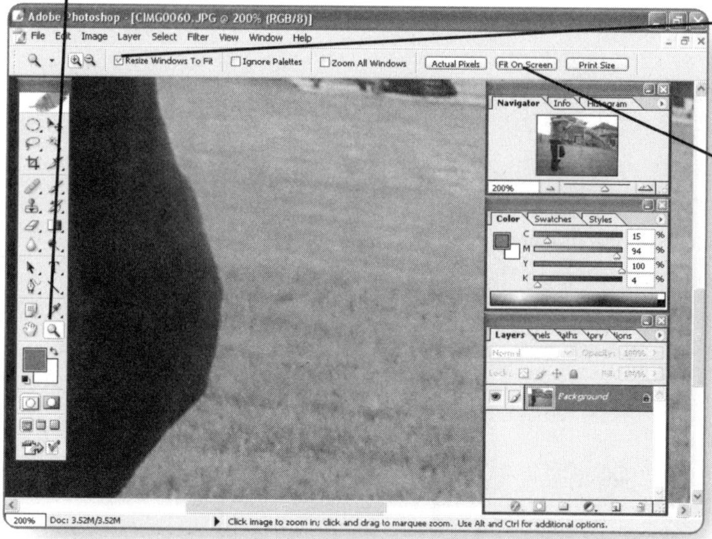

2. **Click** on **Resize Windows To Fit** on the options bar if it is not already selected.

3. **Click** on the **Fit On Screen button**. Photoshop will zoom the image to the largest zoom setting it can have and fit on the screen.

TIP

While the Zoom tool is active, you also can right-click (Control click on Mac OS) on the image to see a shortcut menu with commands for zooming the image.

Changing the View Zone

If you did not opt to resize the image window as you zoomed, zooming in on the image may magnify it to such a size that the image can't fully display in the image window. When this happens, you can use a few different methods to choose which area of the image appears in the image window, thus enabling you to view and work with that portion of the image. This section explores those methods: scroll bars, the Hand tool, and the Navigator.

Using Scroll Bars

Scroll bars appear whenever you've resized the image window so that it can't display all of the image. When this happens, you can use the scroll bars as described next to scroll into view the portion of the image that you'd like to work with.

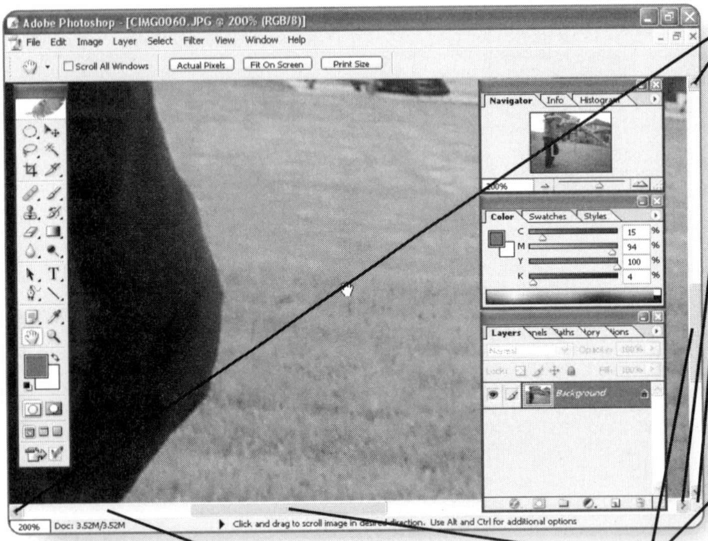

1. **Click** on a **scroll arrow** on either the vertical or horizontal scroll bar. Each time you click, Photoshop will scroll the image by a small increment.

2. **Drag** a **scroll bar** box. Photoshop will scroll the image much more quickly.

3. **Click** on the **scroll bar** itself above or below (or to the left or right of) the scroll box. Depending on the scroll bar and the side of the scroll box on which you click, Photoshop scrolls the image as far as possible in the designated direction.

Using the Hand Tool

You can use the Hand tool to scroll the image in multiple directions at once—much like using both scroll bars simultaneously. The following steps explain how to do so.

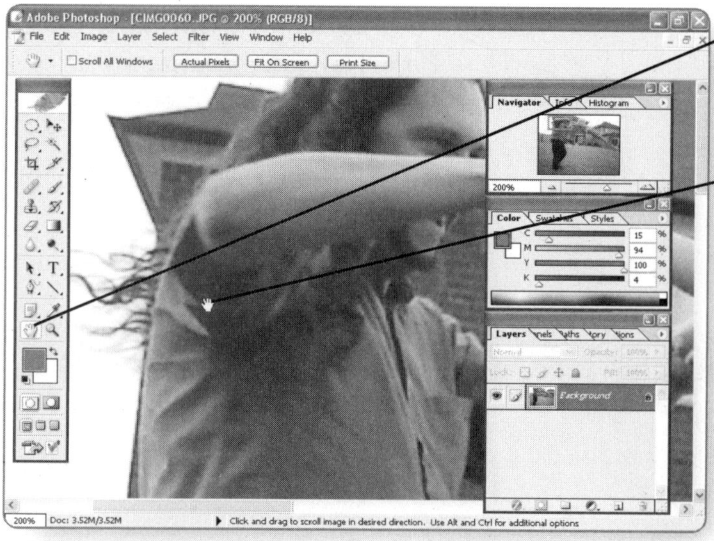

1. **Click** on the **Hand tool** in the toolbox. The mouse pointer will change to a hand pointer.

2. **Click** and **drag** the **image** with the hand pointer. Photoshop will scroll the image in the same direction that you drag.

Using the Navigator

You can use the Navigator palette for multiple purposes—to change the image zoom and to scroll the displayed portion of the image. These steps describe both uses for the palette.

1. **Click** on the **Navigator tab** in the Navigator palette, if necessary. If the palette is not onscreen, it can be opened from the Window menu. The Navigator tab will become active.

2. **Drag** the **zoom slider** in the Navigator palette. Photoshop will zoom the image to the specified size.

NOTE

You also can type a zoom percentage in the text box on the Navigator palette and then press Enter, or you can click on one of the buttons at either end of the zoom slider in the Navigator palette to change the zoom.

3. **Drag** the **red box** on the thumbnail image in the Navigator palette with the hand pointer. Photoshop will scroll the image to display the portion of the image bounded by the red box in the thumbnail.

5

Selecting Image Content

One of the questions I get asked most often during my image-editing training classes is how to take someone's head and put on another person's body. The answer: good selections. Before you can delete, move, fill, or replace part of an image, you have to select the portion of the image with which you want to work. Photoshop offers a number of selection tools that you can use to zero in on an area to edit with precision and control. In this chapter, you'll learn how to:

- Select rectangular or oval shapes
- Make an irregular selection
- Select by color
- Add or remove part of the selection
- Cancel the selection

Using the Marquee Tools

The Marquee tools appear in the upper-left corner of the Photoshop toolbox. Use the Marquee tools to make selections that are regular in shape—rectangles, squares, ovals, circles, or one-pixel borders (also called a row or column selection).

> **NOTE**
>
> If the area to select appears on a particular layer, you need to select that layer in the Layers palette before using any type of tool to make the selection. See Chapter 8, "Working with Layers" to learn more about selecting layers.

Selecting a Rectangle

The following steps show you how easy it is to make a selection that's rectangular in shape:

1. **Press** and **hold** the **mouse button** on the **Marquee tool** in the Photoshop toolbox. The shortcut menu for the Marquee tool will appear.

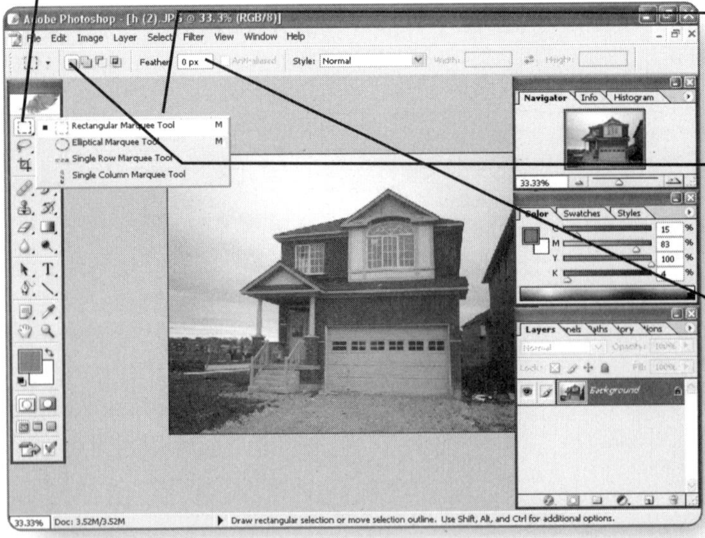

2. **Click** on **Rectangular Marquee Tool**. The Rectangular Marquee tool will become active.

3. **Click** on the **New Selection button** on the options bar, if necessary.

4. **Type** an **entry** (in pixels, up to 250) in the Feather text box on the options bar. The feathering setting will become active.

> **TIP**
>
> Feathering blurs the edges of the selection. The results of feathering become more apparent if you copy and paste the selection.

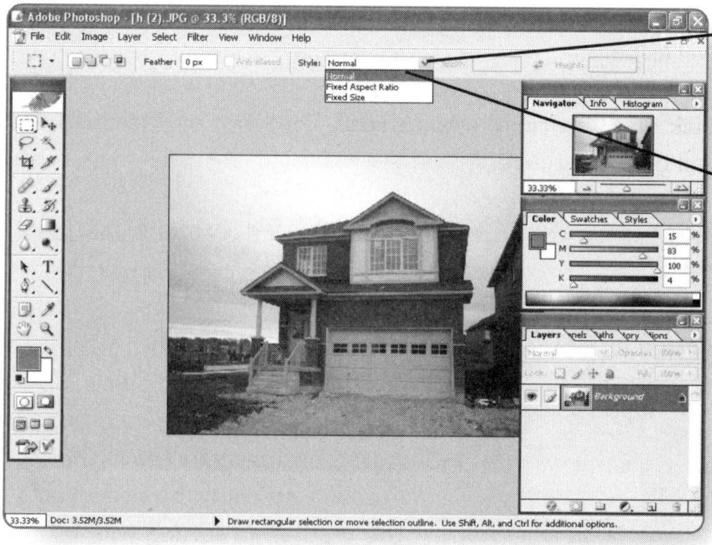

5. **Click** on the **down arrow** next to the Style drop-down list. The list will appear.

6. **Click** on **Normal**. The normal selection method will become active.

> **NOTE**
>
> If you select either the Fixed Aspect Ratio or Fixed Size choice from the Style drop-down list, the Width and Height text boxes become active. Type an entry in one of the text boxes (for Fixed Aspect) or both text boxes to specify a selection size and then click on the image to make the selection.

7. **Drag** on the image over the area to select. (Press and hold Shift as you drag to select a perfect square.)

8. **Release** the **mouse button**. The selection marquee will appear on the image.

Selecting an Ellipse

If you need to make a round or elliptical selection instead, you can use the following steps:

1. **Press** and **hold** the **mouse button** on the **Marquee tool** in the Photoshop toolbox. The shortcut menu for the Marquee tool will appear.

2. **Click** on **Elliptical Marquee Tool**. The Elliptical Marquee tool will become active.

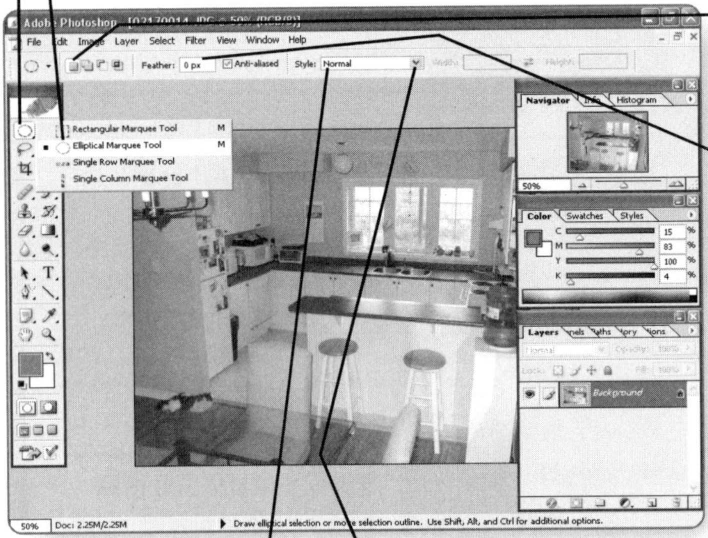

3. **Click** on the **New Selection button** on the options bar, if necessary.

4. **Type** an **entry** (in pixels, up to 250) in the Feather text box on the options bar. Leave the Anti-aliased check box checked. The feathering setting will become active.

5. **Click** on the **down arrow** next to the Style drop-down list. The drop-down list will appear.

6. **Click** on **Normal**. The normal selection method will become active.

> **TIP**
>
> Anti-aliasing fixes jaggedness along the edges of a selection. This occurs when the selection marquee has curves.

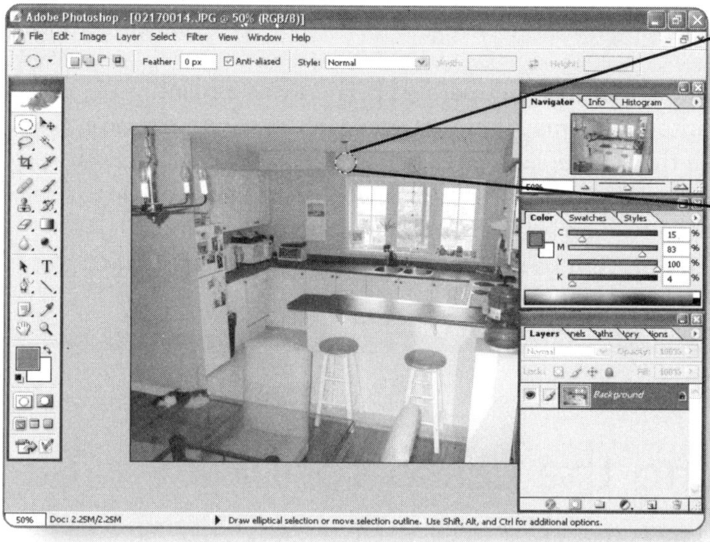

7. **Drag** on the image over the area to select. (Press and hold Shift as you drag to select a perfect circle.)

8. **Release** the **mouse button**. The selection marquee will appear on the image.

Selecting a Row or Column

Use the Single Row Marquee tool or the Single Column Marquee tool to select a one-pixel-wide area in the image. You can then cut or copy and paste the selection to use it as a border in another image.

1. **Press** and **hold** the **mouse button** on the Marquee tool in the Photoshop toolbox. The shortcut menu for the Marquee tool will appear.

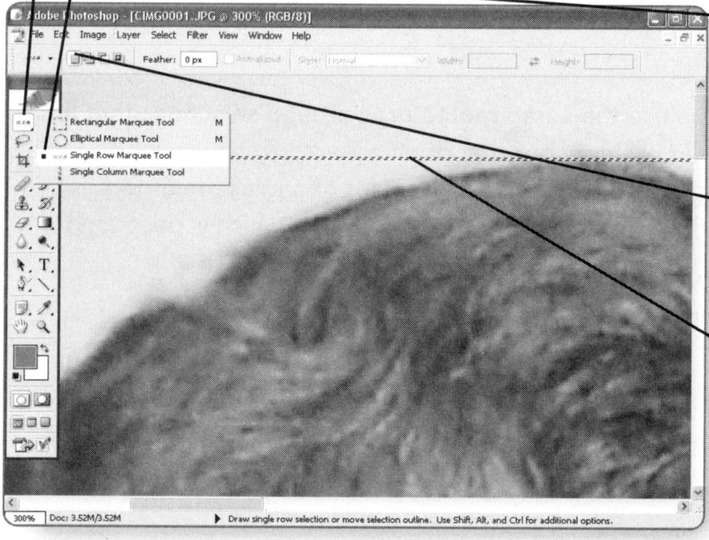

2. **Click** on **Single Row Marquee Tool** or **Single Column Marquee Tool**. The specified marquee tool will become active.

3. **Click** on the **New Selection button** on the options bar, if necessary.

4. **Click** on the **image** over the area to select as a border. The selection marquee will appear on the image.

NOTE

Because Photoshop operates primarily as a paint program, you may find that you can't separate out an area that you'd like to select, no matter which selection technique you use. That's why you retain more editing flexibility in an image if you place the objects for the image on various layers. See Chapter 8 to learn how to create and use layers.

Using the Lasso Tool

Like the Marquee tool, the Lasso tool offers a few different techniques that you can employ to make selections in an image. The Lasso tool's variations enable you to make selections that are not typical or symmetrical in shape. You can select an irregular area by dragging (using the Lasso tool), select a polygon by clicking to place the angles (using the Polygonal Lasso tool), or get help selecting an irregular area (using the Magnetic Lasso tool).

Selecting an Odd Shape

You can use the Lasso tool to drag around selections that are irregular in shape but that don't necessarily have a lot of angle points. (If the shape does have a lot of angles or corners, consider using the Polygonal Lasso tool, which is described next.)

1. **Press** and **hold** the **mouse button** on the **Lasso tool** in the Photoshop toolbox. The shortcut menu for the Lasso tool will appear.

2. **Click** on **Lasso Tool**. The Lasso tool will become active.

3. **Click** on the **New Selection button** on the options bar, if necessary.

4. **Type** an **entry** (in pixels, up to 250) in the Feather text box on the options bar. Leave the Anti-aliased check box checked. The feathering setting will become active.

5. **Drag** around the desired area to select it. A line will appear as you drag.

6. Continue dragging all the way back to the starting point or **release** the **mouse button** to close the selection. The selection marquee will appear on the image.

Selecting a Polygon

Use the Polygonal Lasso tool to select odd shapes that have corners and angles, as the following steps demonstrate:

1. Press and **hold** the **mouse button** on the Lasso tool in the Photoshop toolbox. The shortcut menu for the Lasso tool will appear.

2. Click on **Polygonal Lasso Tool**. The Polygonal Lasso tool will become active.

3. Click on the **New Selection button** on the options bar, if necessary.

4. Type an **entry** (in pixels, up to 250) in the Feather text box on the options bar. Leave the Anti-aliased check box checked. The feathering setting will become active.

5. **Click** around the **desired area** to specify corners for the selection. A line will appear as you click.

6. **Double-click** the **last point** to close the selection. The selection marquee will appear on the image.

> **TIP**
>
> You can press the Alt key while using either the Lasso tool or the Polygonal Lasso tool to switch between freehand drawing and clicking to set corner points. Press Delete while using any Lasso tool to remove the most recently drawn selection segment.

Using the Magnetic Lasso

The Magnetic Lasso tool helps you make a selection by snapping to fastening points along the edge of a shape in an image.

1. **Click** and **hold** the **Lasso tool** in the Photoshop toolbox. The shortcut menu for the Lasso tool will appear.

2. **Click** on **Magnetic Lasso Tool**. The Magnetic Lasso tool will become active.

3. **Click** on the **New Selection** button on the options bar, if necessary.

4. **Change** other **settings** on the options bar as needed:

- **Make** an **entry** (in pixels, up to 250) in the Feather text box on the options bar. Leave the Anti-aliased check box checked. The feathering setting will become active.
- **Change** the **Width** text box entry (in pixels, between 1 and 40) to set the search width for the tool. The tool will look for edges within the specified zone beside the points you identify with the mouse.
- **Change** the **Edge Contrast** text box entry (in percentages between 1 and 100) to identify how much contrast the tool requires. A lower setting will enable the tool to find edges with less contrast, whereas a higher setting will restrict the tool to finding only high-contrast edges.
- **Change** the **Frequency** text box entry (between 0 and 100) if necessary. A higher setting causes the tool to set more fastening points, whereas a lower setting results in fewer fastening points.

5. **Drag** on the **desired area** to specify the selection border. (Click to place a fastening point in a particular location.) The selection marquee will appear on the image.

The Magic Wand

One of the quickest ways to make a selection is to use the Magic Wand tool. If all the pixels in the area you want to select are about the same color and adjoin one another in the image, the Magic Wand tool will select them with one click.

1. **Click** on the **Magic Wand tool** in the Photoshop toolbox. The Magic Wand tool will become active.

2. **Click** on the **New Selection button** on the options bar, if necessary.

3. **Change** other **settings** on the options bar as needed:

- **Change** the **Tolerance text box** entry (between 0 and 255) to specify how much variation can occur between the colors included in the selection. A low entry will result in a smaller selection zone composed of fewer like colors, whereas a higher entry will result in a larger selection zone.
- **Leave** the **Anti-aliased check box** checked. The tool will smooth the edges of the selection.
- Leave the Contiguous check box checked. The tool will select all adjoining pixels of the same (or similar) color, not just the pixel on which you click.
- Click on the Use All Layers check box to check it if desired. The tool will then select the matching colors on all layers in the picture.

4. **Click** on the **color** to select on the image with the Magic Wand tool. The selection marquee will appear on the image.

Selecting by Color Range

Selecting by color works somewhat like the Magic Wand tool, except it enables you to select all the pixels of the specified color in the image—not just adjoining or contiguous pixels.

1. **Click** on **Select**. The Select menu will appear.

2. **Click** on **Color Range**. The Color Range dialog box will open.

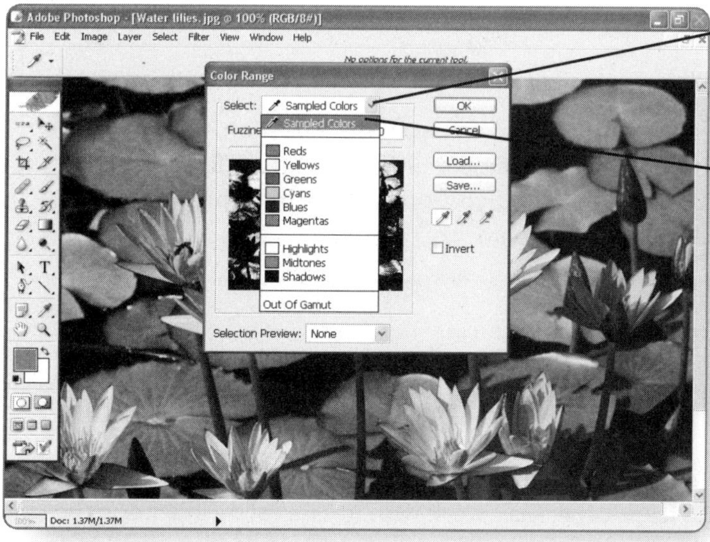

3. **Click** on the **down arrow** beside the Select list. The Select list will open.

4. **Click** on a **selection type** in the list. If you choose anything other than Sampled Colors from the list, Photoshop immediately previews the color selection in the dialog box, and you can skip to step 8. If you choose Sampled Colors, continue with the next step.

5. **Drag** the **Fuzziness slider** to change its setting, if necessary. Increasing this value will cause Photoshop to select colors similar to the color you select for the match.

6. **Click** on the **Eyedropper Tool** button to select it, if necessary. The Eyedropper tool will become active.

7. **Click** on the **desired color** in the picture. If you choose anything other than Sampled Colors from the Select list, Photoshop immediately previews the color selection in the dialog box.

8. **Click** on **OK**. The dialog box will close, and Photoshop will display marquees around the matching selections in the picture.

> **NOTE**
>
> To add or remove colors from the selection, click on either the Add to Sample or Subtract from Sample button (next to the Eyedropper Tool button) and then click a color on the image.

Adjusting a Selection

Once you've made a selection, you can move it, extend it, change it, or otherwise work with it. The following steps run through the possibilities for modifying a selection:

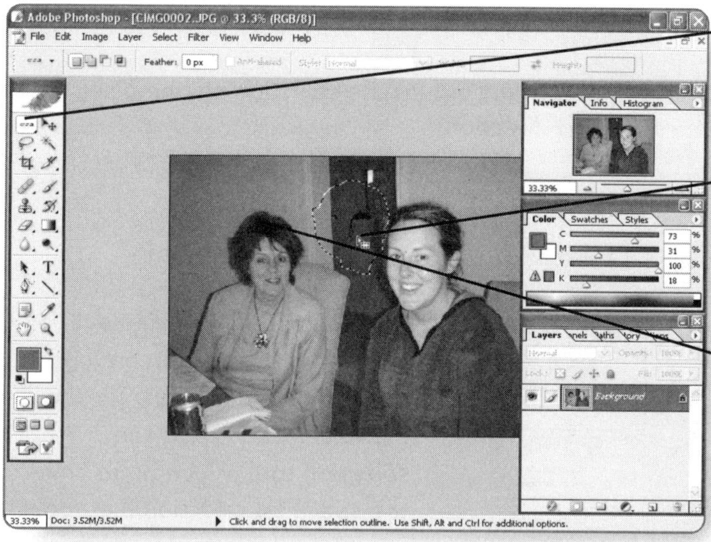

1. Click any of the **Marquee selection tools**. The tool will be highlighted.

2. Position your **mouse pointer** over a selection. The mouse pointer will change to indicate that you are over a selection.

3. Click and **drag** the marquee to a new location. The marquee will move as you drag.

4. Release the **mouse button**. The selection will be moved.

TIP

Pressing an arrow key moves the selection by one pixel in the specified direction.

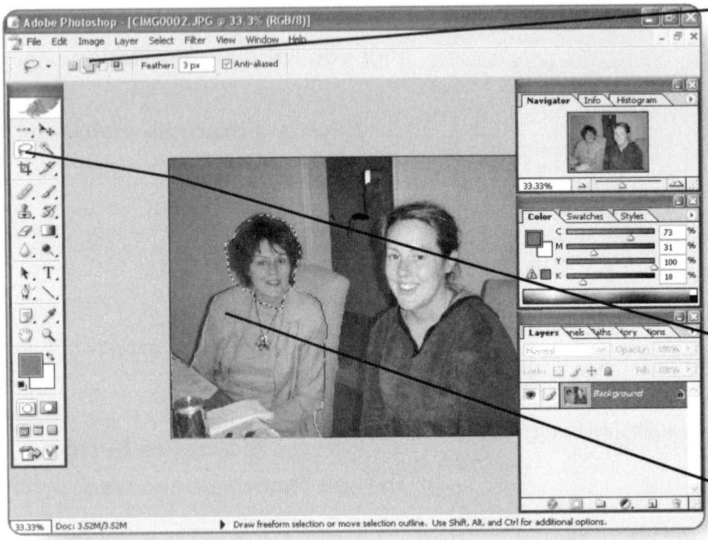

5. Click on the **Add to Selection**, **Subtract from Selection**, or **Intersect with Selection** button on the options bar, if available for the active selection tool. The selection tool will begin to use the specified selection method.

6. Click on the desired **selection tool**. It will be selected.

7. Click and **drag** on the image as required for the active selection tool.

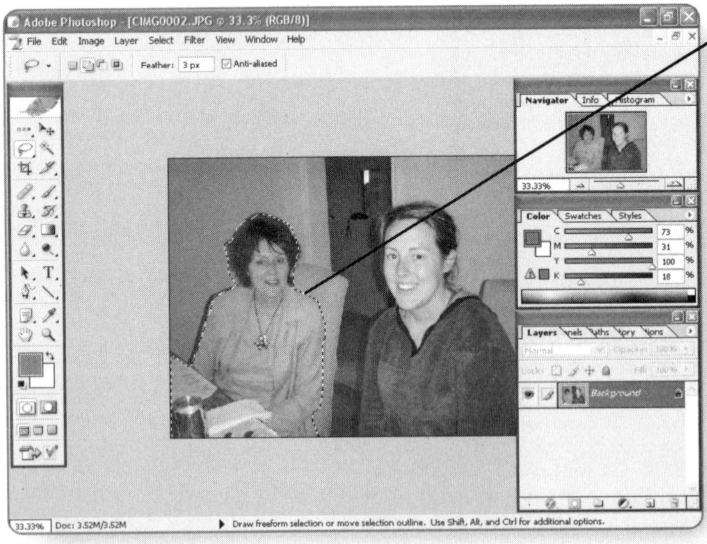

8. Release the **mouse button**. Depending on the selection method selected in step 2, Photoshop adds to, removes from, or crops out the selection.

> **TIP**
>
> You also can press Shift and then use a selection tool to add a selection.

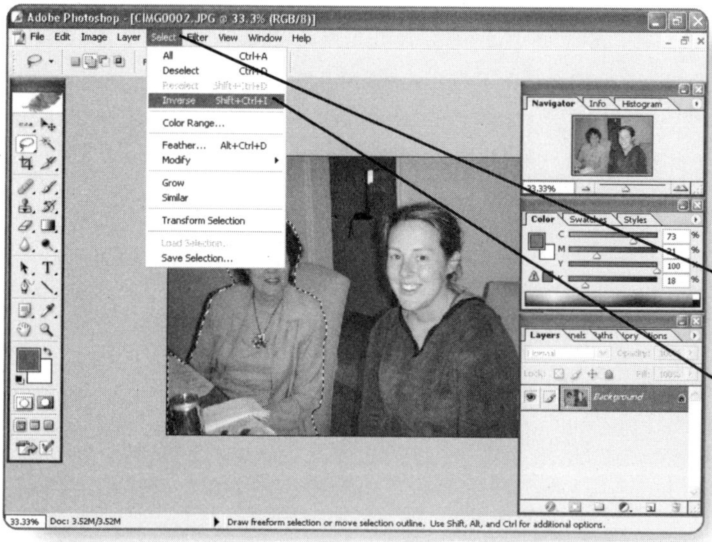

> **TIP**
>
> To remove the latest selection you've added, don't press Delete! Press Ctrl+Z to undo the selection instead.

9. **Click** on **Select**. The Select menu will appear.

10. **Click** on **Inverse**. Photoshop will select the area that previously was not selected in the image and will deselect the area that was selected.

Removing a Selection

When you need to remove or deselect the selection, you can do so with ease.

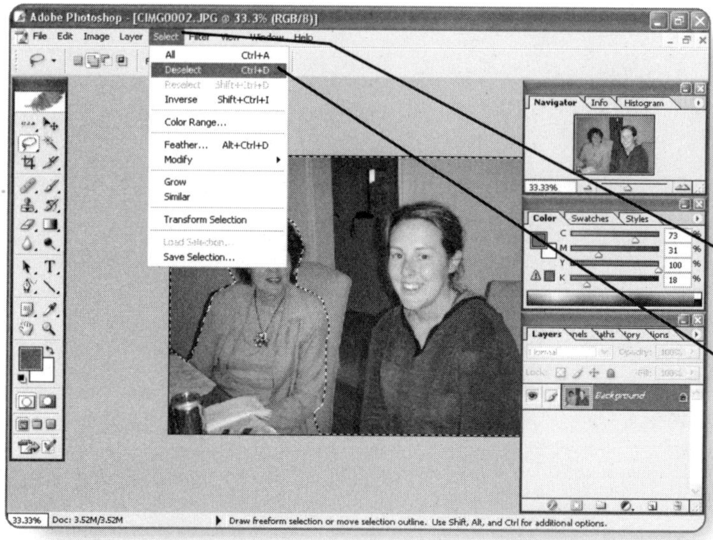

1. **Click** on **Select**. The Select menu will appear.

2. **Click** on **Deselect**. Photoshop will remove the selection immediately, no matter what selection tool or method you used to make the selection.

6

Manipulating Selections

After you've selected part of the image, the fun begins. You can then start manipulating the selection to change the appearance of the image or share information between image files. This chapter introduces you to the basic changes you can make after you've selected part of the information on a layer in the image. (Chapter 8, "Working with Layers," explains how to layer information.) In this chapter, you'll learn how to:

- Delete, move, or copy what you've selected
- Change a selection by transforming or rotating it
- Fine-tune the selection marquee
- Save and reuse a selection
- Undo a change
- Work with the History palette

Deleting a Selection

After you've made a selection, you can remove the contents of the selection by using the Clear command.

1. **Make** a **selection** in the image using the selection tool of your choice. The selection marquee will appear.

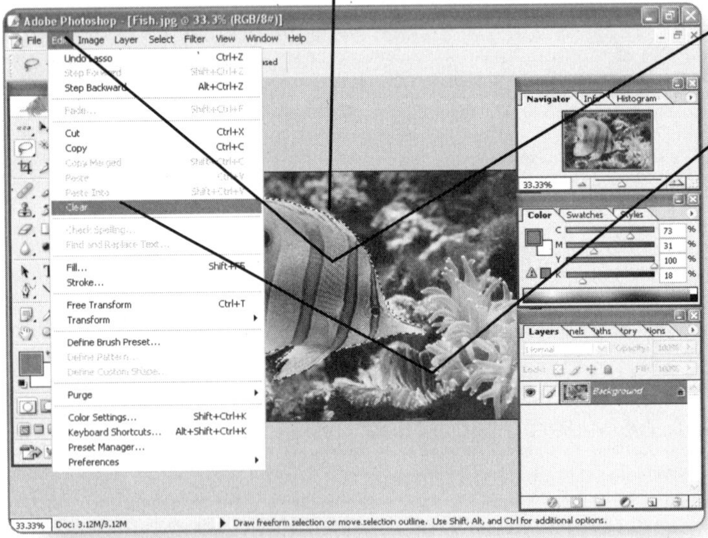

2. **Click** on **Edit**. The Edit menu will appear.

3. **Click** on **Clear**. The selection will disappear completely from the current layer.

> **TIP**
>
> You can press the Delete key in place of steps 2 and 3.

Moving a Selection

Moving a selection requires a tool you haven't used yet—the Move tool. Dragging while the selection tool is active moves the selection marquee only, not the actual image content within that selection. No matter which layer you're working on or what type of content you're dealing with, the Move tool always works in the same way.

1. **Make** a **selection** in the image using the selection tool of your choice. The selection marquee will appear.

2. **Click** on the **Move tool** in the Photoshop toolbox. The Move tool will become active.

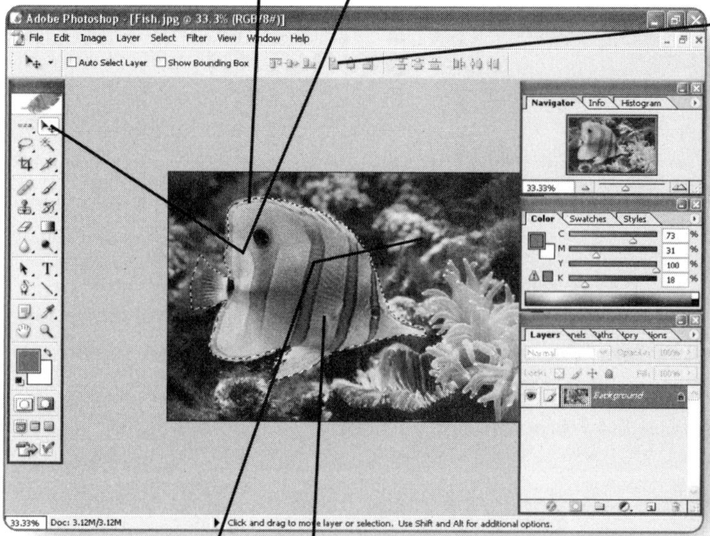

3. **Click** on the desired **options** in the options bar to check them as needed. If you check Auto Select Layer, clicking on an area of the image will select its layer. If you check Show Bounding Box, the selection box may change to show handles.

NOTE

If other buttons become active on the options bar, clicking one of them aligns information within the selection marquee, such as text, relative to the borders of the selection marquee.

4. **Position** the **mouse pointer** over the selection from within the marquee.

5. **Drag** the selection to a new location. The selection will move as you drag.

6. **Release** the **mouse button**. The selection will appear in its final location.

Copying a Selection

You can copy a selection to reuse it in another location, such as on another layer in the image file or in a completely new file. This comes in handy because, once you've drawn or scanned in image content, you can reuse it as often as you need to with a minimum of effort. This example illustrates how to create a new image file from content you copy.

1. **Make** a **selection** in the image using the selection tool of your choice. The selection marquee will appear.

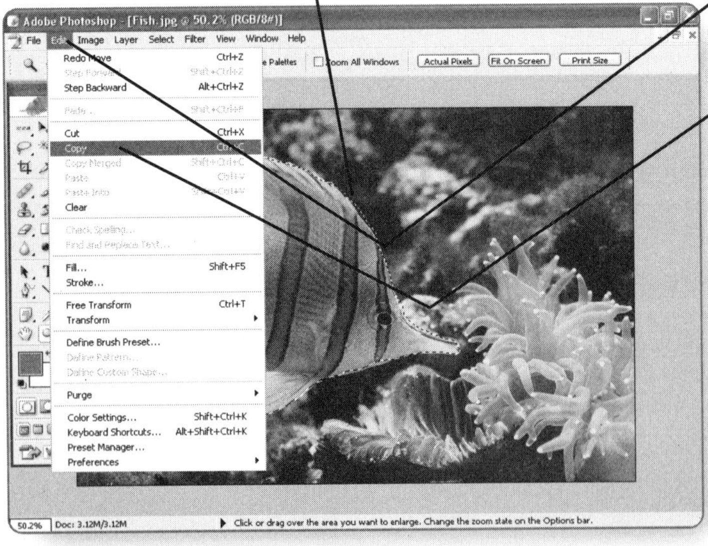

2. **Click** on **Edit**. The Edit menu will appear.

3. **Click** on **Copy**. Photoshop will copy the selection to the Windows Clipboard, a memory holding area.

> **NOTE**
>
> Rather than starting a new image at this point, you could switch to another open image file. If you choose to do that, jump to step 8.

4. **Click** on **File**. The File menu will appear.

5. **Click** on **New**. The New dialog box will open.

6. **Change** the New dialog box **settings** as necessary. The changes you make will affect the size of the new image. You may not need to change the Width and Height entries; typically, they will reflect the size of the copied selection. (See the "Creating a New File" section in Chapter 2, "Working with Image Files," to refresh your memory about the New dialog box settings.)

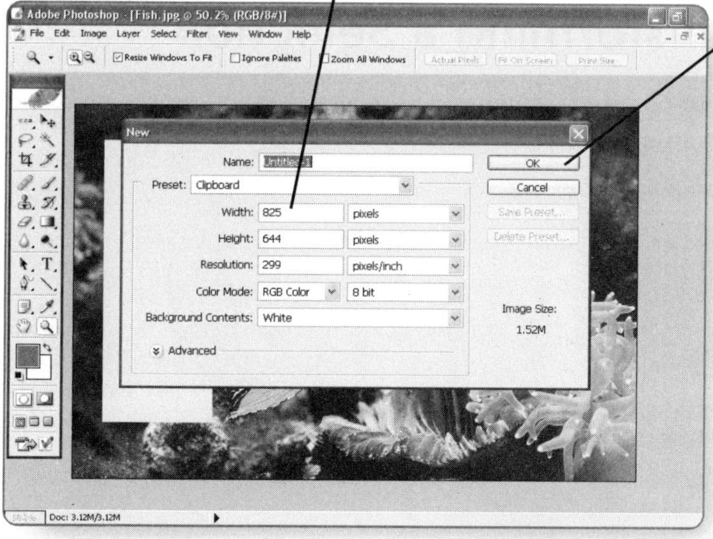

7. **Click** on **OK**. The new image file will open.

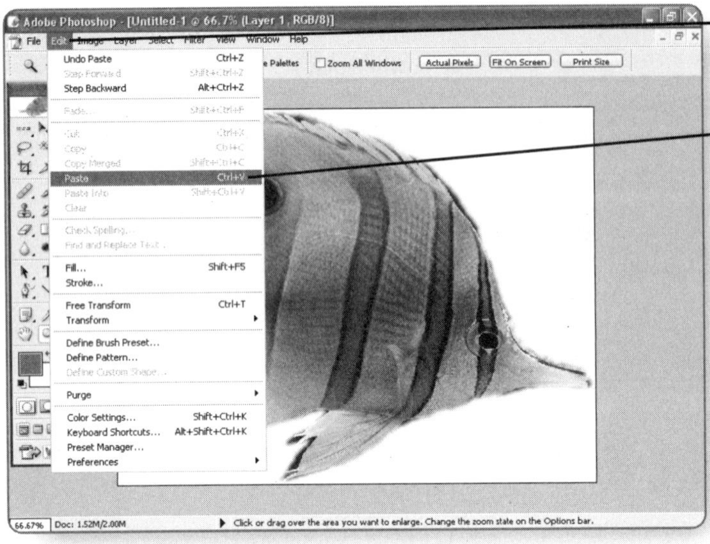

8. Click on **Edit**. The Edit menu will appear.

9. Click on **Paste**. Photoshop will paste the copied selection into the new file.

> **NOTE**
>
> Don't forget to save the new image file after you've pasted the selection into it.

Transforming a Selection

Photoshop offers a number of transformations you can make to affect a selection in an image.

1. **Make** a **selection** in the image using the selection tool of your choice. The selection marquee will appear.

2. **Click** on **Edit**. The Edit menu will appear.

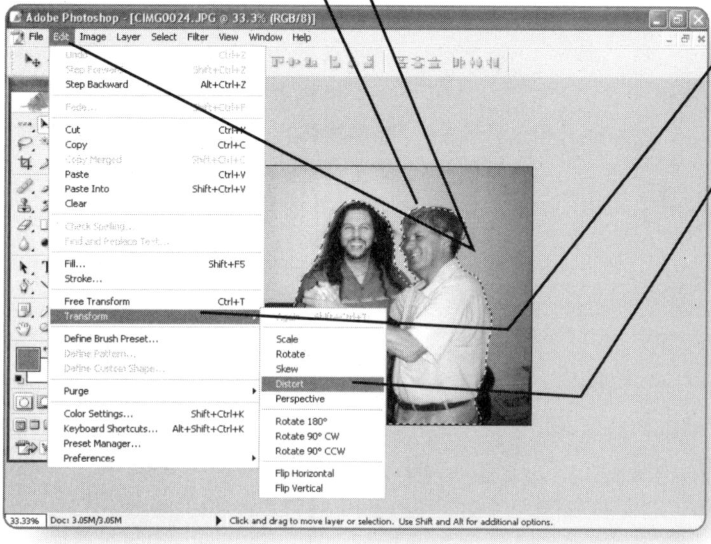

3. **Point** to **Transform**. The Transform submenu will appear.

4. **Click** on the desired **Transform command**. If you choose Rotate 180°, Rotate 90° CW (clockwise), Rotate 90° CCW (counterclockwise), Flip Horizontal, or Flip Vertical, the transformation will appear immediately. If you choose one of the other transforms, proceed to Step 5. The options bar will become active, and special transform handles will appear around the selection.

NOTE

To transform text, you just go to the layer that holds the text; you don't need to select the text itself. The Distort and Perspective transformations aren't available for text.

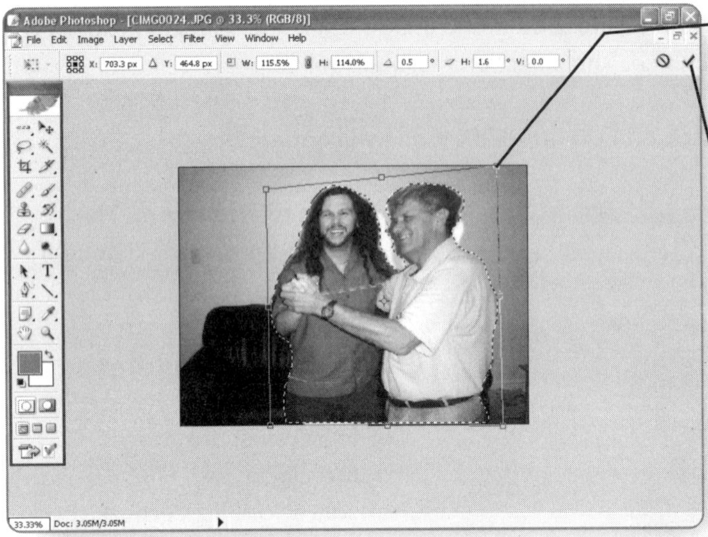

5. **Drag** a **handle**. The transformation will occur. Alternately, you can use the text boxes on the options bar to enter precise transformation settings.

6. **Click** on the **Commit Transform** (check) **button** at the right end of the options bar. Photoshop finalizes the transform.

TIP

Whenever you see a Cancel button (a circle with a slash through it) on the options bar, you can click on that button to cancel the application of the current command or tool settings.

NOTE

You also can choose the Free Transform command from the Edit menu and then drag handles on the selection to transform the selection.

Modifying Part of the Selection

The Select menu gives you a number of commands for adjusting the selection marquee itself. You can use these features before you use other features for altering a selection to be sure that you're working with the proper selection.

Changing the Selection Border

You can add another selection around the current selection marquee so that the specified area within the two marquees becomes the selection. You can then remove that selection or fill it in some way to create a visual border around the selection.

1. **Make** a **selection** in the image using the selection tool of your choice. The selection marquee will appear.

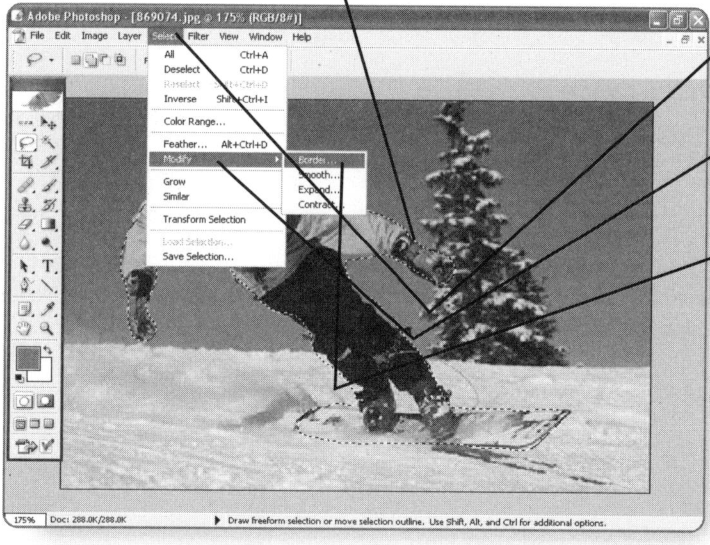

2. **Click** on **Select**. The Select menu will appear.

3. **Point** to **Modify**. The Modify submenu will appear.

4. **Click** on **Border**. The Border Selection dialog box will open.

5. **Type** a new **entry** (between 1 and 64 pixels) for the Width text box. The entry will appear in the text box.

6. **Click** on **OK**. The dialog box will close, and the new border selection will appear.

> **NOTE**
>
> Use the Fill and Stroke commands from the Edit menu to fill in the selected border.

Smoothing the Selection

If you've selected by choosing a color (as described in the "Selecting by Color Range" section in Chapter 5, "Selecting Image Content"), your selection may end up with some stray pixels that are surrounded by a selection marquee. Or, if you've used a Lasso tool, the selection might be a bit more jagged in shape than you now want. To simplify the selection in such instances, you can smooth the selection.

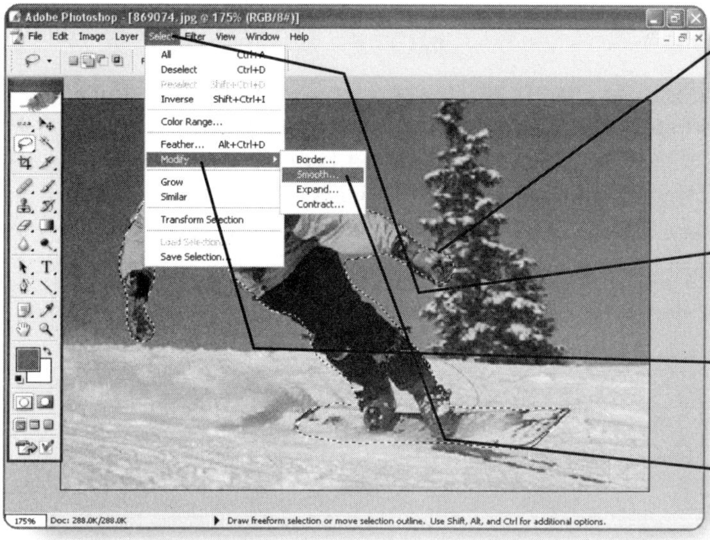

1. **Make** a **selection** in the image by using a color selection method or by using a Lasso tool. The selection marquee or marquees will appear.

2. **Click** on **Select**. The Select menu will appear.

3. **Point** to **Modify**. The Modify submenu will appear.

4. **Click** on **Smooth**. The Smooth Selection dialog box will open.

5. **Type** a new **entry** (between 1 and 16 pixels) for the Sample Radius text box. The entry will appear in the text box.

6. **Click** on **OK**. The dialog box will close, and Photoshop will use the radius setting you entered to add pixels to and eliminate them from the selection.

Photoshop treats each pixel in the selection as the center of a circle with a radius of the width you specified. Depending on whether most of the pixels in the circle are selected, Photoshop will add pixels to the selection (if most are selected) or remove them from the selection (if most aren't selected).

> **NOTE**
>
> You also can use the Grow and Similar commands from the Select menu to expand a selection that you've made by color. The Grow command adds pixels adjoining the current selection that have similar colors to the selection, whereas Similar adds pixels of similar colors from the entire image to the selection.

Expanding or Contracting the Selection

Expanding or contracting the selection really moves the selection marquee rather than affecting the selection itself. Using this method provides more accuracy than dragging or using a color technique (like smoothing) to increase the size of the selection because you specify exactly how many pixels to add or remove from the selection, in terms of height and width.

1. **Make** a **selection** in the image using the selection tool of your choice. The selection marquee will appear.

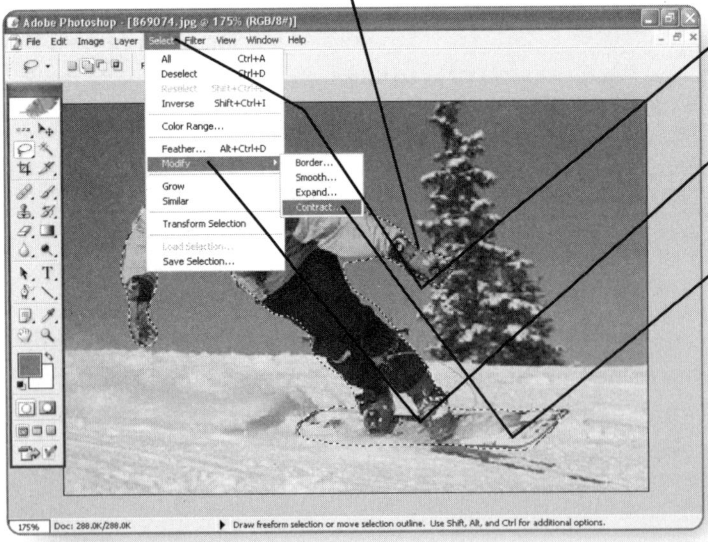

2. **Click** on **Select**. The Select menu will appear.
3. **Point** to **Modify**. The Modify submenu will appear.
4. **Click** on **Expand** or **Contract**. The Expand Selection or Contract Selection dialog box will open.

5. **Type** a **new entry** (between 1 and 100 pixels) in the Expand Selection or Contract Selection text box. The entry will appear in the text box.

6. **Click** on **OK**. The dialog box will close, and the new border selection will appear.

NOTE

You can use the Feather command from the Select menu to feather or soften the edge of the selection. This affects the selection if you copy or paste it or apply another effect like a filter.

Saving a Selection

When you save a selection, you give it a name in the Photoshop file. Then you can easily load the selection in the future. This enables you to repeatedly select exactly the same pixels, which is tough no matter which selection technique you originally used to make the selection.

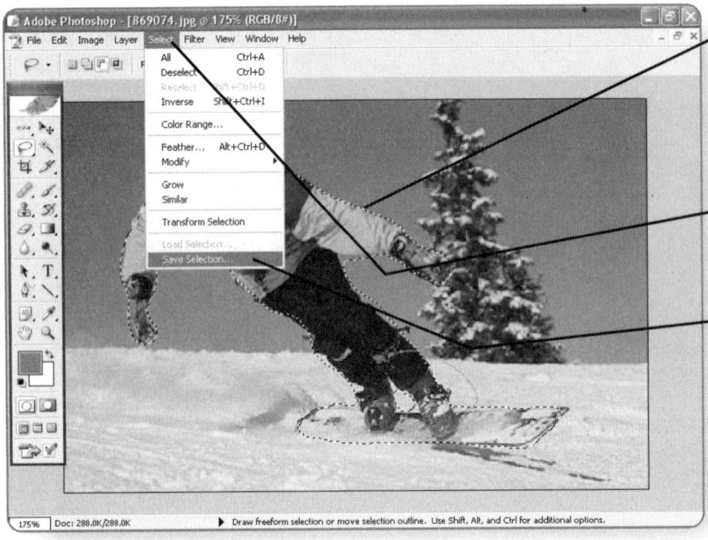

1. **Make** a **selection** in the image using the selection tool of your choice. The selection marquee will appear.

2. **Click** on **Select**. The Select menu will appear.

3. **Click** on **Save Selection**. The Save Selection dialog box will open.

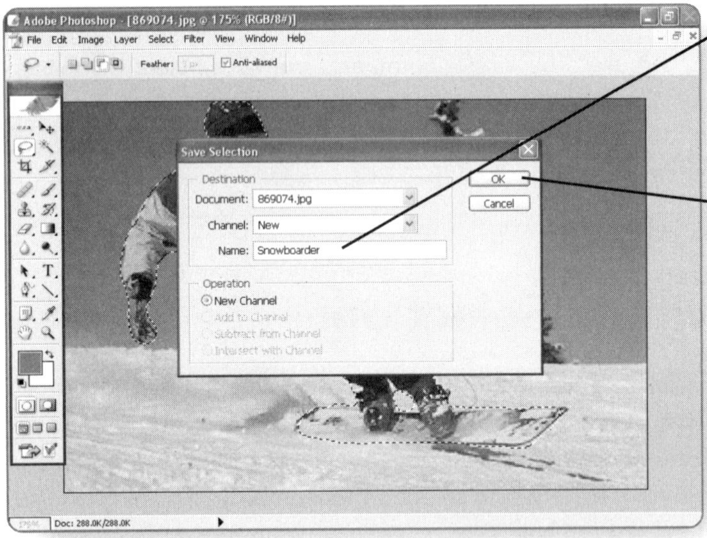

4. **Click** in the **Name text box** and then type a name for the selection. The name will appear in the text box.

5. **Click** on **OK**. The Save Selection dialog box will close, and the saved selection will be added to the file.

NOTE

Be sure to save the file to save the named selection. Also note that saving the selection creates a new channel from the selection. Chapter 15, "Understanding Colors and Channels," explains how to work with channels.

Loading a Selection

When you need to apply a selection that you've previously saved—that is, when you need to reselect a previous selection—you can load the selection.

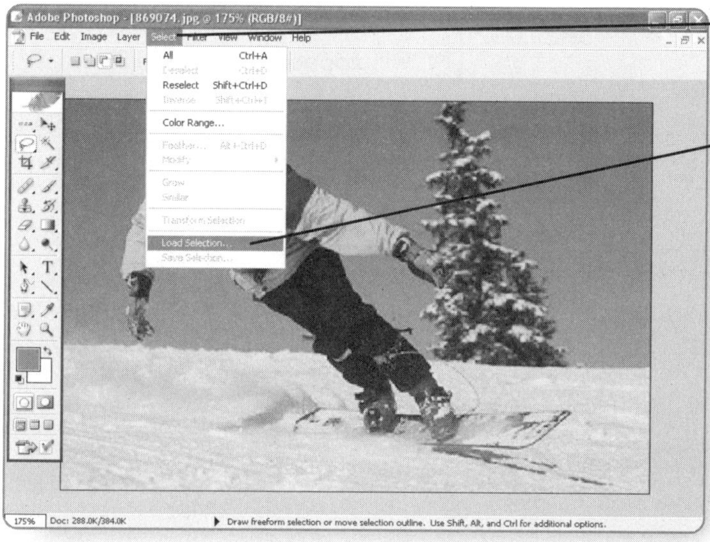

1. **Click** on **Select**. The Select menu will appear.

2. **Click** on **Load Selection**. The Load Selection dialog box will open.

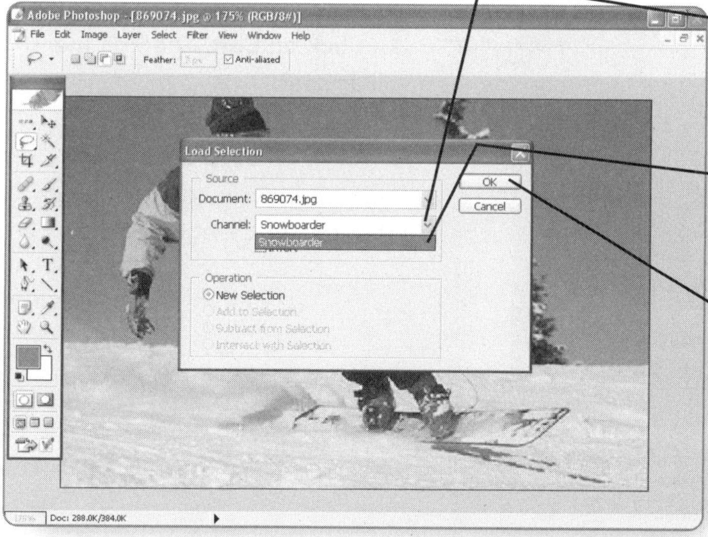

3. **Click** on the **down arrow** next to the Channel box. The list of saved selections will appear.

4. **Click** on the desired **selection**. It will appear as the Channel selection.

5. **Click** on **OK**. The Load Selection dialog box will close, and the selection marquee will appear in the file.

Undoing a Change

The Edit menu offers a number of commands you can use to undo prior changes and actions, such as deselecting a selection.

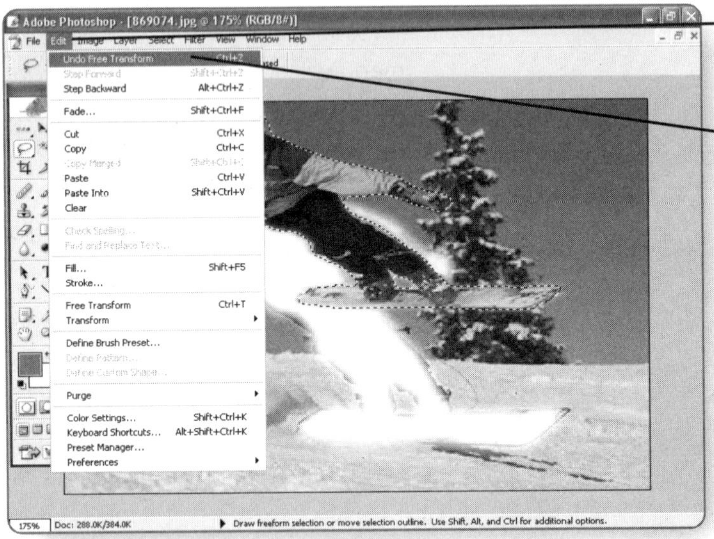

1. **Click** on **Edit**. The Edit menu will appear.

2. **Click** on **Undo** (Action Name). Photoshop will undo your most recent change or action.

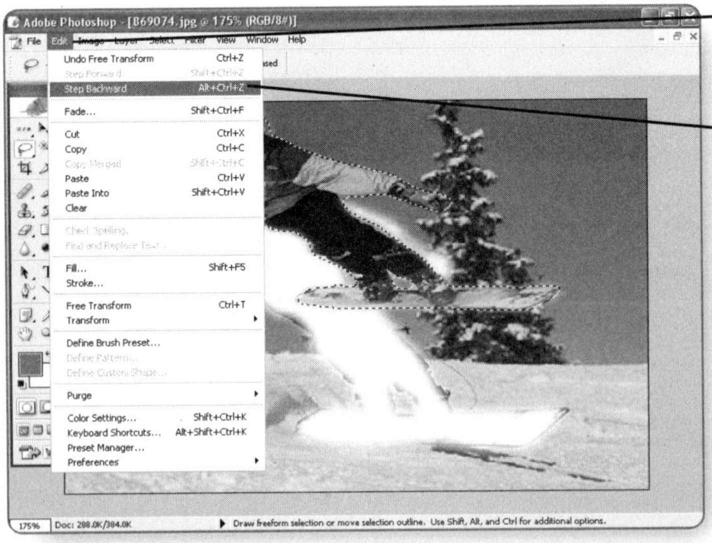

3. **Click** on **Edit**. The Edit menu will appear.

4. **Click** on **Step Backward**. Photoshop will undo your next-most-recent change or action.

> **NOTE**
>
> You should only use the Undo command once. After that, use the Step Backward command (described in steps 3 and 4) as many times as needed to step further backward through your changes. Use the Step Forward command (as in steps 5 and 6) to step further forward. To redo a single change, click on Redo (Action Name) in the Edit menu.

5. **Click** on **Edit**. The Edit menu will appear.

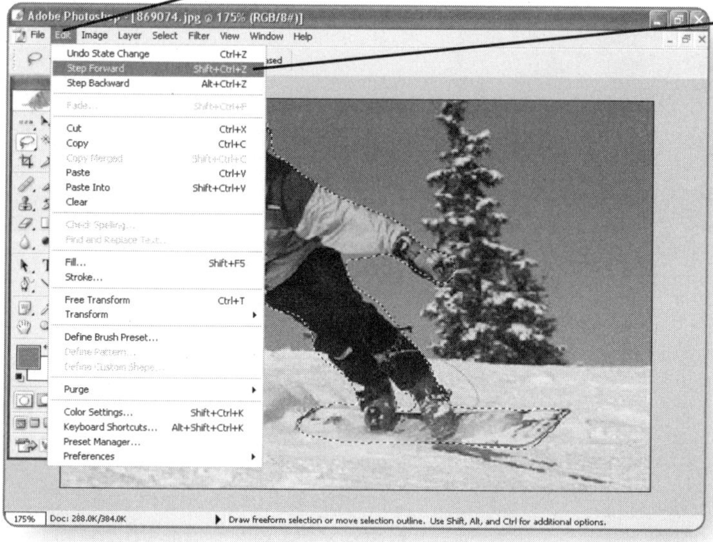

6. **Click** on **Step Forward**. Photoshop will redo the change or action you undid by stepping forward.

Using the History to Undo Changes

The History palette provides one last method for discarding (undoing) actions and changes to a selection that you've made previously. When you use the History palette, you select a change or action out of the sequence of actions you've performed during the current work session with the image file. When you remove that selected action or change, Photoshop undoes that action or change plus all the changes below it in the History list.

1. **Click** on **Window**. The Window menu will appear.

2. **Click** on **History**. The History palette will open.

3. **Click** on the **down scroll arrow** for the scroll bar in the History palette. The list of changes and actions in the History list will scroll down.

4. **Click** on **change** or **action** to undo in the list. The shortcut menu will appear.

5. **Click** on the **Delete** button. A message box asking you to confirm the History deletion will open.

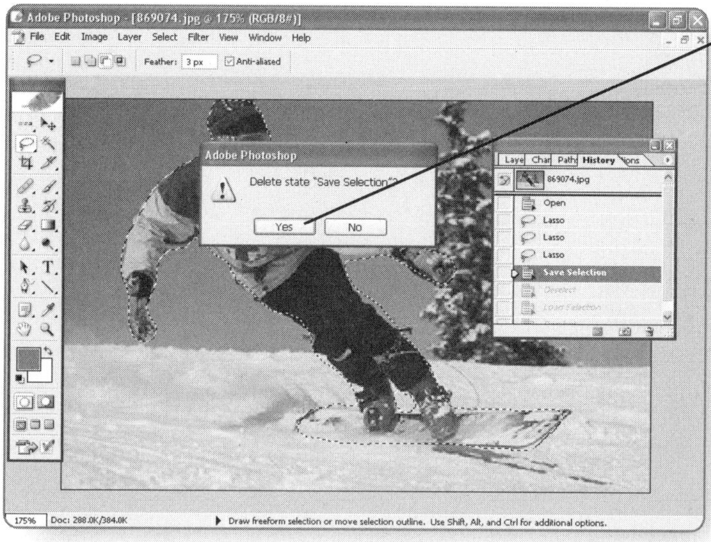

6. Click on **Yes**. Photoshop will close the dialog box and undo the specified change and all the changes below it in the History palette.

Reverting

You can go back to the last saved version of your file using the Revert command. This will undo all the changes you have made since the last time you saved the file.

1. Click on **File**. The File menu will appear.

2. Click on **Revert**. All the changes you have made to the image since the last time you saved it will be undone.

7

Using Positioning Tools and Presets

Photoshop provides more precision editing tools than perhaps any other graphics program. Now that you know how to select and move image content, you may want to try out tools you can exploit to align selections perfectly. Before you start making many moves in your image files, review this chapter to learn the following skills:

- Displaying a grid you can use for alignment
- Displaying rulers you can use for alignment
- Snapping a selection to a guide or grid
- Adding custom alignment guides and locking them in place
- Building presets to customize tools

Showing and Hiding the Grid

You can display nonprinting gridlines in the current image window and then use those gridlines to help you align selections in the image. You can show and hide the grid as needed, turning it on to position selections and then turning it back off when you want to assess the image's background or overall appearance.

> **NOTE**
>
> Remember, you have to be working on the layer that has the image content to select. Chapter 8, "Working with Layers," explains how to navigate to and use layers. In some cases, you can choose the layer and then use the Move tool to move the layer contents without making a selection.

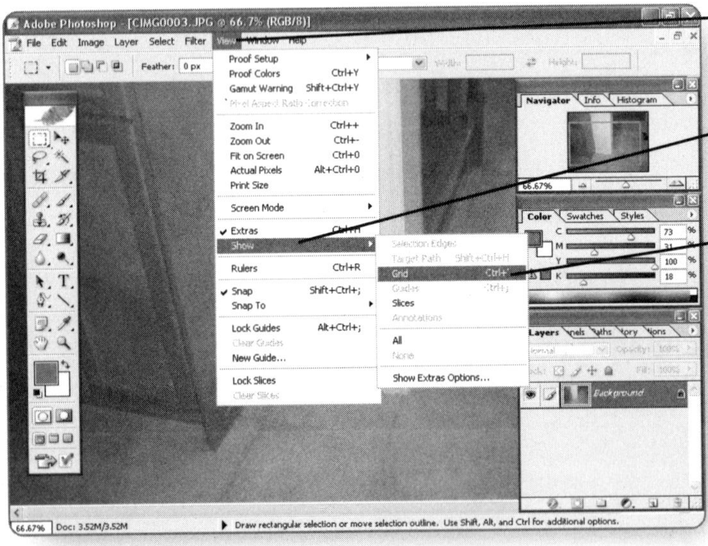

1. **Click** on **View**. The View menu will appear.

2. **Point** to **Show**. The Show submenu will appear.

3. **Click** on **Grid**. The gridlines will appear immediately in the current image file.

4. **Make** a **selection** using one of the selection methods.

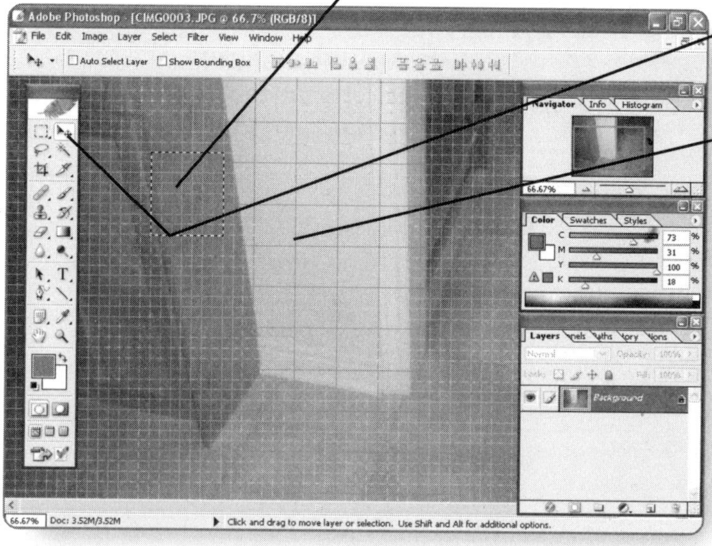

5. **Click** on the **Move tool**. It will be highlighted.

6. **Drag** the selection. You can use the gridline to align the selection.

> **NOTE**
>
> If the selection "jumps around" and won't align as you think it should, the Snap To feature might be active. See the section "Using Snap and Snap To" later in this chapter to learn how to use this feature.

7. **Repeat** steps **1** to **3** to remove the grid.

Showing and Hiding Rulers

The rulers come in handy when you need to position a selection (such as a logo inserted on a new layer) at a precise location within the image. Turn on the rulers when you need to position selections based on measurements and then turn them back off when you no longer need them.

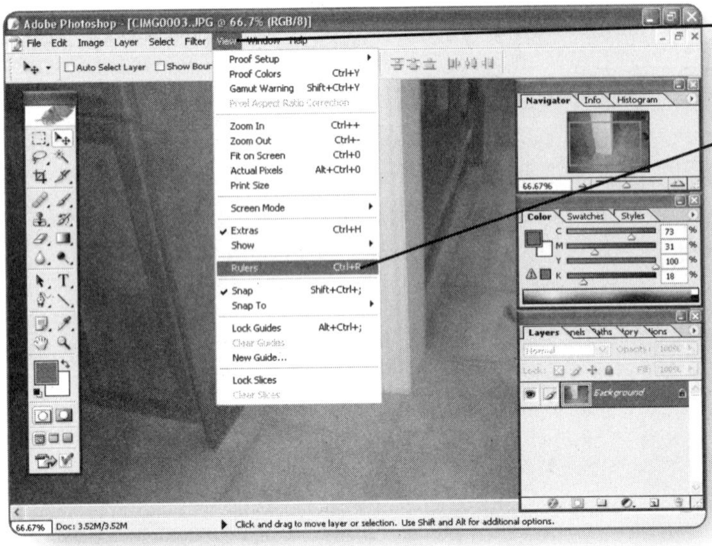

1. **Click** on **View**. The View menu will appear.

2. **Click** on **Rulers**. The rulers will appear immediately in the current image window.

> **NOTE**
>
> The vertical ruler appears along the left side of the image window, and the horizontal ruler appears across the top of the window.

4. **Make** a **selection** using one of the selection methods.

5. **Click** on the **Move tool**. It will be highlighted.

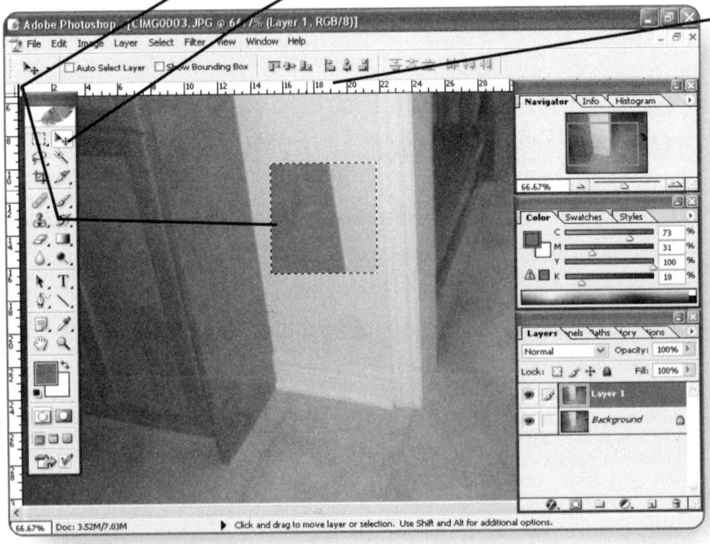

6. **Click** and **drag** the selection. You can use the gridline to align the selection. Watch the dotted gray lines on the rulers to judge position as you drag. The selection will drop into the specified location when you finish dragging.

7. **Repeat** steps **1** to **3** to remove the grid.

Using Snap and Snap To

The Snap To feature in Photoshop ensures that a selection aligns to the grid or to the custom guides that you add as you drag. You can turn snapping to grids or guides off and on individually or use the Snap command to toggle all snapping on and off. By default, snapping to both the grid and guidelines is turned on in Photoshop.

> **NOTE**
>
> The grid must be displayed to enable the command for turning on or off snapping to the grid. In contrast, the command for turning on or off snapping to guidelines is available whether or not you've added guidelines into the image file, as described in the next section.

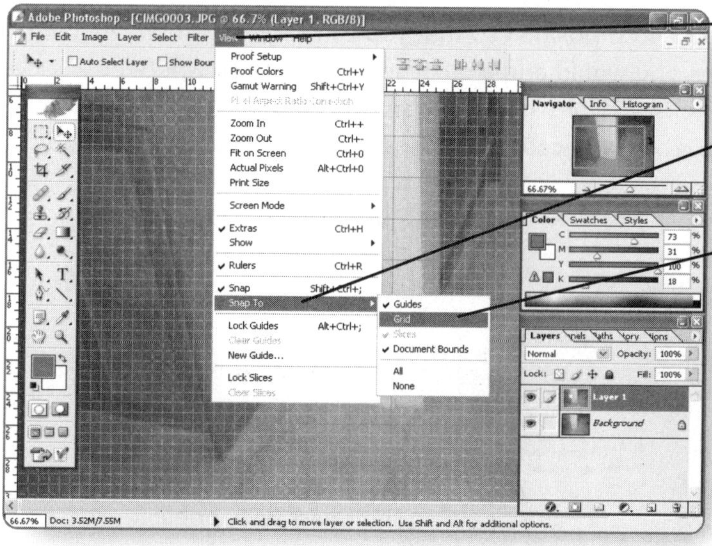

1. **Click** on **View**. The View menu will appear.

2. **Point** to **Snap To**. The Snap To submenu will appear.

3. **Click** on **Guides** or **Grid**. The check beside the feature you clicked will be removed, and the selected Snap To feature will no longer be active. The next time you move a selection, it will not snap into position.

> **NOTE**
>
> Turning off snapping can help when you need to position selections relative to one another rather than relative to a grid.

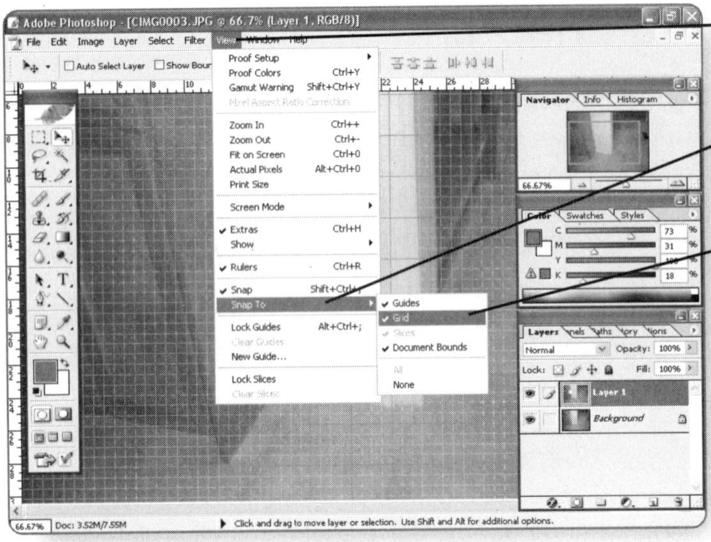

4. **Click** on **View**. The View menu will appear.

5. **Point** to **Snap To**. The Snap To submenu will appear.

6. **Click** on **Guides** or **Grid**. A check will appear beside the feature you clicked, and the selected Snap To feature will become active again. The next time you move a selection, it will snap into position.

Guides

Guides, in a sense, serve as custom gridlines. You put a guideline into position so that you can align selections to it. Ideally, you would add a guideline in a location where no gridline occurs or when you want to use guidelines rather than the grid. Also, because guidelines appear in blue, you can add a guideline to highlight an important grid location. The fastest way to add guidelines is from the ruler.

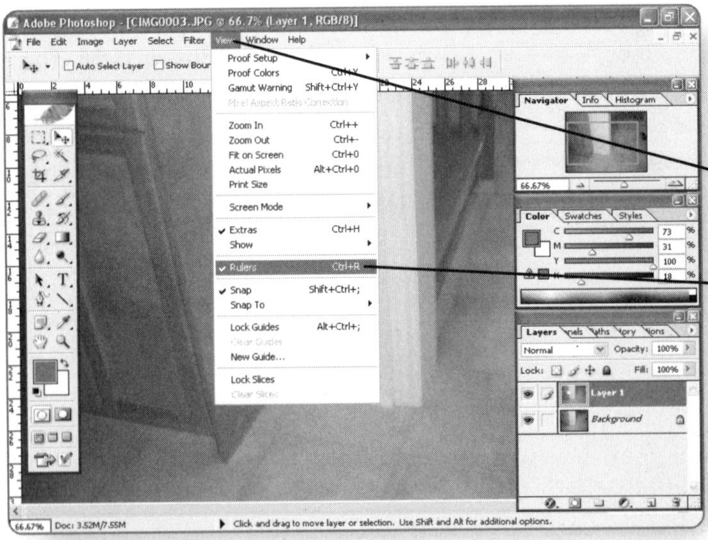

1. **Click** on **View**. The View menu will appear.

2. **Click** on **Rulers** if required. The rulers will appear immediately in the current image window.

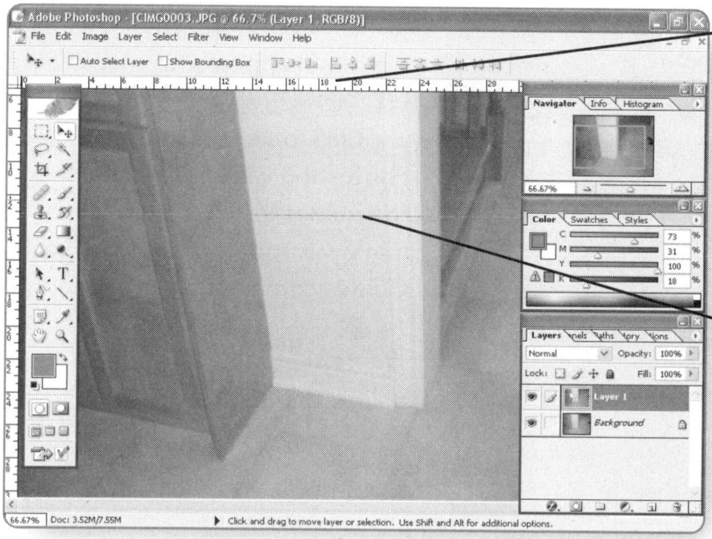

3. **Place** the **mouse pointer** over the vertical or horizontal ruler. Positioning over a horizontal ruler will result in a horizontal guideline, whereas positioning over a vertical ruler will give you a vertical guideline.

4. **Click** and **drag** from the ruler onto your image. A guideline will appear.

Locking Guides

You can lock guides to prevent any accidental guideline changes. (For example, you could mistakenly move a guideline rather than the selection, especially when the selection falls very close to the guideline.) When you need to change guidelines, unlock them first.

> **NOTE**
>
> Locking guidelines doesn't prevent you from clearing them. If you unintentionally clear guidelines, immediately undo the change.

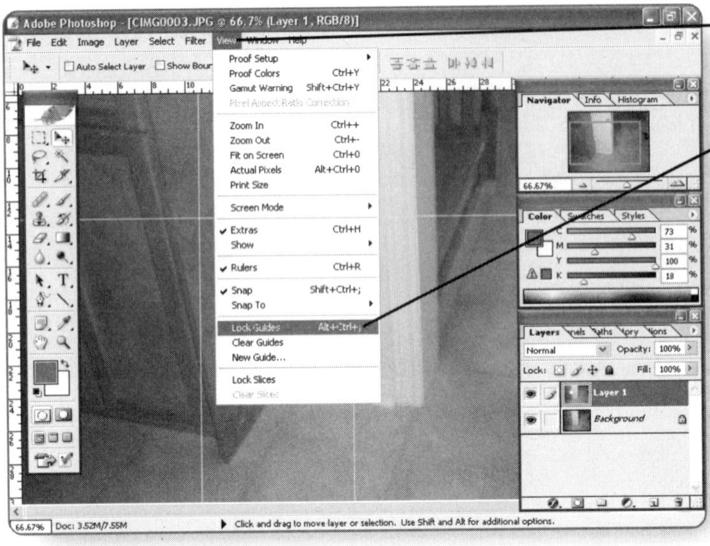

1. Click on **View**. The View menu will appear.

2. Click on **Lock Guides**. Photoshop will immediately lock the guides into position. A check mark will appear beside the Lock Guides command on the menu.

3. **Repeat** steps **1** and **2** to unlock the guides.

Removing Guides

When you are finished using your guides, you can clear them all with the Clear Guides command.

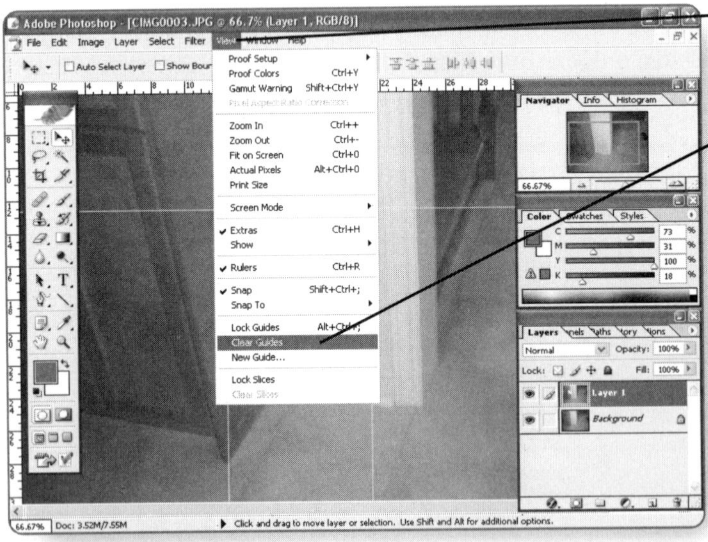

1. Click on **View**. The View menu will appear.

2. Click on **Clear Guides**. The guides will be removed.

Setting Up Your Tools with the Preset Palette

In the "Creating or Displaying a Brush" section in Chapter 3, "Adding Content with Tools," you learned how to create and use your own custom brush in Photoshop. In addition to creating a custom brush, you can create a preset. To make a preset, you select a tool, choose your favorite settings for the tool, and then save the preset. The preset stores your favorite settings for the tool. Later, when you load the preset, the tool and the specified settings immediately become active. This section describes how to create and use presets, as well as how to load additional brush, color, or pattern choices for your tools using the Preset Manager.

Saving a Preset

Because Photoshop offers so many tools and settings, you have nearly unlimited possibilities for editing images. Over time, however, you'll probably develop favorite techniques that involve using a particular tool and particular settings. Rather than having to remember the desired tool and all the associated settings, you can simply save each favorite combination as a preset using the Tool Presets palette.

1. **Click** on the desired **tool**. Its options will become active in the options bar.

2. **Choose** the desired **settings** in the options bar, and choose a foreground or background color if necessary. These settings will become the current settings for the tool.

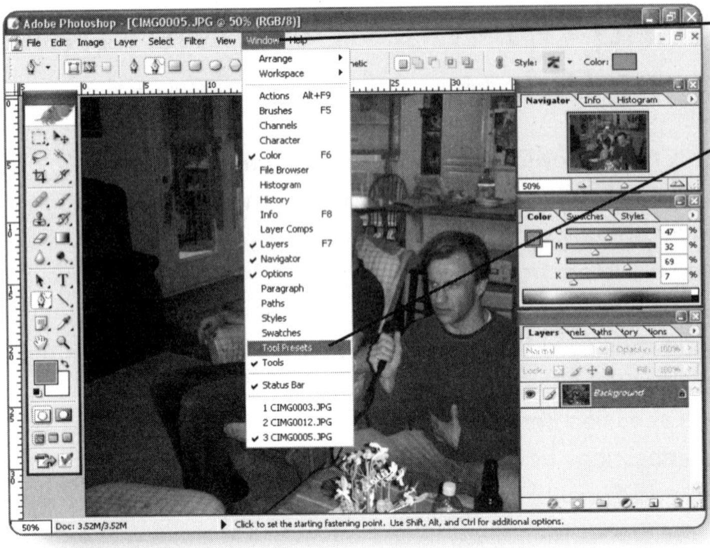

3. Click on **Window**. The Window menu will appear.

4. Click on **Tool Presets**. The Tool Presets palette will open.

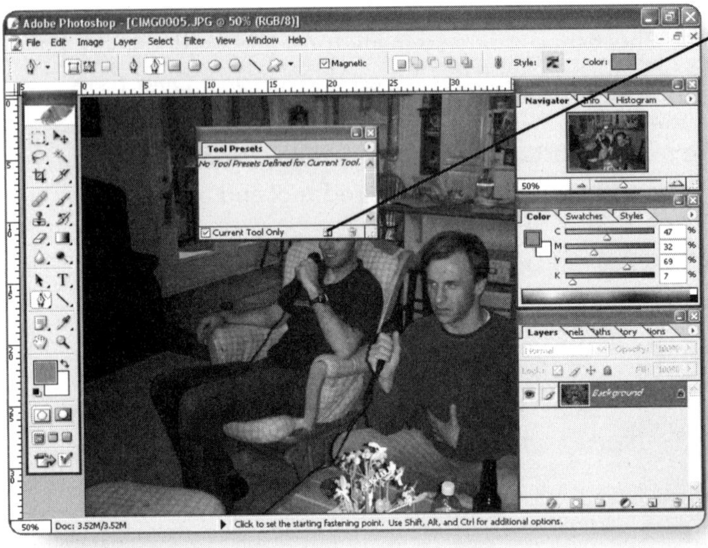

5. Click on the **Create New Tool Preset button** at the bottom of the palette. The New Tool Preset dialog box will open.

6. **Type** a **name** for the preset in the Name text box. The preset name will appear in the dialog box.

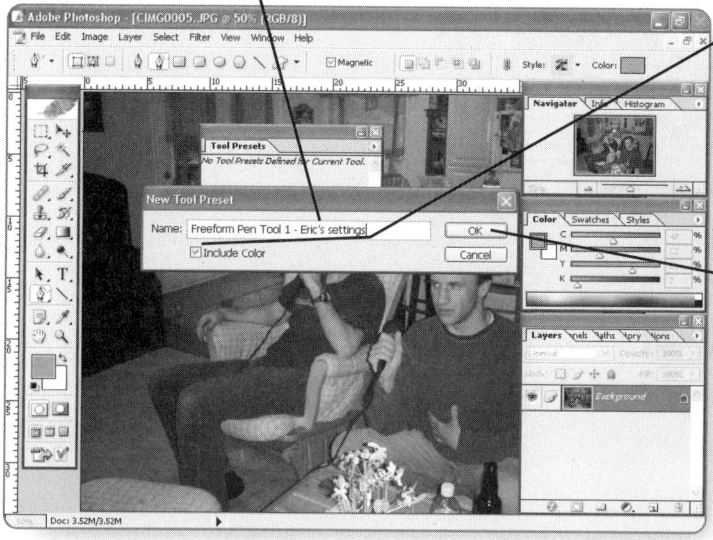

7. **Click** on the **Include Color check box** as necessary. When it's checked, Photoshop will save the current color selections along with the other preset settings.

8. **Click** on **OK**. The dialog box will close, and the new preset will appear in the Tool Presets palette.

Using a Preset

Most presets that you create are available from the options bar for the tool you select.

1. **Click** on the desired **tool**. The option bar will change to match that tool.

2. **Click** on the **Click to open the Tool Presets picker button**. A window with presets for that tool will appear.

3. Double-click on the desired **preset**. It will now be selected, and you can begin using that tool.

Part II Review Questions

1. How do you select a tool? See "Selecting a Tool" in Chapter 3.
2. Which are the painting tools, and which are the drawing tools? See "Working with Painting Tools" and "Working with Drawing Tools" in Chapter 3.
3. What's a fast way to change the portion of the image that appears in the window? See "Using the Hand Tool" and "Using the Navigator" in Chapter 4.
4. What can you select with the Marquee tool? See "Using the Marquee Tool" in Chapter 5.
5. What different selections does the Lasso tool offer? See "Using the Lasso Tool" in Chapter 5.
6. How do you deselect a selection? See "Removing a Selection" in Chapter 5.
7. How do you delete selected image content? See "Deleting a Selection" in Chapter 6.
8. Can you reuse a selection? See "Saving a Selection" and "Loading a Selection" in Chapter 6.
9. What if I need to undo a change? See "Undoing a Change" and "Using the History to Undo Changes" in Chapter 6.
10. Can Photoshop align selections that I move? See "Using Snap and Snap To" in Chapter 7.

PART III

Using Layers, Masks, and Paths

8

Working with Layers

Photoshop allows you to create your images on a variety of different layers. Creating content on separate layers enables you to retain control of the placement and effects for various individual elements in an image. By having your objects on different layers you not only have better control over your image, but you can create some interesting effects. In this chapter, you'll learn how to:

- Use various methods to create a layer
- Select layers
- Create new patterns for use in layers
- Change layer settings
- Arrange layers
- Merge layers to flatten the image

Creating a Layer

Nearly every image file by default has one special layer called the Background layer. (If you create a new transparent image, it starts with Layer 1.) An image can have more layers than your computer's memory can probably handle—up to 8,000. Some actions, such as adding text, create a new layer automatically. In other instances, you might need to create a layer manually before adding elements into it. This section explains how to do so.

> **NOTE**
>
> When you create a new image, it sometimes helps to click on the Transparent option in the New dialog box. This ensures that a white background won't hide other layers you may add.

Making a New Layer

The simplest way to create a layer is to simply add a new, blank layer.

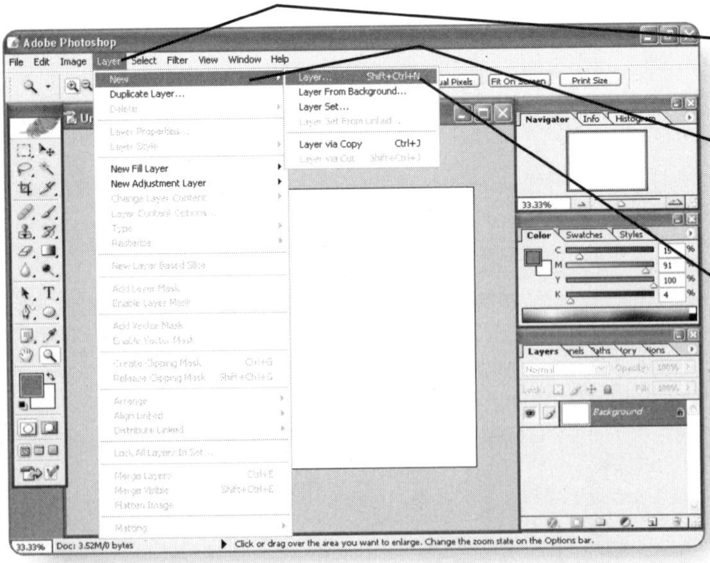

1. **Click** on **Layer**. The Layer menu will appear.
2. Hold the mouse pointer over **New**. The New submenu will appear.
3. **Click** on **Layer**. The New Layer dialog box will open.

TIP

A layer set organizes layers, much as a folder organizes files on a hard disk. Click on Layer, hold the mouse pointer over New, and then click on Layer Set to create a layer set.

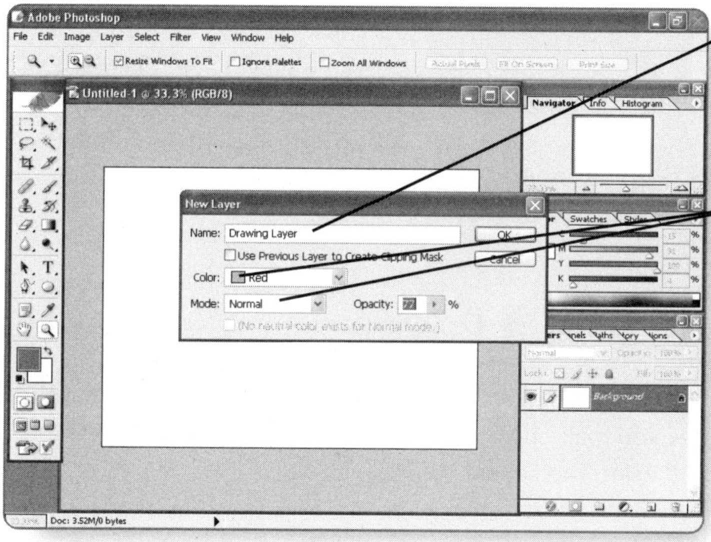

4. **Type** a **name** for the layer into the Name text box. The specified name will be used for the layer.

5. **Choose** an **option** from the Color and Mode lists, if necessary. Making a Color choice will apply a color to the new layer's listing in the Layers palette. Making a Mode choice will apply a layer blending mode, which controls how the individual pixels on the layer blend with pixels on other layers.

TIP

Depending on the choice you make from the Mode list, you may have to make other layers, such as the Background layer, transparent. To do so, double-click on the layer in the Layers palette, change the Opacity setting to 0, and then click on OK.

TIP

Some blending modes enable the Fill with check box. You can click on it to check it and apply the applicable neutral color.

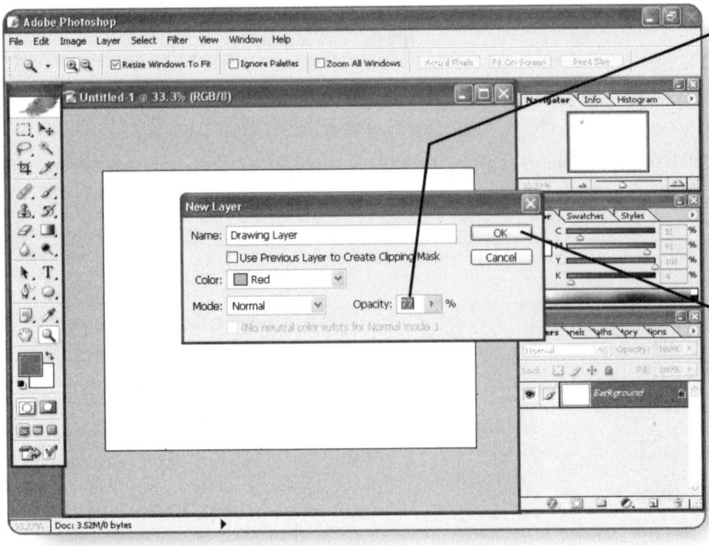

6. **Type** a **new entry** into the Opacity text box, if necessary. (You can also click on its arrow, drag the slider, and click on the arrow again.) Photoshop will make the layer's contents more transparent.

7. **Click** on **OK**. Photoshop will close the New Layer dialog box and create the new layer, which will appear in the Layers palette.

Selecting a Layer

Selecting a layer makes it the current or active layer so that the changes you make next will only apply to that layer. Layers are selected using the Layers palette.

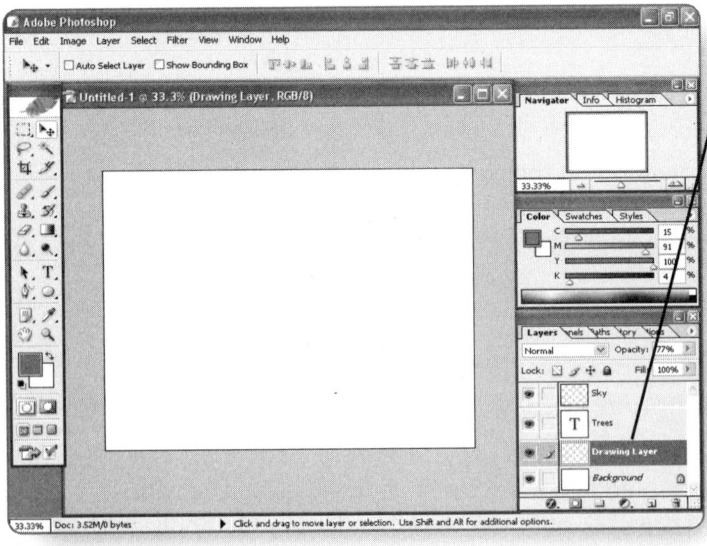

1. **Click** on the **name** of the layer in the Layers palette. The layer will appear selected in the Layers palette, making it the active layer.

TIP

You can hide a layer's contents by clicking on the eye icon to the left of the layer's name in the Layers palette. The layer's content disappears immediately. Click on the spot where the eye icon previously appeared to redisplay the layer.

Duplicating a Layer

When a layer has content that you'd like to reuse, you can duplicate the layer in the image file. Then you can position the layer content or add different effects independently.

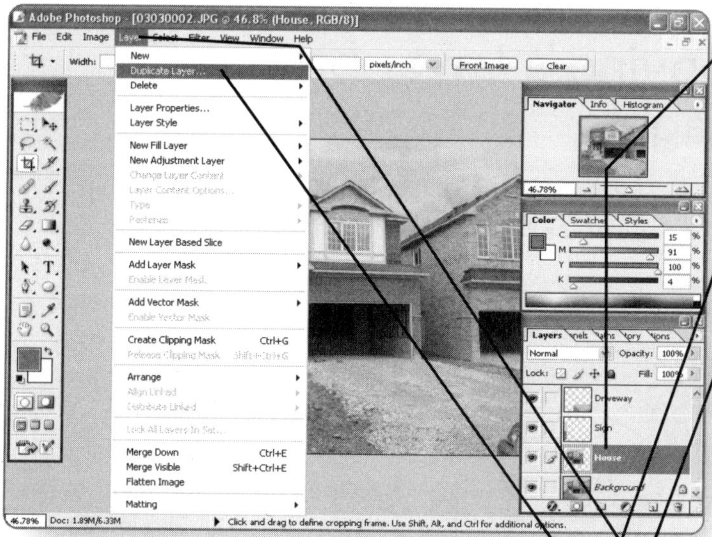

1. **Select** the **layer** to duplicate. The layer's name appears selected in the Layers palette.

2. **Click** on **Layer**. The Layer menu will appear.

3. **Click** on **Duplicate Layer**. The Duplicate Layer dialog box will open.

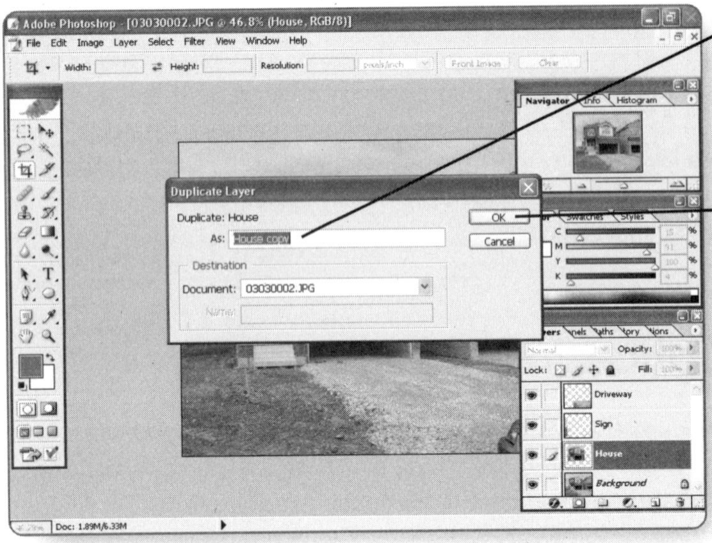

4. **Type** a **name** for the layer into the As text box. The specified name will be used for the layer.

5. **Click** on **OK**. Photoshop will close the Duplicate Layer dialog box and create the new layer, which will appear in the Layers palette.

Copying a Layer between Images

When a layer has content that you'd like to reuse, you can make a copy of the layer and paste it into another image file.

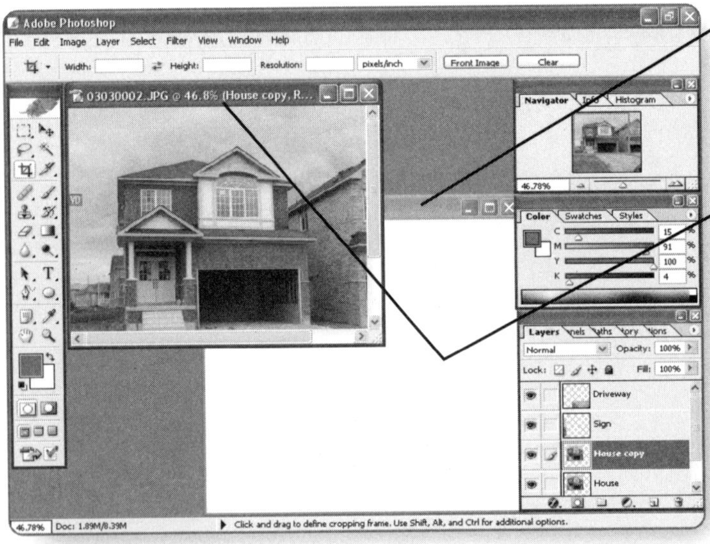

1. **Open** or **create** the **image file** to which you want to copy the layer. The image window appears in Photoshop.

2. **Open** the **image file** that has the layer to copy. The image window appears in Photoshop.

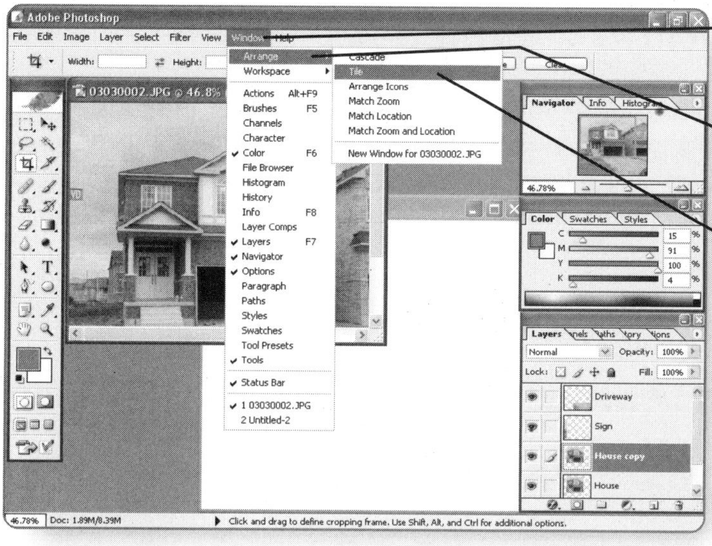

3. Click on **Window**. The window menu will appear.

4. Hold the mouse pointer over **Arrange**. A submenu will appear.

5. Click on **Tile**. The two open files will be tiled.

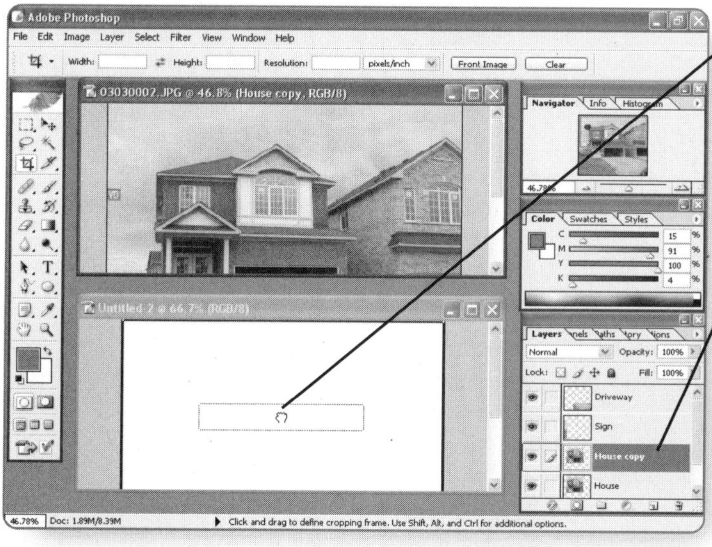

6. Drag the layer from the Layers palette. The layer will appear selected, and the mouse pointer will change to a clenched hand.

7. Drop the **layer** on the window for the file into which you want to copy the layer. The new layer appears immediately in the destination image.

Adding a Fill Layer

You can add a fill layer to color the entire image background. This technique is preferred over drawing a colored box on a layer, which can leave a white edge around the image. These instructions can also be used to create a pattern or gradient fill layer.

1. **Click** on **Layer**. The Layer menu will appear.

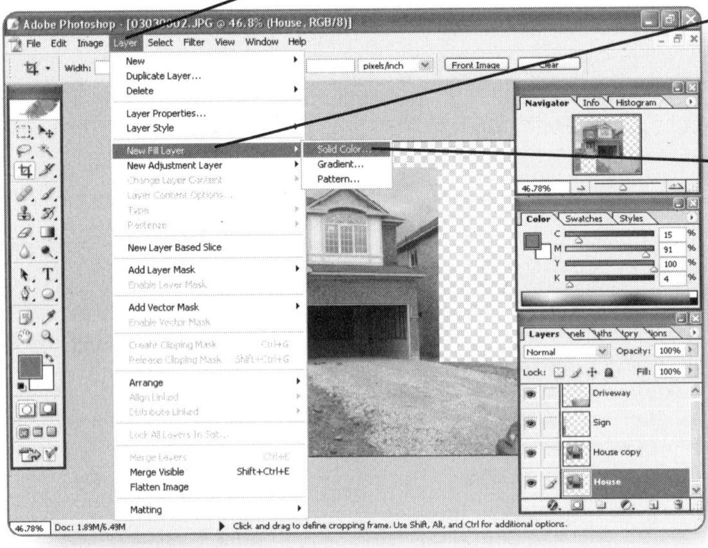

2. **Point** to **New Fill Layer**. The New Fill Layer submenu will appear.

3. **Click** on **Solid Color**. The New Layer dialog box will open.

4. **Type** a **name** for the layer into the Name text box. The specified name will be used for the layer.

5. **Choose** an **option** from the Color and Mode lists, if necessary. Making a Color choice will apply a color to the new layer's listing in the Layers palette. Making a Mode choice will apply a layer blending mode, which controls how the individual pixels on the layer blend with pixels on other layers.

> **TIP**
>
> Depending on the choice you make from the Mode list, you may have to make other layers, such as the Background layer, transparent. To do so, double-click on the layer in the Layers palette, change the Opacity setting to 0, and then click on OK.

6. **Click** on the **arrow** beside the Opacity text box, if necessary. A slider bar will appear that can be used to adjust the opacity level.

7. **Click** on **OK**. Photoshop will close the New Layer dialog box and open the Color Picker dialog box.

8. **Click** on a **color hue** in the narrow band of colors near the middle of the dialog box. Photoshop will display a different range of colors in the Pick a solid color box.

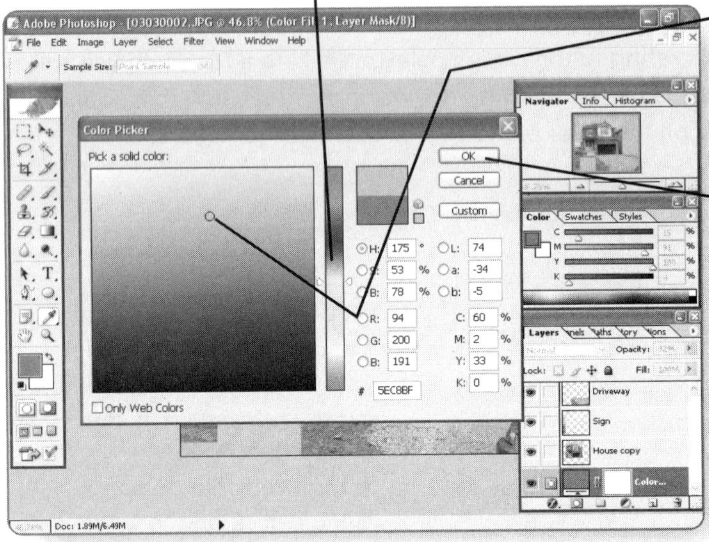

9. **Click** on a **color** in the Pick a solid color box. The color you click on will become the active color.

10. **Click** on **OK**. Photoshop will close the Color Picker dialog box and create the new fill layer. Its name will appear in the Layers palette.

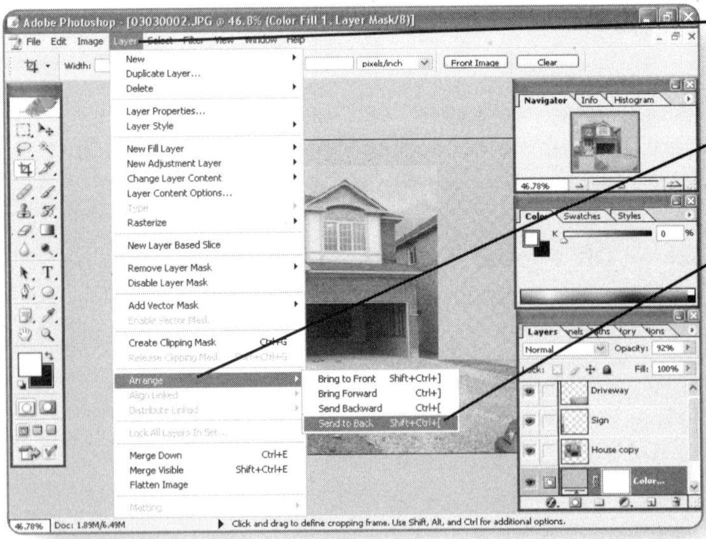

11. **Click** on **Layer**. The Layer menu will appear.

12. **Point** to **Arrange**. The Arrange submenu will appear.

13. **Click** on **Send to Back**. The new layer will shift to the back of the available layers.

> **TIP**
>
> You can change the type of fill for a layer after you create it. To do so, first select the layer. Then click on Layer, point to Change Layer Content, and click on Solid Color, Gradient, or Pattern.

Creating Patterns

If none of the patterns provided with Photoshop suits your needs, you can create your own using one of two methods: sampling a pattern or using the Pattern Maker plug-in.

Sampling a Pattern

You can create a pattern on-the-fly and then use it to create a pattern layer. The new pattern immediately becomes part of the library of available patterns.

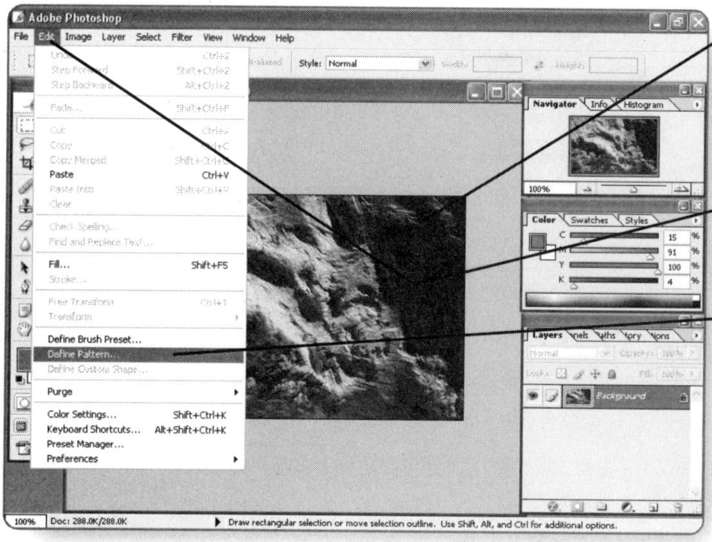

1. **Open** or **create** the **image file** that holds the area to use as the pattern. The image appears in its own window.

2. **Click** on **Edit**. The Edit menu will appear.

3. **Click** on **Define Pattern**. The Pattern Name dialog box will open. This will create a pattern from the entire image. If you want to create a pattern from only part of an image, select that part prior to step 2 using any of the selection tools.

NOTE

If the Define Pattern command is disabled, it's probably because the image bit depth is set to 16 Bits/Channel, the typical setting for many scanners. To enable the Define Pattern command, you have to convert the image to 8 Bits/Channel by choosing Image, Mode, 8 Bits/Channel.

4. **Type** a **name** for the pattern in the Name text box. Photoshop will use the name you specify to identify the pattern.

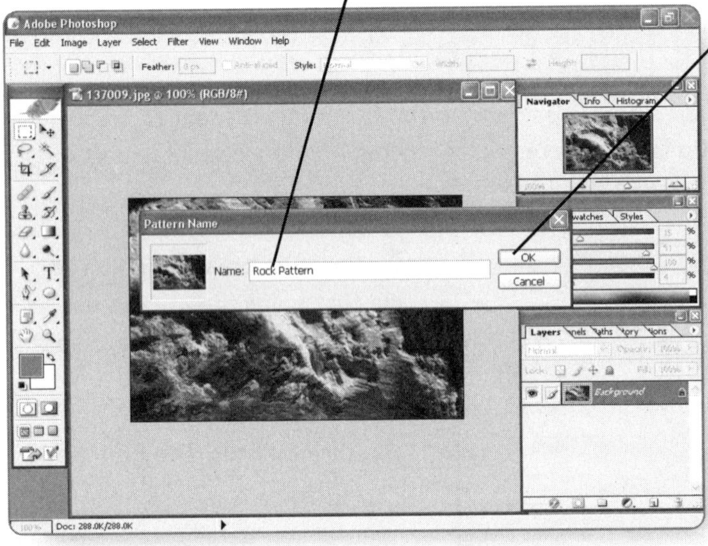

5. **Click** on **OK**. The Pattern Name dialog box will close.

Using the Pattern Maker Plug-In

The Pattern Maker plug-in enables you to preview a pattern and alter it slightly before you save it as a preset. Follow these steps to create a basic pattern with the Pattern Maker plug-in:

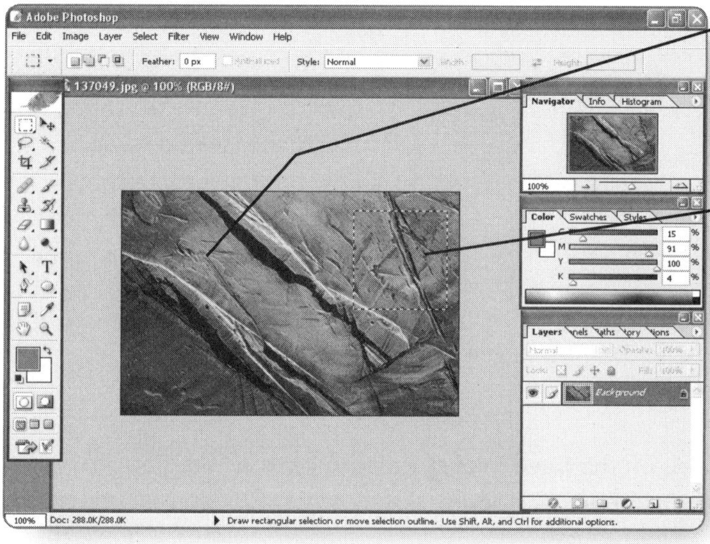

1. **Open** or **create** the **image file** that holds the area to use as the pattern. The image appears in its own window.

2. **Select** the **area** to use as a pattern using the selection tool of your choice. The selection marquee will appear.

3. **Click** on **Filter**. The Filter menu will appear.

4. **Click** on **Pattern Maker**. The Pattern Maker window will open.

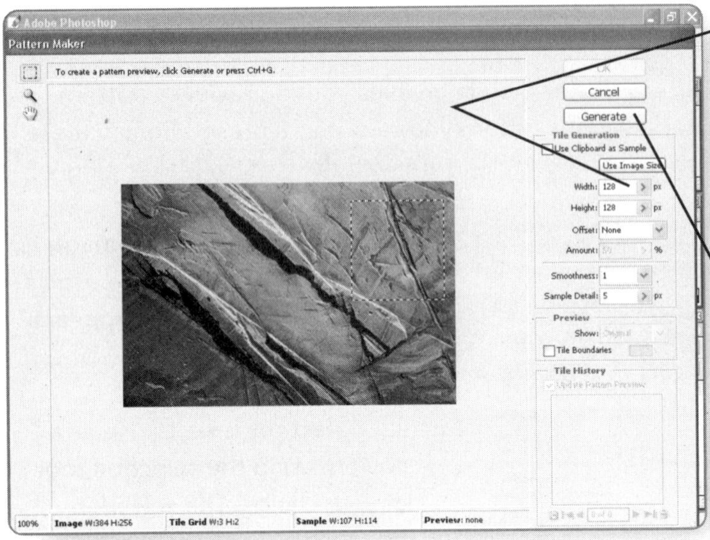

5. Change settings such as the tile's Width, Height, Smoothness, and Sample Detail as necessary. The Pattern Maker will apply those settings when you generate the pattern tile preview.

6. Click on **Generate**. The Pattern Maker window will preview the pattern, both as a single tile in the Tile History area and as an applied pattern in the main portion of the dialog box.

7. Click on the **Save Preset Pattern** button. The Pattern Name dialog box will open.

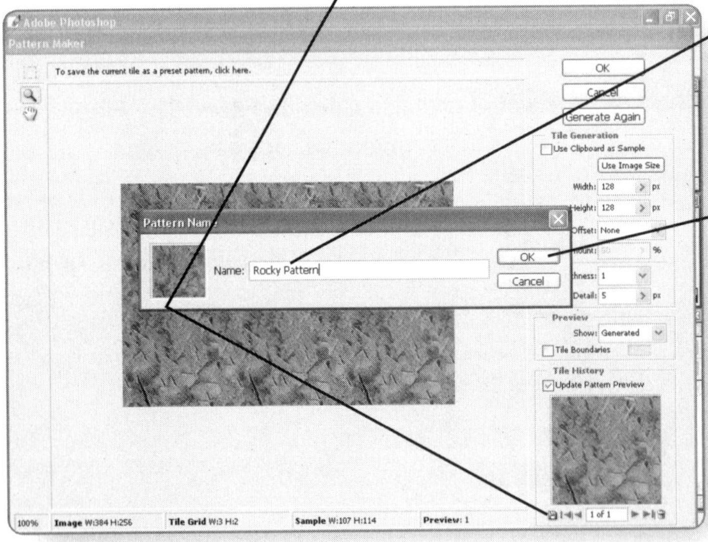

8. Type a **name** for the pattern in the Name text box. Photoshop will use the name you specify to identify the pattern.

9. Click on **OK**. The Pattern Name dialog box will close.

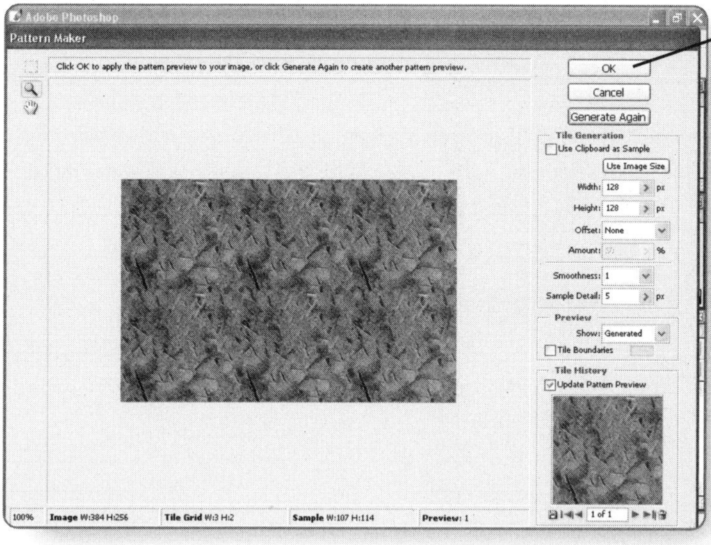

10. **Click** on **OK**. The Pattern Maker window will close, and the pattern will be applied to your current layer.

Deleting a Layer

When you want to remove a layer from an image, it's fastest to use the Layers palette, as detailed here.

1. **Click** on the **layer** to delete in the Layers palette. It will be highlighted.

2. **Click** on the **Delete** layer button. A warning message box will open.

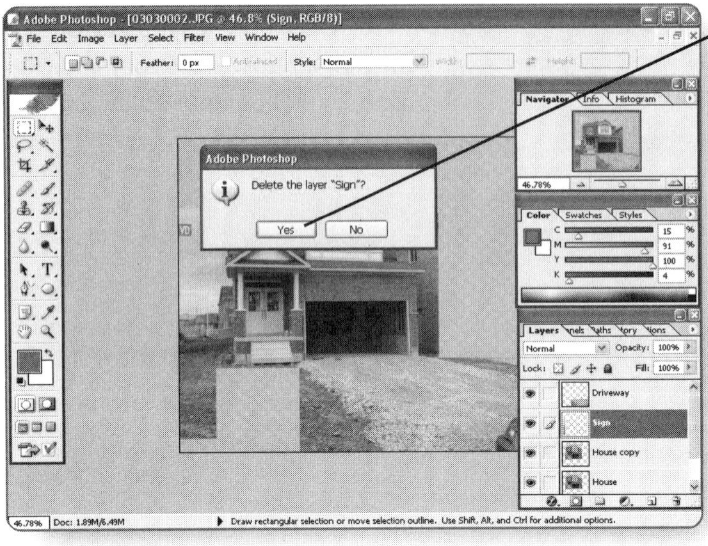

3. Click on **Yes**. Photoshop will complete the deletion.

Grouping and Ungrouping Layers

In order to help you manage your layers you can group them together based on any criteria that makes sense to you. You group layers by creating a layer set and then dragging layers into and out of the set on the Layers palette.

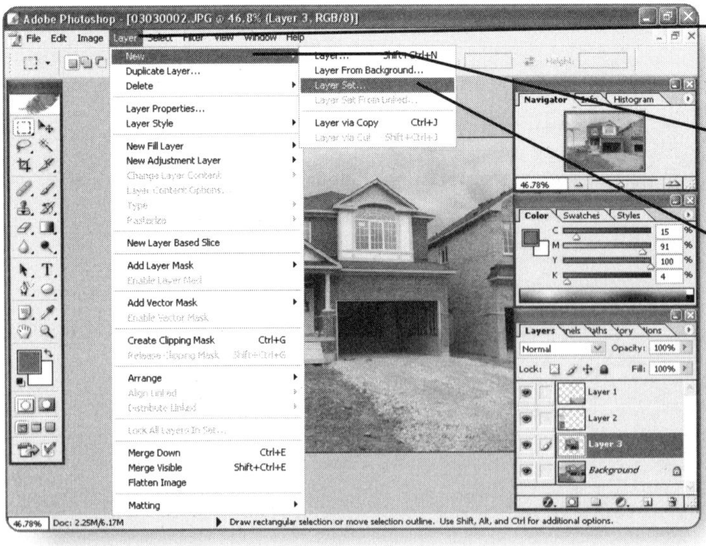

1. Click on **Layer**. The Layer menu will appear.

2. Point to **New**. The New submenu will appear.

3. Click on **Layer Set**. The Layer Set dialog box will appear.

4. **Type** a **name** for the set into the Name text box. The specified name will be used for the set.

5. **Choose** an **option** the Color and Mode lists, if necessary. Making a Color choice will apply a color to the new set's listing in the Layers palette. Making a Mode choice will apply a blending mode, which controls how the individual pixels on the layers in the set blend with pixels on other layers in the set.

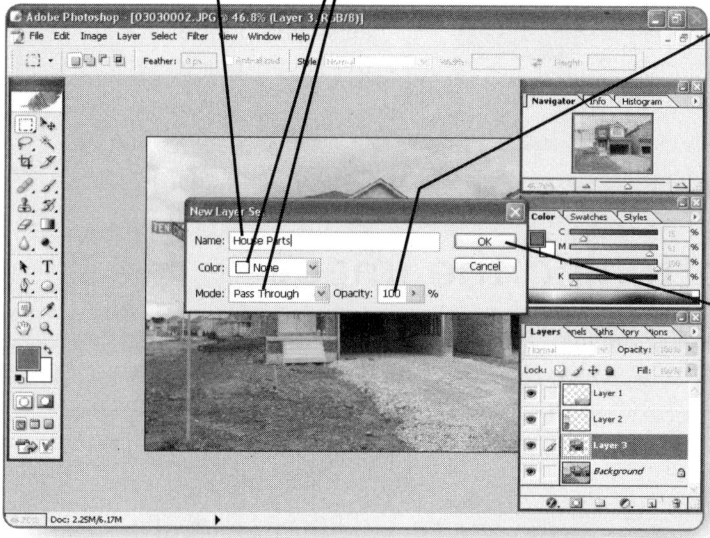

6. **Type** a **new entry** into the Opacity text box, if necessary. (You also can click on its arrow, drag the slider, and then click on the arrow again.) Photoshop will make the set's contents more transparent.

7. **Click** on **OK**. Photoshop will close the New Layer dialog box and create the new layer, which will appear in the Layers palette.

8. **Drag** a **layer name** and **drop** it onto the set name in the Layers palette. The layer will be added into the set.

> **NOTE**
>
> To remove a layer from the set, drag it back off the set and drop it elsewhere in the list on the Layers palette.

Flattening the Image

Flattening the image combines all the layer contents on a single layer, which can make the file size more compact. Use this process only if you've finished editing your image, and undo the action immediately if you've done it by mistake.

1. **Click** on **Layer**. The Layer menu will appear.

2. **Click** on **Flatten Image**. Photoshop immediately combines the contents of all the layers onto a single layer.

9

Adding Variety with Masks

If you've ever taped off an area while you're painting to protect that area from drips and spatters, you've created a mask. In Photoshop, you apply a mask to designate part of an image for changes and to shield (mask) the unselected areas against those changes. In this way, you can apply different effects and filters in varying portions of the image or layer. In this chapter, you'll learn how to:

- Set options for a quick mask
- Work in Quick Mask mode
- Create and use a layer mask
- Explore mask examples

Changing Quick Mask Options

The Quick Mask mode allows you to apply a mask by painting it on your image. Before you change to Quick Mask mode, you can set a few different options that affect how Quick Mask mode behaves.

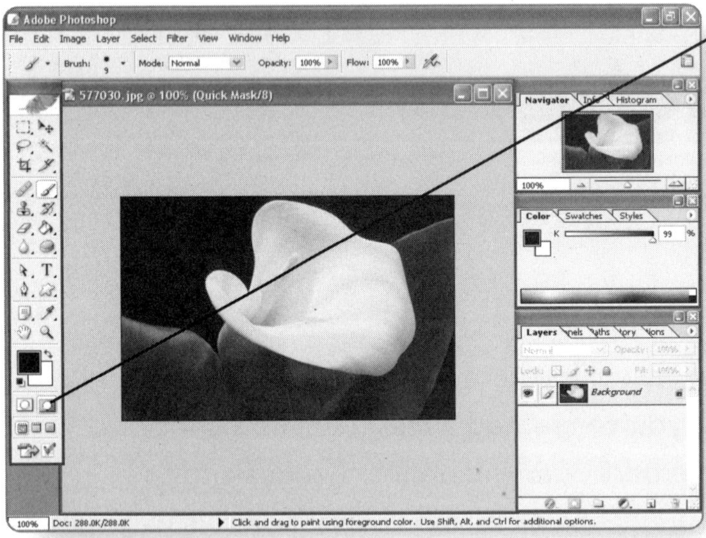

1. **Double-click** on the **Edit in Quick Mask Mode button** on the toolbox. The Quick Mask Options dialog box will open.

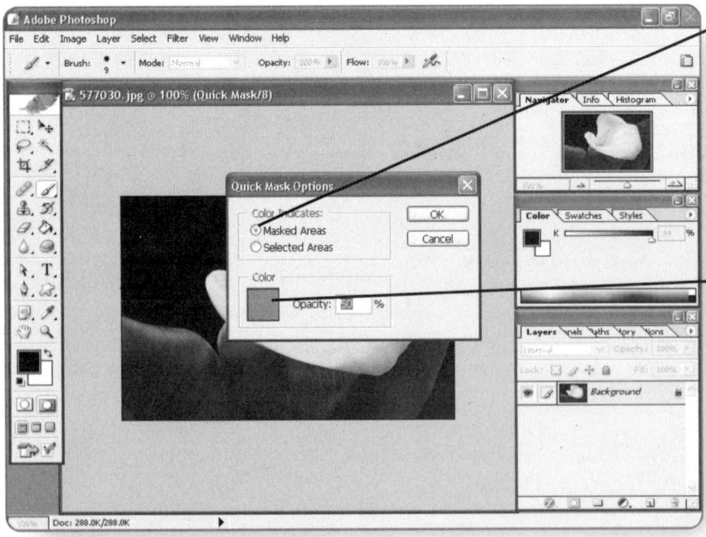

2. **Click** on an **option** in the Color Indicates area. Photoshop will apply the mask color to either the Masked Areas or Selected Areas in the image, depending on your selection.

3. **Click** on the **Color box**. The Color Picker dialog box will open.

4. Click on a **color hue** in the narrow band of colors near the middle of the dialog box. Photoshop will display a different range of colors in the Select Quick Mask color box.

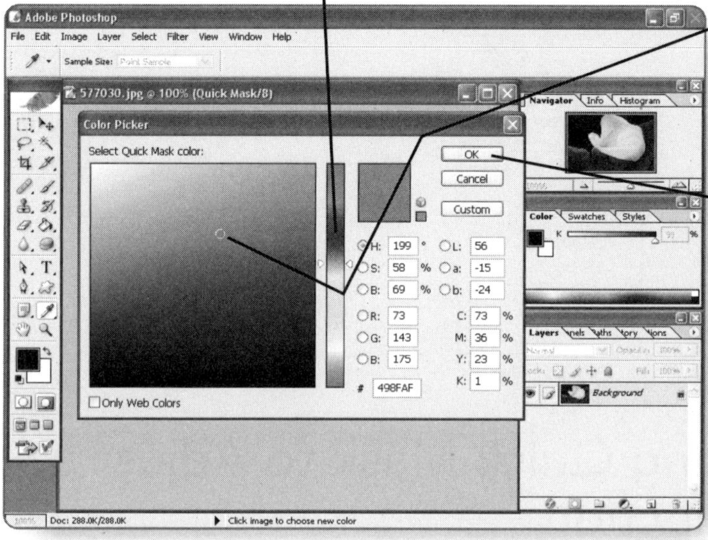

5. Click on a **color** in the Select Quick Mask color box. The color you click on will become the active mask color.

6. Click on **OK**. Photoshop will close the Color Picker dialog box and return to the Quick Mask Options dialog box.

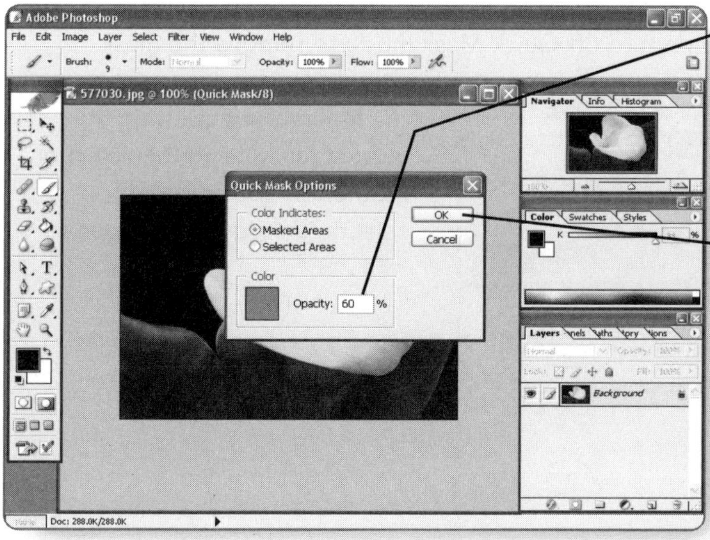

7. Type a new **entry** in the Opacity text box, if necessary. Photoshop will make the mask color more or less transparent, depending on your entry.

8. Click on **OK**. Photoshop will close the Quick Mask Options dialog box and apply the new settings the next time you use Quick Mask mode.

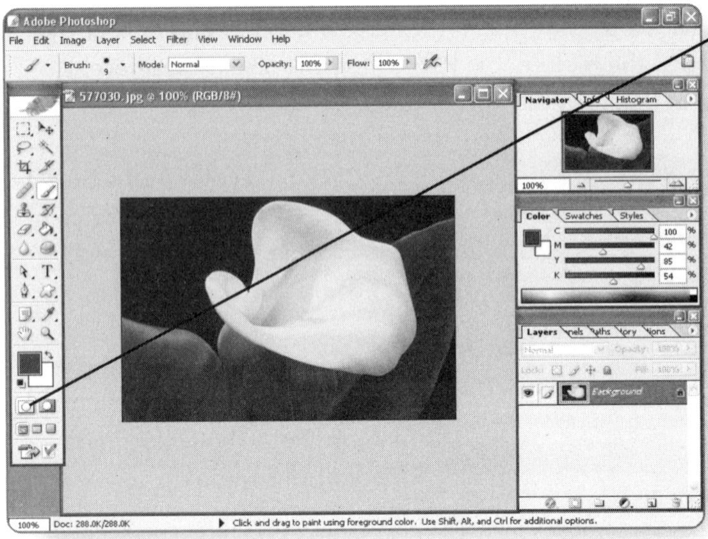

9. **Click** on the **Edit in Standard Mode button** on the toolbox. This turns off Quick Mask mode so that you can make a selection.

Using Quick Mask to Adjust a Selection

Quick Mask mode enables you to use a selection on the current layer as a temporary mask. Once you've masked the area, you can make the needed changes to the unmasked area and then turn off Quick Mask mode to remove the mask.

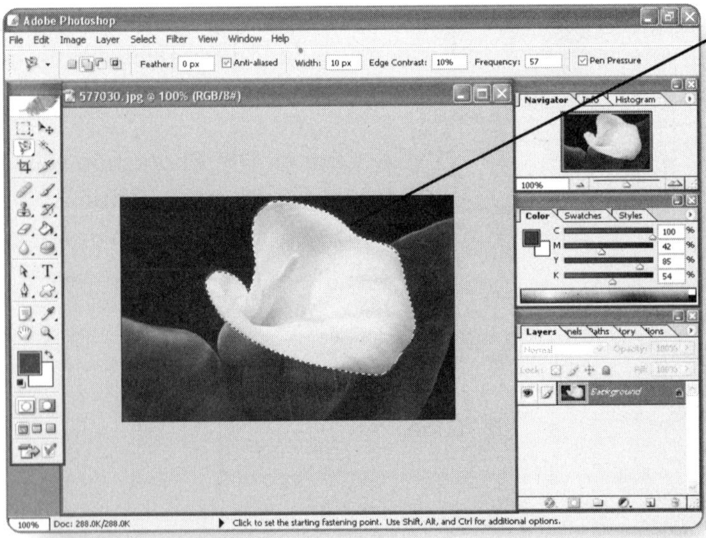

1. **Make** a **selection** on the current layer using the selection method of your choice. The selection marquee will appear.

TIP

See Chapter 5, "Selecting Image Content," to refresh your memory about the various selection methods. One trick is to select the area you don't want to mask, click on Select, and then click on Inverse to select the image areas that previously were not selected. (The figure here shows an inverted selection.)

2. **Click** on the **Quick Mask Mode button** on the toolbox. The Quick Mask mode will become active, and the mask color will appear over the masked area.

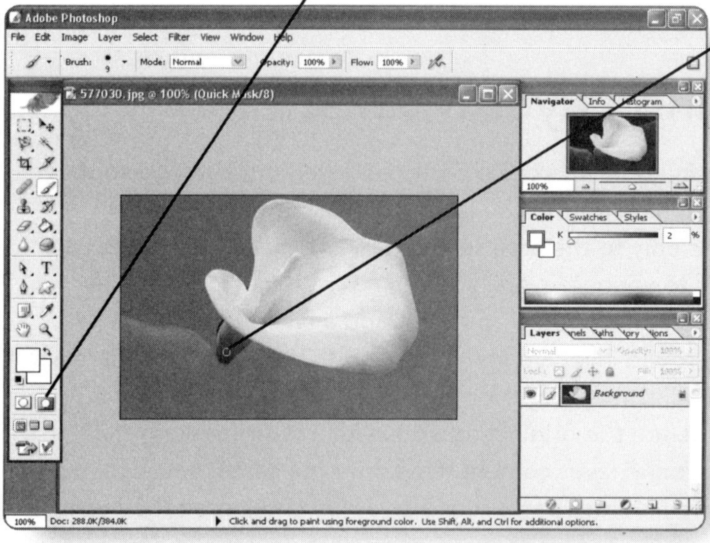

3. **Make** the desired **change** to the masked area, using a toolbox tool or filter. The mask boundaries will change accordingly. This example shows a mask being adjusted using a brush.

NOTE

Paint or draw on the nonmasked area with a color other than white to create a semitransparent masked area. Use white to exclude an area from the mask and black to add area to the mask (the hidden area).

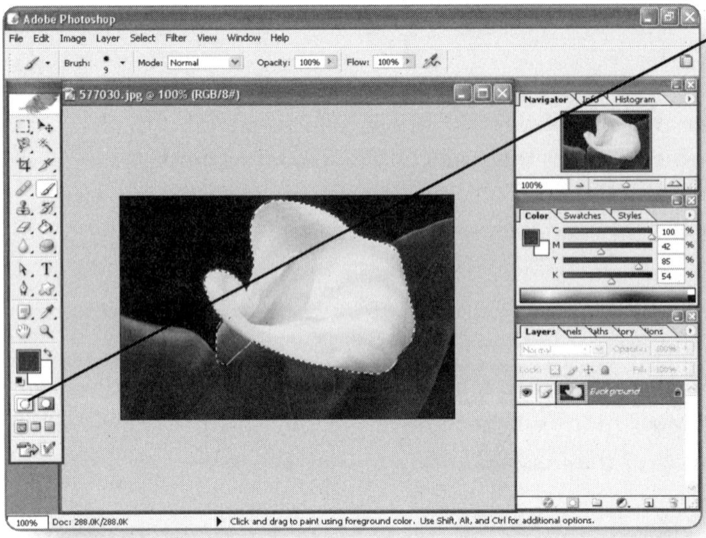

4. **Click** on the **Standard Mode button** on the toolbox. Photoshop will leave Quick Mask mode and return to the altered selection. You can then apply the needed changes to the selected areas, as described later in the section "Putting a Mask to Work."

Using Layer Masks

You can add a mask to a particular layer in the image so that you can hide part of the layer from display or even apply effects only to the area selected by the mask. By adding layer masks to various layers, you can mix and match effects as needed in the image. You can't add a layer mask to the Background layer, so you may need to add another layer such as an adjustment layer or duplicate the Background layer and then delete the original to work with a layer mask on the Background layer content itself. In some cases, you also may want to hide the Background layer (by clicking on the eye icon beside it) to ensure that you can select only the image content that you want.

NOTE

You also can create a special, color-related type of mask called an alpha channel. See "Adding an Alpha Channel" in Chapter 16, "Correcting Image Color," to learn more.

Creating a Mask on a Layer

Adding a mask on a layer will have different effects, depending on the layer's contents. For text layers, it enables you to select text and apply filters without rasterizing the text layer (that is, converting the layer to pixels rather than a vector layer, where objects are based on larger, resizable shapes). For layers with small photos, fills, and other objects, the layer mask excludes the information not contained within the mask area, so it doesn't display in the image. For adjustment layers like a hue/saturation layer, the mask enables you to adjust the image color only within the areas defined by the mask.

> **NOTE**
>
> The examples in this chapter illustrate layer masks. You also can create vector masks to mask sharp shapes based on paths in an image. See Chapter 10, "Using Paths," to learn how to add a path and use it to create a vector mask.

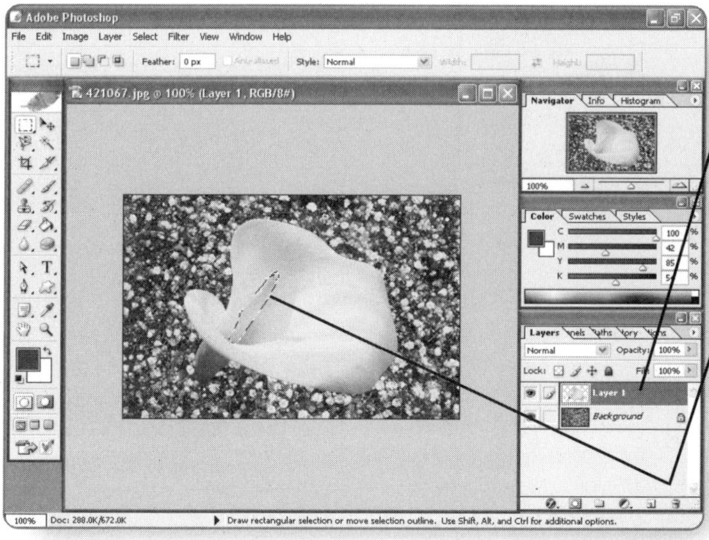

1. **Click** on the **layer** in the Layers palette to which you want to add a mask. The layer will become the current or active layer.

2. **Make** a **selection** on the current layer using the selection method of your choice. The selection marquee will appear.

NOTE

When you add certain types of layers, such as gradient fill layers, they automatically include a mask that includes all the layer content. It's often best to delete this mask by right-clicking on the mask thumbnail in the Layers palette and then clicking on Discard Layer Mask. See the next section, "Changing or Trashing a Mask," for more information. If you try to add another mask without deleting the first one, Photoshop will add a clipping path instead. Chapter 10 describes what a clipping path is and how to use one.

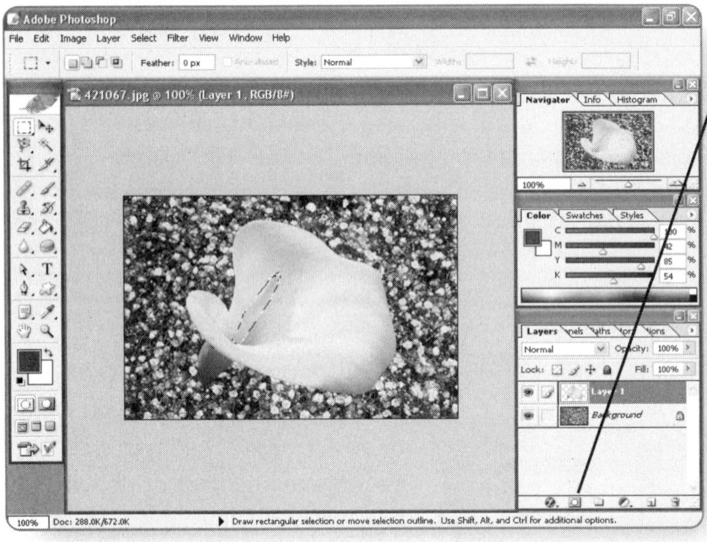

3. **Click** on the **Add Layer Mask button** at the bottom of the Layers palette. Photoshop will create the mask immediately.

TIP

Press and hold the Alt key as you click to invert the selection in the mask.

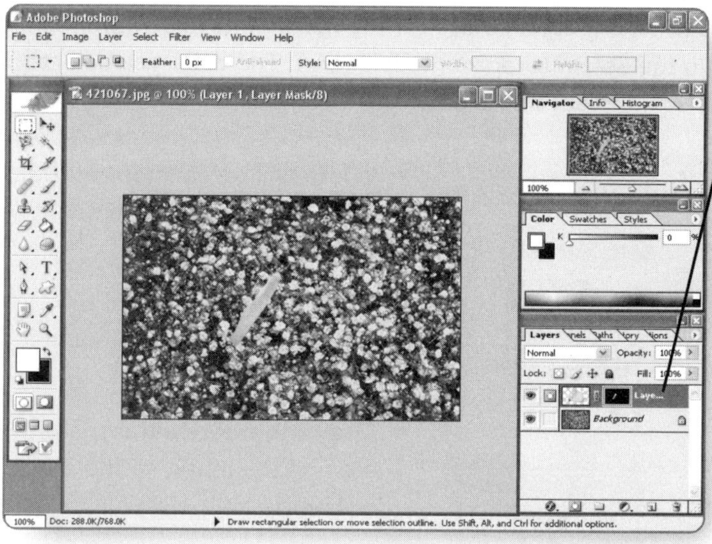

4. Review the **mask thumbnail** in the Layers palette. The black area in the thumbnail will show the zone that the mask hides or excludes.

Changing or Trashing a Mask

The selection on a layer mask isn't permanent once you've made it, so you can adjust the mask at a later time by painting or drawing. You also can delete a mask from a layer altogether.

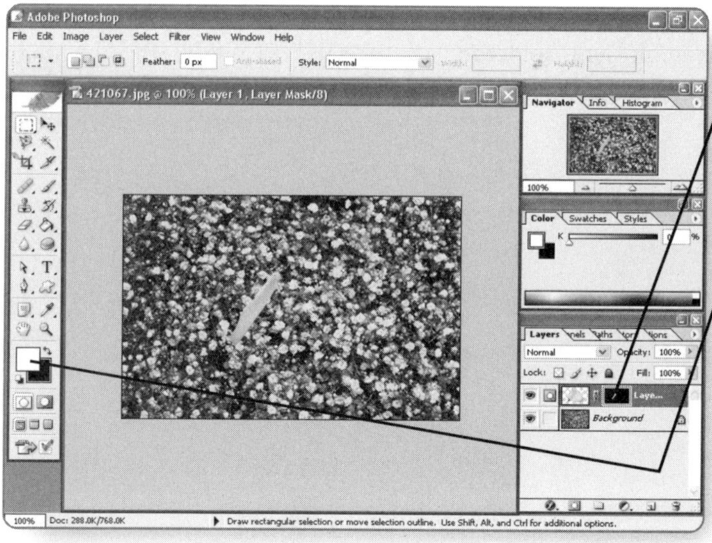

1. Click on the **mask thumbnail** for the desired layer in the Layers palette. The mask (and layer) will become active.

2. Click on the **Set Foreground Color box** at the bottom of the toolbox. The Color Picker dialog box will open.

3. **Click** on the **color** to use for the mask edits (black, white, or gray) in the Select foreground color box. The color you select controls the effect of the edits you will make:

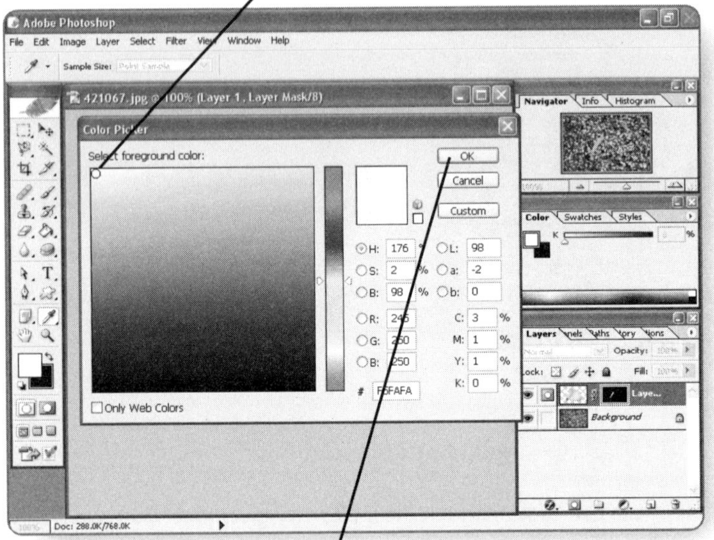

- **White** will reveal more of the layer, decreasing the amount of masked-off area.
- **Black** will hide more of the layer, increasing the amount of masked-off area.
- **Gray** will create a transparent area on the mask, so the area will be partially visible.

4. **Click** on **OK**. The Color Picker dialog box will close, and the color you selected will become active.

NOTE

For solid color, gradient, and pattern fill layers, painting with white has no effect because the entire layer is revealed. Painting with black hides the portion of the fill that you've painted over.

5. **Select** the **tool** to use in the toolbox. The tool will become the active tool.

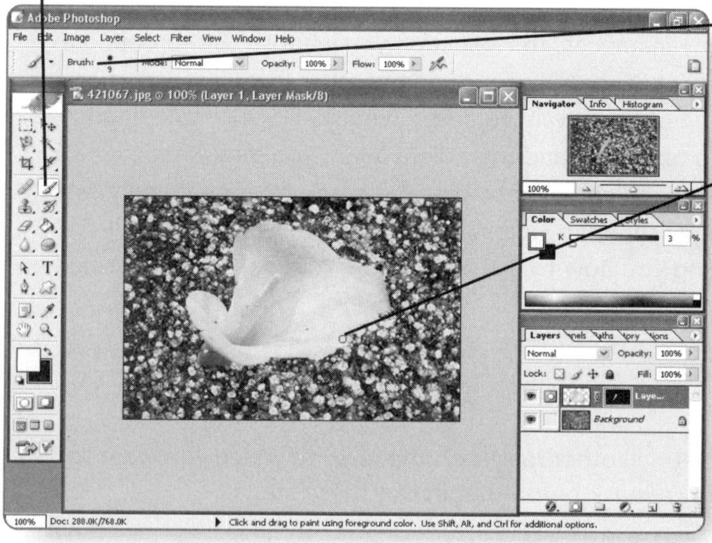

6. **Set** tool **options** on the options bar. The options you specify will become active.

7. **Draw** or **paint** on the **layer**. The mask will be altered accordingly.

8. **Click** on **Layer**. The Layer menu will appear.

9. **Point** to **Remove Layer Mask**. A submenu will appear.

10. **Click** on **Discard**. The Layer Mask will be deleted.

Using a Selection from One Layer as a Mask on Another

In some instances, the selection you want to use to define a mask for a layer may appear on another layer instead of on the layer where you want to add the mask. For example, if you have a text layer and a gradient layer, you may want to mask out the gradient layer so that the gradient appears only over the text. The following steps illustrate this example while showing you how to use a selection from one layer to create a mask on another.

> **CAUTION**
>
> Delete all other masks on the layer to which you want to copy a mask before beginning these steps.

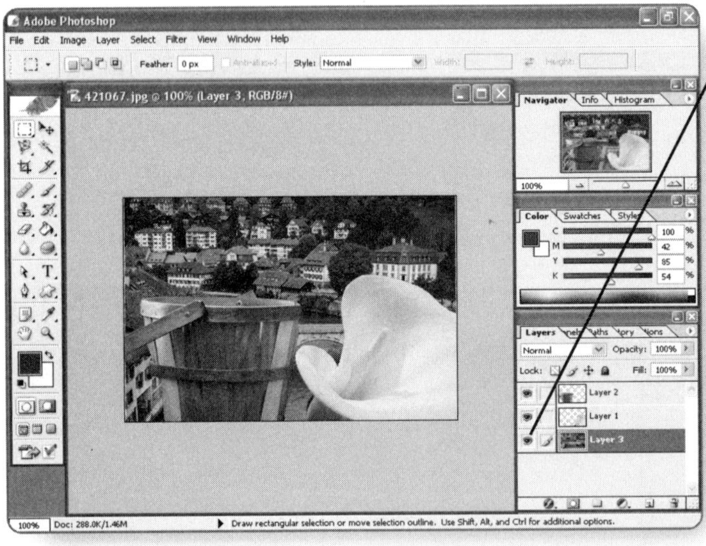

1. **Click** on the **eye icon** beside any layer in the Layers palette. The eye icon will disappear, and the layer will become hidden, making it easier for you to select content on another layer.

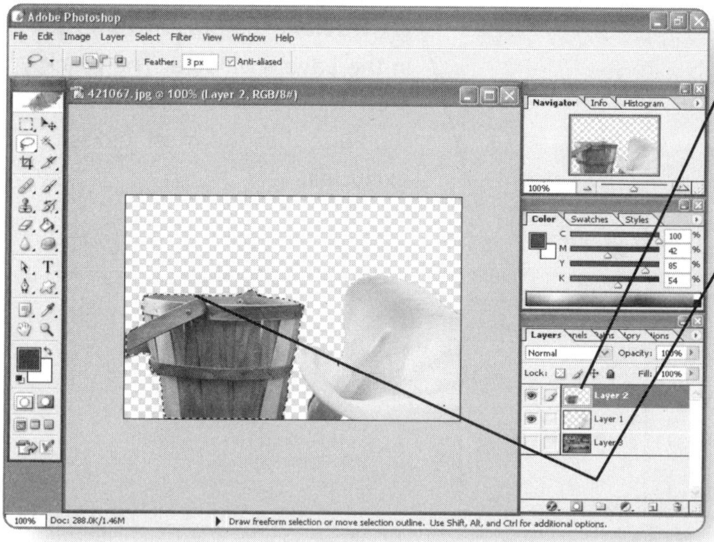

2. Click on the **layer** with the content to select in the Layers palette. The layer will become the current or active layer.

3. Make a **selection** on the current layer using the selection method of your choice. The selection marquee will appear.

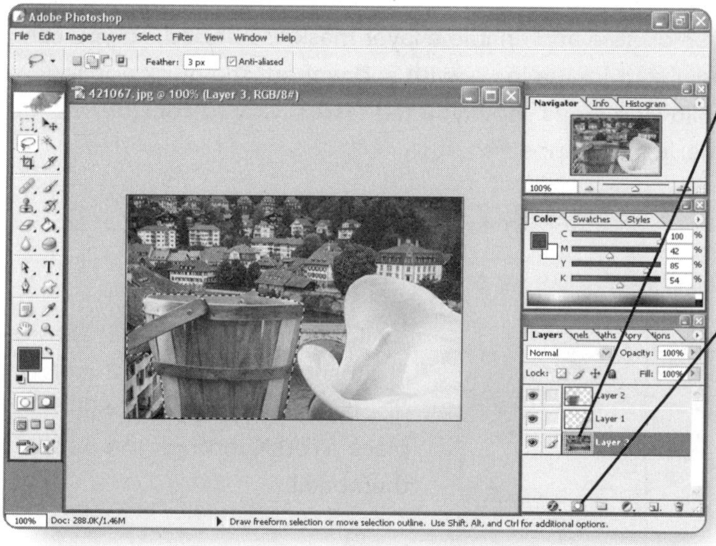

4. Click on the **layer** in the Layers palette to which you want to add the mask. The layer will become the current or active layer, and it should become visible if you hid it in step 1.

5. Click on the **Add Layer Mask button** at the bottom of the Layers palette. Photoshop will create the mask immediately.

6. Review the **mask thumbnail** in the Layers palette. The black area in the thumbnail will show the zone that the mask hides or excludes.

Reviewing the Mask

You can disable and enable a layer mask as needed, so you can see how your image looks with and without the mask applied. The following steps show you the fastest way to control whether a mask appears:

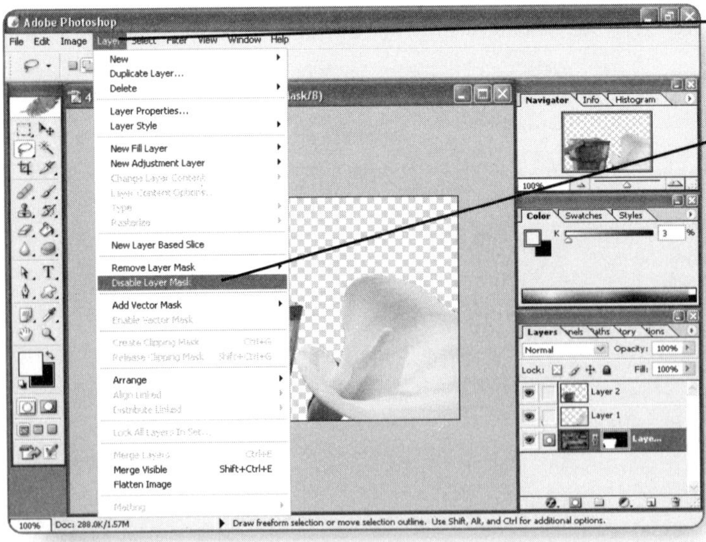

1. Click on **Layer**. The Layer menu will appear.

2. Click on **Disable Layer Mask**. Photoshop will disable the mask display immediately and will place a red X through the mask thumbnail.

3. **Click** on **Layer**. The Layer menu will appear.

4. **Click** on **Enable Layer Mask**. Photoshop will reapply the mask immediately, and the image display will be affected accordingly.

Putting a Mask to Work

As noted earlier in this chapter, a layer mask may behave a bit differently or enable you to do different things, depending on the nature of the layer where you added the mask. This section reviews two examples of how you can use layer masks to adjust or enhance selected content in an image.

Cropping a Photo

To use this technique, make sure the photo to crop appears on its own layer, not on the Background layer.

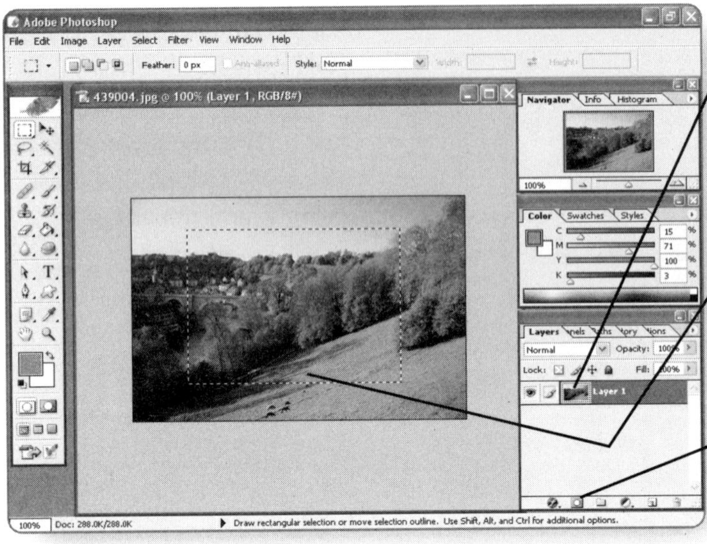

1. Click on the **layer** in the Layers palette to which you want to add the mask. The layer will become the current or active layer.

2. Make a **selection** on the current layer using the selection method of your choice. The selection marquee will appear.

3. Click on the **Add Layer Mask button** at the bottom of the Layers palette. Photoshop will create the mask immediately.

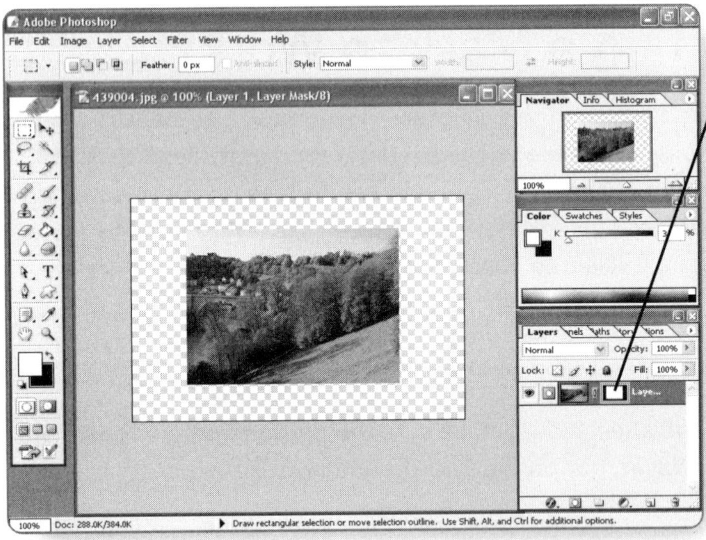

4. Review the **mask results** in the image. Photoshop will mask out the areas not included within the selection from which you created the mask.

Adding a Filter

When you apply a filter, it only affects the currently selected area. Because a mask in effect protects an area like a selection, applying a filter to a layer that has a mask on it filters only the portions of the layer that aren't masked off. This is a particularly vital technique for text layers. With the mask, Photoshop would prompt you to rasterize the text layer, eliminating your ability to edit the text in the future.

1. **Click** on the desired **layer** in the Layers palette. The layer will become the current or active layer.

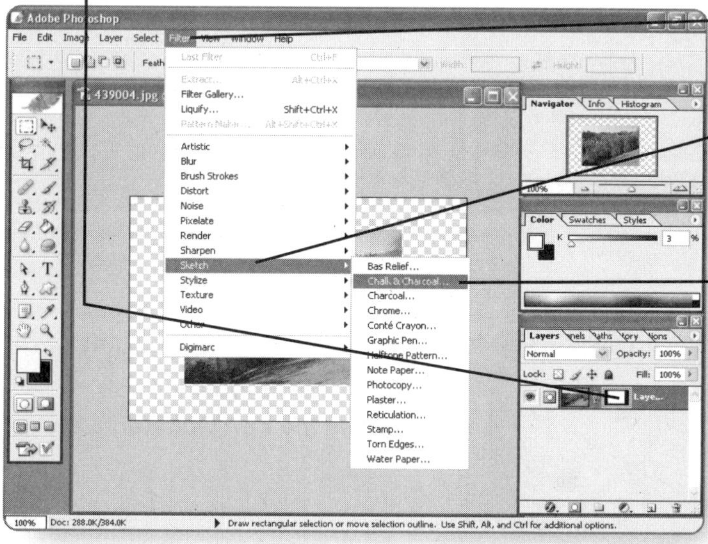

2. **Click** on **Filter**. The Filter menu will appear.

3. **Click** on the **filter command** of your choice. A submenu with specific filter choices will appear.

4. **Click** on a **filter** in the submenu. Depending on the filter you have selected either a dialog box will open allowing you to set options for the filter or the Filter Gallery will open.

5. Set filter **options** as necessary. A preview in the window shows how the filter will look when applied using the settings you specified.

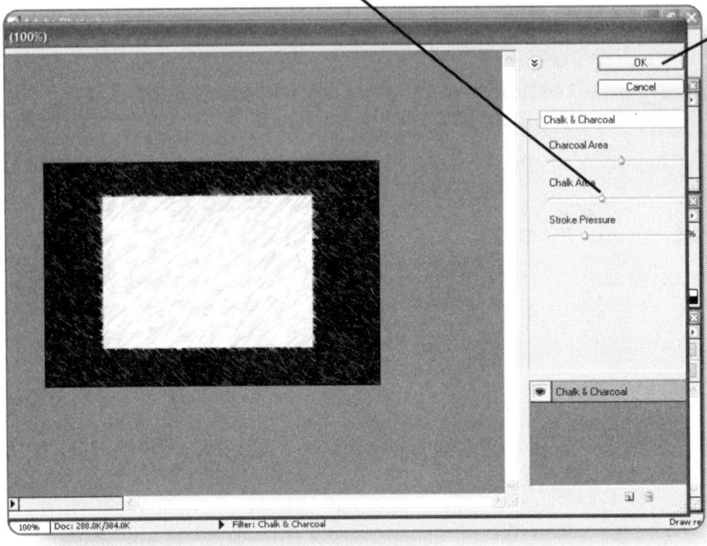

6. Click on **OK**. The Filter Gallery will close, and the filter will be applied to the layer contents not hidden or protected by the mask.

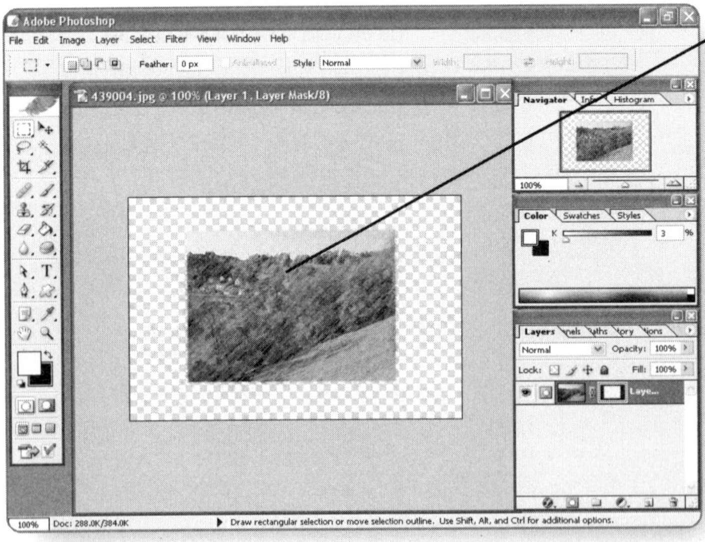

7. Review the filter **results** in the image. Photoshop will display the newly filtered areas.

Recoloring Part of the Image

This mask technique works with a special color-correction layer called an adjustment layer. (You'll learn more about working with colors in Chapters 15 through 17.) It enables you to make a color change on part of an image only. This example shows how to make a hue and saturation change, but you can make other changes depending on the nature of the adjustment layer you choose to use.

1. **Click** on **Layer**. The Layer menu will appear.

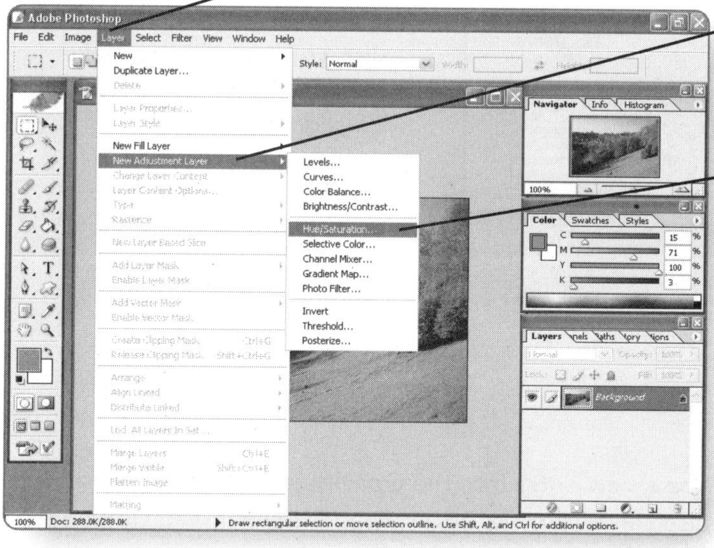

2. **Point** to **New Adjustment Layer**. A submenu with specific layer choices will appear.

3. **Click** on **Hue/Saturation** in the submenu. The New Layer dialog box will appear.

4. **Type** a **name** for the layer into the Name text box. The specified name will be used for the layer.

5. **Click** a **choice** from the Color and Mode lists, if necessary. Making a Color choice will apply a color to the new layer's listing in the Layers palette. Making a Mode choice will apply a layer blending mode, which controls how the individual pixels on the layer blend with pixels on other layers.

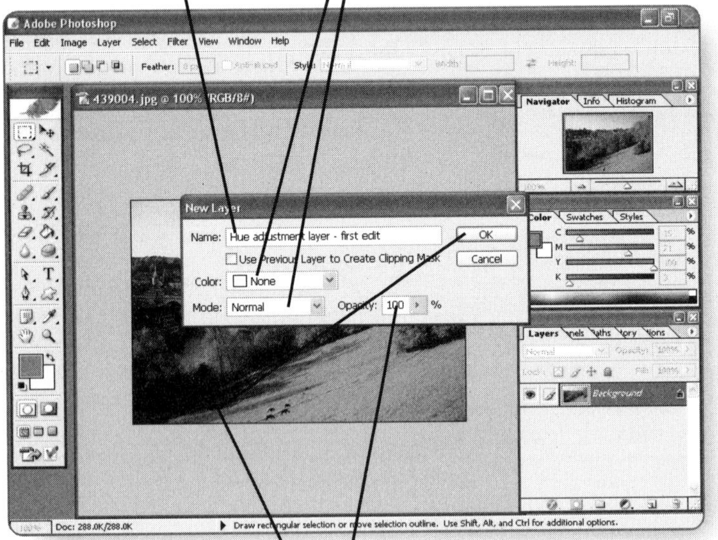

TIP

Depending on the choice you make from the Mode list, you may have to make other layers, such as the Background layer, transparent. To do so, double-click on the layer in the Layers palette, change the Opacity setting to 0, and then click on OK.

6. **Type** a new **entry** into the Opacity text box, if necessary. (You also can click on its arrow, drag the slider, and click on the arrow again.) Photoshop will make the layer's contents more transparent.

7. **Click** on **OK**. Photoshop will close the New Layer dialog box and open the Hue/Saturation dialog box.

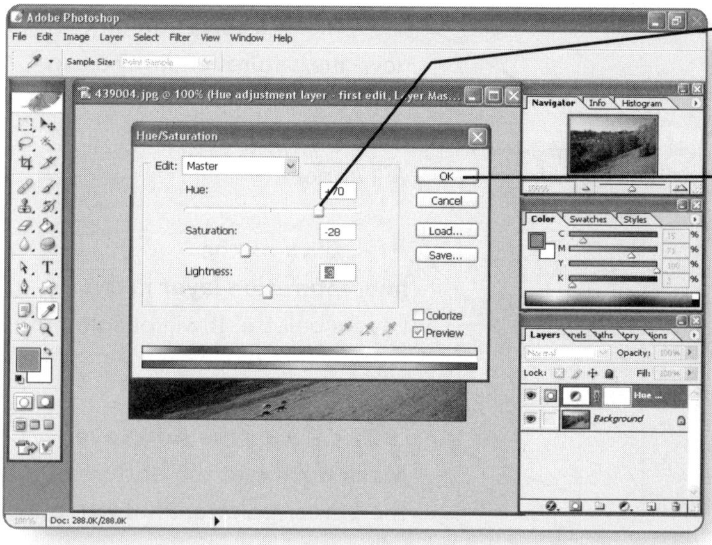

8. **Drag** the **sliders** as necessary. The image will display the corrected color.

9. **Click** on **OK**. The Hue/Saturation dialog box will close.

10. **Click** on **Layer**. The Layer menu will appear.

11. **Click** on **Remove Layer Mask**. A submenu will appear.

12. **Click** on **Discard**. Photoshop will remove the layer mask immediately.

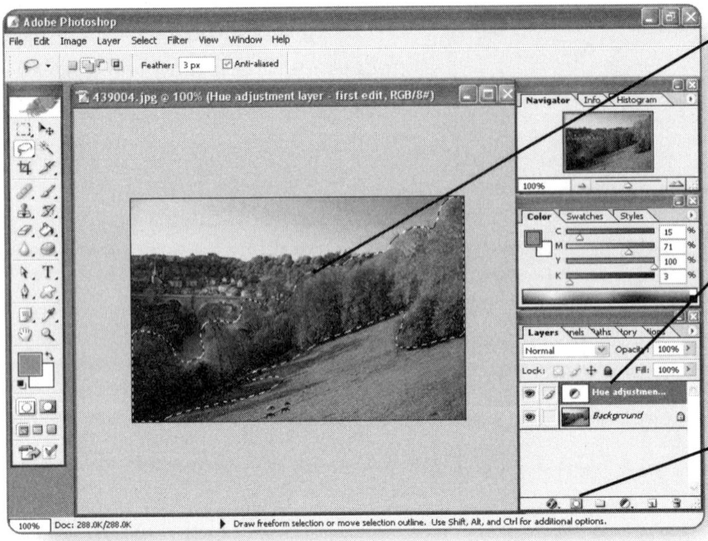

13. Make a **selection** on the new hue/saturation layer using the selection method of your choice. The selection marquee will appear.

14. Click on the **hue/saturation layer** in the Layers palette. It will become the current or active layer.

15. Click on the **Add Layer Mask button** at the bottom of the Layers palette. Photoshop will create the mask immediately.

16. Review the **mask results** in the image. Photoshop will apply the color correction to only the area not blocked by the mask.

NOTE

If you double-click on the layer thumbnail (to the far left) for the hue/saturation layer, the Hue/Saturation dialog box reopens so that you can further adjust the color correction in the areas not blocked by the mask.

10

Using Paths

A path is essentially a vector-based selection outline in Photoshop. Because paths are vector based (an outline rather than a selection of pixels), creating paths rather than saved selections in an image file will have less of a tendency to increase the file size. This can be beneficial if the file is a large scan, has dozens of layers, or is simply large because it's complex. You can use a path as a selection at any time, fill the path or color the path outline, or even use a special type of path to clip image content when you plan to reuse a file. In this chapter, you will learn how to:

- Create various types of paths
- View and work with paths
- Fill a path or color the path outline
- Use a path to define a selection
- Use a clipping path to prepare an image for reuse in other files or settings

Creating Paths

You use the Paths palette to save the paths you create, and you use the Pen tools and Shape tools to actually draw each path. The tool you should use to create the path depends on the desired shape for the path.

> **NOTE**
>
> Paths do not print unless you fill them with color or color their border.

Adding a Shape Path

The "Drawing a Rectangle, Oval, or Other Shape" section in Chapter 3, "Adding Content with Tools," explained how to use the Rectangle tool (and the other shape tools you access via the Rectangle tool) to draw shapes on an image. You also can use these tools to create a path for later use, as described here.

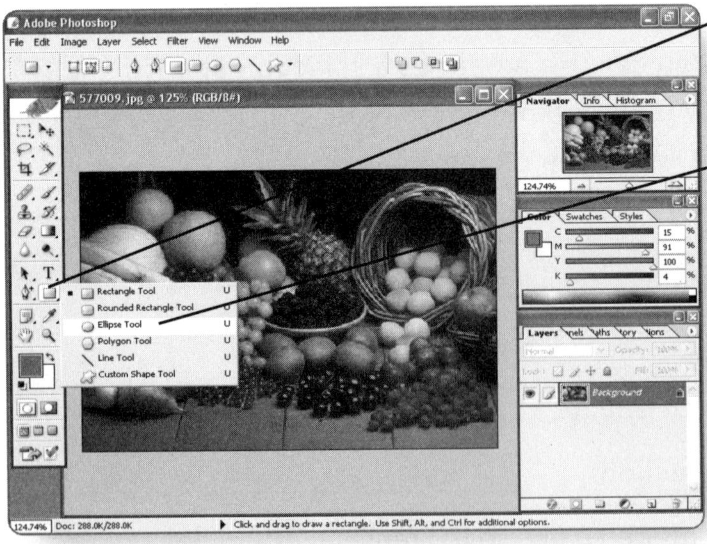

1. **Click** and **hold** the **Rectangle tool** in the toolbox. Its shortcut menu will appear.

2. **Click** on the desired **shape tool** to use in the submenu. The selected tool will become the active tool.

> **NOTE**
>
> If you choose the Custom Shape tool, be sure to use the Shape drop-down list on the options bar to specify which kind of shape to draw.

3. **Click** on the **Paths button** on the options bar. The selected tool will become active for path selection.

4. **Click** and **drag diagonally** on the **picture** in the work area. Keep the mouse button pressed as you drag in any desired direction. When you release the mouse button, the path will appear.

5. **Click** on **Window**. The Window menu will appear.

6. **Click** on **Paths**. The Paths palette will become the active tab in the Layers palette window. The Paths palette will show that the path you've drawn appears as a temporary path called a work path.

> **TIP**
>
> Instead of opening the Window menu and choosing Paths, you can click on the Paths tab in the Layers palette window.

7. Click on the **Paths palette menu button**. The palette menu will appear.

8. Click on **Save Path**. The Save Path dialog box will open.

> **NOTE**
>
> You don't have to save a temporary work path unless you want to reuse it later.

9. Type a **name** for the path in the Name text box. Your new name will replace the temporary name in the text box.

10. Click on **OK**. The Save Path dialog box will close, and Photoshop will finish saving the path under the name you specified.

11. Click on a **blank area** in the Paths palette. Photoshop will deselect the path.

12. Click on the **Layers tab** in the Layers palette window. (Alternately, you can choose Window, Layers.) Photoshop will return to the regular view of layers in the image.

> **NOTE**
>
> If you skip this last step when using a tool to create a path, the path will remain selected, and any further actions you take pertain to that path. For example, if you tried to create a path with another tool, it would simply be added into the current path rather than created as a separate work path.

Making a Pen Path

The Pen tool enables you to create paths with straight lines, curves, and angles. Use this tool when you want to create a path that's irregular in shape or has swooping, controlled curves.

> **NOTE**
>
> You must be careful when using the mouse with the Pen tool. Different mouse actions have different results. The following steps illustrate the various mouse techniques you need to master when using the Pen tool.

1. **Click** on the **Pen tool** in the toolbox. Its options will appear in the options bar.

2. **Click** on the **Paths button** on the options bar. The Pen tool will become active for path selection.

> **NOTE**
>
> If you click on the Shape Layers button (instead of the Paths button) on the options bar for any tool described in this chapter, the tool draws a shape or outline on a new layer in the image rather than simply creating a path.

3. **Click** on the **starting point** for the first segment in the path. An anchor point appears at the location where you clicked.

4. **Click** on the **location** where you want to end the segment. A straight-line segment appears between the anchor points.

5. **Press Ctrl+Z**. This will undo the path segment.

6. **Drag** on the location for the end of the next segment. Because you dragged, Photoshop will create a curved segment.

7. **Drag** the direction **point** at the end of the direction line and then release the mouse button. Photoshop will adjust the depth and direction of the curved segment based on where you drag the direction point.

8. **Drag** in the **opposite direction** on the location for the end of the next segment. Because you dragged in the opposite direction, Photoshop will create a segment that curves in the opposite direction.

> **TIP**
>
> To create a corner point between segments, press and hold the Alt key when you set the anchor point for the next segment. Press and hold the Ctrl key to drag an anchor point or corner point.

9. After you create all the needed segments, finish drawing the path in one of two ways:

- **Click** on the first **anchor** point to close the path shape. Note that when the mouse pointer is over the first anchor point, a small circle appears along with the pointer to tell you that clicking would then close the path.
- **Click** on the **Pen tool** in the toolbox to finish the path without closing the shape.

10. **Click** on the **Paths palette menu button**. The palette menu will appear.

11. **Click** on **Save Path**. The Save Path dialog box will open.

12. **Type** a **name** for the path in the Name text box. Your new name will replace the temporary name in the text box.

13. **Click** on **OK**. The Save Path dialog box will close, and Photoshop will finish saving the path under the name you specified.

14. **Click** on a **blank area** in the Paths palette. Photoshop will deselect the path.

15. **Click** on the **Layers tab** in the Layers palette window. (Alternately, choose Window, Layers.) Photoshop will return to the regular view of layers in the image.

Making a Freeform Path

The Freeform Pen tool enables you to create a path by dragging on the image. In addition, you can turn on the Magnetic option with the Freeform Pen tool to have the path outline "snap to" a shape in the image. This tool comes in handy when you want to create a path around a particular item or region in an image.

1. **Click** and **hold** the **Pen tool** in the toolbox. Its shortcut menu will appear.

2. **Click** on **Freeform Pen Tool**. The Freeform Pen tool will become the active tool.

3. **Click** on the **Paths button** on the options bar. The Freeform Pen tool will become active for path selection.

4. **Click** on the **Magnetic check box** to check it, if desired. Checking this option will cause the Freeform Pen tool to function as the Magnetic Pen tool, and your path will snap to the outline for an item in the image.

> **NOTE**
>
> The Magnetic feature works via color and tone contrast. You can click on the Magnetic check box near the center of the options bar to make the Freeform Pen tool work magnetically.

5. **Drag** on the **picture** in the work area. Keep the mouse button pressed as you drag in any desired direction. When you release the mouse button, the path will appear.

TIP

If you're using the Magnetic Pen tool, you can click to set specific anchor points and press Delete to remove the most recent anchor point. However, with the Freeform Pen tool, you must keep the mouse button pressed as you drag.

6. Finish drawing the path in one of three ways:

- **Click** on the first **anchor** point to close the path shape. Note that when the mouse pointer is over the first anchor point, a small circle appears along with the pointer to tell you that clicking would then close the path.
- **Double-click** on the next-to-last **anchor** point to close the path automatically.
- **Click** on the **Freeform Pen** tool in the toolbox to finish the path without closing the shape.

NOTE

When you're drawing any path, you can press Esc to stop drawing the path.

7. **Click** on the **Paths palette menu button**. The palette menu will appear.

8. **Click** on **Save Path**. The Save Path dialog box will open.

9. **Type** a **name** for the path in the Name text box. Your new name will replace the temporary name in the text box.

10. **Click** on **OK**. The Save Path dialog box will close, and Photoshop will finish saving the path under the name you specified.

11. **Press Esc**. Photoshop will deselect the path.

12. **Click** on the **Layers tab** in the Layers palette window. (Alternately, choose Window, Layers.) Photoshop will return to the regular view of layers in the image.

Viewing and Changing a Path

The Paths palette enables you to view and work with the paths in an image file. When you change a path, you move, add, and delete anchor points.

1. **Click** on **Window**. The Window menu will appear.

2. **Click** on **Paths** if it is not already selected. The Paths palette will become the active tab in the Layers palette window.

> **TIP**
>
> Instead of opening the Window menu and choosing Paths, you can click on the Paths tab in the Layers palette window.

3. **Click** on the desired **path** in the Paths palette tab. The path will become the active path.

4. **Use** the **Navigator** to pan the path into view, if necessary. The path will become visible in the work area.

5. **Click** and **hold** the **Pen tool** in the toolbox. Its shortcut menu will appear.

6. **Click** on **Add Anchor Point Tool**. The Add Anchor Point tool will become the active tool.

7. Click on the **path** at the location where you want to add the new anchor point. The anchor point will appear.

8. Drag the **new anchor point** (and any others) to the desired location. The path will reshape accordingly.

9. Click once on an **anchor point** that you want to delete. It will appear filled in.

10. Press Delete on your keyboard. The Anchor Point will be deleted, and the path will reshape accordingly.

11. **Click once** on an **anchor point** that you want to modify. It will appear filled in.

12. **Drag anchor points** to reposition them as needed. Again, the path will reshape accordingly, but in this case, you didn't have to add new anchor points.

13. **Press Esc**. The path will be deselected, but your changes will remain in the path. From here, you can click on the Layers tab in the Layers palette or choose Window, Layers to resume working with layers.

Filling or Coloring a Path

You can fill a path with color to add a blotch of color in an image, or you can "stroke" the path outline with color to add a subtle outline of color in the image. Although by default a path doesn't print, it will print after you fill or stroke it with color. These steps explain how to use color with a path.

1. **Click** on the desired **fill or outline color** in the color ramp at the bottom of the Color palette. The color will become the active foreground color.

2. **Click** on **Window**. The Window menu will appear.

3. **Click** on **Paths**. The Paths palette will become the active tab in the Layers palette window.

> **TIP**
>
> Instead of opening the Window menu and choosing Paths, you can click on the Paths tab in the Layers palette window.

4. **Click** on the desired **path** to color in the Paths palette. The path will become the active path.

5a. **Click** on the **Fill Path with Foreground Color button** at the bottom of the Paths palette. Photoshop will fill the path with the color you selected in step 1.

OR

5b. **Click** on the **Stroke Path with Brush button** at the bottom of the Paths palette. Photoshop will apply a very thin outline of the foreground color to the path outline.

6. **Review** the resulting **color**. This example shows the path filled with color. If you merely stroked the path with color, the result could be fairly subtle and may not be visible until you finish working with the Paths palette.

> **NOTE**
>
> At this point, you can click on the Layers tab in the Layers palette or choose Window, Layers to finish working with paths.

Using a Path to Make a Selection

As noted earlier in this chapter, you can use a path as a selection at any time, making it easy for you to work with the path area later, applying a filter or other effect.

1. **Click** on **Window**. The Window menu will appear.

2. **Click** on **Paths** if the Paths palette is not already open. The Paths palette will become the active tab in the Layers palette window.

3. **Click** on the desired **path**. The path will become the active path.

4. **Click** on the **Load Path as a Selection button** at the bottom of the Paths palette tab. A selection marquee will appear around the path. You then can work with the selection just as you would any other selection.

Using a Path to Create a Vector Mask

A vector mask enables you to define a mask based on an outline (rather than based on image pixels and colors, as for a layer mask). You base a vector mask on a work path that you've previously created. Once you've created the vector mask, you can move or resize it as needed to adjust the masked area—something you can't easily do with a layer mask.

> **NOTE**
>
> Vector masking does not work on the Background layer, so right-click on the Background layer and click Duplicate Layer. Enter a name for the new layer in the Duplicate Layer dialog box and then click on OK. Finally, click the eye icon beside the original Background layer in the Layers palette to hide that layer so you can see the effects of your vector mask.

1. **Click** on **Window**. The Window menu will appear.

2. **Click** on **Paths** if the Paths palette is not already open. The Paths palette will become the active tab in the Layers palette window.

3. **Click** on the desired **path**. The path will become the active path.

4. **Click** on the **Layers tab** in the Layers palette window. Photoshop will return to the regular view of layers in the image.

5. **Click** on the **layer** with the content to mask. The layer will become the active layer.

6. **Click** on **Layer**. The Layer menu will appear.

7. **Point** to **Add Vector Mask**. The Add Vector Mask submenu will appear.

8. **Click** on **Current Path**. The mask will be created and applied immediately.

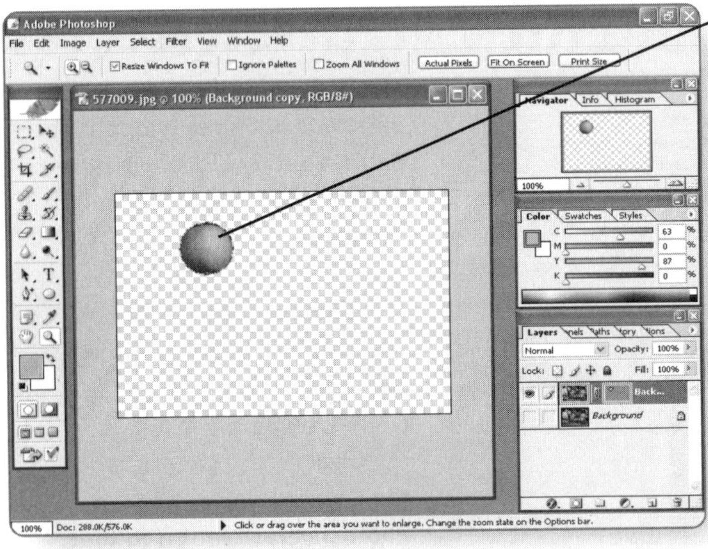

9. **Review** the resulting **mask**. Layer content outside the mask (path) will be hidden.

NOTE

At this point, you could use the Path Selection tool to move the mask around on the layer or to adjust the shape of the mask. To turn off the mask, right-click on the mask thumbnail in the Layers palette and then click on Disable Vector Mask. Right-click again and then click on Enable Vector Mask to reapply the mask.

Part III Review Questions

1. How do you add a new layer? See "Making a New Layer" in Chapter 8.
2. How do you go to a layer to work with it? See "Selecting a Layer" in Chapter 8.
3. What other kinds of layers can you add? See "Adding a Fill Layer," "Adding a Gradient Layer," and "Adding a Pattern Layer" in Chapter 8.
4. What do you do if one layer is hiding part of another? See "Arranging Layer Order" in Chapter 8.
5. Why do you use a mask? See "Using Layer Masks" in Chapter 9.
6. Can you convert a selection to a mask? See "Using a Selection from One Layer as a Mask on Another" in Chapter 9.
7. What can you do once you've created a mask? See "Putting a Mask to Work" in Chapter 9.
8. How and why do you create a path? See "Adding a Shape Path," "Making a Pen Path," and "Making a Freeform Path" in Chapter 10.
9. How do you convert a selection to a path? See "Using a Path to Make a Selection" in Chapter 10.
10. How do you create and use a clipping path? See "Using Clipping Paths" in Chapter 10.

PART IV

Fine-Tuning Your Image

11

Using Other Editing Tools

Photoshop includes a number of editing tools that you can use to touch up specific areas of an image or layer. Many of the techniques resemble traditional techniques used to correct a photo during development. You can adjust the focus of a particular area, enhance its intensity, or use other techniques such as filling an area with color. In this chapter, you will learn how to:

- Add blurring or smudging to an area
- Sharpen an area
- Use the Eraser tools to erase to the background color or transparency
- Erase all of a particular color on a layer using the Magic Eraser
- Add a gradient or fill an area with color
- Dodge, burn, or sponge an area
- Use tools to fix scratches, spots, and imperfections

Blurring an Area

I'm sure you've seen many infomercials for products that can make you look younger and that get rid of wrinkles and other skin imperfections. The truth is that Photoshop can actually make you look younger! It may seem contrary to your needs in most cases, but blurring part of an image can help camouflage an imperfection or achieve an effect.

These effects are broken down into filters and tools. Use a filter when you want to change the appearance of a selection or a layer. Use a tool when you want to "paint" on a particular area to make a correction.

1. **Click** on the **layer** in the Layers palette that holds the content you want to blur. The selected layer will become the active layer.

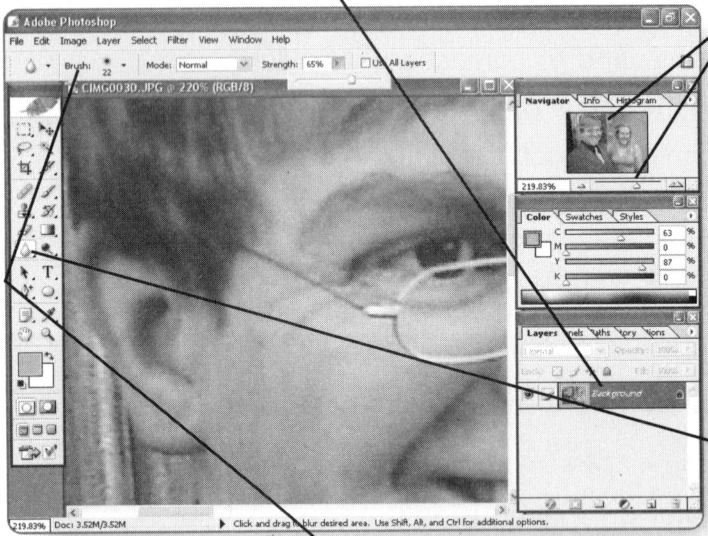

2. **Use** the **Navigator** to zoom in on and display the desired area. The selected area will become more visible.

3. **Click** on the **Blur tool** in the toolbox. The Blur tool will become the active tool.

4. **Choose** a **Brush style** on the options bar. The selected brush will become active for the Blur tool.

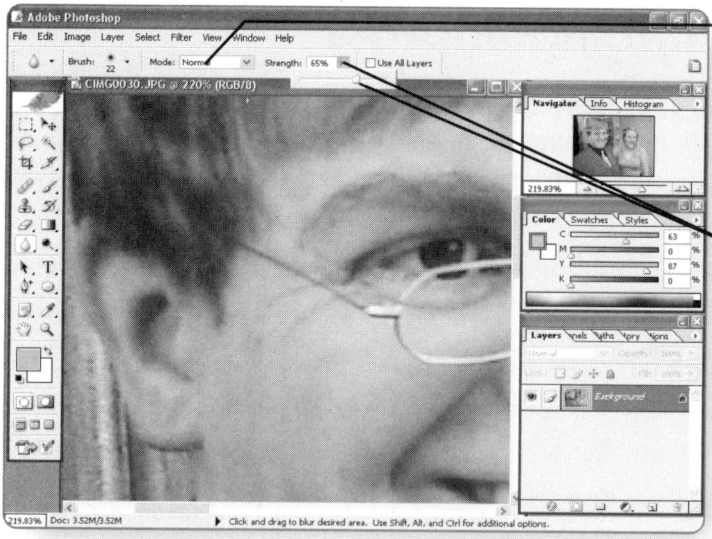

5. **Select** an **option** from the Mode drop-down list on the options bar. The selected mode will become active for the Blur tool.

6. **Select** the **Strength text box contents**, **type** a new **entry**, and **press Enter**. (Alternately, click on the right arrow beside the Strength choice, drag the slider, and then click on the right arrow again.) The strength setting will become active for the Blur tool.

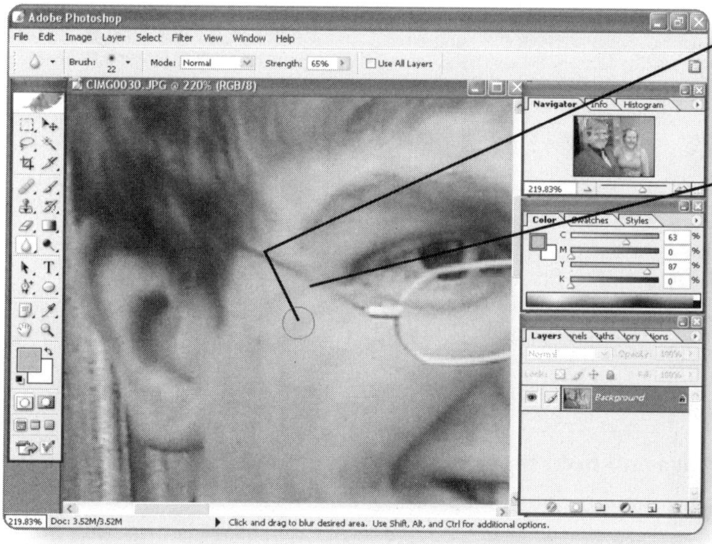

7. **Click** and **drag** on the **layer** to apply the blur. Blurring will begin to appear.

8. **Drag** as much as necessary. Photoshop will continue to add more blurring, but it may take quite a bit of dragging. When you finish, you can continue working with another tool or operation in Photoshop.

Smudging an Area

The Smudge tool helps you drag color from one area into another, much as you can with a paintbrush full of wet paint. You can use the Smudge tool to add a painted effect in a very specific area of the image. Smudging resembles blurring but has a much more dramatic effect. Follow these steps to practice smudging:

1. **Click** on the **layer** in the Layers palette that holds the content you want to smudge. The selected layer will become the active layer.

2. **Use** the **Navigator** to zoom in on and display the area to smudge. The selected area will become more visible.

3. **Press** and **hold** the **mouse button** on the Blur tool in the toolbox. A submenu will appear.

4. **Click** on **Smudge Tool**. The Smudge tool will become the active tool.

5. Choose a **Brush style** on the options bar. The selected brush will become active for the Smudge tool.

6. Make a **choice** from the Mode drop-down list on the options bar. The selected mode will become active for the Smudge tool.

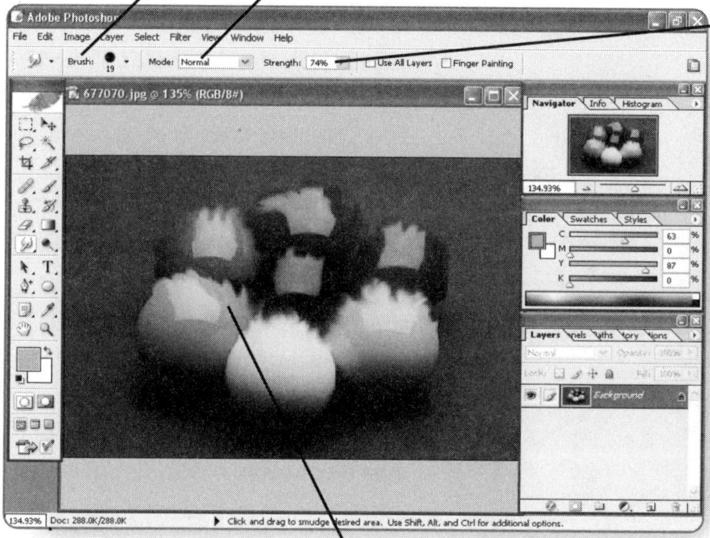

7. Select the **Strength text box contents**, **type** a new **entry**, and **press Enter**. (Alternately, click on the right arrow beside the Strength choice, drag the slider, and then click on the right arrow again.) The strength setting will become active for the Smudge tool.

8. Drag on the **layer** over two contrasting colors to make the smudge. Smudging will begin to appear. When you finish creating all the necessary smudges, you can continue working with another tool or operation in Photoshop.

NOTE

If you click on the Finger Painting check box in the options bar to check it, dragging with the Smudge tool will paint using the currently selected foreground color.

NOTE

You can make the effects of the Blur, Smudge, or Sharpen tool partially transparent after you use the tool. To do so, click on Edit and then click on Fade (Tool Name). Specify an Opacity setting in the Fade dialog box that appears and then click on OK.

Sharpening an Area

The Sharpen tool works in the opposite way as the Blur tool: It tries to improve the focus of edges that are soft so that the image appears clearer. So, for example, you might want to use this tool if one small spot on a layer looks out of focus.

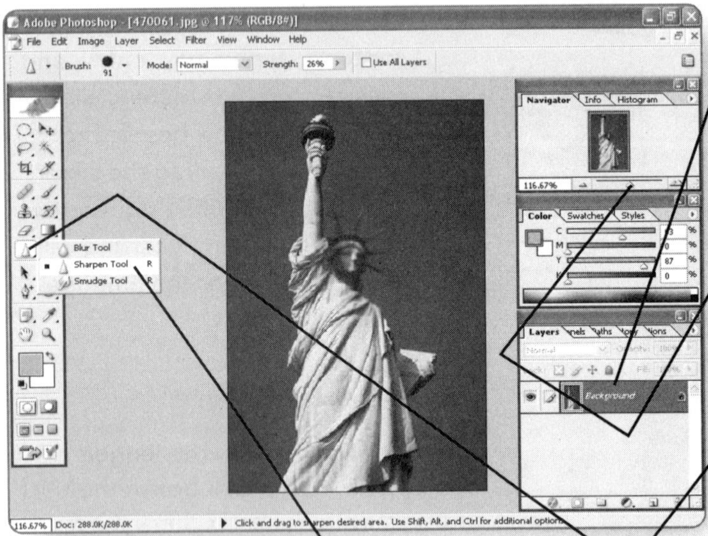

1. **Click** on the **layer** in the Layers palette that holds the content you want to sharpen. The selected layer will become the active layer.

2. **Use** the **Navigator** to zoom in on and display the area to sharpen. The selected area will become more visible.

3. **Click** and **hold** the **Blur tool** in the toolbox. A submenu will appear.

4. **Click** on **Sharpen Tool**. The Sharpen tool will become the active tool.

5. **Choose** a **Brush style** on the options bar. The selected brush will become active for the Sharpen tool.

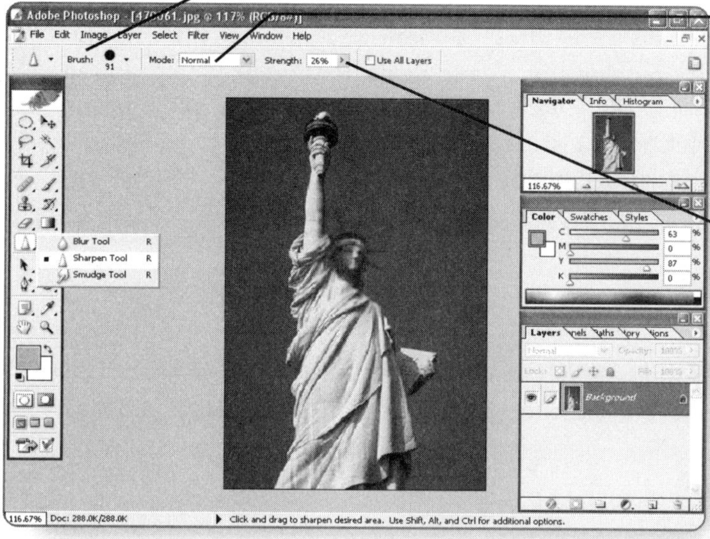

6. **Make** a **choice** from the Mode drop-down list on the options bar. The selected mode will become active for the Sharpen tool.

7. **Select** the **Strength text box contents**, **type** a new **entry**, and **press Enter**. (Alternately, click on the right arrow beside the Strength choice, drag the slider, and then click on the right arrow again.) The strength setting will become active for the Sharpen tool.

8. **Drag** on the **layer** to apply the sharpening. Sharpening will begin to appear. When you finish adding all the necessary sharpening, you can continue working with another tool or operation in Photoshop.

NOTE

If you use a large, sharp brush and a higher Strength setting with the Sharpen tool, clicking or dragging can have unwanted effects beyond sharpening—the color of pixels outside the area to be sharpened may be changed dramatically. Even though the impact of sharpening can be subtle, you still want to use the Sharpen tool sparingly to avoid those unwanted changes.

Erasing Image Content

Photoshop offers three different eraser tools so you can achieve the exact erasing effect you need in any particular situation.

Using the Eraser

The standard Eraser tool erases color or content on a layer, enabling the background layer in the image to show through to varying degrees, depending on the opacity you specify. If you're working on the background layer itself, using the standard Eraser actually paints or draws the currently selected background color rather than erasing layer content. The following steps show an example of each of these uses for the Eraser tool.

CAUTION

The Eraser tools don't work on shape layers. To work around this issue, create a new layer using the Layer, New, Layer command. Choose the shape layer in the Layers palette and select and copy its content using the Edit, Copy Merged command. Then choose the new layer you created in the Layers palette and use the Edit, Paste command to paste the content onto it. You can then delete the shape layer and erase as necessary on the new layer.

1. Click on the **layer** in the Layers palette that holds the content you want to erase. (In this case, click on any regular layer except the Background layer.) The selected layer will become the active layer.

2. Use the **Navigator** to zoom in on and display the area to erase. The selected area will become more visible.

3. Click on the **Eraser tool**. The Eraser tool will become the active tool.

4. Make a **choice** from the Mode drop-down list on the options bar. The selected mode will become active for the Eraser tool.

NOTE

Because the Mode choice affects the available Brush choices in this case, choose the Mode first. If you choose the Block mode, you cannot choose a brush shape.

5. Choose a **Brush style** on the options bar. The selected brush will become active for the Eraser tool. Note that selecting certain brush styles enables airbrush capabilities for the Eraser tool.

6. Select the **Opacity text box contents**, **type** a new **entry**, and **press Enter**. (Alternately, click on the right arrow beside the Opacity choice, drag the slider, and then click on the right arrow again.) The opacity setting will become active for the Eraser tool.

7. If available, **select** the **Flow text box contents**, **type** a new **entry**, and **press Enter**. (Alternately, click on the right arrow beside the Flow choice, drag the slider, and then click on the right arrow again.) The flow setting will become active for the Eraser tool, controlling how quickly the eraser works.

8. Drag on the desired layer. Photoshop will erase the current layer's content and reveal the content on the Background layer.

Using the Background Eraser

The Background Eraser tool erases the content on any layer, including both the foreground and background colors on the layer. Areas you erase with this tool become transparent so that content on other layers in the image can show through. If the image has only one layer, or if you're erasing the background layer and there's no content in front of it, the areas erased with this tool will be transparent if the image file is placed in a document.

1. **Click** on the **layer** in the Layers palette that holds the content you want to erase. The selected layer will become the active layer.

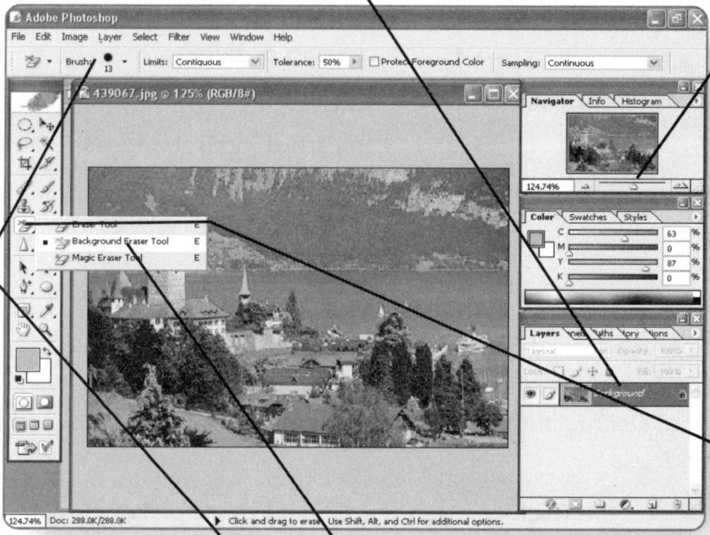

2. **Use** the **Navigator** to zoom in on and display the area to erase. The selected area will become more visible.

3. **Click** and **hold** on the **Eraser tool**. A shortcut menu will appear.

4. **Click** on **Background Eraser Tool**. The Background Eraser tool will become the active tool.

5. **Click** on the **Click to open the Brush Preset picker button** on the options bar. A palette of brush options will appear.

6. **Make Diameter**, **Hardness**, **Spacing**, **Angle**, and **Roundness choices** in the palette. The selected choices will affect the shape of the eraser brush as follows:

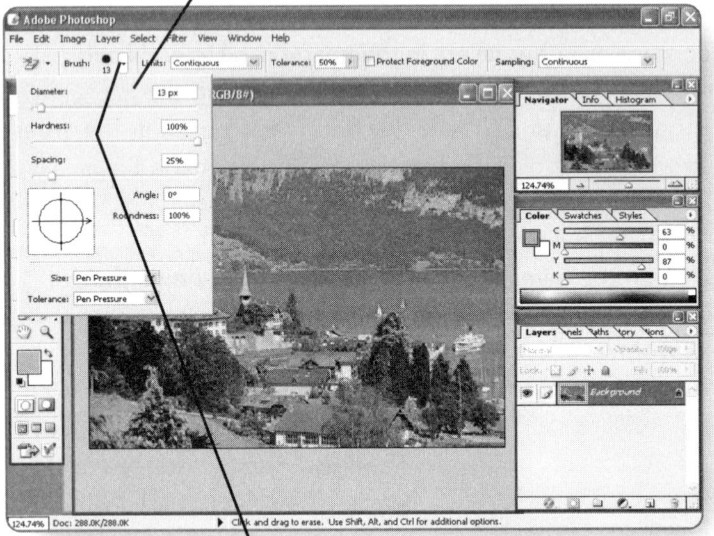

- **Diameter.** Enables you to specify the size of the brush (the area to be erased).
- **Hardness.** Enables you to specify the size of the brush's hard center, as a percentage of the total diameter.
- **Spacing.** If you want eraser brush strokes to be noncontiguous as you erase, increase this setting to add spacing or skips.
- **Angle.** This setting works with the specified Roundness value to tip the brush shape. You can either enter a value in the Angle text box or drag the arrow axis on the brush preview.
- **Roundness.** Enables you to specify whether a brush is round. Decrease this value to less than 100% to decrease roundness.

7. **Click** on the **Click to open the Brush Preset picker down arrow**. The palette of brush settings will close.

NOTE

Use the bottom two settings, Size and Tolerance, to further control the brush when you're using a graphics tablet with Photoshop.

8. **Make Limits**, **Tolerance**, and **Sampling choices** on the options bar. The selected choices will affect the erasing as follows:

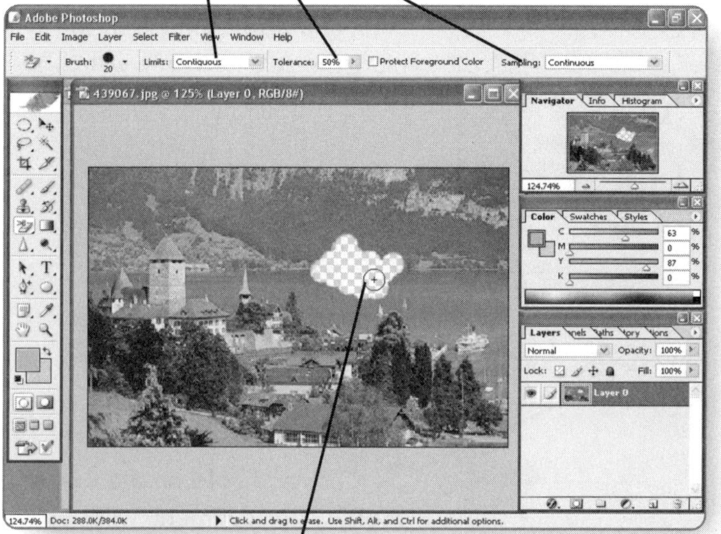

- **Limits.** Controls how far the erasing can spread, based on dragging over similar colors.
- **Tolerance.** Controls whether the eraser will erase only pixels of alike colors (lower settings) or similar colors.
- **Sampling.** Determines whether erasing tests matching colors continuously or by the color initially selected.

9. **Click** or **drag** on the layer to erase. Photoshop will erase the current layer's content, leaving a transparent area behind.

Using the Magic Eraser

Use the Magic Eraser tool when you want to erase a contiguous area of color on a layer. You can either completely erase the area of color or make the erasure less opaque so that only part of the color area is erased.

1. Click on the **layer** that holds the content to erase in the Layers palette. The selected layer will become the active layer.

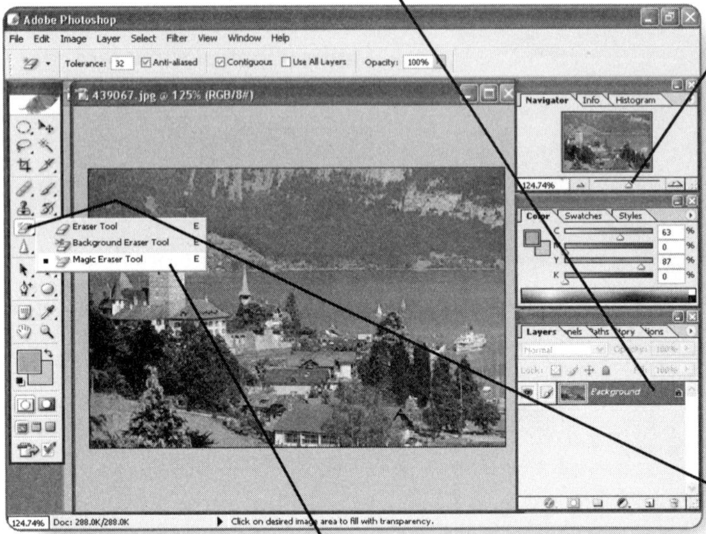

2. Use the **Navigator** to zoom in on and display the area to blur. The selected area will become more visible.

3. Click and **hold** on the **Eraser tool**. A shortcut menu will appear.

4. Click on **Magic Eraser Tool**. The Magic Eraser tool will become the active tool.

5. **Enter** a **Tolerance setting** on the options bar. The specified setting will become active for the Magic Eraser tool. Lower settings will tell the tool to erase only colors that are a closer match; higher settings will enable the tool to erase less similar colors.

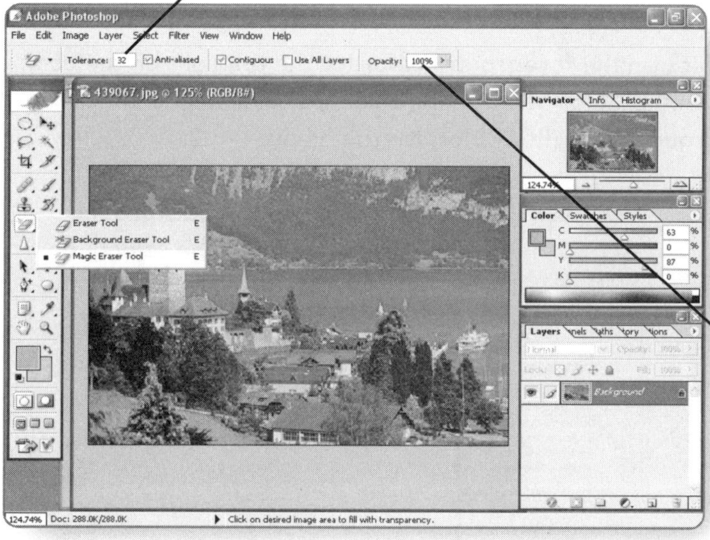

TIP

To enter a Tolerance setting, highlight the contents of that text box, type a new entry, and press Enter.

6. **Select** the **Opacity text box contents**, **type** a new **entry**, and **press Enter**. (Alternately, click on the right arrow beside the Opacity choice, drag the slider, and then click on the right arrow again.) The Opacity setting will become active for the Magic Eraser tool.

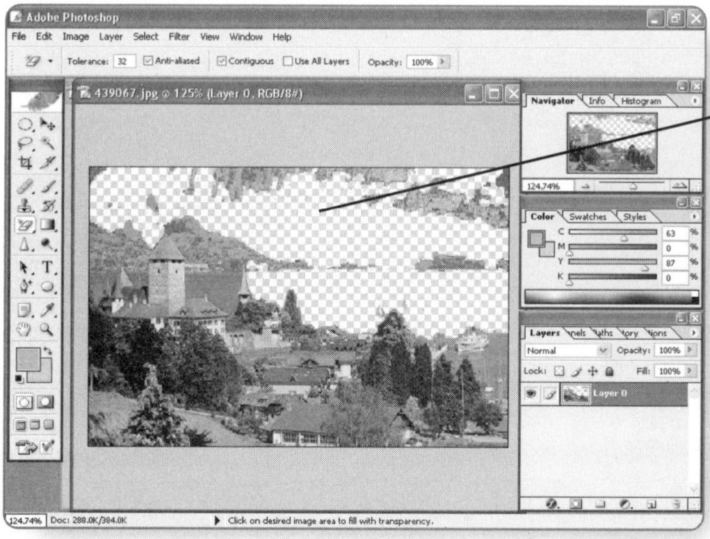

7. **Click** or **drag** on the area with the color to erase on the current layer. Photoshop will erase the selected color and any matching adjacent areas, applying transparency if specified.

TIP

No matter what types of changes you're making, don't forget to save your file from time to time.

Adding a Gradient

You can add a gradient onto most layers, except for layers that hold text. When you add a gradient, you can specify which colors to blend within the gradient. You can great a gradient fill for an entire layer or for a selection on that layer.

1. **Click** on the **foreground color** for the gradient on the color ramp in the Color palette. The selected color will become the foreground color (first color) for the blend.

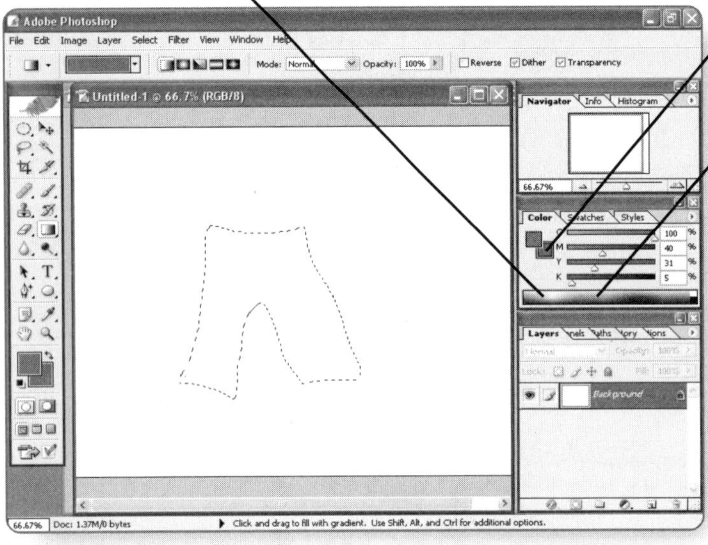

2. **Click** on the **background color box**. It will be selected.

3. **Click** on a **color** for the background on the color ramp in the Color palette.

4. **Click** on the **layer** to which you want to add the gradient in the Layers palette. The selected layer will become the active layer.

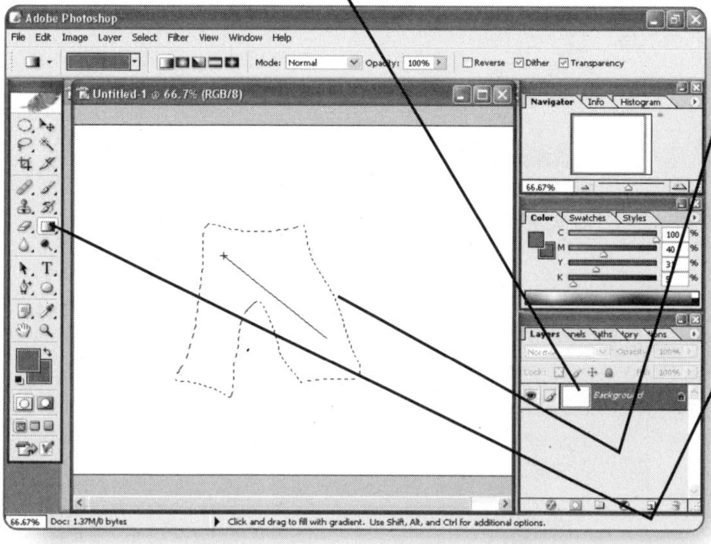

5. **Select** the **area** first (either manually or with a path) or **use** a **mask** to prevent Photoshop from displaying the gradient in the affected area. If you don't select an area, the entire layer will be filled.

6. **Click** on the **Gradient tool** in the toolbox. The Gradient tool will become the active tool.

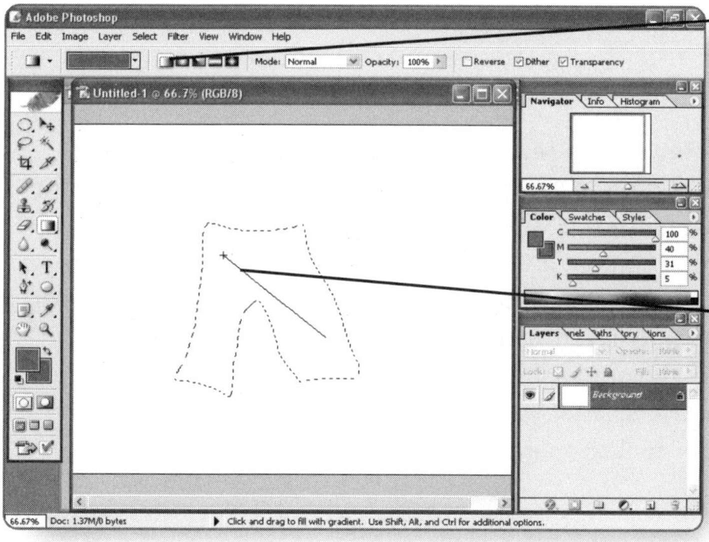

7. **Click** on a **gradient style button**. (The available choices include Linear Gradient, Radial Gradient, Angle Gradient, Reflected Gradient, and Diamond Gradient.) Photoshop will apply the selected style.

8. **Select** the **Opacity text box contents**, **type** a new **entry**, and **press Enter**. (Alternately, click on the right arrow beside the Opacity choice, drag the slider, and then click on the right arrow again.) The Opacity setting will become active for the Gradient tool.

NOTE

Changing the Mode setting can allow the Gradient tool (and the Paint Bucket tool, which is described in the next section) to apply a different behavior, such as dissolving the image.

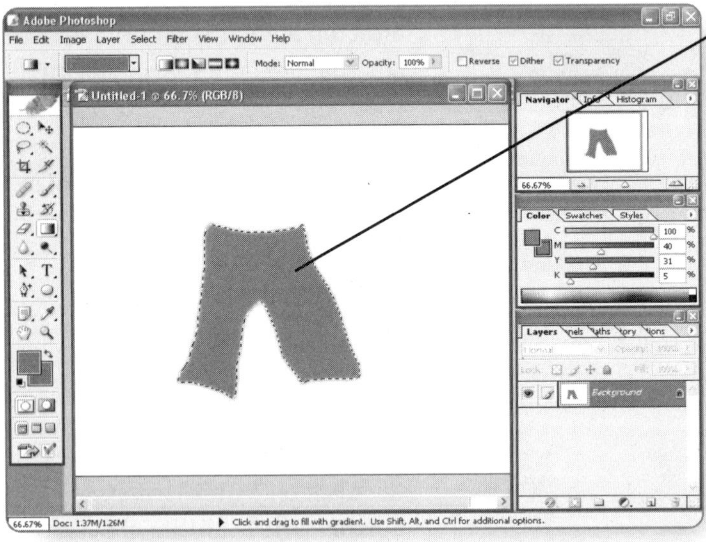

9. **Click** and **drag** on the **layer** to set the angle or center point for the gradient (depending on the style you selected in step 6). Photoshop applies the gradient immediately.

10. **Review** the **results**. (If you made a selection, you can deselect it first.) As with other types of effects you create, the gradient interacts with other content on the layer, blending with that content if the gradient wasn't 100% opaque. Note that, in this instance, because the text and leaf images appear on separate layers and those layers are in the front of the image, the gradient doesn't fill or overlay the content of the other layers. After you finish the gradient, you can work with another tool or operation in Photoshop.

Filling with the Paint Bucket

Use the Paint Bucket tool to fill a contiguous area of color (or similar colors) with the current foreground color.

> **CAUTION**
>
> The Paint Bucket tool doesn't work on shape layers. To work around this issue, create a new layer using the Layer, New Layer command. Choose the shape layer in the Layers palette and select and copy its content using the Edit, Copy Merged command. Then choose the new layer you created in the Layers palette and use the Edit, Paste command to paste the content onto it. You can then delete the shape layer and erase as necessary on the new layer.

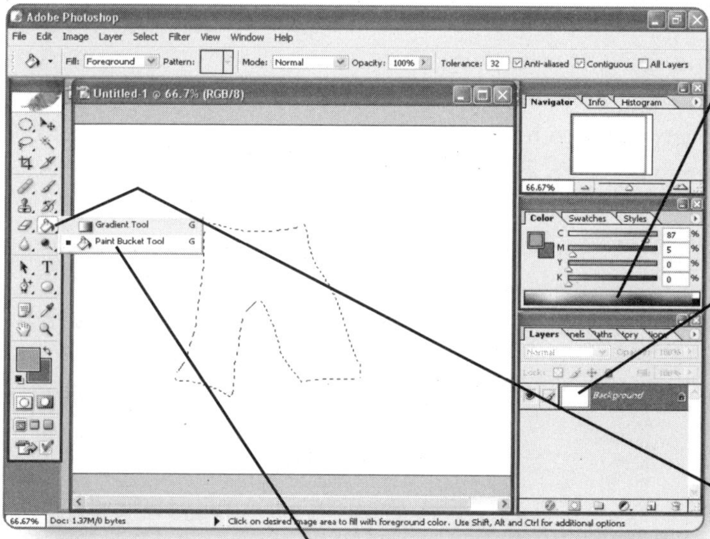

1. **Click** on the **foreground color** for the fill on the color ramp in the Color palette. The selected color will become the fill color for the Paint Bucket tool.

2. **Click** on the **layer** in the Layers palette that includes the area you want to fill. The selected layer will become the active layer.

3. **Click** and **hold** on the **Gradient tool** in the toolbox. A shortcut menu will appear.

4. **Click** on **Paint Bucket Tool**. The Paint Bucket tool will become the active tool.

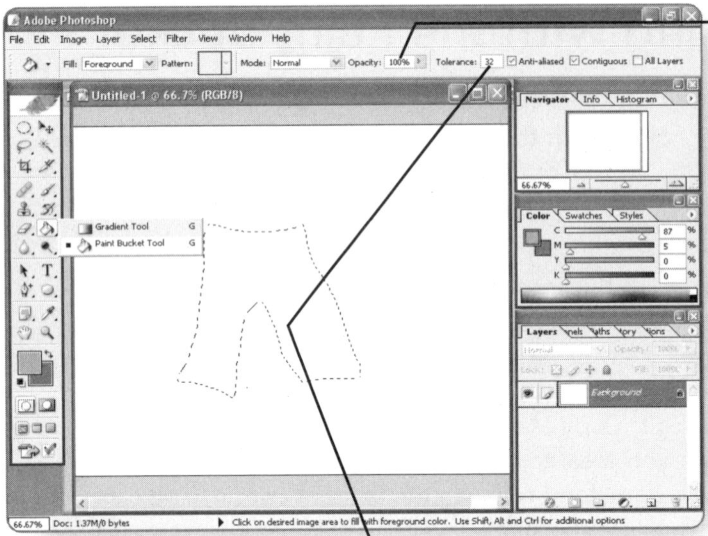

5. Select the **Opacity text box contents**, **type** a new **entry**, and **press Enter**. (Alternately, click on the right arrow beside the Opacity choice, drag the slider, and then click on the right arrow again.) The Opacity setting will become active for the Paint Bucket.

6. Select the **Tolerance text box contents**, **type** a new **entry**, and **press Enter**. The Tolerance setting will become active for the Paint Bucket tool. (Remember, tolerance refers to how carefully a tool must match the color of an area in order to identify which pixels to fill or erase.)

> **TIP**
>
> If you want to use the Paint Bucket to fill an area with a pattern, choose Pattern from the Fill drop-down list and then choose a pattern from the Pattern drop-down list.

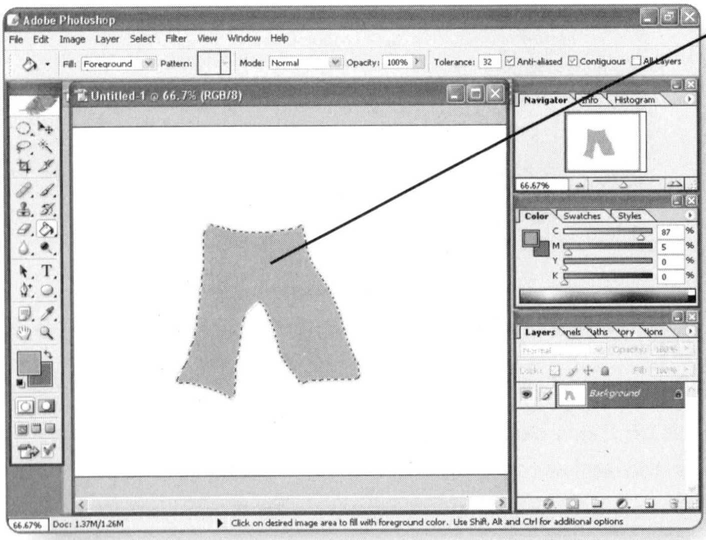

7. Click on the **area** to fill with the foreground color you selected. Photoshop applies the gradient immediately. Even if the layer includes other areas with the same color, those areas will not be filled if they are not contiguous. After you finish filling, you can work with another tool or operation in Photoshop.

Using Photo Techniques

In the past, one of the benefits of using a professional photographer was the photographer's (or the photo lab's) ability to manipulate lighting—both when shooting the initial photo and when creating the prints. The Dodge, Burn, and Sponge tools in Photoshop help you mimic a photographer's tricks in correcting lighting in an image. The Healing Brush and Patch tools can help you repair an image, such as a scanned image of a photo with spots, scratches, and other blemishes.

Dodging an Area

Use the Dodge tool to lighten an area that's too dark in your image. In the case of scanned content or a photo downloaded from a digital camera, dodging can actually reveal detail that previously wasn't visible in the image. Follow these steps to work with dodging:

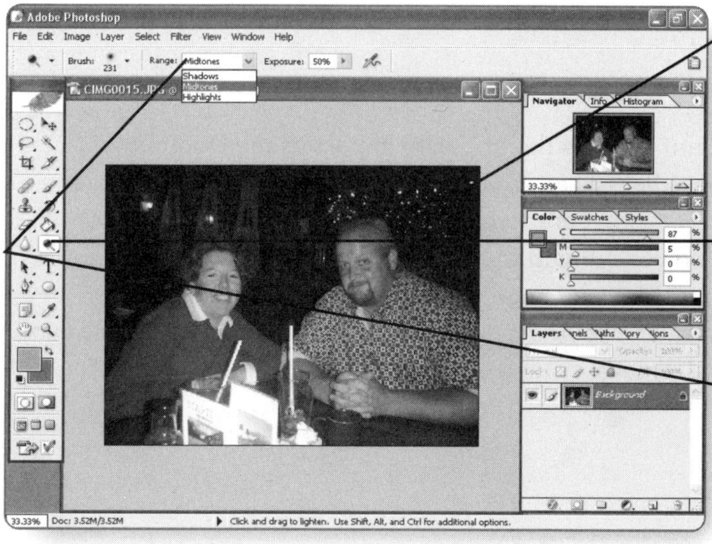

1. **Open** the **image** to correct and select the desired layer and zoom, if necessary. The image (and layer) will become active or current.

2. **Click** on the **Dodge tool** in the toolbox. The Dodge tool will become the active tool.

3. **Choose options** on the options bar as needed. The options for the Dodge tool are:

- **Brush.** Designates the brush style for the tool.
- **Range.** Specifies whether the Dodge tool affects shadows, midtones, or highlights in the areas over which you drag.

- **Exposure.** Identifies how much of a change the Dodge tool makes as you drag.
- **Airbrush.** Enables the airbrush effect for the tool.

4. Click on or **drag** over the area(s) to dodge. Photoshop makes the corrections immediately. After you finish dodging, you can work with another tool or operation in Photoshop.

Burning an Area

The Burn tool has the opposite impact as the Dodge tool. Burning darkens an area in the image, as if more light were directed to that area when the "photo" was being developed. You can use burning to help balance an area that seems weak or too light in an image or to emphasize a particular area. In the case of a color image, burning can intensify the color in an area and make it stand out from its background a bit more.

1. Open the **image** to correct and select the layer to burn, if necessary. The image (and layer) will become active or current.

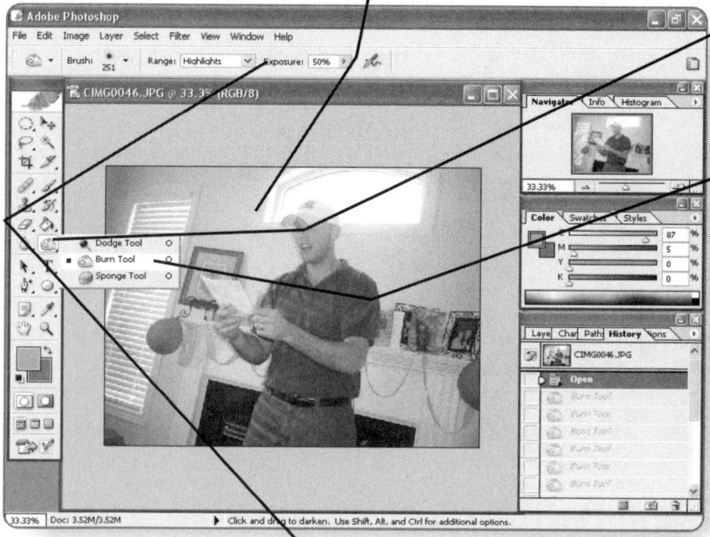

2. Click and **hold** on the **Dodge tool** in the toolbox. A shortcut menu will appear.

3. Click on **Burn Tool**. The Burn tool will become the active tool.

4. Choose options on the options bar as necessary. The options for the Burn tool are:

- **Brush.** Designates the brush style for the tool.
- **Range.** Specifies whether the Burn tool affects shadows, midtones, or highlights in the areas over which you drag.
- **Exposure.** Identifies how much of a change the Burn tool makes as you drag.
- **Airbrush.** Enables the airbrush effect for the tool.

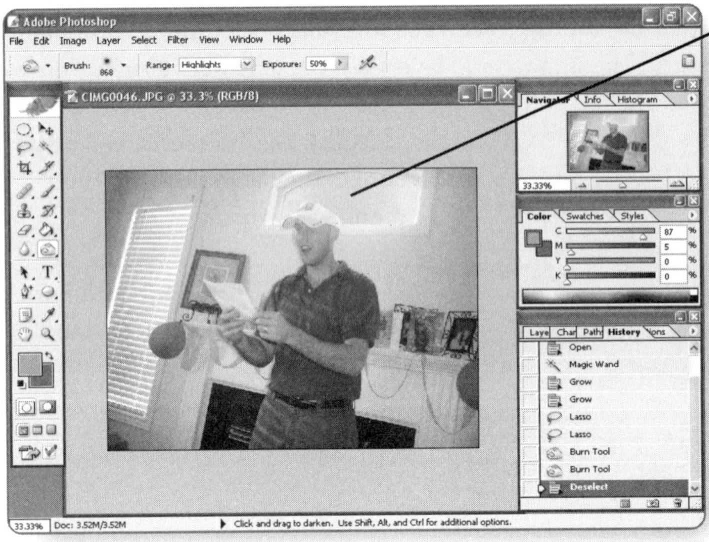

5. **Click** on or **drag** over the area(s) to burn. Photoshop makes the corrections immediately. After you finish burning, you can work with another tool or operation in Photoshop.

Sponging an Area

The Sponge tool (sponging) changes color saturation in a color image and contrast in a grayscale image. In either case, using the Sponge tool helps make the area you're correcting appear more bright or crisp, to help it stand out from surrounding content in the image.

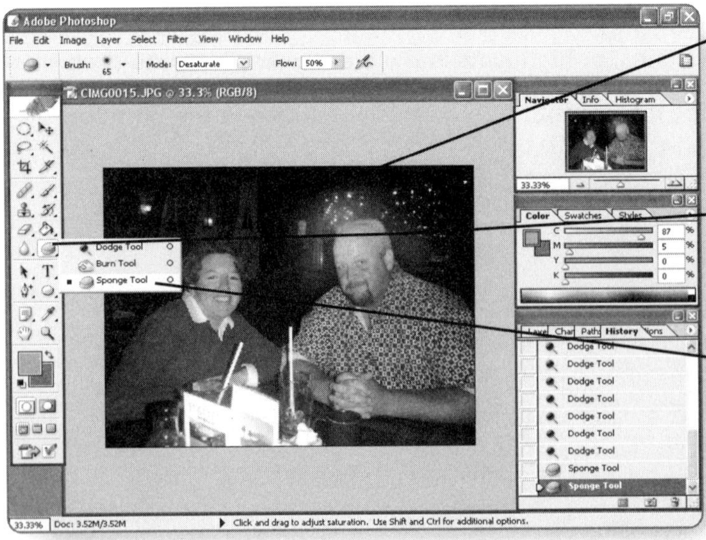

1. **Open** the desired **image** and select the layer to correct, if necessary. The image (and layer) will become active or current.

2. **Click** and **hold** on the **Dodge tool** in the toolbox. A shortcut menu will appear.

3. **Click** on **Sponge Tool**. The Sponge tool will become the active tool.

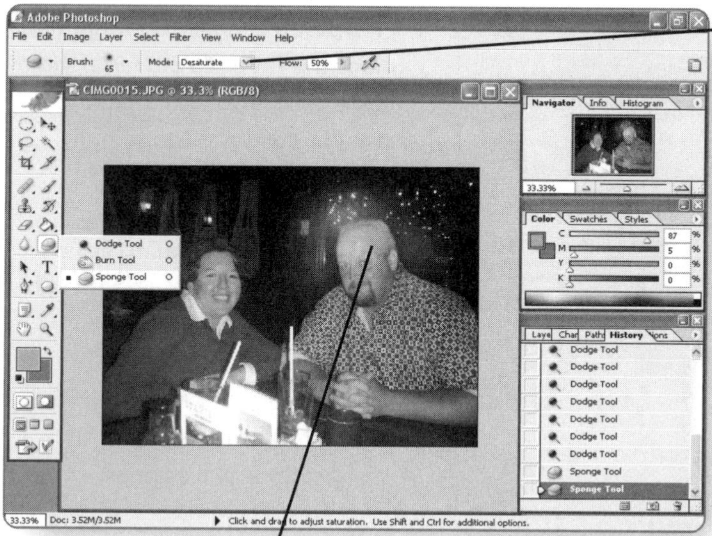

4. **Choose options** on the options bar as necessary. The options for the Sponge tool are:

- **Brush.** Designates the brush style for the tool.
- **Mode.** Specifies whether the Sponge tool saturates (adds more color intensity) or desaturates (decreases color intensity) in the area you drag over.
- **Flow.** Identifies how much of a change the Sponge tool makes as you drag.
- **Airbrush.** Enables the airbrush effect for the tool.

5. **Click** on or **drag** over the area(s) to sponge. Photoshop makes the corrections immediately. After you finish sponging, you can work with another tool or operation in Photoshop.

Using the Healing Brush

The Healing Brush is an amazing tool for getting rid of unwanted areas in photos. It can be used to clean up dirt marks, scratches, holes, tears, or other imperfections that can arise on photos. In this example, we will remove a logo from the sleeve of a t-shirt using the Healing Brush.

1. Open the desired **image** and **select** the **layer** to correct. The image (and layer) will become active or current. Zoom in, if needed.

2. Click on the **Healing Brush** tool. The Healing Brush tool will become the active tool.

3. Click on the **Brush style** on the options bar. A palette of brush options will appear.

4. Make Diameter, **Hardness**, **Spacing**, **Angle**, and **Roundness choices** in the palette. The selected choices will affect the shape of the Healing Brush tool as follows:

- **Diameter.** Enables you to specify the size of the brush (the area to be "healed").
- **Hardness.** Enables you to specify the size of the brush's hard center, as a percentage of the total diameter.
- **Spacing.** If you want erasure brush strokes to be noncontiguous as you heal, increase this setting to add spacing or skips.

- **Angle.** This setting works with the Roundness value you specify to tip the brush shape. You can either enter a value in the Angle text box or drag the arrow axis on the brush preview.

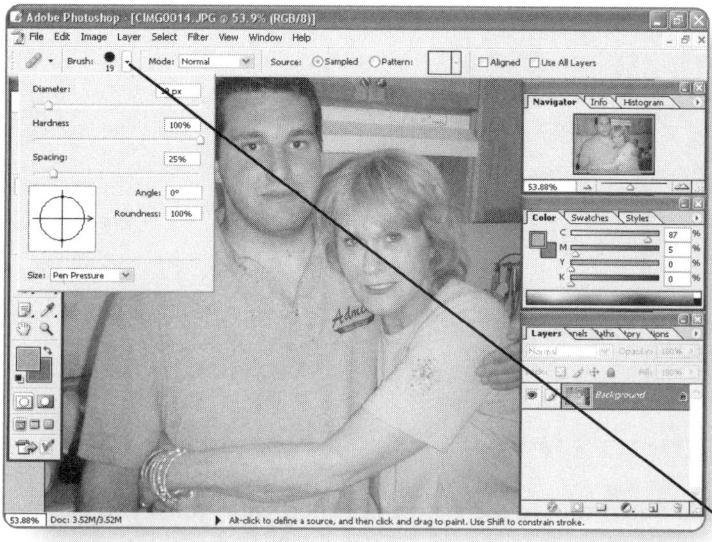

- **Roundness.** Enables you to specify whether a brush is round. Decrease this value to less than 100% to decrease roundness.

> **NOTE**
>
> Use the bottom setting, Size, to further control the brush when you're using a graphics tablet with Photoshop.

5. **Click** on the **Brush style down arrow**. The palette of brush settings will close.

6. **Click** on the **Sampled option button** to select it, if necessary. The Healing Brush tool will use the area you sample in the image to make the needed repair.

7. **Alt+click** on the **area** to sample. (Of course, you should sample an area that looks like the area to patch.) The target mouse pointer will appear to verify that you are sampling, and the sample will be loaded after you click.

8. **Click again** or **drag** on the area to repair. Photoshop will cover the flaw using the sampled content.

Patching a Flaw

Use the Patch tool to increase the speed with which you can make even more complicated repairs. With this tool, rather than painting over an area with sampled material, you select a patch area from the image and then drag that patch over the area to repair. This tool works particularly well when the area to repair has a pattern, striping, or some other type of texture that the Healing Brush tool cannot capture. Use the following steps to create a patch and use it to repair an image:

1. **Open** the desired **image** and select the layer to correct. The image (and layer) will become active or current. Zoom in, if necessary.

2. **Click** and **hold** on the **Healing Brush tool** in the toolbox. A shortcut menu will appear.

3. **Click** on **Patch Tool**. The Patch tool will become the active tool.

4. **Click** on the **Destination option button** on the options bar. This will set up the Patch tool so that you will first select the sample to use as the patch and then drag it over the area to be patched.

5. **Drag** on the **image** to select the source area (patch). The area you drag around will be selected so that you can use it as the patch.

> **TIP**
>
> It's important to select a patch source area that's large enough to cover the flaw but not so large that it will cover mismatching areas around the flaw.

6. **Drag** the **patch** from the source location over the flaw; release the mouse button only when you've positioned the patch as necessary. The patch will cover the flaw.

TIP

As long as the patch remains selected, you can move it and reposition it. You also can rotate the patch (Edit, Transform, Rotate) and make other changes to ensure a precise fit.

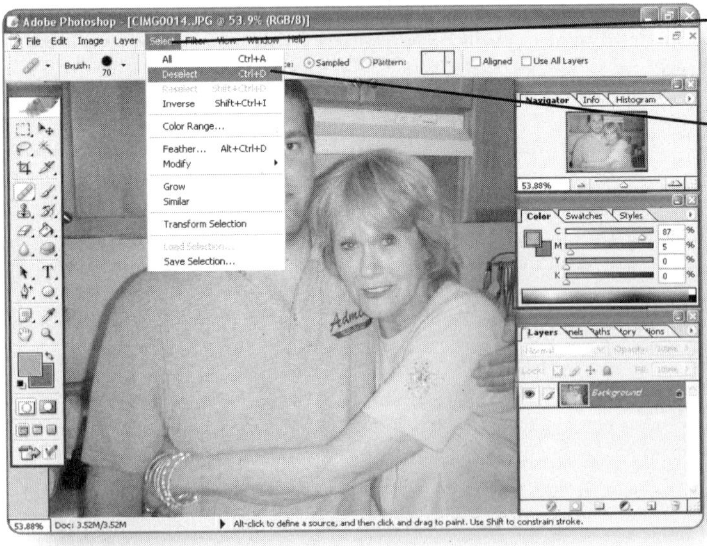

7. **Click** on **Select**. The Select menu will appear.

8. **Click** on **Deselect**. The patch selection marquee will disappear. Depending on how close the patch was to the area to be repaired, the repair will be totally or nearly impossible to see.

12

Working with Image Size and Orientation

When you create a new image file, you specify its size. When you import an image from a scanner or digital camera, you have less control over the size and orientation of the image. In either case, you can use some tricks to tweak the size and orientation of the image so that it suits your purpose. In this chapter, you'll learn how to:

- Use the Crop tool to crop an image
- Resize the image
- Adjust the image canvas
- Rotate the entire canvas
- Trim the edges of the image
- Automatically crop and straighten images

Cropping the Image

When you crop the image, you select the area of the image that you want to keep, and then you have Photoshop hide or remove the unselected portions of the image. You can crop if an image's subject is off-center, if you need to eliminate a distracting element from the image, or if you need to fit the image to a particular height and width.

1. **Click** on the **Crop tool** on the toolbox. The Crop tool will become active.

2. **Type entries** in the Width and Height text boxes, if necessary. When you use these text boxes, Photoshop will resize the cropped material to the specified dimensions (in addition to performing the crop).

3. **Type** an **entry** in the Resolution text box, if necessary. If you make an entry, Photoshop will resample the cropped material to the specified resolution.

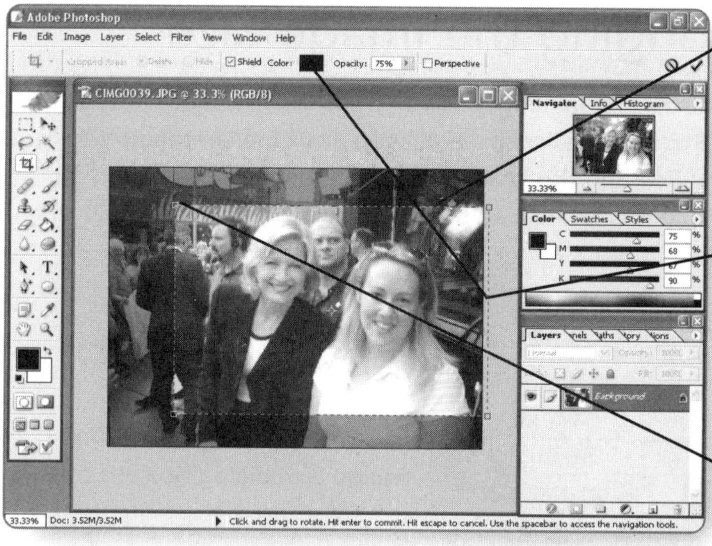

4. **Drag** on the **image to create a selection to crop**. This will select the area to keep; the area outside the selection will be shielded or grayed out.

5. **Adjust shield settings**, if necessary. Photoshop will change the temporary shading used to mask the areas to be cropped out of the image.

6. **Drag** the **crop selection** to resize or rotate the crop zone. Dragging a corner will resize the crop zone; dragging a side will rotate the crop zone.

> **NOTE**
>
> If you click on the Crop tool again at this point, a message box appears to ask whether you want to crop the image. You can click on Crop to proceed, Cancel to stop the crop operation, or Don't Crop to remove the cropping selection.

7. **Click** on the **Commit (check) button** on the options bar or press Enter. Photoshop will crop the image to the specified zone.

Changing the Image Size

You can resize an image file when you want to both fit the image to a particular size and keep all of the content in the image. Resizing the image also gives you the opportunity to resample it or change to the resolution (pixels per inch) in the image.

1. Click on **Image**. The Image menu will appear.

2. Click on **Image Size**. The Image Size dialog box will open.

> **TIP**
>
> To see the current image size before you display the Image Size dialog box, press and hold the Alt key and then click and hold on the Doc size indicator near the bottom-left corner of the Photoshop window.

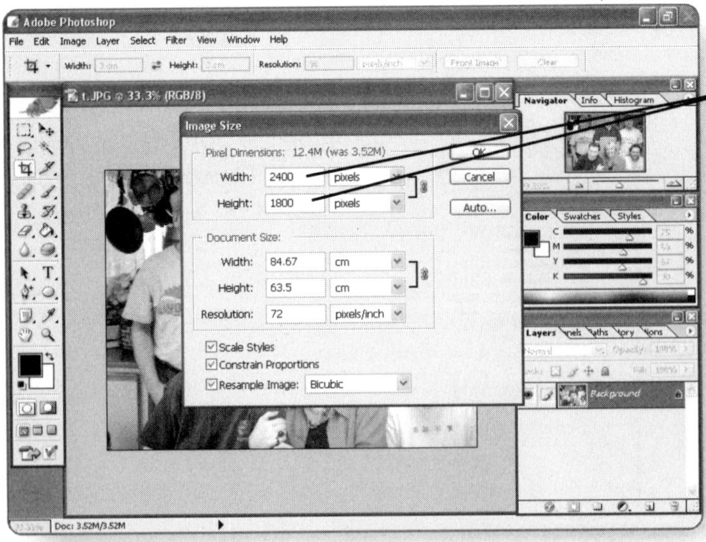

3. Enter a new **Width** or **Height** under either Pixel Dimensions or Document Size. Photoshop will adjust the other three text box entries to keep them proportional.

TIP

Click on the Constrain Proportions check box to clear the check if you want to resize only one image dimension. Otherwise, changing a Height entry automatically adjusts the Width and vice versa.

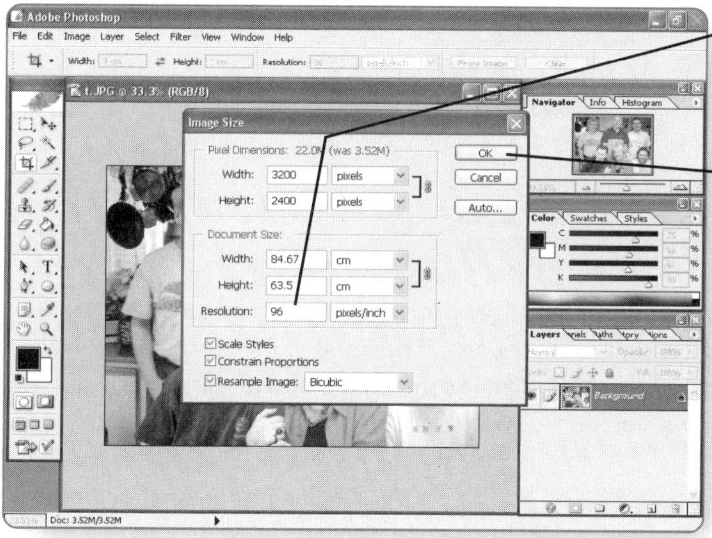

4. **Enter** a new **Resolution**. Photoshop will apply the new resolution setting.

5. **Click** on **OK**. The settings you have entered will take effect.

Changing the Canvas Size

The canvas size and image size always use the same dimensions. Thus, changing the canvas size changes the image size, but not in the same way that using the Image Size command does. When you change to a canvas size that's smaller than the current image/canvas size, Photoshop crops out part of the image. When you change to a canvas size that's larger than the current image/canvas size, Photoshop adds space around the image.

1. **Click** on **Image**. The Image menu will appear.

2. **Click** on **Canvas Size**. The Canvas Size dialog box will open.

3. **Enter** a new **Width** and/or **Height** and choose another measurement unit for each, if necessary. Photoshop will display the projected New Size for the image above those measurements.

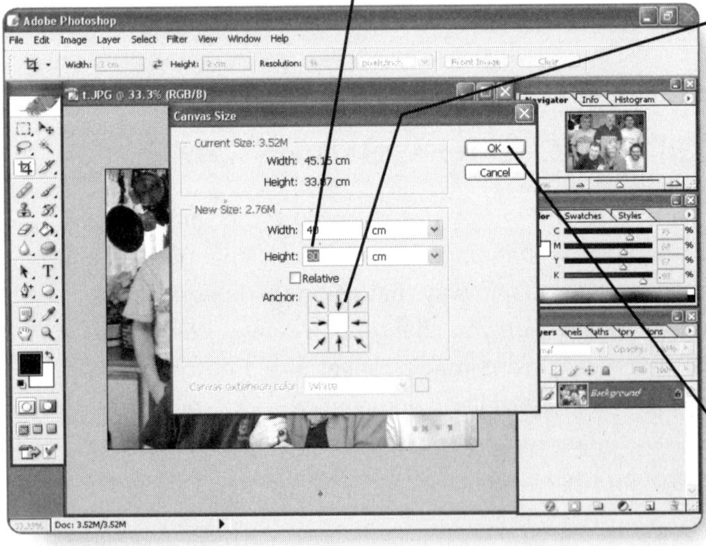

4. **Click** another **Anchor point**, if necessary. When you're increasing the canvas size, the selected anchor point will control where white space will be added around the image. When you're decreasing the canvas size, the selected anchor point will designate which part of the image to keep and which to crop out.

5. **Click** on **OK**. Photoshop will apply the new canvas size, unless it needs to display a warning regarding the size change, as shown in step 6.

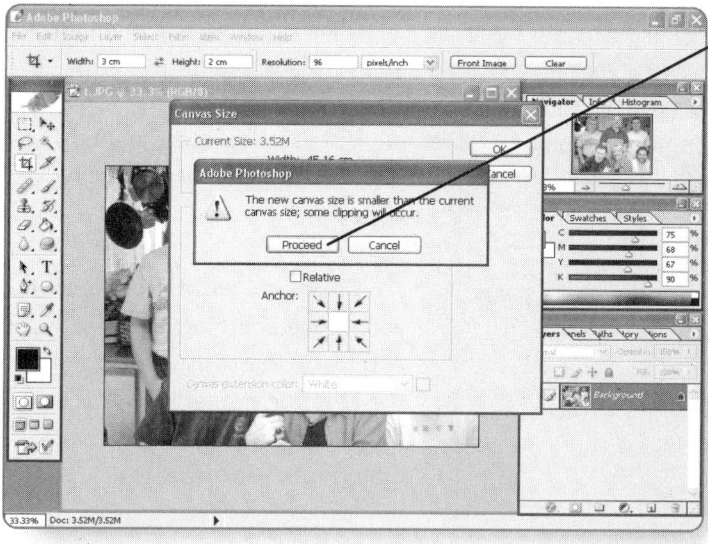

6. **Click** on **Proceed** in the warning dialog box, if it appears. Photoshop will finish resizing the canvas.

Rotating the Canvas

You can rotate the canvas to rotate the entire image—all the content on all the layers. Photoshop provides these rotation options:

- **180°.** Rotates the canvas so that the top of the image becomes the bottom.
- **90° CW.** Rotates the canvas one quarter turn in the clockwise direction.
- **90° CCW.** Rotates the canvas one quarter turn in the counterclockwise direction.
- **Arbitrary.** Displays the Rotate Canvas dialog box so that you can specify a precise rotation amount and direction.
- **Flip Canvas Horizontal.** Flips the image right to left.
- **Flip Canvas Vertical.** Flips the image top to bottom.

Use the following steps when you're ready to rotate the image:

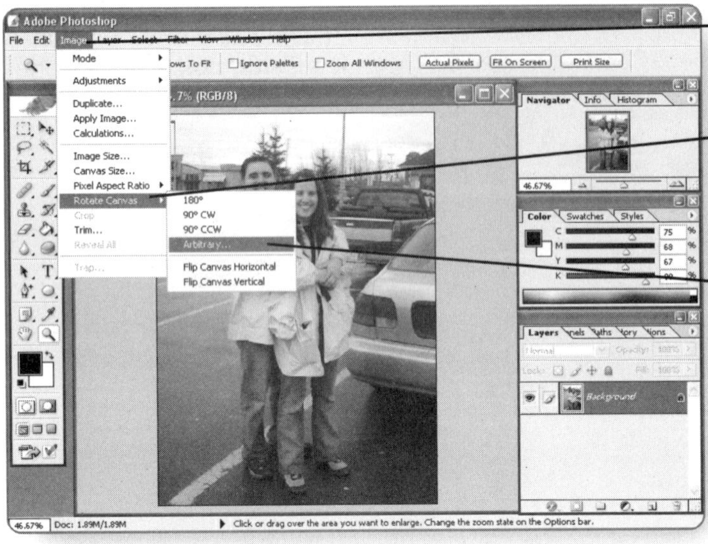

1. **Click** on **Image**. The Image menu will appear.

2. **Point** to **Rotate Canvas**. The Rotate Canvas submenu will appear.

3. **Click** on a **rotation choice**. If you chose anything but Arbitrary, Photoshop will apply the rotation immediately. Otherwise, the Rotate Canvas dialog box will appear.

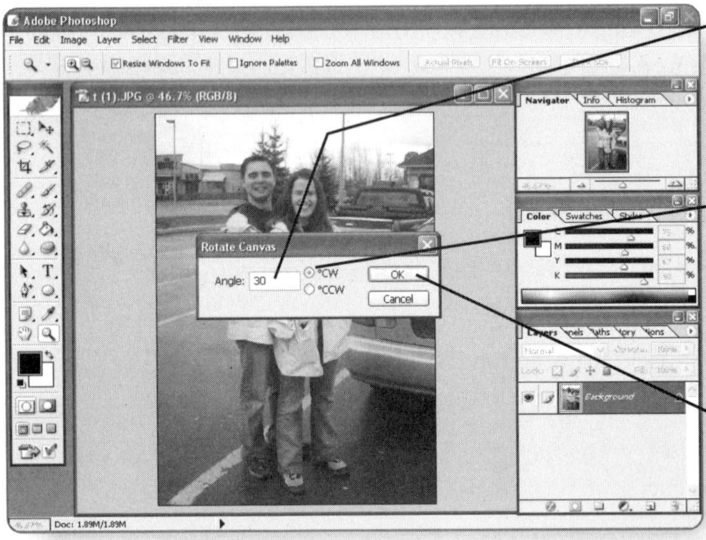

4. **Type** an **entry** in the Angle text box. Your entry will specify how much rotation Photoshop applies.

5. **Click** on the **°CW** or **°CCW** option. Your choice will specify either the clockwise or counterclockwise rotation direction.

6. **Click** on **OK**. Photoshop will rotate the image as specified by the rotation settings you entered.

Trimming the Canvas

You can use the trim feature to crop out unnecessary information around the edge of an image, such as a white photo print border, blank canvas space that's no longer needed, or discolored areas around an image from a contact sheet fading or folding. For the trim feature to work, the area to be trimmed must all be the same color.

1. **Click** on **Image**. The Image menu will appear.

2. **Click** on **Trim**. The Trim dialog box will open.

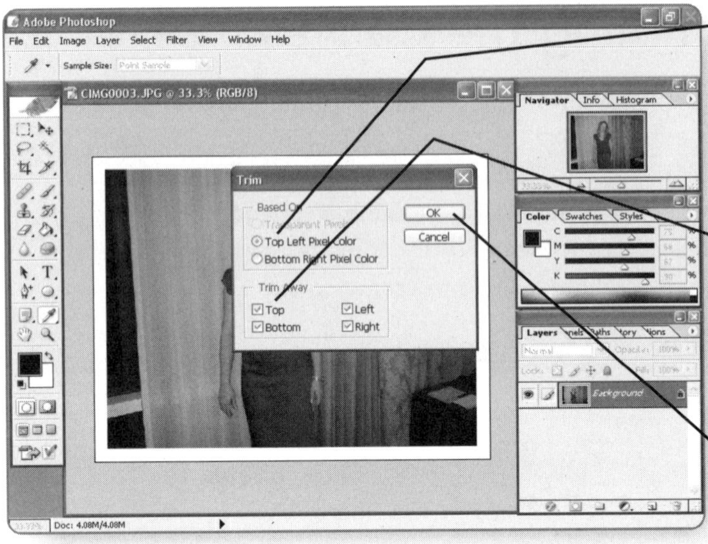

3. Click on a **Based On option button**. Photoshop will use the specified setting to identify which pixels to trim from the image.

4. Click on the **Trim Away check boxes** as needed. Clearing a Trim Away check box tells Photoshop not to trim the designated portion of the image.

5. Click on **OK**. Photoshop will perform the image trim.

Automatically Cropping and Straightening Images

One of the problems when scanning in images is that it is difficult to get a perfectly straight scan. In addition, if you are scanning multiple images at a time, you traditionally have had to individually crop and save each image. Photoshop CS has a new autocrop feature that will automatically straighten and crop your scanned images.

1. Open or **scan in** the **image** you would like to automatically crop and straighten.

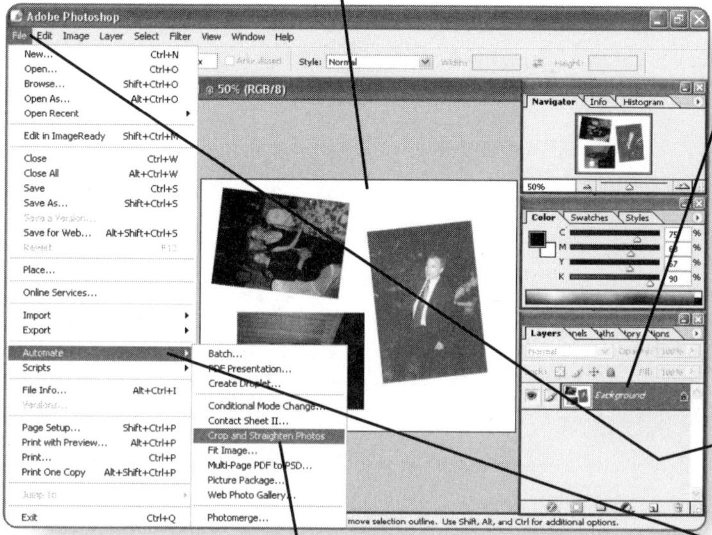

2. Click on the **layer** that contains those images. Alternatively, you can create a selection around the images for which you would like to create separate files.

3. Click on **File**. The file menu will appear.

4. Click on **Automate**. A submenu will appear.

5. Click on **Crop and Straighten Photos**. All of the images on the layer will be straightened, cropped, and opened in their own separate window.

13

Applying Filters

What's the big draw of most movies we go to today? It's the special effects. Within Photoshop CS, there are dozens of different special effects, called filters, that you can apply to your images. Filters can be used to correct problems with images or just to add artistic flare. Photoshop CS adds a new Filter Gallery that makes applying filters even easier. The goal of this chapter is to have you:

- Understand the available filters
- Apply a filter when you need it
- Adjust the filter
- Use the Filter Gallery

Previewing the Filters

The default Photoshop installation installs dozens of filters. The Filter menu groups the filters on several submenus. Table 13-1 lists the submenus and gives a description of the types of filters found in each submenu group.

Table 13-1 ***Reviewing Filter Groups***

Group	Includes Filters That
Artistic	Make the image look like it was created with watercolors or pastels, has a film grain, has poster edges, and so on.
Blur	Add blurs to simulate movement, such as in a single direction or rotation.
Brush Strokes	Apply a brush stroke effect in one of various available shapes.
Distort	Give the appearance of natural or artificial distortions caused by shape and light, such as a ripple, glass, or twirl effect.
Noise	Apply noise (white speckling) to affect the image appearance or to fix spots and scratches.
Pixelate	Apply one of several dotted effects to the image, such as simulating the Pointillism technique.
Render	Let you change the fill, add a lighting effect, apply 3D, and more.
Sharpen	Improve image sharpness.
Sketch	Apply a drawing effect in one of various available techniques.
Stylize	Make a number of changes, like glowing edges or embossing, that lend a modern effect.
Texture	Convert the image's appearance to make it consistent with the selected texture.
Video	Change the color method used in a video still.
Other	Create a custom filter or work with other custom filters.

NOTE

Photoshop applies the filter effect only to the current layer and current selection (if any).

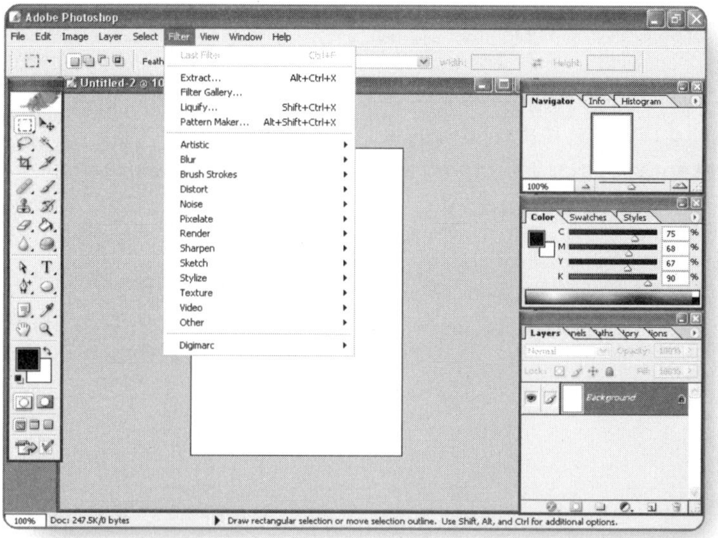

The Filter Gallery

A new addition to Photoshop CS is the Filter Gallery. The Filter Gallery offers a one-stop location for you to apply and manipulate filters. The Filter Gallery not only displays all of the available filters, it also allows you to apply multiple filters to an image.

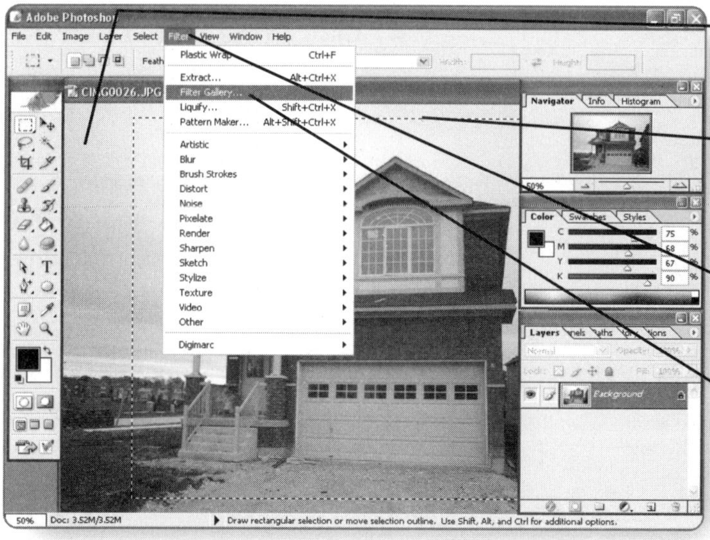

1. **Open** the **image** to which you would like to apply a filter.

2. **Create** a **selection** if you only want to apply the filter to a particular area of your image.

3. **Click** on **Filter**. The Filter menu will appear.

4. **Click** on **Filter Gallery**. The Filter Gallery window will open. Alternatively, you can select a specific filter from the list in the menu.

Applying Filters

The Filter Gallery enables you to preview, adjust, and apply filters to images. It provides you with generic thumbnail representations of effects so that you can quickly select the filter you would like to apply.

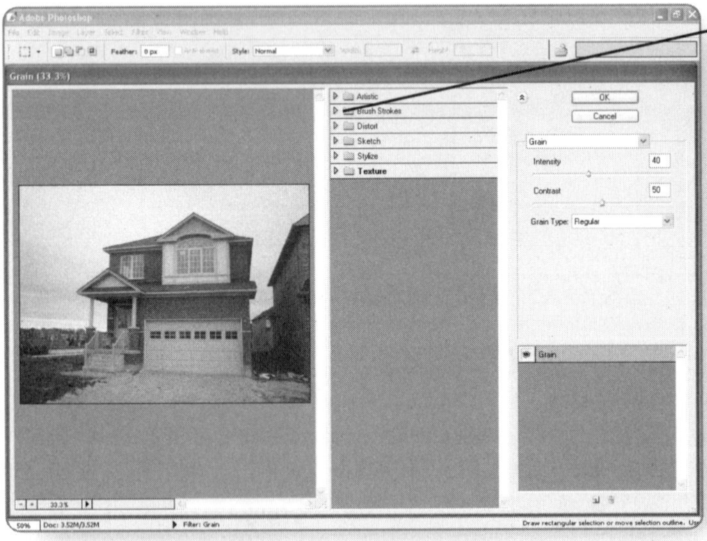

1. **Click** on the **triangle** beside the filter category to display the filters that fall within that category.

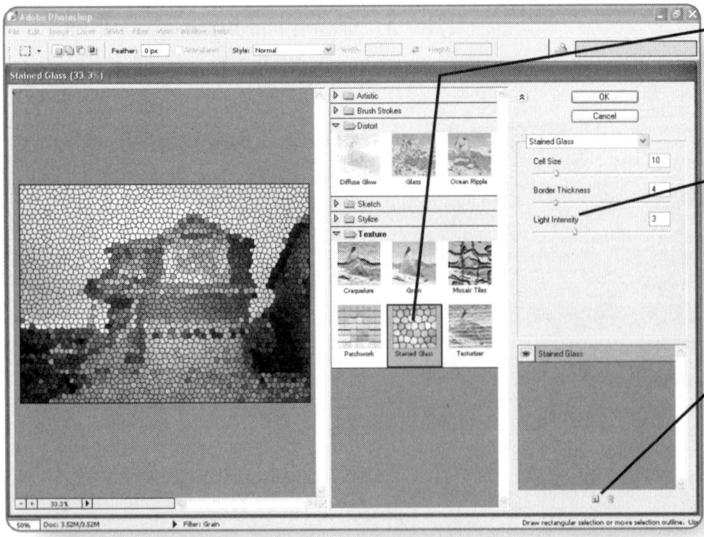

2. **Click** on the desired **filter**. A preview of the effect will appear on your image.

3. **Adjust** any of the **settings** for that filter. The changes to the filter will appear as you make the adjustments.

4. **Click** on the **New Effect Layer button**. This will allow you to apply multiple filters to the same image.

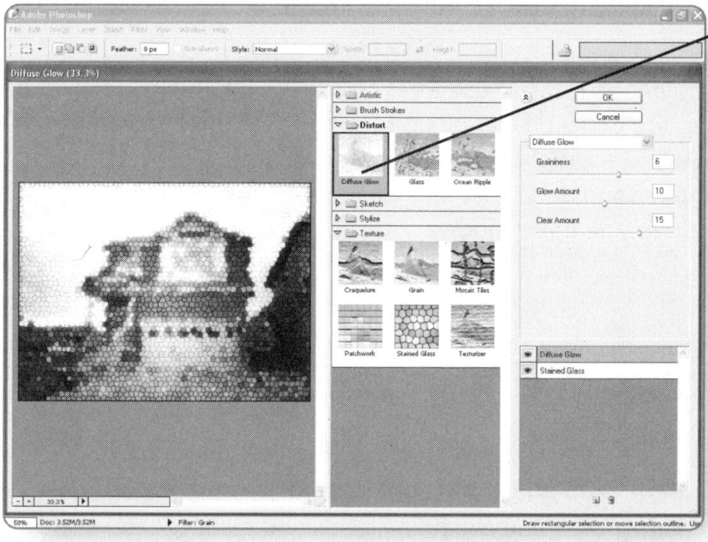

5. **Click** on the desired **filter**. A preview of the effect will appear on your image.

6. **Repeat** steps **4** and **5** until you have completed adding all the filters to your image.

7. **Click** on an **effect layer** that you would like to delete. It will be selected.

8. **Click** on the **Delete effect layer button** to remove the unwanted layer.

9. **Click** on **OK**. The Filter Gallery will close, and the filtered image will appear in the Photoshop CS window.

NOTE

If the image doesn't use RGB color or is a bitmapped, indexed, or 16-bit-per-channel image, Photoshop won't allow you to apply a filter to it. See Chapter 15, "Understanding Colors and Channels," to learn more about image color modes.

Fading a Filter

Fading a filter enables you to make the filter effect more transparent or to adjust the light or color density for the filter effect. Using the Fade capability gives you even greater control over how the filter affects the image.

NOTE

The Fade command may not be available for all filters. It also is not available after you save and close the image; you must use it during the current image-editing session. It is, however, available for some of the painting tools in Photoshop and works for those just as described here.

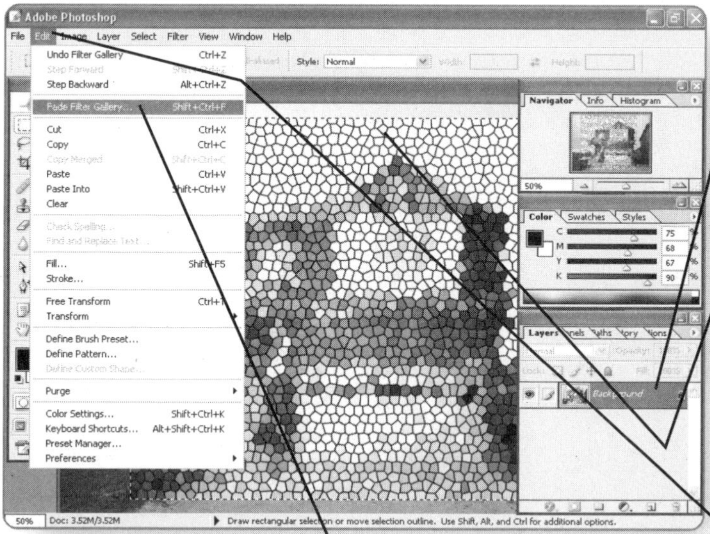

1. Display the **layer** that holds the filtered image content. The selected layer's content will appear.

2. Select the **filtered area**, if necessary. A selection marquee will appear.

3. Click on **Edit**. The Edit menu will appear.

4. Click on **Fade (Filter Name** or Filter Gallery**)**. The Fade dialog box will open.

5. Drag the **Opacity slider**. The Opacity setting will adjust accordingly.

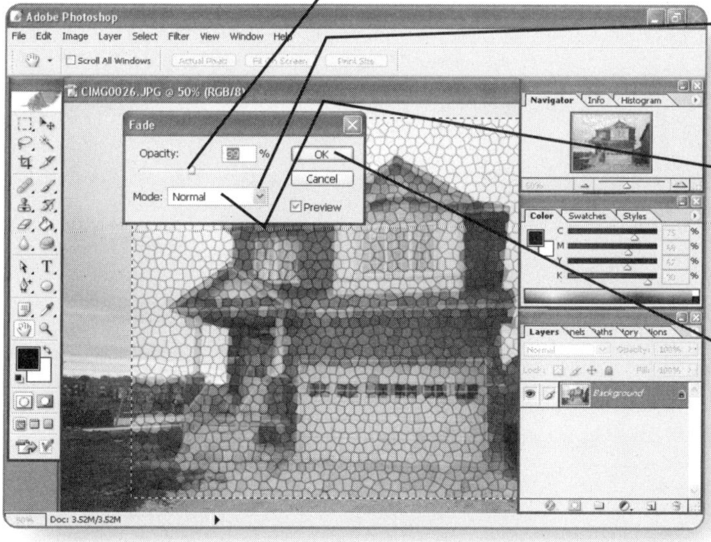

6. Click on the **down arrow** beside the Mode list. The Mode list will open.

7. Click on a **mode** in the list. The image or selection will preview the selected Opacity and Mode settings.

8. Click on **OK**. The dialog box will close, and Photoshop will apply the fade.

14

Printing and Other Outputs

What good is an image if you can't print it out and attach it to the front of your refrigerator for all to see? Photoshop CS adds a number of printing features that you may not have seen before if your previous computer experience has been limited to word processors and spreadsheets. In addition to printing your images, there are a variety of other options for outputting your images. In this chapter, you will learn how to:

- Create a PDF slideshow
- Create a contact sheet
- Use Photomerge to create panoramas
- Choose the printer to use
- Choose print scaling options
- Add a border and background for the printout
- Send the print job
- Print multiple copies of an image on a page with the Picture Package feature

Creating a PDF Slideshow

One of the new features that Photoshop CS offers is the capability to create a PDF slideshow. PDF (*Portable Document Format*) provides an efficient way of viewing and sharing documents. The beauty of this feature is that you can create a digital slideshow without needing any additional software.

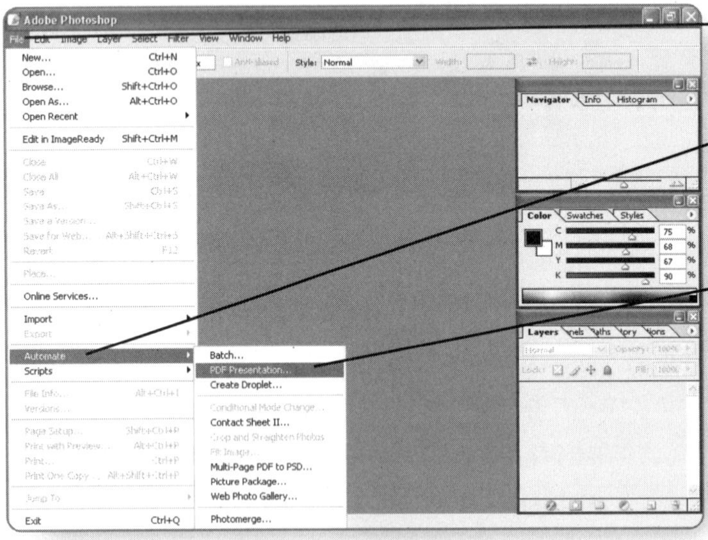

1. **Click** on **File**. The file menu will appear.

2. **Click** on **Automate**. A submenu of different options will appear.

3. **Click** on **PDF Presentation**. The PDF Presentation dialog box will open, where you can set the options for your slideshow.

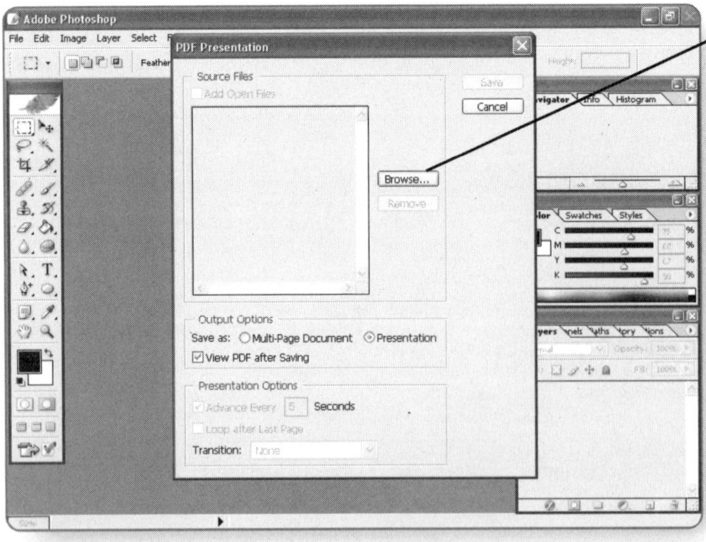

4. **Click** on **Browse**. You can now select which image files you want to be a part of your slideshow.

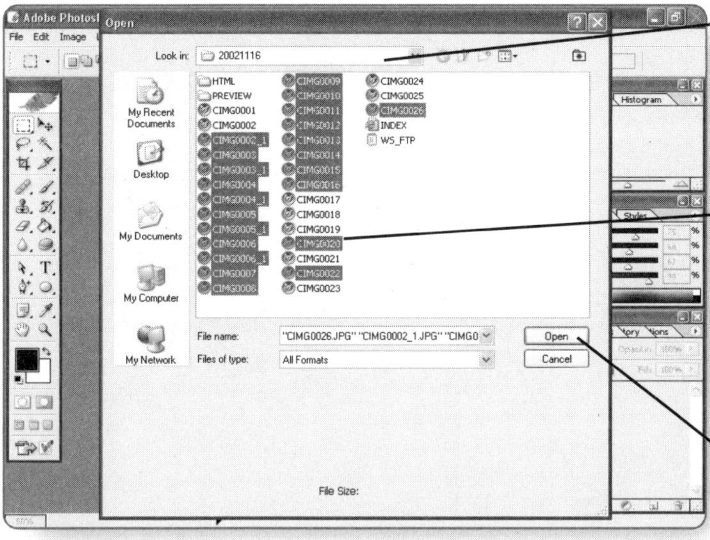

5. Navigate your **computer** to the location of the images you would like to use in the slideshow.

6. Ctrl-click on the **files** you want to include in the slideshow. Alternatively, you can Shift-click to select contiguous files. The files will be highlighted once selected.

7. Click on **Open**. You will return to the PDF Presentation dialog box.

8. Click on the **Presentation** option to save the file as a slideshow.

9. Click in the **View PDF after Saving check box** if you want to preview the slideshow after it has been saved.

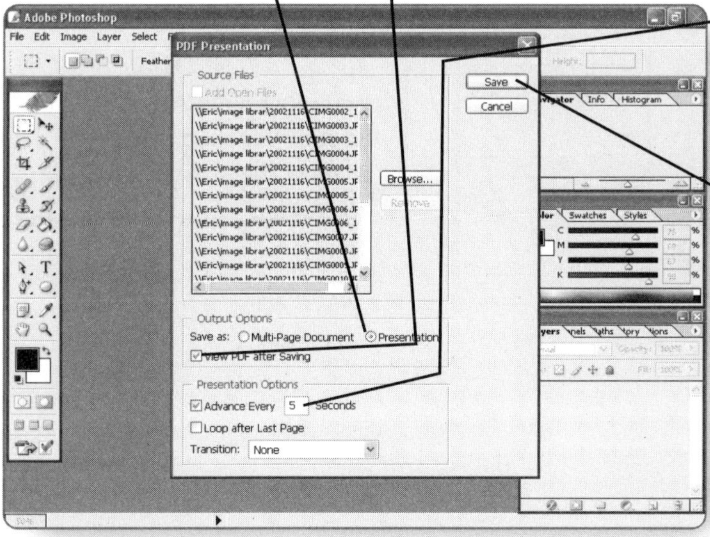

10. Adjust the **settings** for the Presentation Options, including the length of time spent on each slide and looping options.

11. Click on **Save**. The Save dialog box will open.

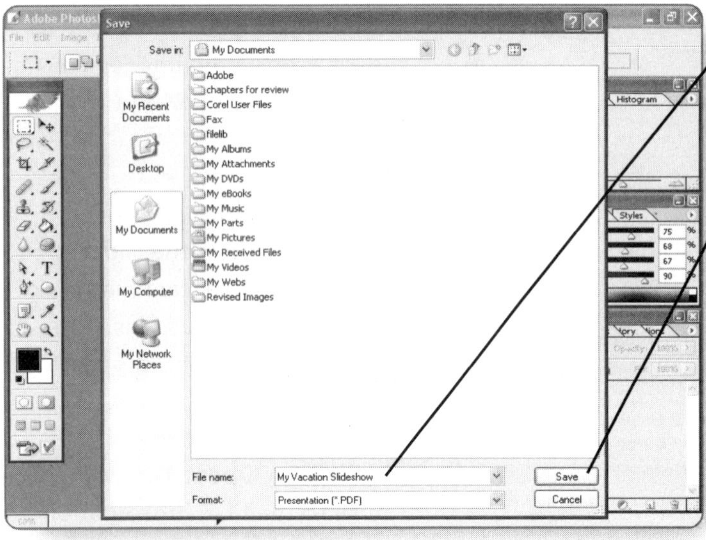

12. Type a **name** for your file. You can give it any name you want.

13. Click on **Save**. The slideshow will be saved.

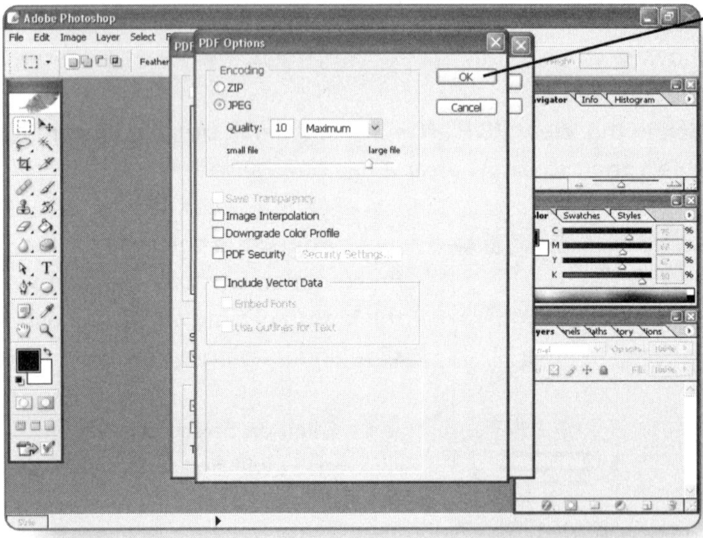

14. Click on **OK** to accept the default settings in the PDF Options dialog box. If you chose to preview the slideshow, it will now play.

NOTE

You must have Acrobat Reader installed in order to view the slideshow.

Creating a Contact Sheet

In traditional photography, a contact sheet is a sheet of thumbnail-size images that enables you to view images from more than one negative. Photoshop CS allows you to create a contact sheet from your digital images. Before you create a contact sheet, it's a good idea to place all of the photos that you want to appear on the sheet into a specific folder on your computer.

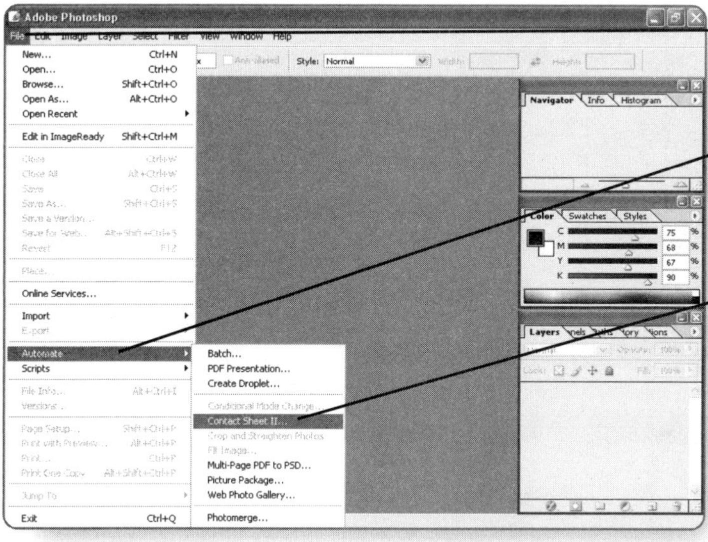

1. **Click** on **File**. The file menu will appear.
2. **Click** on **Automate**. A submenu of different options will appear.
3. **Click** on **Contact Sheet II**. The Contact Sheet II dialog box will appear, where you can set the options for your Contact Sheet.

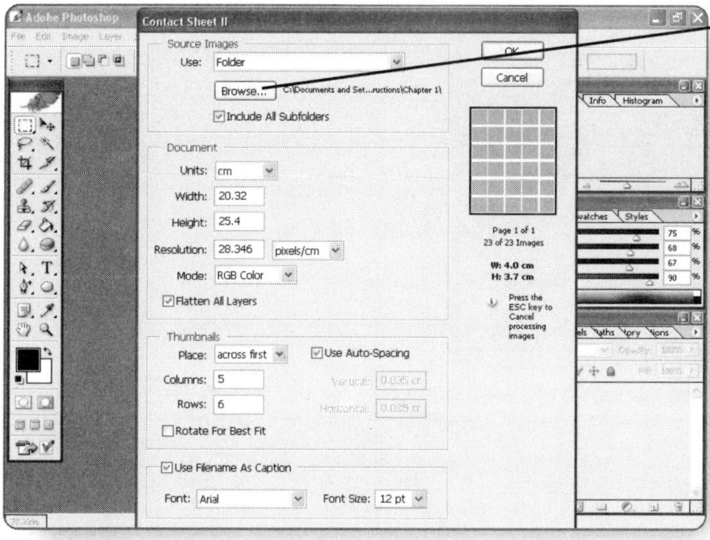

4. **Click** on the **Browse button** to select the folder containing the images that will appear on the contact sheet.

5. **Click** on the **+** beside a folder to view any subfolders.

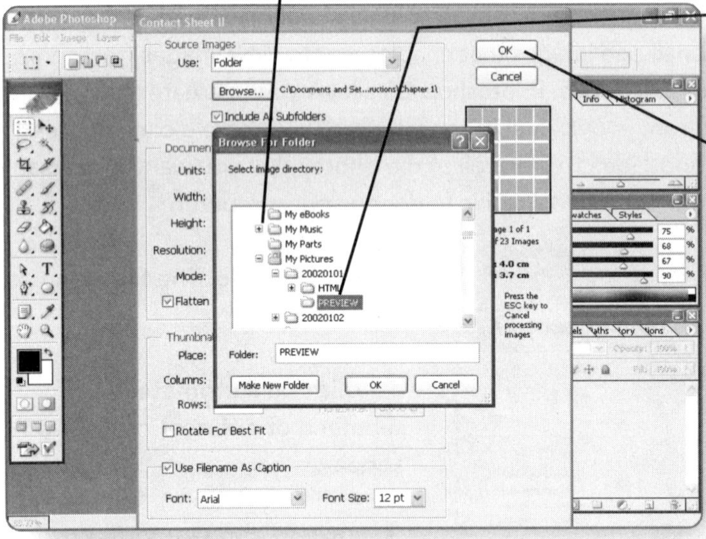

6. **Click** on the **folder** that contains the images to be displayed on the contact sheet.

7. **Click** on **OK**. The folder will be selected.

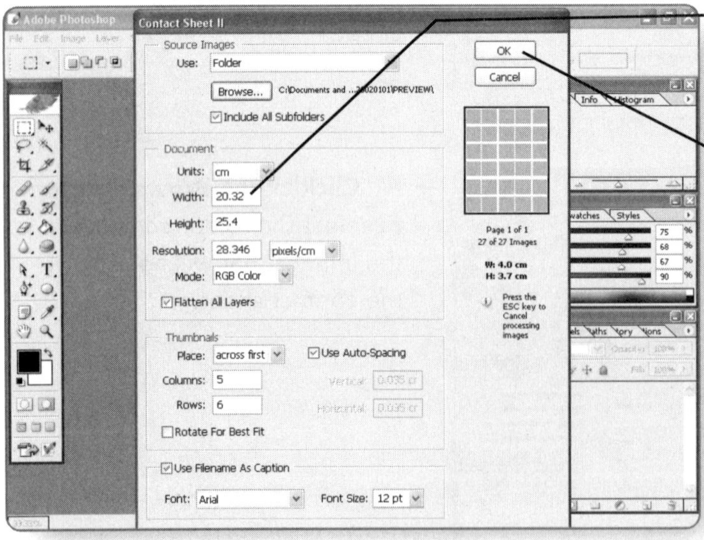

8. **Adjust** the **settings** for the Document and Thumbnail options.

9. **Click** on **OK**. The contact sheet will be created.

Creating Panoramas

The big rage a few years ago was cameras that allowed you to create panoramic images. They basically just stretched and cropped a photo to make it look like it was panoramic. Although that fad may have somewhat faded, you can still create panoramic images using Photoshop CS. Photoshop will actually analyze your images, see how they best fit together, and make a panoramic image that can then be modified.

1. **Open** all of the **images** that you would like to be a part of the panorama.

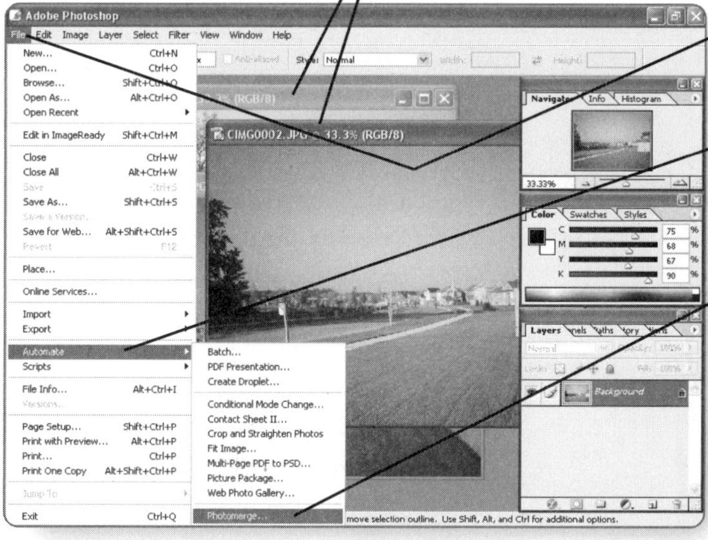

2. **Click** on **File**. The File menu will appear.

3. **Click** on **Automate**. A submenu of different options will appear.

4. **Click** on **Photomerge**. The Photomerge dialog box will appear, where you can set the options for your panoramic image. The files you have open will be listed in the dialog box.

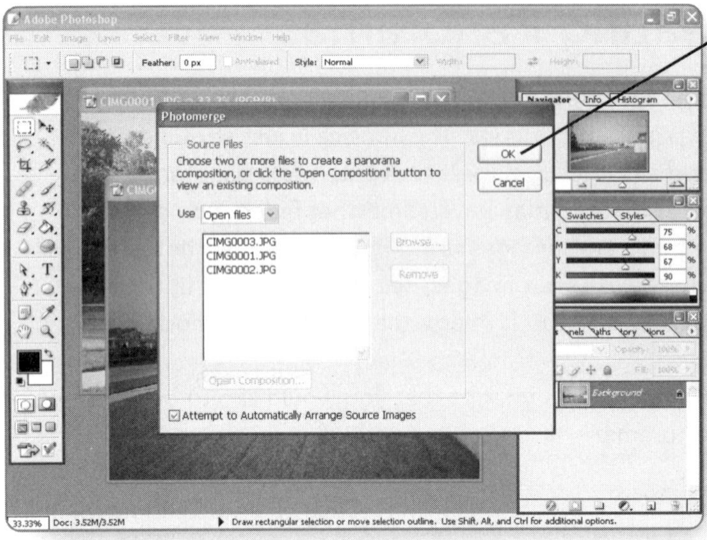

5. **Click** on **OK**. Photoshop will analyze the images and attempt to make a panoramic image from them. The Photomerge window will open.

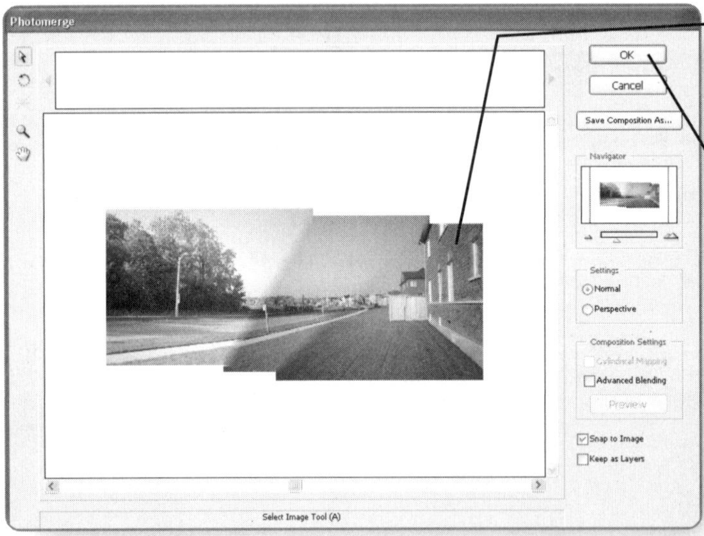

6. **Drag** any **image** to adjust it. You can drag images from the top of the window to the main window.

7. **Click** on **OK**. The Panoramic image will be created and will appear in the Photoshop window.

Printing

When you've finished editing your document, you'll probably want to print it. A huge range of options is available when it comes to printing your image files in Photoshop CS.

Choosing a Printer

Stating the obvious, different printers offer different capabilities. You may use a black-and-white laser printer for basic document printouts and image proofing and use a color printer for sales documents and final image printouts. You need to select the printer to use to print the current image from among those installed on your system, as described here. Once you've selected the printer, you can set available page setup options, which will vary depending on the capabilities of the printer. For example, the software with many printers now calculates margins for you, so the margin choices may be disabled in the Page Setup dialog box.

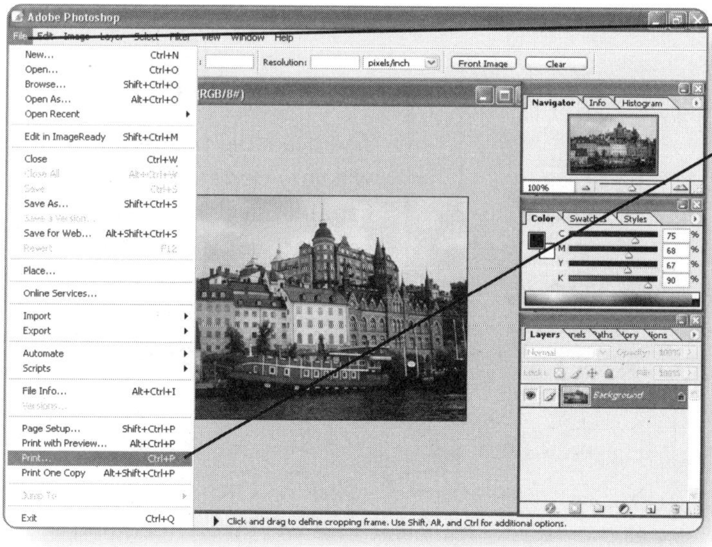

1. **Click** on **File**. The File menu will appear.

2. **Click** on **Print**. The Print dialog box will open.

3. **Click** on the **down arrow** beside the Name drop-down list. The Name drop-down list will open.

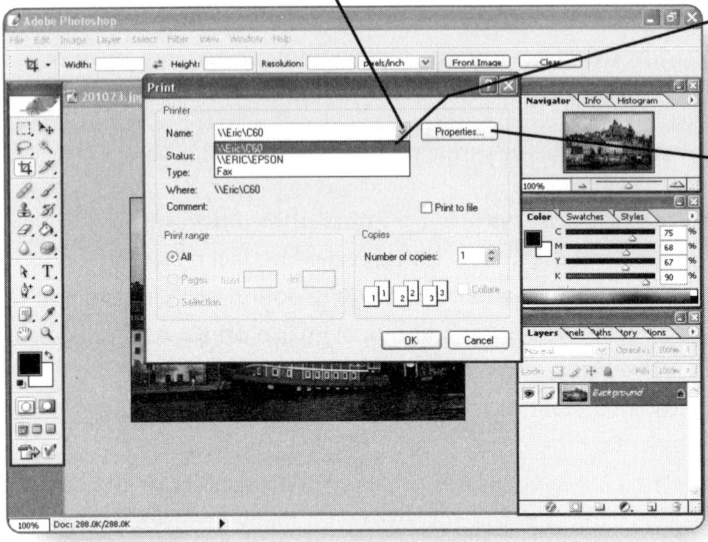

4. **Click** on the desired **printer** in the list. The printer will become the active printer.

5. **Click** on **Properties**. The Properties dialog box for the selected printer will appear.

6. **Choose options** for the printer as necessary. Your choices will become the active choices.

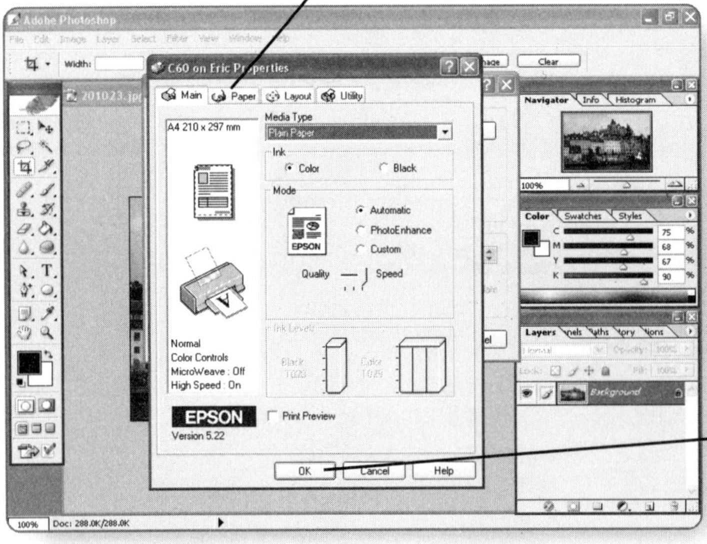

NOTE

The available properties will vary depending on the capabilities and driver software for the printer you selected in step 5, so it's not possible to cover available settings in detail.

7. **Click** on **OK**. Your printer settings will take effect, and the Properties dialog box will close.

Changing the Print Settings

Photoshop offers a variety of other print settings via the Print with Preview command on the File menu. These settings have an impact on how Photoshop prepares an image for printing. In the dialog box where you work with these print settings, a preview image shows the impact of your choices, helping you to better fine-tune the printout. This section shows you how to find the various settings you may need to prepare the current image for printing.

> **NOTE**
>
> You must save an image to save your print setup choices for it. Use the Save As command on the File menu to save a Photoshop file as an .eps file. The "Saving to Another Format" section in Chapter 2 explains how to save a Photoshop file in another format.

Centering and Scaling the Image

For each printout, you can choose how to position the image on the paper relative to the edges of the paper. You also can scale the image to a larger or smaller size so that it better fits the paper. (Note that the scaling is only a temporary printing change and does not affect the size of the saved image.) The following steps review the options for positioning and scaling the image:

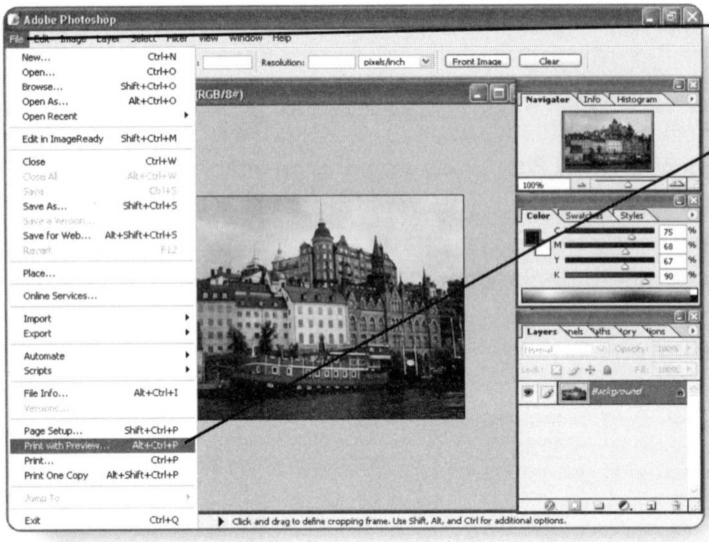

1. **Click** on **File**. The File menu will appear.

2. **Click** on **Print with Preview**. A large Print dialog box will open. (A different Print dialog box appears when you choose the File, Print command.)

3. **Click** on the **Center Image check box** to clear it. The Top and Left choices will become active.

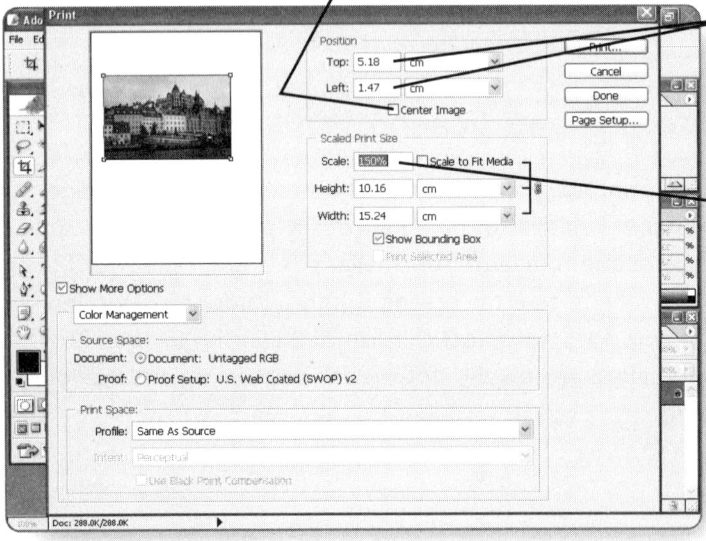

4. **Enter Top** and **Left entries** and measurement units. The image will reposition on the paper as specified.

5. **Change** the **Scale text box entry** if you want to increase or decrease the size of the image in the printout. The image will resize accordingly.

> **NOTE**
>
> If you scale the image, you may need to readjust the Top and Left position entries when the Center Image check box is unchecked. You also can drag the image in the preview area to adjust its position if the Show Bounding Box check box is checked.

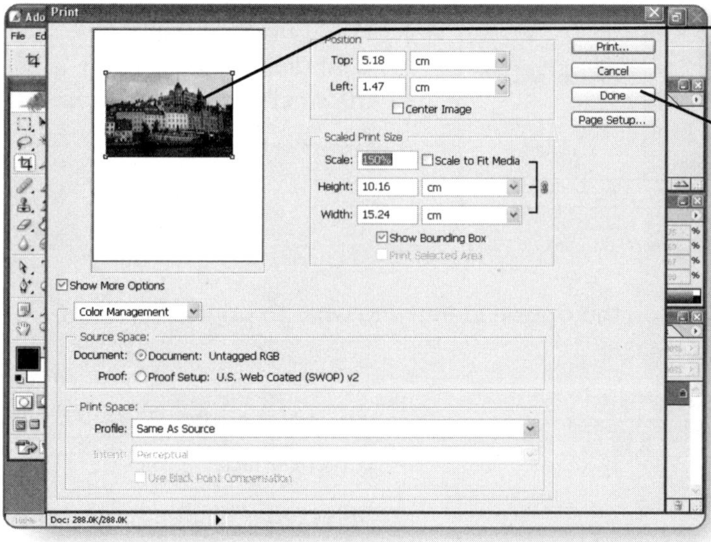

6. **Drag** the **preview** to move the image on the page.

7. **Click** on **Done**. The Print dialog box will close.

Printing the Image

You should at last be ready for the moment of truth—sending your final image to the printer. Follow these steps to get the job done, so to speak.

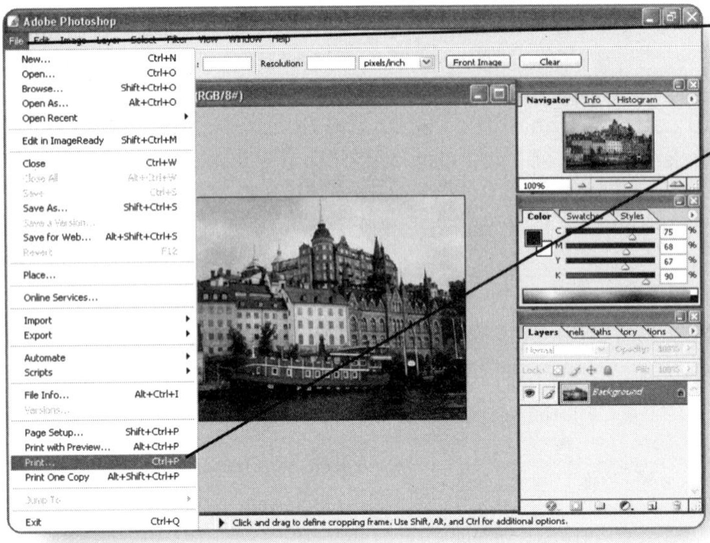

1. **Click** on **File**. The File menu will appear.

2. **Click** on **Print**. The (small) Print dialog box will open.

> **TIP**
>
> You also can click on the Print button in the large Print dialog box to open the small Print dialog box.

3. **Click** on the **option** identifying what to print in the Print Range area:

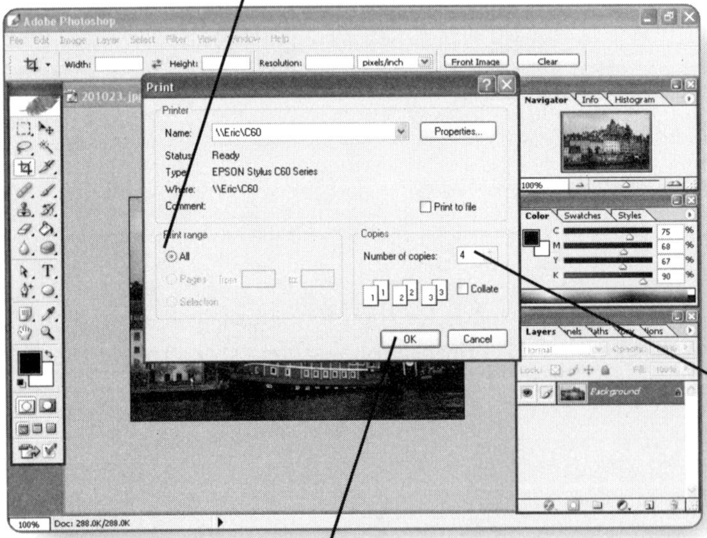

- **All.** Will print the entire current image.
- **Selected.** Will print only the area that's selected in the current image.
- **Pages.** Will print only the pages you identify by making entries in the From and To text boxes.

4. **Change** the **entry** in the Number of copies text box, if necessary. Photoshop will print multiple copies of the image if you change this setting.

5. **Click** on **OK**. Photoshop will send the print job to the printer and close the Print dialog box.

Printing Multiple Images with Picture Package

Photoshop CS includes an enhanced feature called the Picture Package that enables you to create a single sheet that prints multiple copies of an image at various sizes. (Each picture package resembles the print sheets you received for school photos as a kid.) With the Picture Package feature, you select the image to package, choose how to lay out the duplicates on the page, and then specify any additional information you'd like to include with each photo duplicate. Use these steps to create a picture package:

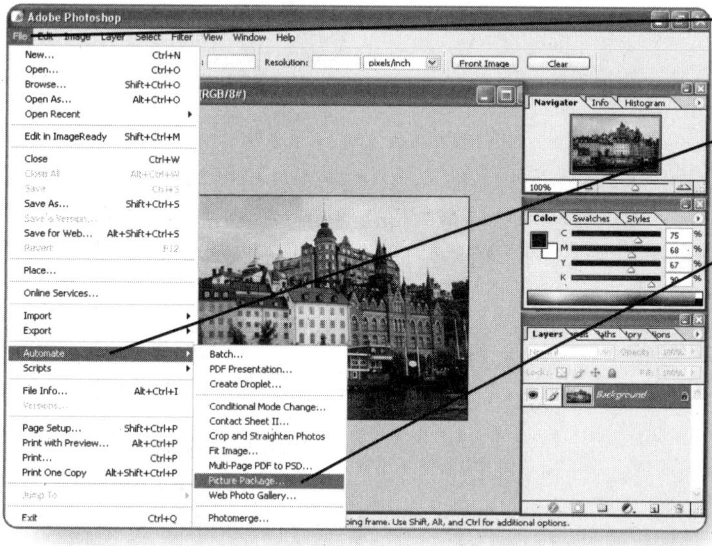

1. **Click** on **File**. The File menu will appear.

2. **Click** on **Automate**. The Automate submenu will appear.

3. **Click** on **Picture Package**. The Picture Package dialog box will open.

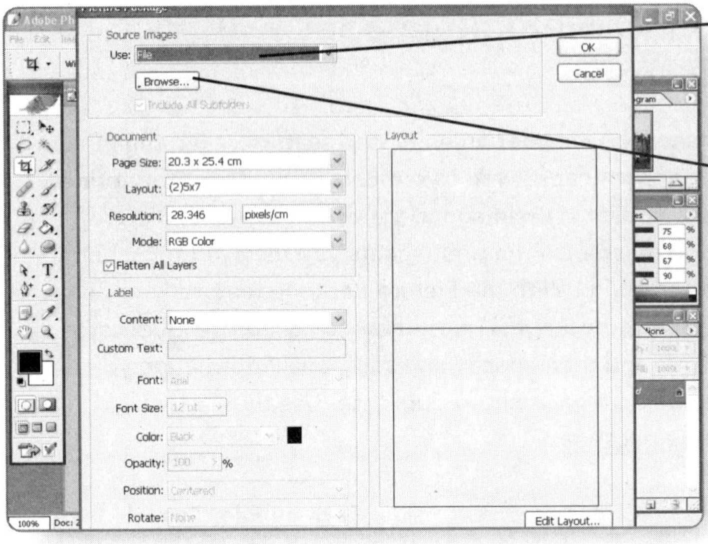

4. Choose File from the Use drop-down list. File will become the active choice.

5. Click on the **Browse button**. The Select an Image File dialog box opens.

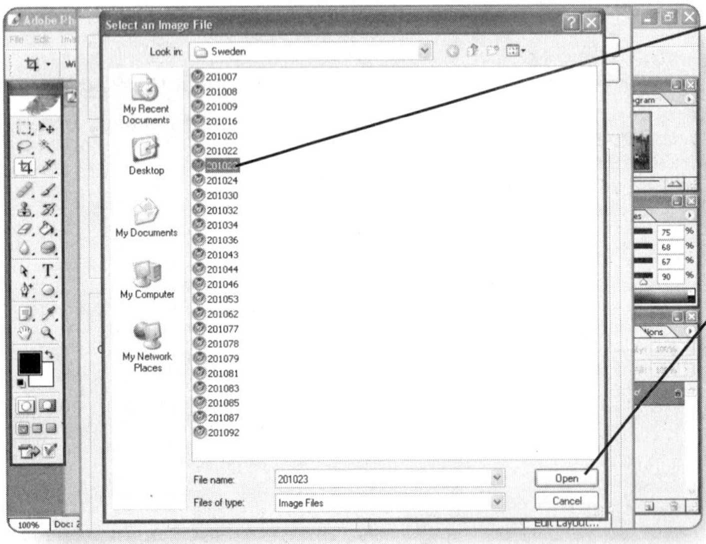

6. Click on the **file** to use for the picture package, using the Look In drop-down list to navigate to the proper disk and folder first, if necessary. The file will be selected.

7. Click on the **Open button**. The selected image appears in the preview area of the Picture Package dialog box.

8. **Choose** the **Document settings** to use for the picture package. The Page Size, Resolution, and Mode choices work as previously discussed with regard to adjusting the image and printout. The Layout choice determines how many duplicates each page will hold, as well as their size. The preview area of the Picture Package dialog box shows the specified layout.

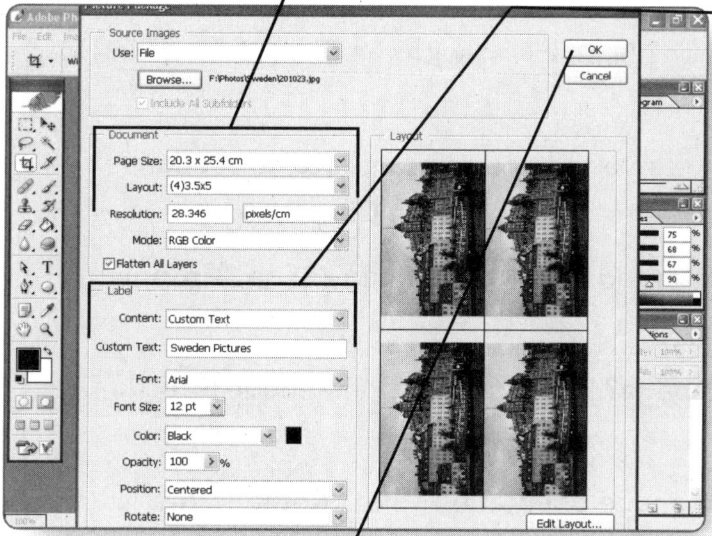

9. **Specify** the **Label settings** to use for the picture package. The Font, Font Size, Color, and Opacity settings work just as for adding text to an image. You can choose a Position for the label on each duplicate, as well as choosing whether to Rotate the label text. To control what actually appears as the label, you can either choose Custom Text from the Content drop-down list and then add your own text into the Custom Text text box, or you can choose one of the other file info options from the Content drop-down list.

10. **Click** on **OK**. Photoshop will generate the picture package in its own image window. Make sure you save the picture package document in order to use it in the future.

Part IV Review Questions

1. How can you correct an area that's too sharp or fuzzy? See "Blurring an Area," "Smudging an Area," and "Sharpening an Area" in Chapter 11.
2. How do you fill a selection? See "Filling with the Paint Bucket" in Chapter 11.
3. Which toolbox tool enables you to access pro photo correction techniques? See "Using Photo Techniques" in Chapter 11.
4. How do you remove unwanted parts of the image? See "Cropping the Image" in Chapter 12.
5. How do you resize the image? See "Changing the Image Size" in Chapter 12.
6. How do you change the image orientation? See "Rotating the Canvas" in Chapter 12.
7. What kinds of filters are available? See "Previewing the Filters" in Chapter 13.
8. How do you apply a filter to an image? See "Applying a Filter" in Chapter 13.
9. What print choices can you adjust before printing? See "Choosing a Printer" and "Changing the Print Settings" in Chapter 14.
10. How do you finish a print job? See "Printing the Image" in Chapter 14.

PART V

Using More Advanced Techniques

15

Understanding Colors and Channels

When you're preparing images for professional printing, color management becomes an important issue. That's because there are differences between how colors are composed onscreen (out of light) and when printed (out of ink). This chapter helps you explore issues surrounding working with color in Photoshop. In this chapter, you will learn how to:

- Use the available color modes
- View and use color channels
- Convert an image to another type of color
- Control bit depth
- Proof the image color

Reviewing the Color Modes

As you learned in Chapter 2, "Working with Image Files," when you create a new image in Photoshop, you can choose the color mode it should use. When you're creating an image for onscreen use, you can typically stick with the default mode, RGB color. However, you might want to choose another of the color modes for special situations. Alternatively, you can convert an image to a particular color mode later, after you've created or scanned it. Table 15-1 details the available color modes in Photoshop so that you can understand color basics while working with color choices in this chapter.

Table 15-1 ***Image Color Modes***

Mode	Description
Bitmap	This mode enables you to create a black-and-white image only. Because it provides for only two tones, you can't convert a full-color image to this mode because too much image information would need to be discarded.
Grayscale	This mode provides for 256 shades of gray in the image, offering enough variation to facilitate clear detail in the image.
Duotone	This mode prepares an image for traditional duotone printing, which uses two solid ink colors such as a dark gray and a blue, yielding a nicely tinted image. You also can construct images with three ink colors (tritones) and four ink colors (quadtones).
Indexed Color	This mode converts an image to a more limited palette of 256 colors, using the matching or lookup system that you specify. You may want to convert to indexed color, for example, for images to be used on a Web page or in a presentation because this mode dramatically decreases the file size while maintaining image appearance. (In fact, this is the preferred setting for Web graphics.)
RGB	This mode mimics visual light—composing images of red, green, and blue—and works best for images to be viewed onscreen, such as those ultimately to be saved for use in a presentation.
CMYK	This mode optimizes images to be printed because cyan, magenta, yellow, and black are the ink colors used for color printing. This mode tries to compensate for the fact that paper absorbs some of the ink, affecting the appearance of colors.

Mode	Description
Lab	This mode uses luminance and brightness settings to help balance the image for all types of devices—printers, monitors, and scanners.
Multichannel	This mode allows you to convert color images for special printing situations. This mode converts the various color channels to channels with 256 colors of gray, with each channel having variations in the distribution of gray tones, according to the original colors.

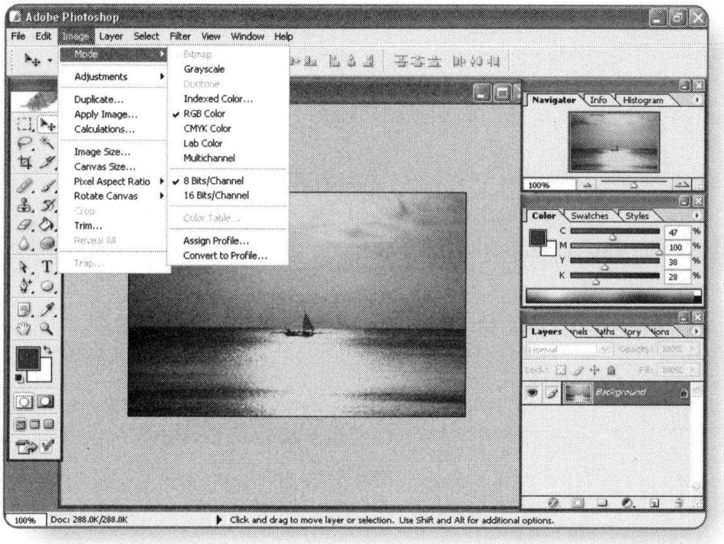

Using Color Channels

When an image uses one of the color modes that has color (for example, not bitmap or grayscale mode), Photoshop displays each color to be displayed or printed as a separate channel. You can work with the image information for a particular channel to edit only that color in the image. This section shows you how to display a channel and gives an example of working with channel content.

NOTE

Bitmap, grayscale, duotone, and indexed images have a single channel. You can add more channels, called alpha channels, to any type of image but bitmaps. (See the "Adding an Alpha Channel" section in the next chapter to learn how to add an alpha channel.) The alpha channels you add can hold masks or add separate colors to be printed in the image.

Changing to a Channel

You use the Channels palette to work with the various color channels in a Photoshop image. Follow these steps when you want to display a particular channel only:

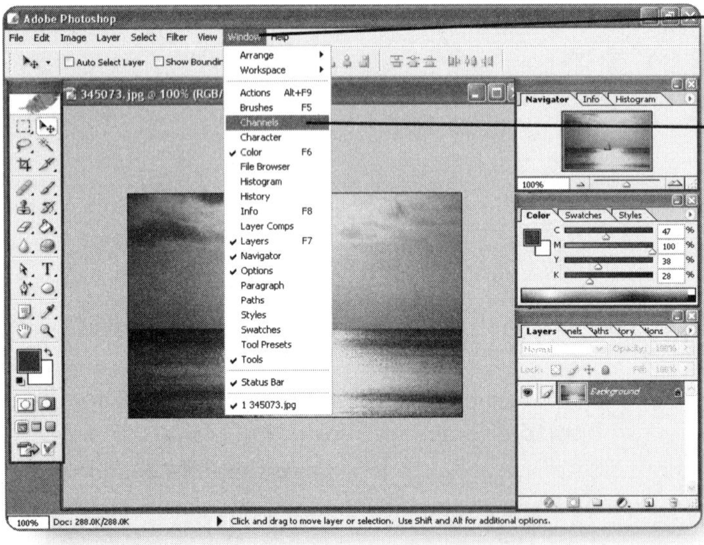

1. **Click** on **Window**. The Window menu will appear.
2. **Click** on **Channels**. The Channels palette will become the active palette.

TIP

You also can click on the Channels tab, if it's visible in the Layers palette. The Layers palette window holds five tabs, making it tough to see the tab to click. You can either resize the palette window to make the tabs accessible or use the Window menu as noted in the steps in this book.

3. Click on the desired **channel**. The channel will become the current or active channel, and its content will appear in the image window.

> **TIP**
>
> To hide a channel, click on the eye icon to the left of the channel name. To redisplay the change, click on the empty box to redisplay the eye icon.

Working on a Channel

You can edit the content on a single color channel just as you can edit the content of a single layer. You can make a selection on the channel, use editing tools such as the Airbrush, delete selected channel content, apply a filter, and so on. The following steps show just one example of the editing possibilities:

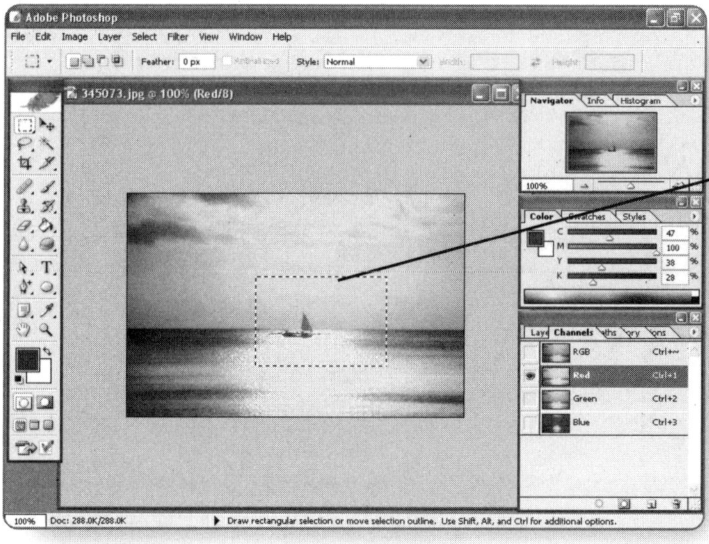

1. Make a **selection** on the current channel using the tool of your choice, if necessary. The selection will become active.

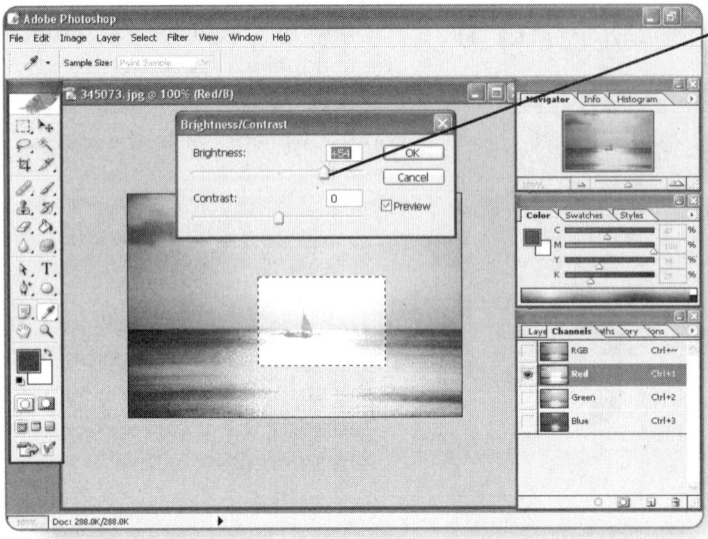

2. Make changes to the **channel content** using the tool or filter of your choice. This example shows brightness being adjusted. The changes will appear on the channel immediately.

3. Click on the **composite channel**. The composite channel will become the current or active channel, and all the image color content will reappear in the image window. From this point, you can continue working with other Photoshop tools.

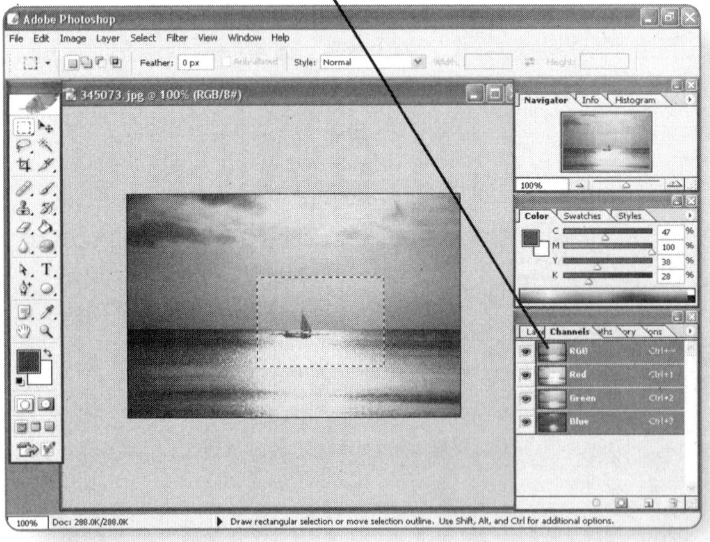

NOTE

If you experiment with color channel changes, you'll find that they can be very subtle. Although the average person might not catch all your channel changes, being able to control and manipulate colors is essential if you plan to use your images for professional-level output.

Converting Images

Images you create don't have to remain in the original color mode. Photoshop makes it easy to convert to another color mode when necessary. This section walks you through a few of the more common color-mode-conversion scenarios.

Choosing CMYK

Adobe recommends that you perform most color corrections (and other edits) to an image before you convert the image to CMYK color for professional printing. (Adobe also recommends that you save a copy of the image file before converting to CMYK so that you can work with the original colors in the image, if necessary, at a later time.) You convert to CMYK when the image is ready for a print shop to create color separations—a separate piece of film for each ink color, used for creating a plate to print each color ink. Typically, you'll convert to CMYK color from RGB color, as in the following steps:

1. **Click** on **Layer**. The Layer menu will appear.

2. **Click** on **Flatten Image**. Photoshop will merge all the separate layers onto a single layer so that you can convert the image to CMYK color. (This is another reason why you should complete your edits in RGB color before converting to CMYK.)

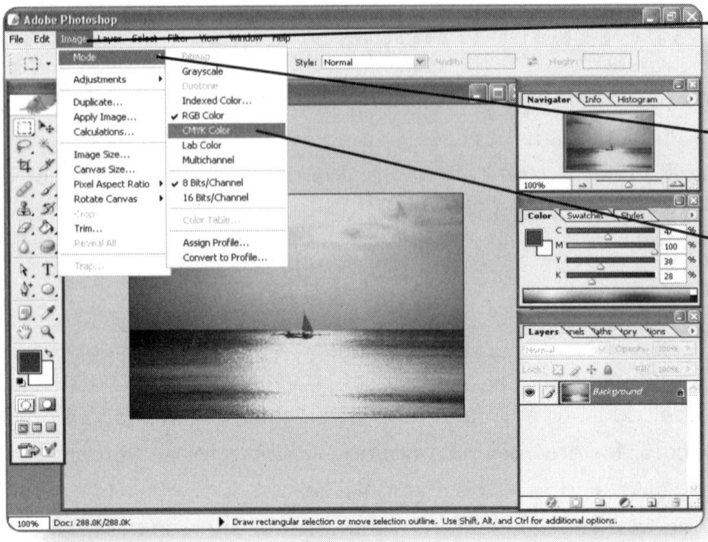

3. **Click** on **Image**. The Image menu will appear.

4. **Point** to **Mode**. The Mode submenu will appear.

5. **Click** on **CMYK Color**. Photoshop will convert the image to CMYK color immediately. If you display the Colors palette, you will see the new channels.

> **NOTE**
>
> You use the Mode submenu of the Image menu to convert between all color modes.

Working with Bit Depth

In Photoshop, bit depth refers to the amount of color information each pixel can hold per color channel. For example, an image set to 16 bits per channel (the default for many scanners) would have an overall color depth of 48 bits (16 x 3) for an RGB image. The higher the bit depth, the greater the possible variation of colors in the image, and the more detail the image can appear to have. On the other hand, an image set to 8 bits per channel provides a much smaller file size, which may work best for certain publications and applications. The following steps show you how to convert from 8 bits per channel to 16 bits per channel and back again:

NOTE

In some cases, when you add layers and masks to a scanned image, Photoshop automatically converts the image from 16 bits to 8 bits, so you have to manually adjust the bit depth later.

1. **Click** on **Layer**. The Layer menu will appear.

2. **Click** on **Flatten Image**. Photoshop will merge all the separate layers onto a single layer so that you can convert an image from 8 bits per channel to 16 bits per channel.

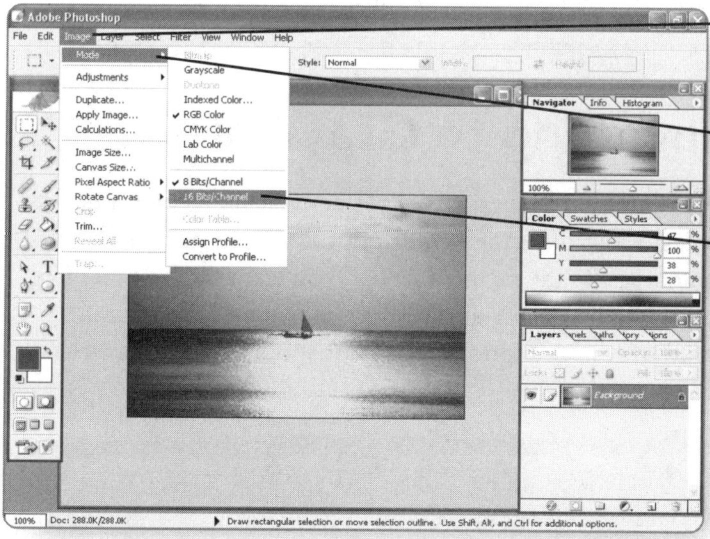

3. **Click** on **Image**. The Image menu will appear.

4. **Point** to **Mode**. The Mode submenu will appear.

5. **Click** on **16 Bits/Channel**. Photoshop will convert the image to 16 bits of color information per channel immediately.

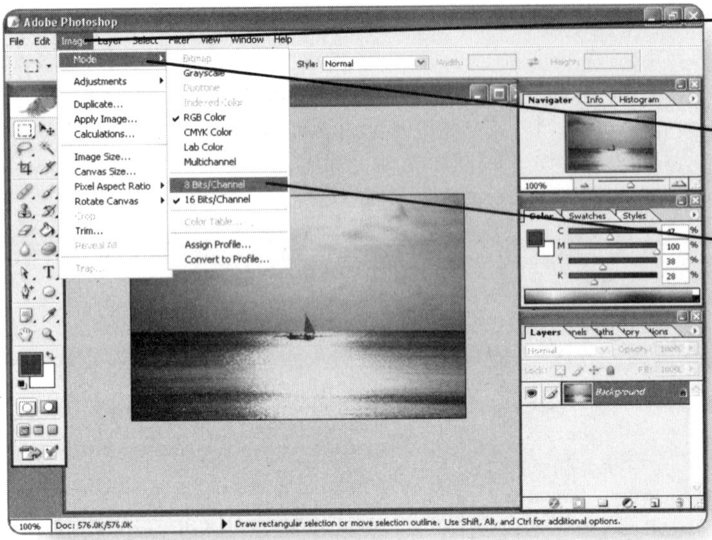

6. **Click** on **Image**. The Image menu will appear.

7. **Point** to **Mode**. The Mode submenu will appear.

8. **Click** on **8 Bits/Channel**. Photoshop will convert the image to 8 bits of color information per channel immediately.

> **NOTE**
>
> Some tools and features, such as the Text tool, don't work in an image set to 16 bits of color. If you try to use an unavailable tool or feature while the image is set to 16 bits, Photoshop will display a message telling you to convert the image to 8 bits per channel.

Converting to Grayscale

Another common scenario involves converting a color image to grayscale. Most of us take color photos with either our traditional or digital cameras. When you want to use one of those images in a black-and-white publication, convert the image to grayscale mode using Photoshop, as described here:

1. **Click** on **Image**. The Image menu will appear.
2. **Point** to **Mode**. The Mode submenu will appear.
3. **Click** on **Grayscale**. A dialog box will appear to ask whether you want to complete the conversion by discarding color information.

NOTE

It's not necessary to flatten the image before converting to grayscale. However, if you do not flatten the image first and the image contains a color adjustment layer, the wording of the dialog box that appears after step 3 will be slightly different, asking if you want to discard the adjustment layer information.

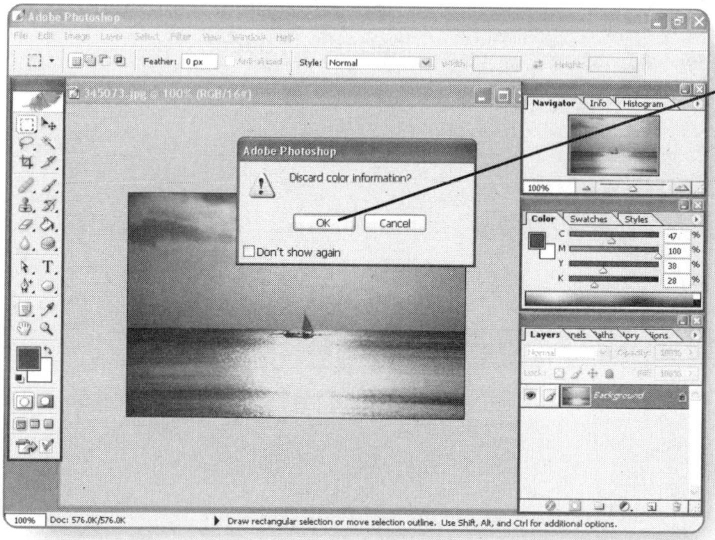

4. **Click** on **OK**. Photoshop will complete the grayscale conversion.

NOTE

If you convert from grayscale back to one of the color modes, Photoshop won't be able to re-create the original color information. For that reason, it's a good idea to save a copy of your image file before converting to grayscale, so that you can continue working with the color version of the image whenever you need it.

Proofing Colors

Photoshop provides you with the means to proof the appearance of the various color plates (Cyan, Magenta, Yellow, and blacK) after you've converted an image to CMYK color. You might want to do this, for example, to look for small specks of color that you want to clean up by erasing them from the applicable channel. The following steps explain how to get started proofing a color plate:

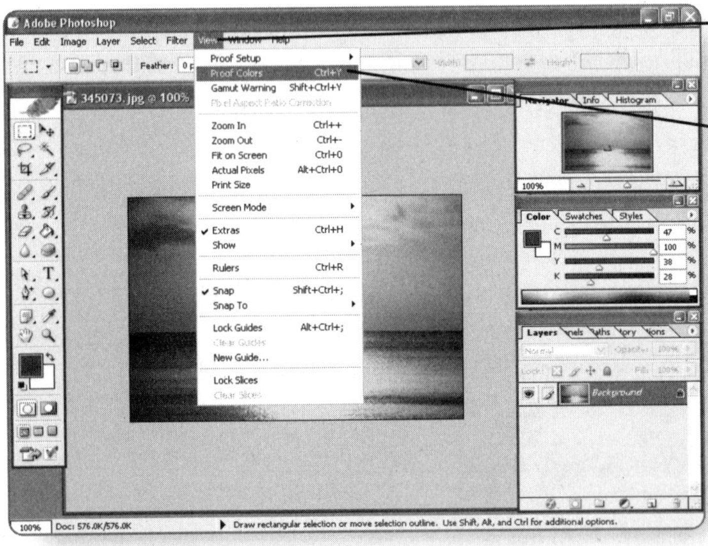

1. **Click** on **View**. The View menu will appear.

2. **Click** on **Proof Colors** (to check it). The color-proofing feature will become active.

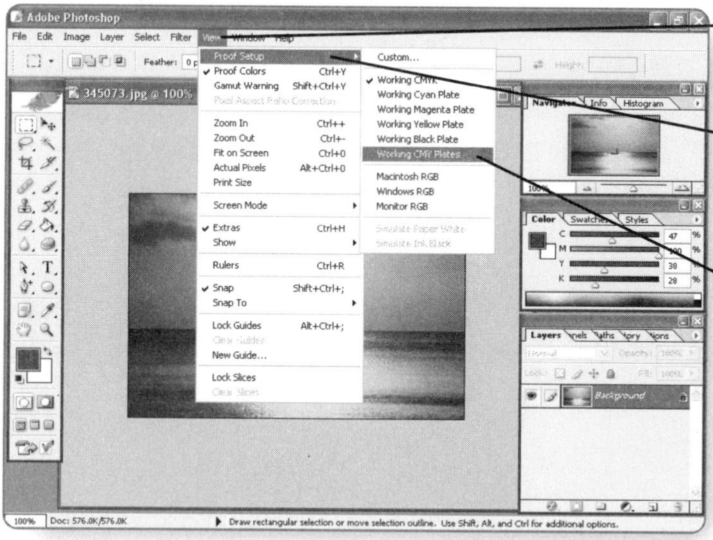

3. **Click** on **View**. The View menu will appear.

4. **Point** to **Proof Setup**. The Proof Setup submenu will appear.

5. **Click** on one of the **Working (Color) Plate** choices.

NOTE

You can repeat steps 3 through 5 to proof other plates.

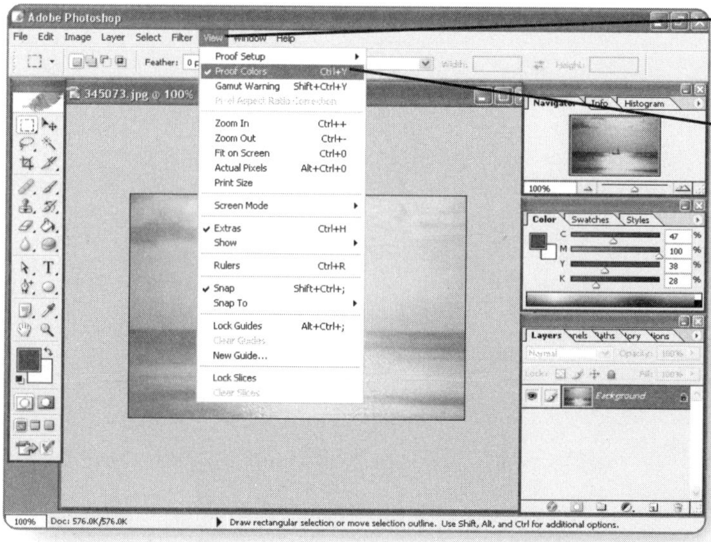

6. **Click** on **View**. The View menu will appear.

7. **Click** on **Proof Colors** (to uncheck it). The color-proofing feature will be disabled, and all the colors will reappear in the image.

16

Correcting Image Color

Let's face it, we're not all professional photographers. The truth is that many of the digital images we take have some technical flaw in them, one way or another. By using a few straightforward commands, you can make color corrections to your photos that once required quite a bit of time in the photo lab. This chapter introduces you to basic color-correction techniques in Photoshop. In this chapter, you'll learn how to:

- Make quick color corrections
- Adjust image tones
- Rebalance the image color
- Change image brightness and contrast
- Use a special color effect
- Use the new Histogram palette
- Create an alpha channel

Using the Auto Color Command

If you want to improve the appearance of your image without working in depth with color settings, you can use the Auto Color command. This command searches the image content and improves the contrast and colors. The following steps show how to use the Auto Color command to adjust an image's color and contrast with ease.

> **NOTE**
>
> The changes that the Auto Color command makes are based on the settings in the Auto Color Corrections Options dialog box. You can access this dialog box by choosing Image, Adjustments, Curves. Then click on the Options button in the Curves dialog box.

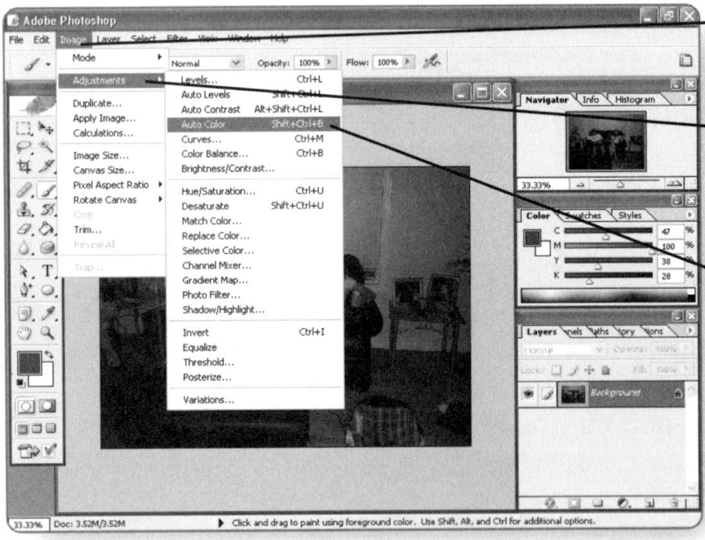

1. **Click** on **Image**. The Image menu will appear.
2. **Point** to **Adjustments**. The Adjustments submenu will appear.
3. **Click** on **Auto Color**. The image color and contrast will be adjusted.

Changing the Tonal Quality

The tonal quality settings in Photoshop enable you to manipulate the image's appearance by adjusting highlights or shadows. This can make the image appear a bit lighter or darker if you adjust all the colors in the image, or it can make more subtle changes if you adjust one channel only. Follow these steps to work with the image tone:

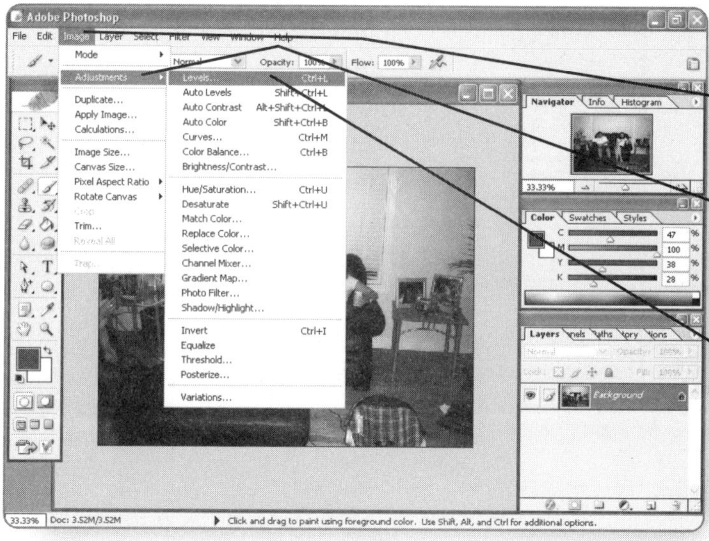

1. **Click** on **Image**. The Image menu will appear.

2. **Point** to **Adjustments**. The Adjustments submenu will appear.

3. **Click** on **Levels**. The Levels dialog box will open.

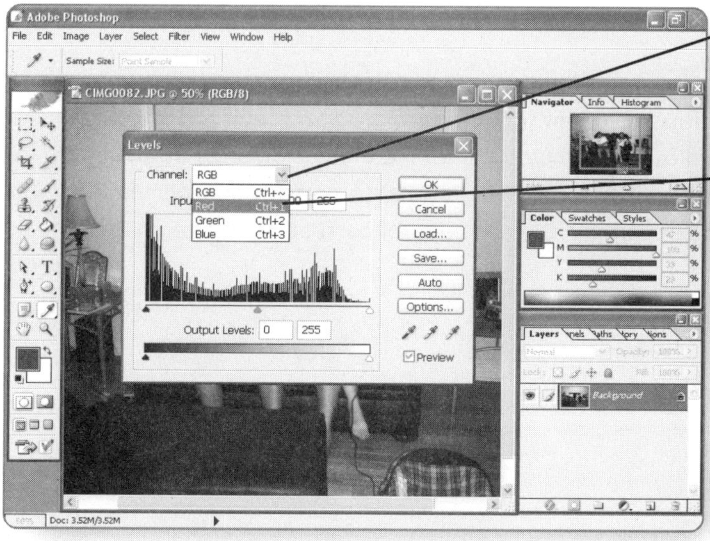

4. **Click** on the **down arrow** beside the Channel drop-down list. A list of options will appear.

5. **Click** on the desired **channel** in the list. The desired channel will be selected for tonal adjustments.

6. **Drag** the **Input Levels sliders** as necessary to adjust the tone. The left slider affects shadows, the middle slider affects midtones, and the right slider affects highlights. The image window will preview the changes.

7. **Drag** the **Output Levels sliders** as necessary to further adjust the tone for the selected channel. The left slider adjusts shadows, and the right slider adjusts highlights. The image window will preview the changes.

8. **Click** on **OK**. Photoshop will close the Levels dialog box and apply the tonal changes.

Correcting the Color Balance

The color balance in an image refers to the overall proportion of various colors in the image. For example, if a photo looks too yellow to you, you can make a color balance adjustment (as described in the following steps) to correct that problem. Color balance changes make a general correction to the image color.

1. **Click** on **Image**. The Image menu will appear.

2. **Point** to **Adjustments**. The Adjustments submenu will appear.

3. **Click** on **Color Balance**. The Color Balance dialog box will open.

4. **Click** on the **option button** for the tonal range to correct in the Tone Balance area, if necessary. The color balance changes you make will be applied to the specified tonal range.

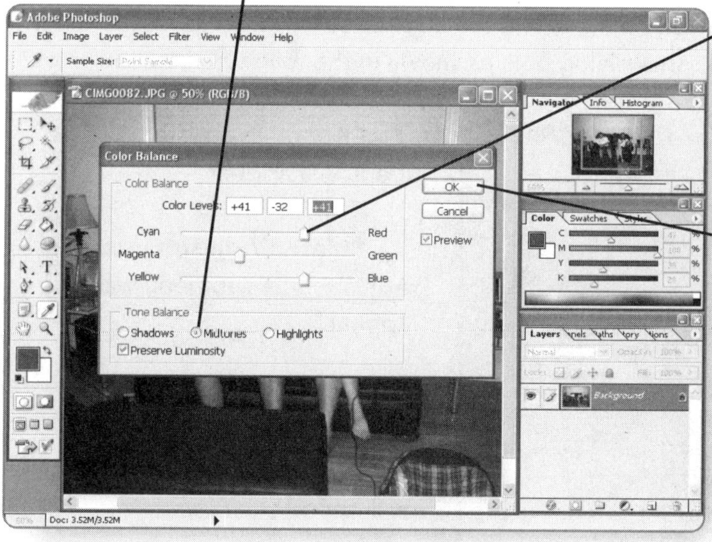

5. **Drag** the **Color Balance sliders** as necessary to change the amount of color in an image. The image window will preview the changes.

6. **Click** on **OK**. Photoshop will close the Color Balance dialog box and apply the color changes.

NOTE

You also can make various color corrections and apply various color special effects by adding an adjustment layer to the image. The adjustment layer enables you to display the color correction or effect when needed and hide it when not needed. Use the New Adjustment Layer submenu of the Layer menu to add an adjustment layer.

Correcting Brightness and Contrast

The most typical problem with photos taken by amateur photographers is that the brightness and contrast levels are off. Brightness generally refers to the amount of light (overall lightness) in the image, and contrast refers to the difference between the lightest points and the darkest points in the image. Adding brightness to an image can soften its appearance, whereas increasing contrast can make an image appear a bit more well-defined. You can adjust both brightness and contrast in the same dialog box, as shown in the following steps.

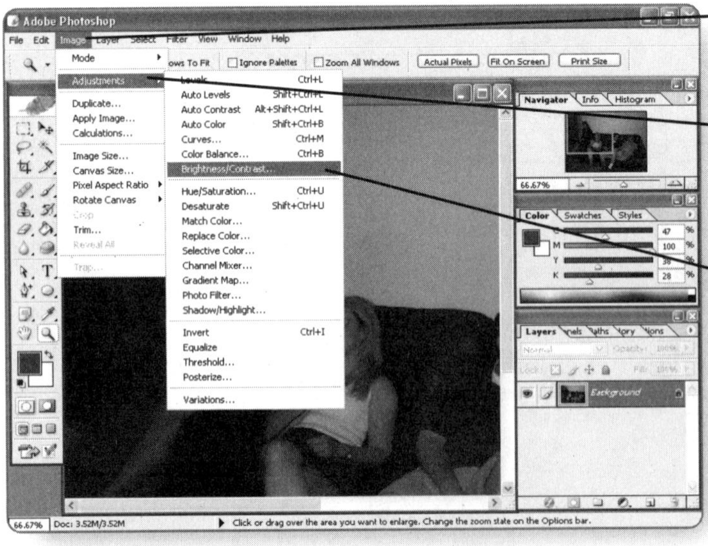

1. **Click** on **Image**. The Image menu will appear.
2. **Point** to **Adjustments**. The Adjustments submenu will appear.
3. **Click** on **Brightness/Contrast**. The Brightness/Contrast dialog box will open.

4. **Drag** the **Brightness slider**. The image window will preview the changes.

5. **Drag** the **Contrast slider**. The image window will preview the changes.

6. **Click** on **OK**. Photoshop will close the Brightness/Contrast dialog box and apply the changes.

Applying a Special Color Effect

Some of the commands on the Adjustments submenu of the Image menu—specifically the Invert, Equalize, Threshold, and Posterize choices—apply special color effects. Each of these commands works a bit differently and applies a slightly different effect, so the following steps provide an example of using one of them—the Posterize choice. The posterizing effect reduces the number of colors used in the image so that the image becomes composed of larger color areas, much like paint-by-number pictures or the way posters used to be designed.

NOTE

The Invert Image command reverses the colors in an image, creating a negative effect. Equalize finds the lightest and darkest pixels in the image and sets them to white and black, respectively. It then distributes the brightness values for the remaining pixels between the two extremes. Finally, the Threshold command converts any image to a high-contrast, black-and-white image.

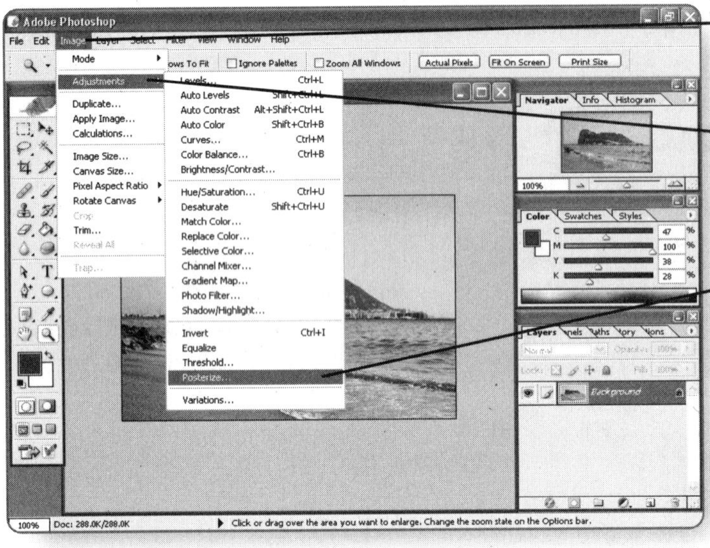

1. **Click** on **Image**. The Image menu will appear.
2. **Point** to **Adjustments**. The Adjustments submenu will appear.
3. **Click** on **Posterize**. The Posterize dialog box will open.

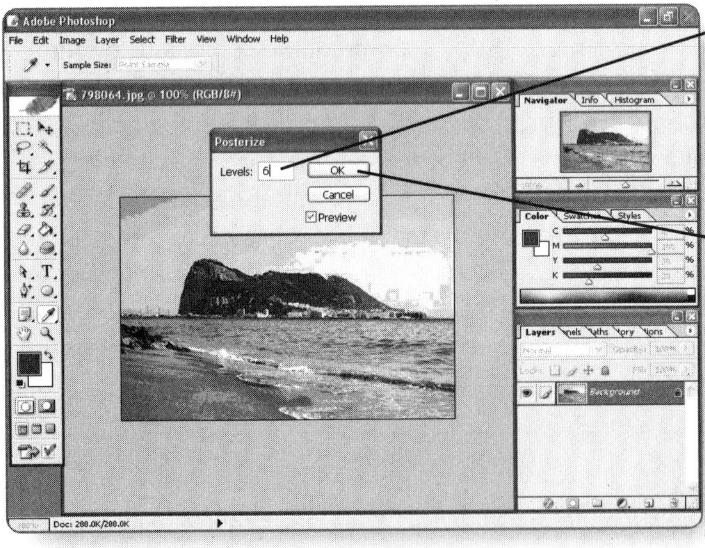

4. **Type** a new **Levels text box entry**, if necessary. The image window will preview the specified degree of posterization.
5. **Click** on **OK**. Photoshop will close the Posterize dialog box and apply the special effect.

Using The Histogram Palette

New to Photoshop CS is a Histogram palette that continually updates itself as you work on your image. A Histogram provides a graphical representation of the tonal and color information in your image.

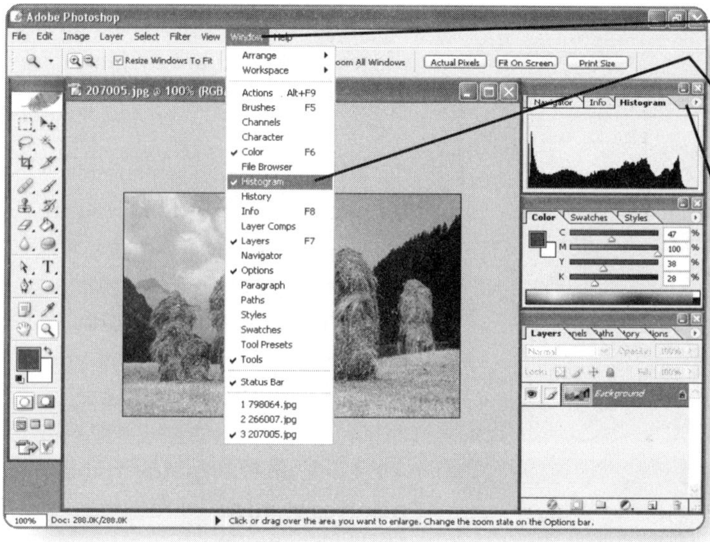

1. **Click** on **Window**. The Window menu will appear.
2. **Click** on **Histogram**. The Histogram palette will become active.
3. **Click** on the **Histogram palette menu button**. A list of options will appear.

4. **Click** on **Expanded View**. This will expand the size of your histogram and provide you with additional color and tonal information about your image.

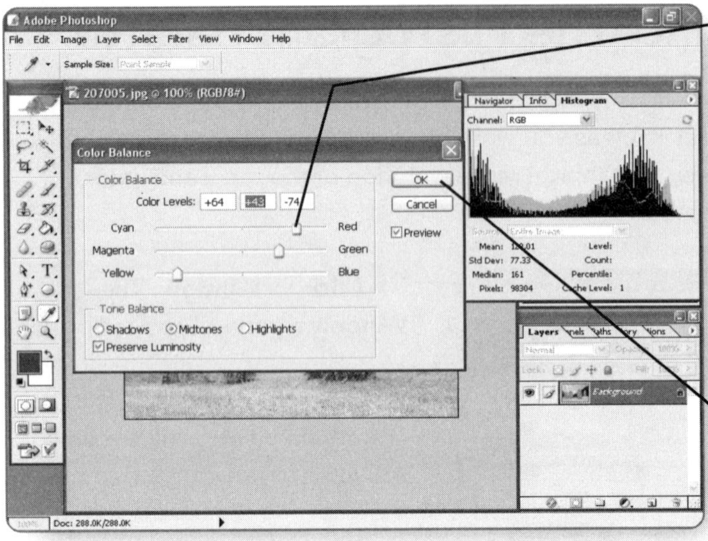

5. **Make** a **color** or **tonal change** to your image. In this example, we are adjusting the color balance. As you make changes, they are reflected in the histogram. The previous histogram appears in light gray, and the new histogram based on the changes you are making appears in black.

6. **Click** on **OK** in whichever tonal or color change dialog box you are using. As soon as you finish applying your color or tonal changes, the light gray histogram disappears, and you are left with the black one.

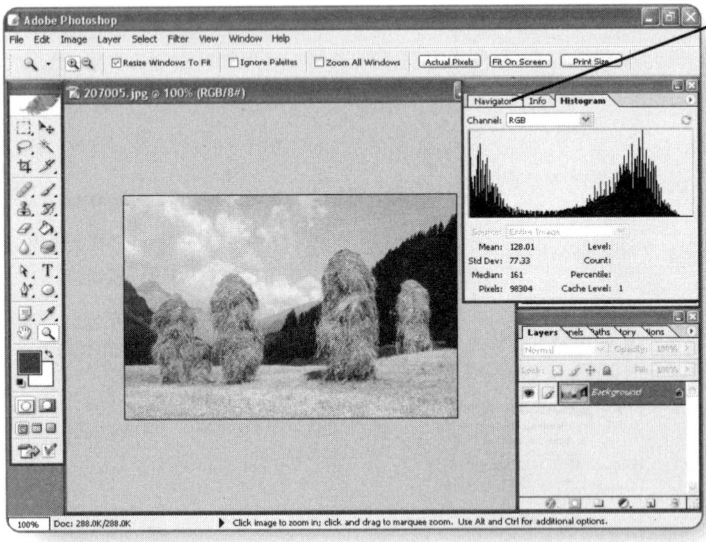

7. **Click** on **Navigator** in the palettes window to return to the Navigator palette.

Adding an Alpha Channel

An alpha channel is an extra channel that you use to store a selection in an image. You can easily reload the selection from the channel or even convert the channel to a spot-color treatment, as described in the section "Adding Spot Color" in the next chapter. The steps that follow explain the easiest way to save a spot channel—by saving a selection as a spot channel.

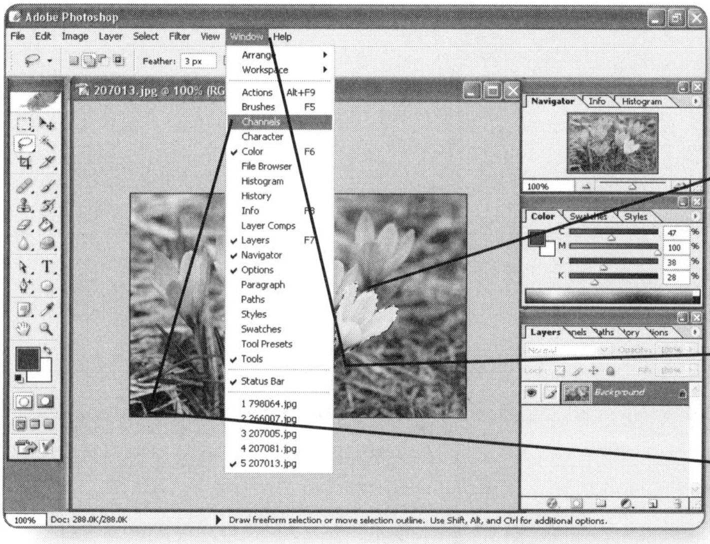

1. **Make** a **selection** on a layer using the selection tool of your choice. The selection will appear in the image.

2. **Click** on **Window**. The Window menu will appear.

3. **Click** on **Channels**. The Channels palette will become active.

4. **Click** on the **Save Selection as Channel button** at the bottom of the Channels palette. The new channel will appear immediately in the Channels palette.

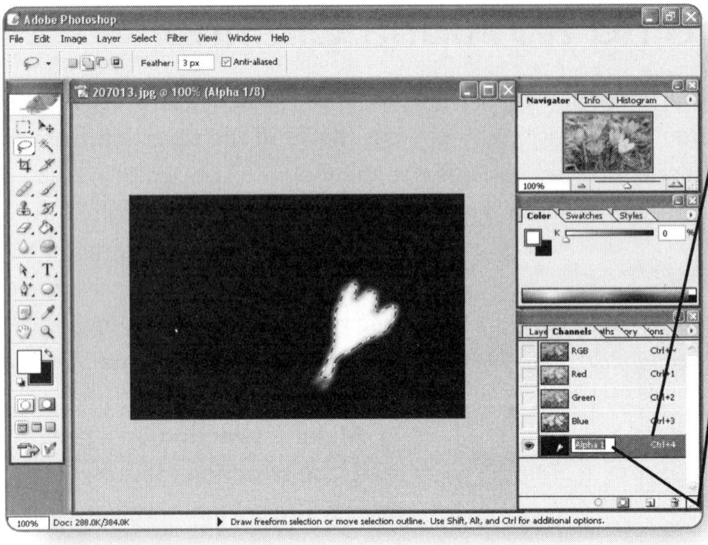

5. **Click** on the **new channel** in the palette. The new channel will be selected.

6. **Double-click** on the **Name** of the channel. It will appear highlighted in a box.

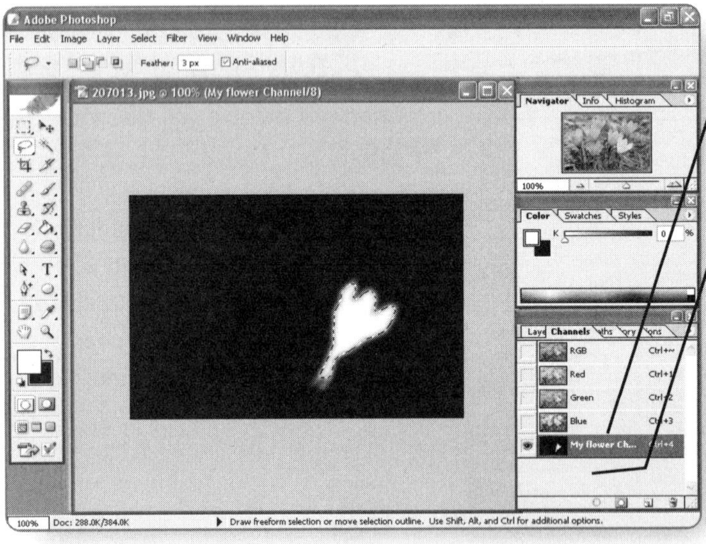

7. **Type** a **name** for the channel. Your new name will replace the temporary name in the box.

8. **Click** on any **blank area** in the palette. Photoshop will save the channel under the name you specified.

> **NOTE**
>
> To load the selection from a channel, click on the channel in the Channels palette and then click on the Load Channel as Selection button at the bottom of the Channels palette.

Correcting Overexposure

A common problem with digital camera pictures is that they are over- or underexposed. This problem can be easily corrected with the new Shadow/Highlight adjustment dialog box.

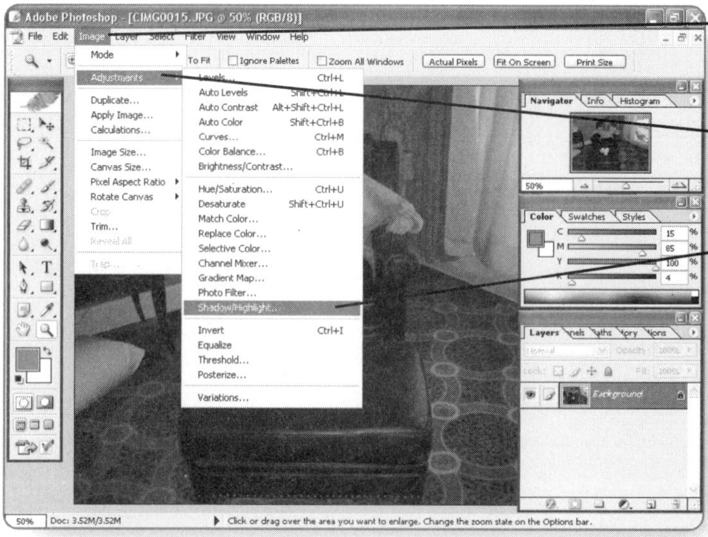

1. **Click** on **Image**. The Image menu will appear.
2. **Point** to **Adjustments**. A submenu will appear.
3. **Click** on **Shadow/Highlight**. The Shadow/Highlight dialog box will open.

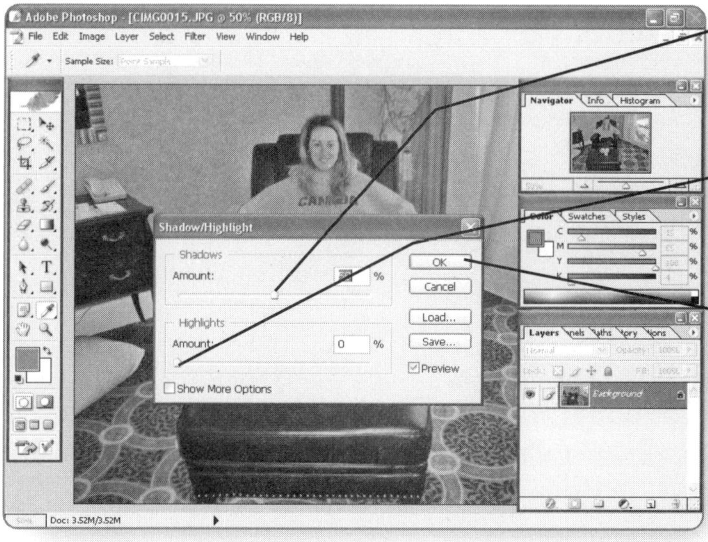

4. **Drag** to adjust the **shadows level**. As you drag, the changes will appear on your image.
5. **Drag** to adjust the **highlight level**. As you drag, the changes will appear on your image.
6. **Click** on **OK**. The adjustments will be implemented.

17

Having Fun with Color

Why have boring, regular old photos when you can spice them up with color. Photoshop CS provides you with a variety of ways in which you can adjust and add color to your images to make them interesting and unique. In this chapter, you'll learn how to:

- Create a duotone image
- Convert a color image to sepia tones
- Match colors

Creating a Duotone Image

A nice effect to add to a photo is a duotone. Basically, a duotone is a grayscale image to which you add a second printed color to tint the image overall. (You can add two tint colors to create a tritone image or three tint colors to create a quadtone image.) The steps here illustrate converting a grayscale image to a duotone for a nicely tinted printout.

> **NOTE**
>
> Remember, some tools and conversions aren't available for images using 16 bits of color information per channel, so convert to 8 bits per channel. To convert to a duotone, the image must be set to 8 bits per channel. Refer to the "Working with Bit Depth" section in Chapter 15, "Understanding Colors and Channels," to see how to make this change.

1. **Click** on **Image**. The Image menu will appear.
2. **Point** to **Mode**. The Mode submenu will appear.
3. **Click** on **Duotone**. The Duotone Options dialog box will open.

> **NOTE**
>
> If the Duotone option isn't available, you must first convert your image to grayscale.

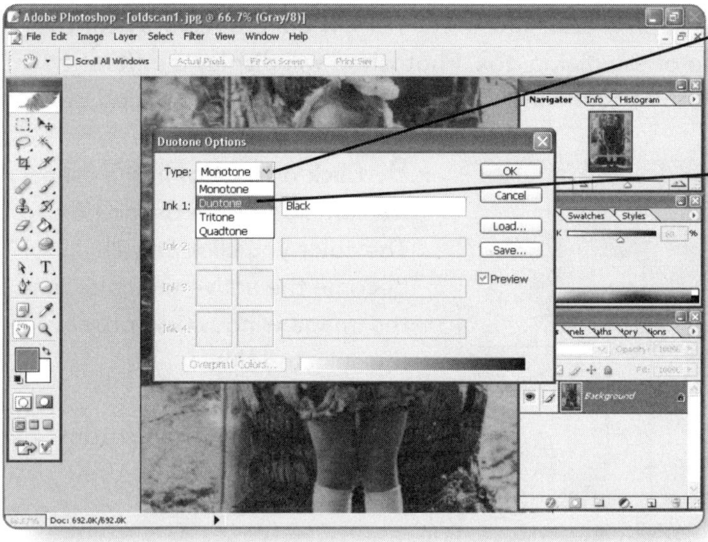

4. Click on the **down arrow** beside the Type drop-down list. A list of options will appear.

5. Click on **Duotone** in the list. The second ink color will become active for the image.

NOTE

You would click on Tritone or Quadtone to add more than one tint color to the image.

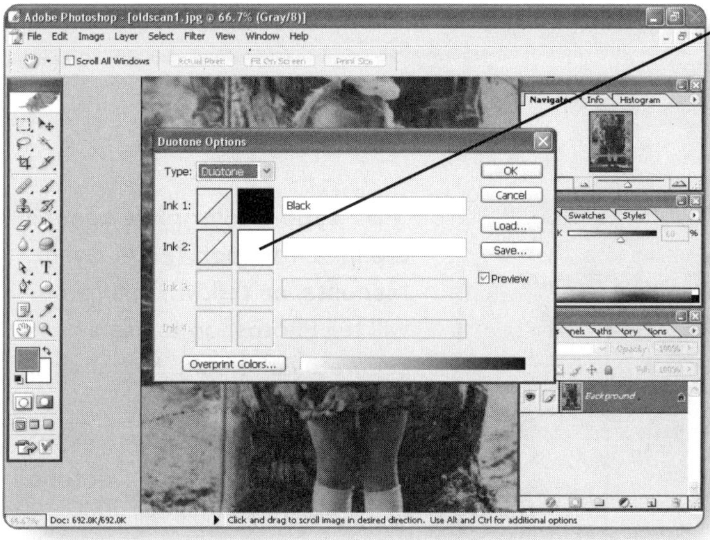

6. Click on the **white Ink 2 box**. The Custom Colors dialog box will open.

7. **Click** on a **color hue** in the narrow band of colors near the middle of the dialog box. Photoshop will display a different selection of colors in the list at the left side of the dialog box.

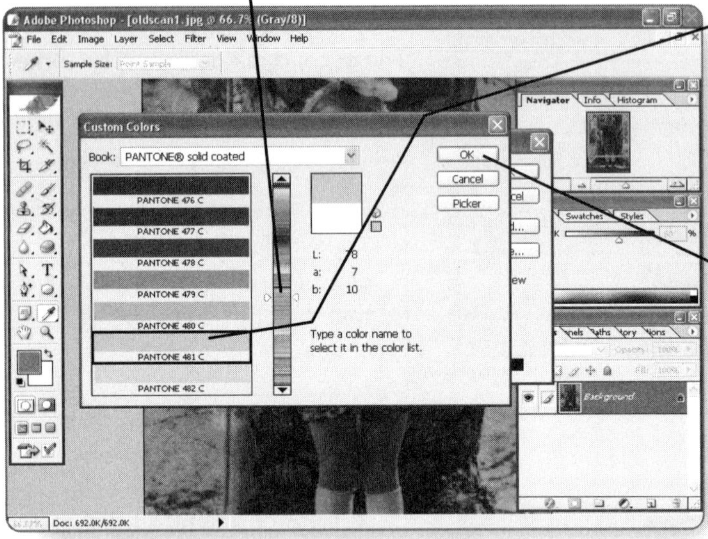

8. **Click** on a **color** in the list at the left side of the dialog box. The color you click on will become the active tint color, and the image window will preview the selected tint.

9. **Click** on **OK**. The Custom Colors dialog box will close.

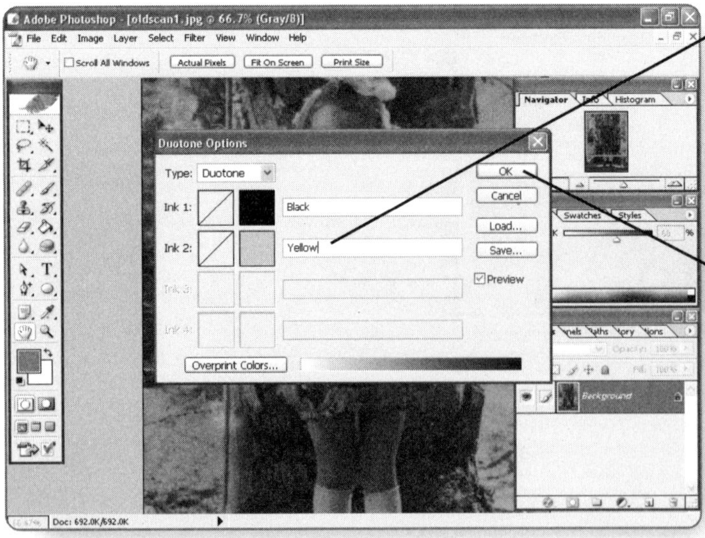

10. **Type** a **color plate name** in the Ink 2 text box. (Enter Cyan, Magenta, or Yellow.) The name will tell Photoshop to use a separate color plate for the tint ink color.

11. **Click** on **OK**. The Duotone Options dialog box will close, finishing the duotone creation.

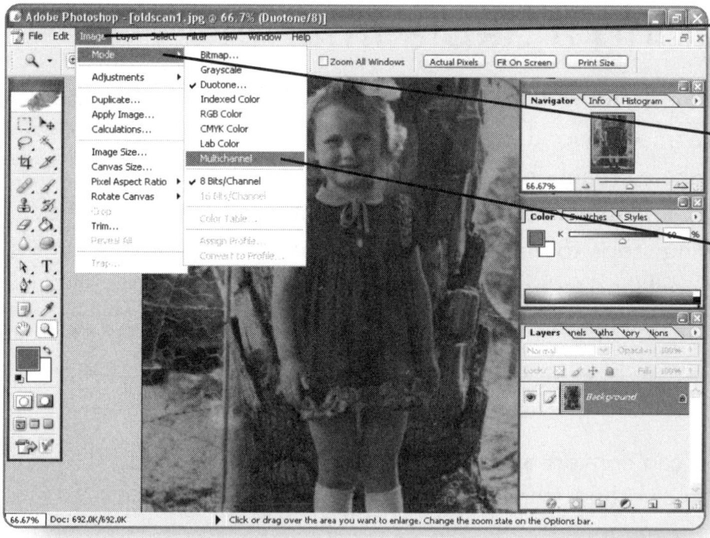

12. **Click** on **Image**. The Image menu will appear.

13. **Point** to **Mode**. The Mode submenu will appear.

14. **Click** on **Multichannel**. Photoshop separates the single duotone color channels into multiple channels so that you can preview individual colors.

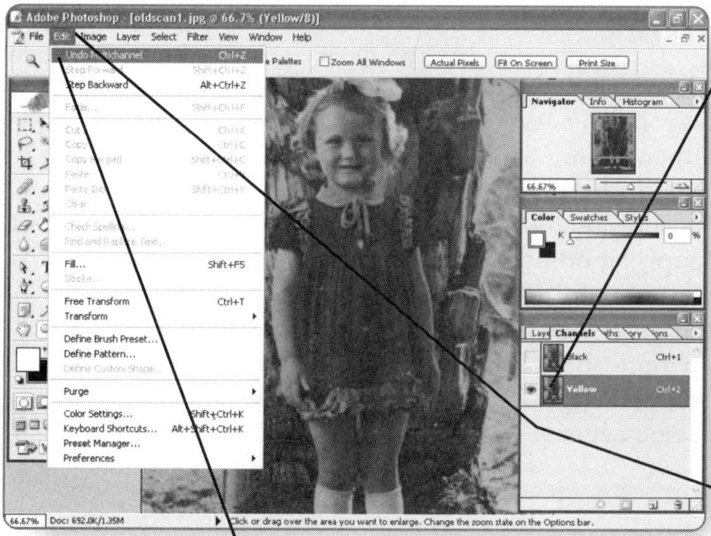

15. **Click** on the **color channel** to preview in the Channels palette. Photoshop will display the ink areas to be printed with that color in the image window.

16. **Click** on **Edit**. The Edit menu will appear.

17. **Click** on **Undo Multichannel**. Photoshop removes the multichannel mode and redisplays the single duotone color channel.

Making a Sepia Image

You'll typically work in the opposite direction when you create a sepia image, working from a color image to one that appears more like a creamy brown grayscale. (But you can make a "sepia" image with any mix of color that you prefer.) Use the following steps to make your favorite color image appear as a traditional (and trendy) sepia image.

TIP

You can convert a grayscale image to RGB color and then use the techniques described here to make it a sepia image.

NOTE

Photoshop includes an action you can use to create a sepia tone on a layer. (Choose File, Automate, Batch, and then choose Sepia Toning from the Action drop-down list. Use the other Batch dialog box settings to finish applying the automation.) There are also actions for applying other color effects, and you can download actions for applying sepia tone and other effects from the Internet. See Chapter 19, "Working with Actions," to learn more about actions, and see Appendix D, "Online Resources," for sources for downloadable goodies, including actions.

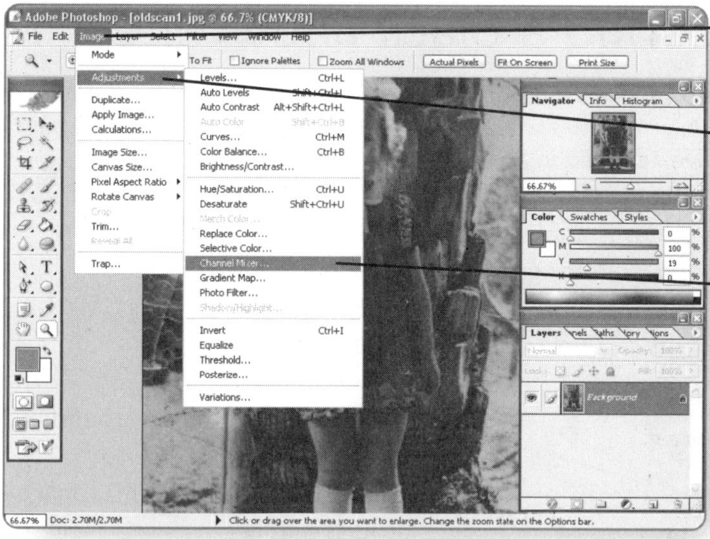

1. Click on **Image**. The Image menu will appear.

2. Point to **Adjustments**. The Adjustments submenu will appear.

3. Click on **Channel Mixer**. The Channel Mixer dialog box will appear.

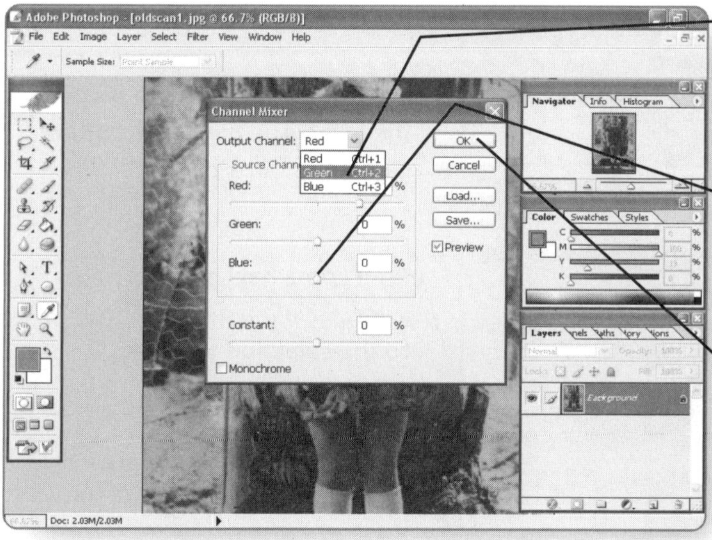

4. Choose a **channel** from the Output Channel drop-down list. The selected color channel will be ready for adjustment.

5. Drag the **Source Channels slider** for the selected color. The image window will preview the color change in the image.

6. Click on **OK** after you have adjusted the mix for each channel. The Channel Mixer dialog box will close so that you can review the final tint.

Coloring a Black and White Photo

If you've scanned in an old black-and-white image and you want to colorize it, you can take advantage of Photoshop CS's layers to easily apply color. If the image was scanned in as a black-and-white or grayscale image, it will have to first be converted to an RGB or CMYK color mode.

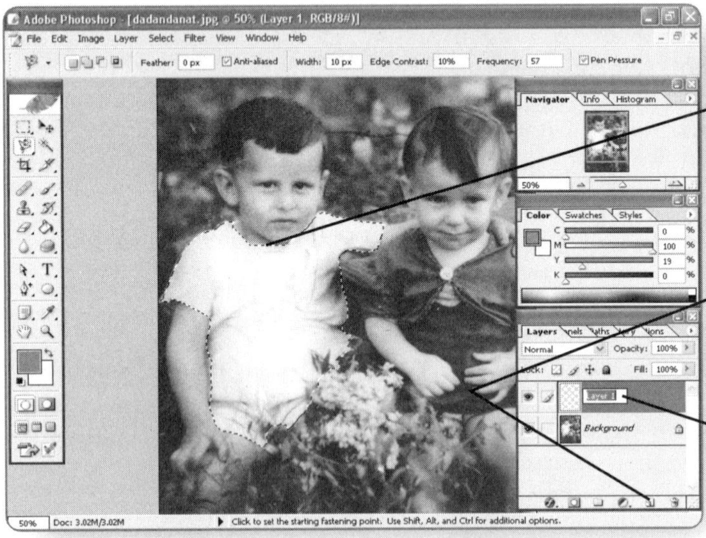

1. **Create** a **selection** around the area you would like to colorize. A marquee will appear around that area.

2. **Click** on the **New Layer button** in the Layers palette. A new layer will appear.

3. **Double-click** on the **name** of the layer. The name will appear highlighted in a box.

4. **Type** a new **name** for the layer. Give it a name appropriate to the selection you are colorizing.

5. **Click** on any **blank area** of the palette. The layer will now have a new name.

6. **Click** on a **color** in the Color palette that you would like to apply to the selection.

7. **Click** on the **Paint Bucket tool**. It will be selected.

8. **Click once** within the selection. The selection will be filled with the color you selected. It doesn't look very realistic at this point, but it will after we adjust the opacity of the layer.

9. **Click** on the **down arrow** beside the Opacity number box. A slider bar will appear.

10. **Drag** the **slider bar** to the appropriate level. Typically, this would be anywhere from 20% to 30% for colorizing a black-and-white photo.

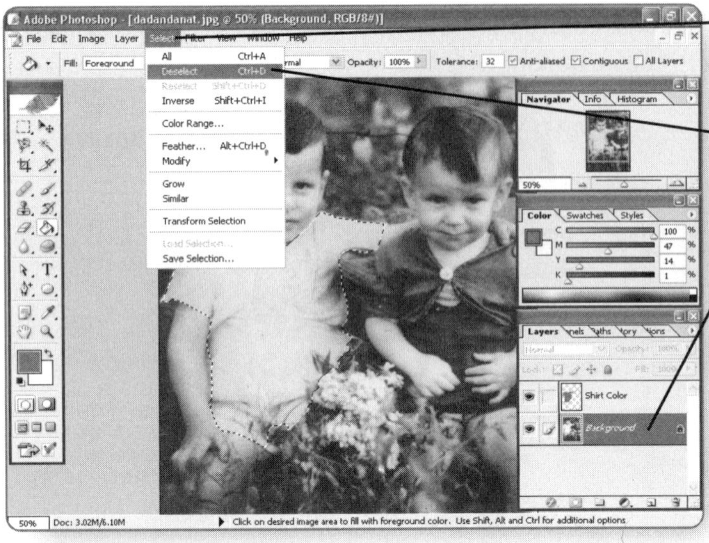

11. **Click** on **Select**. The Select menu will appear.

12. **Click** on **Deselect**. The selection will be removed.

13. **Click** on the **Layer** that contains the original image. It will be selected.

14. **Repeat** steps **1** through **13** for the rest of the image.

Matching Colors

As I mentioned in an earlier chapter, one of the biggest questions I get in my training classes is how to remove someone's head in a picture and put it on someone else's body. You've already learned that a selection can be made, copied, and pasted onto a new image. One of the problems that arises is that skin tones from the source image don't necessarily match the tones of the target image, so it won't end up looking realistic. This problem can be solved with Photoshop CS's new Match Color feature, which will take the color scheme from one image and apply it to another.

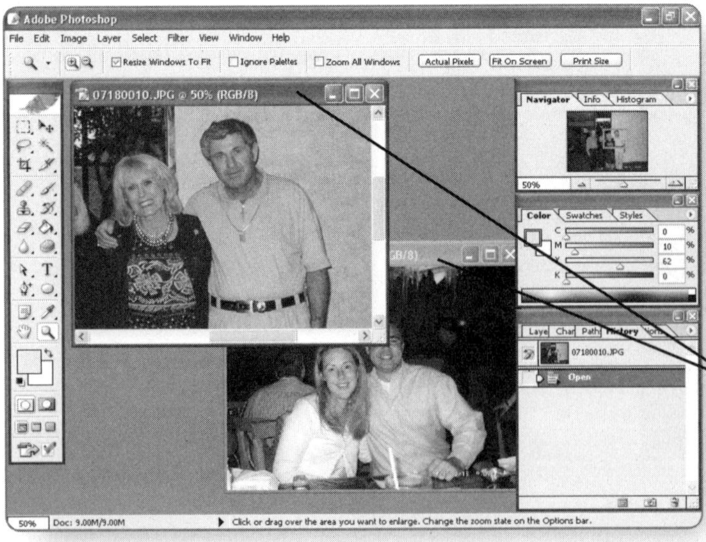

1. **Open** both the **source** and **target images** for your color match.

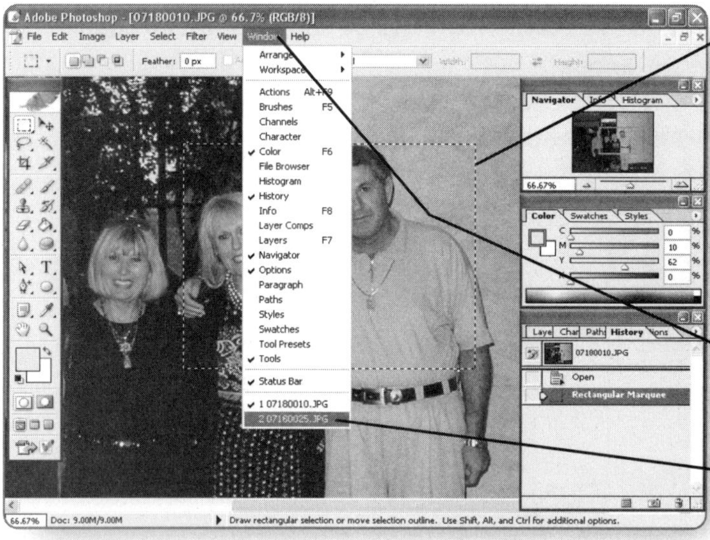

2. Create a **selection** around the area containing the colors you would like to match in the source image. This step is optional; if you don't make a selection, the color scheme from the entire photo will be matched.

3. Click on **Window**. The Window menu will appear.

4. Click on the **target image**. It will become the active window.

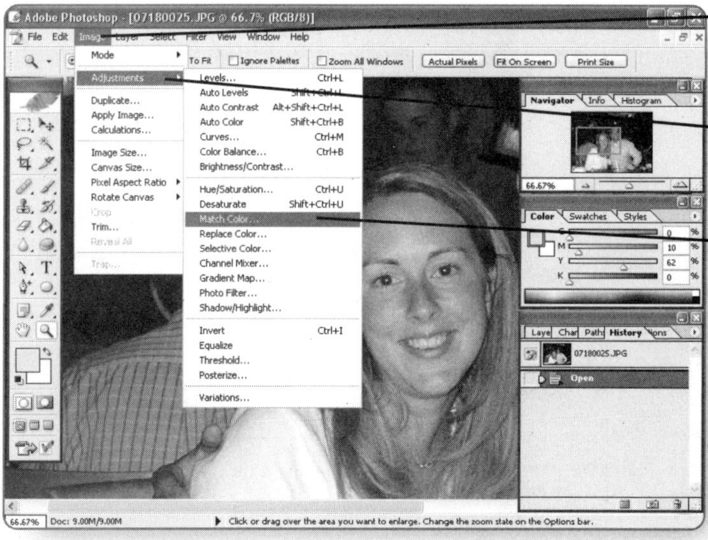

5. Click on **Image**. The Image menu will appear.

6. Click on **Adjustments**. A submenu will appear.

7. Click on **Match Color**. The Match Color dialog box will open.

8. Click on the **down arrow** beside source. A list of open images will appear.

9. Click the desired **source image**. It will be selected.

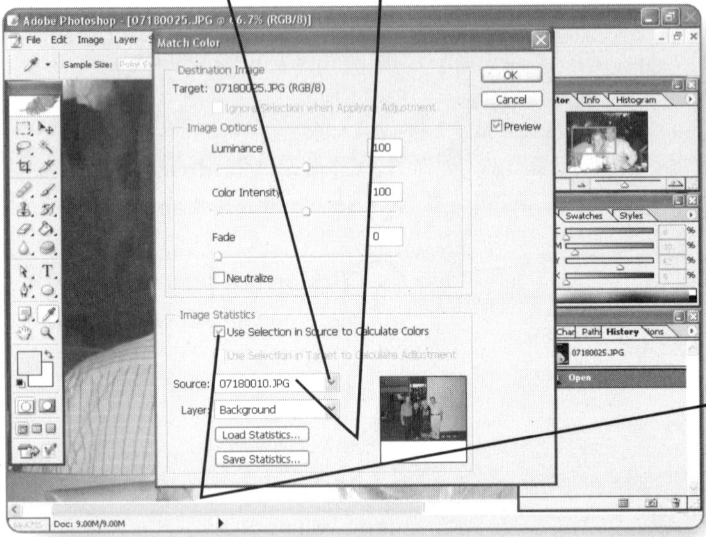

10. Click the Use Selection in Source to Calculate Colors **check box** if you made a selection within the source that you would like to use to match colors.

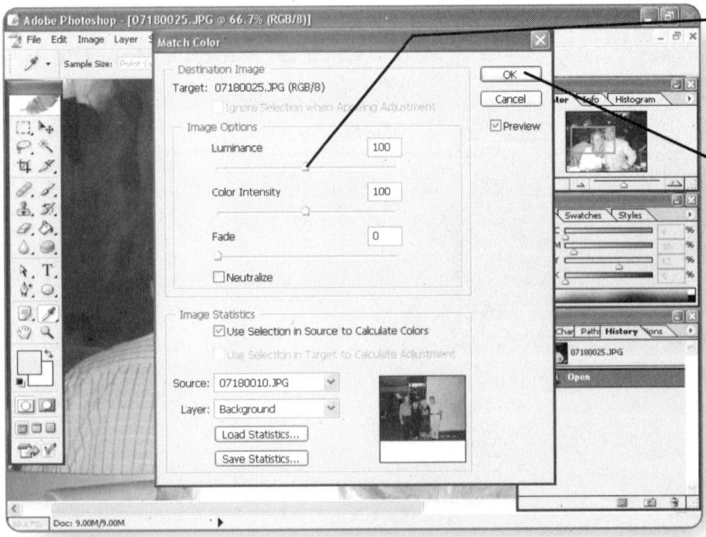

11. Drag the various **image options**. They will adjust as you drag.

12. Click on **OK**. The color scheme from the source will be applied to the target image.

18

Working with Plug-Ins

Simply stated, a plug-in is a mini program that extends the capabilities of Photoshop (or its companion program ImageReady). Each plug-in functions in one of three ways: as a filter, as an additional import or export choice, or as a file format choice in the Save As or Open dialog box. This chapter shows you how to take advantage of plug-ins. In this chapter, you'll learn how to:

- Install a plug-in you've purchased or downloaded
- Use a plug-in that performs a special action
- Use a filter plug-in

Installing Plug-Ins

By default, the plug-ins that come with Photoshop install to various subfolders of the Program Files\Adobe\Photoshop CS\Plug-Ins\ folder. You can purchase additional plug-ins or download a variety of freeware and shareware plug-ins from a number of sources online. If you download a particular type of plug-in, you typically can just move or copy the plug-in file (after decompressing it, unzipping it, or renaming it, if indicated by the instructions accompanying the plug-in) to the folder that holds similar plug-in files, assuming the plug-in doesn't include its own installer program. In other cases, you may want to store your third-party plug-ins in a separate folder to distinguish them from the plug-ins provided with Photoshop. If you choose this route, you need to specify the alternate plug-in location, as described next.

NOTE

If a plug-in was written for Photoshop only, copy it to the appropriate subfolder of C:\Program Files\Adobe\Photoshop CS\Plug-Ins\Adobe Photoshop Only\. If a plug-in was written for ImageReady only, copy it to the appropriate subfolder of C:\Program Files\Adobe\Photoshop CS\Plug-Ins\Adobe ImageReady Only\.

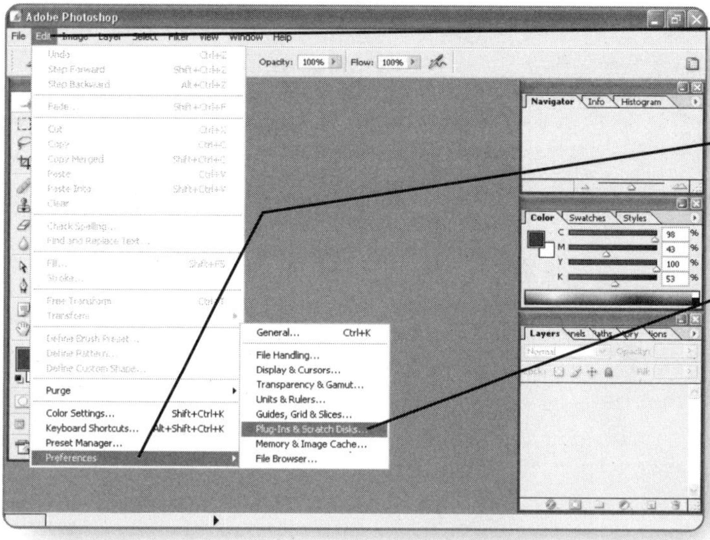

1. **Click** on **Edit**. The Edit menu will appear.

2. **Point** to **Preferences**. The Preferences submenu will appear.

3. **Click** on **Plug-Ins & Scratch Disks**. The Preferences dialog box will appear with its Plug-Ins & Scratch Disks settings displayed.

> **NOTE**
>
> In ImageReady, you would choose Edit, Preferences, Plug-Ins to start specifying another plug-ins folder.

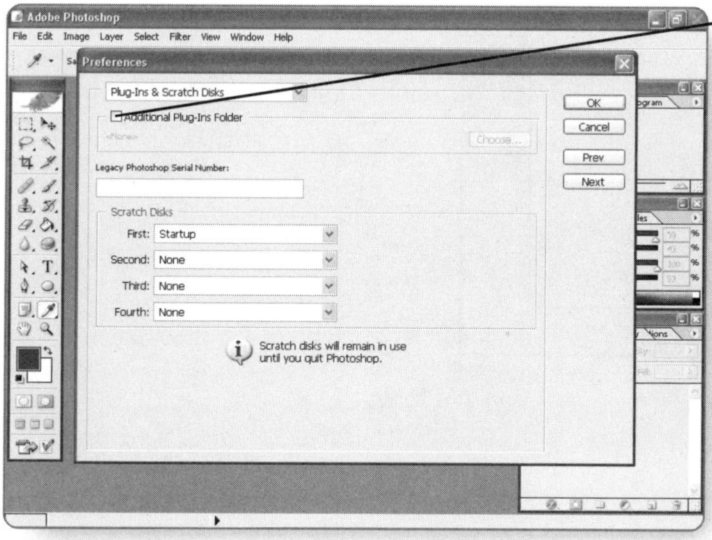

4. **Click** on the **Additional Plug-Ins Folder** check box. The check box will be checked, and the Browse for Folder dialog box will open.

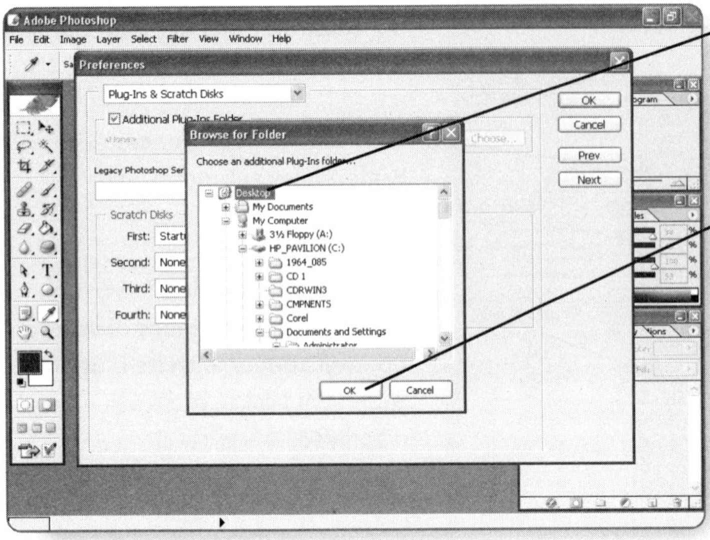

5. **Select** the **folder** that holds the plug-ins in the folder tree. The specified folder will become active as a plug-in folder.

6. **Click** on **OK**. The Browse for Folder dialog box will close.

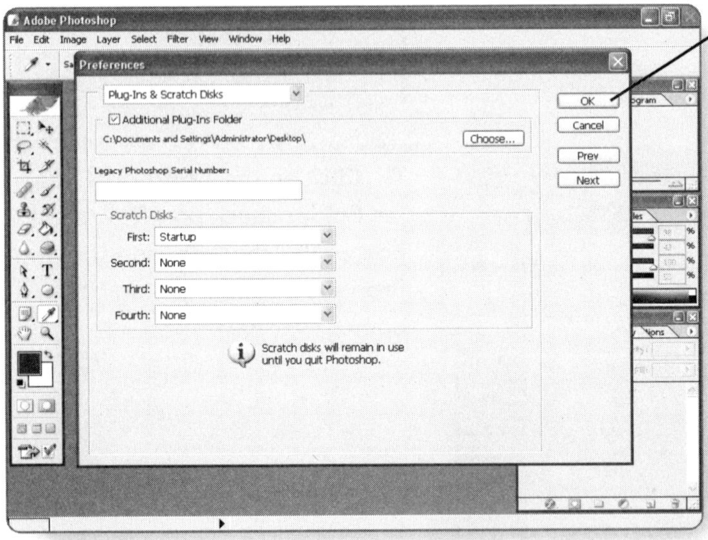

7. **Click** on **OK**. The Preferences dialog box will close.

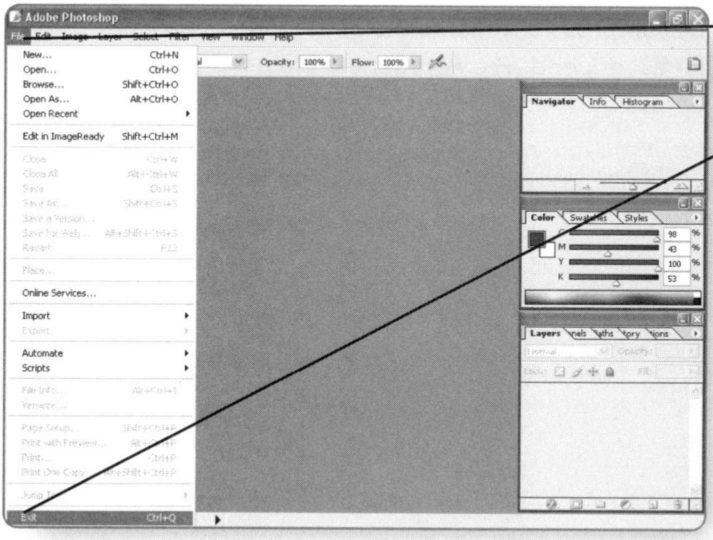

8. **Click** on **File**. The File menu will appear.

9. **Click** on **Exit**. Photoshop will close.

NOTE

When you close Photoshop, save changes to any open file, if prompted. You must exit and restart Photoshop (or ImageReady) for the new plug-ins folder to take effect.

10. **Open** the newly specified plug-ins **folder** on the desktop.

11. **Decompress** or **rename** the **plug-in file** or **run** its **installer** as required. The appropriate plug-in files will decompress or be installed in the appropriate folder location.

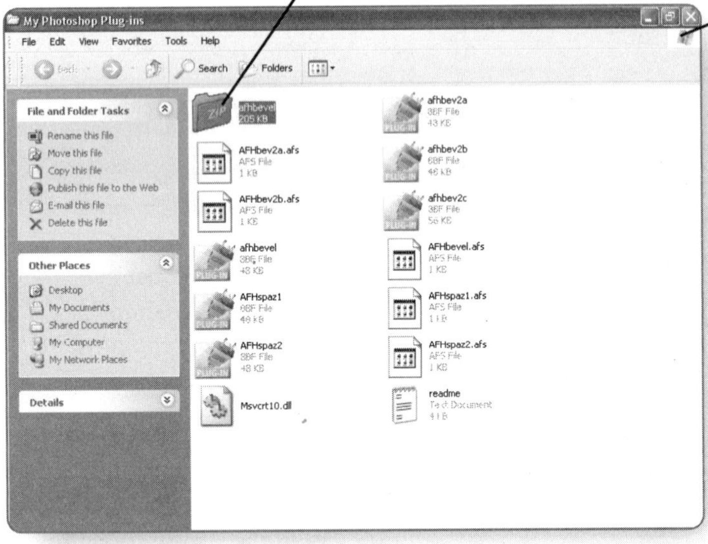

12. **Close** the **folder** on the desktop.

> **NOTE**
>
> In some cases, you may have to move the plug-ins to C:\Program Files\Adobe\Photoshop CS\Plug-Ins\ rather than running them from the alternate folder. Be sure to read any Readme file that comes with a plug-in to verify how to install it, particularly if the plug-in creates one or more folders when you unzip or decompress it.

13. **Click** on **Start**. The Start menu will appear. If using Mac OX, double-click on the Photoshop icon to start the program.

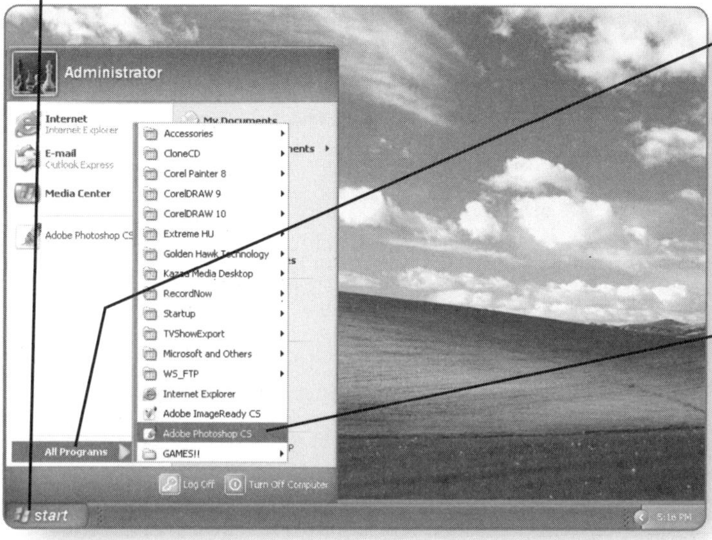

14. **Point** to **All Programs** (or Programs in Windows versions prior to XP). The Programs submenu will appear. If you are using Mac OS, simply double-click on the Photoshop CS icon to launch the program.

15. **Click** on **Adobe Photoshop CS**. The Photoshop program will load with the added plug-ins newly active. You can now open files as needed and use the plug-ins.

Applying a Plug-In to a File

As noted at the very beginning of this chapter, plug-ins generally work in limited ways, enabling you to open or save files in different formats or to apply custom filters to an image. This section shows an example of using a filter that falls into each category.

Applying by Opening or Saving

If a filter enables you to use Photoshop to work with files of different formats, the filter typically adds the format into the Files of Type list of the Open dialog box or the Format list of the Save As dialog box. The following steps show one example—using a filter that enables you to save files in the Windows icon format (.ico). Before you begin the steps, be sure you open the file to which you want to apply the plug-in.

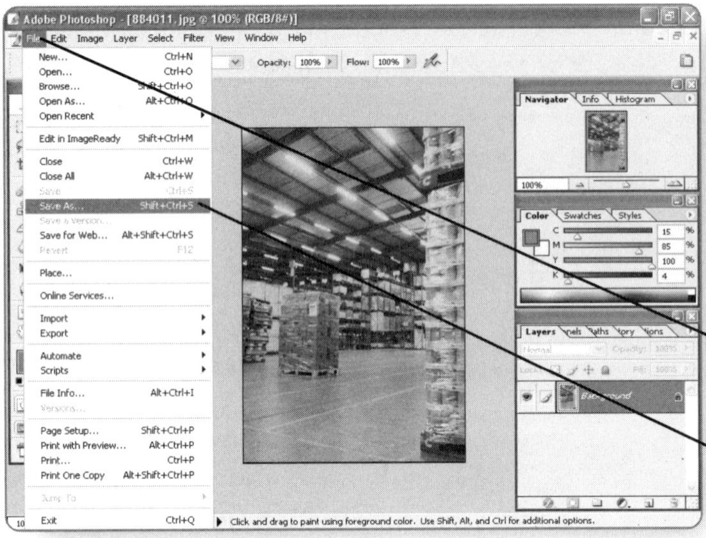

NOTE

In other cases, plug-ins that work with file formats appear on the Import or Export submenus of the File menu.

1. **Click** on **File**. The File menu will appear.

2. **Click** on **Save As**. The Save As dialog box will open.

3. **Click** on the **down arrow** beside the Format drop-down list and then **click** on the **file format** provided by the plug-in (in this case, BoxTop ProJPEG 5.0). The selected format will be used for the save operation.

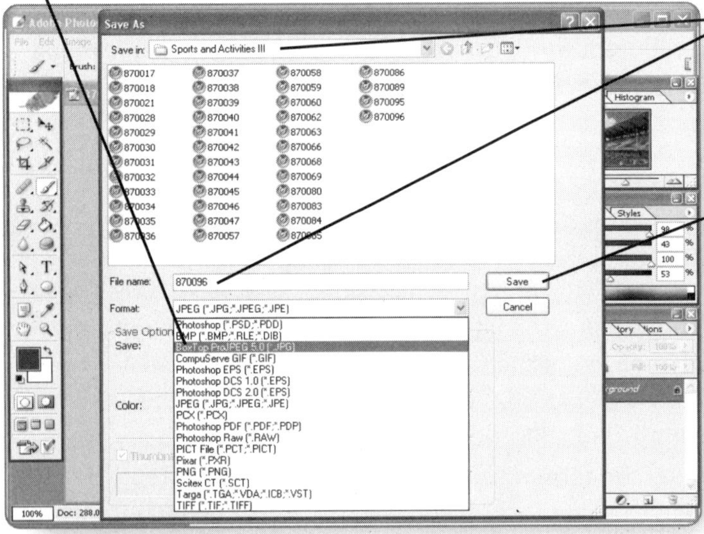

4. **Change** the **File name** and **Save in location**, if necessary. The newly saved file will use the name and location you specify.

5. **Click** on **Save**. The Save As dialog box will close, and one of two things will happen. Either the file will be saved immediately in the new format, or a dialog box for the plug-in will appear to prompt you to specify additional settings for the saved file.

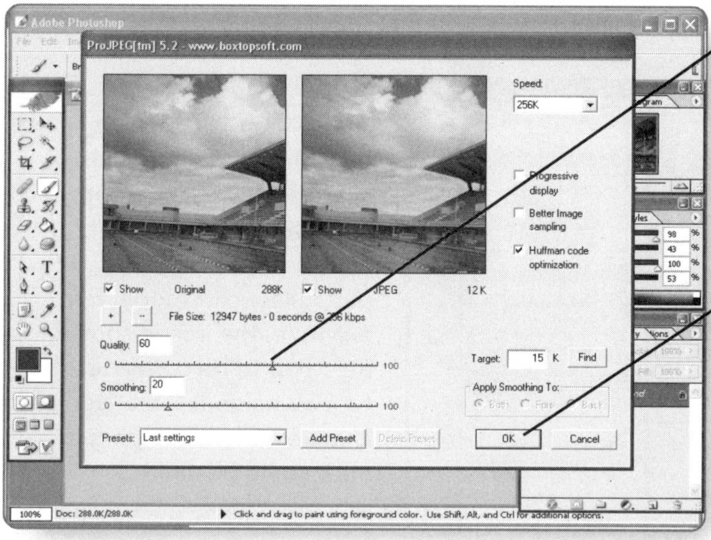

6. Adjust settings as necessary. In many cases, an image preview or output settings will change to show the impact of the new settings on the image file that will be created.

7. Click on **OK** or **Save**. The dialog box will close, and the image will be saved. You can then close and use the image.

Applying a Filter Plug-In

In most cases, installing a plug-in installs a new filter or group of filters. Photoshop typically adds the new filter choices or groups (submenus) to the bottom of the Filter menu, making added filters as easy to access as default filters. Like the default filters, some plug-in filters will display a dialog box prompting you to choose additional settings, whereas others will take effect immediately. The following steps show an example of a freeware plug-in filter.

1. Click on **Filter**. The Filter menu will appear.

> ## NOTE
>
> As with other commands and effects in Photoshop, many filters require that an image be using a particular color mode. For example, the image shown here had to be converted to RGB color at 8 bits per channel before the plug-in filter could be used.

2. Point to the **name** for the filter group, if necessary. The group submenu will appear.

3. Click on a **filter**. The filter will appear, or the filter dialog box will open.

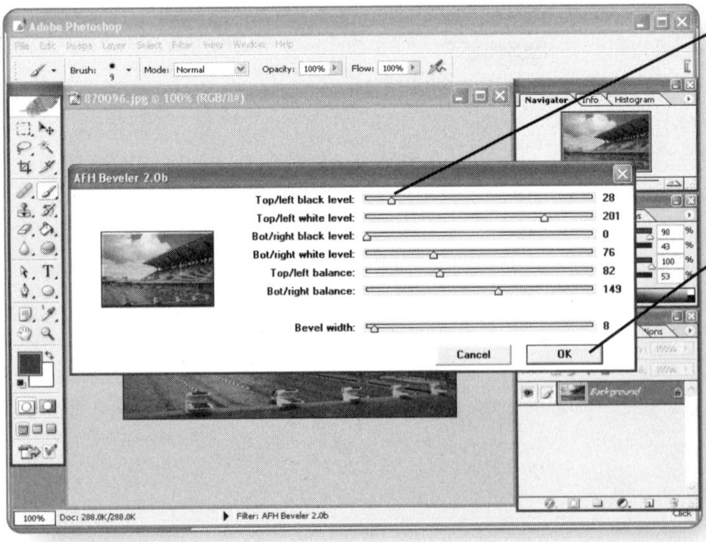

4. Adjust filter settings as necessary. Either a preview area in the filter dialog box or the image window itself will preview the filter changes.

5. Click on **OK**. Photoshop will apply the filter settings to the image.

Using the Liquify Plug-In

The Liquify plug-in appears as a standalone command (rather than as part of a submenu) on the Filter menu. The Liquify plug-in offers a variety of settings for distorting and manipulating an image. The Turbulence tool represents one new enhancement to this filter, enabling you to place distortion along with a "jitter" effect. You can view a mesh that illustrates the distortion as well. The following steps illustrate some of the basics for working with this important plug-in.

1. **Click** on **Filter**. The Filter menu will appear.

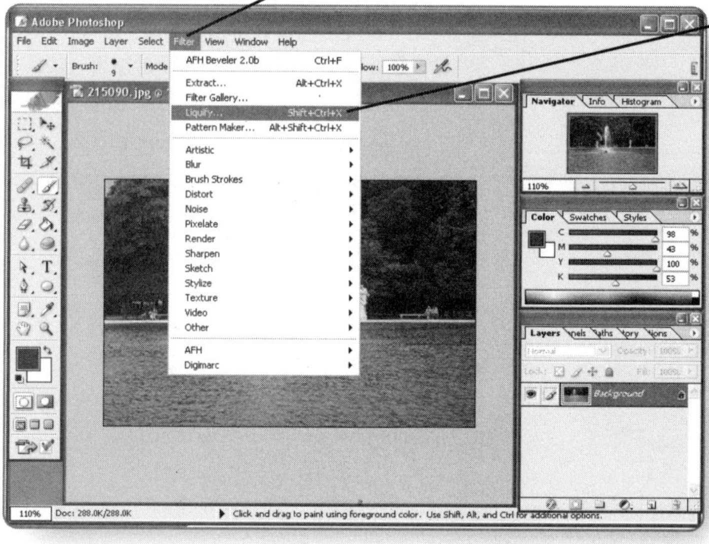

2. **Click** on **Liquify**. The Liquify dialog box will open.

3. Adjust the **zoom setting** for the image, if necessary. The image will appear at the new zoom.

4. Click on the desired **tool**. The tool will be selected. In this example, the Turbulence tool is selected.

5. Adjust the tool **options** as needed. The mouse pointer will change in size or appearance accordingly when you move the pointer over the image.

6. Drag on the **image** at the desired location(s). The image will be distorted according to the selected tool, its settings, and the amount of dragging.

7. Click on **OK**. The Liquify dialog box will close, and the image will appear with its new distortion in Photoshop.

19

Working with Actions

If you've made it this far along in the book, you can see that the possible combinations of Photoshop features and filters are endless, not to mention the sheer number of specific settings you can use with each feature or filter. In Photoshop, you can create actions and droplets to store a series of commands and settings that you choose. This chapter shows you how to save yourself some work in Photoshop. You will learn how to:

- Record an action
- Play an action
- Make a droplet from an action
- Use a droplet

Creating an Action

If you've ever created a macro in an application, you'll have an easy time creating an action. Like a macro, an action is a series of steps and settings that you save so that you can repeat them quickly later. Saving and using the action eliminates the need to remember the filter settings you prefer, for example, or the color adjustment choices to use. Actions come in handy when you need to prepare multiple images using the same settings—for example, if you're converting a series of grayscale images to duotones using a particular Pantone color for inclusion in the same publication. The following steps show you how to use the Actions palette to record a new action.

1. **Click** on **Window**. The Window menu will appear.

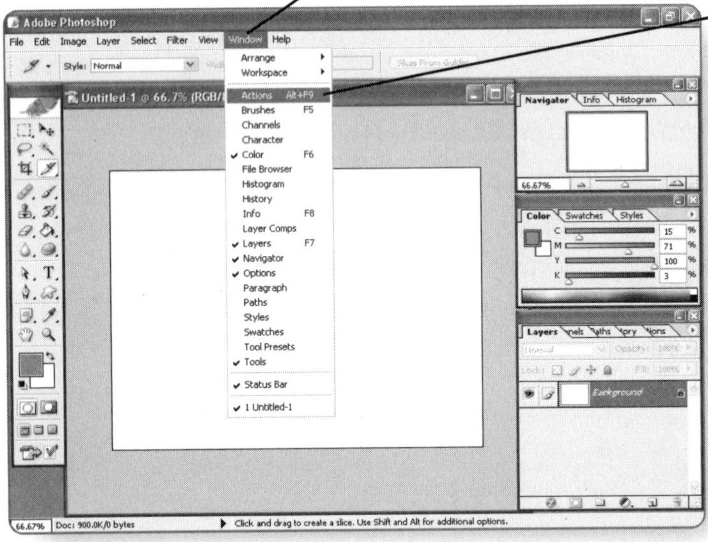

2. **Click** on **Actions**. The Actions palette will become active.

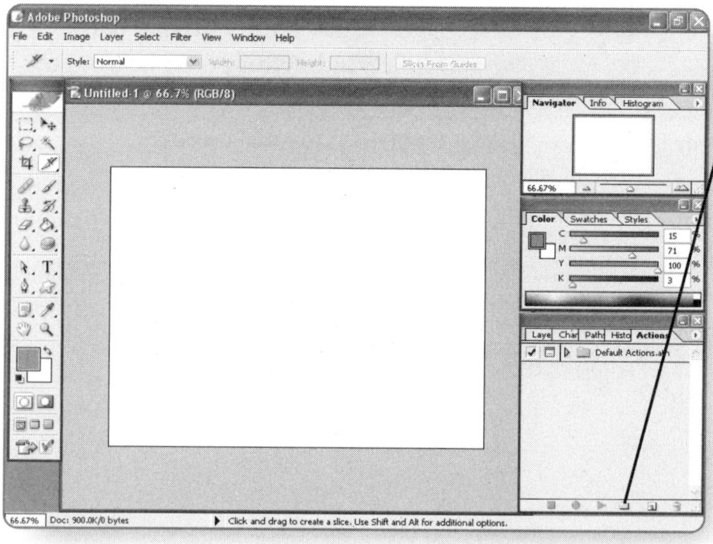

3. Click on the **Create New Set button** at the bottom of the palette. The New Set dialog box will appear.

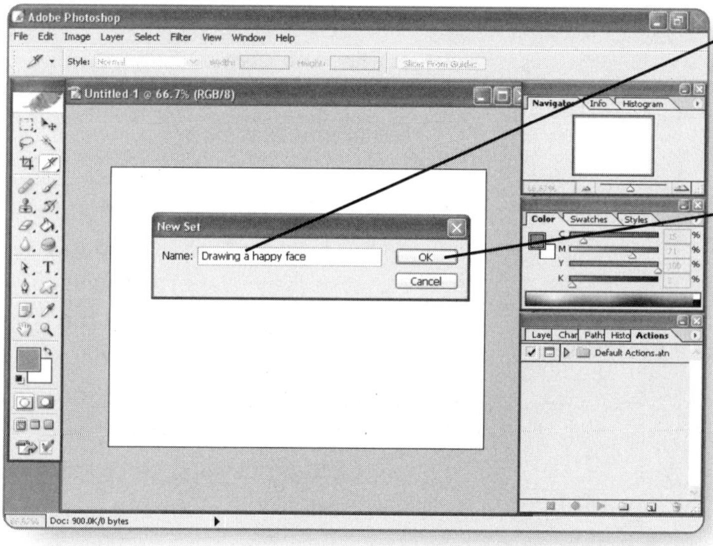

4. Type a **name** for the new set. The name you type will replace the placeholder entry in the Name text box.

5. Click on **OK**. The new set will appear in the Actions palette and will be selected by default.

NOTE

To add a new action to an existing set, click on the set name in the Actions palette and then follow the rest of the steps here.

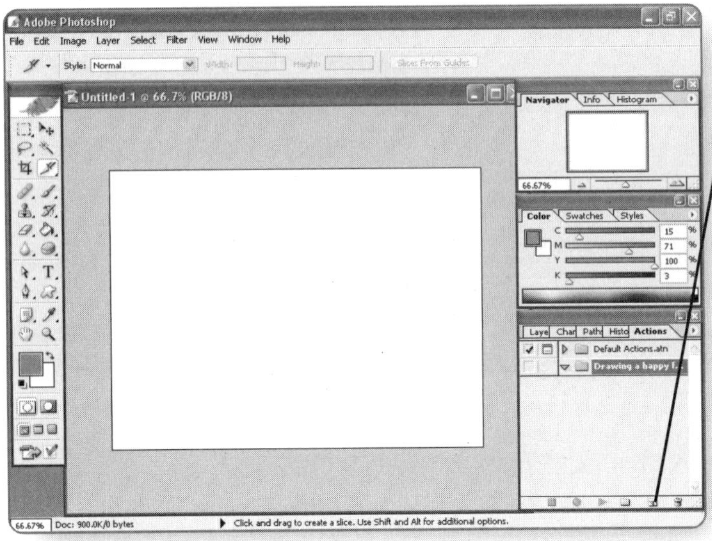

6. **Click** on the **Create New Action button** at the bottom of the palette. The New Action dialog box will appear.

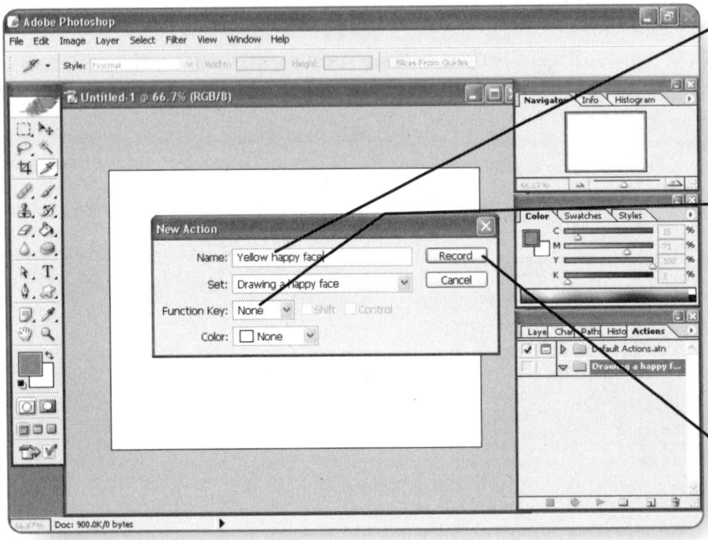

7. **Type** a **name** for the new action. The name you type will replace the placeholder entry in the Name text box.

8. **Specify** other **settings** in the dialog box, such as adding a Function Key (a shortcut key combination) to play back the action. The remaining settings will be added for the function.

9. **Click** on **Record**. Recording will start.

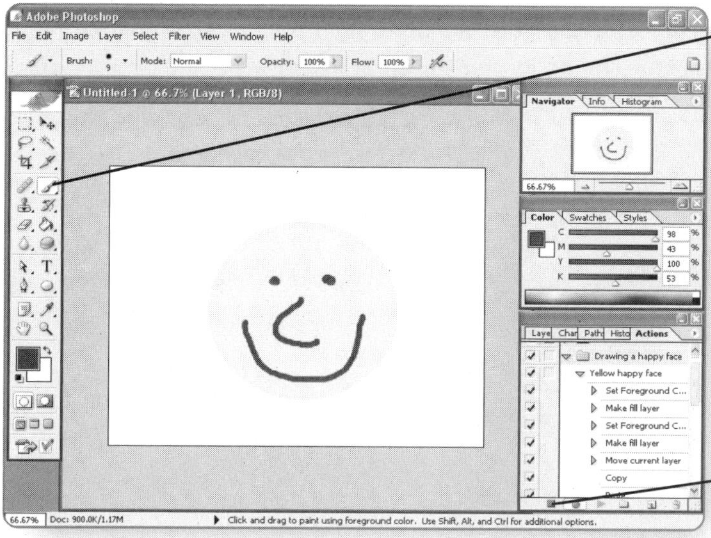

10. Perform the **steps** to record. The steps will be added to the named action.

> **NOTE**
>
> If a particular feature can't be recorded, either it will be unavailable or you'll see a warning message.

11. Click on the **Stop Playing/Recording button** at the bottom of the Actions palette. Photoshop will stop recording your steps, finishing the action.

Using an Action

Much as you use a recording process to create an action, you use a playback process to run the action. Before you run the action, open the file to which you want to apply the action and perform any preliminary steps to prepare for the action, such as making a selection or converting to the proper color mode. Then use the steps that follow:

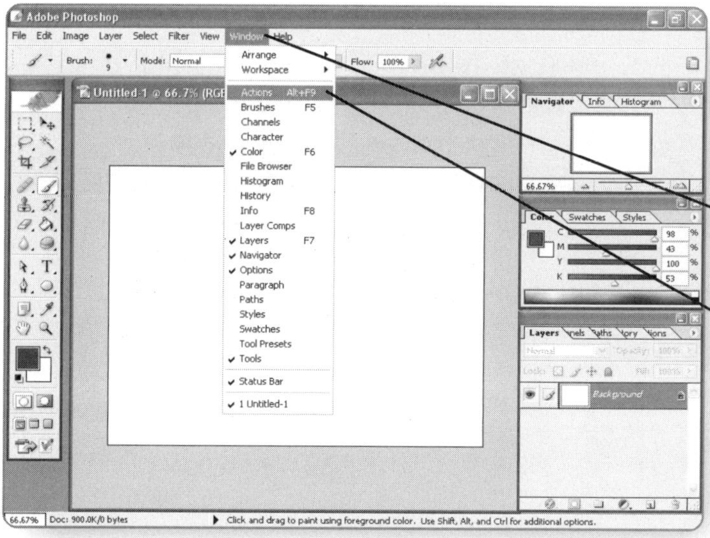

1. Click on **Window**. The Window menu will appear.

2. Click on **Actions**. The Actions palette will become active.

3. Scroll to **display** the **set** that holds the action to perform in the palette. The actions will appear in the palette.

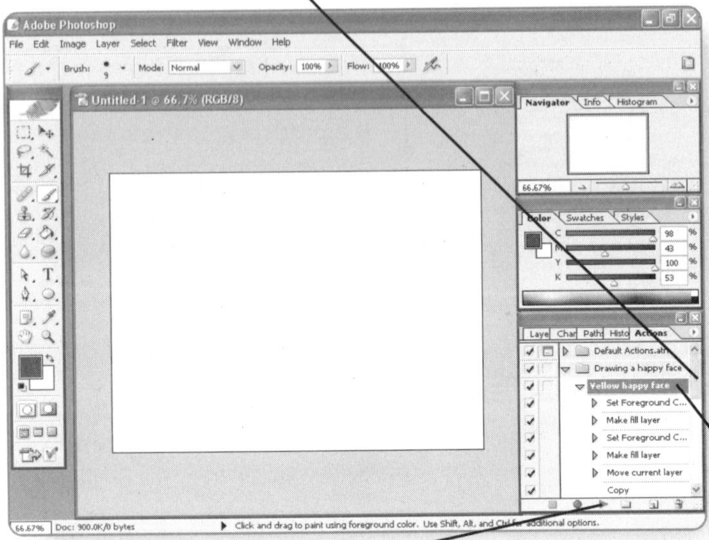

NOTE

Click on the right arrow to the left of the set name if you don't see its actions.

4. Click on the **action** to perform. The action will be selected.

5. Click on the **Play Selection button** at the bottom of the palette. The action plays immediately.

Batch Processing

There may be times when you want to apply an action to a series of images. Rather than having to apply the action to each image one at a time, you can take advantage of Photoshop CS's batch processing, which allows you to apply an action to multiple images in one step. It's a good idea to put all of the images you would like to batch process in one folder before you begin the process.

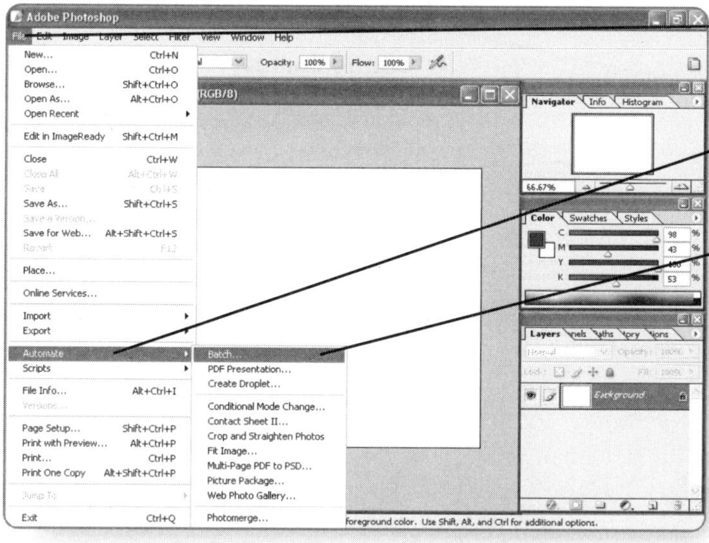

1. **Click** on **File**. The file menu will appear.
2. **Click** on **Automate**. A submenu will appear.
3. **Click** on **Batch**. The Batch dialog box will open.

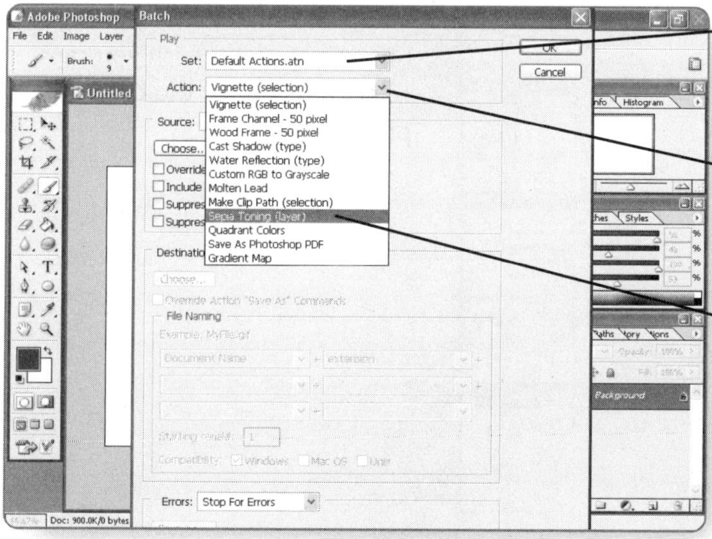

4. **Click** on the **down arrow** beside Set and choose the desired set of actions.
5. **Click** on the **down arrow** beside Action. A menu will appear.
6. **Click** on the **desired action** that you would like to apply to your images.

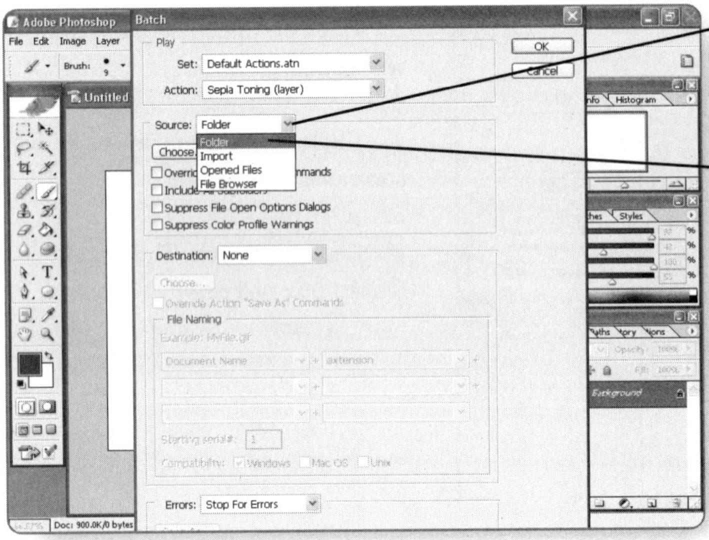

7. **Click** on the **down arrow** beside **Source**. A menu of options will appear.

8. **Click** on **Folder**. Photoshop will apply the actions to all the images within a folder that you specify.

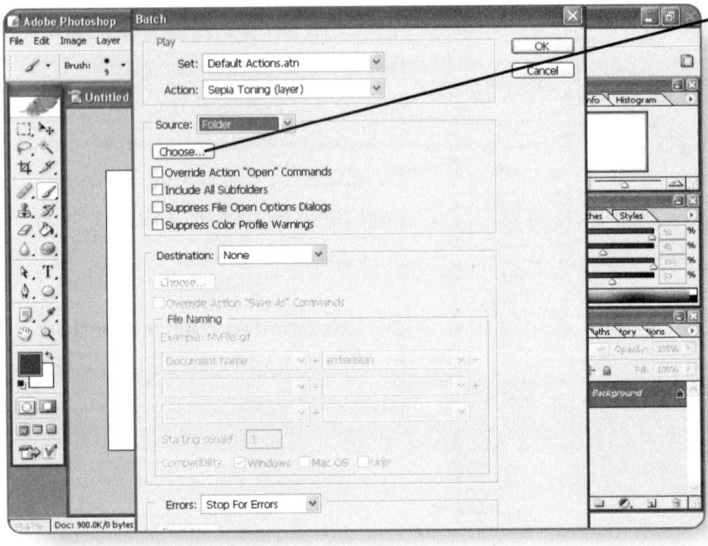

9. **Click** on **Choose**. A dialog box will open in which you can select a folder for the batch processing.

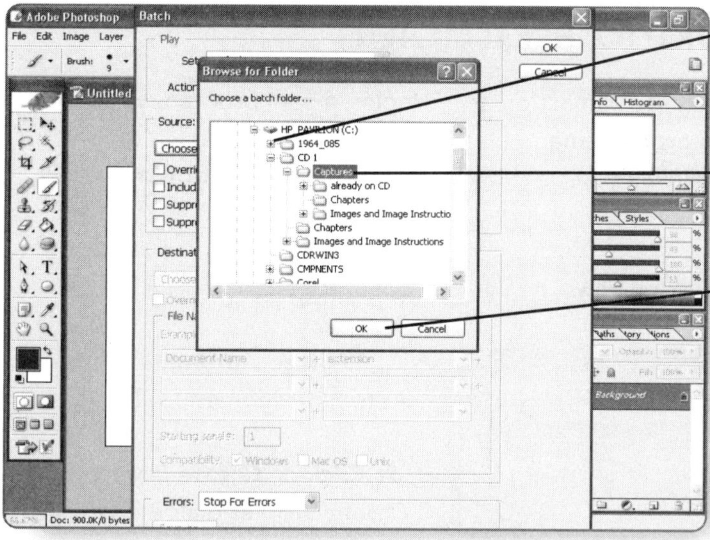

10. **Click** on the **+** to expand a folder. All of the folders within that folder will appear.

11. **Click** the desired **folder**. It will be highlighted.

12. **Click** on **OK**. The folder will be selected.

13. **Click** on the desired **Source options**. A check mark will appear in the boxes you have selected.

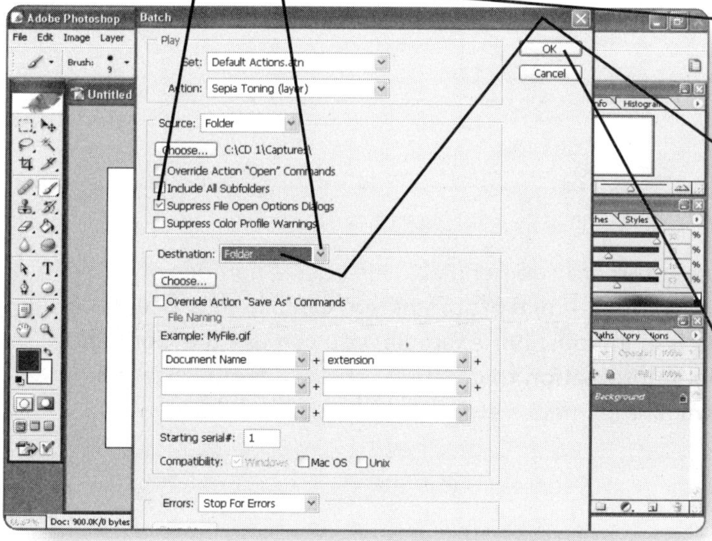

14. **Click** on the **down arrow** beside Destination. A menu of options will appear.

15. **Click** on the desired **Destination option**. This determines what will be done to the image after the batch process is complete.

16. **Click** on **OK**. The batch process will take place based on the settings you have entered.

Making a Droplet

You can save an action as a droplet, a mini program you can use to process image files even when Photoshop isn't running. The following steps show you how to create a droplet using default droplet settings.

1. **Click** on **File**. The File menu will appear.

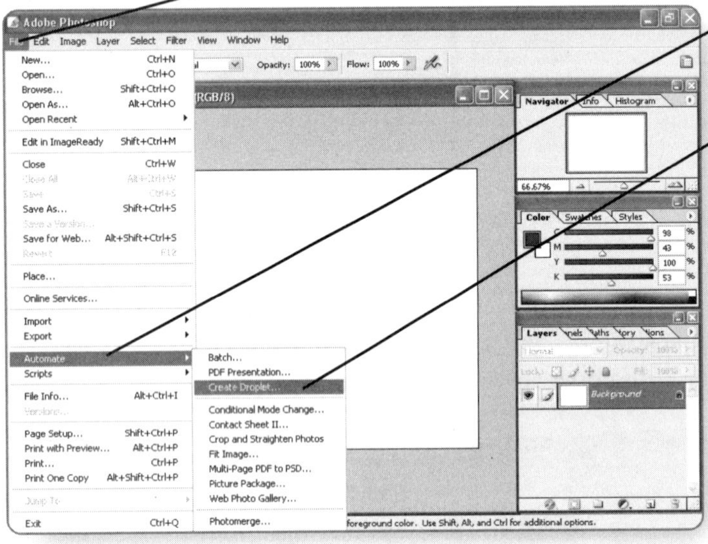

2. **Point** to **Automate**. The Automate submenu will appear.

3. **Click** on **Create Droplet**. The Create Droplet dialog box will open.

> **NOTE**
>
> The Automate submenu also includes a number of preset automations—mini programs you can use to process a batch of images. For example, you can use the Contact Sheet automation to create a contact sheet image file from all the images stored in a particular folder.

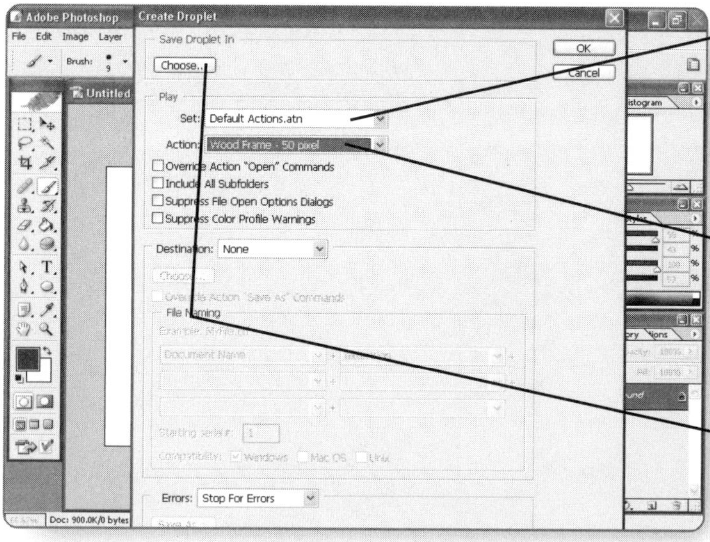

4. Choose the **set** that holds the action to convert from the Set drop-down list. The set's actions will become available in the Action drop-down list.

5. Choose the **action** to save as a droplet from the Action drop-down list. The selected action appears.

6. Click on **Choose**. The Save dialog box will open.

7. Navigate to the **folder** where you want to save the droplet. It will become the active folder.

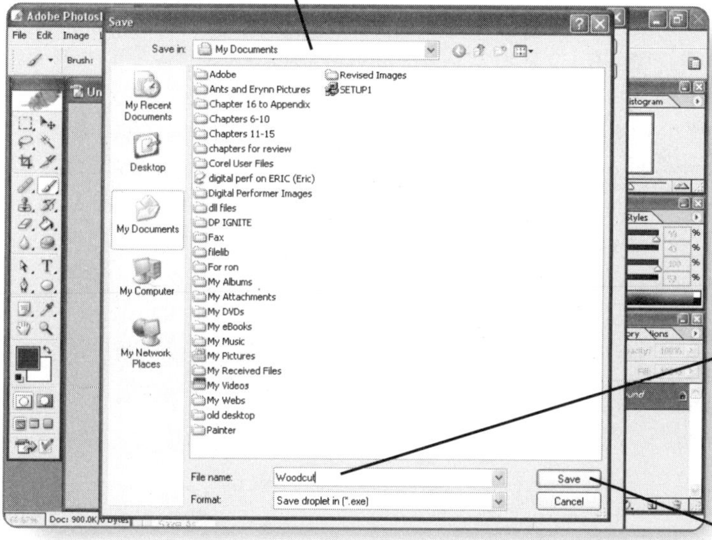

NOTE

By default, the Save dialog box displays the My Documents folder, but you can save a droplet in any location you prefer.

8. Type a **name** for the new droplet file. The name you type will replace the placeholder entry in the File name text box.

9. Click on **Save**. The Save dialog box will close, and the name you specified will appear in the Create Droplet dialog box.

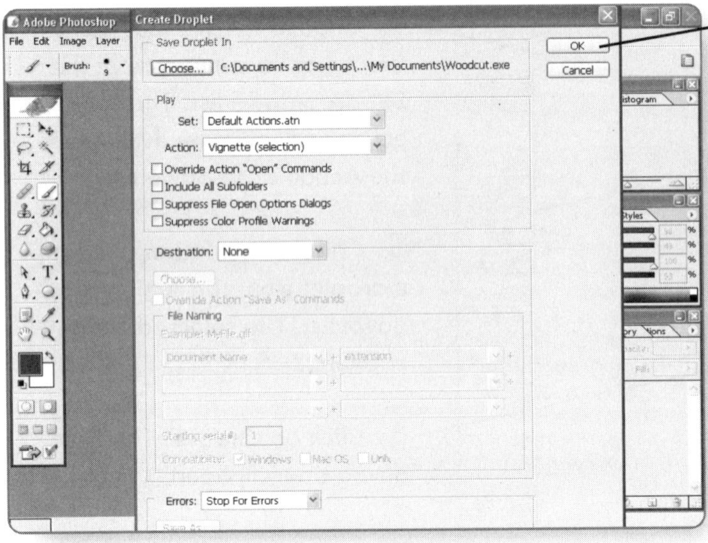

10. Click on **OK**. Photoshop will close the Create Droplet dialog box and finish saving the droplet.

Using a Droplet

As you saw in the preceding section, Photoshop saves a droplet you create as an .exe file. The Photoshop program doesn't have to be open for you to use the droplet. You can use the droplet from the folder where you saved it, or you can copy the .exe file to any other folder, including the Windows desktop—shown in the following steps—for convenient use. You don't have to open Photoshop, so the droplet provides a fast alternative for making changes to a number of files because you also don't have to open the individual image files in Photoshop. Using the droplet is an easy drag-and-drop operation, as illustrated in the following steps.

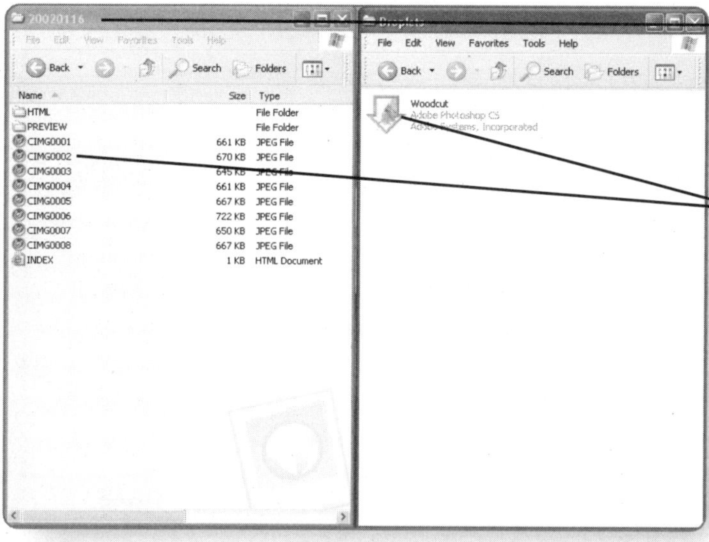

1. **Open** the **folder** that holds the file to process with the automation. The folder will appear in Windows.

2. **Drag** the **file** to process from its folder and **drop** it onto the icon for the droplet file (on the desktop or in another folder). The droplet's actions will be performed on the file. You can repeat the process for as many files as need to be processed.

NOTE

The file(s) to be processed must use the correct color mode and other settings; otherwise, the droplet will stop and display an error message.

Part V Review Questions

1. How do I choose what type of image colors to use? See "Reviewing the Color Modes" in Chapter 15.
2. What's a color channel, and how do I select one? See "Using Color Channels" in Chapter 15.
3. What are the most common color mode conversions? See "Converting Images" in Chapter 15.
4. What do I do if my image is too dark? See "Correcting Brightness and Contrast" in Chapter 16.
5. What's a duotone, and how do you create one? See "Creating a Duotone Image" in Chapter 17.
6. How do you create a Sepia image? See "Making a Sepia Image" in Chapter 17.
7. How do you add plug-ins to Photoshop? See "Installing Plug-Ins" in Chapter 18.
8. What methods do you use to employ a plug-in? See "Applying a Plug-In to a File" in Chapter 18.
9. How do you create an action? See "Creating an Action" in Chapter 19.
10. How do you use an action? See "Using an Action" in Chapter 19.

PART VI

Prepping Images for the Web

20

Creating Web Images

Because Photoshop provides some of the best tools for creating and editing images in general, it's not surprising that it offers superior options for preparing images for use in Web pages. This chapter walks you through the basic skills for preparing images for the Web. You'll learn how to:

- Use Web graphic formats
- Utilize the Save As command
- Create an optimized JPEG image
- Create an optimized GIF image
- Create a WBMP image
- Generate a Web photo gallery

Reviewing Web Graphic Formats

The HTML Web page format spurred the growth of the Internet not only because it could present information in an attractive graphic format, but also because its files were relatively compact in size for reasonable download times. In the spirit of preserving those download times, a few different new formats for graphics files also emerged. Through special compression technology, these file formats preserve color and detail while dramatically reducing file size—sometimes eliminating megabytes in file size. Table 20-1 lists the most common Web graphic file formats and their features.

Table 20-1 ***Web Graphic File Formats***

Format	Description
Compuserve GIF (.gif)	This mode requires conversion to Indexed Color mode (which limits the image to 256 colors) and enables you to preserve transparency so that the Web page background shows through.
JPEG (.jpe, .jpg, or .jpeg)	This mode does not preserve transparency, but it does enable you to specify the amount of compression to use so you can control file size and quality.
PNG (.png)	Portable Network Graphics (PNG) mode enables you to preserve transparency and choose specific methods for reducing colors and handling dithering in the image. This format isn't used often.
WBMP	This 1-bit color format optimizes images for wireless devices. Converting an image to this format converts it to simplified black and white.

> **TIP**
>
> Remember, when you create a new image with the File, New command, you click on the Transparent option button to set up an image with a transparent background. If you scan an image or download it from a digital camera, you cannot specify a transparent background, so it's best to copy a selection from such an image, create a new image with a transparent background, and then paste the copied selection into it.

Using Save As

You can use the Save As command on the File menu to save an image in the common Web graphic formats. When you use the Save As command and choose one of the Web file formats, you'll be prompted to make various changes depending on the selected format.

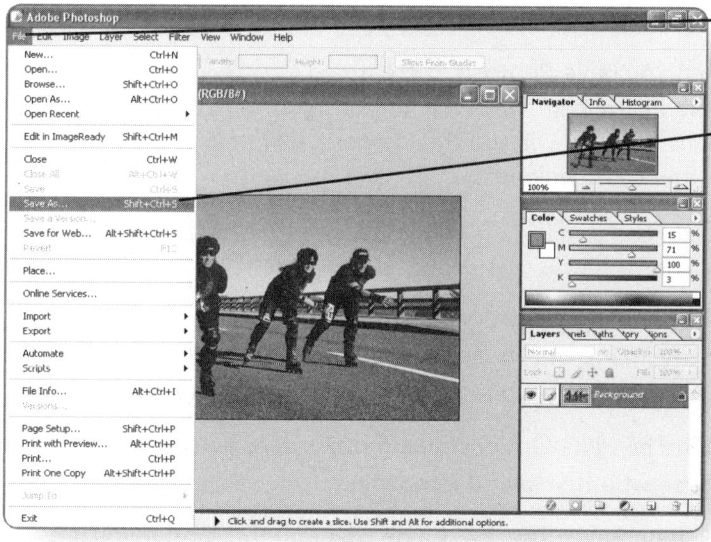

1. **Click** on **File**. The File menu will appear.

2. **Click** on **Save As**. The Save As dialog box will open.

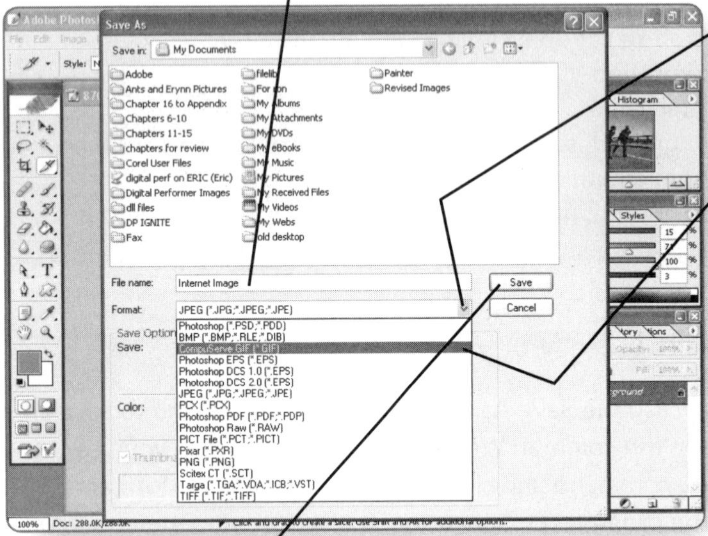

3. Type a **name** for your file in the File name field. It will appear as you type.

4. Click on the **down arrow** beside the Format field. A list of formats will appear.

5. Click on the desired **format** for the Web:

- **GIF.** The Indexed Color dialog box opens to specify color palette, transparency, and matte settings, and then the GIF Options dialog box opens to prompt you whether to choose an interlaced GIF format.

NOTE

When you have Photoshop create an interlaced file, part of the image can "preload" on the Web page. This means the user will see the image at low resolution until the full file downloads.

- **JPEG.** The JPEG Options dialog box opens so you can specify image quality and matte options. Transparent areas will be filled with white when you finish the save.
- **PNG.** The PNG Options dialog box opens so you can choose whether to add interlacing.

6. Click on **Save**. The file will be saved in the format you selected. Depending on the type of file you specified, another dialog box may open in which you can configure the settings for that type of file.

Save an Optimized Image File

To see all the settings for Web graphic file formats in a single dialog box, use the Save for Web command on the File menu. This command enables you to select a Web file format, specify settings for the format, and then proceed with the save. The rest of this section shows you how to use the Save for Web command to optimize and save a file in the three most common Web graphic formats—JPEG, GIF, and WBMP.

Saving a JPEG

These steps show you how to use the Save for Web command to save a JPEG file so that you can choose the optimum compression for your image.

1. Click on **File**. The File menu will appear.

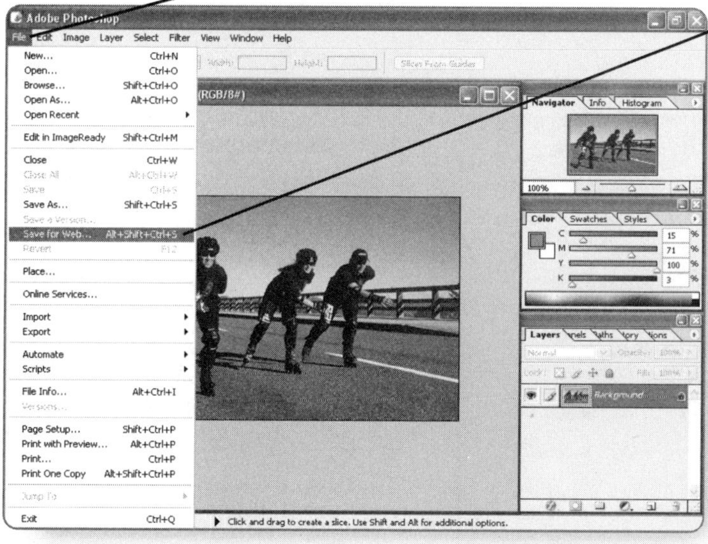

2. Click on **Save for Web**. The Save For Web dialog box will open with its Optimized tab selected.

3. Click on the **down arrow** beside the file format drop-down list and then click on JPEG. The JPEG choices will appear in the settings box.

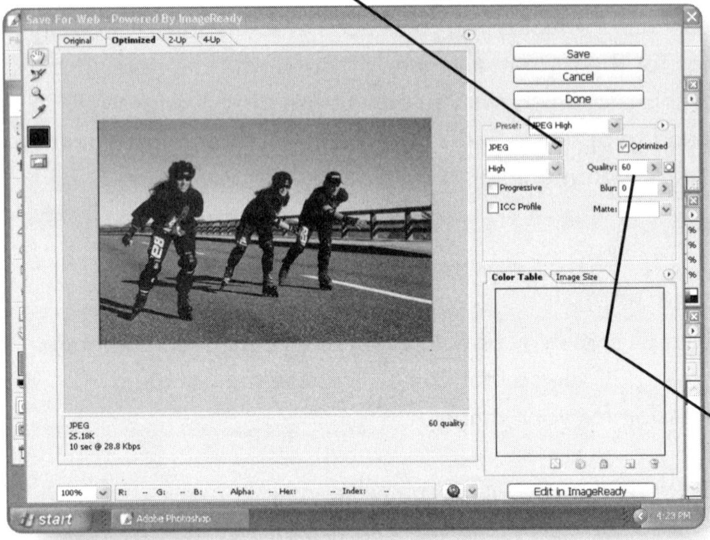

NOTE

You can use the drop-down list labeled Preset the top of the Settings box to choose a presaved set of optimization settings, such as JPEG High or GIF 32 Dithered.

4. Type an **image quality setting**. The higher the setting, the lower the file compression and vice versa.

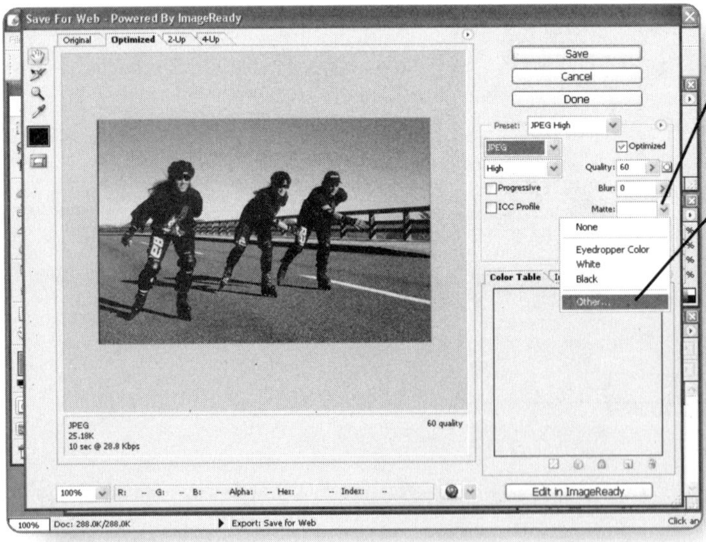

5. Click on the **down arrow** beside the Matte drop-down list. A menu will appear.

6. Click on **Other**. The Color Picker dialog box will appear so that you can use it to specify a matte for the image.

NOTE

A matte color in a GIF or PNG Web graphic helps the edges of transparent areas blend with the Web page background. In a JPEG image, it fills areas that were originally transparent with the specified color for blending.

7. **Click** on a **color hue** in the narrow band of colors near the middle of the dialog box. Photoshop will display a different range of colors in the Choose a color box.

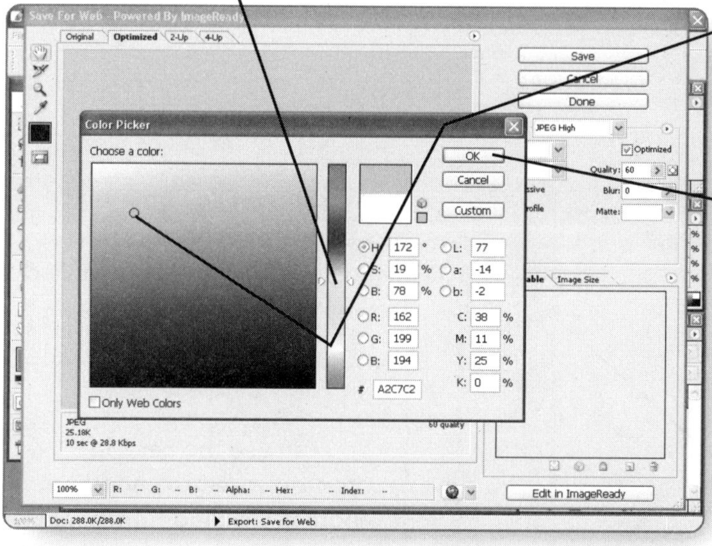

8. **Click** on a **color** in the Choose a color box. The color you click on will become the active matte color.

9. **Click** on **OK**. The Color Picker dialog box will close.

10. **Click** on **Save**. The Save Optimized As dialog box will appear.

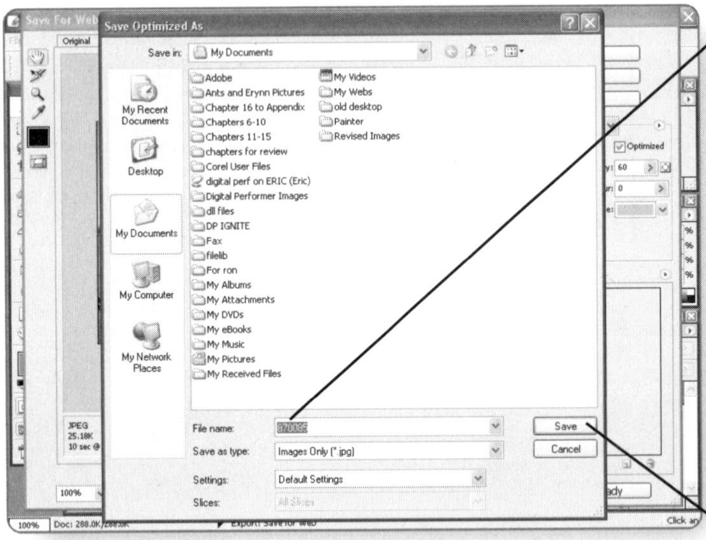

11. **Edit** the **File name text box** entry as necessary. The name you specify will be applied to the Web graphic file.

> **NOTE**
>
> You can use the Save In drop-down list to choose another disk and folder location for the saved file, if necessary.

12. **Click** on **Save**. The Save Optimized As and Save For Web dialog boxes will close. Only the original image will be open in Photoshop. You can find the new, optimized Web graphic file in the folder where you saved it.

Saving a GIF

Saving an optimized GIF file follows much the same process as saving an optimized JPEG file. Get started with the process now.

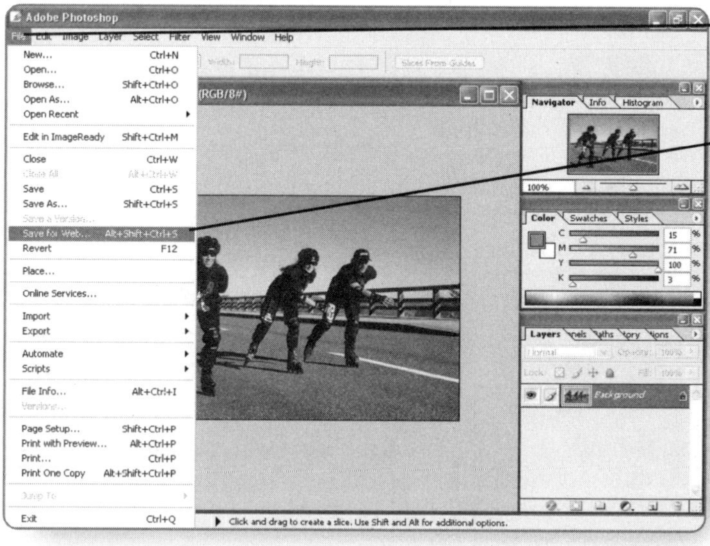

1. Click on **File**. The File menu will appear.

2. Click on **Save For Web**. The Save For Web dialog box will open with its Optimized tab selected.

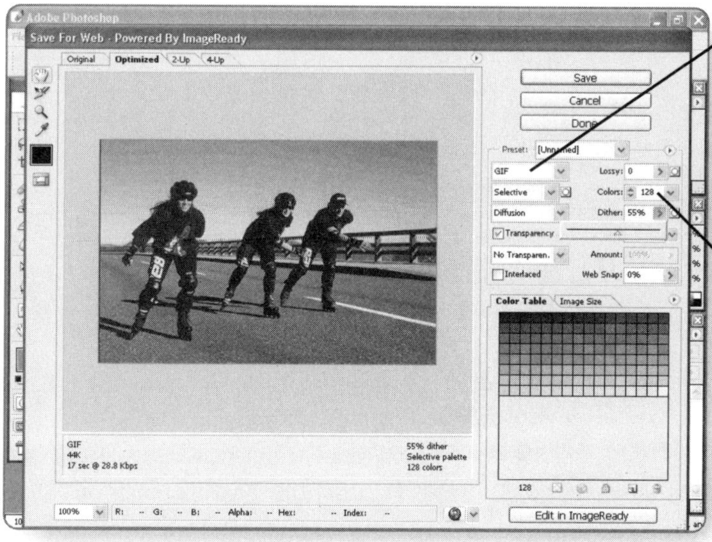

3. Click on the **down arrow** beside the drop-down list in the upper-left corner of the Settings box and then click on GIF. The GIF choices will appear in the Settings box.

4. Choose image color settings. This represents the maximum number of colors in the image.

5. **Choose image dithering settings**, both by choosing a dithering method from the drop-down list and by choosing the amount of dithering using the slider that appears when you click on the down arrow beside Dither. The statistics in the lower-right corner of the preview area will change to show the specified dithering method.

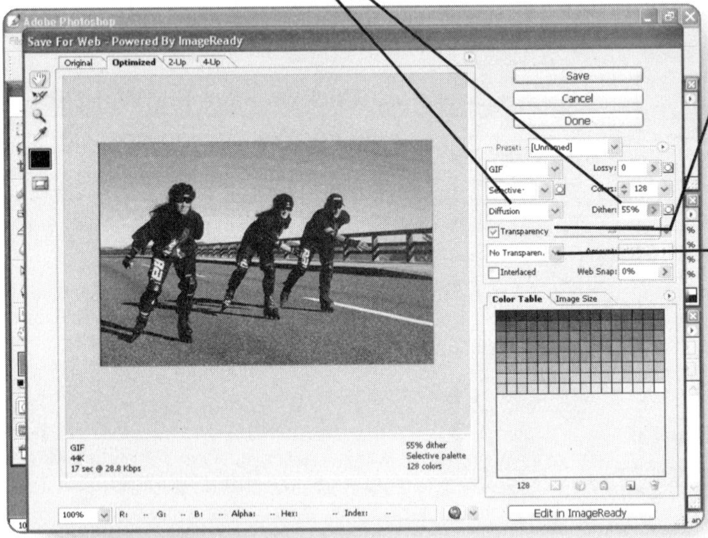

6. **Leave** the **Transparency check box checked**. This ensures that the transparent areas in the image will remain transparent in the final GIF file.

7. **Click** on the **down arrow** beside the drop-down list below the Transparency check box. A menu of transparency dithering algorithms will appear.

8. Click on the desired **algorithm**. The preview will show the impact of the selected algorithm.

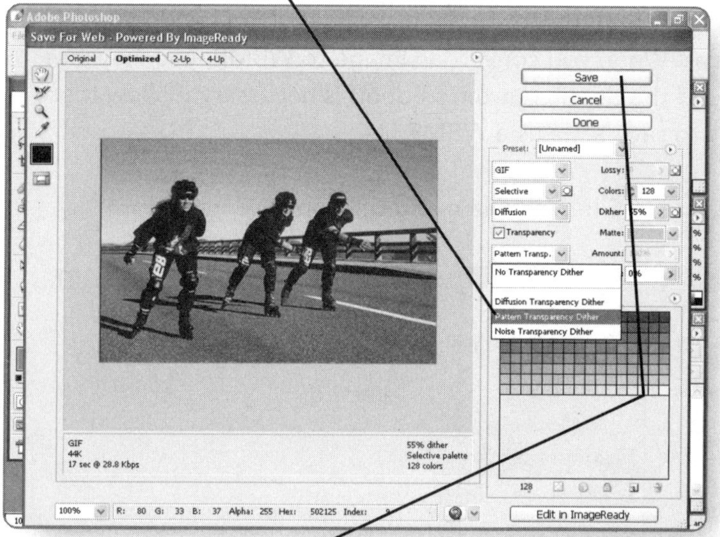

9. Click on **Save**. The Save Optimized As dialog box will open.

NOTE

Specifying the transparency dither algorithm will be necessary for images with semitransparent areas, such as gradients or bleeds.

You also can add a matte for the GIF, but it won't be as obvious in the preview. That's because the matte for a GIF image serves more as a blending zone between the image content and the Web page background.

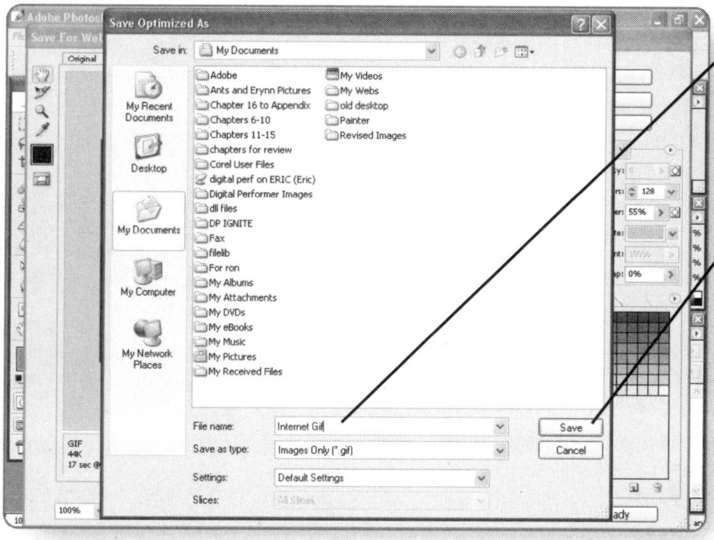

10. Edit the **File name text box entry** as necessary. The name you specify will be applied to the Web graphic file.

11. Click on **Save**. The Save Optimized As and Save For Web dialog boxes will close. Only the original image will be open in Photoshop. You can find the new, optimized Web graphic file in the folder where you saved it.

Saving a WBMP

As noted earlier in this chapter, a WBMP file is a black-and-white file created specifically for wireless (and handheld) devices. When you convert an image to WBMP, you may lose some of the detail, but the tradeoff is necessary. Follow these steps to save a file as a WBMP file.

1. **Click** on **File**. The File menu will appear.

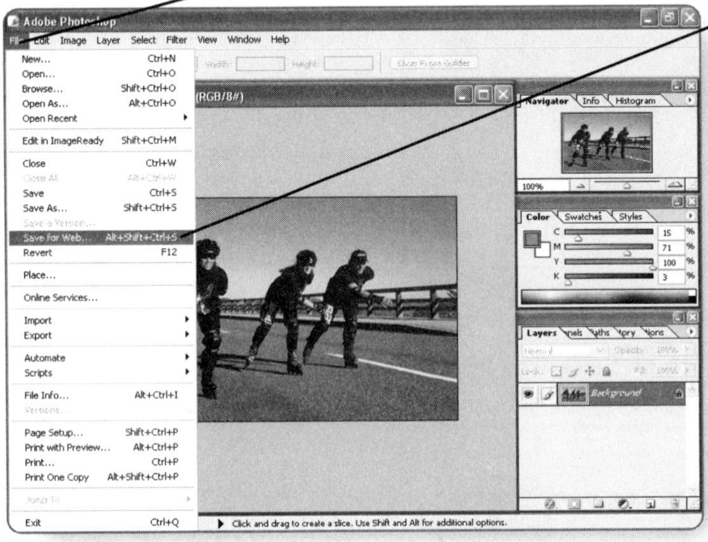

2. **Click** on **Save for Web**. The Save For Web dialog box will open with its Optimized tab selected.

3. **Click** on the **down arrow** beside the drop-down list and then click on WBMP. The WBMP choices will appear in the Settings box.

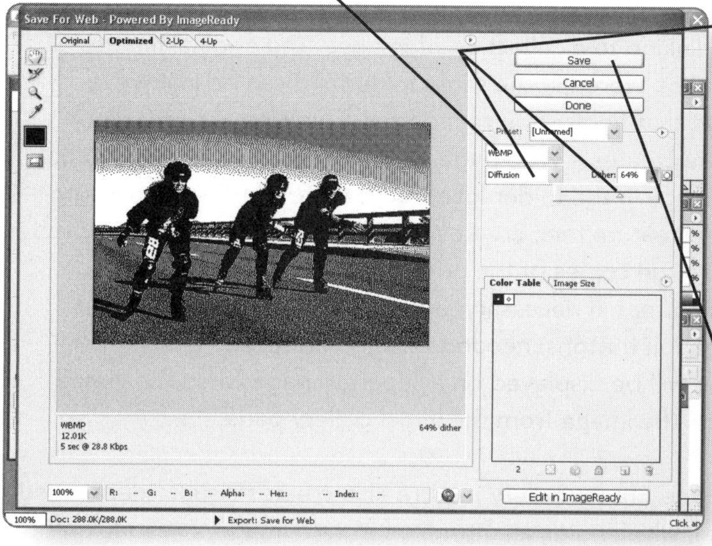

4. **Choose** image **dithering settings**, both by choosing a dithering method setting from the drop-down list on the left and by choosing the amount of dithering using the Dither choice on the right. The statistic in the lower-right corner of the preview area will change to show the specified dithering method.

5. **Click** on **Save**. The Save Optimized As dialog box will open.

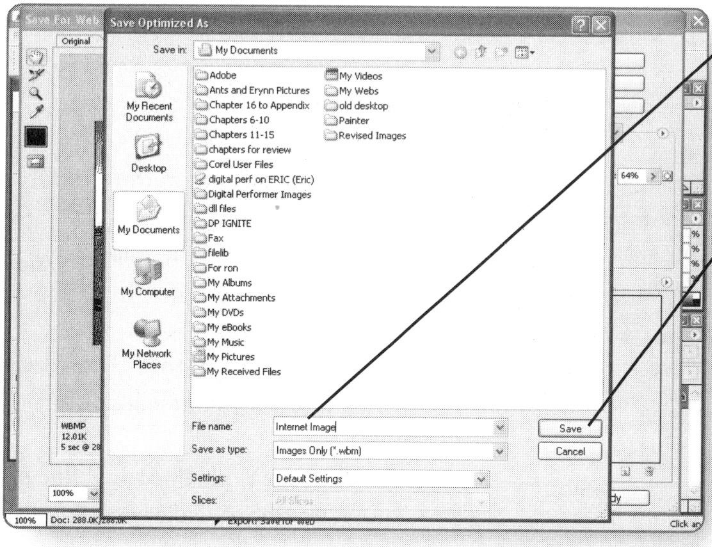

6. **Edit** the **File name text box entry** as necessary. The name you specify will be applied to the Web graphic file.

7. **Click** on **Save**. The Save Optimized As and Save For Web dialog boxes will close. Only the original image will be open in Photoshop. You can find the new, optimized Web graphic file in the folder where you saved it.

Setting Up a Web Photo Gallery

The Web Photo Gallery feature enables you to create a Web page linking to a collection of images. The original images all should be stored in the same folder and can be in any file format that Photoshop recognizes. The Web Photo Gallery feature creates a Web page named index.htm and stores that Web page in the folder location you specify. The Web Photo Gallery feature then creates a subfolder named images, which holds large copies of the original image files (converted to JPEG format, if necessary) as well as other images (such as navigation buttons) needed for the Web photo gallery. Each image will be displayed on a separate page when the viewer selects the image from the initial gallery page.

The Web Photo Gallery feature also creates a subfolder named pages, which holds an .htm file for each image. The index.htm file has a link to each of these .htm files. Finally, a newthumbnails subfolder holds a smaller version of each image in the gallery for display on the index.htm page. Follow these steps to create a basic Web photo gallery. Before you begin these steps, you must move or copy the images for the gallery into a single folder in Windows. The images will appear in that folder.

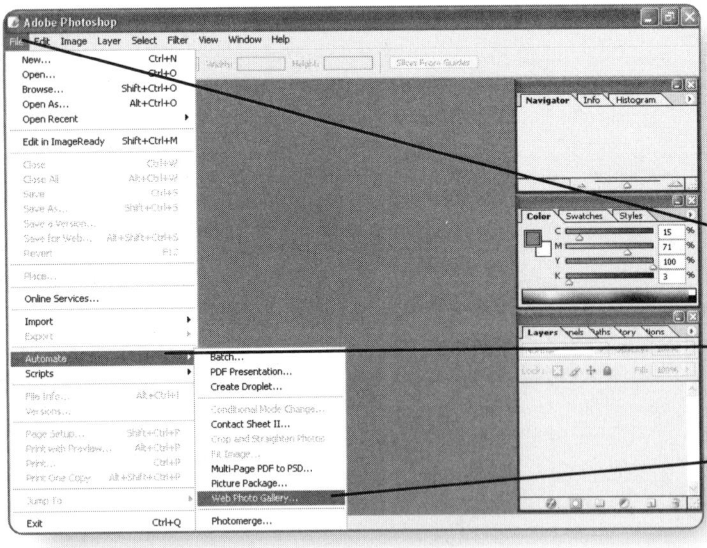

1. **Click** on **File**. The File menu will appear.

2. **Point** to **Automate**. The Automate submenu will appear.

3. **Click** on **Web Photo Gallery**. The Web Photo Gallery dialog box will open.

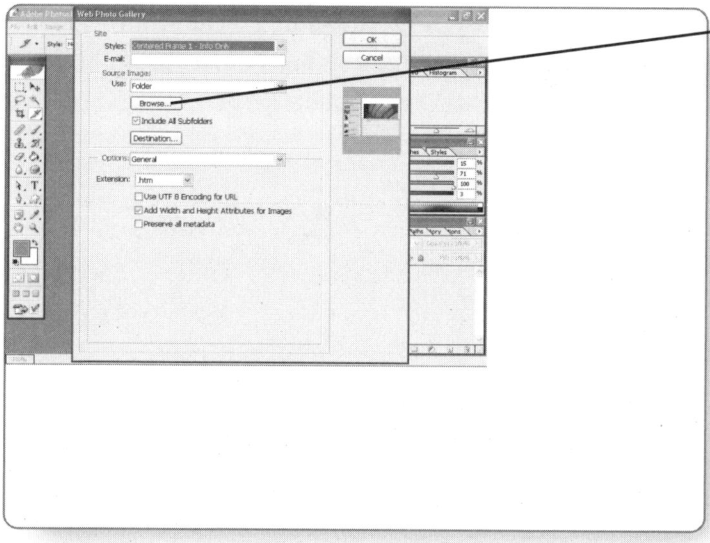

4. **Click** on **Browse**. The Browse For Folder dialog box will open.

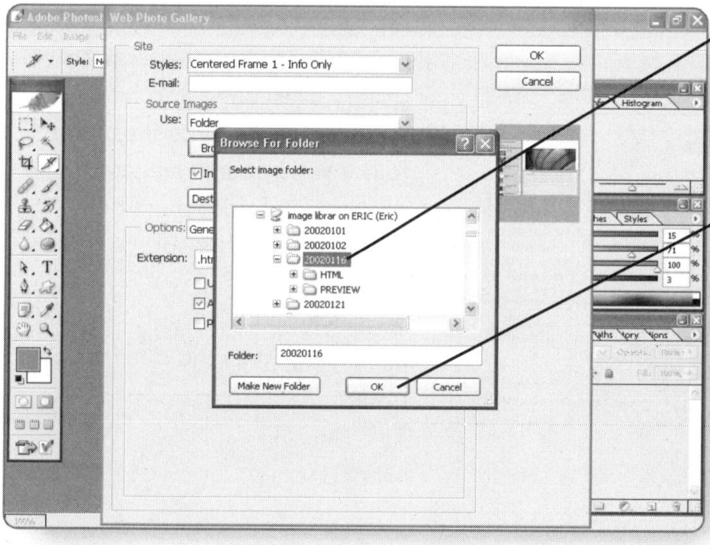

5. **Select** the **folder** that holds the images to include in the photo gallery. The folder will become selected.

6. **Click** on **OK**. The folder will be displayed as the source folder.

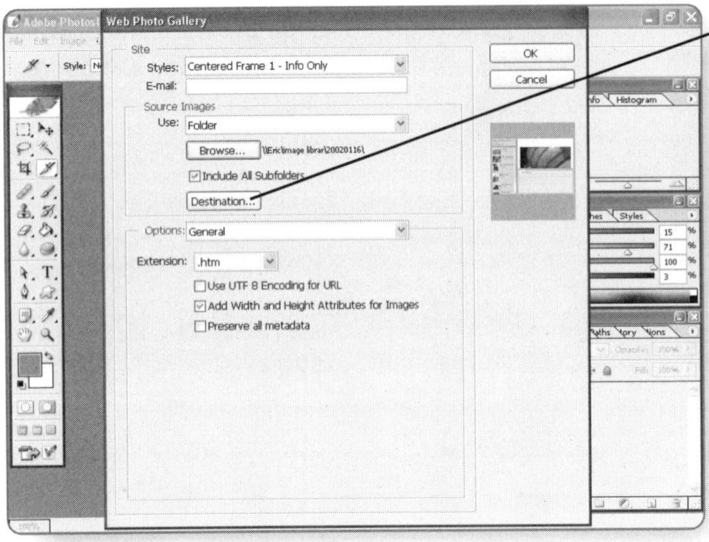

7. **Click** on **Destination**. The Browse For Folder dialog box will open.

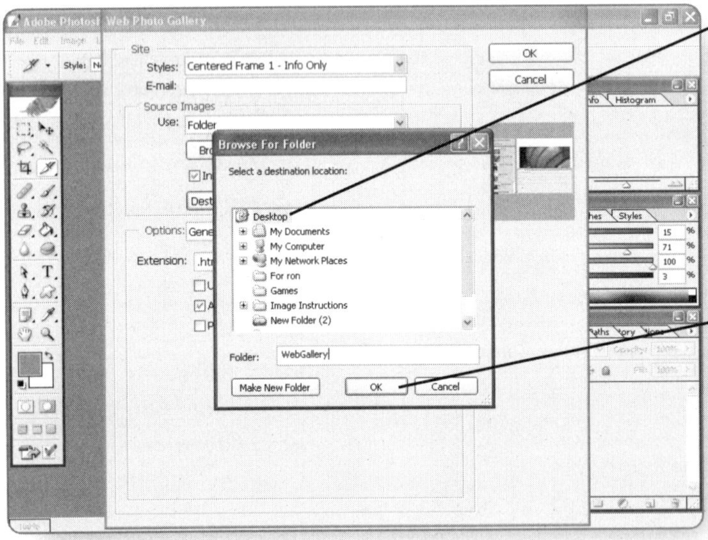

8. **Select** the **folder** where you would like to store the photo gallery Web page and its subfolders of source files. The folder will become selected. The destination folder must be different from the source folder.

9. **Click** on **OK**. The folder will be displayed as the destination folder.

10. Click the **down arrow** beside the Styles field to choose from a variety of different templates.

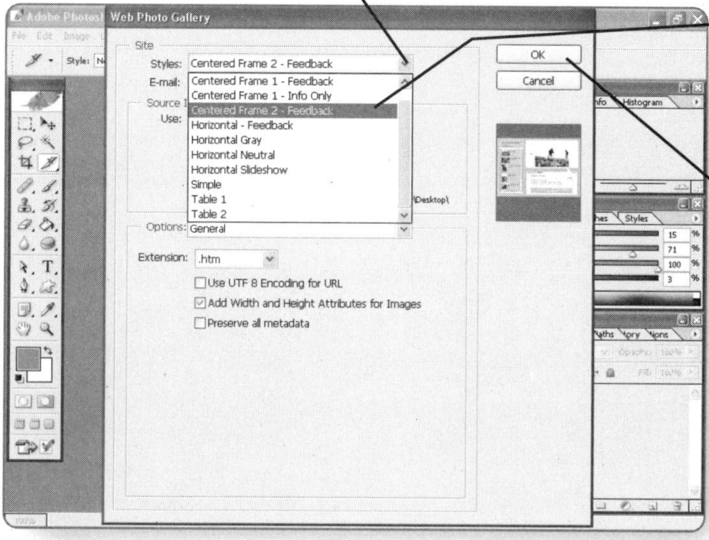

11. Click on the desired **template**. It will be selected, and a preview of the template will appear in the dialog box.

12. Click on **OK**. Photoshop will generate the Web Photo Gallery, launch your Web browser, and display the initial page. The page will show thumbnail images.

13. Click on an **image link** or **thumbnail**. The Web Photo Gallery page for that image will open. From this point, you can continue browsing images in the gallery or close your Web browser.

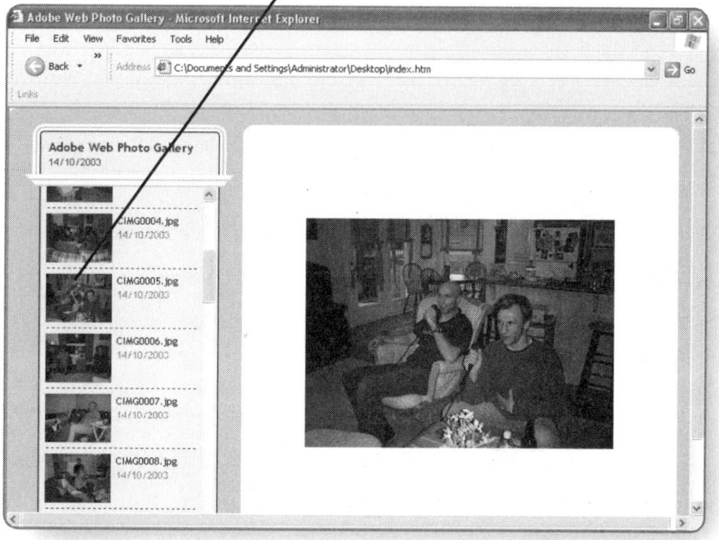

NOTE

If you move or copy the Web Photo Gallery to another location, you must move all the elements—the index.htm file, the images folder, the pages folder, and the thumbnails folder.

21

Adding Hotspots

Web browsing hinges on the ability to navigate by following links. You can use the Slice tool to identify areas for linking in an image and then save that image as a Web (HTML) file so that an image with the links can be incorporated into an overall Web site. This chapter introduces you to the basics of the slice feature. You'll learn how to:

- Add a slice and set its options
- Work with existing slices
- Save the sliced image in HTML format

Adding Slices or "Hotspots"

The Slice tool on the Photoshop toolbox adds slices into an image file, dividing your images into various sections. By then specifying the slice options, you create a link to a particular Web address called a URL (*Uniform Resource Locator*). After you save the image as an HTML file (as described in the final section of this chapter, "Saving the Sliced File in HTML"), users can click on the area defined by the slice to follow the link. That's why such linked areas are called "hotspots." The steps that follow explain how to add a slice and set it up as a hotspot, after you've performed all the necessary edits in Photoshop.

1. **Click** on the **Slice tool** in the toolbox. The Slice tool will become active.

2. **Drag** on the **image** to define the slice. (You don't really need to select a layer first.) When you release the mouse button, the new slice will appear. The slice appears as a box.

3. **Double-click** on the **slice number** for the new slice. The Slice Options dialog box will open.

> **NOTE**
>
> In addition to the slice you drew, called a user slice, Photoshop divides the rest of the image into slices called auto slices. Typically, Photoshop draws vertical slice lines continuing from one or both corners of the slice you drew, depending on its location. It also may draw horizontal slice lines from the top or bottom of the slice.

4. **Specify options**, as follows:

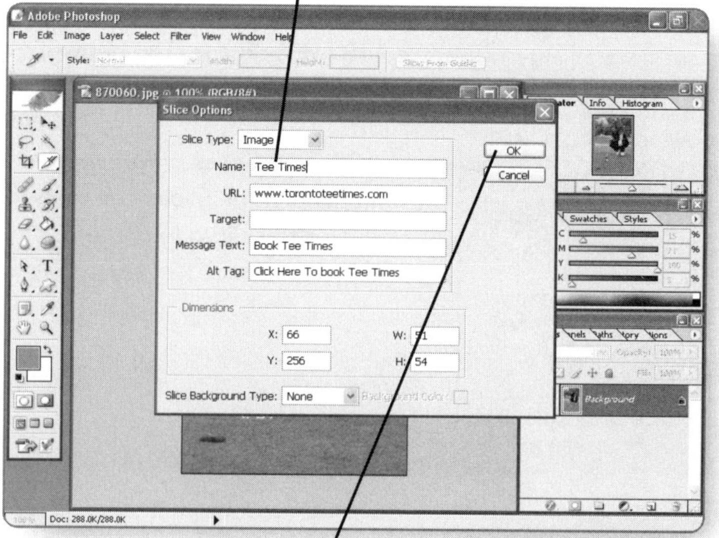

- **URL.** Enter the URL for the Web page that will appear when the user clicks on the hotspot. To enter an absolute address (not just a relative address on the server holding the page), be sure to include http:// at the start of your entry.
- **Target.** Specify the frame in which the linked page will appear, if applicable. (Consult the Help system for your Web authoring software to learn more about working with frames.)
- **Message Text.** Enter more descriptive information about the linked Web page. The description will appear in the Web browser status bar when the user hovers the mouse pointer over the hotspot.
- **Alt Tag.** Enter a description to appear in place of the image content if the page is displayed in a nongraphical Web browser.

5. **Click** on **OK**. The Slice Options dialog box will close, and the specified settings will be applied to the slice.

Viewing and Hiding Slices

If it so happens that you need to make further edits to the sliced image before you save it as an HTML file, you can hide the slice lines so that they won't distract you. Then you can redisplay the slices later as necessary.

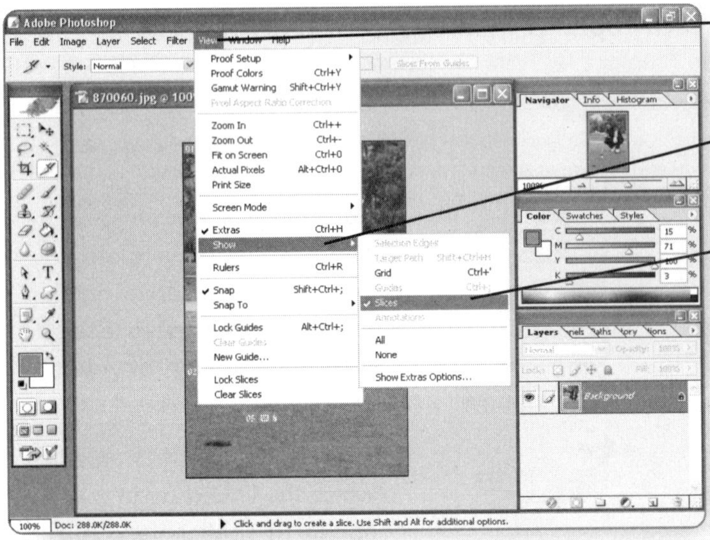

1. **Click** on **View**. The View menu will appear.
2. **Point** to **Show**. The Show submenu will appear.
3. **Click** on **Slices**. Photoshop will uncheck the Slices command and hide the slices in the image file.

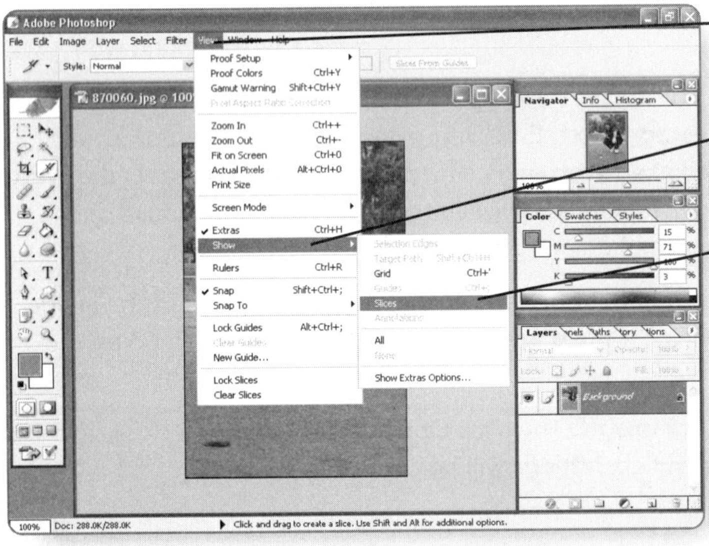

4. **Click** on **View**. The View menu will appear.
5. **Point** to **Show**. The Show submenu will appear.
6. **Click** on **Slices**. Photoshop will check the Slices command and redisplay the slices in the image file.

NOTE

If you need to resize a slice, click and hold the Slice tool and then click on Slice Select Tool in the shortcut menu that appears. Then drag the corner of the slice area to resize it.

Saving the Sliced File in HTML

When you need to save the sliced file in HTML format, use the Save for Web command on the File menu, as demonstrated here.

1. **Click** on **File**. The File menu will appear.

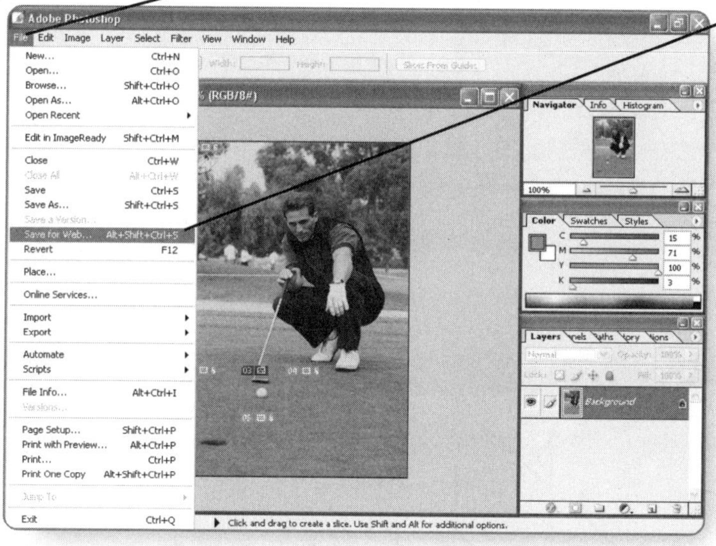

2. **Click** on **Save for Web**. The Save For Web dialog box will open, with its Optimized tab selected.

TIP

If you previously used the Save For Web command to save a JPEG or GIF image and specified a matte, you're going to want to be sure to remove that matte color. Click on the Optimize menu button (the round button with the arrow on it) in the Save For Web dialog box and then click on Edit Output Settings in the menu. Open the drop-down list that has HTML selected in it by default and then click on Background. Open the Color drop-down list, click on None, and then click on OK to return to the Save For Web dialog box.

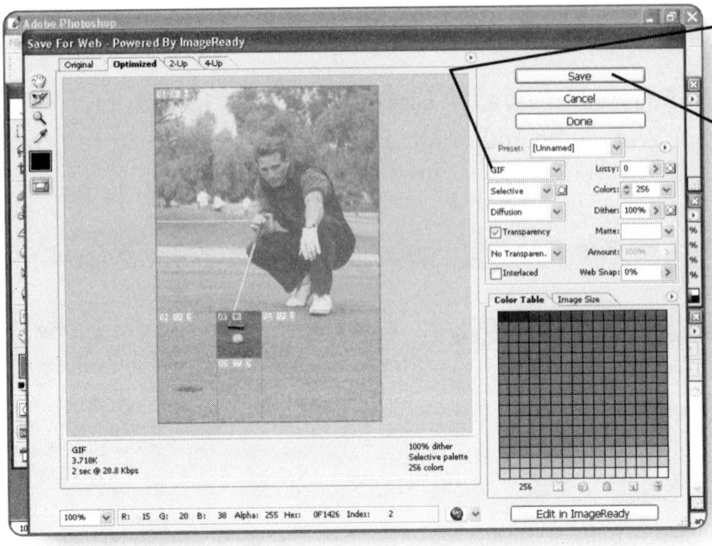

3. **Click** the desired **Optimized file format**. It will be selected.

4. **Click** on **Save**. The Save Optimized As dialog box will open.

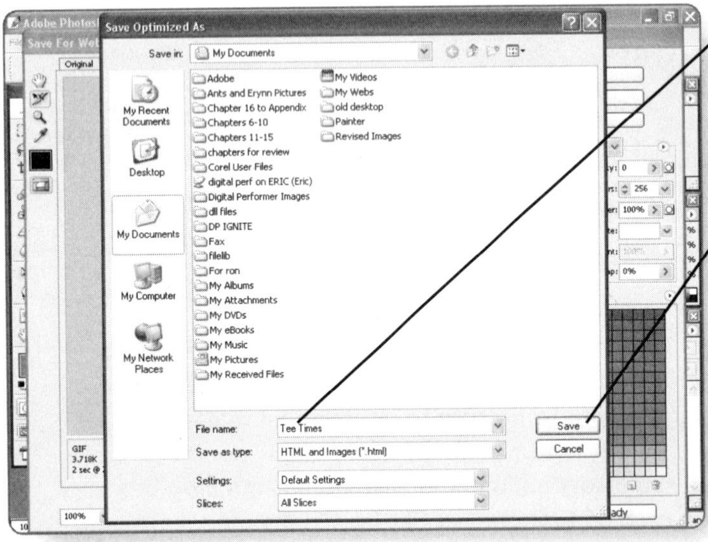

5. **Edit** the **File name text box entry** as necessary. The name you specify will be applied to the HTML file.

6. **Click** on **Save**. The Save Optimized As and Save For Web dialog boxes will close. Only the original image will be open in Photoshop. You can find the new HTML file in the folder where you saved it.

TIP

Use the File, Open command in your Web browser to open and preview the new HTML file. (Note that you can use Save As to resave the file using the shorter .htm extension instead.) You can even click on the hotspot to test the link. When you copy or move the Web page, be sure to copy or move the accompanying images folder created by the HTML saving process. That folder holds the actual sliced image content.

22

Getting Help

The goal of this book is to give you a solid foundation in Photoshop so that you can begin the process of creating your digital masterpieces. Photoshop is an enormous application with thousands of different commands and features geared toward specific uses and users. If you need answers to questions that are beyond the scope of this book, Photoshop CS provides you with a variety of tools for getting help. In this chapter, you'll learn how to:

- Use the new Welcome Screen
- Access the Help index
- Search for topic-specific help
- Use and create How To's

The Welcome Screen

New to Photoshop CS is a Welcome Screen that provides you with a variety of options for getting help. When you launch Photoshop, the Welcome Screen appears before you can begin working in the program. The Welcome Screen also can be opened at any time using the Help menu.

1. **Click** on **Start** at the left end of the Windows Taskbar. The Start menu will appear. If you are using Mac OS, find the Photoshop icon and double-click on it to launch the program.

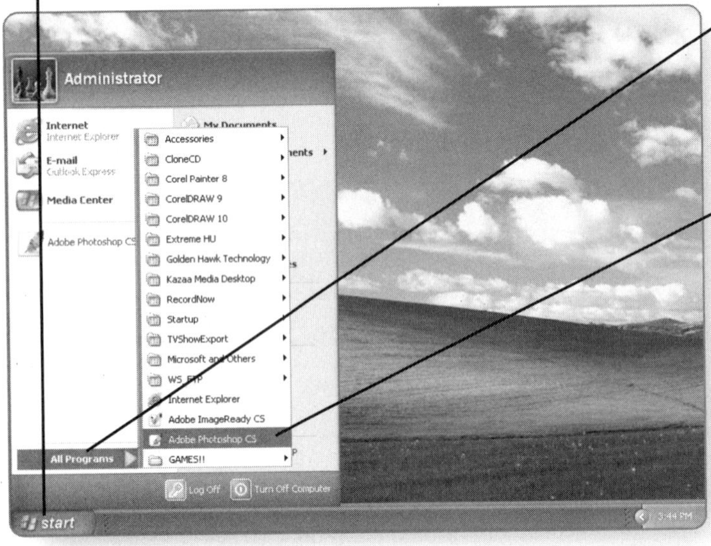

2. Place the mouse pointer over All Programs (or Programs for Windows versions prior to XP). The Programs menu will appear.

3. **Click** on **Adobe Photoshop CS**. The new Photoshop CS Welcome Screen will appear.

TIP

If you don't want the Welcome Screen to appear whenever you start Photoshop CS, uncheck the box in the lower-left corner of the Welcome Screen entitled Show this dialog at startup.

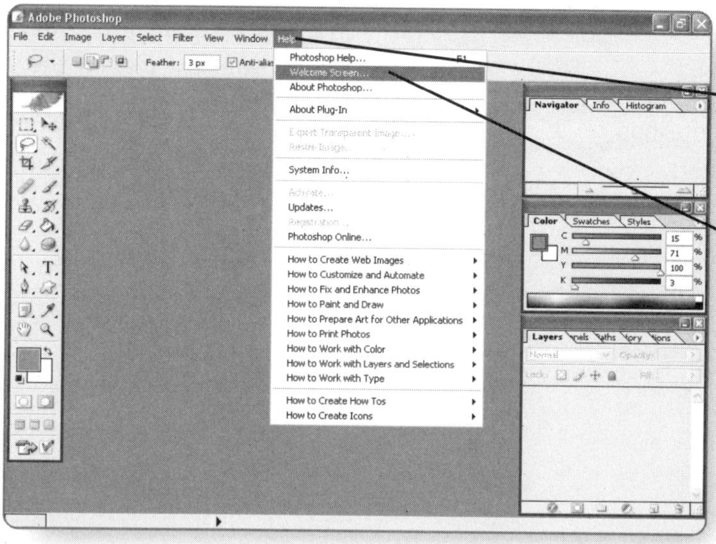

or

1. **Click** on **Help** from within Photoshop. The Help menu will appear.

2. **Click** on **Welcome Screen.** The Welcome Screen will open.

Using the Welcome Screen Tutorials

Photoshop CS comes with six project tutorials that cover certain common tasks like removing red eyes from a photograph or correcting image levels.

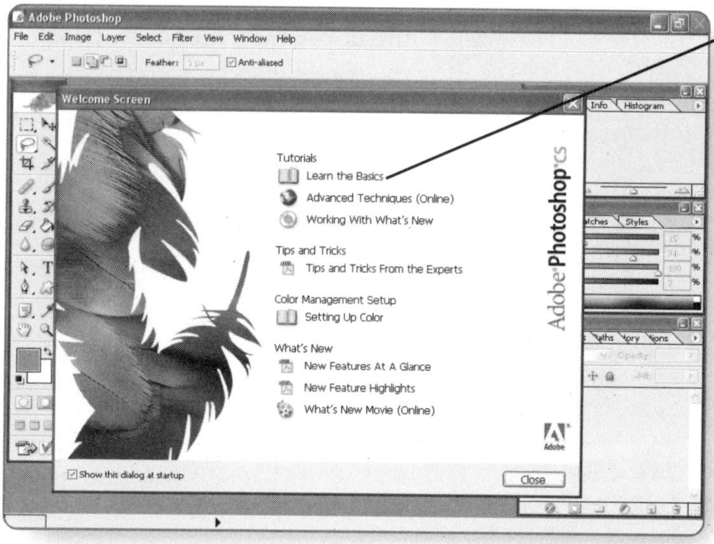

1. **Click** on **Learn the Basics.** Your Internet browser program will launch.

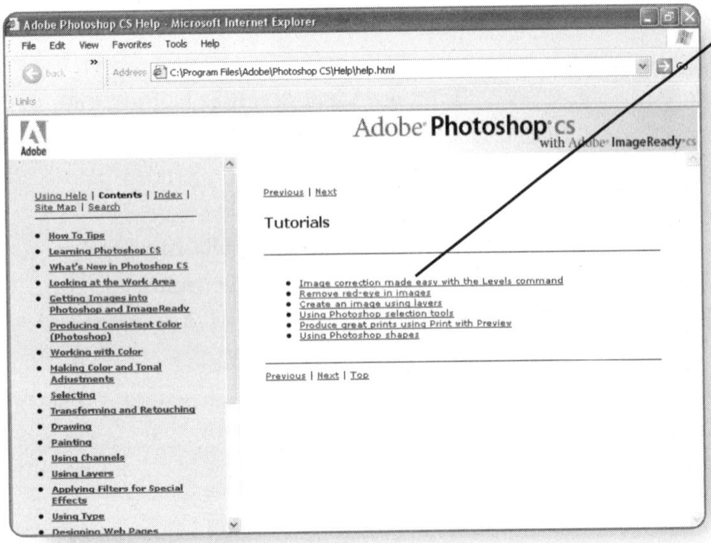

2. **Click** on the desired **tutorial**. The window will now display the steps for that tutorial.

3. **Scroll through** the **steps** to follow the tutorial. You can drag the scroll box or click on the scroll buttons to move through the topic.

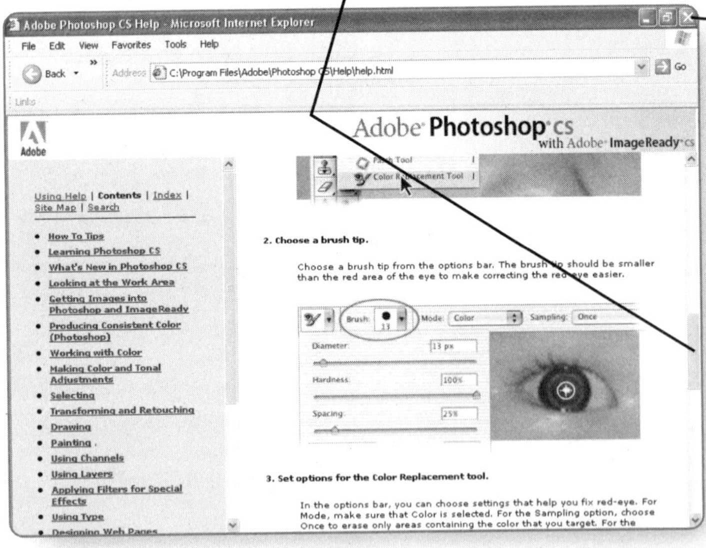

4. **Click** on the **close button** in the upper-right corner to close the window and return to Photoshop.

Watching Tutorial Movies

Adobe provides a Web site that contains tutorials in the form of movies for a variety of advanced topics. This Web site is constantly being updated, so the tutorials found there may change from time to time. You can access these tutorials directly from the Welcome Screen.

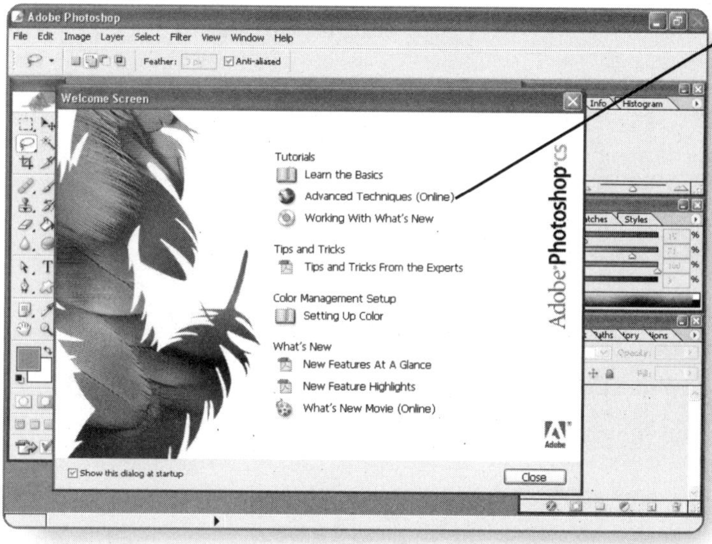

1. Click on **Advanced Techniques (Online)**. Your Internet browser program will launch.

> **NOTE**
>
> You must be connected to the Internet to take advantage of this feature.

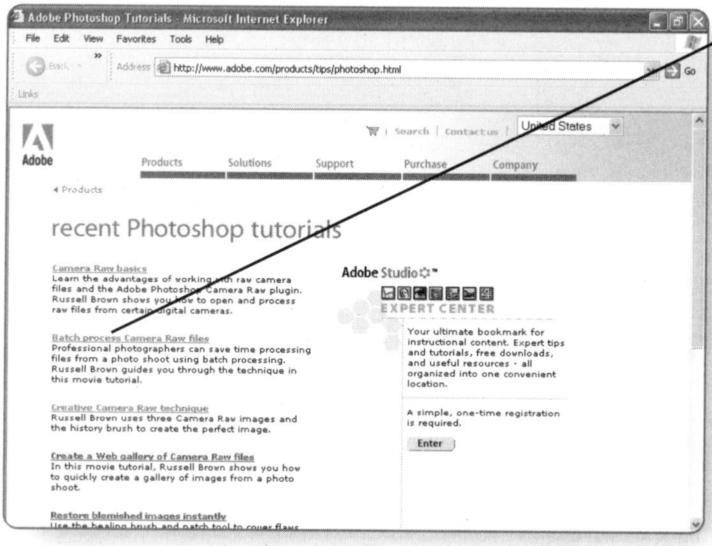

2. Click on the desired **tutorial**. The window will now change to give you a full description of the tutorial.

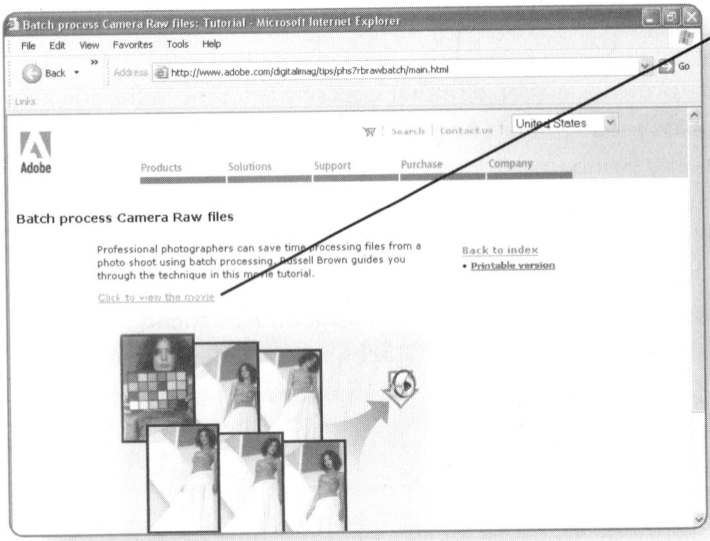

3. Click on the **Click to view the movie link**. A new window will launch, and the tutorial will begin playing.

You must have the QuickTime plug-in installed on your Internet browser to watch the tutorial movies.

4. Click on the **x** in the upper-right corner of the window to close the movie.

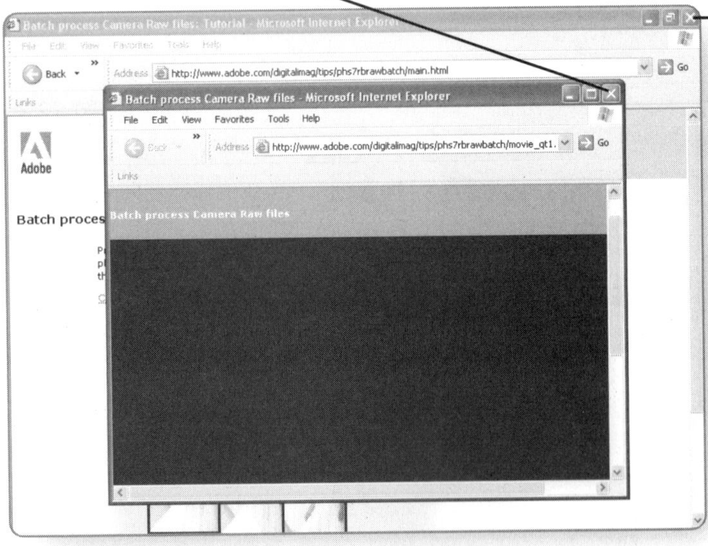

5. Click on the **x** in the upper-right corner to close the browser window and return to Photoshop.

Tips and Tricks

Photoshop CS comes with a PDF (*Portable Document Format*) file that contains a variety of tips, tricks, and projects that you can take advantage of.

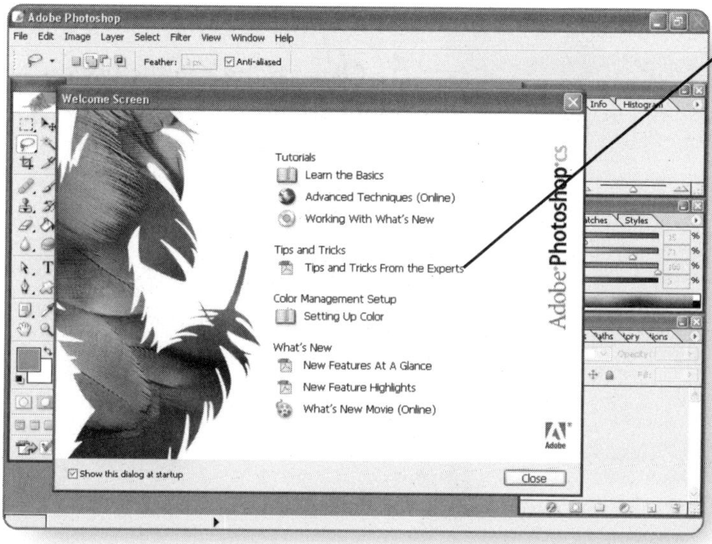

1. **Click** on **Tips and Tricks From the Experts**. Adobe Acrobat Reader will open.

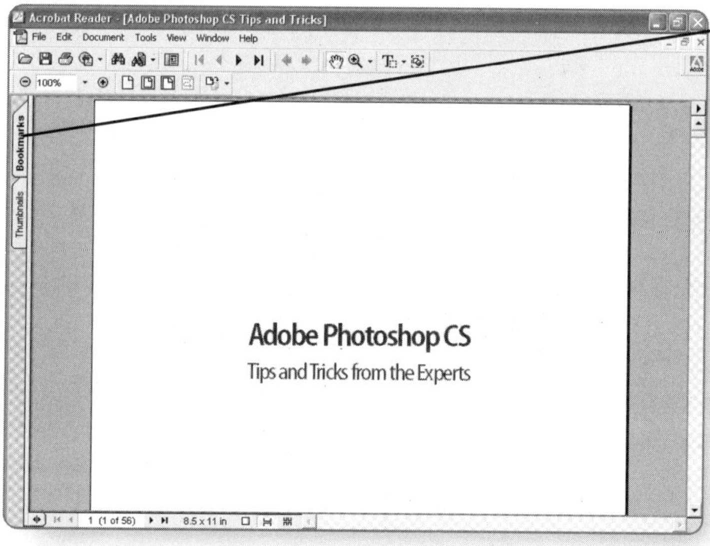

2. **Click** on the **Bookmarks** tab if it is not already selected. The Bookmarks window will open.

3. **Click** on the desired **tutorial**. It will be selected, and the tutorial will appear in the window.

4. **Scroll through** the **steps** of the tutorial. You can drag the scroll box or click on the scroll buttons to move through the topic.

5. **Click** on the **x** in the upper-right corner of the Acrobat window to close the file and return to Photoshop.

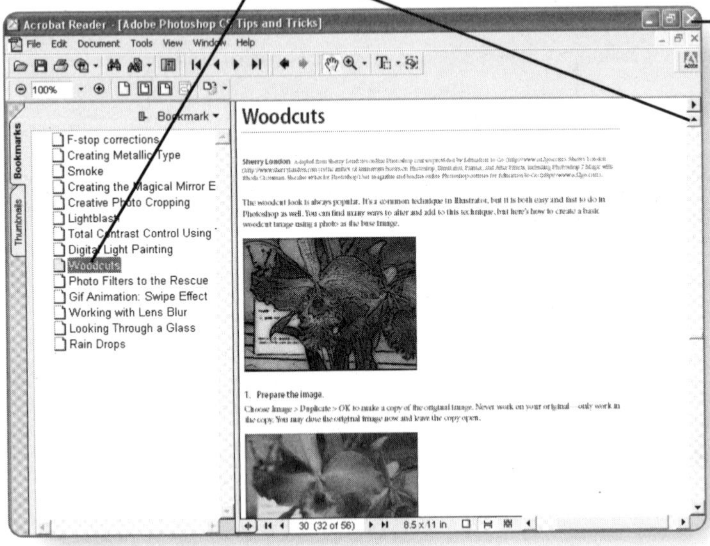

Color Management Help

Color management is an integral part of image design and output. In a nutshell, color management is the process of matching the appearance of colors on all your devices. In other words, it's making sure that the colors you see on your screen match the colors on your printed output. Although specific programs and hardware devices are designed for professional designers and printers to calibrate their equipment, Photoshop has a variety of tools to help with the color management process. Getting help with color management is available directly through the Welcome Screen.

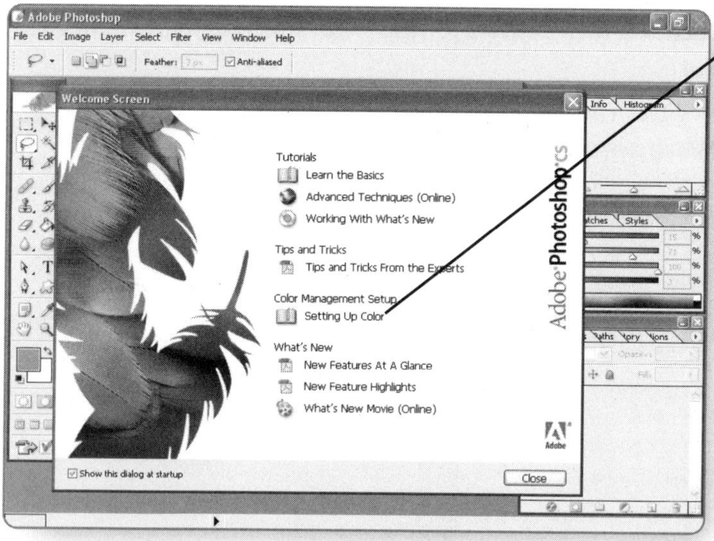

1. Click on **Setting Up Color**. Your Internet browser program will launch.

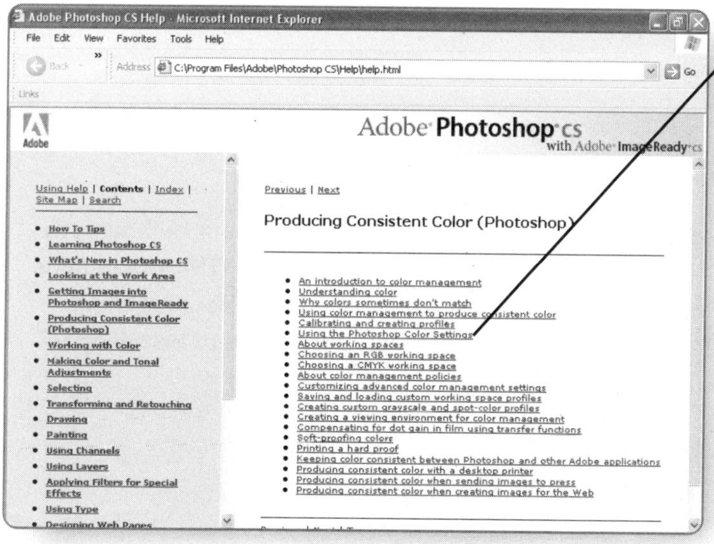

2. Click on the desired **color management topic**. The topic help will open in the window.

3. **Read** the **instructions** for the help topic you have selected.

4. **Click** on one of the **navigational links** at the bottom of the page.

5. **Click** on the **x** in the upper-right corner to close the window and return to Photoshop.

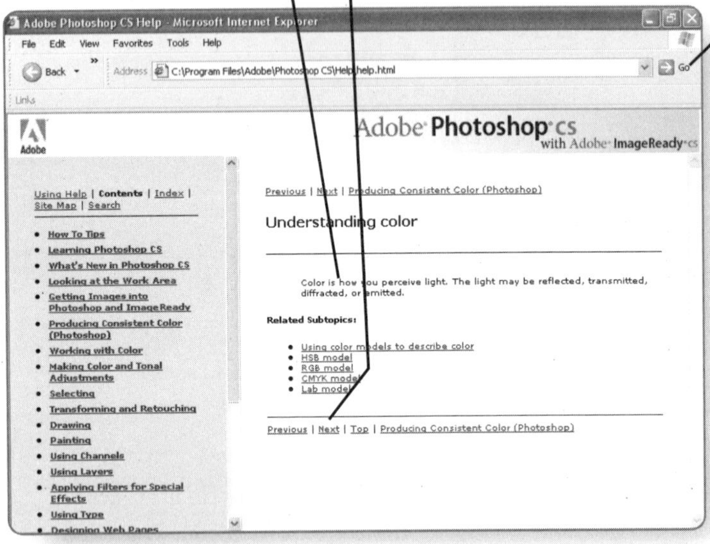

Photoshop Help

Photoshop has a comprehensive help document built directly into the program. The help files are actually HTML documents that are viewed from your Internet browser. Because these files reside on your computer, you don't have to be online to view them.

Accessing Help

Some of the help files in Photoshop can be accessed through the Welcome Screen, as you learned earlier. The Help menu serves as a central location for you to find help on almost every Photoshop topic.

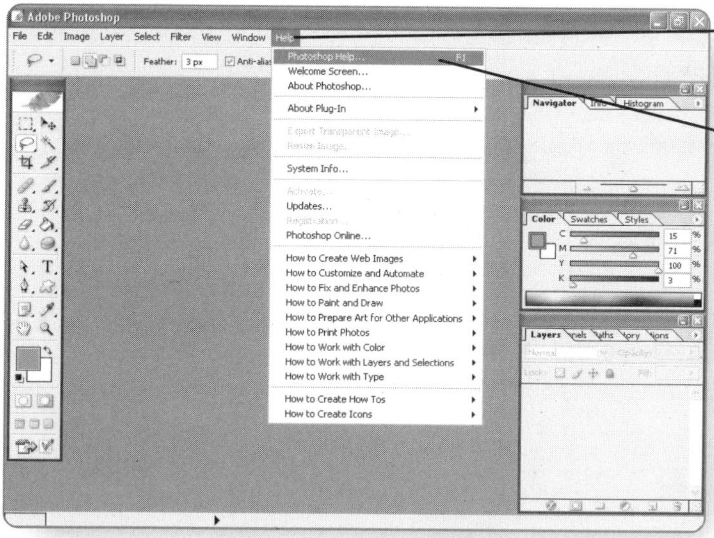

1. **Click** on **Help**. The Help menu will appear.

2. **Click** on **Photoshop Help**. Your Internet browser program will launch with the Adobe help file.

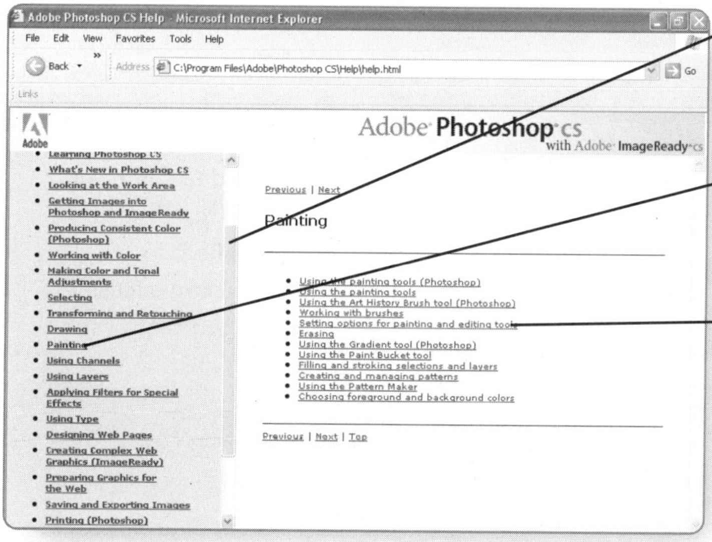

3. **Scroll through** the various **topics**. You can drag the scroll bar or use the scroll buttons.

4. **Click** on the desired **topic**. The help topics relating to the topic you selected will appear.

5. **Click** on the desired **topic**. The help associated with that topic will appear in the window.

6. **Click** on the desired **navigation control** at the bottom of the window.

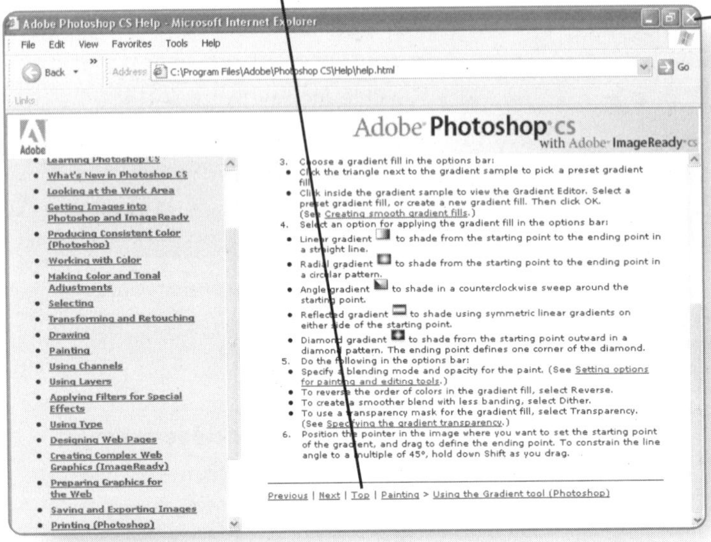

7. **Click** on the **close button** in the upper-right corner to close the window and return to Photoshop.

The Help Index

If you wanted to access a specific topic in this book, you'd probably turn to the back, open the index, and find the topic you are looking for. The same holds true with help in Photoshop. You can access the index to get a complete list of help topics.

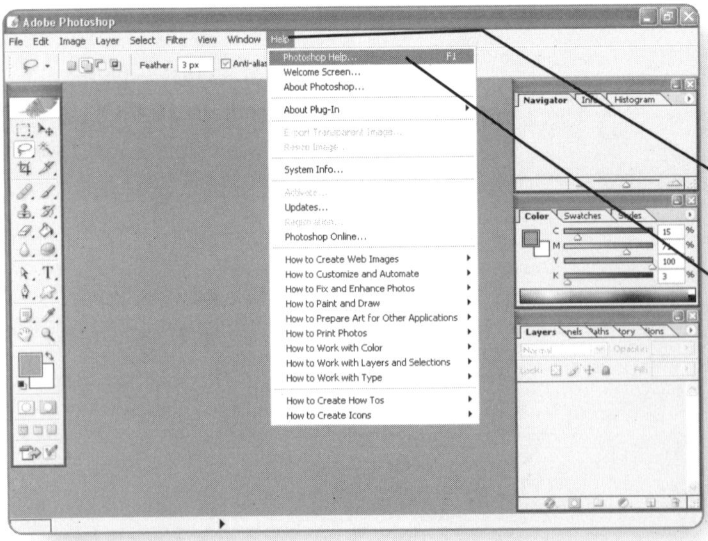

1. **Click** on **Help**. The Help menu will appear.

2. **Click** on **Photoshop Help**. Your Internet browser program will launch with the Adobe help file.

3. **Click** on **Index**. An alphabetical list of all of the help files will appear.

4. **Click** on a **letter** to jump to topics that begin with that letter.

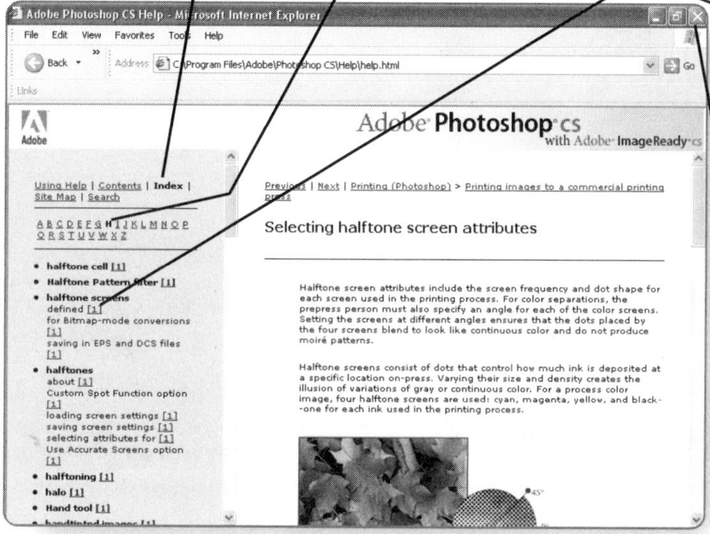

5. **Click** on the **number** beside the help topic you would like to view. The topic will appear in the window. Topics with multiple numbers beside them indicate that more than one help option is available.

6. **Click** on the **close button** in the upper-right corner to close the window and return to Photoshop.

Searching for Help

Rather than having to sort through the index to find help, you can search for particular topics. In your search, you can either use keywords or ask a question.

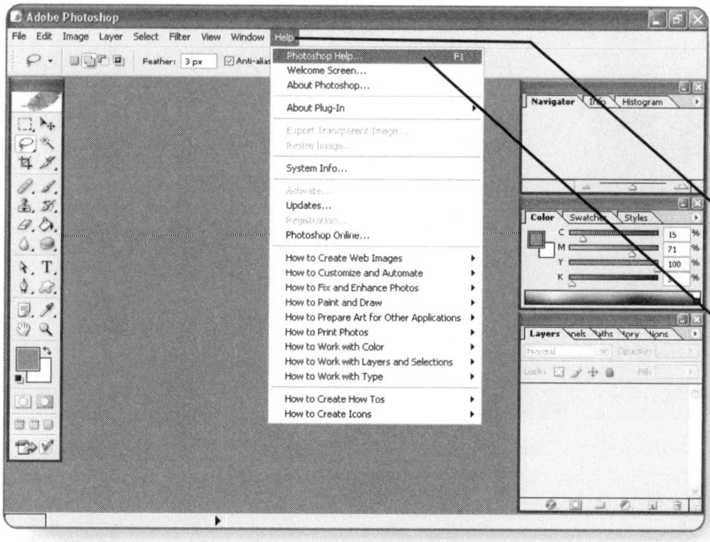

1. **Click** on **Help**. The Help menu will appear.

2. **Click** on **Photoshop Help**. Your Internet browser program will launch with the Adobe help file.

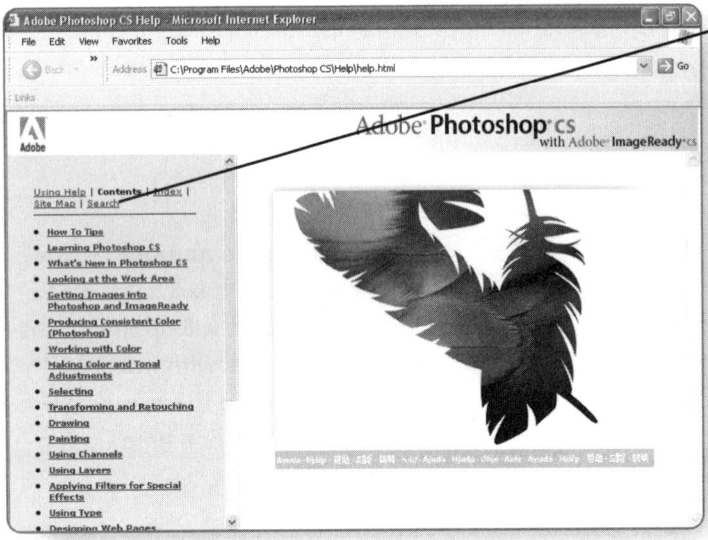

3. **Click** on **Search**. A text box will appear where you can enter your search.

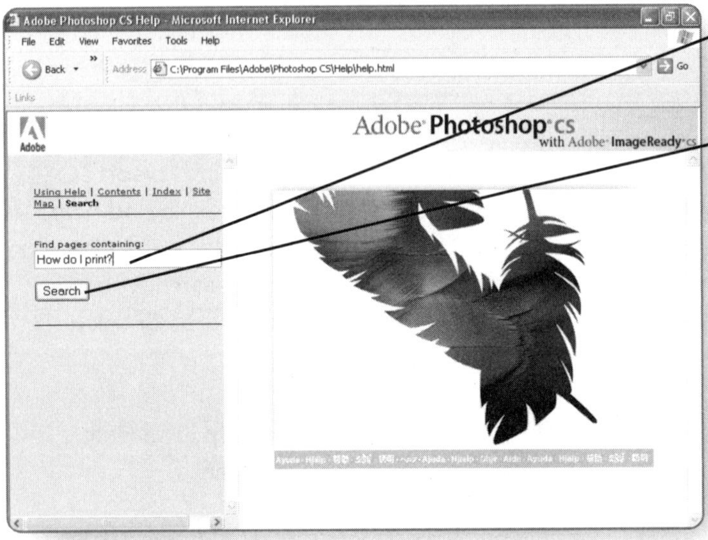

4. **Type** the **keywords** or **question** for your search.

5. **Click** on the **Search button**. The Search will be conducted, and topics matching your search criteria will appear below the search button.

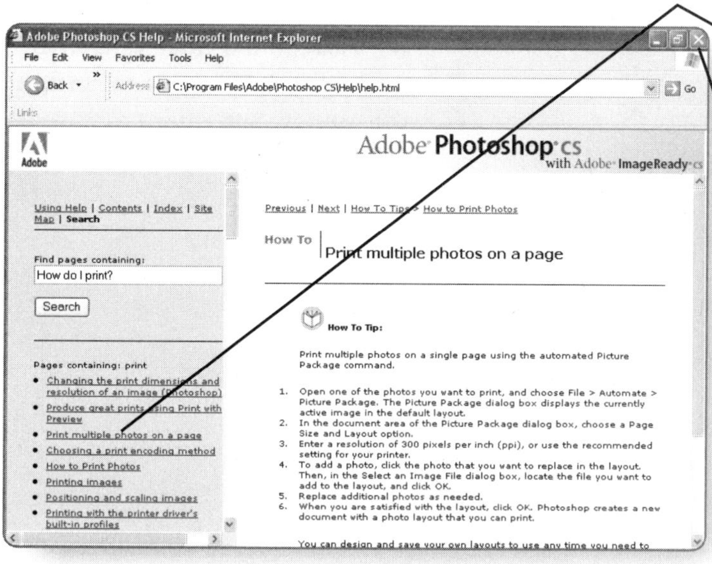

6. **Click** on the desired **topic**. Its contents will appear in the window.

7. **Click** on the **close button** in the upper-right corner to close the window and return to Photoshop.

How To's

Within the Help menu, there are a variety of How To options that allow you to jump to certain help topics that cover commonly asked questions. Not only can you access these How To's, you can also create your own.

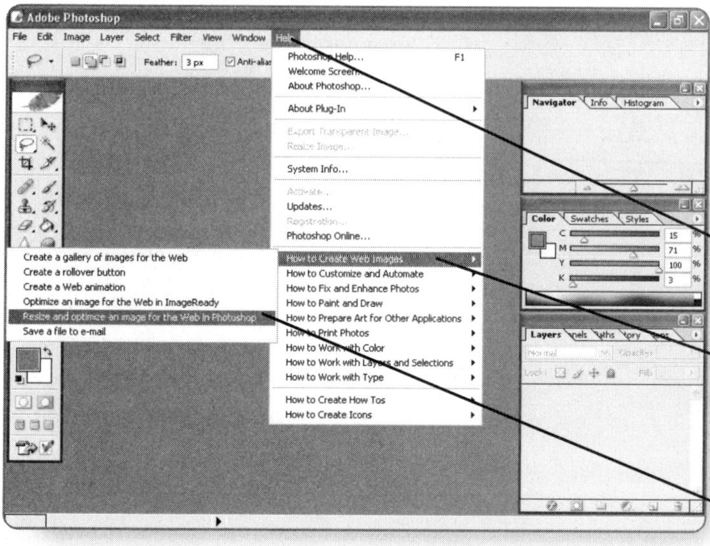

Accessing How To's

Accessing a How To is simply a matter of clicking on the desired category and then selecting the specific help file.

1. **Click** on **Help**. The Help menu will appear.

2. **Point** to the desired **How To category**. A submenu will appear.

3. **Click** on the desired **How To topic**. The help file will launch in your Internet Browser.

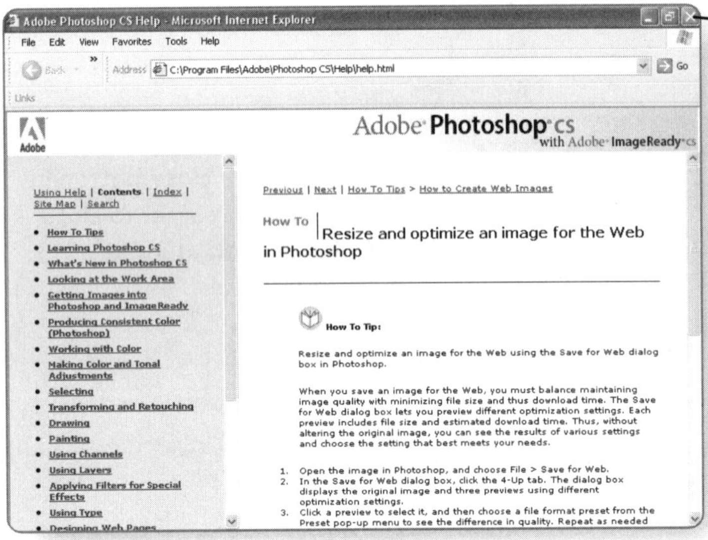

4. Click on the **close button** in the upper-right corner to close the window and return to Photoshop.

Creating How To's

Because the help files in Photoshop CS are HTML files, you can create your own categories and topics of How To's. Because so many resources are available on the Web for Photoshop, you can copy the HTML code from one of these pages and create your own How To. Alternatively, you can have your How To link to a specific Web page.

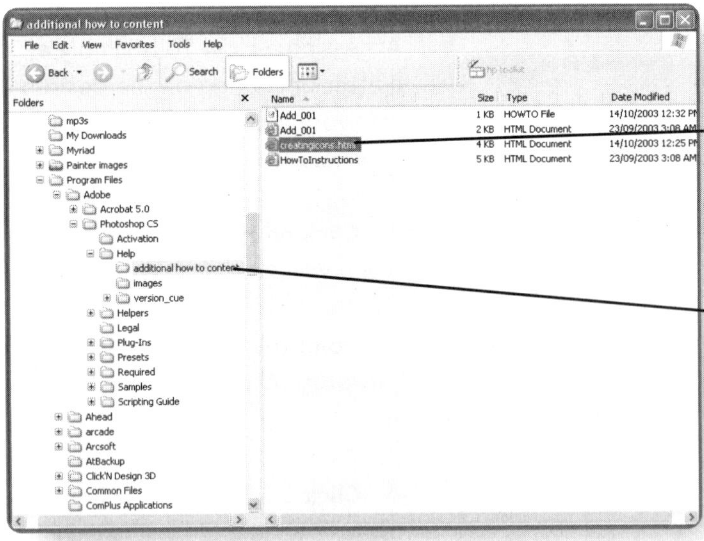

1. Create your **HTML file** by either creating one from scratch or copying it from an existing site.

2. Save your **HTML file** to the folder \PhotoshopCS\Help\Additional How To Content.

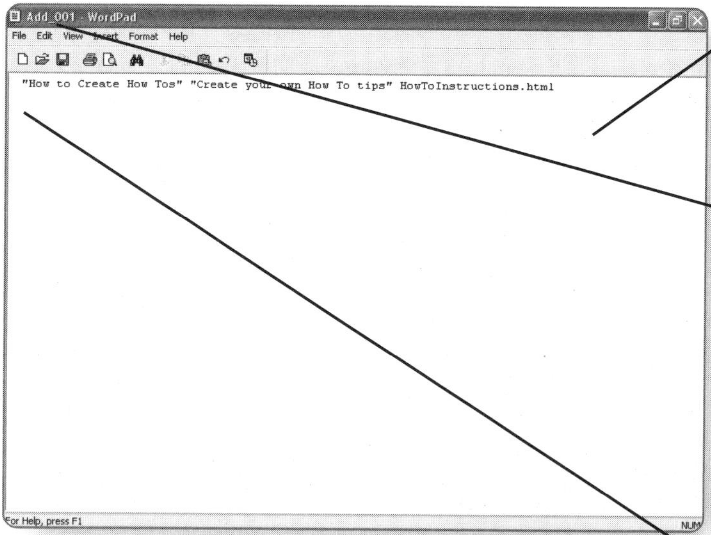

3. Open a **text editor**. You can use any text editor that comes with your computer, including Notepad, Write, or WordPad.

4. Open the file **Add_001.howto** in your text editor. The file can be found in the folder \PhotoshopCS\Help\Additional How To Content\. Depending on the text editor you have selected, there will be different methods for opening the file.

5. Click on a **new line**. The insertion point will be flashing.

6. Type the following, including the quotation marks: **"How To Category" "My How To Topic" myfile.html**. (Replace How To Category with the actual category you would like to create. Replace My How To Topic with the actual topic you'd like to create. Replace myfile.html with the name of the HTML file you saved in step 2.)

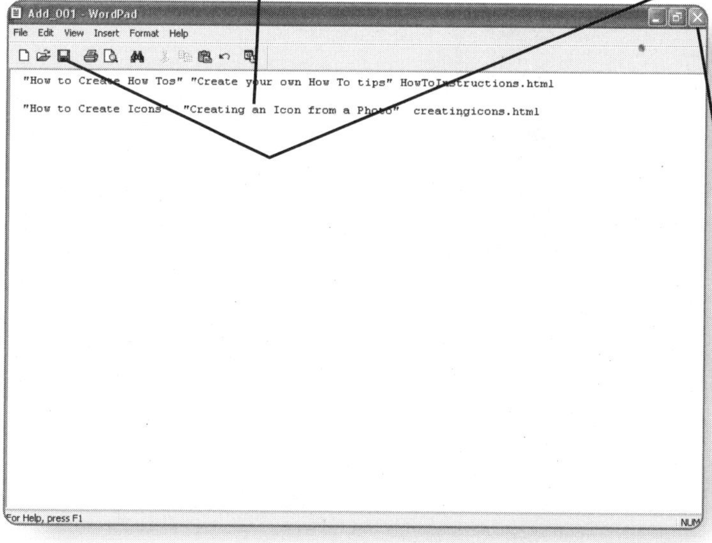

7. Save the **changes** you have made. Depending on the text editor you are using, the methods of saving will differ.

8. Click on the **close button** in the upper-right corner to close the text editor. For Mac OS, click on the red circle in the upper left of the window.

9. **Click** on **Start** at the left end of the Windows Taskbar. The Start menu will appear. If you are using Mac OS, find the Photoshop icon and double-click on it to launch the program.

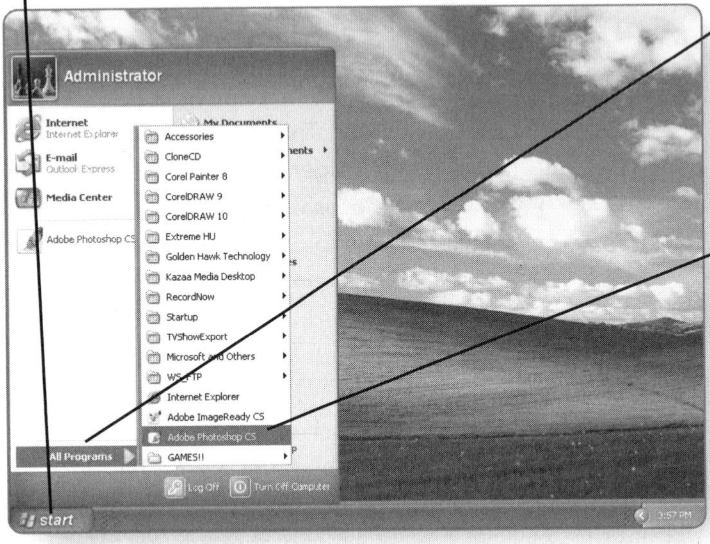

10. Place the mouse pointer over All Programs (or Programs for Windows versions prior to XP). The Programs menu will appear.

11. **Click** on **Adobe Photoshop CS**. The new Photoshop CS Welcome Screen will appear.

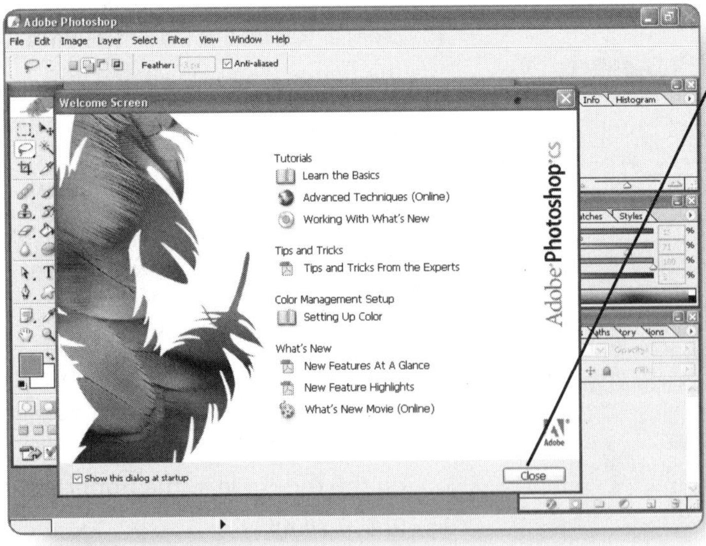

12. **Click** on **Close**. The Welcome Screen will close.

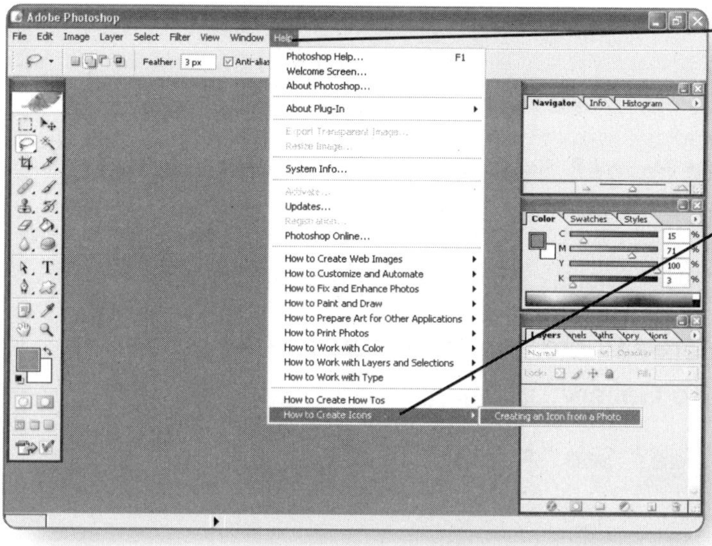

13. **Click** on **Help**. The Help menu will appear, and the category you created will appear at the bottom of the list.

14. **Point** to the **category** you created. The topic you created for this category will appear.

Part VI Review Questions

1. How do you save a .jpeg image? See "Saving a JPEG" in Chapter 20.
2. What is a WBMP file? See "Saving a WBMP" in Chapter 20.
3. What are the steps required to create a photo web gallery. See "Setting Up a Web Photo Gallery" in Chapter 20.
4. How do you slice an image? See "Adding Slices or "Hotspots" in Chapter 21.
5. How do you hide a slice? See "Viewing and Hiding Slices" in Chapter 21.
6. How do you launch a tutorial? See "Using the Welcome Screen Tutorials" in Chapter 22.
7. How do you get help with color management? See "Color Management Help" in Chapter 22.
8. Other than the Welcome Screen, what is another way to access help in Photoshop? See "Accessing Help" in Chapter 23.
9. What is the result of clicking on a letter in the Help index? See "The Help Index" in Chapter 22.
10. How do you create your own How To's? See "Creating How To's" in Chapter 22.

Index

A

B

C

T

Adobe® Photoshop® CS

fast&easy®

Adobe® Photoshop® CS

fast&easy®

Eric Grebler

Premier Press

Publisher: Stacy L. Hiquet

Senior Marketing Manager: Sarah O'Donnell

Marketing Manager: Heather Hurley

Associate Marketing Manager: Kristin Eisenzopf

Manager of Editorial Services: Heather Talbot

Senior Acquisitions Editor: Kevin Harreld

Project Editor: Argosy Publishing

Technical Reviewer: Lisa Bucki

Retail Market Coordinator: Sarah Dubois

Copy Editor: Amy Lepore

Interior Layout: Argosy Publishing

Cover Designer: Mike Tanamachi

Indexer: Larry Sweazy

Proofreader: Heather Moehn

ISBN: 1-59200-345-1

Library of Congress Catalog Card Number: 2003115739

Printed in the United States of America

04 05 06 07 08 BH 10 9 8 7 6 5 4 3 2 1

Premier Press, a division of Course Technology
25 Thomson Place
Boston, MA 02210

Acknowledgments

Putting together a book like this is truly a group effort and thanks must be extended to the entire Premier Press team. In particluar I would like to point out the efforts of Amy Lepore for making up for my lack of spelling and grammar skills and Lisa Bucki for technically editing the book. Thanks also go to Sally Boylan, Stacy Hiquet, and Kevin Harreld for help in bringing this book together.

Who I am today is a result of the upbringing by my parents, Ricky and Victor, and the relationships with my brothers, Oren, Leor, and Ron. I thank them for the giant contribution they have made to my life. Thanks also to my wife Kara for her constant love and devotion and to the rest of my friends and family for the wonderful dynamic they add.

About the Author

Eric Grebler is an IT professional, author, and certified trainer who has demystified the world of computers for thousands of people. Originally from Ottawa, he currently resides in Toronto, Canada. Eric has developed curriculum and resource material on a wide range of technical topics, including desktop publishing, audio sequencing, graphics, XML, and operating systems.

When he's not writing books, Eric moonlights as a general contractor whose attention to detail is matched by no other. His natural talent for carpentry first appeared when he started making stereo boxes, and it continues to this day as he specializes in curved walls, warped wood, and uneven drywall. Eric takes great pride in rarely having used any of his father's best wood.

Contents at a Glance

PART IV
FINE-TUNING YOUR IMAGE. 209

PART V
USING MORE ADVANCED TECHNIQUES. 279

PART VI
PREPPING IMAGES FOR THE WEB. 347

Contents

Introduction

This *Fast & Easy* book from Premier Press will help you understand, use, and explore the world of Adobe Photoshop CS. Photoshop is the industry standard when it comes to digital imaging, and this latest version, called CS (*Creative Suite*), continues the tradition of providing powerful image-manipulation tools. In this latest version, many changes have been made to simplify the user experience, to increase the functionality of different tools, brushes, and effects, and to make publishing to the Web as easy as possible.

Being a suite means that there is more than one program in the box. In addition to Photoshop, the other main program in the suite is ImageReady. ImageReady primarily is designed to help get images ready for the Internet and is not covered in this book.

Obviously, no book can teach you everything there is to know about one topic. The goal of this book is to give you a solid introduction to the world of Photoshop and to teach you how to use most of the different tools it has to offer. Along the way, you'll learn a variety of tips for creating your work faster and some creative tricks to make your artwork stand out.

The battles between good vs. evil, wrong vs. right, Coke vs. Pepsi, and Big Mac vs. Whopper are rivaled only by the age-old debate of PC vs. Mac. To avoid getting in the middle of the conflict, Adobe Photoshop CS rides the fence by being available on both platforms. The program works almost identically on both operating systems, with the exception of keyboard shortcuts. Throughout this book, whenever a keyboard shortcut is mentioned, both the PC and the Mac version of the shortcut is mentioned.

Who Should Read This Book?

If you are ready to explore the world of photo editing and digital art, this book is for you. Whether you are a seasoned veteran of Photoshop or just getting started, this book can be of benefit to you. New users can take advantage of the step-by-step, illustrated instructions of common tasks, while veteran users can use the book as a reference for new tools as well as old ones you might have forgotten.

Some Helpful Hints

In addition to the step-by-step instructions, you'll notice that there are three other elements designed to help you:

TIP

Tips provide quick ways or shortcuts to perform certain tasks.

NOTE

Notes provide additional information or background on a particular topic.

CAUTION

Cautions warn you about a particular step or function that might have some detrimental consequences.

PART I

Getting Started with the Basics

1

Touring the Work Area

Imagine going on a long road trip to a place you've never been before without bothering to bring along a map. In no time, you'd be lost, confused, frustrated, or even angry. The same could be true the first time you use Photoshop. It's a very powerful application for creating, correcting, and enhancing image files, but at the same time, it can be very confusing if you don't know your way around. This first chapter acts as your roadmap by leading you through the basics of navigating the Photoshop work area. You'll learn how to:

- Start and exit Photoshop
- Use the toolbox
- Work with a palette or context menu
- View and hide screen elements

Starting Photoshop

As with other applications, you must start Photoshop to be able to work with its tools and create a new image. Use the following steps to start Photoshop:

1. **Click** on **Start** at the left end of the Windows Taskbar. The Start menu will appear. If you are using Mac OS, find the Photoshop icon and double-click on it to launch the program. You can then skip to Step 4.

2. **Move** the **mouse pointer** to All Programs (or **Programs** for Windows versions prior to XP). The Programs menu will appear.

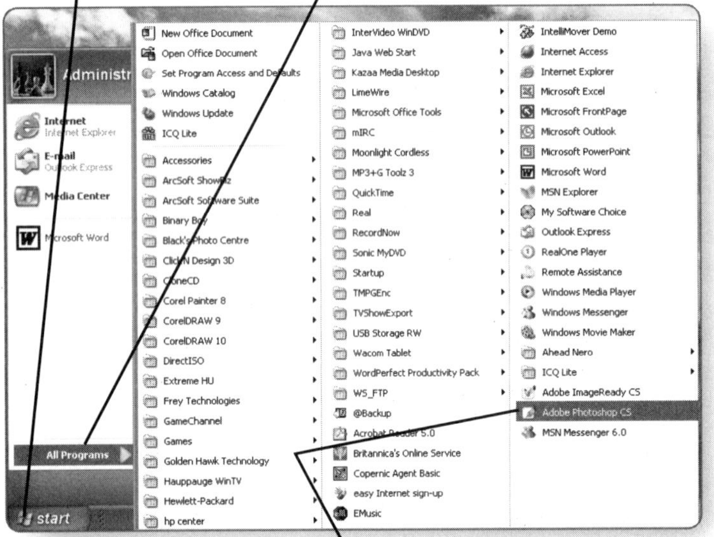

> **TIP**
>
> After you click on Start, you can point to a menu choice with a right-pointing triangle beside it by moving the mouse pointer over it. Pointing will highlight that menu choice and open a submenu. When you see the name of the program you want to start, click on the program name.

3. **Click** on **Adobe Photoshop CS**. The new Photoshop CS Welcome Screen will appear. The Weclome Screen will be covered in detail in Chapter 22, "Getting Help".

4. **Click** on **Close**. The Welcome Screen will close, and the Photoshop CS application window will appear, and you can begin using the program.

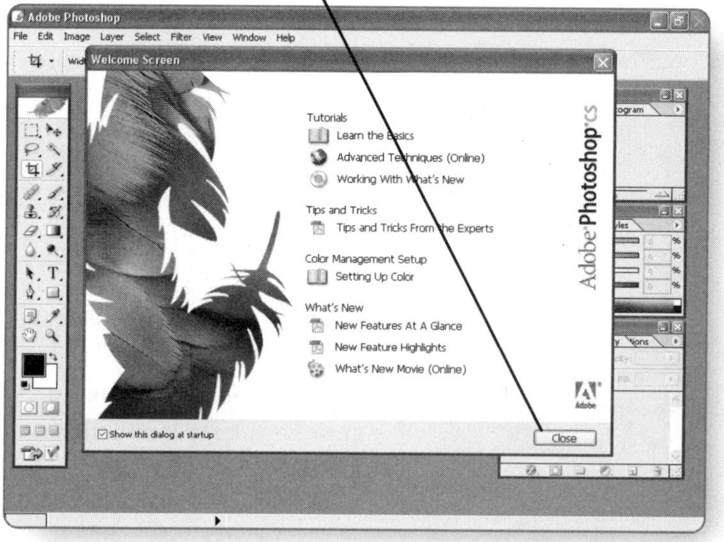

Accessing Photoshop Tools

The work area in Photoshop includes a menu bar like other Windows applications, as well as a few windows that organize the tools you use to do your work. Although later chapters will cover these tools in greater detail, familiarize yourself now with menus and tools and how to use them.

Using Menus

The menus in Photoshop work the same as in most other applications.

1. **Click** on a **menu name**. The menu will open.

2. **Click** on a **command**. The result will differ depending on the nature of the command on which you clicked:

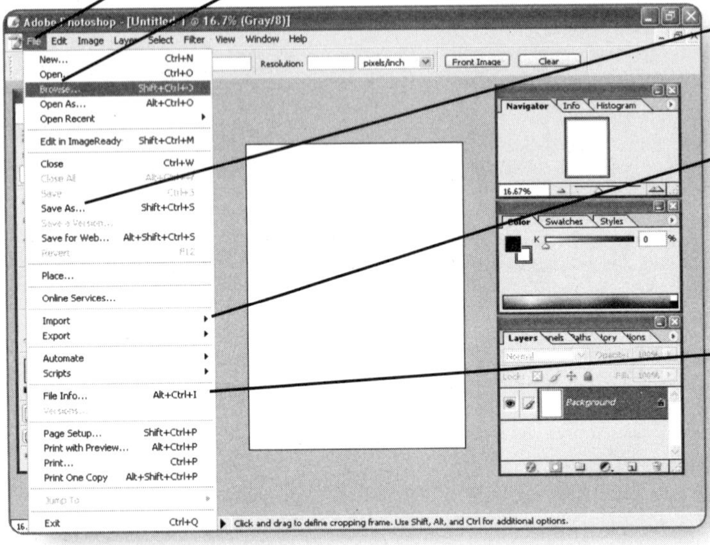

- If the command name is followed by an ellipsis (...), a dialog box will open.
- If the command name has a triangle beside it, a submenu will appear. You can then click on a command in the submenu.
- If the command name has a set of keystroke instructions beside it, this keystroke combination can be used to execute the command at any time.

> **NOTE**
>
> You can't use the various Photoshop tools until you create or open a new file. Chapter 2, "Working with Image Files," explains how to create new files in Photoshop. The illustrations here include a blank file strictly as an example.

Using Dialog Boxes

Dialog boxes are mini windows that allow you to provide Photoshop with information for a particular task.

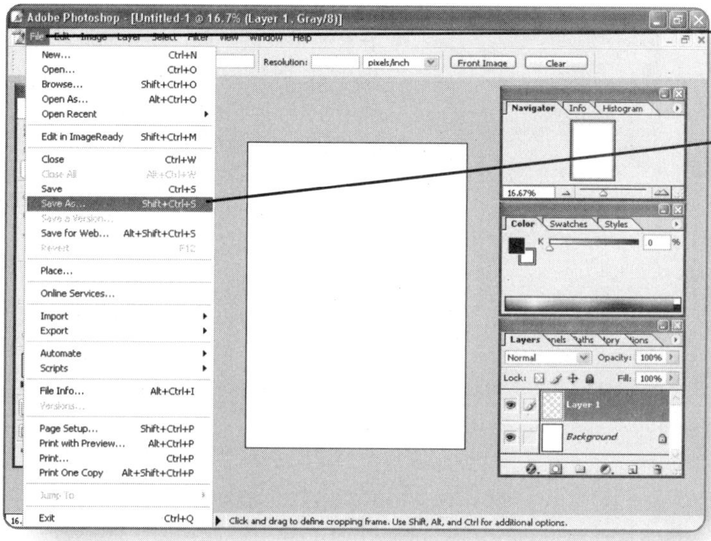

1. Click on a **menu name**. The menu will open.

2. Click on a **command** that has three dots beside it. A dialog box will open.

3. Make selections in the dialog box. Typical dialog box choices include the following:

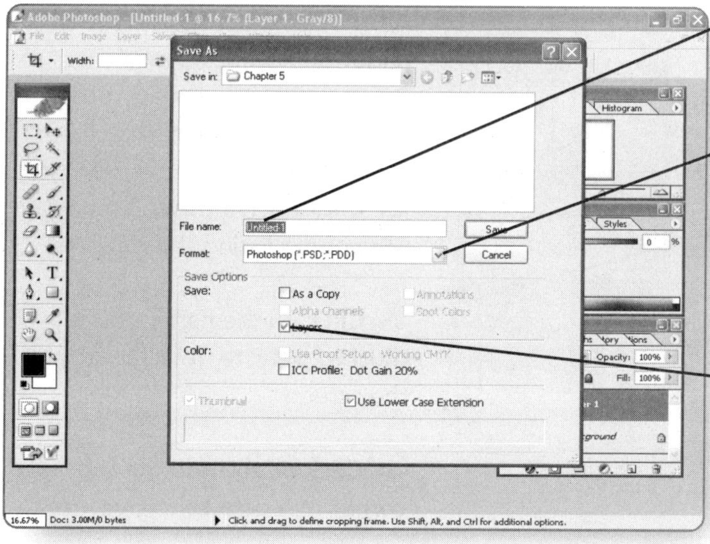

- **Text box.** Drag over a text box entry to select it and then type a new entry.
- **Drop-down list box.** Click on the down arrow or scroll arrow to open a drop-down list or to scroll through a list's choices. Then click on the list item you want.
- **Check box.** Click on a check box to select (check) or deselect (uncheck) it.

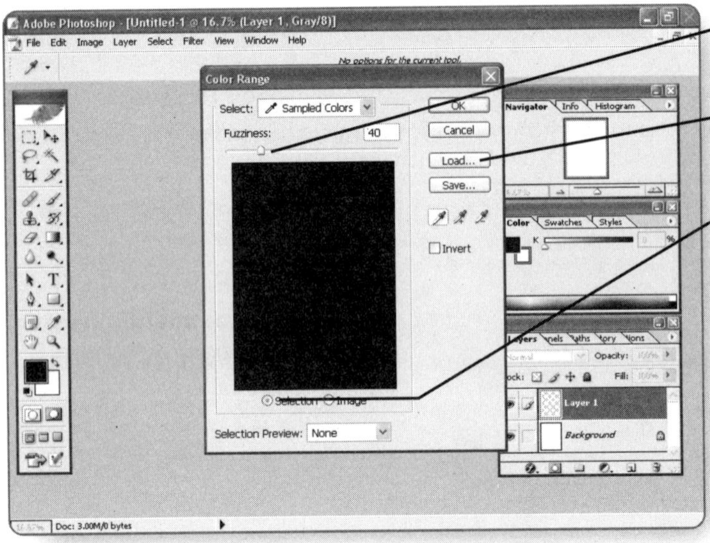

- **Slider.** Drag a slider to choose another setting.
- **Command button.** Click on a command button to choose it.
- **Option button.** Click on an option button to choose it and deselect other option buttons in the group.

Palettes

Palettes are floating windows that can be opened and closed as needed and repositioned anywhere on the screen. They provide additional tools and settings for your projects.

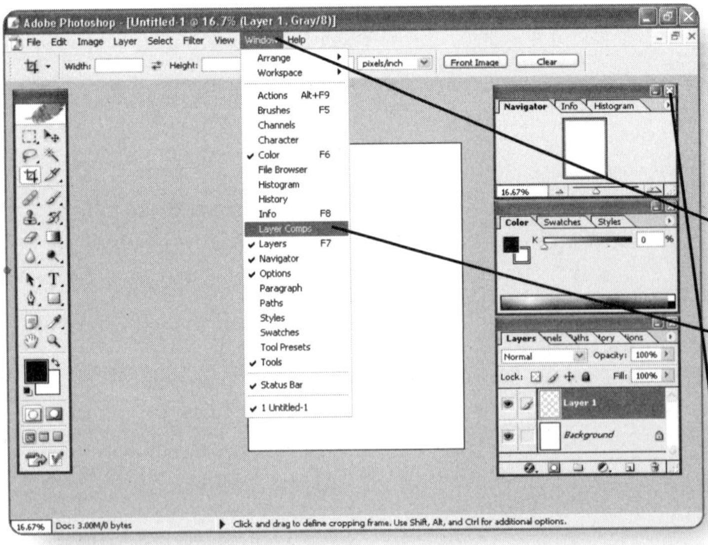

Selecting Palettes

A list of palettes can be found under the Windows menu. Palettes that are already open have a check mark beside them.

1. **Click** on **Window**. A menu will appear listing the palettes.
2. **Click** on the name of the **desired palette**. It will open on the screen.
3. **Click** on the **x** in the top right corner of a palette to close it.

Moving Palettes

If you have a number of palettes open on your page, you may want to move them to avoid potential clutter on your screen.

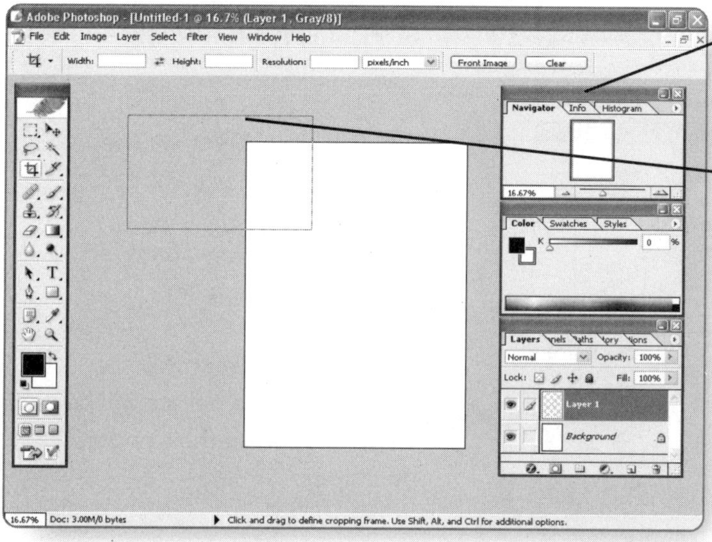

1. **Position** your **mouse pointer** over the **title bar** of the palette you would like to move.
2. **Drag** the **palette** to the desired new location. As you drag, an outline of the palette will appear to indicate its location.

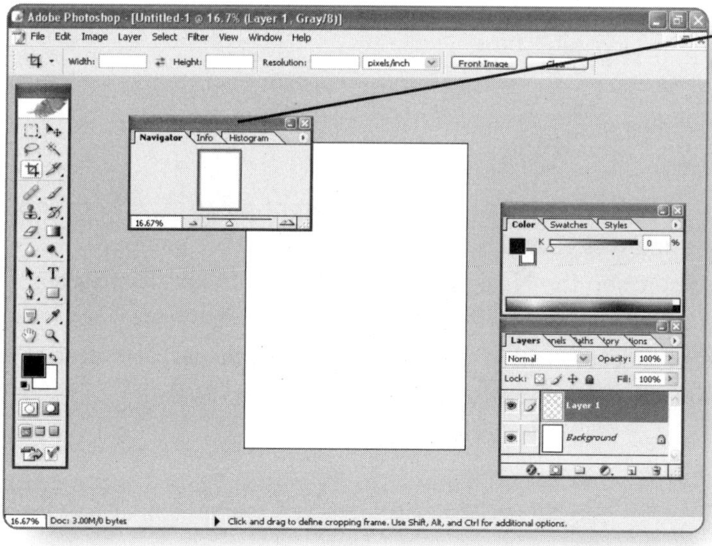

3. **Release** the **mouse button**. The palette will be in its new location.

Resetting Palettes

So you've gone and made a mess of things. Palettes are strewn all over the place, and some have inadvertently been deleted. There's no need to panic, however, because with a few clicks of the mouse button you can reset the palettes to their default look.

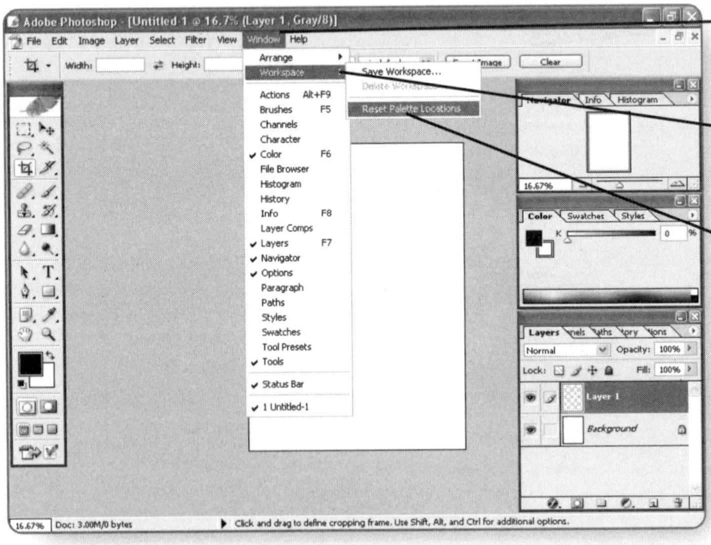

1. **Click** on **Window**. The Window menu will appear.
2. **Click** on **Workspace**. A submenu will appear.
3. **Click** on **Reset Palette Locations**. The pallets will be repositioned to their original locations.

Using Palettes

Rather than having several dozen different palettes, Photoshop groups palettes to make them easier to use. For example, when you open the Navigator palette, the Info and Histogram palettes will also be available. You not only can select from different palettes within a palette window, you can also access a variety of menus and tools.

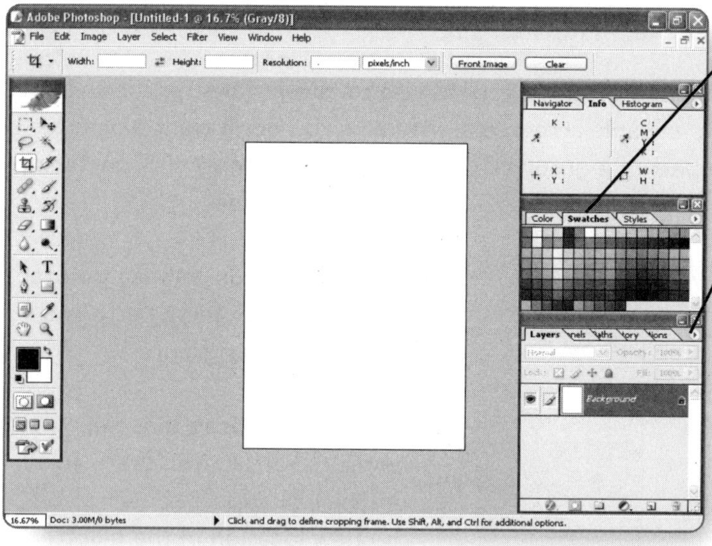

1. Click on the **tab** of the palette you would like to open. The palette will appear in front of all others in that group.

2. Click on the Display palette menu button in the top right corner of the palette. A menu will appear with different options.

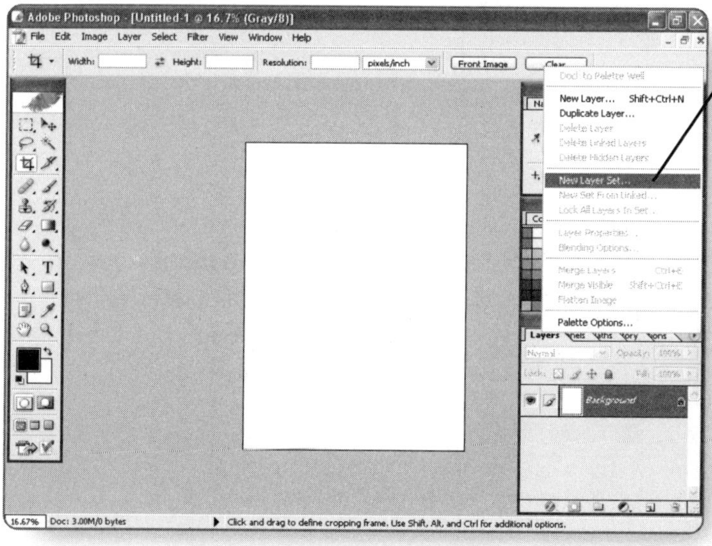

3. Click on the **desired option**. The command will be executed.

Ungrouping Palettes

Palettes are grouped together in small windows for the sake of saving valuable screen real estate. If you don't want a palette to be part of a group of palettes, you can simply click and drag it out of the group to have it appear on its own.

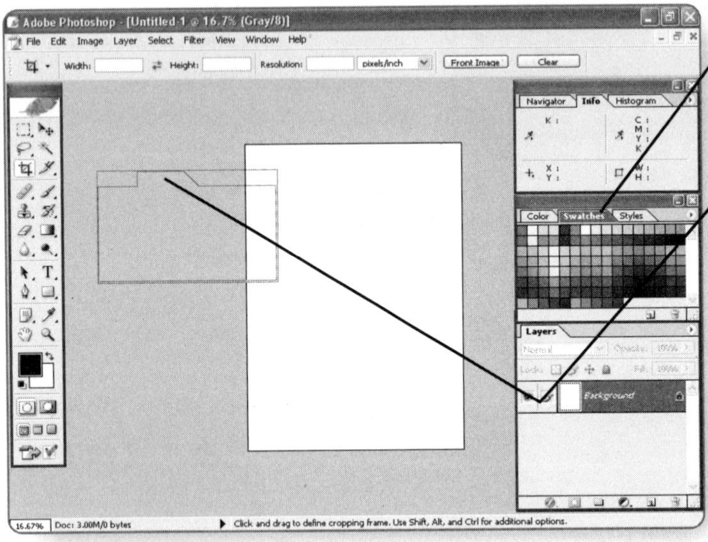

1. **Position** your **mouse pointer** over the **tab** of the palette you would like to ungroup.

2. **Click** and **drag** that **tab** to a new location. As you drag, an outline will appear showing you the new location of the palette.

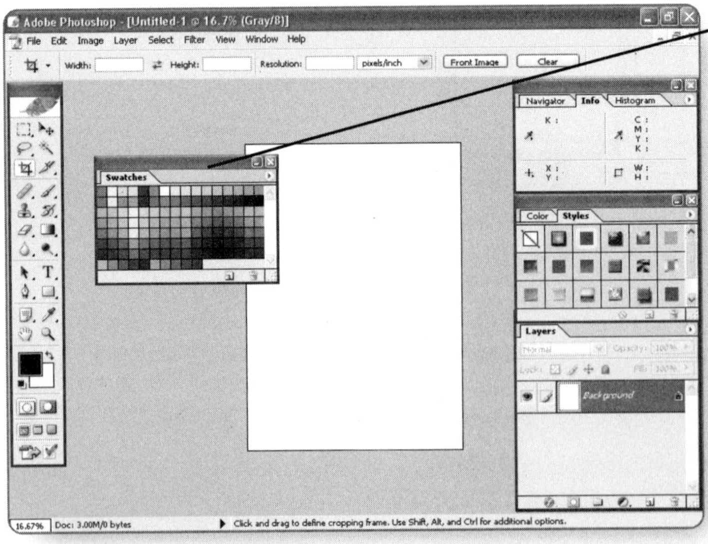

3. **Release** the **mouse** button. The palette will no longer be part of that group.

The Toolbox

The toolbox provides a central location for the equipment needed to get most of your work done in Photoshop. The toolbox contains many of the tools you will be using while editing your image files.

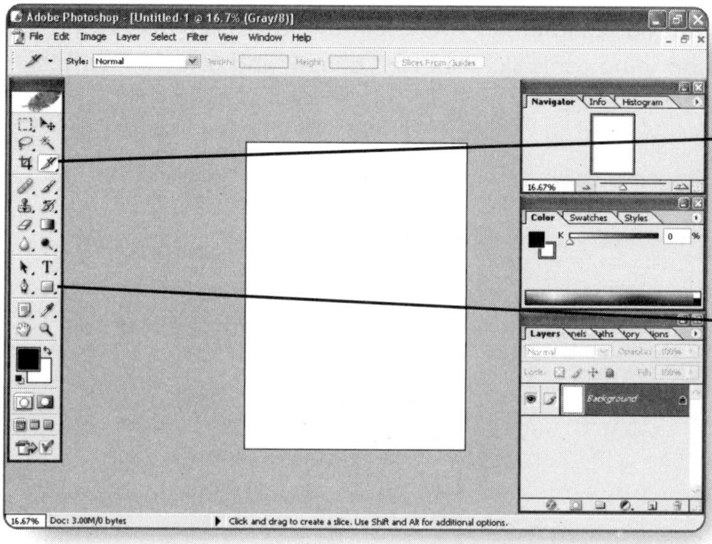

1. **Click** on a **toolbox button**. The button will appear highlighted to indicate that it is selected.

2. **Click** and **hold** on any **button** with a triangle on it. The triangle indicates that there are more tools in that location than can currently be seen. A list of tools will appear.

3. **Click** on the **desired tool**. It will be selected.

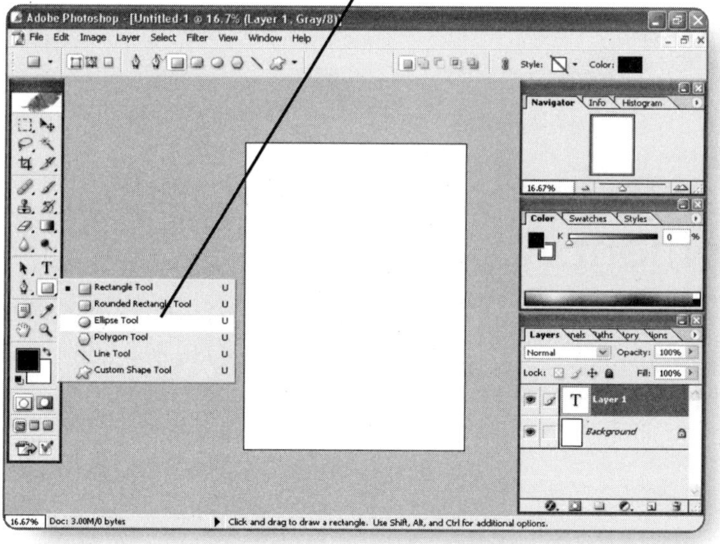

> **NOTE**
>
> If you have certain toolbox tools selected when you right-click on the image, a pop-up palette of settings for the tool appears instead. You'll learn more about using a palette like this in Chapter 3, "Adding Content with Tools."

The Options Bar

Rather than having to search around for different tools, the context-sensitive Options bar allows you to select corresponding elements to the particular tool you have selected. For example, if you select the Text tool, corresponding tools like font size, shape, and color will appear in the Options bar.

1. **Click** on a **tool** in the toolbox. It will be selected.

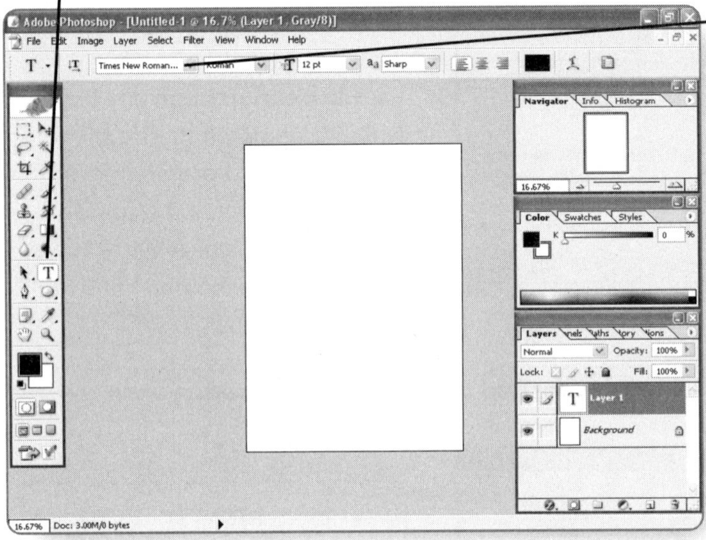

2. **Review** the **options** in the Options bar. They will change to correspond with the tool you have selected.

Hiding and Showing Screen Elements

Most of the elements on your screen can be found under the Window menu. Using that menu, not only can you open and close palettes, you can also show and hide other screen elements including toolbars.

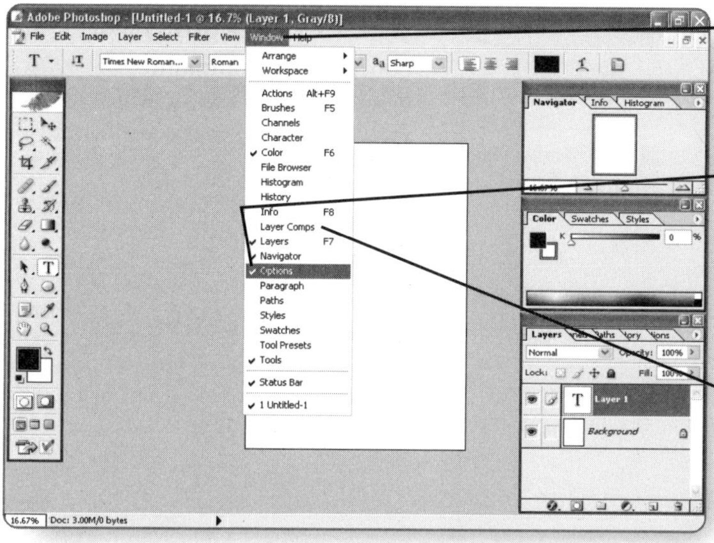

1. **Click** on **Window**. A menu will appear listing the screen elements.

2. **Click** on the **desired palette** or **toolbar**. It will open on the screen. Elements with a check mark beside them are already open.

3. **Repeat Steps 1** and **2** to remove a screen element.

Keyboard Shortcuts

Keyboard shortcuts are commands you can execute from your keyboard rather than having to use menus or dialog boxes. Photoshop has assigned a variety of keyboard shortcuts to various tasks within the program. New to Photoshop CS is the capability to customize any and all of these keyboard shortcuts.

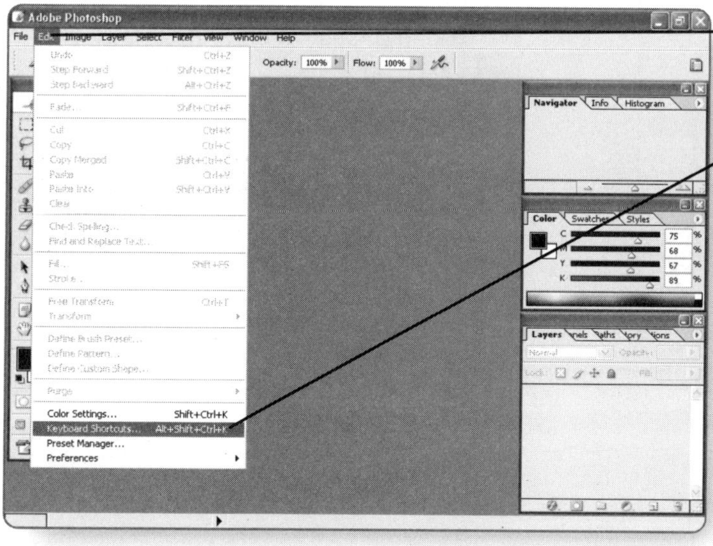

1. **Click** on **Edit**. The Edit menu will appear.

2. **Click** on **Keyboard Shortcuts**. A dialog box will open, allowing you to customize your keyboard shortcuts.

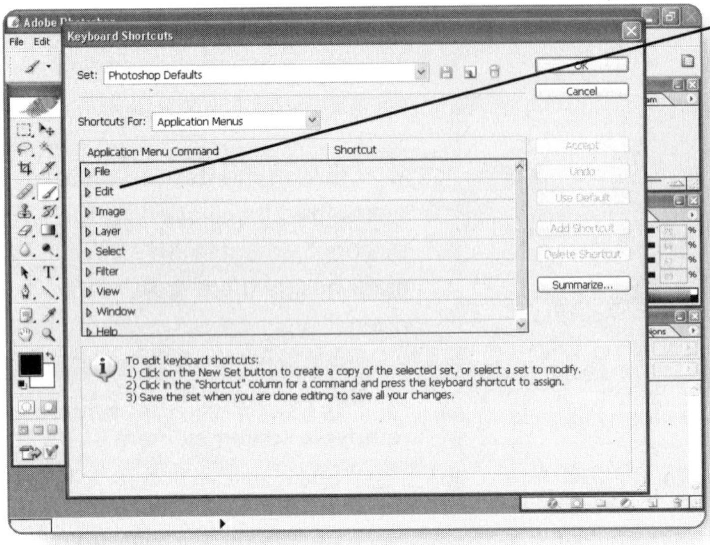

3. **Click** on the **group** that contains the command you would like to modify. A list of the commands that fall within that group will appear.

4. **Click** on the **desired command**. It will be selected, and the keyboard shortcut for that command will appear highlighted.

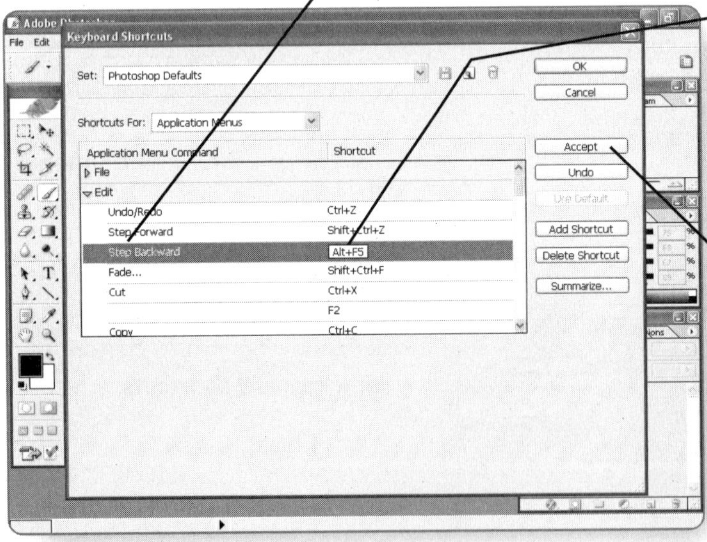

5. **Type** a **new keyboard shortcut**. For example, if you want the new shortcut to be Alt+5, hold down the Alt key and the 5 key at the same time. The new shortcut will appear.

6. **Click** on **Accept**. The keyboard shortcut for that command will be selected.

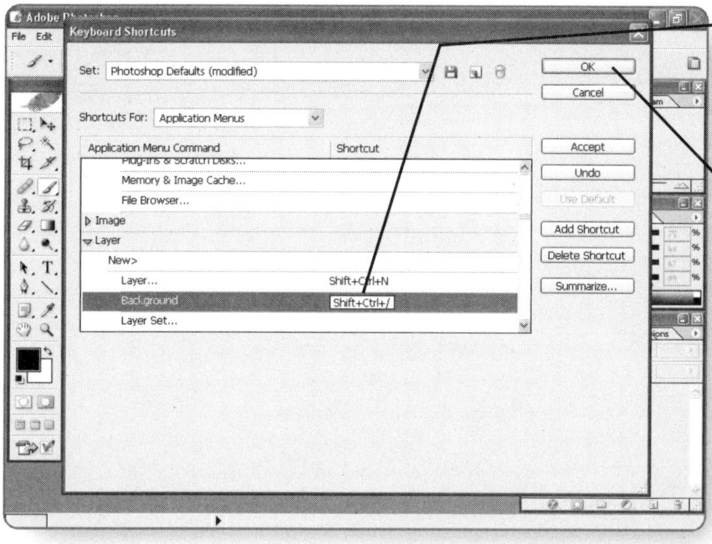

7. **Repeat Steps 3** to **6** for any other commands to which you would like to assign new keyboard shortcuts.

8. **Click** on **OK**. Your changes will be accepted.

Exiting Photoshop

When you finish working in Photoshop or want to shut down your system altogether, you need to exit the Photoshop program. It takes just a few brief steps, as detailed here.

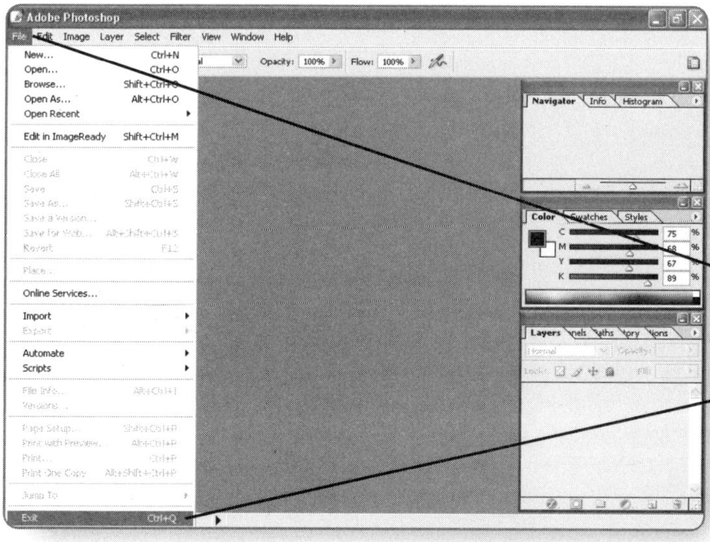

1. **Save** the currently open **file**. Photoshop will preserve the latest changes to the file. The "Saving a File" section in Chapter 2 will explain how to save a file.

2. **Click** on **File**. The File menu will open.

3. **Click** on **Exit**. The Photoshop application window will close.

2

Working with Image Files

Everything that you do in Photoshop is done to an image file. You can either use an existing image file or create one from scratch. Photoshop gives you a variety of methods to open, create, or import images so that they can be further manipulated. In this chapter, you'll learn how to:

- Create a new image file
- Open a file
- Import a scanner or digital camera image
- Add file info
- Save and close a file
- Use the enhanced File Browser
- Save your workspace

Creating a New File

In some cases, you may want to start the creative process with a blank canvas—a new, blank image file. Photoshop doesn't open a blank file by default when you start the program, so you must do it manually. When you create a new file in Photoshop, you can specify the file size, whether it includes a background color, and more.

1. **Click** on **File**. The File menu will appear.

2. **Click** on **New**. The New dialog box will open.

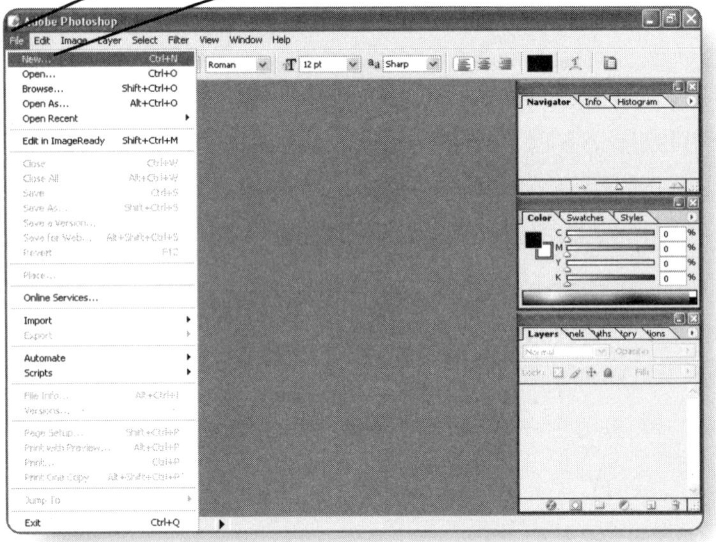

3. **Type** a **name** for your file in the Name text box.

4. **Set** the **image settings** in the Preset box as follows:

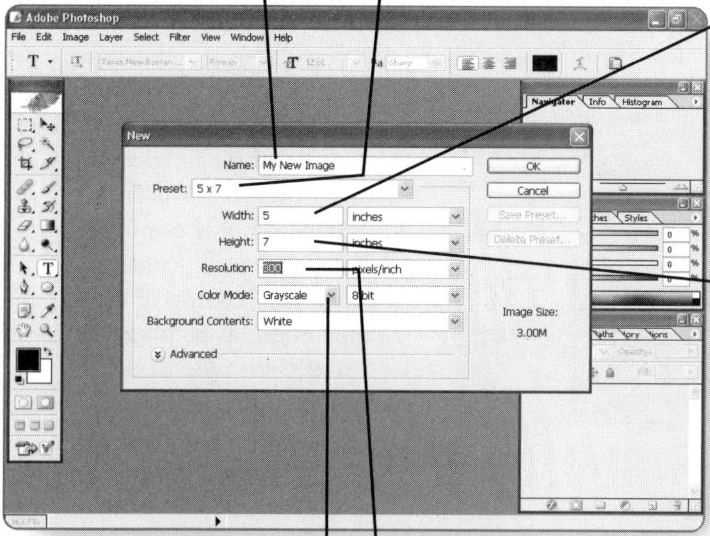

- Double-click on the Width text box contents and type a new image width value. If necessary, click on the down arrow for the unit list and then select another measurement unit.
- Double-click on the Height text box contents and type a new image height value. If necessary, click on the down arrow for the unit list and select another measurement unit.
- Double-click on the Resolution text box contents and type a new resolution value. If necessary, click on the down arrow for the unit list and select another resolution unit.
- Click on the down arrow for the Color Mode list and then click on the color mode to use.

TIP

Rather than specifying image dimensions, you can opt to choose a predefined image size from the Preset drop-down list.

5. **Click** on the down arrow beside the **Background Contents box option**. A list of options will appear.

6. Click on the desired option. The options work as follows:

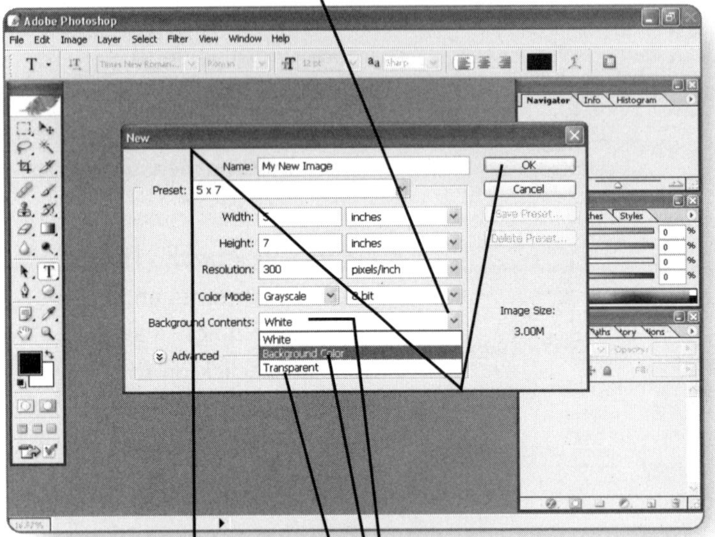

> ### NOTE
> Resolution refers to the number of pixels (dots) printed per measurement unit (commonly per inch). The color mode controls how many colors define the image, as required by a particular type of display and output. See Chapter 15, "Understanding Colors and Channels," to learn more about color modes.

- **White.** Fills the image with a default white background.
- **Background Color.** Fills the image with the background color currently selected in the Photoshop toolbox.
- **Transparent.** Gives the image a transparent background so that, when you use the image in a document or Web page, the page background and page elements can show through the image file.

7. **Click** on **OK**. The New dialog box will close, and the new image file will open onscreen.

Opening an Existing File

If you've already saved an image file, you can reopen it at any time to make changes and improvements. You can open not only images that have been created in Photoshop, but almost any other type of image file.

1. **Click** on **File**. The File menu will appear.

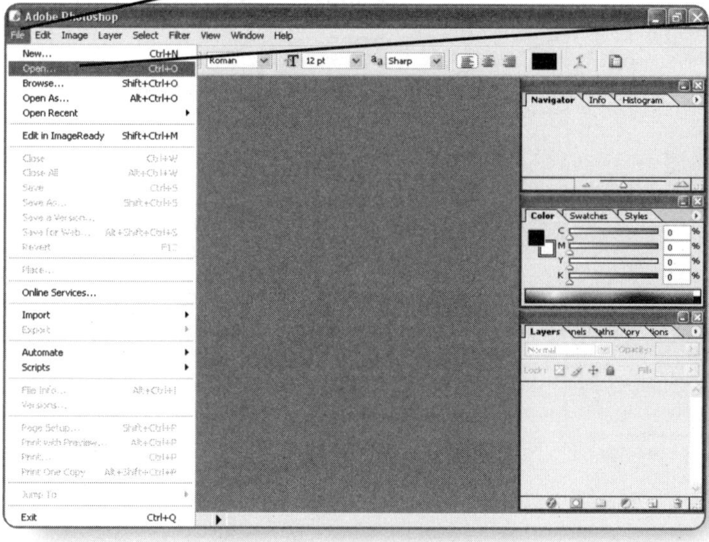

2. **Click** on **Open**. The Open dialog box will open.

> **TIP**
>
> To open a file you've used recently, click on the File menu, drag the mouse pointer down to the Open Recent command, and then click on the name of the file you want to open in the submenu that appears.

3. **Navigate** to the **file location**. The desired file will be displayed in the file list. You may need to do one or more of the following to locate the file:

- Click on the down arrow to the right of the Look In list, then click on the icon for the disk that holds the file.

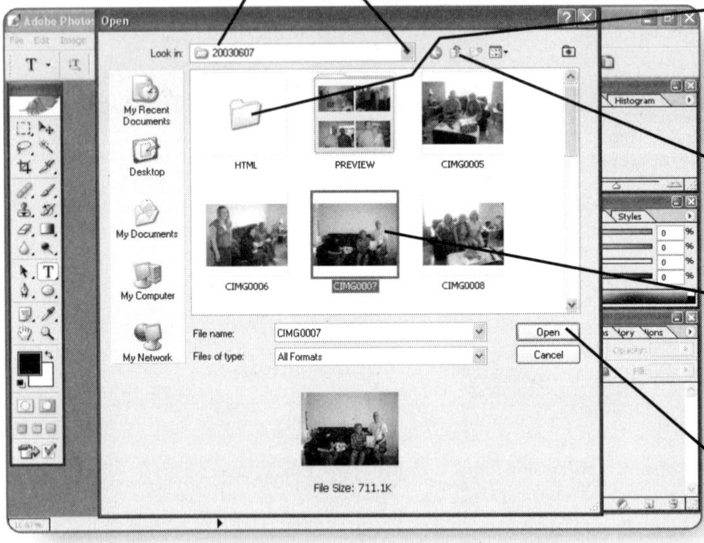

- Double-click on folder icons in the list to navigate to the folder that holds the file to open.
- Click on Up One Level to return to a folder that's one level higher.

4. **Click** on the **file** you want to open. A preview of the file will appear at the bottom of the Open dialog box.

5. **Click** on **Open**. The file will appear onscreen.

Opening and Accessing Multiple Files

You can have a variety of images open at any given time in Photoshop. You can open additional files all at once or one by one. Once you have multiple images open, you can toggle between them during the editing process.

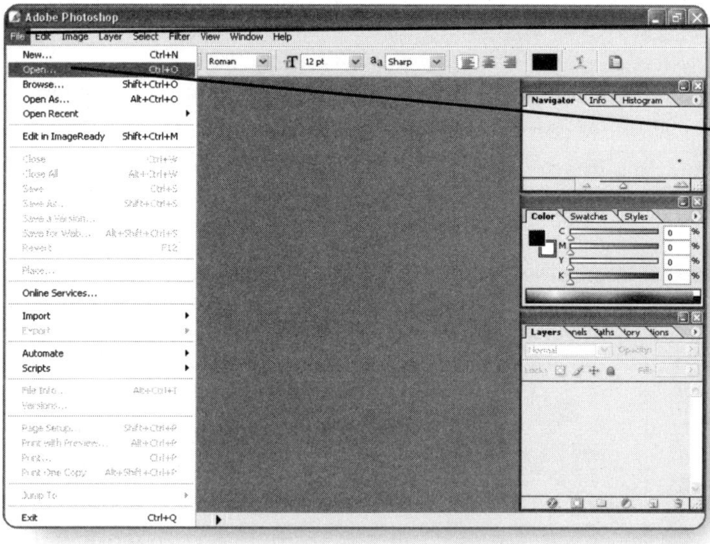

1. Click on **File**. The File menu will appear.

2. Click on **Open**. The Open dialog box will open.

3. Click on one of the **files** you would like to open. It will be highlighted.

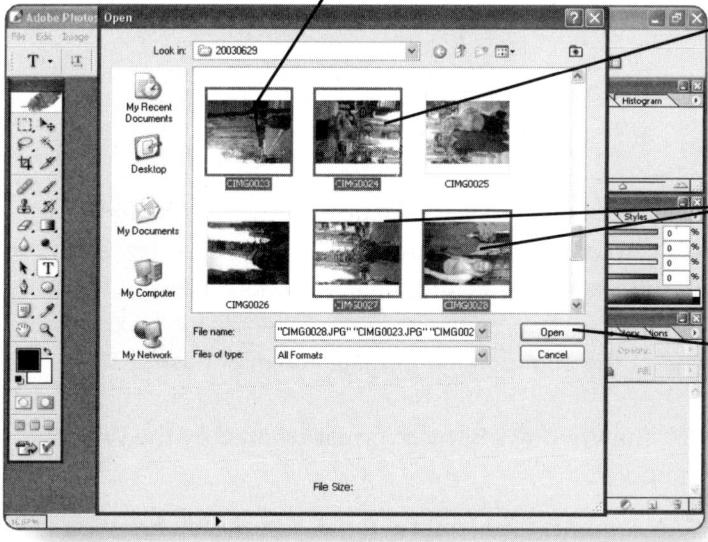

4. Hold down the **Ctrl** key (**Command** key for Mac OS) and **click** another file you would like to open.

5. Repeat step **4** until you have selected all of the files you would like to open.

6. Click on **Open**. All of the files you selected will now open in Photoshop.

Accessing Files

To toggle back and forth between your open images, you can use the Window command in Photoshop. Although you can have multiple images open at any time, you can only work on them one at a time.

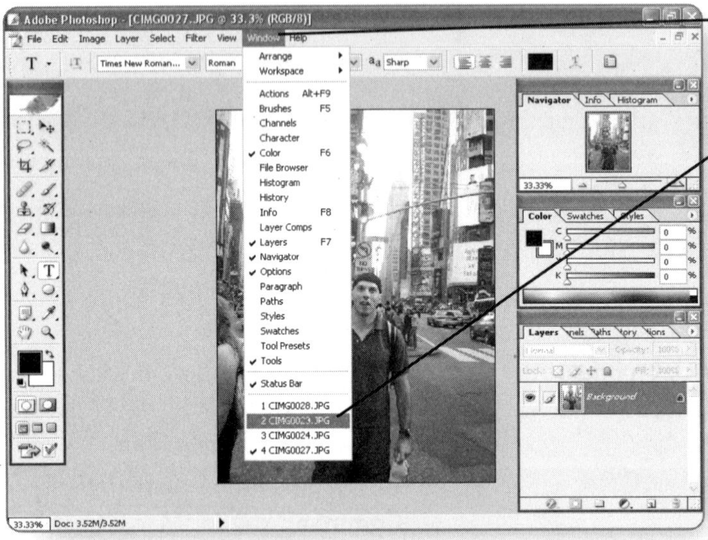

1. **Click** on **Window**. The Window menu will appear.

2. **Click** on the **file name** for the file to display. The file's window moves to the top of other open files and becomes the active image so that you can work with the file.

Using File Formats in Photoshop

Photoshop supports more than a dozen different file formats by default, so chances are you can open an image created in another program by selecting the appropriate file type from the Files of type drop-down list in the Open dialog box. Here are some of the common file formats you might use:

- **.BMP.** The Windows Bitmap format created by the Windows Paint applet.
- **.GIF.** A compact file format often used for Web graphics.
- **.PDF.** The Adobe Acrobat file transfer format. Photoshop CS now supports password protection for .PDF files, so you may be prompted to enter a password when you open a .PDF file.

- **.JPG or JPEG.** Another file format often used for Web graphics.
- **.PCX.** An alternate to the Windows Bitmap format that was originally popularized via the PC Paintbrush program.
- **Photo CD.** A format originally developed by Kodak.
- **PICT.** A Macintosh graphics format.
- **.TIF or TIFF.** A common format for scanned images.
- **.PNG.** Another format for Web graphics.

Importing an Image

You may want to use Photoshop to improve images you generate from another source, such as a scanner or digital camera. Assuming you've installed the Windows software driver that came with the scanner or camera, Photoshop should be able to recognize the device and import images directly from it.

Grabbing a Scanner Image

Impressive scanners costing $300 or less have become widely available. You can use Photoshop to scan hard-copy photos and other graphics for modifications and editing. When you're ready to scan an image, turn on the scanner and position the image on the scanner bed before continuing with the following steps. If you're not sure how to position it correctly, consult the scanner's user manual.

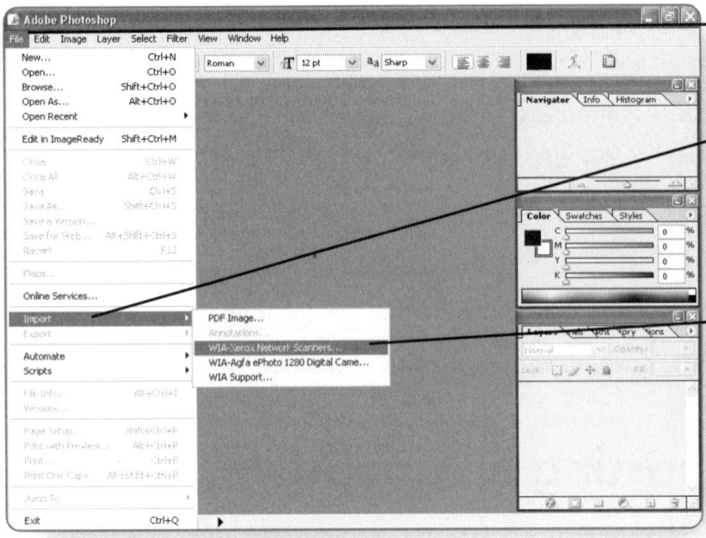

1. Click on **File**. The File menu will appear.

2. Drag the **mouse pointer** down to the Import command. (That is, point to the command.) A submenu will appear.

3. Click on the **name** of your scanner in the submenu. The scanner software (TWAIN or WIA [*Windows Image Acquisition*] software) for your scanner will load.

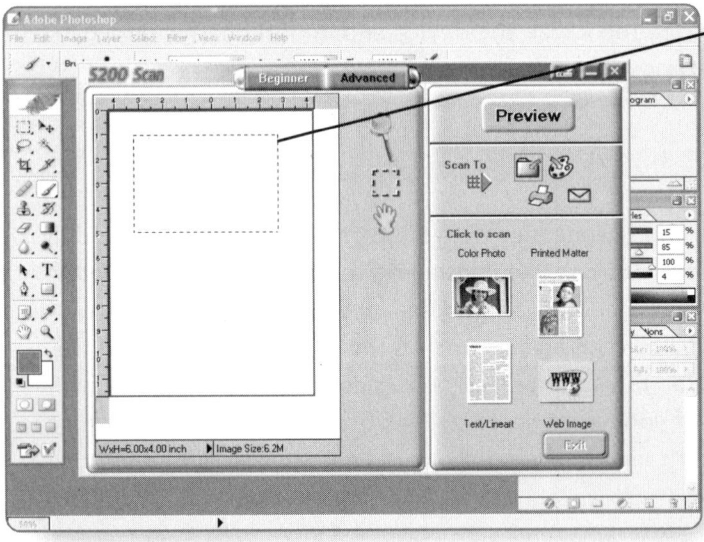

4. Follow the **on-screen instructions** for your scanner. Depending on the type of scanner you have installed, different on-screen options will appear for scanning your image. Once you have finished scanning the image, it will appear in Photoshop and be ready for editing.

Grabbing a Digital Camera Image

My mother recently got a digital camera and can use it like a pro. The reason I mention this is that, if she can work with her digital camera and edit the images in Photoshop, just about anyone else can as well. Digital cameras skip the film and hard-copy stage, storing images digitally directly within the camera. To work with the images, you need to install the camera software, connect the camera to your system via the applicable cable, and place the camera in its playback mode. From there, you use the following procedure to copy images from the camera into Photoshop.

> **NOTE**
>
> Some cameras do not enable you to import images directly into Photoshop. In such cases, an icon for a removable disk representing the camera's removable media appears in the My Computer window, and you can copy the images from that "disk" to the system's hard disk to work with the images.

1. **Click** on **File**. The File menu will appear.

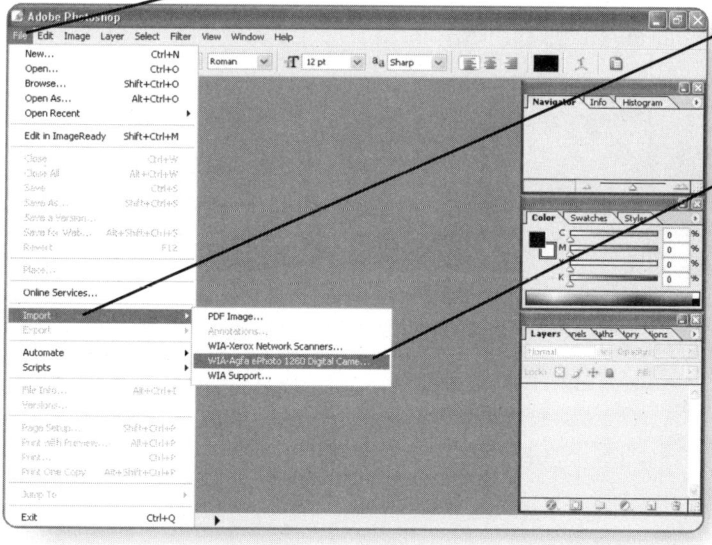

2. **Drag** the **mouse pointer** down to the Import command. A submenu will appear.

3. **Click** on the **name** of your digital camera in the submenu. The software (TWAIN or WIA software) for your camera will load.

4. **Follow** the **on-screen instructions** for your digital camera. Depending on the type of camera, different on-screen

options will appear for scanning your image. Once you have finished scanning the image, it will appear in Photoshop and be ready for editing.

Adding Information

The name of the file alone does not have to be the only way it is identified. You can save special information with an image file to give it a caption, describe its origin, identify who created or shot it, and so on. The information follows professional image identification standards, but even home users may find this information useful in building a digital "photo album."

Embedding Information in the File

Use the following process to store file info for the current file:

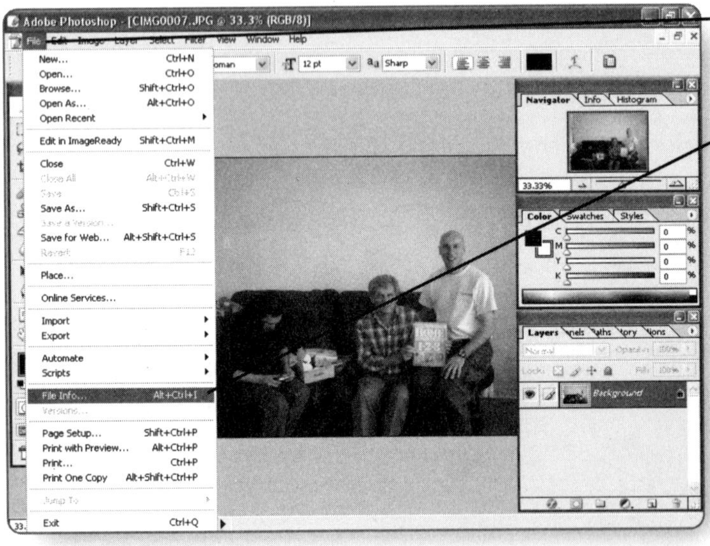

1. Click on **File**. The File menu will appear.

2. Click on **File Info**. The File Info dialog box will open.

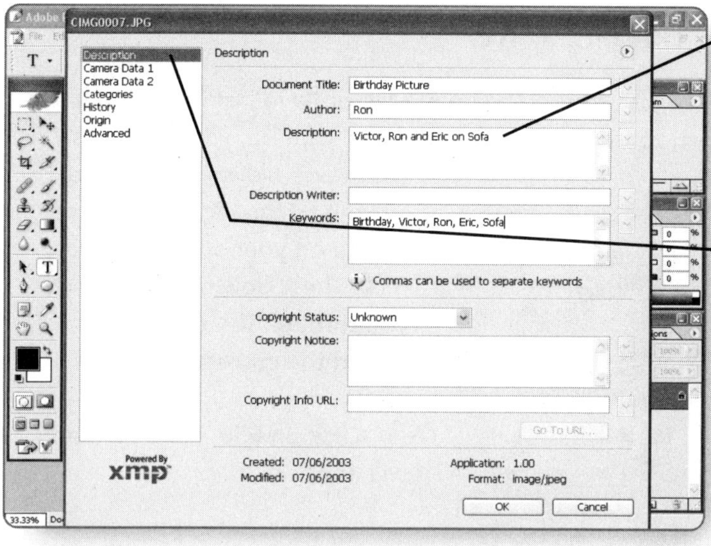

3. Type entries as desired in the text boxes. Of course, you don't have to use all the entries. You can opt to use only those that are relevant to you.

4. Click on a different **category**. A new list of boxes will appear.

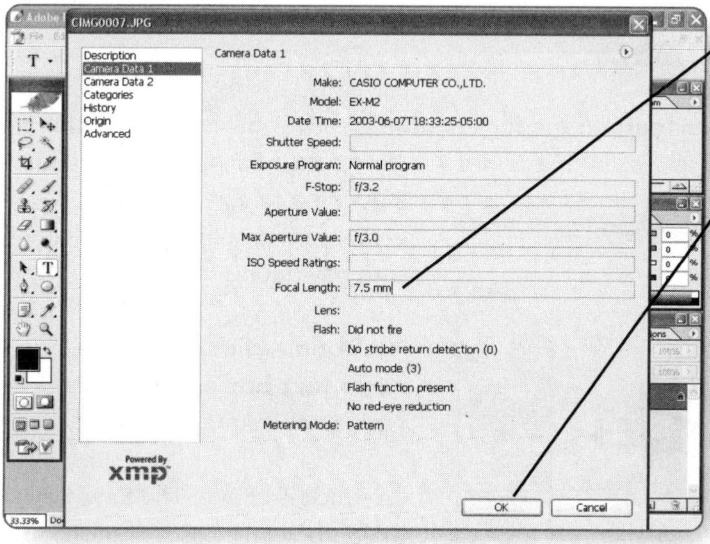

5. Repeat steps **3** and **4** to enter information for other categories of file info.

6. Click on **OK**. The File Info dialog box closes, adding the information to the file.

Saving a File

If you've just created an image file or have just imported it into Photoshop from a scanner or digital camera, you need to save the image file to name it and store it to the location of your choice on your system's hard disk. The following steps lead you through the process for saving the current file:

1. Click on **File**. The File menu will appear.

2. Click on **Save As**. The Save As dialog box will open.

3. Navigate to the **file location** where you want to save the file. The files in that folder will be displayed in the file list. (See "Opening an Existing File" earlier in this chapter for help with navigating folders.)

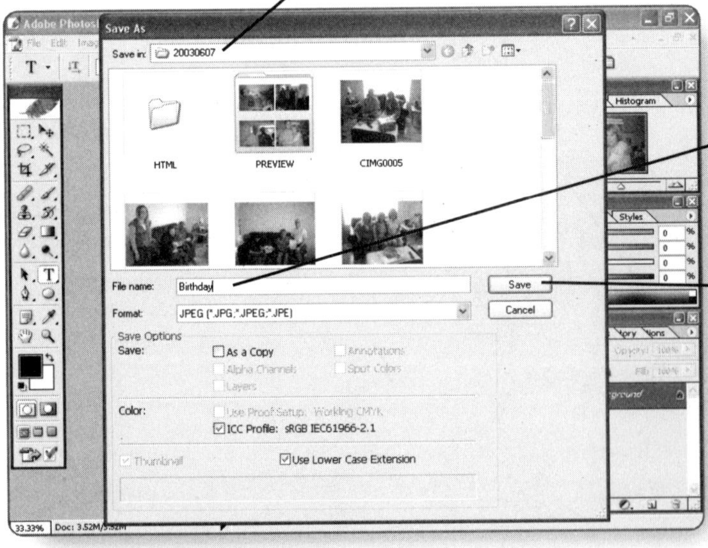

4. Double-click on the **File name text box entry** and then type a new name for the file.

5. Click on **Save**. The Save As dialog box will close. Photoshop saves the file and leaves it open onscreen for further work.

> **NOTE**
>
> If you make changes to the file, be sure to click on File and then click on Save to save your changes. The Save As dialog box will not appear for subsequent saves unless you click Save As rather than Save on the File menu.

Saving to Another Format

By default, Photoshop saves new images in its Photoshop (.PSD or .PDD) format. However, you may need to save an image in another format. For example, you might want to save the file in the Windows Bitmap (.BMP) or Paint (.PCX) format to use the file in a word processor document. Photoshop enables you to save images in more than a dozen formats.

Using Save As

Use the following process to save the current file to one of the available graphics formats. (The Adobe .PDF format will be covered in the next section.)

1. **Click** on **File**. The File menu will appear.

2. **Click** on **Save As**. The Save As dialog box will open.

3. **Navigate** to the **location** where you want to save the file. The files in that folder will be displayed in the file list.

4. **Double-click** on the **File name text box entry**. The name will be selected.

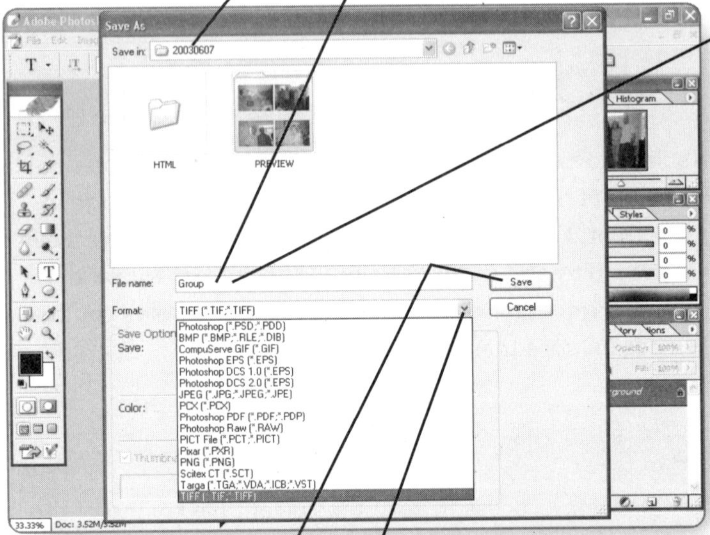

5. **Type** an **alternate name**, if needed, for the converted file. The new name will be displayed.

> **TIP**
>
> To save a copy of the current file (in the same file format) rather than the original, click on the As a Copy check box to place a check in it. Then skip to step 7.

6. **Click** on the **down arrow** for the Format list, then click on the format to use for the converted file in the list. The list will close, and the format will be selected.

7. **Click** on **Save**. The Save As dialog box will close.

8. Set needed **options** if an Options dialog box appears. An Options dialog box appears only for certain types of conversions, and the options vary depending on the conversion format.

9. Click on **OK**. Photoshop converts and saves the file, closing the original file. The converted file remains open in Photoshop for further work.

Saving a Password-Protected .PDF File

PDF (*Portable Document Format*) is one of the most convenient ways to send files to other people electronically. You can password protect your PDF file to prevent others from making changes to the file or from doing certain other things with the file.

1. Click on **File**. The File menu will appear.

2. Click on **Save As**. The Save As dialog box will open.

3. **Navigate** to the **location** where you want to save the file. The files in that folder will be displayed in the file list.

4. **Double-click** on the **File name text box entry**. The name will be selected.

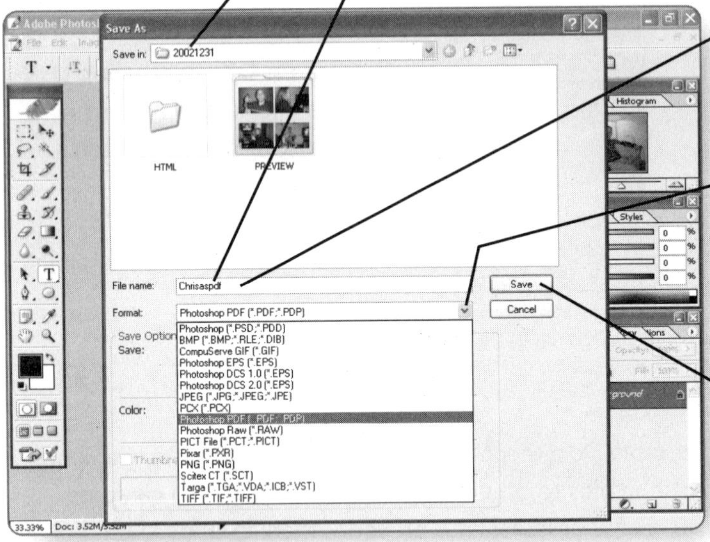

5. **Type** an **alternate name**, if needed, for the converted file. The new name will be displayed.

6. **Click** on the **down arrow** for the Format list and then click on Photoshop PDF. The list will close, and that format will be specified for the converted file.

7. **Click** on **Save**. The Save As dialog box will close, and the PDF Options dialog box will open.

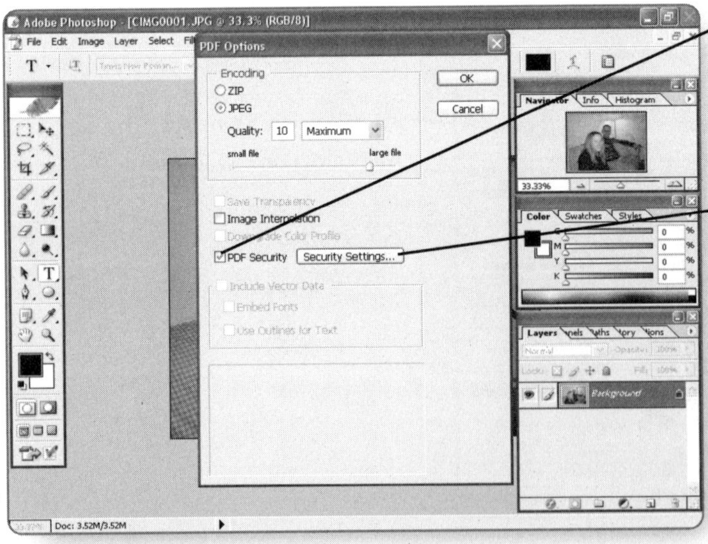

8. **Click** on the **PDF Security** check box. It will be checked, and the Security Settings button will become active.

9. **Click** on **Security Settings**. The PDF Security dialog box will open.

10. **Click** on the **Password Required to Open Document** check box. It will be checked, and the Document Open Password text box will become active.

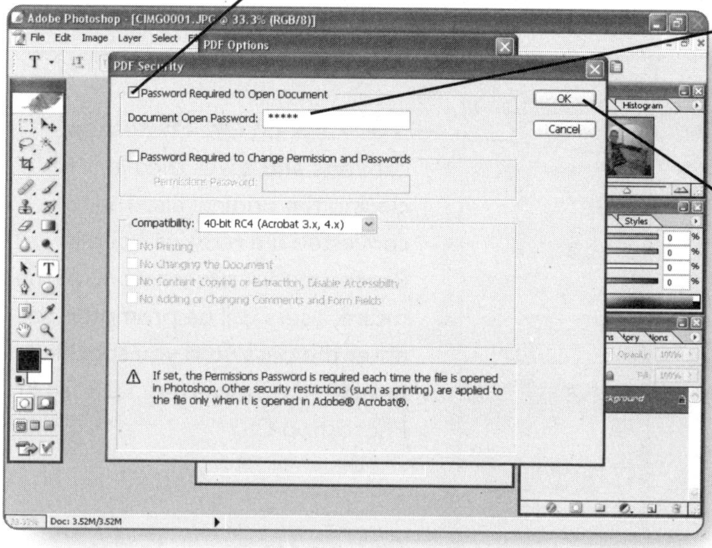

11. **Type** a **password** in the Document Open Password text box. An asterisk will appear for each character you type.

12. **Click** on **OK**. The Confirm Password dialog box will open.

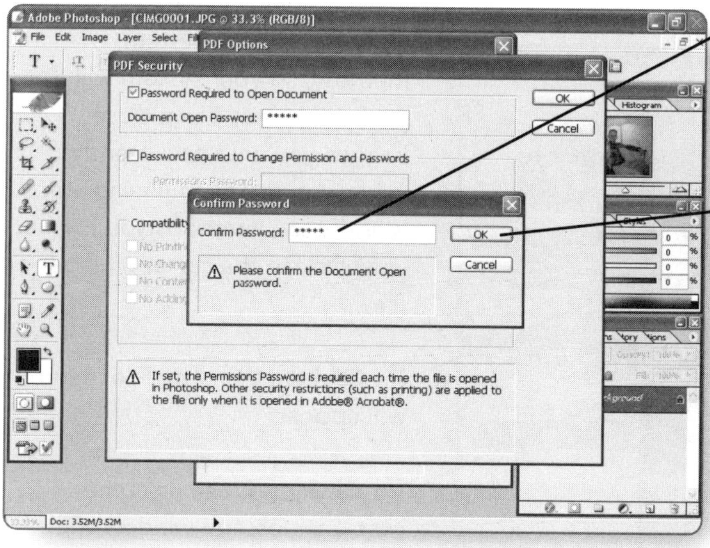

13. **Type** the **password** again in the Confirm Password text box. An asterisk will appear for each character you type.

14. **Click** on **OK**. The Confirm Password and PDF Security dialog boxes will close.

TIP

At this point, you could click on the Security Settings button in the PDF Options dialog box to reopen the PDF Security dialog box and specify additional security settings.

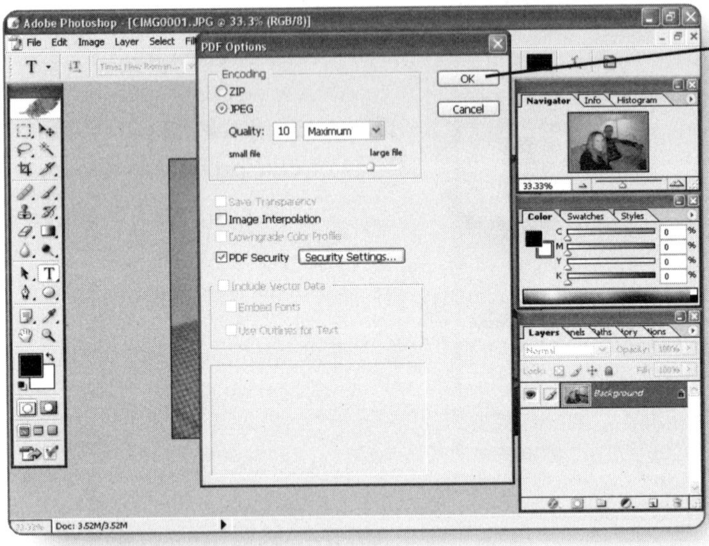

15. Click on **OK**. Photoshop converts and saves the file, closing the original file. The converted file remains open in Photoshop for further work. In the future, users will be prompted to enter the password you specified to open the converted .PDF file in Photoshop CS.

Closing a File

Although you can have multiple images open, image files tend to consume a lot of system memory, so your system will perform better if you close images you are not currently using. Again, the following steps identify two methods you can use to close the current image file.

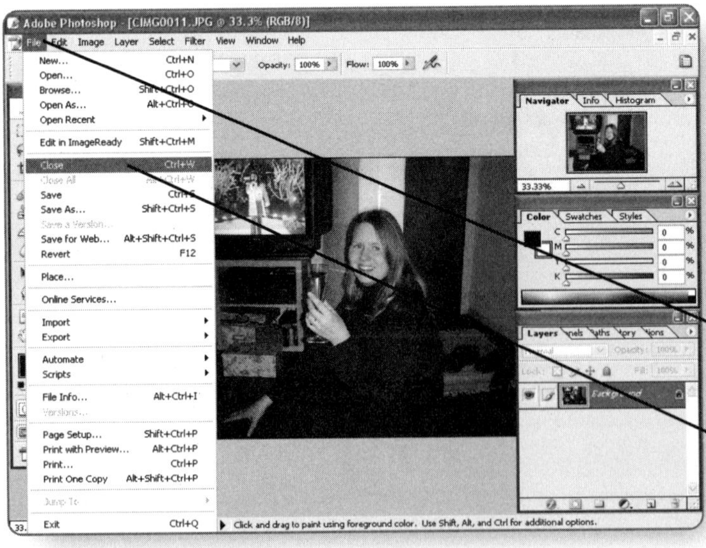

1. Click on **File**. The File menu will appear.

2. Click on **Close**. In some cases, a message window will open.

NOTE

If you added a new text layer, a dialog box may first prompt you to commit (finish) the layer. Click on Commit to do so.

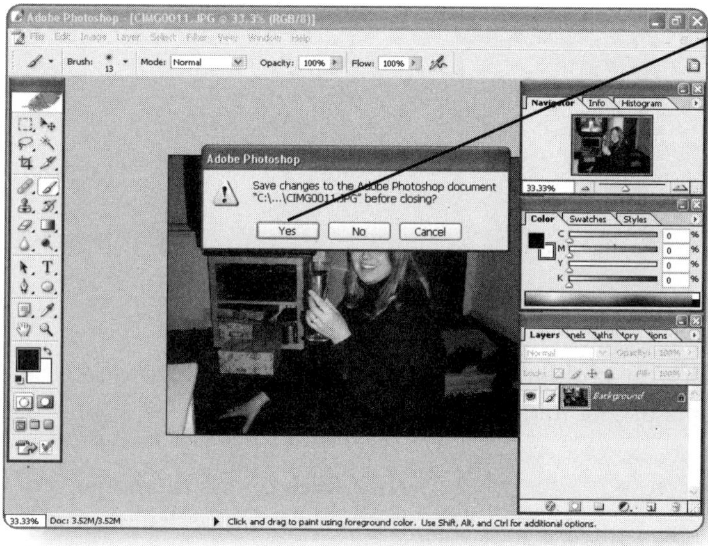

3a. **Click** on **Yes** if you see a message window prompting you to save the file. Photoshop will finish saving it, and the file will close.

OR

3b. **Click** on **Close** for the window of the image file to close. If prompted, save your changes as described in step 3a. Photoshop closes the image window.

The File Browser

Photoshop CS includes an enhanced feature called the File Browser. The File Browser acts as a separate program running from within Photoshop. With it, you can manage all of your image files, including naming files, organizing them, deleting them, and renaming and then performing edits without having to open an image.

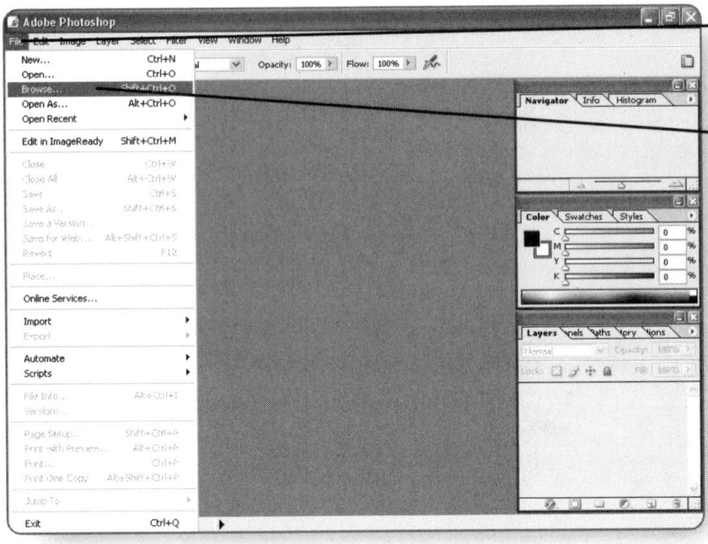

1. **Click** on **File**. The File menu will appear.

2. **Click** on **Browse**. The File Browser window will open.

3. **Click** on a **folder** in the upper-left pane of the window. The contents of that folder will appear.

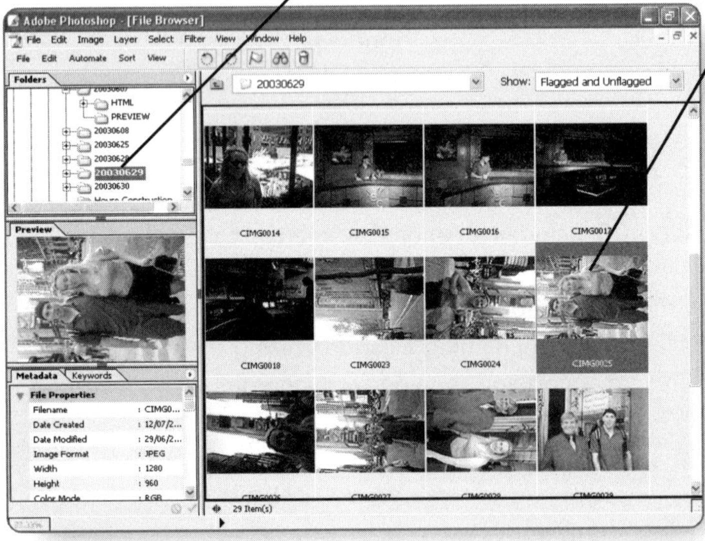

4a. **Click** on the **thumbnail** for the desired image. Its metadata will appear in the lower-left pane of the File Browser for you to review as needed.

OR

4b. **Double-click** on the **desired image**. It will open immediately in Photoshop.

Editing Files

Using the File Browser window, you can quickly do minor editing of your image files. One of the editing options includes rotating files. This is perfect for manipulating pictures that were taken in landscape mode, but that you would like to appear in portrait mode or vice versa.

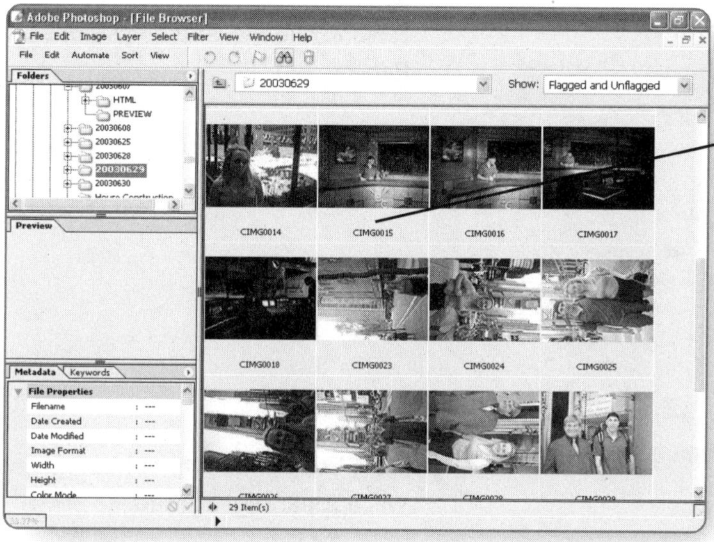

1. **Click** on the **name** of a file. A box will appear around the name of the file, and it will be highlighted.

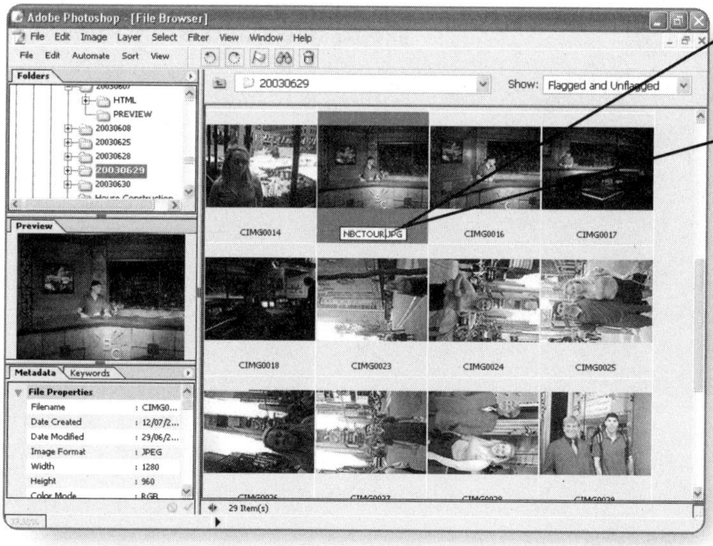

2. **Type** a **new name** for your file. It will appear as you type.

3. **Press Enter**. The file will have a new name.

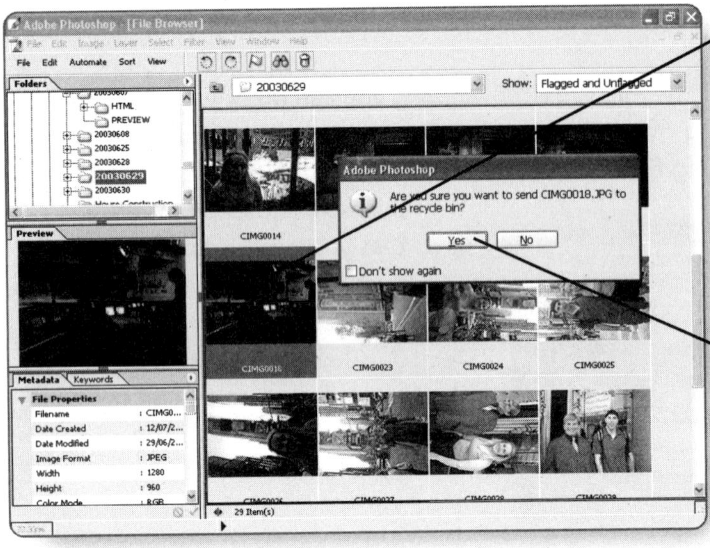

4. Click on a **file**. It will appear highlighted.

5. Press Delete on your keyboard. A dialog box will appear, confirming that you want to send the file to the system's Recycle Bin.

6. Click on **Yes**. The file will be sent to the Recycle Bin.

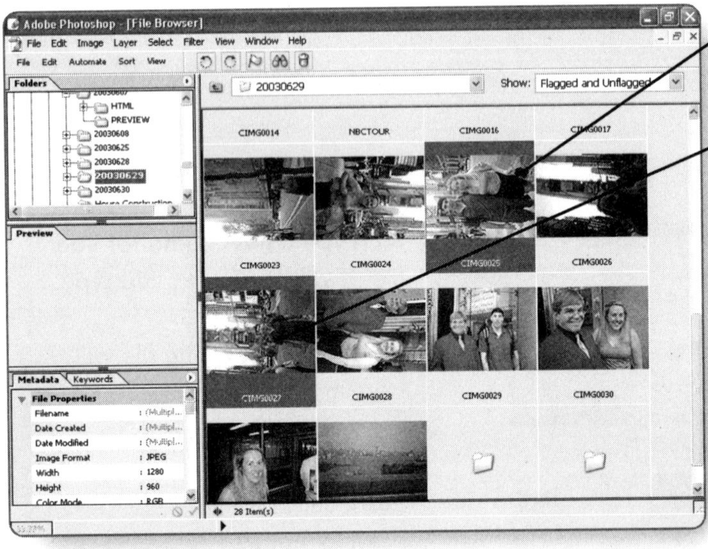

7. Click on a **file** to select it. It will appear highlighted.

8. Hold down the **Ctrl** key (**Command** key Mac OS) and **click** on any other files you would like to select at the same time.

9. **Click** on one of the **Rotate buttons** to rotate the files you have selected. They can be rotated clockwise or counterclockwise by 90 degrees.

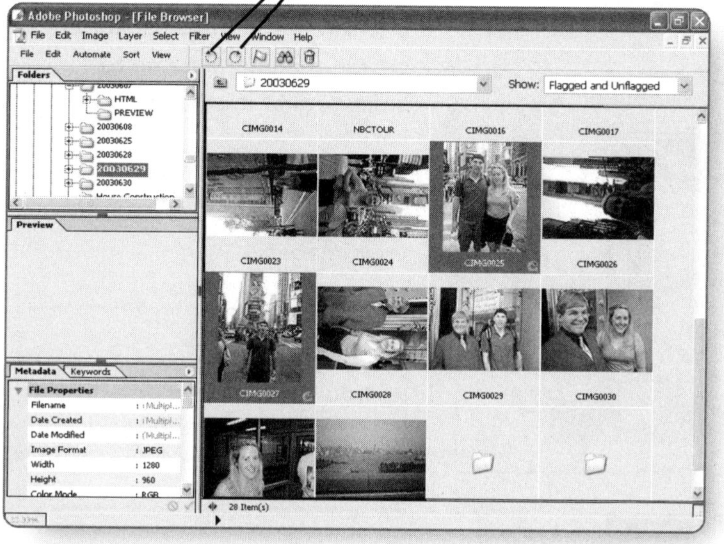

Managing Files

Once you get the hang of your digital camera, your image collection can easily become quite large. The File Browser is a great tool for helping you manage your collection of images. With it, you can mark certain images, add keywords to images, and search for particular files.

Flagging and Accessing Images

The File Browser allows you to mark certain images so that they can be quickly accessed. Imagine flipping through a photo album and placing sticky notes on the pages of the images you would like to go back to. That's pretty much how the Markers in the File Browser work. You simply select the images you would like to mark, and then you can choose how you would like to view those images.

1. **Click** on an **image** you would like to flag. The image will be highlighted.

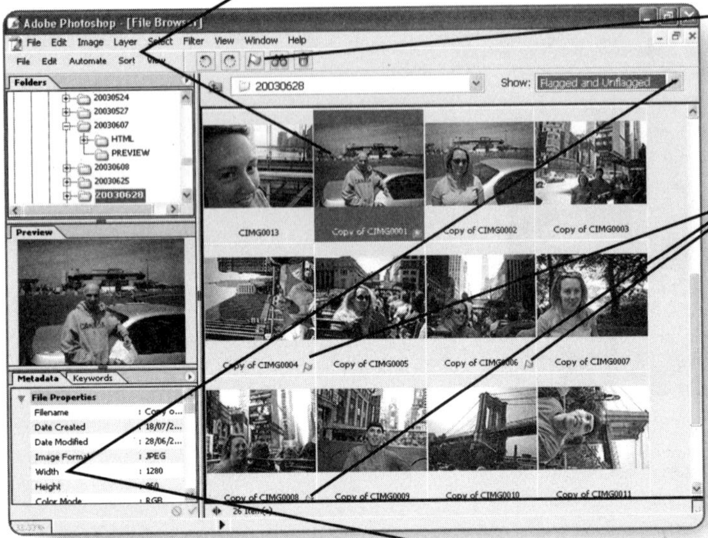

2. **Click** on the **Flag File button**. A little flag will appear beside the image name to indicate that it is flagged.

3. **Repeat** steps **1** and **2** until you have completed flagging your images.

TIP

You can deflag an image by selecting it and clicking on the Flag button.

4. **Click** on the Show drop-down list **arrow** in the top-right corner. A list of viewing options will appear.

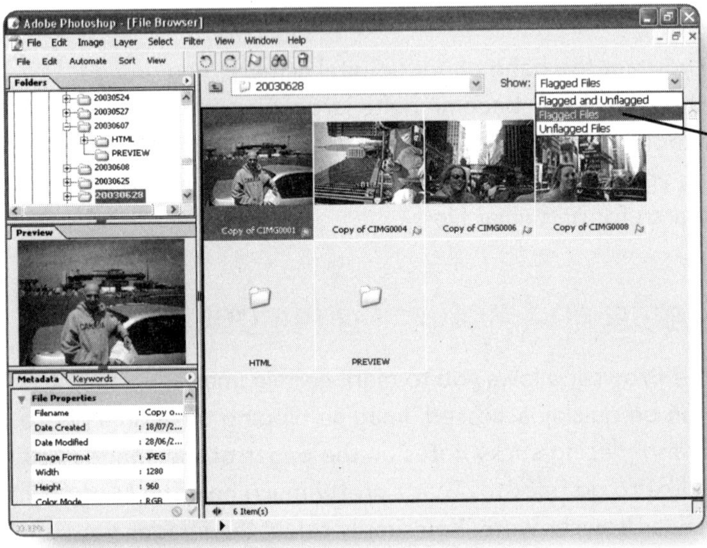

5. **Click** on the **desired option**. You can choose to view all of the flagged images, all of the unflagged images, or simply all of the images.

Searching Files

The File Browser has a built-in search engine that will allow you to find specific photos based on the criteria you set.

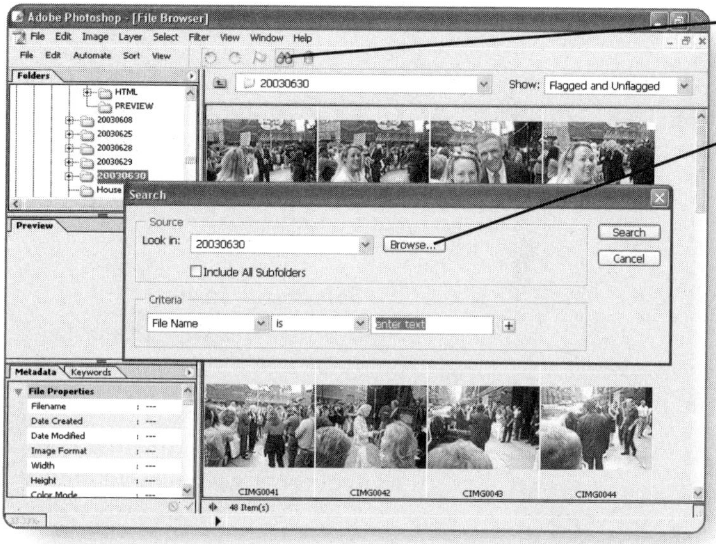

1. **Click** on the **Search** button. The Search dialog box will open.

2. **Click** on the **Browse** button. A Browse for Folder dialog box will open in which you can select where you would like to conduct the search.

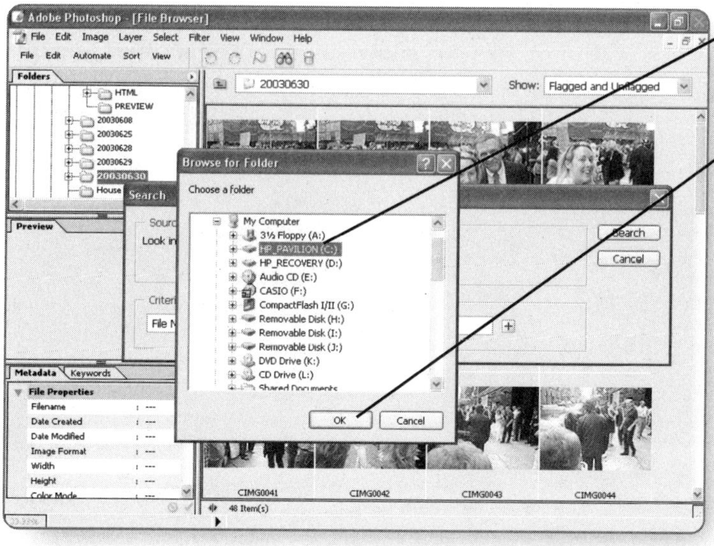

3. **Click** on the desired **drive** or **folder**. It will be selected.

4. **Click** on **OK**. The dialog box will close, and you will now be able to set the criteria for your search.

5. Click on the **down arrow** beside the first box in the Criteria area. A list of different criteria will appear.

6. Click on the desired **criteria**. It will be selected. Depending on the criteria you select, different parameter options will be available in the next two boxes.

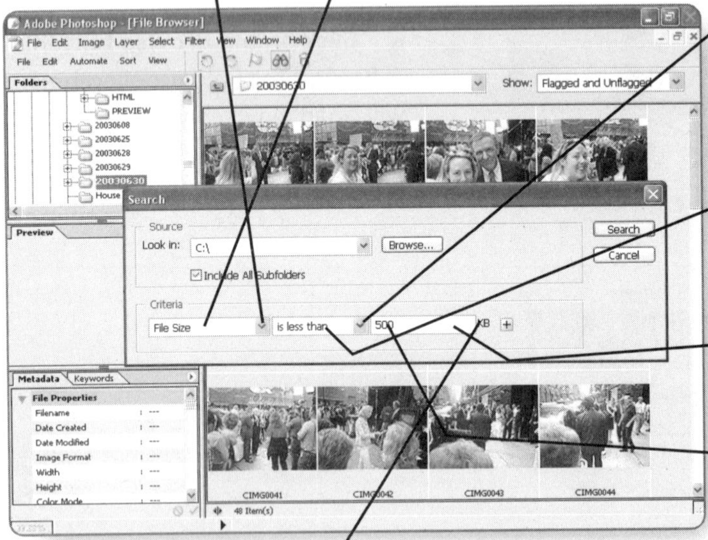

7. Click on the **down arrow** beside the next box. This will allow you to set the conditions of your criteria.

8. Select the desired **conditions**. This will appear in the box.

9. Double-click in the **last box**. The contents will be highlighted.

10. Type the **data criteria** for your search. It will appear as you type.

11. Click on the **+**. This will allow you to enter another line of criteria for your search.

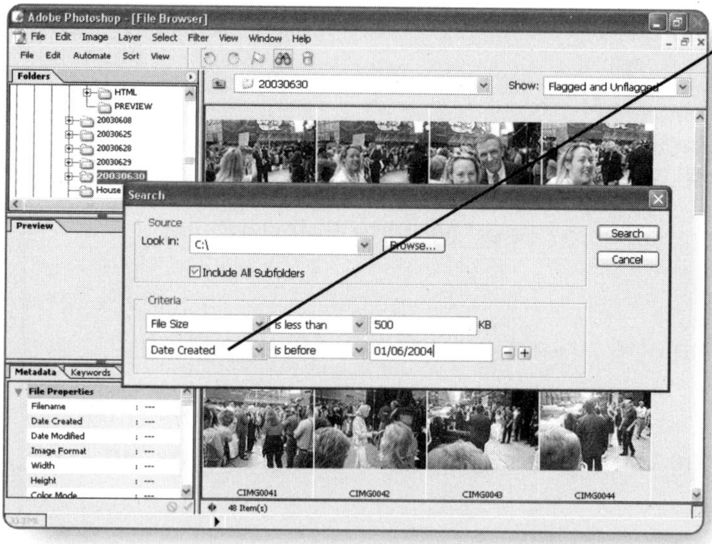

12. Repeat steps **5** to **11** for the next line of criteria.

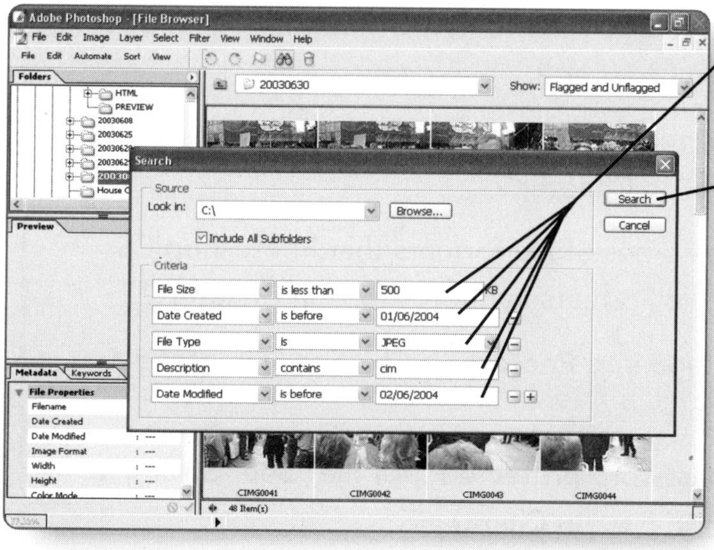

13. Repeat step **12** until you are finished adding lines of criteria for your search.

14. Click on **Search**. The images that match the criteria you have set will appear in the File Browser.

Part I Review Questions

1. How do you open a palette? See "Selecting Palettes" in Chapter 1.
2. How can you reposition a palette? See "Moving Palettes" in Chapter 1.
3. How do you remove a palette from a group? See "Ungrouping Palettes" in Chapter 1.
4. How do you reveal all the tools in one location? See "Toolbox" in Chapter 1.
5. How do you create a keyboard shortcut? See "Keyboard Shortcuts" in Chapter 1.
6. What are the steps required to make a new blank document? See "Creating a New File" in Chapter 2.
7. How do you open more than one file at a time? See "Opening and Accessing Multiple Files" in Chapter 2.
8. What are three different types of file formats that Photoshop CS supports? See "Using File Formats in Photoshop" in Chapter 2.
9. How do you scan an image into Photoshop CS? See "Grabbing a Scanner Image" in Chapter 2.
10. How do you create a password protected .pdf file? See "Saving a Password-Protected .PDF File" in Chapter 2.

PART II

Making Basic Edits

3

Adding Content with Tools

When most people think of Photoshop, they think of it as a photo-editing application. Although it is very strong in that department, it also has a full range of tools to help you add content to a blank image or to an image you've created or opened from another source. Painting and drawing with your computer may take some practice, but like any other skill, the results are worth the effort. In this chapter, you'll learn how to:

- Select colors for painting
- Paint with the painting tools
- Draw with the drawing tools
- Add and improve text
- Create your own brushes

Choosing Colors

Color can bring your images and creations to life, and Photoshop gives you abundant options when it comes to selecting colors. Typically, you will be setting two types of colors, one for the foreground and one for the background. Photoshop generally uses the selected foreground color when you draw lines and the background color for gradient fills and erased areas. The Foreground Color, Background Color box near the bottom of the toolbox shows the currently selected foreground and background colors. The following steps detail the numerous methods you can use to select a new foreground or background color. You should first ensure that the color palette is open before you attempt to change colors.

1. **Click** on **Window**. The Window menu will appear.

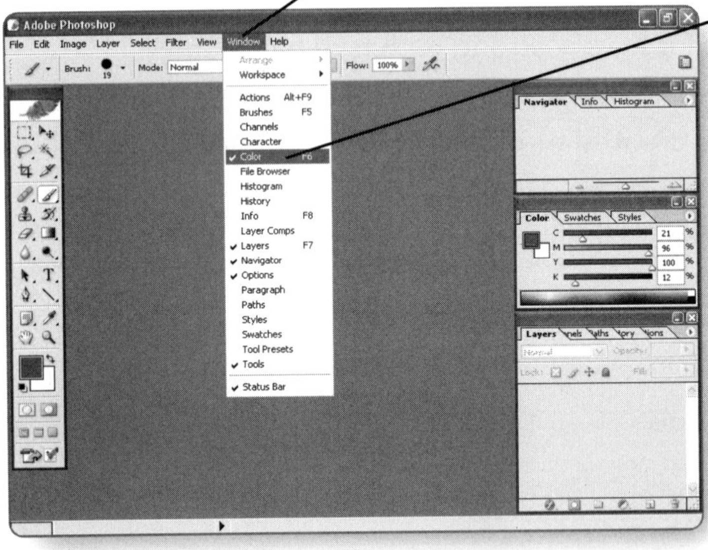

2. **Click** on **Color** if it is not already selected. The color palette will appear.

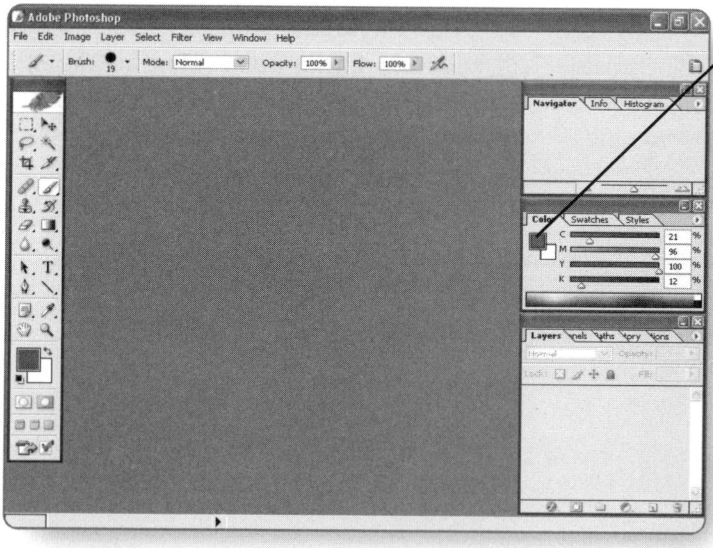

3. Double-click on the Set **Foreground color box**. A Color Picker dialog box will open in which you can select a foreground color.

4. Click on a **hue level**. You can click anywhere along the hue line. Alternatively, you can enter a value for the hue in the hue box.

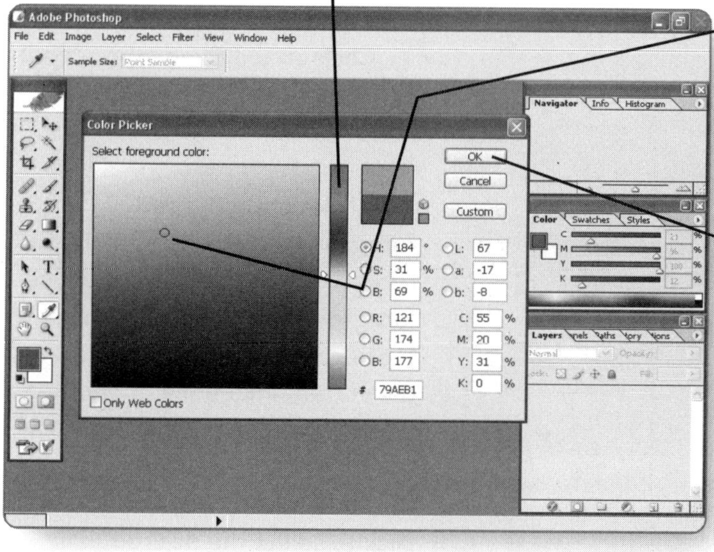

5. Click anywhere in the Select foreground color area to choose a saturation and brightness level. The color will be selected when you click.

6. Click on OK. The foreground color will be set.

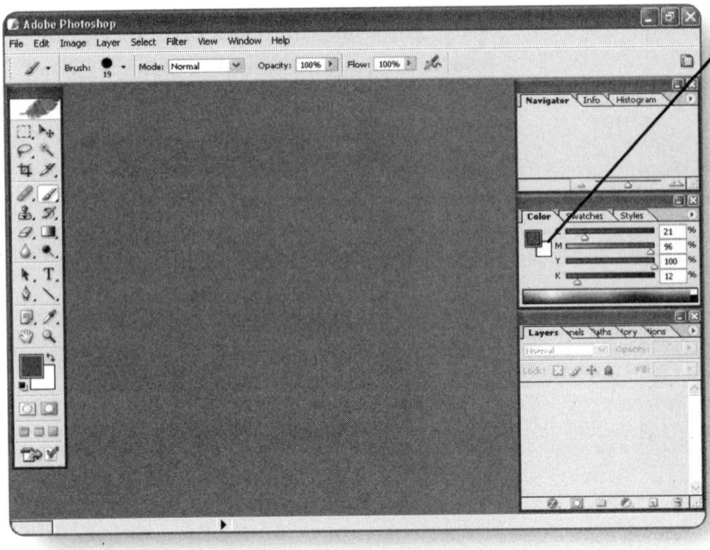

7. **Repeat** steps **3** through **6** for the background color. In Step 3, double click the Set background color box rather than the foreground color box.

Choosing Colors from Images

Rather than selecting a color from a color palette, you can choose specific colors from within your images. The Eyedropper tool enables you to pick a color from your image that can then be used when painting.

1. **Click** on the **Eyedropper tool** in the toolbox. The Eyedropper tool will become the active tool.

2. **Click** on the desired **foreground color**. The color you clicked on will become the active foreground color. You can use those colors to paint and draw in the current image file or another file.

3. **Hold** the **Alt key** and then click to select the desired background color.

Working with Painting Tools

You can bring out your inner Rembrandt with the painting tools you are provided with in Photoshop. You can choose to either paint an image from scratch or paint onto an existing image file.

> **NOTE**
>
> Photoshop places painted information on the background layer by default. You can separate painted information by placing it on different layers in the file; this enables you to move and work with the painted information independent of other information in the image. See Chapter 8, "Working with Layers," to learn how to place content on different layers in an image.

Painting with the Paintbrush

The Brush tool enables you to use the mouse to create freehand strokes with any of a number of brush shapes. Photoshop CS includes a large variety of different brushes for you to choose from. These brushes include both traditional strokes and some more unique brushes including star-, grass-, and leaf-shaped brushes.

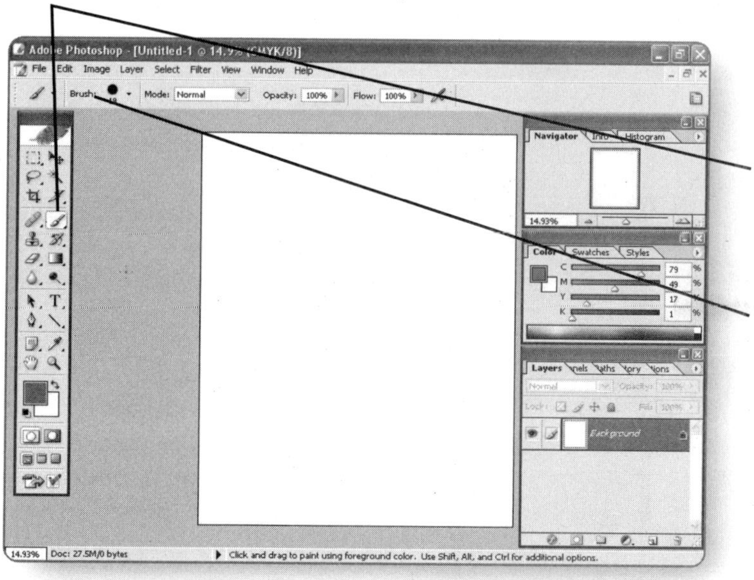

1. **Click** on the **Brush tool** in the toolbox. It will become the active tool.

2. **Click** on the **Brush Preset picker button** in the options bar. A list of different brush options will appear.

3. **Click** on the **scroll buttons** to browse the different brushes.

4. **Click** on the desired **brush**. It will be selected.

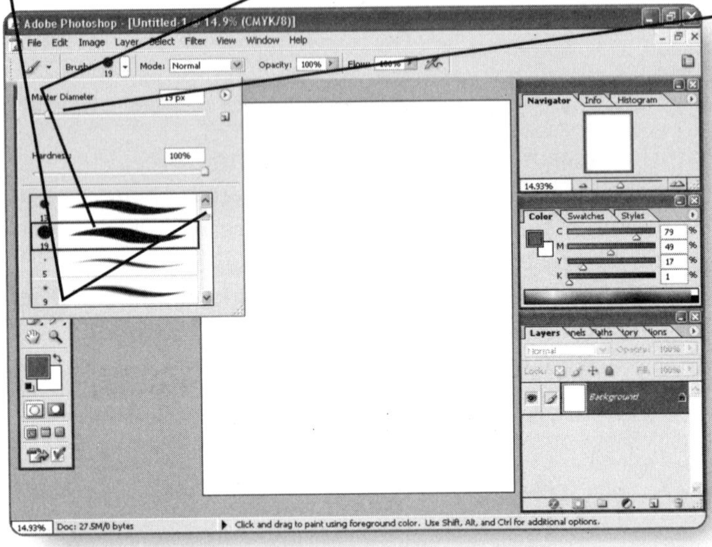

5. **Press** and **hold** the **mouse button** and then **drag** the **slider** to adjust the size of the brush.

6. **Select** the **foreground color** using the method of your choice. The color you select will become active for the paintbrush.

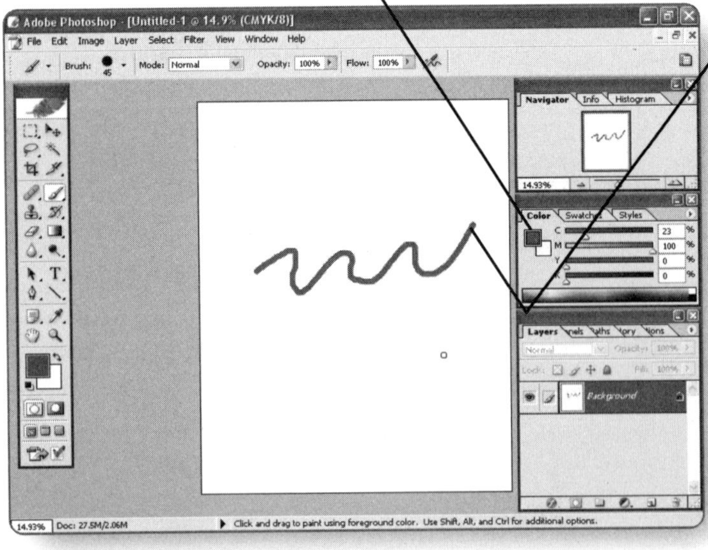

7. **Drag** on the picture in the work area. As you drag, your brush stroke will appear.

TIP

If you paint or draw on the image and make a mistake, immediately press Ctrl+Z or choose the Undo (tool) command on the Edit menu to undo the mistake.

Painting with the Pencil

Technically speaking, the Pencil tool functions as a drawing tool in Photoshop, recoloring pixels as you drag along with the tool. The following example illustrates how to use the Pencil tool:

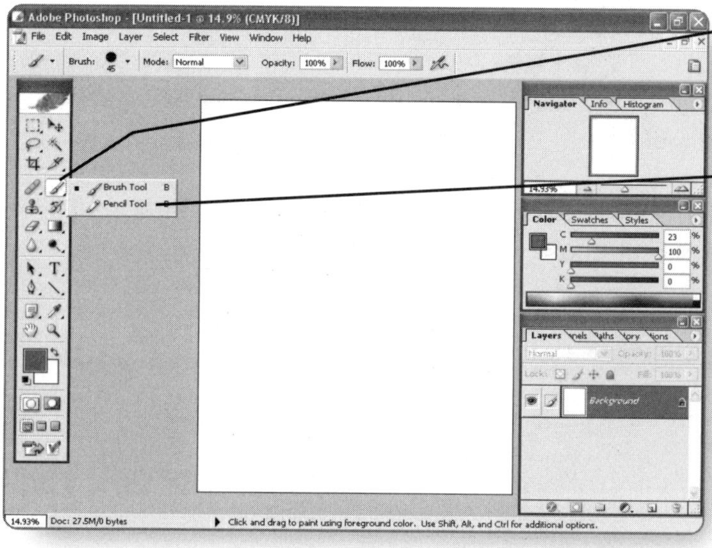

1. **Press** and **hold** the **mouse button** over the **Brush tool** in the toolbox. A list of tools will appear.

2. **Click** on the **Pencil tool**. The Pencil tool will become the active tool.

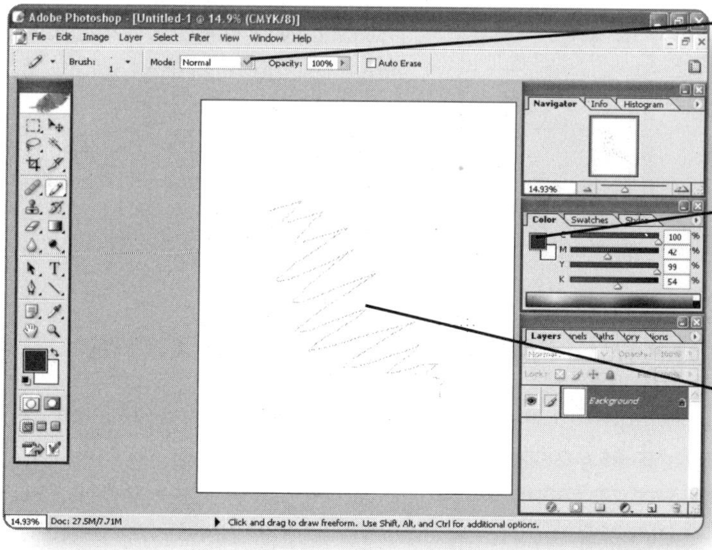

3. **Choose** the desired **settings** in the options bar. Your selections will become the active settings for the tool.

4. **Select** the **foreground color** using the method of your choice. The color you select will become active for the Pencil tool.

5. **Drag** on the picture in the work area. As you drag, your brush stroke will appear.

Painting with the Airbrush

We've all been to a county fair or amusement park where there was a carnie airbrushing t-shirts with people's names or caricatures. Your dreams of being a carnie can now come true because there is an Airbrush tool in Photoshop that mimics real-life airbrushing.

1. **Click** on the **Brush tool** in the toolbox. It will become the active tool.

2. **Choose** a **brush** and other desired **settings** in the options bar. Your selections will become the active settings for the tool.

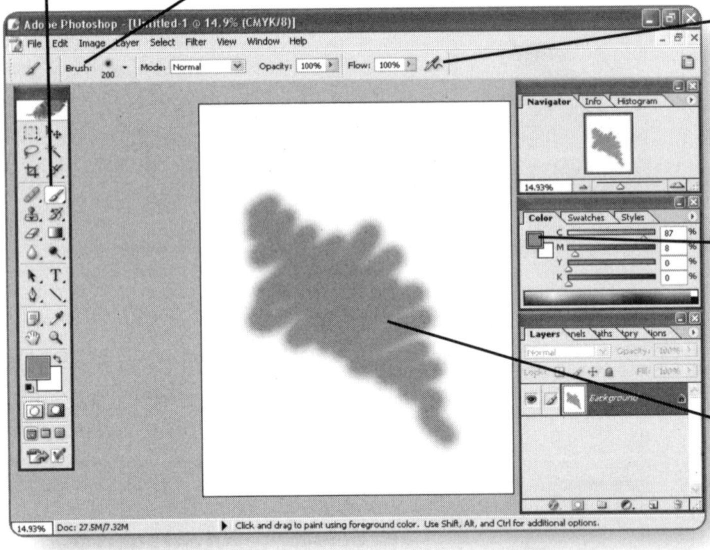

3. **Click** on the **Set to Enable Airbrush Capabilities** button on the options bar. The button will appear pressed, and the airbrush will become active.

4. **Select** the **foreground color** using the method of your choice. The color you select will become active for the Airbrush tool.

5. **Drag** in the work area. As you drag, your brush stroke will appear.

Working with Drawing Tools

The drawing tools enable you to create regular shapes in an image such as a rectangle, rounded rectangle, ellipse, polygon, line, or custom shape. When you draw a shape, Photoshop by default places the shape on its own layer in the image, so refer to Chapter 8 if you have a question about working with layers.

> **NOTE**
>
> The Pen tool is for creating paths, not drawing lines. Chapter 10, "Using Paths," explains how to work with paths.

Drawing a Line

As you might expect, you use the Line tool to draw lines. The following steps explain how to use this tool:

1. **Press** and **hold** the **mouse button** over the Rectangle tool in the toolbox. A list of tools will appear.

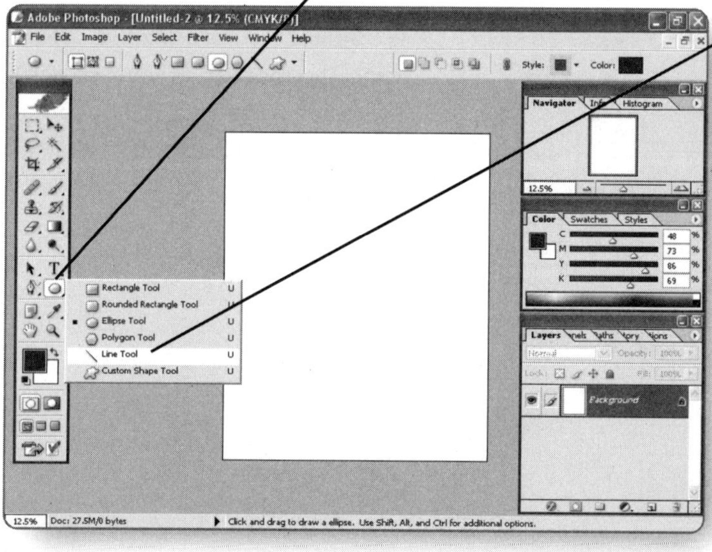

2. **Click** on the **Line tool**. The Line tool will become the active tool.

3. **Choose** the desired **settings** in the options bar. Your selections will become the active settings for the tool.

> **TIP**
>
> Click on the Fill Pixels button on the options bar if you want to place the drawing on the background layer rather than on a new layer in your image. Otherwise, leave the Shape Layers button selected. If you instead click on the Paths button, Photoshop will create a path and not a line. (You can find these buttons together in a group near the left end of the options bar.) Chapter 10 explains what paths are and how to use them.

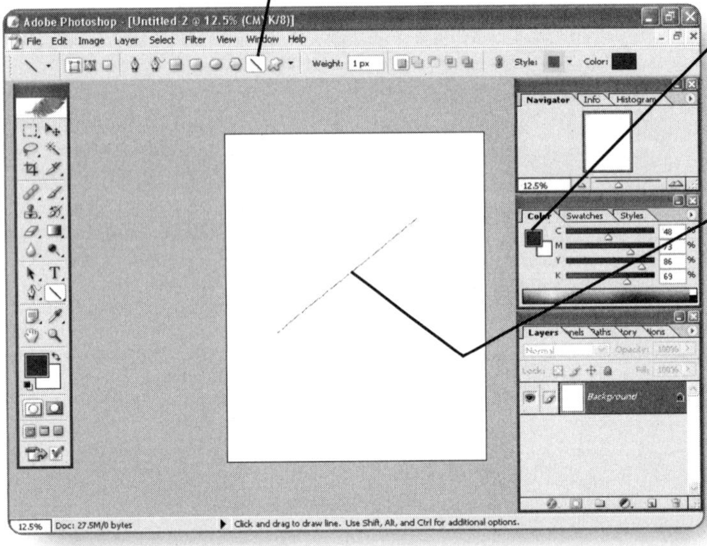

4. **Select** the **foreground color** using the method of your choice. The color you select will become active for the Line tool.

5. **Drag** in the work area. As you drag, your line will appear.

Drawing a Rectangle, Oval, or Other Shape

As you may have noticed from the preceding set of steps, the Shape tools are grouped with the Line tool on the Photoshop toolbox. The following set of steps demonstrates how to use one of the Shape tools. (They all basically work in the same way.)

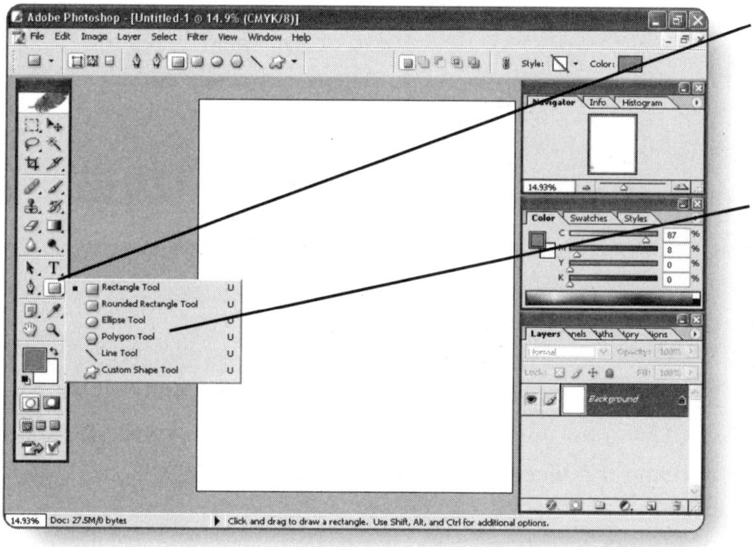

1. **Press** and **hold** the **mouse button** over the Rectangle tool in the toolbox. A list of tools will appear.

2. **Click** on the desired **Shape tool** in the submenu. The selected tool becomes the active tool.

3. **Choose** the desired **settings** in the options bar. Your selections will become the active settings for the tool.

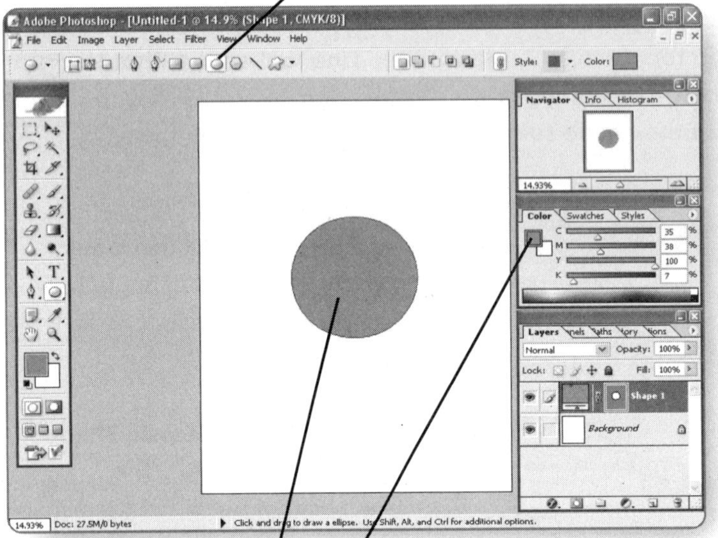

> **NOTE**
>
> If you choose the Custom Shape tool, be sure to use the Shape drop-down list on the options bar to specify which kind of shape to draw. Again, leave the Shape Layers button selected unless you want to add the shape to the current layer (whether it's the background layer or another layer).

4. **Select** the **foreground color** using the method of your choice. The color you select will become active for the tool and will become the fill color for the drawn object.

5. **Drag** in the work area. As you drag, your shape will appear.

Transforming Objects

Once you have created your shapes you can manipulate them into other forms by using one of the Transform Path settings. You'll learn more about Paths in Chapter 10. These transformations aren't limited to just basic shapes as they can be used to manipulate lines, text, and other objects.

Scaling Objects

You can quickly change the size of the shapes that you have created by using the scaling option.

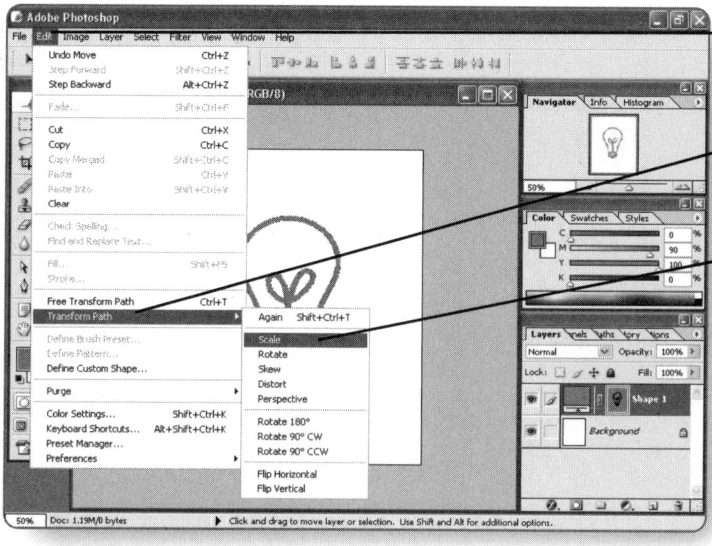

1. **Click** on **Edit**. The Edit menu will appear.
2. **Click** on **Transform Path**. A submenu of options will appear.
3. **Click Scale**. A series of handles will appear around your object.

If an option in the Transform Path menu appears gray, then it is not available for that particular object.

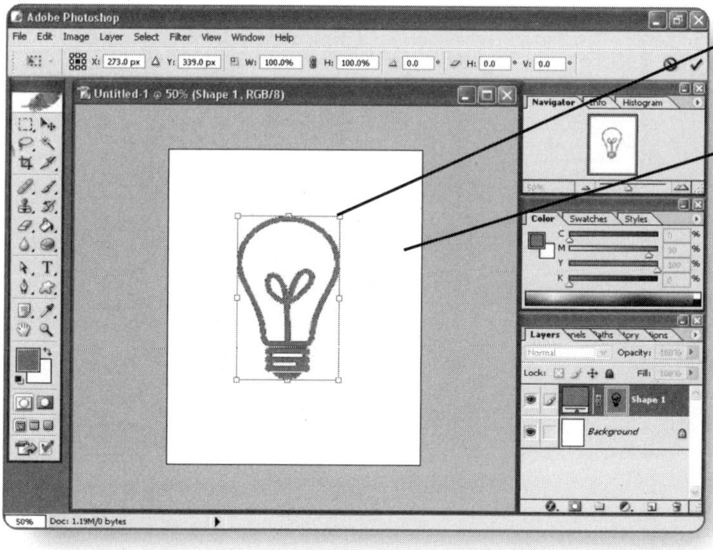

4. **Position** your **mouse pointer** over one of the handles.
5. **Click** and **drag** to change the size of your shape. As you drag, the shape will change size.

6. **Click** on the **Commit** button to finalize the transformation.

Rotating Objects

1. **Click** on **Edit**. The Edit menu will appear.

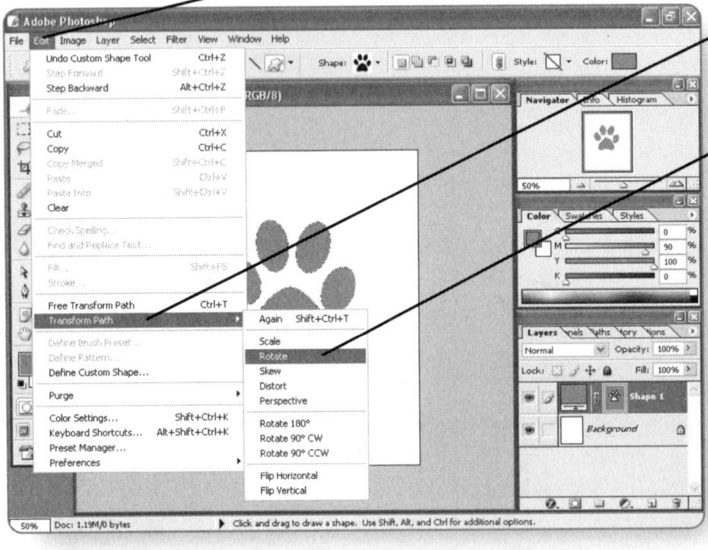

2. **Click** on **Transform Path**. A submenu of options will appear.

3. **Click Rotate**. A series of handles will appear around your object.

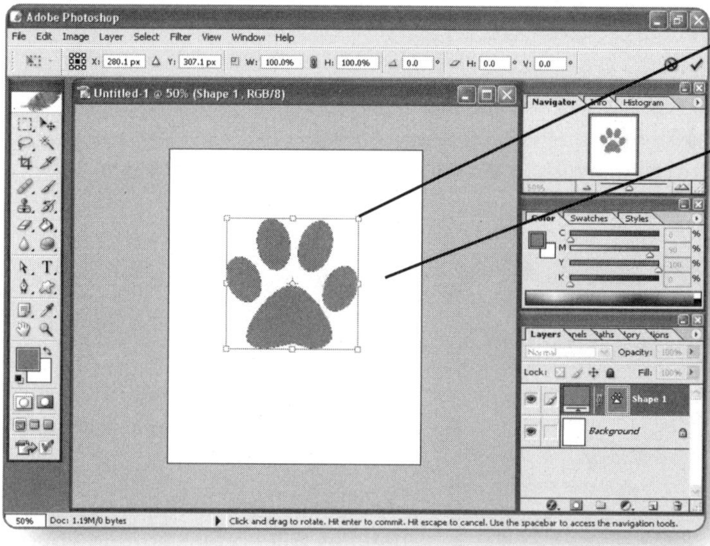

4. **Position** your **mouse pointer** over one of the handles.

5. **Click** and **drag** to rotate your shape. As you drag, the shape will be rotated.

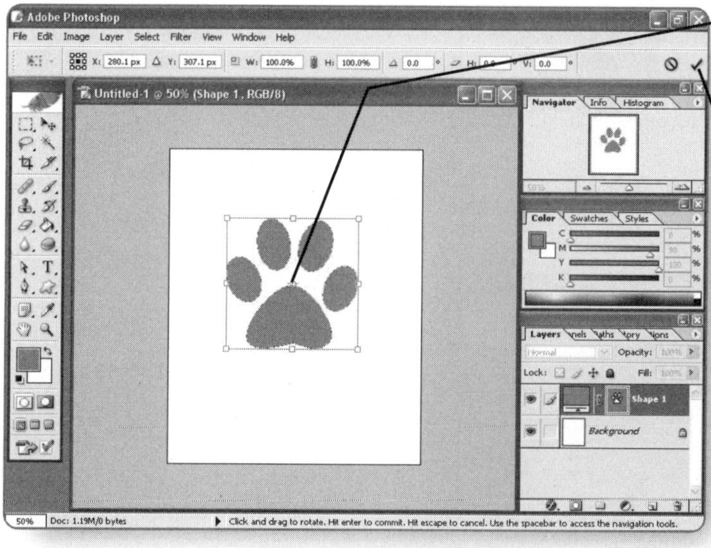

6. **Drag** the **center of rotation icon** in the middle of the shape to change the center of rotation and repeat rotation as required.

7. **Click** on the **Commit** button to finalize the transformation.

Skewing Objects

You're probably familiar with the concept of italizing text. When you apply italics to text, it slants the text forward, which is a form of skewing. You can skew any of your objects in Photoshop CS in any direction.

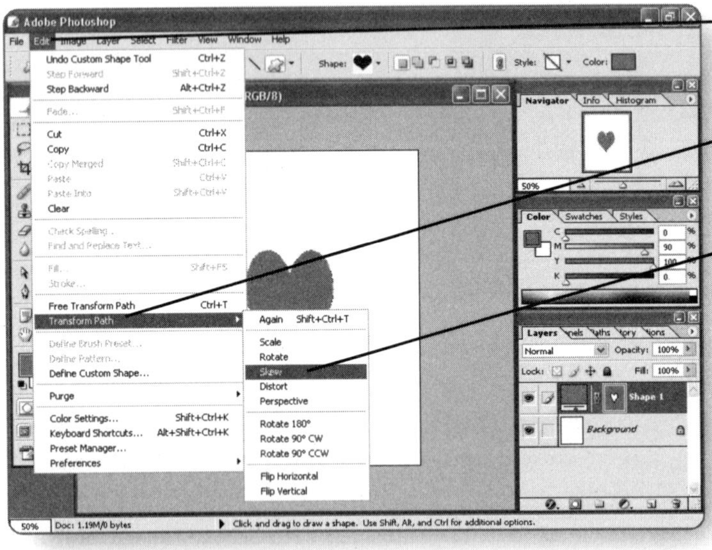

1. **Click** on **Edit**. The Edit menu will appear.

2. **Click** on **Transform Path**. A submenu of options will appear.

3. **Click Skew**. A series of handles will appear around your object.

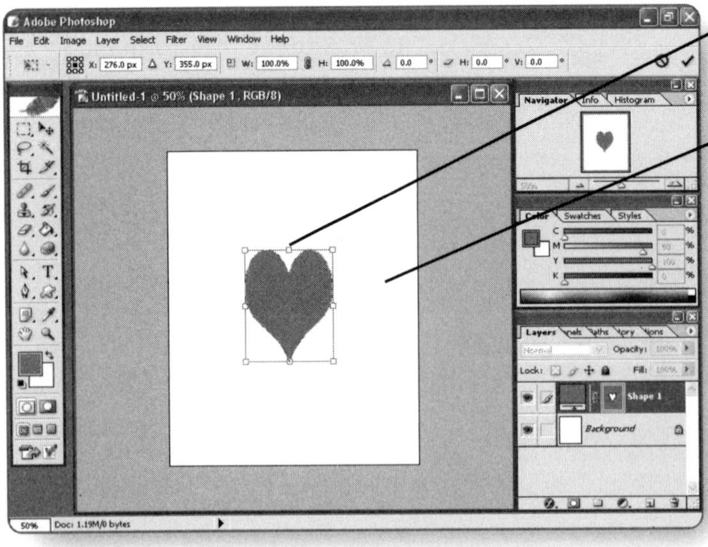

4. **Position** your **mouse pointer** over one of the handles.

5. **Click** and **drag** to skew your shape. As you drag, the shape will be skewed.

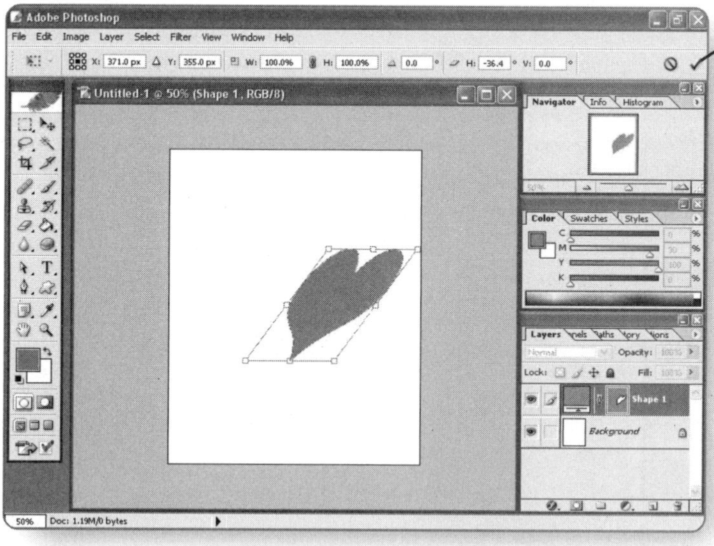

6. Click on the **Commit** button to finalize the transformation.

Distorting Objects

The Distort feature allows you to change the dimension of the shape you are manipulating. By dragging on the handles you can change the length and position of each side of your shape.

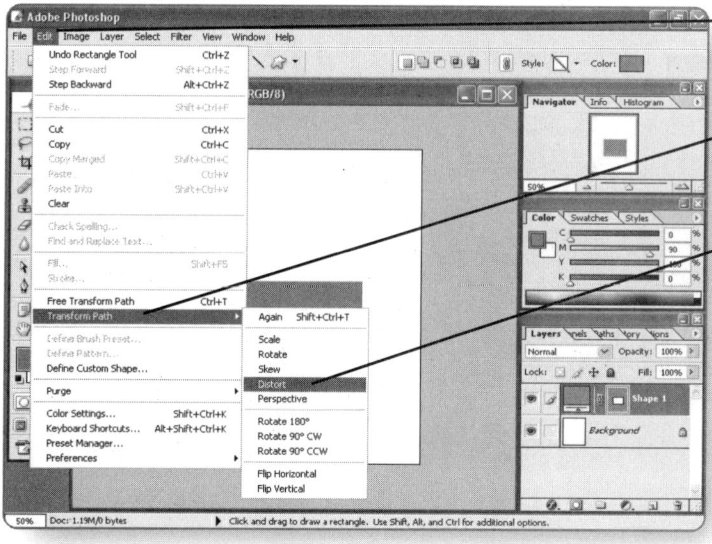

1. Click on **Edit**. The Edit menu will appear.

2. Click on **Transform Path**. A submenu of options will appear.

3. Click Distort. A series of handles will appear around your object.

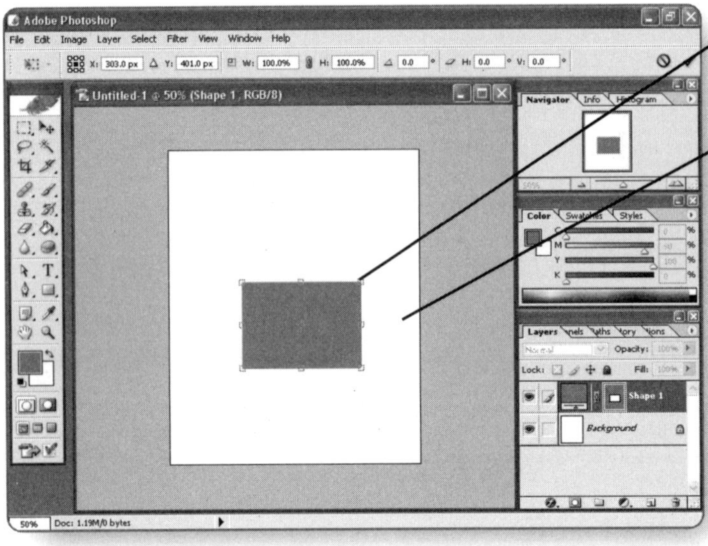

4. **Position** your **mouse pointer** over one of the handles.

5. **Click** and **drag** to distort your shape. As you drag, the shape will be distorted.

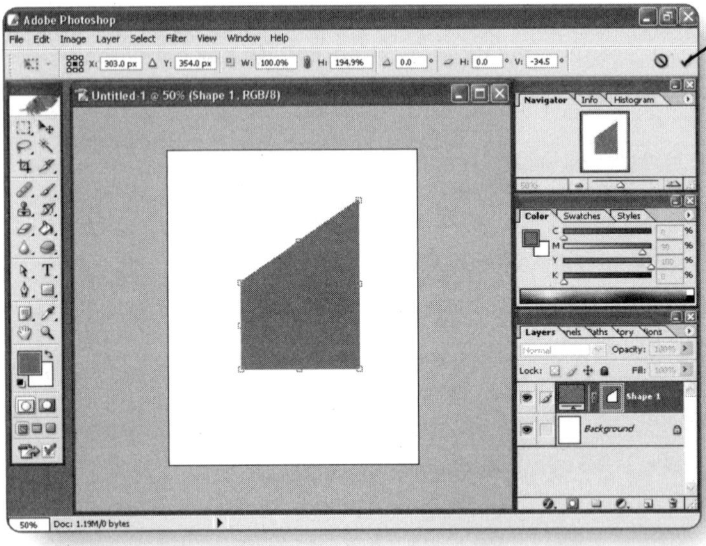

6. **Click** on the **Commit** button to finalize the transformation.

Adding Perspective

You can add perspective to your objects to give them the illusion of three dimensions.

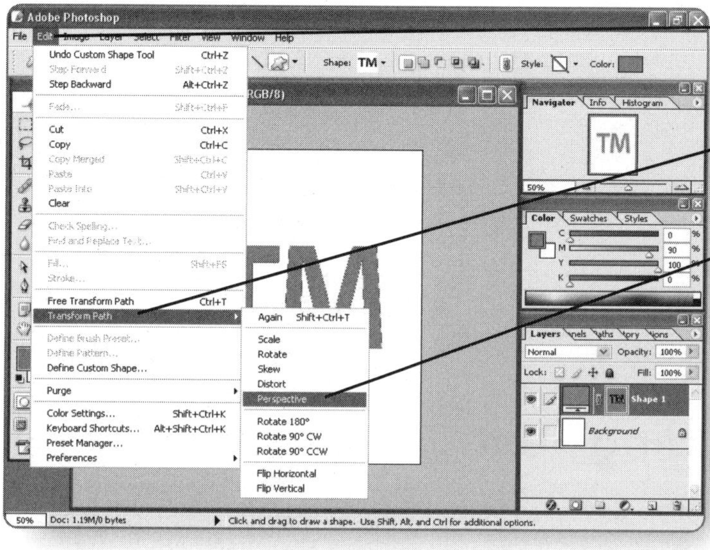

1. **Click** on **Edit**. The Edit menu will appear.

2. **Click** on **Transform Path**. A submenu of options will appear.

3. **Click Perspective**. A series of handles will appear around your object.

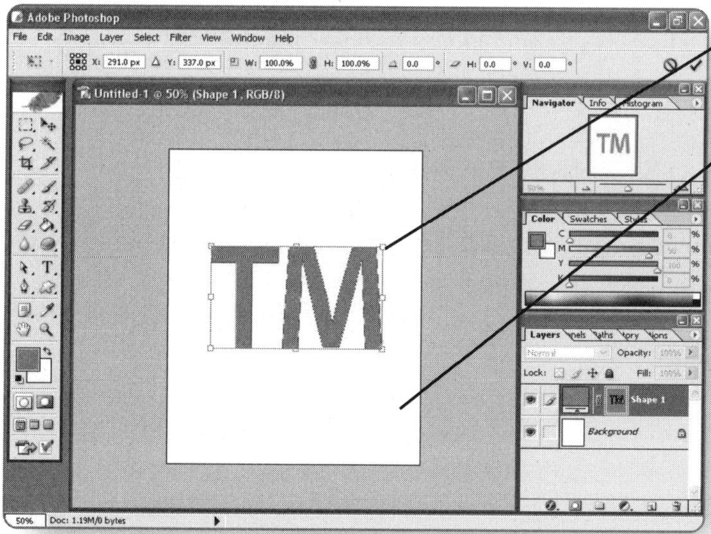

4. **Position** your **mouse pointer** over one of the handles.

5. **Click** and **drag** to ad perspective your object. As you drag, the object will change.

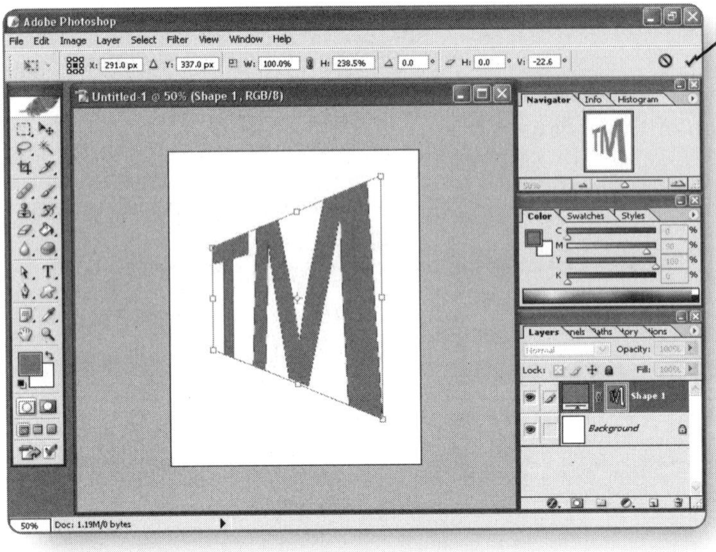

6. **Click** on the **Commit** button to finalize the transformation.

Adding Text

Photoshop CS has enhanced the way in which you work with text, including adding a new editable text on a path feature that allows your text to follow a path as you type. All text that you create appears on a new layer in the image. Photoshop CS offers a variety of tools, such as a spell checker and a find-and-replace feature, to enable you to fine-tune the text in your image.

Creating the Text Layer

Whenever you apply text, it is created on its own separate text layer. By using the options bar, you have a number of choices to customize the text for fun and interesting text treatments in an image.

1. Click on the **Horizontal Type** (or **Vertical Type**) **tool** in the toolbox. It will become the active tool.

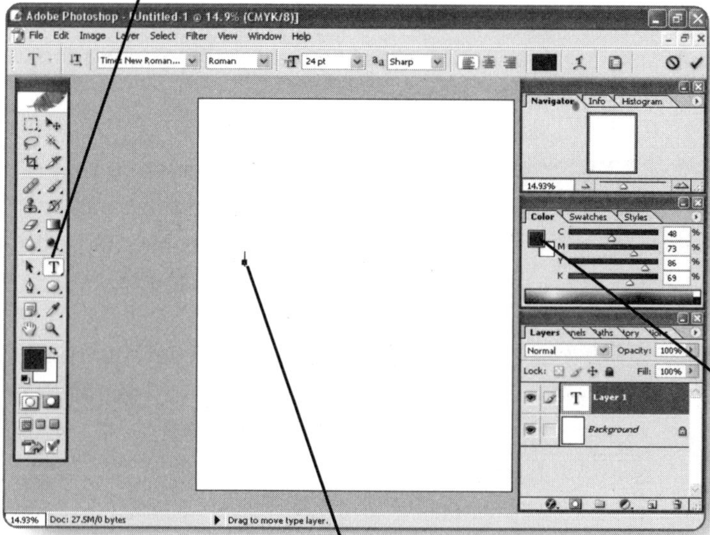

NOTE

To switch between horizontal and vertical type, press and hold the mouse button over the currently selected Type tool and then click on the desired option.

2. Select the desired **foreground color** using the method of your choice. The color you select will become active for the tool and will become the fill color for the text.

3. Click once on the page. An insertion point will appear where you can begin to type.

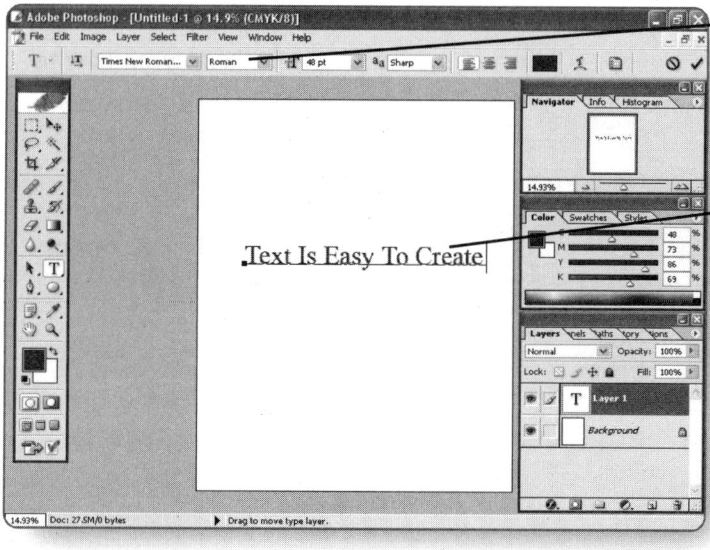

4. Choose the desired **settings** in the options bar. Your selections will become the active settings for the tool.

5. Type the desired **text**. Your text will appear in the text box.

Warping Text

Photoshop CS comes with a variety of warp options for distorting the look of your text. After you've created your text, manipulating it with a warp is simply a matter of selecting the type of warp you'd like to apply.

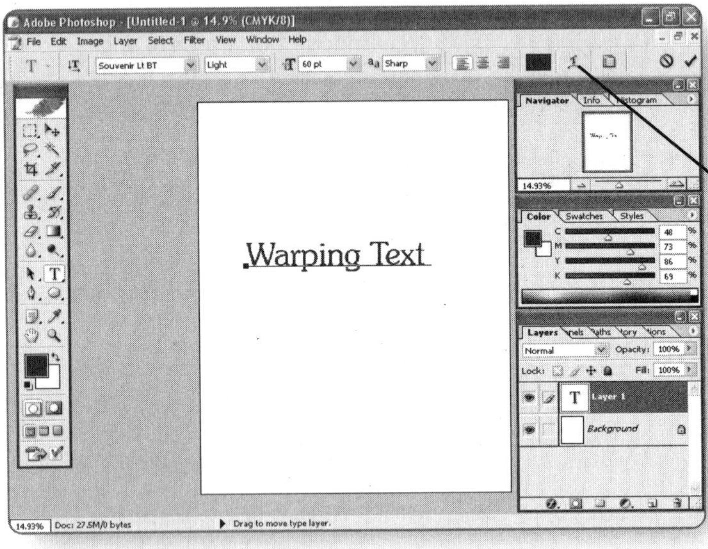

Ensure that you have the text layer selected and the text tool enabled before proceeding with the steps to warp the text.

1. **Click** on the **Create warped text** button. A Warp Text dialog box will open.

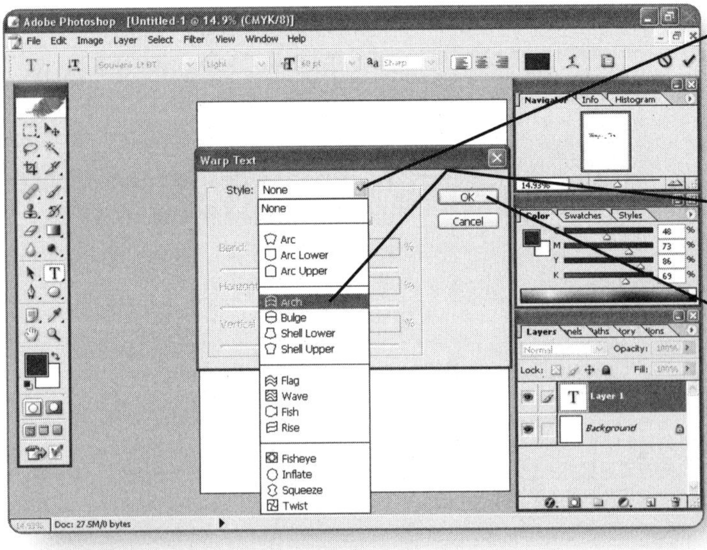

2. **Click** on the **down arrow** to open the Style drop-down list that contains different warp options.

3. **Click** on the desired **option**. It will be selected.

4. **Click** on **OK**. The warp will be applied to your text.

TIP

Once you have warped a piece of text, you are not stuck with that distortion. You can always go back and apply a different warp to the text. You start by selecting the desired text layer, then select any Type tool to bring up the options bar which contains the Warp options that can be reapplied.

Fit Text to Path

One of the enhanced features in Photoshop CS is the capability to create editable text on a path. To do this, you must first create a path. Paths will be covered in detail in Chapter 10, but for now, we will use a simple path for this example.

1. **Click** on the **Pen tool**. It will be selected.

2. **Click** on the **Paths button** in the options bar. It will be activated.

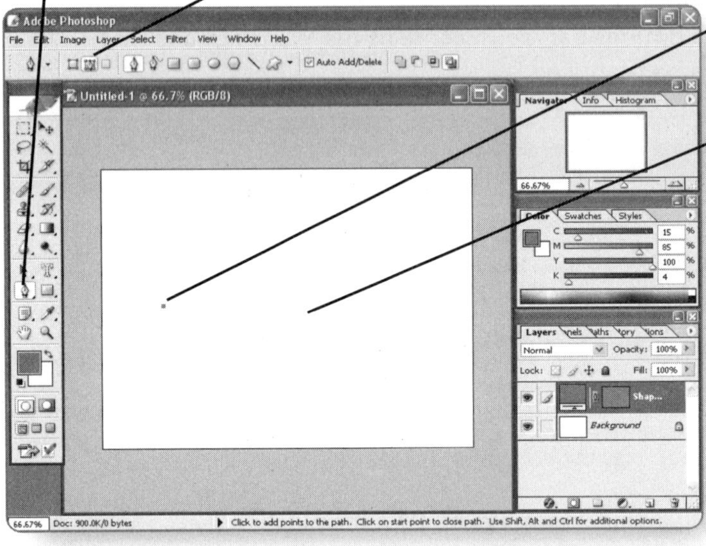

3. **Click once** on the page. A dot will appear.

4. **Position** the **mouse pointer** to the **right** of the dot you have created.

5. **Drag** downward. A path will appear.

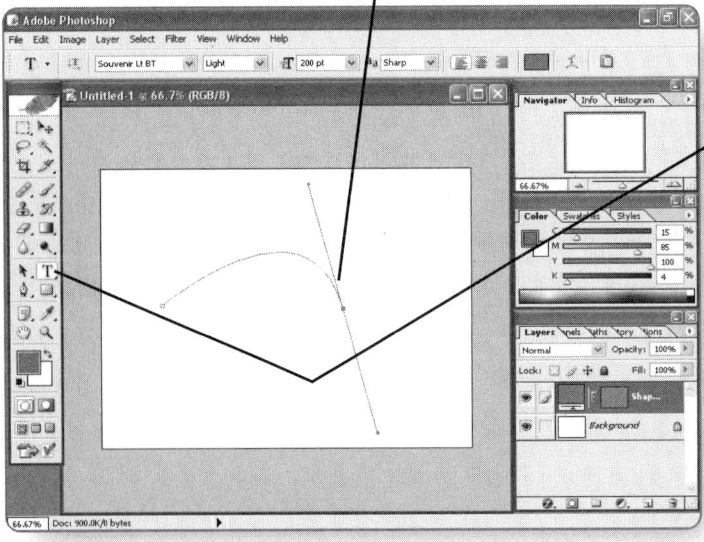

6. **Release** the **mouse button**. A path will now be created.

7. **Click** on the **Horizontal Type** (or **Vertical Type**) **tool** in the toolbox. It will become the active tool.

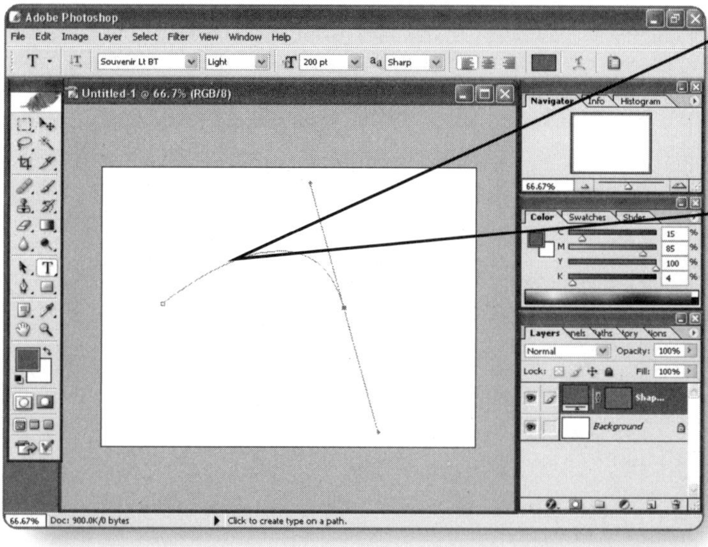

8. **Position** the **mouse pointer** over the **path**. The cursor will have a little line through it when it is over a path.

9. **Click once**. You can now begin typing on the path.

10. **Type** the desired **text**. As you type, the text will appear along the path.

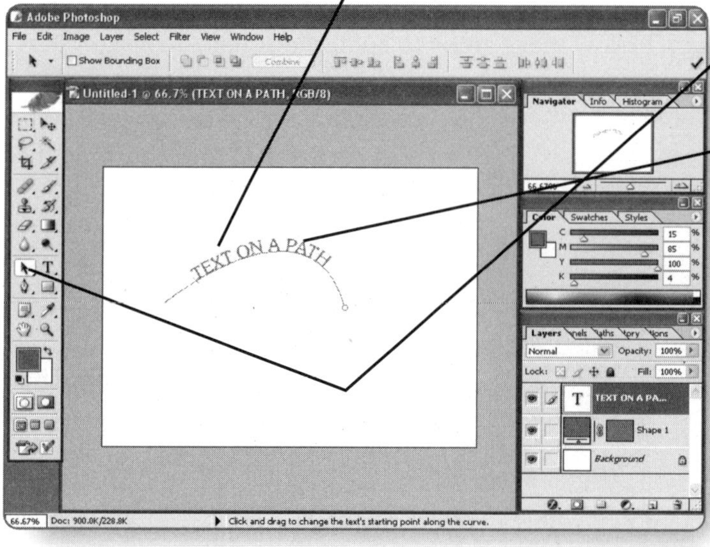

11. **Click** the **Path Selection tool**. It will be activated.

12. **Position** the **mouse pointer** directly over the text on the path.

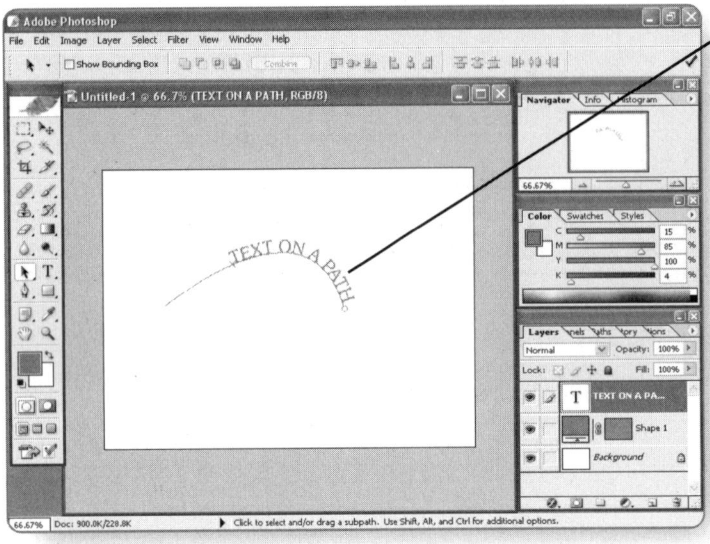

13. **Drag** to the **left** or **right** to reposition the text along the path.

Spell-Checking Text

You'll be investing a lot of time to add professional polish to the images you create and edit in Photoshop. To ensure that you put your best foot forward in your work, you can spell-check the text you've included in the image to ensure its accuracy. Follow these steps to spell-check text.

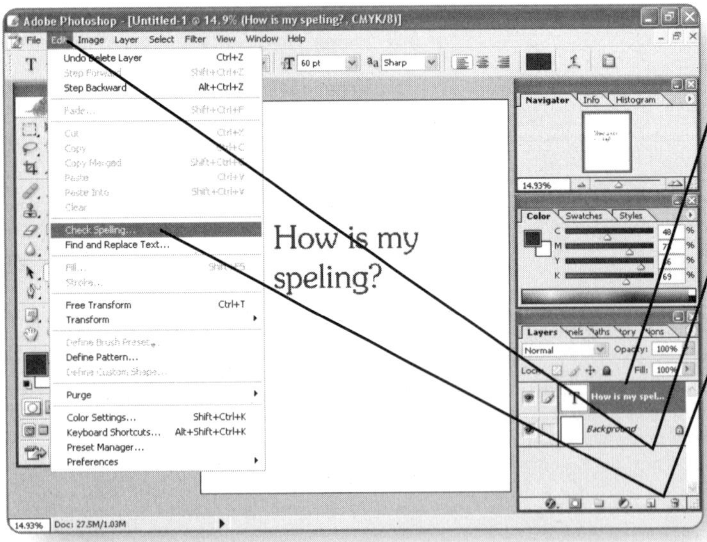

1. **Click** on the **text layer** in the Layers palette. It will become the active layer.

2. **Click** on **Edit**. The Edit menu will appear.

3. **Click** on **Check Spelling**. The Check Spelling dialog box will open and display the first word not found in the spell checker's dictionary.

4a. **Click** on the **replacement** to use in the Suggestions list. The replacement word will be selected.

4b. **Click** on **Change**. The spell checker will replace the word in the image file.

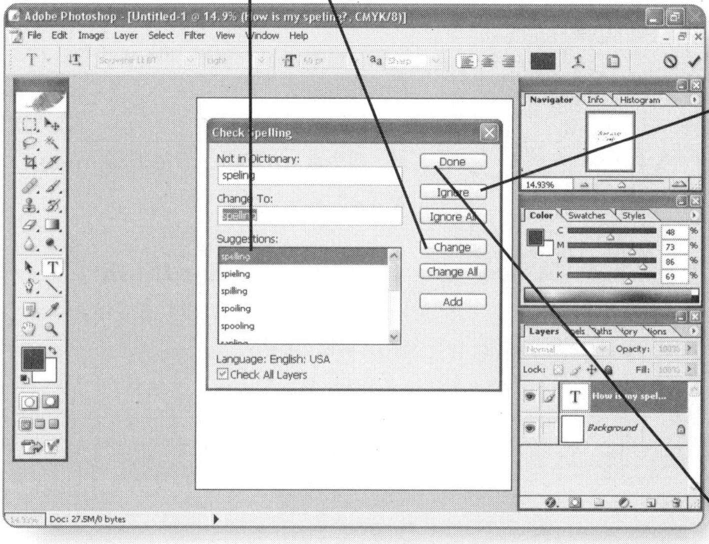

OR

4c. **Click** on **Ignore**. The spell checker will skip the word without replacing it.

5. **Repeat** step **4** as necessary. The spell-checking will continue until the spell checker finds no additional unrecognized words, at which point it will display a message telling you that the spell check is complete.

6. **Click** on **Done**. The Check Spelling dialog box will close.

Creating or Displaying a Brush

Photoshop CS enables you to create your own custom brushes, giving you maximum creative power for editing and developing image files. This section looks at how to create your own brushes and how to use the new Brushes palette to find and work with available brushes.

Sampling a New Brush

The fastest way to create a new brush is to base it on a shape available in your image. To sample a brush, you have to select a portion of the image on a layer. Chapter 5, "Selecting Image

Content," will explain in detail how to make selections. You can refer to that chapter if you need help with step 1 here. The following steps show you how to create your own brush in Photoshop:

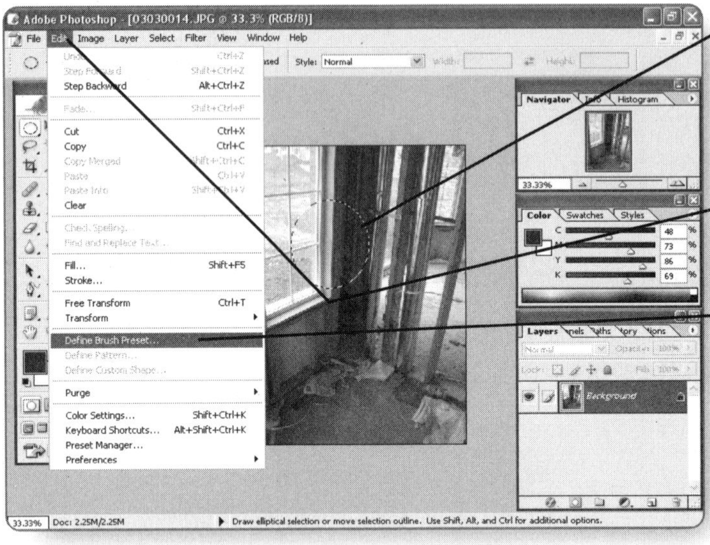

1. **Select** the **image content** to save as a new brush shape. The selection marquee will appear in the image.

2. **Click** on **Edit**. The Edit menu will appear.

3. **Click** on **Define Brush Preset**. The Brush Name dialog box will open.

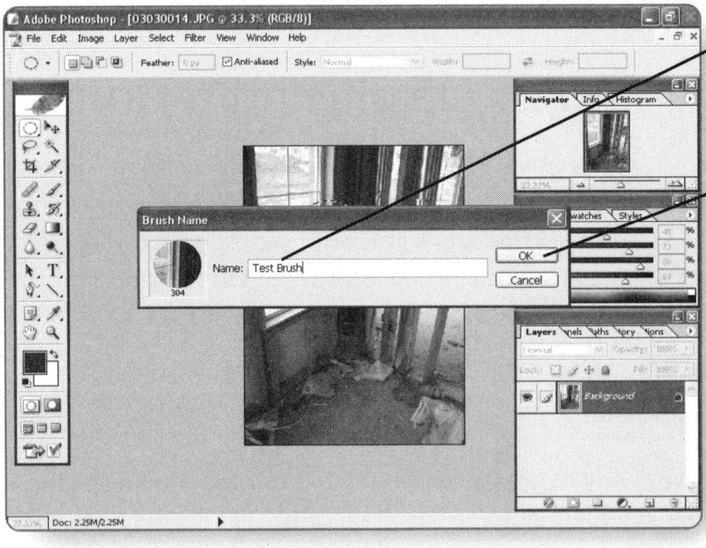

4. **Type** a **brush name**. The name will appear in the Name text box.

5. **Click** on **OK**. The brush will be created and will be included in the Brush drop-down list on the options bar choices for painting tools.

Opening the Brushes Palette

Photoshop CS offers a Brushes palette that you can use to work with available brushes, including custom brushes you've created. The easiest way to access the Brushes palette is from the options bar when you have the Brush tool selected.

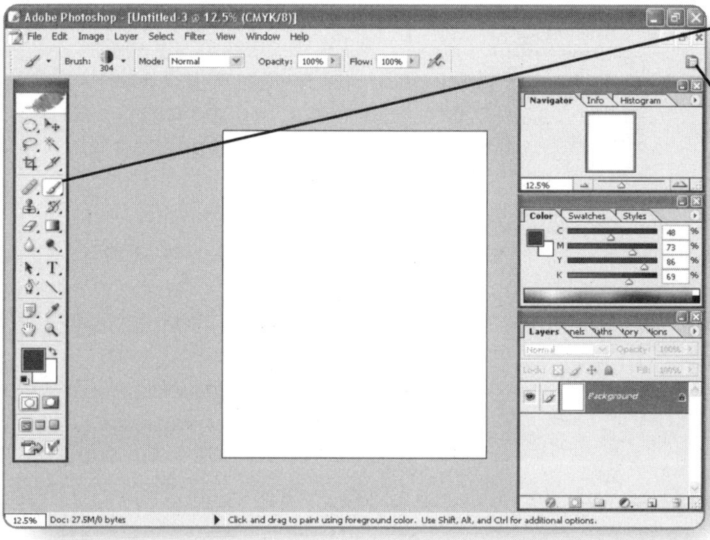

1. **Click** on the **Brush tool**. It will be selected.
2. **Click** on **Toggle the Brush Palette** button in the options bar.

Deleting a Brush

You might create a brush and find that it doesn't offer the effect you had hoped for. In such an instance, you can delete the brush so that it no longer takes up space among the brush choices. Follow these steps to use the Brushes palette to delete a brush.

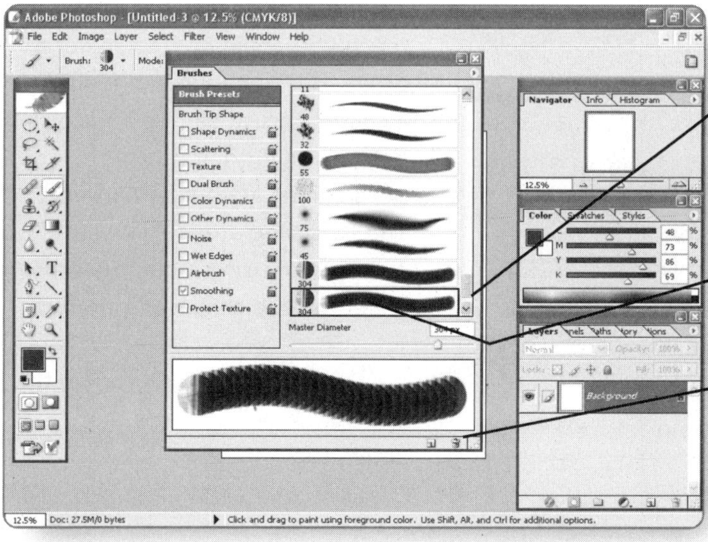

1. **Scroll down** to view additional brushes, if necessary. You will see the brush to delete among the choices.
2. **Click** on the **brush** to delete. It will be selected.
3. **Click** on the **Delete Brush** button in the lower-right corner of the Brushes palette. A message will appear to prompt you to confirm the deletion.

4. **Click** on **OK**. The brush will be deleted.

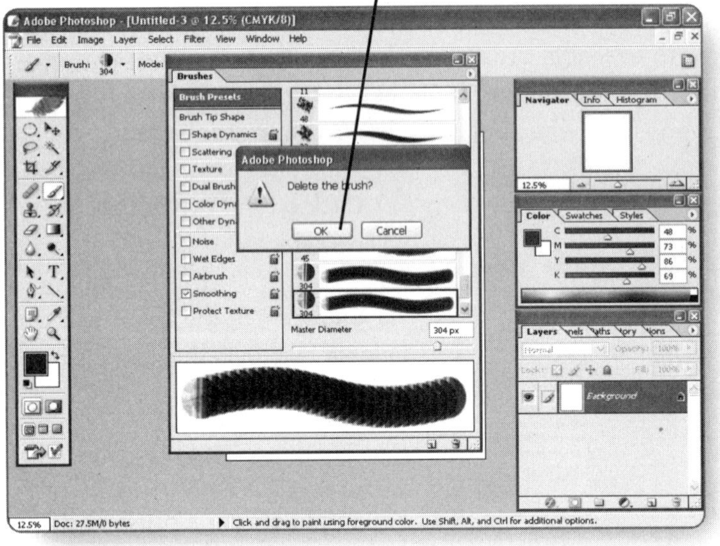

> **TIP**
>
> As with other palettes, the Brushes palette features a menu you can display if you click on the button with the right triangle in the upper-right corner of the palette. You can use the choices on the menu that appears to create, rename, and otherwise work with brushes. The menu also offers a variety of additional brush collections that you can select and display in Photoshop.

Using a Custom Brush

Using a custom brush shape is just like using any other brush shape provided with Photoshop. This final set of steps shows a sample custom brush, not to teach you again how to select a brush, but to show you how cool a custom brush can be and to get you excited about the possibilities in your own work. The following steps show an example of using a custom brush based on the shape of a daffodil.

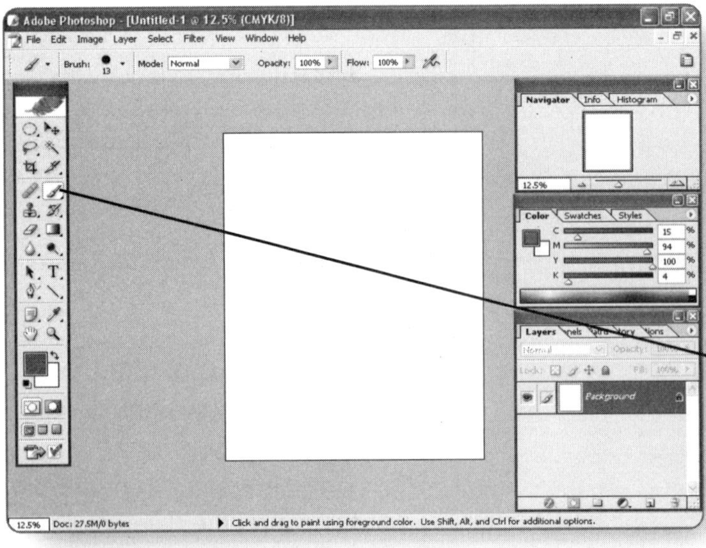

1. **Click** on the **Brush tool** in the toolbox. It will become the active tool.

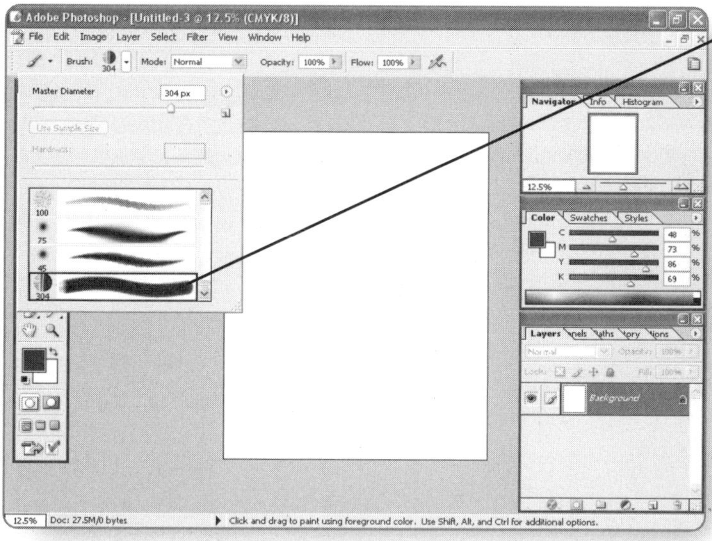

2. **Open** the **Brush** Preset Picker **drop-down list** on the options bar, click on the custom brush to use, and then close the drop-down list. The custom brush you selected will become the active brush shape.

> **TIP**
>
> Custom brushes typically appear at the bottom of the list of brush choices.

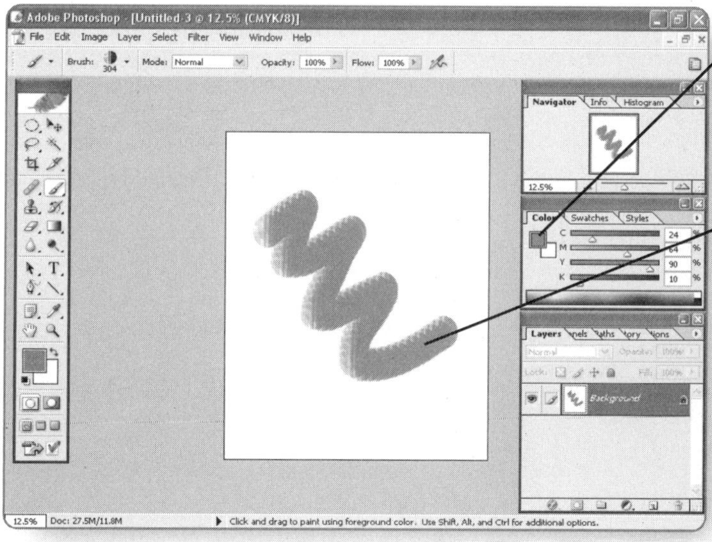

3. **Select** the **foreground color** using the method of your choice. The color you select will become active for the paintbrush.

4. **Drag** in the work area. A paint stroke in the shape of the brush will appear.

4

Zooming and Panning

As you're working with your image, you may need to zoom in to make minute changes, zoom out to see how your image looks overall, and otherwise move around to ensure that you're working with just the image area you need. Photoshop offers a number of techniques you can use to change your view of the image. In this chapter, you'll learn how to:

- Zoom in and out of an image
- View the actual pixel size or print size
- Fit the image to the screen
- Scroll with the scroll bar
- Move around with the Hand tool and Navigator

Using the Zoom Tool

You may have worked with a zoom tool in another program, clicking on a file to zoom in and then clicking again to zoom back out. Photoshop's Zoom tool offers the same behavior plus some additional features to help you quickly display an image in the view that works best. Note that zooming merely adjusts the size of the image file onscreen so that you can work more effectively. Zooming does not adjust the dimensions of the file itself and therefore does not affect the size at which the file prints.

Zooming In and Out

The most common zoom operations are to zoom in (to get a closer view of the image) and to zoom out (to get a farther, more overall view of the image). The steps here illustrate these common uses for the Zoom tool:

1. **Click** on the **Zoom tool** in the Photoshop toolbox. The mouse pointer will change to a magnifying glass, and the options bar will show the options for the Zoom tool.

2. **Click** on the **image**, near the spot you want to magnify. Each time you click with the default zoom pointer (a magnifying glass with a plus sign in it), Photoshop will zoom in on the image by one zoom increment.

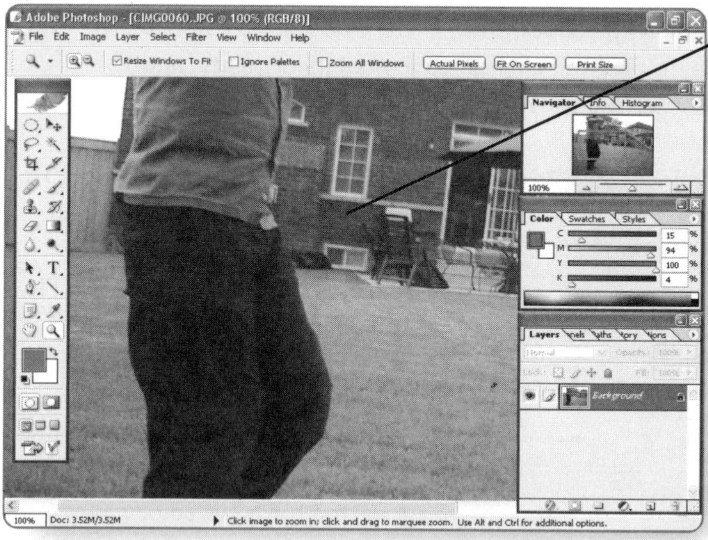

3. Press and **hold** the **Alt key** and then **click** on the **image**. Photoshop will zoom out by one zoom increment each time you Alt+click with the mouse pointer for zooming out (a magnifying glass with a minus sign).

> **NOTE**
>
> The remainder of this book will use the phrase Alt+click to indicate when you should press and hold the Alt key while clicking on a screen item.

Zooming to Print and Pixel Size

You also can use the Zoom tool to zoom the image to one of two predetermined sizes: its pixel size (100%) or the actual print size (if you've used the Page Setup commands to change the size for the printout). You'll learn about these two zoom types next.

1. **Click** on the **Zoom tool** in the Photoshop toolbox. The mouse pointer will change to a magnifying glass, and the options bar will show the options for the Zoom tool.

2. **Click** on **Resize Windows To Fit** on the options bar. A check will appear in the box. When checked, Resize Windows To Fit will change the window size to accommodate the zoomed image. Also, leave Ignore Palettes unchecked. (It should be unchecked by default.) Ignore Palettes turns off color palette features that may change the image's appearance as you zoom.

> **TIP**
>
> Double-clicking on the Zoom tool in the toolbox zooms to 100% size.

3. **Click** on **Print Size button** on the options bar. Photoshop will zoom the image to the actual size it will be when printed.

Fitting the Image to the Screen

To take advantage of all the workspace available in Photoshop, you can zoom the image to the screen size using the Zoom tool, as explained here.

1. **Click** on the **Zoom tool** in the Photoshop toolbox. The mouse pointer will change to a magnifying glass, and the options bar will show the options for the Zoom tool.

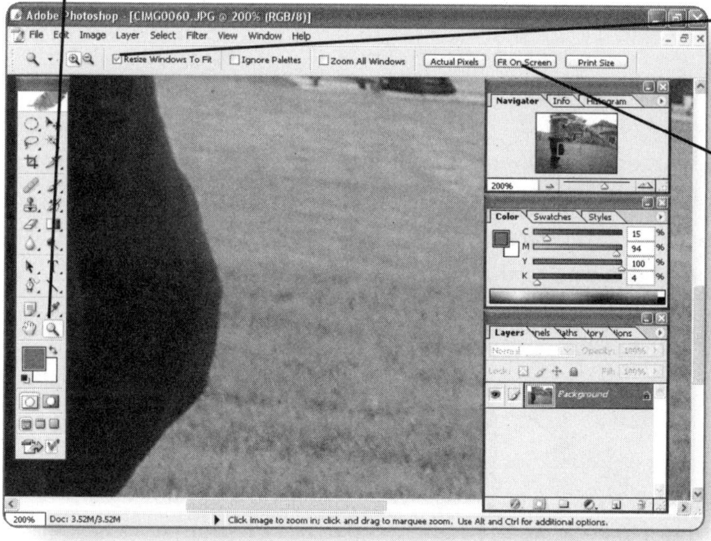

2. **Click** on **Resize Windows To Fit** on the options bar if it is not already selected.

3. **Click** on the **Fit On Screen button**. Photoshop will zoom the image to the largest zoom setting it can have and fit on the screen.

> **TIP**
>
> While the Zoom tool is active, you also can right-click (Control click on Mac OS) on the image to see a shortcut menu with commands for zooming the image.

Changing the View Zone

If you did not opt to resize the image window as you zoomed, zooming in on the image may magnify it to such a size that the image can't fully display in the image window. When this happens, you can use a few different methods to choose which area of the image appears in the image window, thus enabling you to view and work with that portion of the image. This section explores those methods: scroll bars, the Hand tool, and the Navigator.

Using Scroll Bars

Scroll bars appear whenever you've resized the image window so that it can't display all of the image. When this happens, you can use the scroll bars as described next to scroll into view the portion of the image that you'd like to work with.

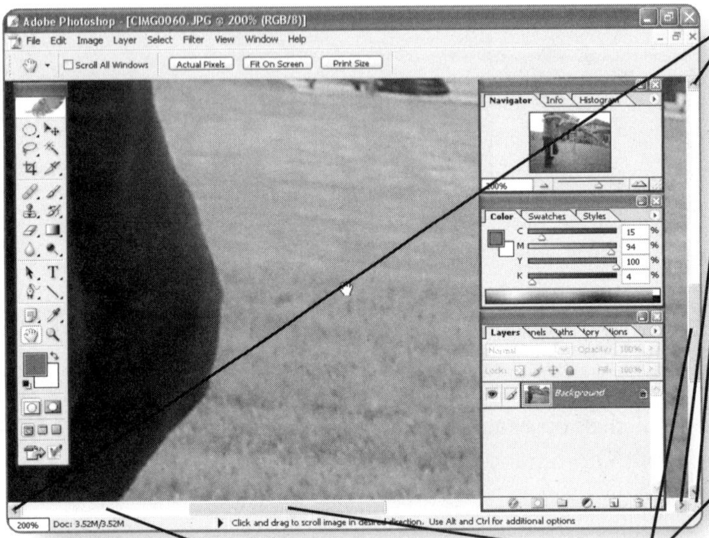

1. Click on a **scroll arrow** on either the vertical or horizontal scroll bar. Each time you click, Photoshop will scroll the image by a small increment.

2. Drag a **scroll bar** box. Photoshop will scroll the image much more quickly.

3. Click on the **scroll bar** itself above or below (or to the left or right of) the scroll box. Depending on the scroll bar and the side of the scroll box on which you click, Photoshop scrolls the image as far as possible in the designated direction.

Using the Hand Tool

You can use the Hand tool to scroll the image in multiple directions at once—much like using both scroll bars simultaneously. The following steps explain how to do so.

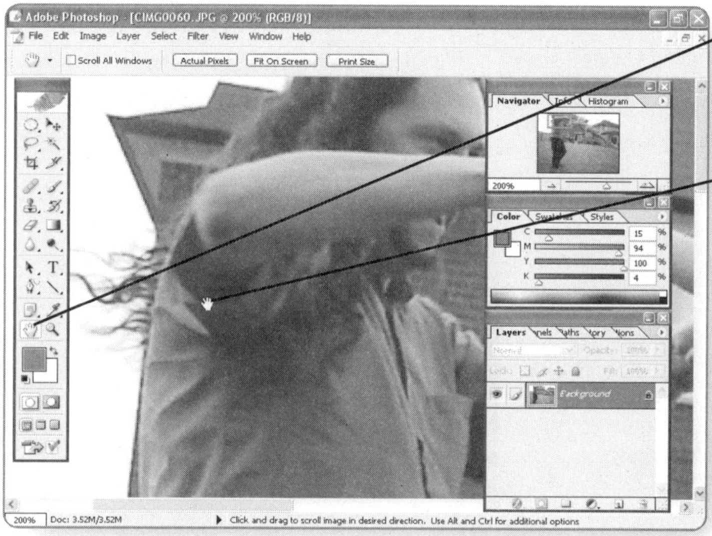

1. **Click** on the **Hand tool** in the toolbox. The mouse pointer will change to a hand pointer.

2. **Click** and **drag** the **image** with the hand pointer. Photoshop will scroll the image in the same direction that you drag.

Using the Navigator

You can use the Navigator palette for multiple purposes—to change the image zoom and to scroll the displayed portion of the image. These steps describe both uses for the palette.

1. **Click** on the **Navigator tab** in the Navigator palette, if necessary. If the palette is not onscreen, it can be opened from the Window menu. The Navigator tab will become active.

2. **Drag** the **zoom slider** in the Navigator palette. Photoshop will zoom the image to the specified size.

> **NOTE**
>
> You also can type a zoom percentage in the text box on the Navigator palette and then press Enter, or you can click on one of the buttons at either end of the zoom slider in the Navigator palette to change the zoom.

3. **Drag** the **red box** on the thumbnail image in the Navigator palette with the hand pointer. Photoshop will scroll the image to display the portion of the image bounded by the red box in the thumbnail.

5

Selecting Image Content

One of the questions I get asked most often during my image-editing training classes is how to take someone's head and put on another person's body. The answer: good selections. Before you can delete, move, fill, or replace part of an image, you have to select the portion of the image with which you want to work. Photoshop offers a number of selection tools that you can use to zero in on an area to edit with precision and control. In this chapter, you'll learn how to:

- Select rectangular or oval shapes
- Make an irregular selection
- Select by color
- Add or remove part of the selection
- Cancel the selection

Using the Marquee Tools

The Marquee tools appear in the upper-left corner of the Photoshop toolbox. Use the Marquee tools to make selections that are regular in shape—rectangles, squares, ovals, circles, or one-pixel borders (also called a row or column selection).

> **NOTE**
>
> If the area to select appears on a particular layer, you need to select that layer in the Layers palette before using any type of tool to make the selection. See Chapter 8, "Working with Layers" to learn more about selecting layers.

Selecting a Rectangle

The following steps show you how easy it is to make a selection that's rectangular in shape:

1. **Press** and **hold** the **mouse button** on the **Marquee tool** in the Photoshop toolbox. The shortcut menu for the Marquee tool will appear.

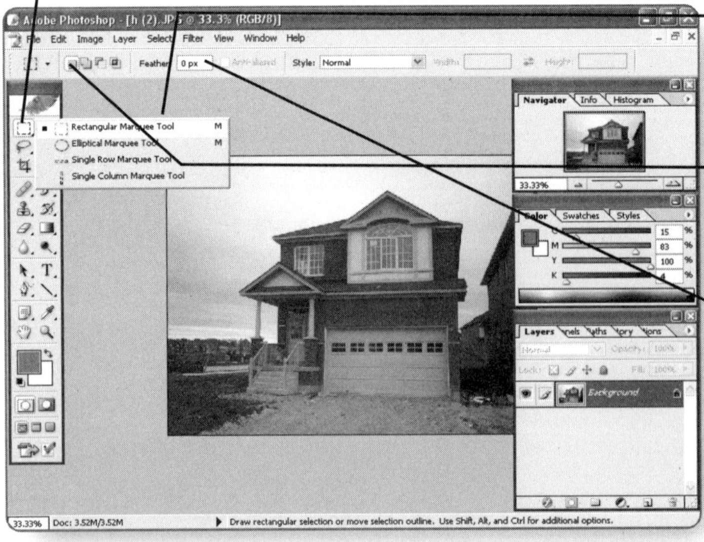

2. **Click** on **Rectangular Marquee Tool**. The Rectangular Marquee tool will become active.
3. **Click** on the **New Selection button** on the options bar, if necessary.
4. **Type** an **entry** (in pixels, up to 250) in the Feather text box on the options bar. The feathering setting will become active.

TIP

Feathering blurs the edges of the selection. The results of feathering become more apparent if you copy and paste the selection.

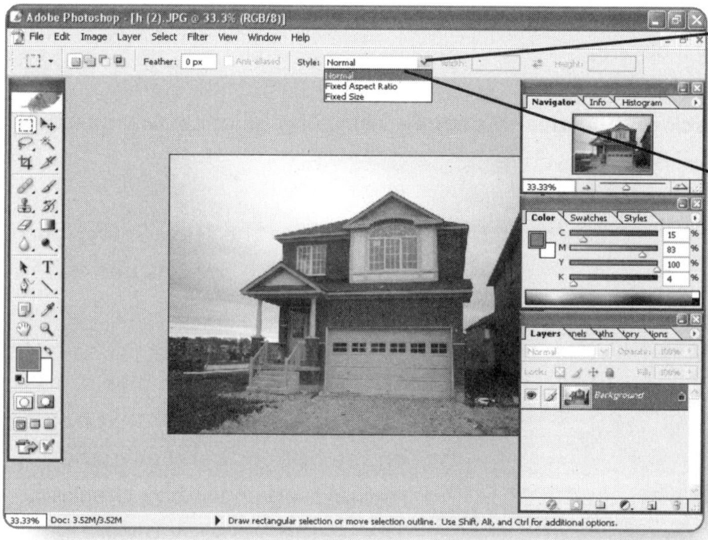

5. Click on the **down arrow** next to the Style drop-down list. The list will appear.

6. Click on **Normal**. The normal selection method will become active.

NOTE

If you select either the Fixed Aspect Ratio or Fixed Size choice from the Style drop-down list, the Width and Height text boxes become active. Type an entry in one of the text boxes (for Fixed Aspect) or both text boxes to specify a selection size and then click on the image to make the selection.

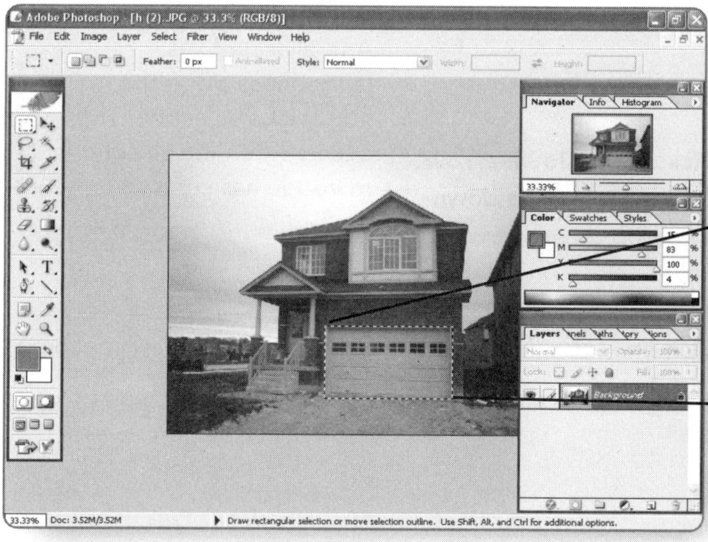

7. Drag on the image over the area to select. (Press and hold Shift as you drag to select a perfect square.)

8. Release the **mouse button**. The selection marquee will appear on the image.

Selecting an Ellipse

If you need to make a round or elliptical selection instead, you can use the following steps:

1. **Press** and **hold** the **mouse button** on the **Marquee tool** in the Photoshop toolbox. The shortcut menu for the Marquee tool will appear.

2. **Click** on **Elliptical Marquee Tool**. The Elliptical Marquee tool will become active.

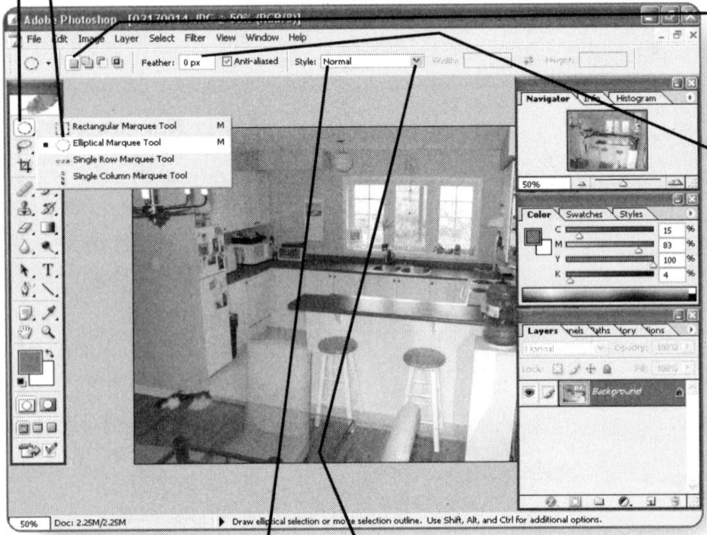

3. **Click** on the **New Selection button** on the options bar, if necessary.

4. **Type** an **entry** (in pixels, up to 250) in the Feather text box on the options bar. Leave the Anti-aliased check box checked. The feathering setting will become active.

> **TIP**
>
> Anti-aliasing fixes jaggedness along the edges of a selection. This occurs when the selection marquee has curves.

5. **Click** on the **down arrow** next to the Style drop-down list. The drop-down list will appear.

6. **Click** on **Normal**. The normal selection method will become active.

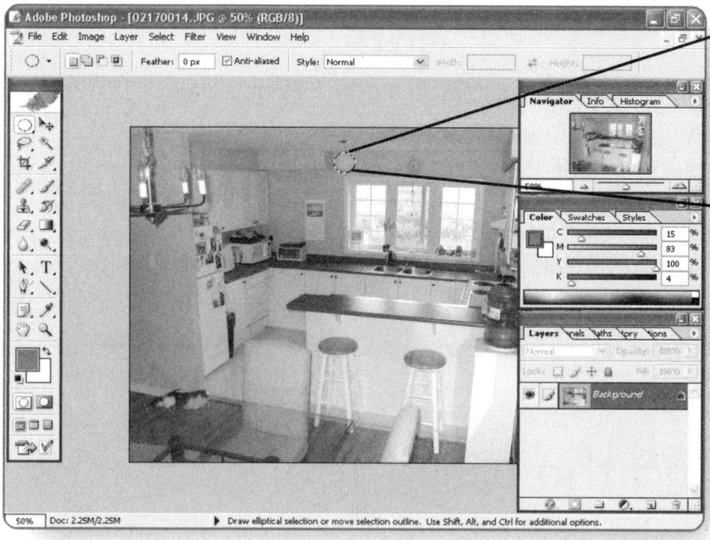

7. **Drag** on the image over the area to select. (Press and hold Shift as you drag to select a perfect circle.)

8. **Release** the **mouse button**. The selection marquee will appear on the image.

Selecting a Row or Column

Use the Single Row Marquee tool or the Single Column Marquee tool to select a one-pixel-wide area in the image. You can then cut or copy and paste the selection to use it as a border in another image.

1. **Press** and **hold** the **mouse button** on the Marquee tool in the Photoshop toolbox. The shortcut menu for the Marquee tool will appear.

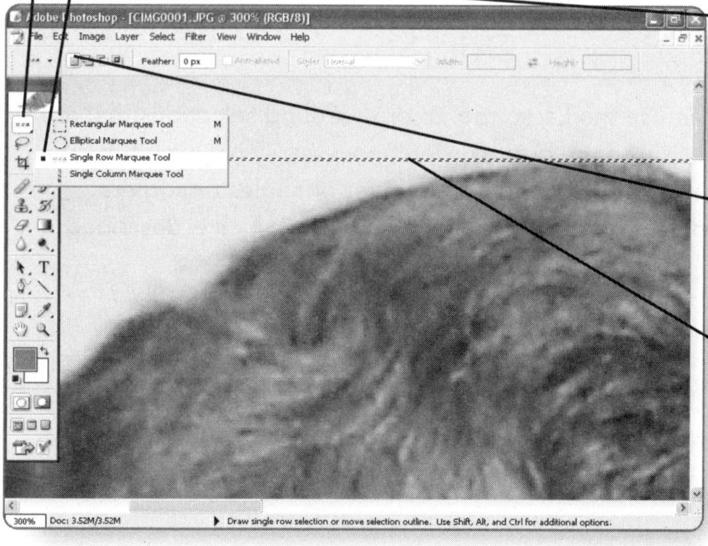

2. **Click** on **Single Row Marquee Tool** or **Single Column Marquee Tool**. The specified marquee tool will become active.

3. **Click** on the **New Selection button** on the options bar, if necessary.

4. **Click** on the **image** over the area to select as a border. The selection marquee will appear on the image.

NOTE

Because Photoshop operates primarily as a paint program, you may find that you can't separate out an area that you'd like to select, no matter which selection technique you use. That's why you retain more editing flexibility in an image if you place the objects for the image on various layers. See Chapter 8 to learn how to create and use layers.

Using the Lasso Tool

Like the Marquee tool, the Lasso tool offers a few different techniques that you can employ to make selections in an image. The Lasso tool's variations enable you to make selections that are not typical or symmetrical in shape. You can select an irregular area by dragging (using the Lasso tool), select a polygon by clicking to place the angles (using the Polygonal Lasso tool), or get help selecting an irregular area (using the Magnetic Lasso tool).

Selecting an Odd Shape

You can use the Lasso tool to drag around selections that are irregular in shape but that don't necessarily have a lot of angle points. (If the shape does have a lot of angles or corners, consider using the Polygonal Lasso tool, which is described next.)

1. **Press** and **hold** the **mouse button** on the **Lasso tool** in the Photoshop toolbox. The shortcut menu for the Lasso tool will appear.

2. **Click** on **Lasso Tool**. The Lasso tool will become active.

3. **Click** on the **New Selection button** on the options bar, if necessary.

4. **Type** an **entry** (in pixels, up to 250) in the Feather text box on the options bar. Leave the Anti-aliased check box checked. The feathering setting will become active.

5. **Drag** around the desired area to select it. A line will appear as you drag.

6. **Continue dragging** all the way back to the starting point or **release** the **mouse button** to close the selection. The selection marquee will appear on the image.

Selecting a Polygon

Use the Polygonal Lasso tool to select odd shapes that have corners and angles, as the following steps demonstrate:

1. **Press** and **hold** the **mouse button** on the Lasso tool in the Photoshop toolbox. The shortcut menu for the Lasso tool will appear.

2. **Click** on **Polygonal Lasso Tool**. The Polygonal Lasso tool will become active.

3. **Click** on the **New Selection button** on the options bar, if necessary.

4. **Type** an **entry** (in pixels, up to 250) in the Feather text box on the options bar. Leave the Anti-aliased check box checked. The feathering setting will become active.

5. **Click** around the **desired area** to specify corners for the selection. A line will appear as you click.

6. **Double-click** the **last point** to close the selection. The selection marquee will appear on the image.

TIP

You can press the Alt key while using either the Lasso tool or the Polygonal Lasso tool to switch between freehand drawing and clicking to set corner points. Press Delete while using any Lasso tool to remove the most recently drawn selection segment.

Using the Magnetic Lasso

The Magnetic Lasso tool helps you make a selection by snapping to fastening points along the edge of a shape in an image.

1. **Click** and **hold** the **Lasso tool** in the Photoshop toolbox. The shortcut menu for the Lasso tool will appear.

2. **Click** on **Magnetic Lasso Tool**. The Magnetic Lasso tool will become active.

3. **Click** on the **New Selection** button on the options bar, if necessary.

4. **Change** other **settings** on the options bar as needed:

- **Make** an **entry** (in pixels, up to 250) in the Feather text box on the options bar. Leave the Anti-aliased check box checked. The feathering setting will become active.
- **Change** the **Width** text box entry (in pixels, between 1 and 40) to set the search width for the tool. The tool will look for edges within the specified zone beside the points you identify with the mouse.
- **Change** the **Edge Contrast** text box entry (in percentages between 1 and 100) to identify how much contrast the tool requires. A lower setting will enable the tool to find edges with less contrast, whereas a higher setting will restrict the tool to finding only high-contrast edges.
- **Change** the **Frequency** text box entry (between 0 and 100) if necessary. A higher setting causes the tool to set more fastening points, whereas a lower setting results in fewer fastening points.

5. Drag on the **desired area** to specify the selection border. (Click to place a fastening point in a particular location.) The selection marquee will appear on the image.

The Magic Wand

One of the quickest ways to make a selection is to use the Magic Wand tool. If all the pixels in the area you want to select are about the same color and adjoin one another in the image, the Magic Wand tool will select them with one click.

1. **Click** on the **Magic Wand tool** in the Photoshop toolbox. The Magic Wand tool will become active.

2. **Click** on the **New Selection button** on the options bar, if necessary.

3. **Change** other **settings** on the options bar as needed:

- **Change** the **Tolerance text box** entry (between 0 and 255) to specify how much variation can occur between the colors included in the selection. A low entry will result in a smaller selection zone composed of fewer like colors, whereas a higher entry will result in a larger selection zone.
- **Leave** the **Anti-aliased check box** checked. The tool will smooth the edges of the selection.
- Leave the Contiguous check box checked. The tool will select all adjoining pixels of the same (or similar) color, not just the pixel on which you click.
- Click on the Use All Layers check box to check it if desired. The tool will then select the matching colors on all layers in the picture.

4. **Click** on the **color** to select on the image with the Magic Wand tool. The selection marquee will appear on the image.

Selecting by Color Range

Selecting by color works somewhat like the Magic Wand tool, except it enables you to select all the pixels of the specified color in the image—not just adjoining or contiguous pixels.

1. **Click** on **Select**. The Select menu will appear.

2. **Click** on **Color Range**. The Color Range dialog box will open.

3. **Click** on the **down arrow** beside the Select list. The Select list will open.

4. **Click** on a **selection type** in the list. If you choose anything other than Sampled Colors from the list, Photoshop immediately previews the color selection in the dialog box, and you can skip to step 8. If you choose Sampled Colors, continue with the next step.

5. **Drag** the **Fuzziness slider** to change its setting, if necessary. Increasing this value will cause Photoshop to select colors similar to the color you select for the match.

6. **Click** on the **Eyedropper Tool** button to select it, if necessary. The Eyedropper tool will become active.

7. **Click** on the **desired color** in the picture. If you choose anything other than Sampled Colors from the Select list, Photoshop immediately previews the color selection in the dialog box.

8. **Click** on **OK**. The dialog box will close, and Photoshop will display marquees around the matching selections in the picture.

NOTE

To add or remove colors from the selection, click on either the Add to Sample or Subtract from Sample button (next to the Eyedropper Tool button) and then click a color on the image.

Adjusting a Selection

Once you've made a selection, you can move it, extend it, change it, or otherwise work with it. The following steps run through the possibilities for modifying a selection:

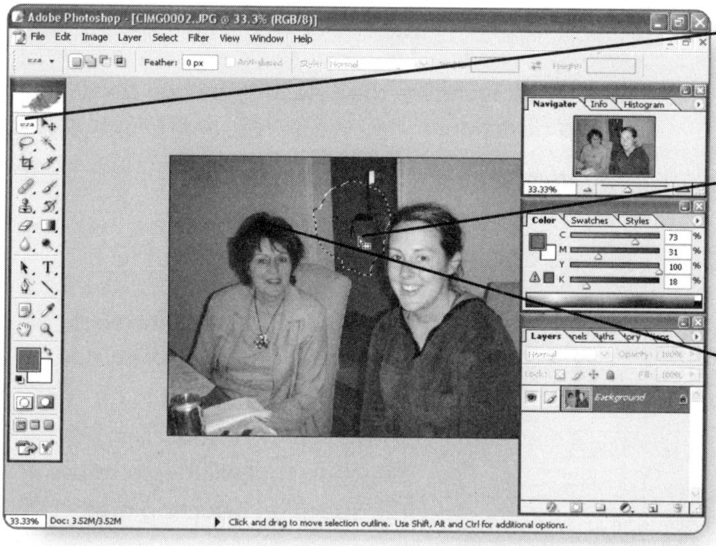

1. Click any of the **Marquee selection tools**. The tool will be highlighted.

2. Position your **mouse pointer** over a selection. The mouse pointer will change to indicate that you are over a selection.

3. Click and **drag** the marquee to a new location. The marquee will move as you drag.

4. Release the **mouse button**. The selection will be moved.

TIP

Pressing an arrow key moves the selection by one pixel in the specified direction.

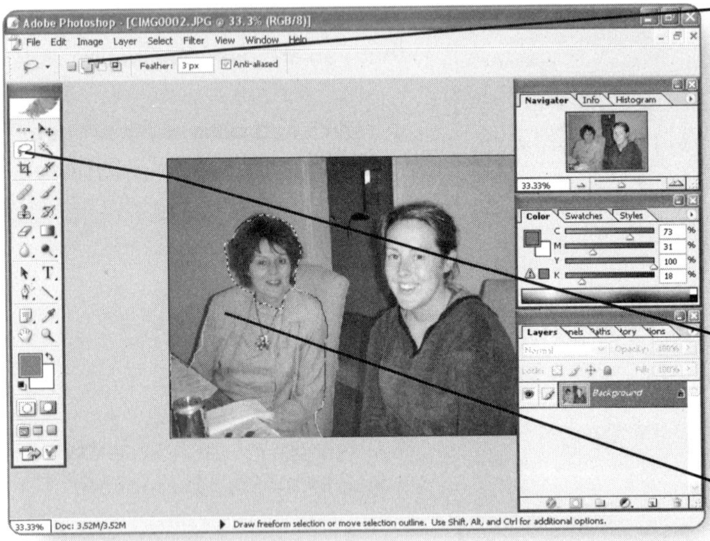

5. **Click** on the **Add to Selection**, **Subtract from Selection**, or **Intersect with Selection** button on the options bar, if available for the active selection tool. The selection tool will begin to use the specified selection method.

6. **Click** on the desired **selection tool**. It will be selected.

7. **Click** and **drag** on the image as required for the active selection tool.

8. **Release** the **mouse button**. Depending on the selection method selected in step 2, Photoshop adds to, removes from, or crops out the selection.

> **TIP**
> You also can press Shift and then use a selection tool to add a selection.

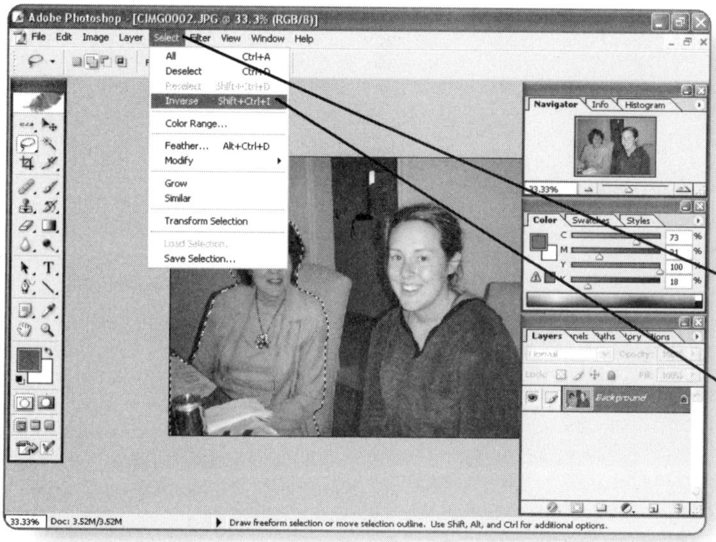

> **TIP**
> To remove the latest selection you've added, don't press Delete! Press Ctrl+Z to undo the selection instead.

9. **Click** on **Select**. The Select menu will appear.

10. **Click** on **Inverse**. Photoshop will select the area that previously was not selected in the image and will deselect the area that was selected.

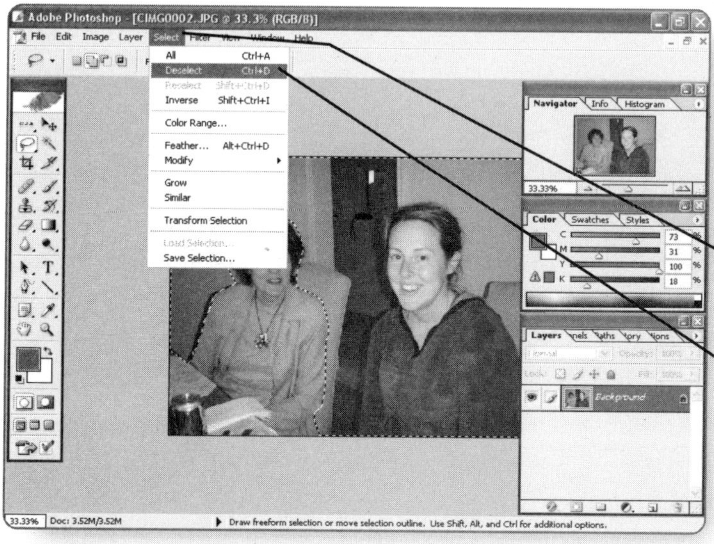

Removing a Selection

When you need to remove or deselect the selection, you can do so with ease.

1. **Click** on **Select**. The Select menu will appear.

2. **Click** on **Deselect**. Photoshop will remove the selection immediately, no matter what selection tool or method you used to make the selection.

6

Manipulating Selections

After you've selected part of the image, the fun begins. You can then start manipulating the selection to change the appearance of the image or share information between image files. This chapter introduces you to the basic changes you can make after you've selected part of the information on a layer in the image. (Chapter 8, "Working with Layers," explains how to layer information.) In this chapter, you'll learn how to:

- Delete, move, or copy what you've selected
- Change a selection by transforming or rotating it
- Fine-tune the selection marquee
- Save and reuse a selection
- Undo a change
- Work with the History palette

Deleting a Selection

After you've made a selection, you can remove the contents of the selection by using the Clear command.

1. **Make** a **selection** in the image using the selection tool of your choice. The selection marquee will appear.

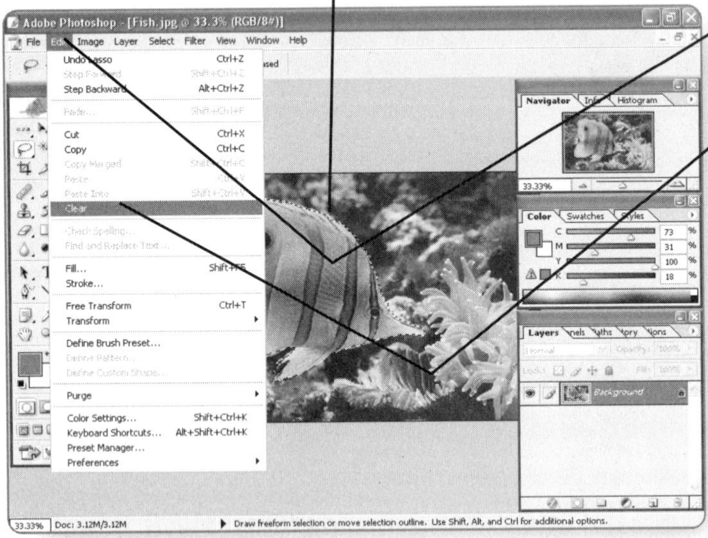

2. **Click** on **Edit**. The Edit menu will appear.

3. **Click** on **Clear**. The selection will disappear completely from the current layer.

> **TIP**
>
> You can press the Delete key in place of steps 2 and 3.

Moving a Selection

Moving a selection requires a tool you haven't used yet—the Move tool. Dragging while the selection tool is active moves the selection marquee only, not the actual image content within that selection. No matter which layer you're working on or what type of content you're dealing with, the Move tool always works in the same way.

1. **Make** a **selection** in the image using the selection tool of your choice. The selection marquee will appear.

2. **Click** on the **Move tool** in the Photoshop toolbox. The Move tool will become active.

3. **Click** on the desired **options** in the options bar to check them as needed. If you check Auto Select Layer, clicking on an area of the image will select its layer. If you check Show Bounding Box, the selection box may change to show handles.

> **NOTE**
>
> If other buttons become active on the options bar, clicking one of them aligns information within the selection marquee, such as text, relative to the borders of the selection marquee.

4. **Position** the **mouse pointer** over the selection from within the marquee.

5. **Drag** the selection to a new location. The selection will move as you drag.

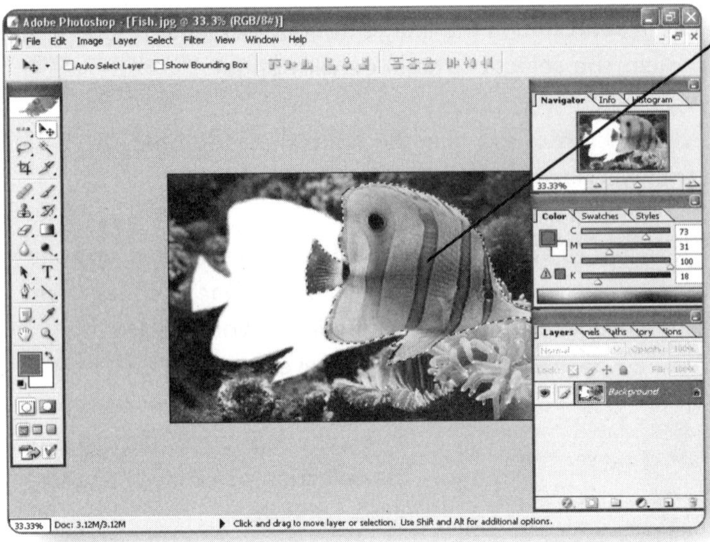

6. **Release** the **mouse button**. The selection will appear in its final location.

Copying a Selection

You can copy a selection to reuse it in another location, such as on another layer in the image file or in a completely new file. This comes in handy because, once you've drawn or scanned in image content, you can reuse it as often as you need to with a minimum of effort. This example illustrates how to create a new image file from content you copy.

1. **Make** a **selection** in the image using the selection tool of your choice. The selection marquee will appear.

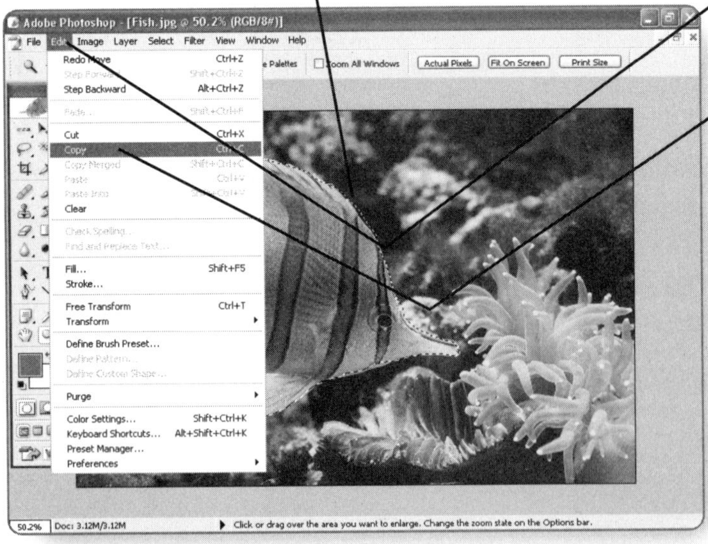

2. **Click** on **Edit**. The Edit menu will appear.

3. **Click** on **Copy**. Photoshop will copy the selection to the Windows Clipboard, a memory holding area.

> **NOTE**
>
> Rather than starting a new image at this point, you could switch to another open image file. If you choose to do that, jump to step 8.

4. Click on **File**. The File menu will appear.

5. Click on **New**. The New dialog box will open.

6. Change the New dialog box **settings** as necessary. The changes you make will affect the size of the new image. You may not need to change the Width and Height entries; typically, they will reflect the size of the copied selection. (See the "Creating a New File" section in Chapter 2, "Working with Image Files," to refresh your memory about the New dialog box settings.)

7. Click on **OK**. The new image file will open.

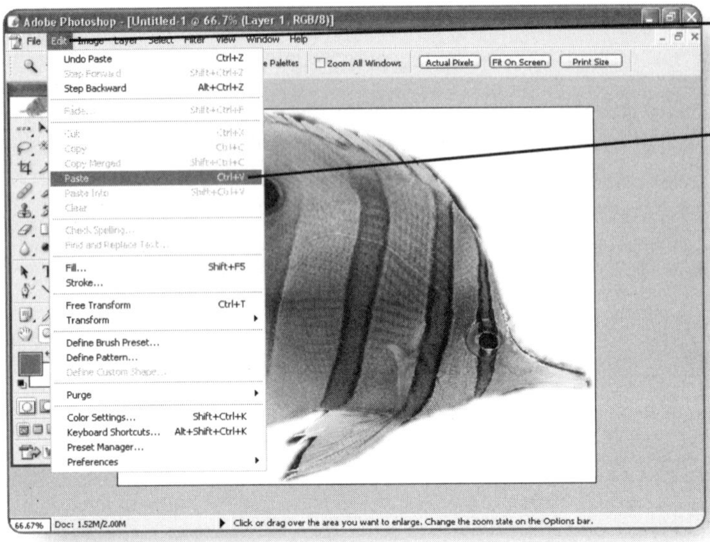

8. **Click** on **Edit**. The Edit menu will appear.

9. **Click** on **Paste**. Photoshop will paste the copied selection into the new file.

> **NOTE**
>
> Don't forget to save the new image file after you've pasted the selection into it.

Transforming a Selection

Photoshop offers a number of transformations you can make to affect a selection in an image.

1. **Make** a **selection** in the image using the selection tool of your choice. The selection marquee will appear.

2. **Click** on **Edit**. The Edit menu will appear.

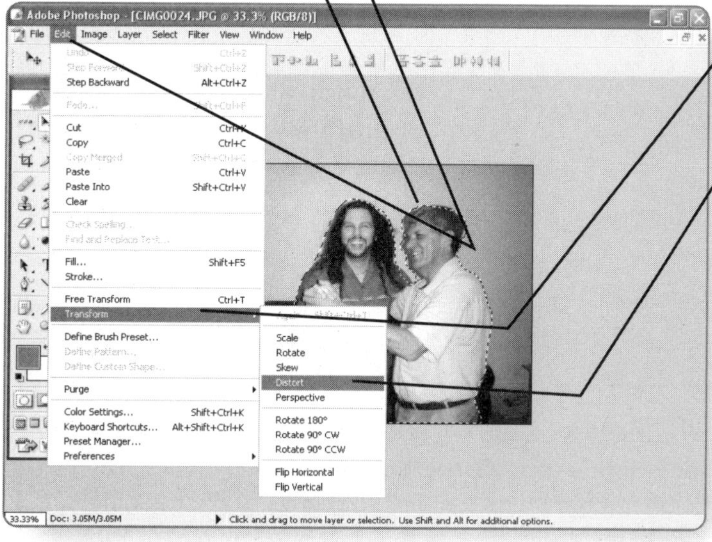

3. **Point** to **Transform**. The Transform submenu will appear.

4. **Click** on the desired **Transform command**. If you choose Rotate 180°, Rotate 90° CW (clockwise), Rotate 90° CCW (counterclockwise), Flip Horizontal, or Flip Vertical, the transformation will appear immediately. If you choose one of the other transforms, proceed to Step 5. The options bar will become active, and special transform handles will appear around the selection.

NOTE

To transform text, you just go to the layer that holds the text; you don't need to select the text itself. The Distort and Perspective transformations aren't available for text.

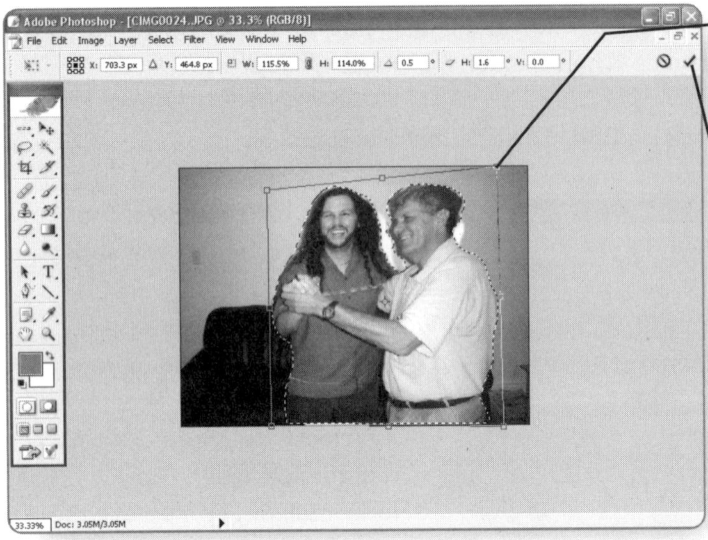

5. **Drag** a **handle**. The transformation will occur. Alternately, you can use the text boxes on the options bar to enter precise transformation settings.

6. **Click** on the **Commit Transform** (check) **button** at the right end of the options bar. Photoshop finalizes the transform.

TIP

Whenever you see a Cancel button (a circle with a slash through it) on the options bar, you can click on that button to cancel the application of the current command or tool settings.

NOTE

You also can choose the Free Transform command from the Edit menu and then drag handles on the selection to transform the selection.

Modifying Part of the Selection

The Select menu gives you a number of commands for adjusting the selection marquee itself. You can use these features before you use other features for altering a selection to be sure that you're working with the proper selection.

Changing the Selection Border

You can add another selection around the current selection marquee so that the specified area within the two marquees becomes the selection. You can then remove that selection or fill it in some way to create a visual border around the selection.

1. **Make** a **selection** in the image using the selection tool of your choice. The selection marquee will appear.

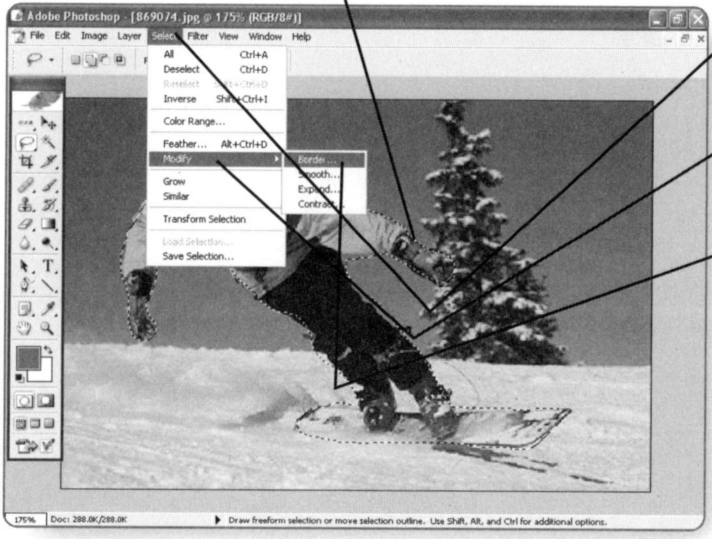

2. **Click** on **Select**. The Select menu will appear.

3. **Point** to **Modify**. The Modify submenu will appear.

4. **Click** on **Border**. The Border Selection dialog box will open.

5. **Type** a new **entry** (between 1 and 64 pixels) for the Width text box. The entry will appear in the text box.

6. **Click** on **OK**. The dialog box will close, and the new border selection will appear.

NOTE

Use the Fill and Stroke commands from the Edit menu to fill in the selected border.

Smoothing the Selection

If you've selected by choosing a color (as described in the "Selecting by Color Range" section in Chapter 5, "Selecting Image Content"), your selection may end up with some stray pixels that are surrounded by a selection marquee. Or, if you've used a Lasso tool, the selection might be a bit more jagged in shape than you now want. To simplify the selection in such instances, you can smooth the selection.

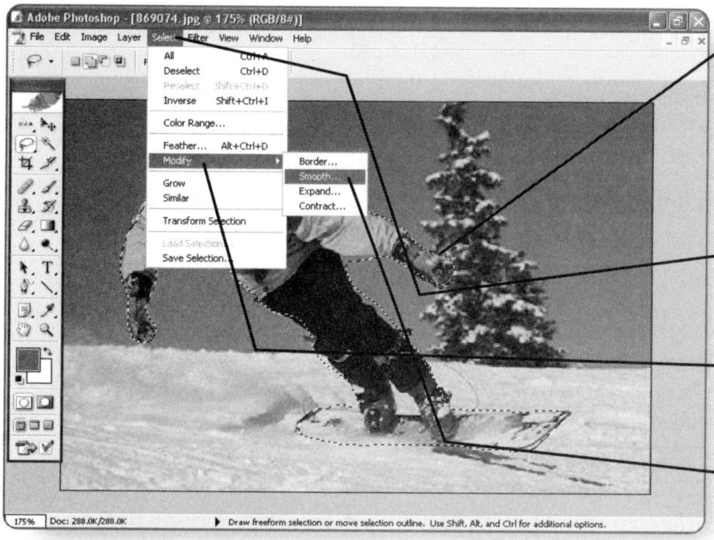

1. **Make** a **selection** in the image by using a color selection method or by using a Lasso tool. The selection marquee or marquees will appear.

2. **Click** on **Select**. The Select menu will appear.

3. **Point** to **Modify**. The Modify submenu will appear.

4. **Click** on **Smooth**. The Smooth Selection dialog box will open.

5. **Type** a new **entry** (between 1 and 16 pixels) for the Sample Radius text box. The entry will appear in the text box.

6. **Click** on **OK**. The dialog box will close, and Photoshop will use the radius setting you entered to add pixels to and eliminate them from the selection.

Photoshop treats each pixel in the selection as the center of a circle with a radius of the width you specified. Depending on whether most of the pixels in the circle are selected, Photoshop will add pixels to the selection (if most are selected) or remove them from the selection (if most aren't selected).

NOTE

You also can use the Grow and Similar commands from the Select menu to expand a selection that you've made by color. The Grow command adds pixels adjoining the current selection that have similar colors to the selection, whereas Similar adds pixels of similar colors from the entire image to the selection.

Expanding or Contracting the Selection

Expanding or contracting the selection really moves the selection marquee rather than affecting the selection itself. Using this method provides more accuracy than dragging or using a color technique (like smoothing) to increase the size of the selection because you specify exactly how many pixels to add or remove from the selection, in terms of height and width.

1. **Make** a **selection** in the image using the selection tool of your choice. The selection marquee will appear.

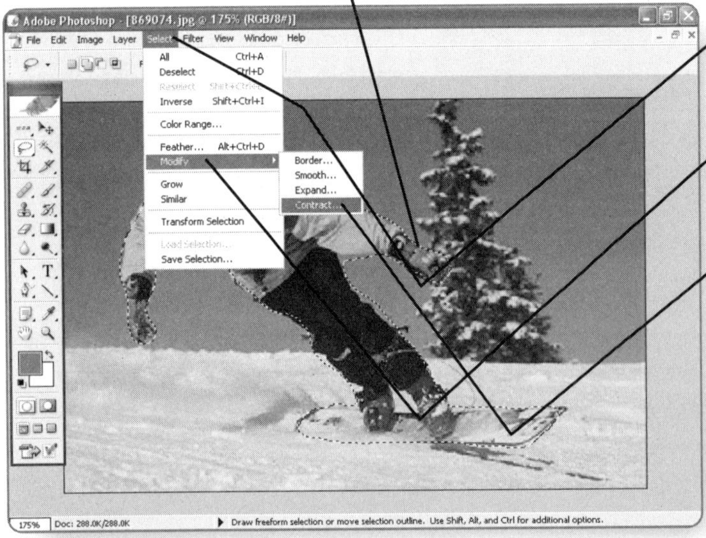

2. **Click** on **Select**. The Select menu will appear.

3. **Point** to **Modify**. The Modify submenu will appear.

4. **Click** on **Expand** or **Contract**. The Expand Selection or Contract Selection dialog box will open.

5. **Type** a **new entry** (between 1 and 100 pixels) in the Expand Selection or Contract Selection text box. The entry will appear in the text box.

6. **Click** on **OK**. The dialog box will close, and the new border selection will appear.

NOTE

You can use the Feather command from the Select menu to feather or soften the edge of the selection. This affects the selection if you copy or paste it or apply another effect like a filter.

Saving a Selection

When you save a selection, you give it a name in the Photoshop file. Then you can easily load the selection in the future. This enables you to repeatedly select exactly the same pixels, which is tough no matter which selection technique you originally used to make the selection.

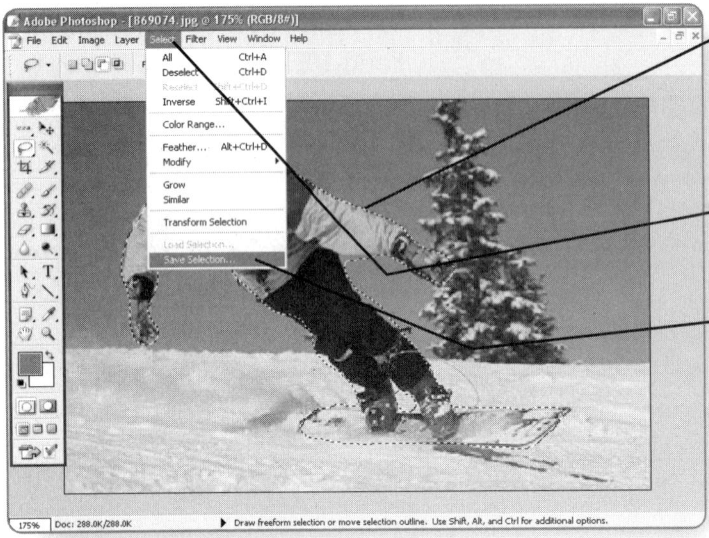

1. **Make** a **selection** in the image using the selection tool of your choice. The selection marquee will appear.

2. **Click** on **Select**. The Select menu will appear.

3. **Click** on **Save Selection**. The Save Selection dialog box will open.

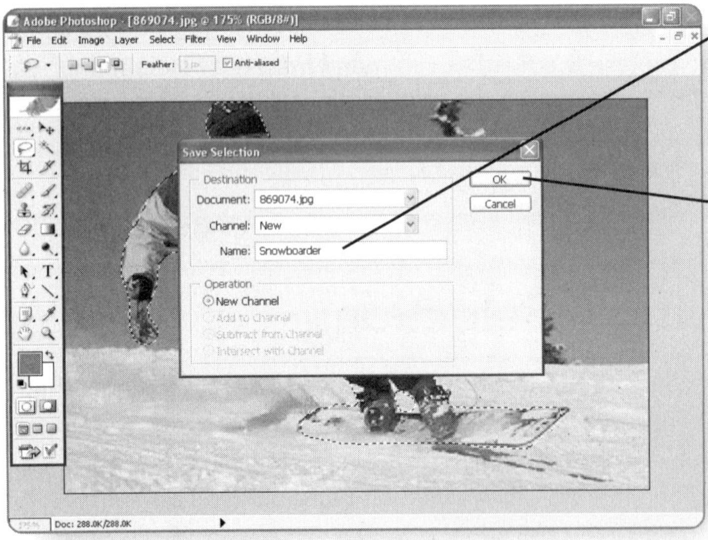

4. **Click** in the **Name text box** and then type a name for the selection. The name will appear in the text box.

5. **Click** on **OK**. The Save Selection dialog box will close, and the saved selection will be added to the file.

NOTE

Be sure to save the file to save the named selection. Also note that saving the selection creates a new channel from the selection. Chapter 15, "Understanding Colors and Channels," explains how to work with channels.

Loading a Selection

When you need to apply a selection that you've previously saved—that is, when you need to reselect a previous selection—you can load the selection.

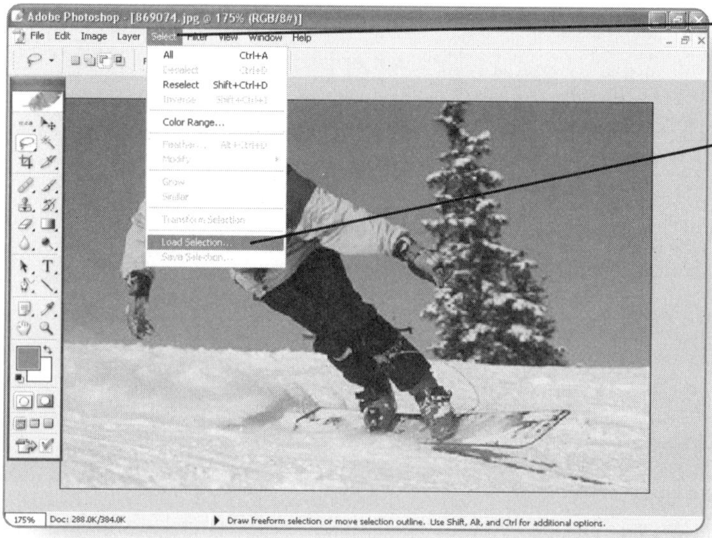

1. **Click** on **Select**. The Select menu will appear.

2. **Click** on **Load Selection**. The Load Selection dialog box will open.

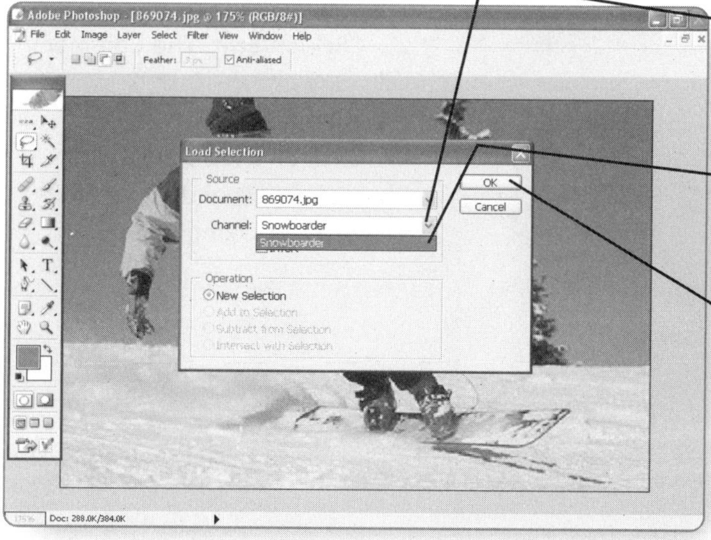

3. **Click** on the **down arrow** next to the Channel box. The list of saved selections will appear.

4. **Click** on the desired **selection**. It will appear as the Channel selection.

5. **Click** on **OK**. The Load Selection dialog box will close, and the selection marquee will appear in the file.

Undoing a Change

The Edit menu offers a number of commands you can use to undo prior changes and actions, such as deselecting a selection.

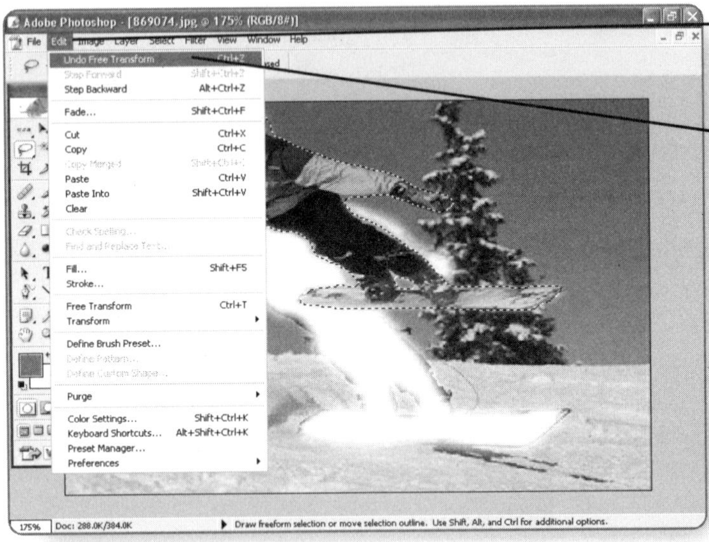

1. Click on **Edit**. The Edit menu will appear.

2. Click on **Undo** (Action Name). Photoshop will undo your most recent change or action.

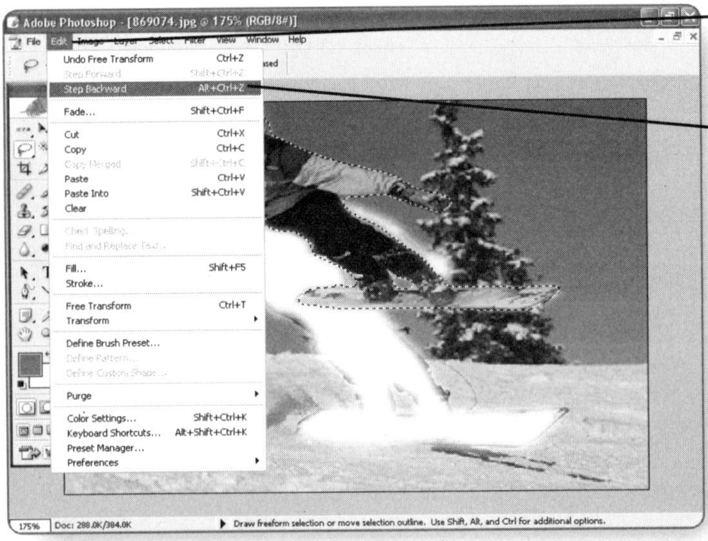

3. Click on **Edit**. The Edit menu will appear.

4. Click on **Step Backward**. Photoshop will undo your next-most-recent change or action.

> **NOTE**
>
> You should only use the Undo command once. After that, use the Step Backward command (described in steps 3 and 4) as many times as needed to step further backward through your changes. Use the Step Forward command (as in steps 5 and 6) to step further forward. To redo a single change, click on Redo (Action Name) in the Edit menu.

5. **Click** on **Edit**. The Edit menu will appear.

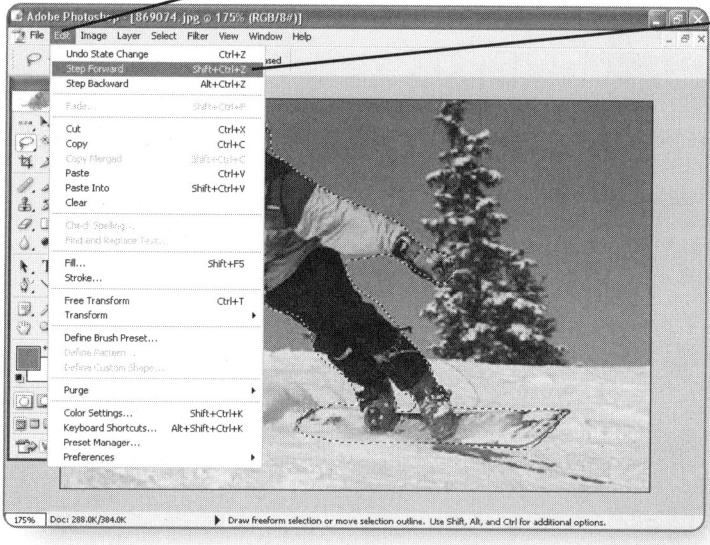

6. **Click** on **Step Forward**. Photoshop will redo the change or action you undid by stepping forward.

Using the History to Undo Changes

The History palette provides one last method for discarding (undoing) actions and changes to a selection that you've made previously. When you use the History palette, you select a change or action out of the sequence of actions you've performed during the current work session with the image file. When you remove that selected action or change, Photoshop undoes that action or change plus all the changes below it in the History list.

1. **Click** on **Window**. The Window menu will appear.

2. **Click** on **History**. The History palette will open.

3. **Click** on the **down scroll arrow** for the scroll bar in the History palette. The list of changes and actions in the History list will scroll down.

4. **Click** on **change** or **action** to undo in the list. The shortcut menu will appear.

5. **Click** on the **Delete** button. A message box asking you to confirm the History deletion will open.

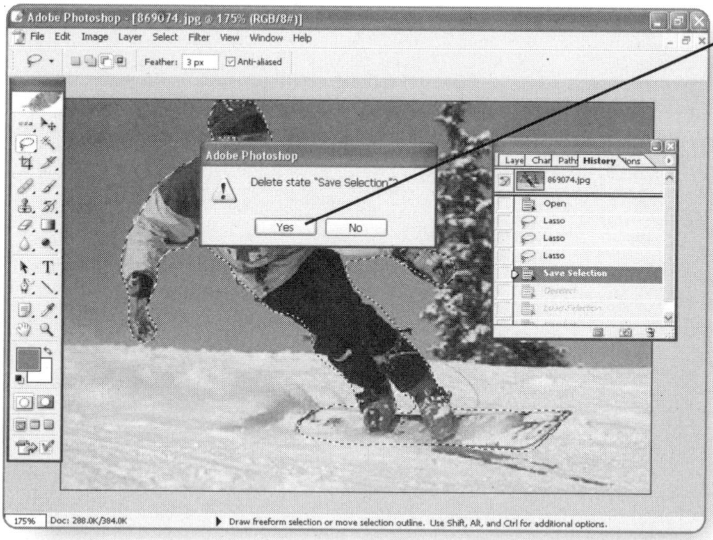

6. Click on **Yes**. Photoshop will close the dialog box and undo the specified change and all the changes below it in the History palette.

Reverting

You can go back to the last saved version of your file using the Revert command. This will undo all the changes you have made since the last time you saved the file.

1. Click on **File**. The File menu will appear.

2. Click on **Revert**. All the changes you have made to the image since the last time you saved it will be undone.

7

Using Positioning Tools and Presets

Photoshop provides more precision editing tools than perhaps any other graphics program. Now that you know how to select and move image content, you may want to try out tools you can exploit to align selections perfectly. Before you start making many moves in your image files, review this chapter to learn the following skills:

- Displaying a grid you can use for alignment
- Displaying rulers you can use for alignment
- Snapping a selection to a guide or grid
- Adding custom alignment guides and locking them in place
- Building presets to customize tools

Showing and Hiding the Grid

You can display nonprinting gridlines in the current image window and then use those gridlines to help you align selections in the image. You can show and hide the grid as needed, turning it on to position selections and then turning it back off when you want to assess the image's background or overall appearance.

> **NOTE**
>
> Remember, you have to be working on the layer that has the image content to select. Chapter 8, "Working with Layers," explains how to navigate to and use layers. In some cases, you can choose the layer and then use the Move tool to move the layer contents without making a selection.

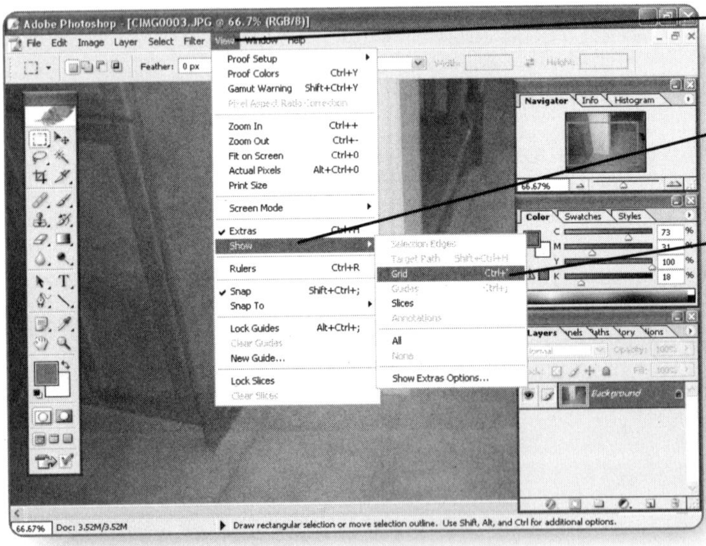

1. **Click** on **View**. The View menu will appear.
2. **Point** to **Show**. The Show submenu will appear.
3. **Click** on **Grid**. The gridlines will appear immediately in the current image file.

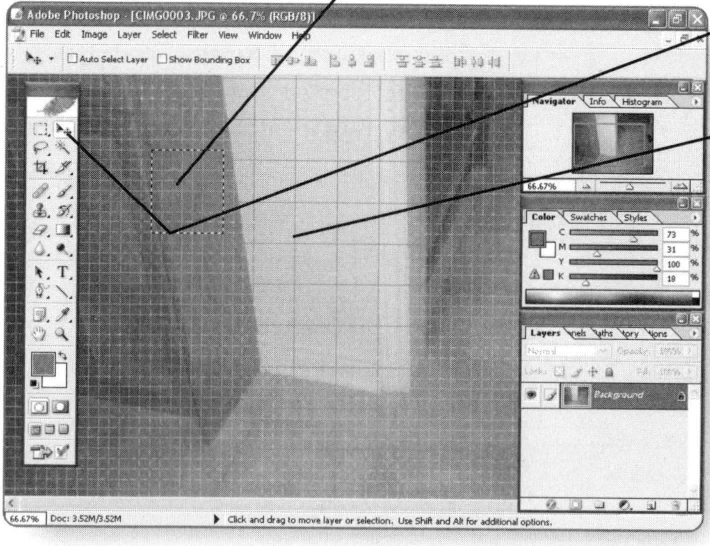

4. **Make** a **selection** using one of the selection methods.

5. **Click** on the **Move tool**. It will be highlighted.

6. **Drag** the selection. You can use the gridline to align the selection.

> **NOTE**
>
> If the selection "jumps around" and won't align as you think it should, the Snap To feature might be active. See the section "Using Snap and Snap To" later in this chapter to learn how to use this feature.

7. **Repeat** steps **1** to **3** to remove the grid.

Showing and Hiding Rulers

The rulers come in handy when you need to position a selection (such as a logo inserted on a new layer) at a precise location within the image. Turn on the rulers when you need to position selections based on measurements and then turn them back off when you no longer need them.

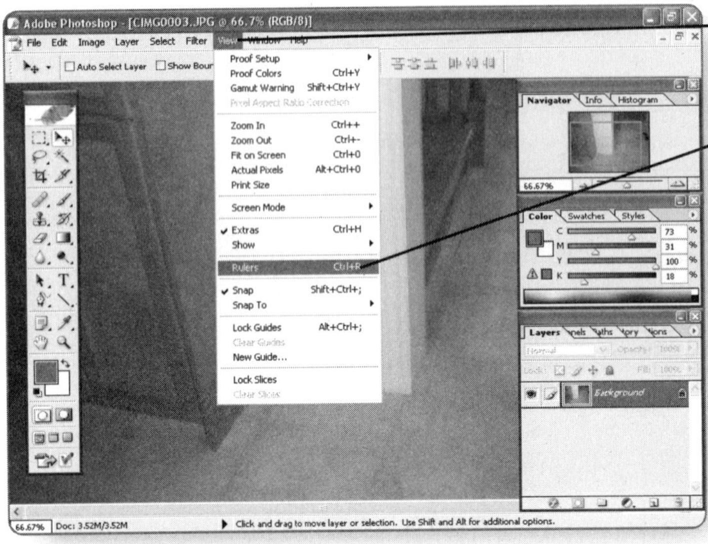

1. **Click** on **View**. The View menu will appear.

2. **Click** on **Rulers**. The rulers will appear immediately in the current image window.

> **NOTE**
>
> The vertical ruler appears along the left side of the image window, and the horizontal ruler appears across the top of the window.

4. **Make** a **selection** using one of the selection methods.

5. **Click** on the **Move tool**. It will be highlighted.

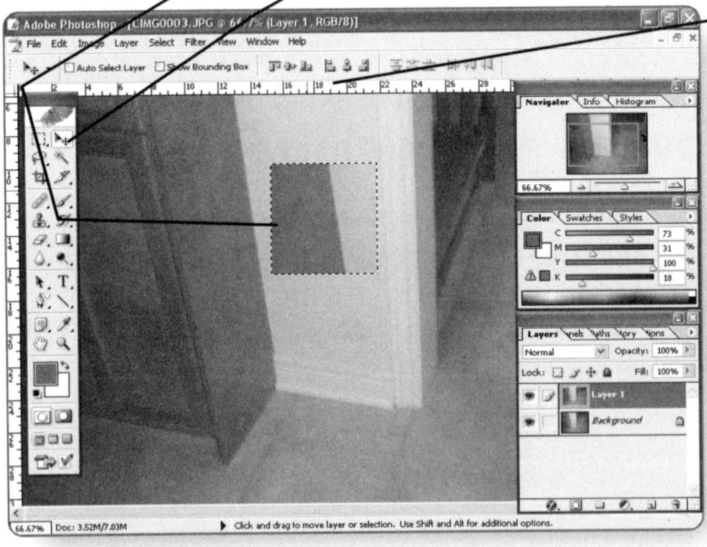

6. **Click** and **drag** the selection. You can use the gridline to align the selection. Watch the dotted gray lines on the rulers to judge position as you drag. The selection will drop into the specified location when you finish dragging.

7. **Repeat** steps **1** to **3** to remove the grid.

Using Snap and Snap To

The Snap To feature in Photoshop ensures that a selection aligns to the grid or to the custom guides that you add as you drag. You can turn snapping to grids or guides off and on individually or use the Snap command to toggle all snapping on and off. By default, snapping to both the grid and guidelines is turned on in Photoshop.

NOTE

The grid must be displayed to enable the command for turning on or off snapping to the grid. In contrast, the command for turning on or off snapping to guidelines is available whether or not you've added guidelines into the image file, as described in the next section.

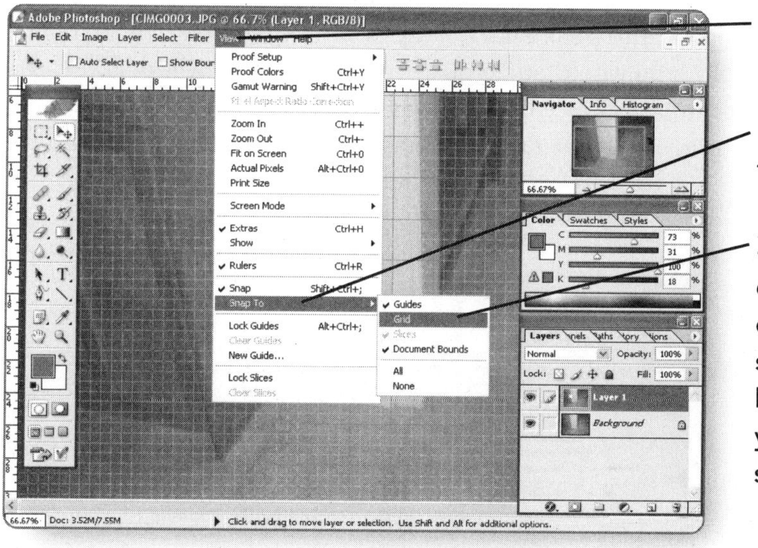

1. **Click** on **View**. The View menu will appear.
2. **Point** to **Snap To**. The Snap To submenu will appear.
3. **Click** on **Guides** or **Grid**. The check beside the feature you clicked will be removed, and the selected Snap To feature will no longer be active. The next time you move a selection, it will not snap into position.

NOTE

Turning off snapping can help when you need to position selections relative to one another rather than relative to a grid.

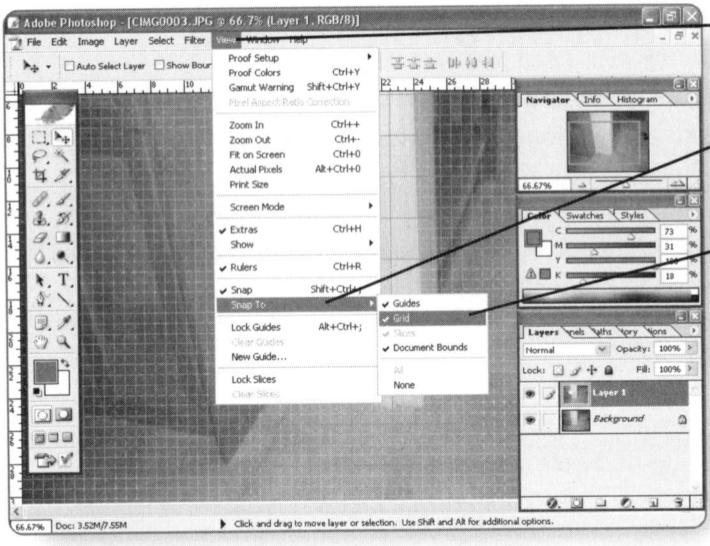

4. Click on **View**. The View menu will appear.

5. Point to **Snap To**. The Snap To submenu will appear.

6. Click on **Guides** or **Grid**. A check will appear beside the feature you clicked, and the selected Snap To feature will become active again. The next time you move a selection, it will snap into position.

Guides

Guides, in a sense, serve as custom gridlines. You put a guideline into position so that you can align selections to it. Ideally, you would add a guideline in a location where no gridline occurs or when you want to use guidelines rather than the grid. Also, because guidelines appear in blue, you can add a guideline to highlight an important grid location. The fastest way to add guidelines is from the ruler.

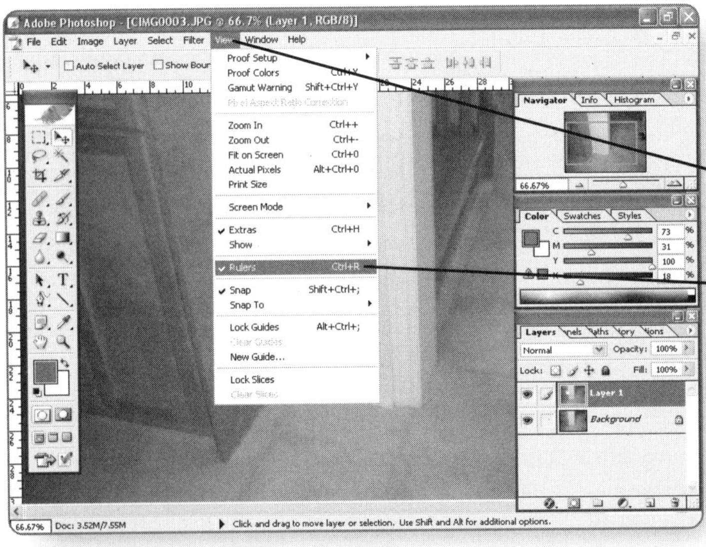

1. Click on **View**. The View menu will appear.

2. Click on **Rulers** if required. The rulers will appear immediately in the current image window.

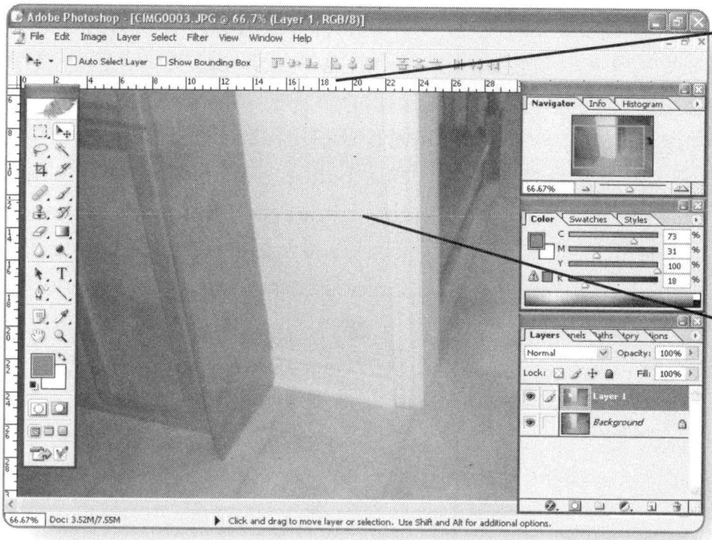

3. **Place** the **mouse pointer** over the vertical or horizontal ruler. Positioning over a horizontal ruler will result in a horizontal guideline, whereas positioning over a vertical ruler will give you a vertical guideline.

4. **Click** and **drag** from the ruler onto your image. A guideline will appear.

Locking Guides

You can lock guides to prevent any accidental guideline changes. (For example, you could mistakenly move a guideline rather than the selection, especially when the selection falls very close to the guideline.) When you need to change guidelines, unlock them first.

> **NOTE**
>
> Locking guidelines doesn't prevent you from clearing them. If you unintentionally clear guidelines, immediately undo the change.

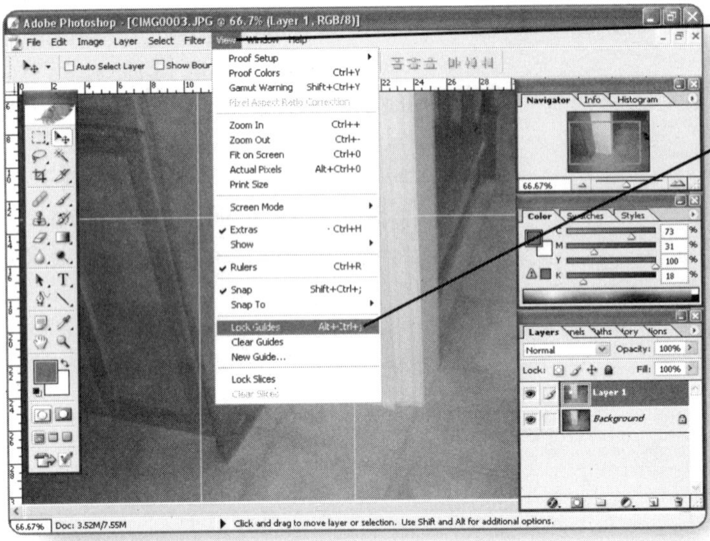

1. **Click** on **View**. The View menu will appear.
2. **Click** on **Lock Guides**. Photoshop will immediately lock the guides into position. A check mark will appear beside the Lock Guides command on the menu.
3. **Repeat** steps **1** and **2** to unlock the guides.

Removing Guides

When you are finished using your guides, you can clear them all with the Clear Guides command.

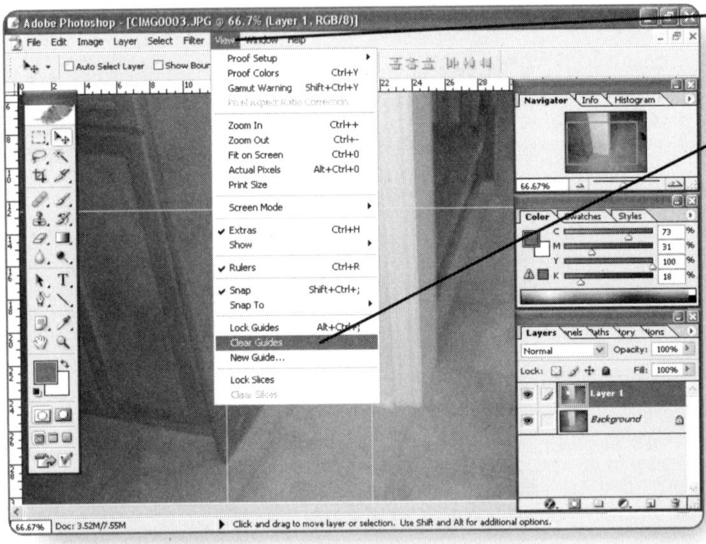

1. **Click** on **View**. The View menu will appear.
2. **Click** on **Clear Guides**. The guides will be removed.

Setting Up Your Tools with the Preset Palette

In the "Creating or Displaying a Brush" section in Chapter 3, "Adding Content with Tools," you learned how to create and use your own custom brush in Photoshop. In addition to creating a custom brush, you can create a preset. To make a preset, you select a tool, choose your favorite settings for the tool, and then save the preset. The preset stores your favorite settings for the tool. Later, when you load the preset, the tool and the specified settings immediately become active. This section describes how to create and use presets, as well as how to load additional brush, color, or pattern choices for your tools using the Preset Manager.

Saving a Preset

Because Photoshop offers so many tools and settings, you have nearly unlimited possibilities for editing images. Over time, however, you'll probably develop favorite techniques that involve using a particular tool and particular settings. Rather than having to remember the desired tool and all the associated settings, you can simply save each favorite combination as a preset using the Tool Presets palette.

1. **Click** on the desired **tool**. Its options will become active in the options bar.

2. **Choose** the desired **settings** in the options bar, and choose a foreground or background color if necessary. These settings will become the current settings for the tool.

3. Click on **Window**. The Window menu will appear.

4. Click on **Tool Presets**. The Tool Presets palette will open.

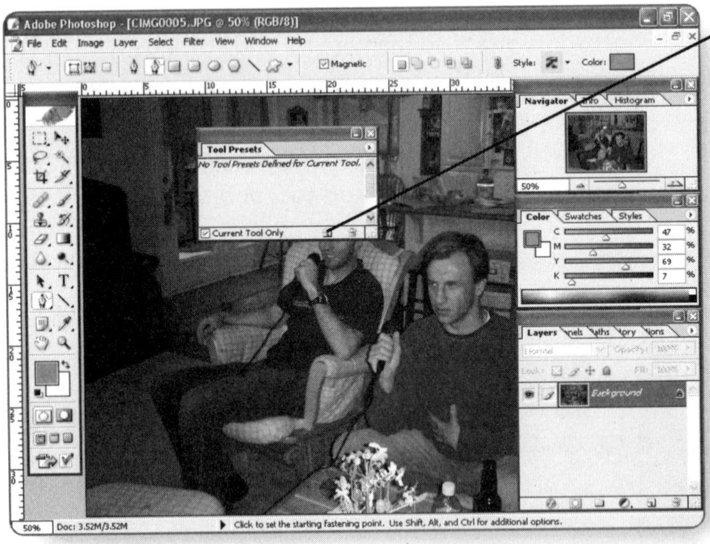

5. Click on the **Create New Tool Preset button** at the bottom of the palette. The New Tool Preset dialog box will open.

6. Type a **name** for the preset in the Name text box. The preset name will appear in the dialog box.

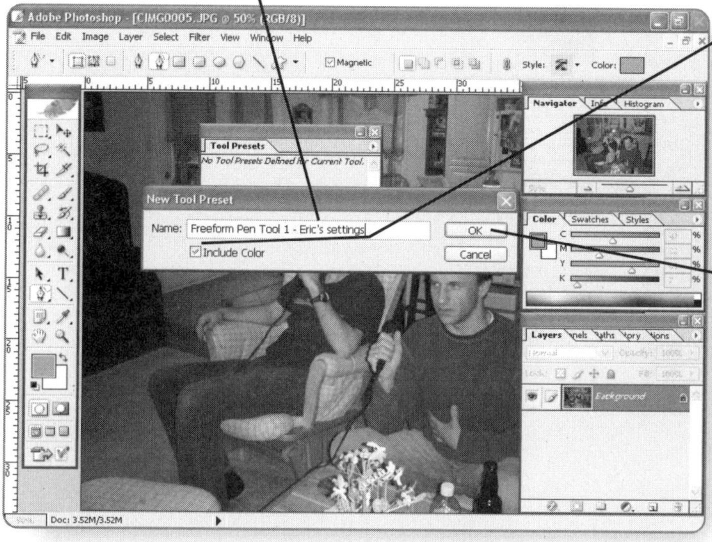

7. Click on the **Include Color check box** as necessary. When it's checked, Photoshop will save the current color selections along with the other preset settings.

8. Click on **OK**. The dialog box will close, and the new preset will appear in the Tool Presets palette.

Using a Preset

Most presets that you create are available from the options bar for the tool you select.

1. Click on the desired **tool**. The option bar will change to match that tool.

2. Click on the **Click to open the Tool Presets picker button**. A window with presets for that tool will appear.

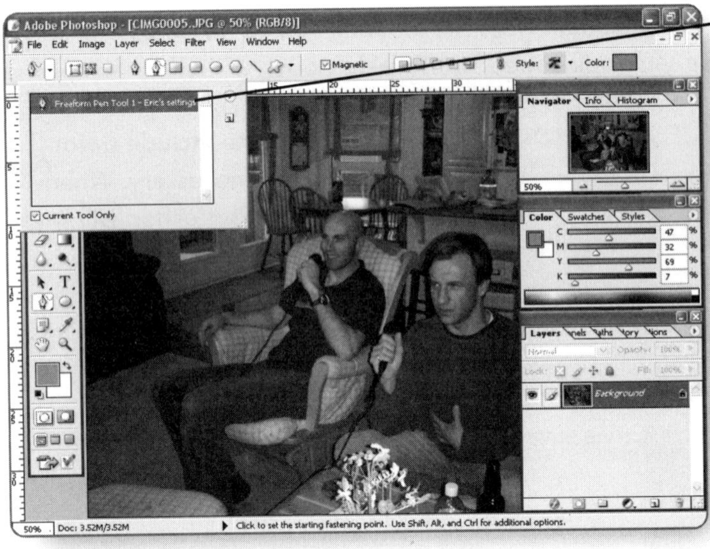

3. **Double-click** on the desired **preset**. It will now be selected, and you can begin using that tool.

Part II Review Questions

1. How do you select a tool? See "Selecting a Tool" in Chapter 3.
2. Which are the painting tools, and which are the drawing tools? See "Working with Painting Tools" and "Working with Drawing Tools" in Chapter 3.
3. What's a fast way to change the portion of the image that appears in the window? See "Using the Hand Tool" and "Using the Navigator" in Chapter 4.
4. What can you select with the Marquee tool? See "Using the Marquee Tool" in Chapter 5.
5. What different selections does the Lasso tool offer? See "Using the Lasso Tool" in Chapter 5.
6. How do you deselect a selection? See "Removing a Selection" in Chapter 5.
7. How do you delete selected image content? See "Deleting a Selection" in Chapter 6.
8. Can you reuse a selection? See "Saving a Selection" and "Loading a Selection" in Chapter 6.
9. What if I need to undo a change? See "Undoing a Change" and "Using the History to Undo Changes" in Chapter 6.
10. Can Photoshop align selections that I move? See "Using Snap and Snap To" in Chapter 7.

PART III

Using Layers, Masks, and Paths

8

Working with Layers

Photoshop allows you to create your images on a variety of different layers. Creating content on separate layers enables you to retain control of the placement and effects for various individual elements in an image. By having your objects on different layers you not only have better control over your image, but you can create some interesting effects. In this chapter, you'll learn how to:

- Use various methods to create a layer
- Select layers
- Create new patterns for use in layers
- Change layer settings
- Arrange layers
- Merge layers to flatten the image

Creating a Layer

Nearly every image file by default has one special layer called the Background layer. (If you create a new transparent image, it starts with Layer 1.) An image can have more layers than your computer's memory can probably handle—up to 8,000. Some actions, such as adding text, create a new layer automatically. In other instances, you might need to create a layer manually before adding elements into it. This section explains how to do so.

> **NOTE**
>
> When you create a new image, it sometimes helps to click on the Transparent option in the New dialog box. This ensures that a white background won't hide other layers you may add.

Making a New Layer

The simplest way to create a layer is to simply add a new, blank layer.

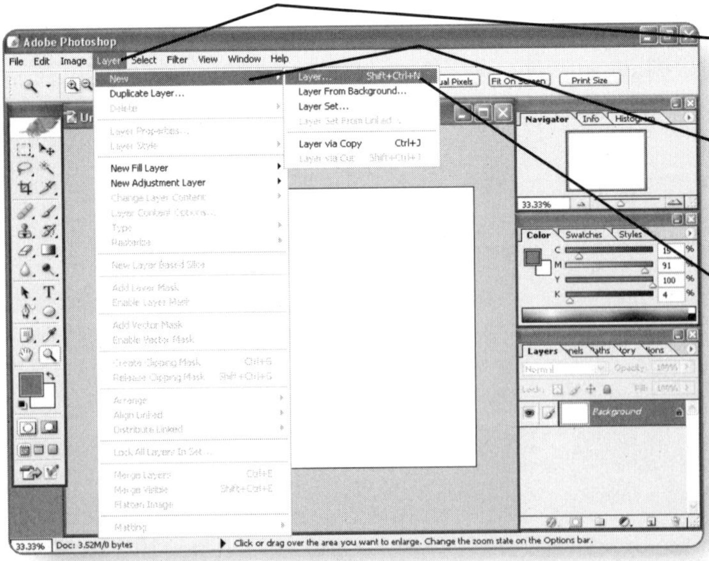

1. **Click** on **Layer**. The Layer menu will appear.
2. Hold the mouse pointer over **New**. The New submenu will appear.
3. **Click** on **Layer**. The New Layer dialog box will open.

TIP

A layer set organizes layers, much as a folder organizes files on a hard disk. Click on Layer, hold the mouse pointer over New, and then click on Layer Set to create a layer set.

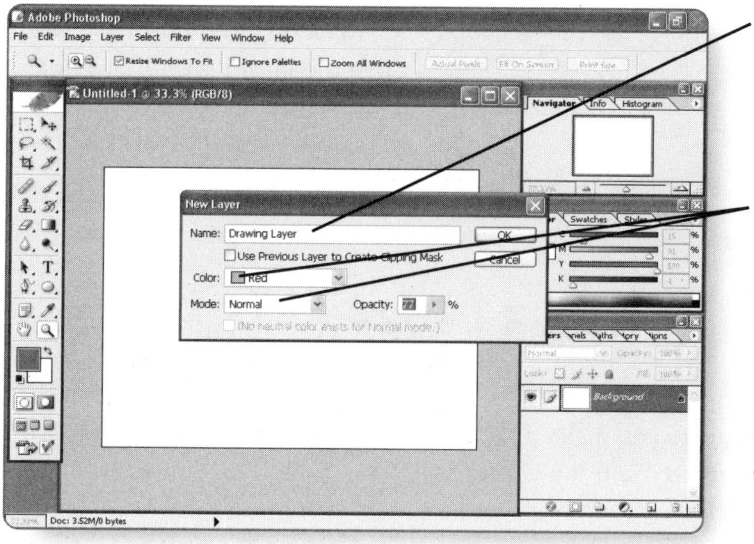

4. **Type** a **name** for the layer into the Name text box. The specified name will be used for the layer.

5. **Choose** an **option** from the Color and Mode lists, if necessary. Making a Color choice will apply a color to the new layer's listing in the Layers palette. Making a Mode choice will apply a layer blending mode, which controls how the individual pixels on the layer blend with pixels on other layers.

TIP

Depending on the choice you make from the Mode list, you may have to make other layers, such as the Background layer, transparent. To do so, double-click on the layer in the Layers palette, change the Opacity setting to 0, and then click on OK.

TIP

Some blending modes enable the Fill with check box. You can click on it to check it and apply the applicable neutral color.

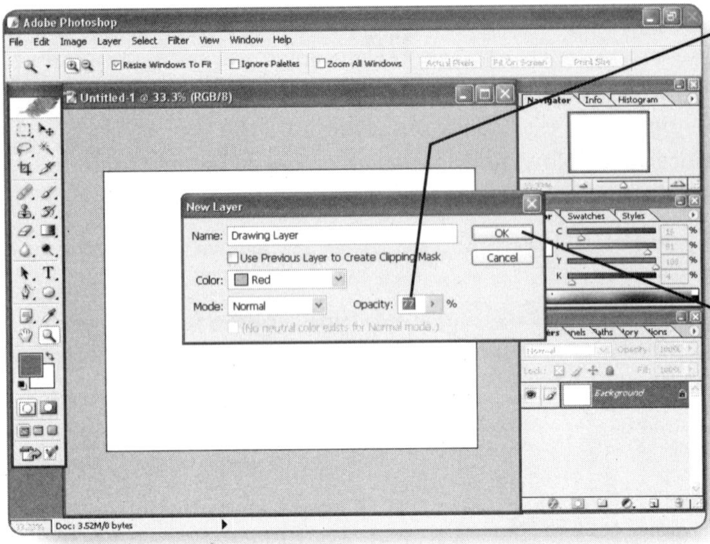

6. **Type** a **new entry** into the Opacity text box, if necessary. (You can also click on its arrow, drag the slider, and click on the arrow again.) Photoshop will make the layer's contents more transparent.

7. **Click** on **OK**. Photoshop will close the New Layer dialog box and create the new layer, which will appear in the Layers palette.

Selecting a Layer

Selecting a layer makes it the current or active layer so that the changes you make next will only apply to that layer. Layers are selected using the Layers palette.

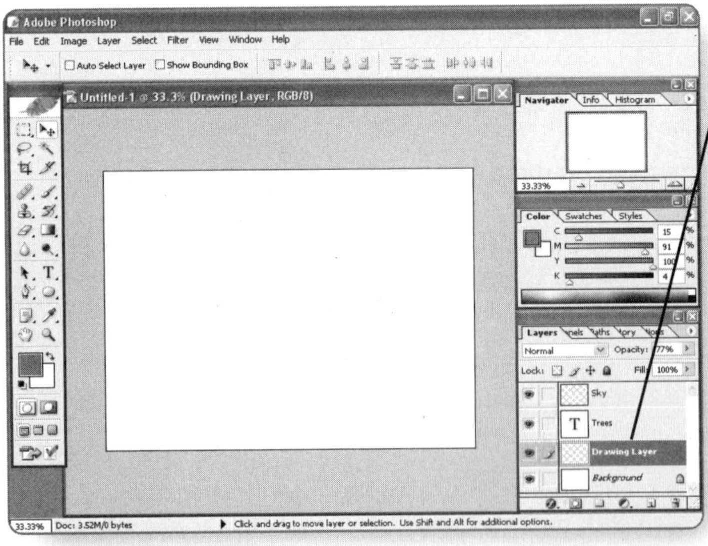

1. **Click** on the **name** of the layer in the Layers palette. The layer will appear selected in the Layers palette, making it the active layer.

TIP

You can hide a layer's contents by clicking on the eye icon to the left of the layer's name in the Layers palette. The layer's content disappears immediately. Click on the spot where the eye icon previously appeared to redisplay the layer.

Duplicating a Layer

When a layer has content that you'd like to reuse, you can duplicate the layer in the image file. Then you can position the layer content or add different effects independently.

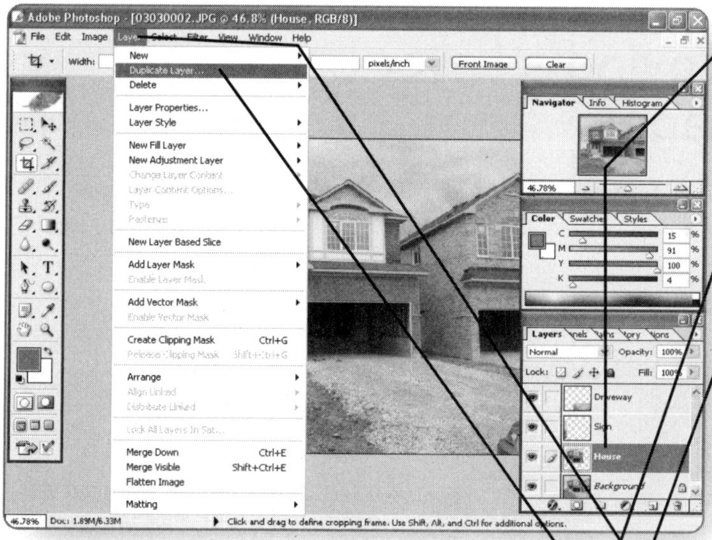

1. **Select** the **layer** to duplicate. The layer's name appears selected in the Layers palette.
2. **Click** on **Layer**. The Layer menu will appear.
3. **Click** on **Duplicate Layer**. The Duplicate Layer dialog box will open.

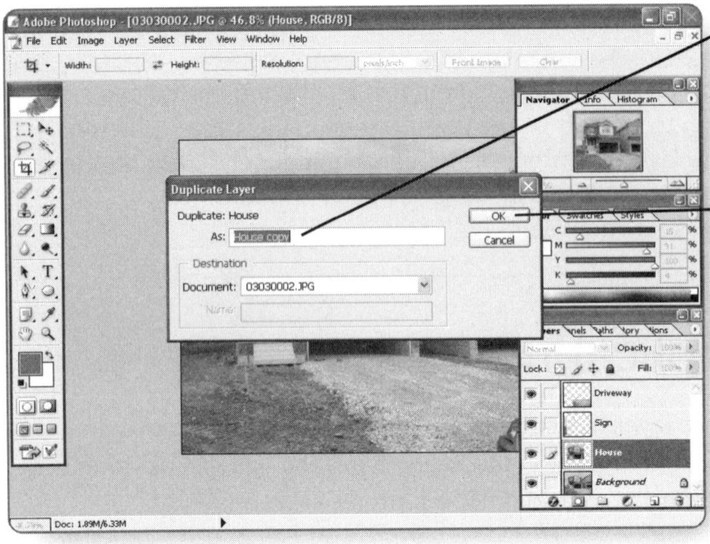

4. **Type** a **name** for the layer into the As text box. The specified name will be used for the layer.

5. **Click** on **OK**. Photoshop will close the Duplicate Layer dialog box and create the new layer, which will appear in the Layers palette.

Copying a Layer between Images

When a layer has content that you'd like to reuse, you can make a copy of the layer and paste it into another image file.

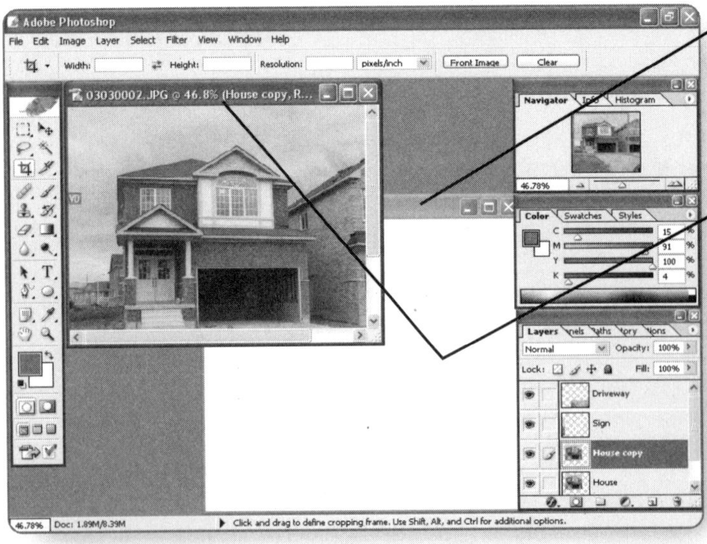

1. **Open** or **create** the **image file** to which you want to copy the layer. The image window appears in Photoshop.

2. **Open** the **image file** that has the layer to copy. The image window appears in Photoshop.

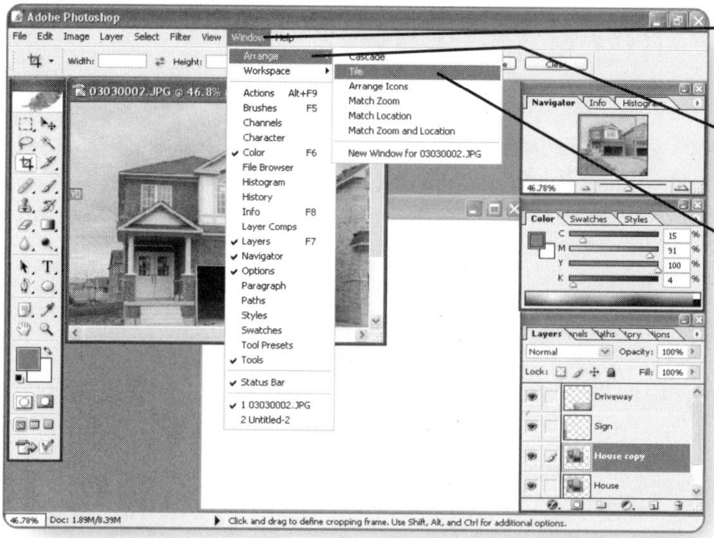

3. **Click** on **Window**. The window menu will appear.

4. **Hold** the mouse pointer over **Arrange**. A submenu will appear.

5. **Click** on **Tile**. The two open files will be tiled.

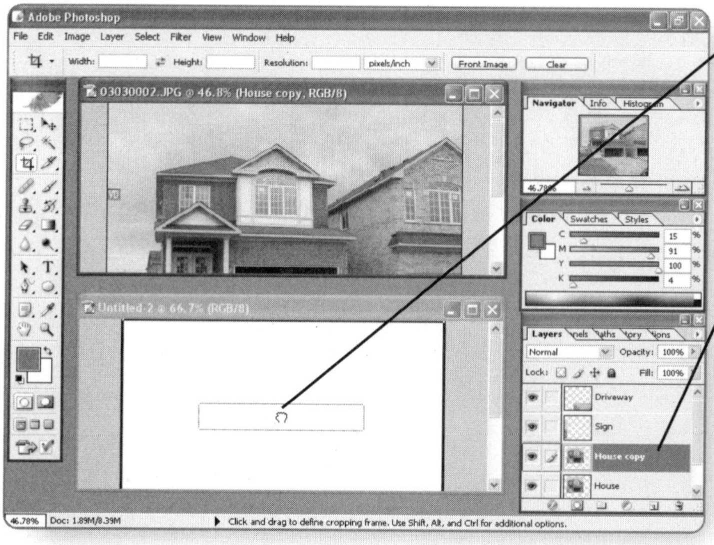

6. **Drag** the layer from the Layers palette. The layer will appear selected, and the mouse pointer will change to a clenched hand.

7. **Drop** the **layer** on the window for the file into which you want to copy the layer. The new layer appears immediately in the destination image.

Adding a Fill Layer

You can add a fill layer to color the entire image background. This technique is preferred over drawing a colored box on a layer, which can leave a white edge around the image. These instructions can also be used to create a pattern or gradient fill layer.

1. **Click** on **Layer**. The Layer menu will appear.

2. **Point** to **New Fill Layer**. The New Fill Layer submenu will appear.

3. **Click** on **Solid Color**. The New Layer dialog box will open.

4. **Type** a **name** for the layer into the Name text box. The specified name will be used for the layer.

5. **Choose** an **option** from the Color and Mode lists, if necessary. Making a Color choice will apply a color to the new layer's listing in the Layers palette. Making a Mode choice will apply a layer blending mode, which controls how the individual pixels on the layer blend with pixels on other layers.

TIP

Depending on the choice you make from the Mode list, you may have to make other layers, such as the Background layer, transparent. To do so, double-click on the layer in the Layers palette, change the Opacity setting to 0, and then click on OK.

6. **Click** on the **arrow** beside the Opacity text box, if necessary. A slider bar will appear that can be used to adjust the opacity level.

7. **Click** on **OK**. Photoshop will close the New Layer dialog box and open the Color Picker dialog box.

8. **Click** on a **color hue** in the narrow band of colors near the middle of the dialog box. Photoshop will display a different range of colors in the Pick a solid color box.

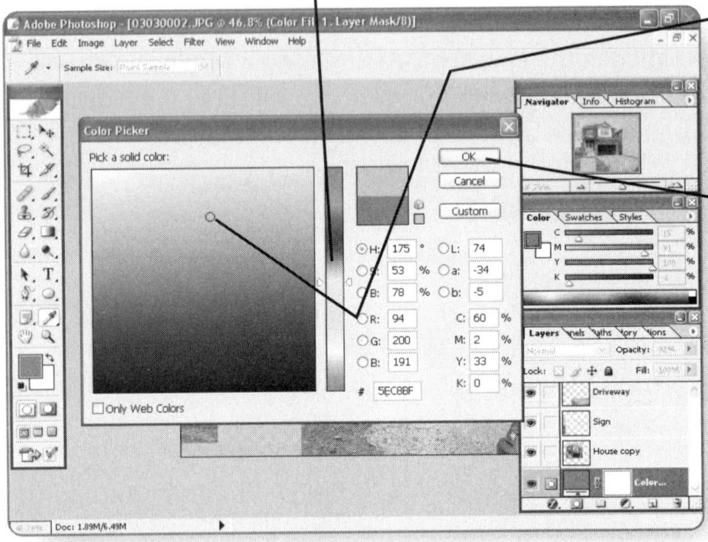

9. **Click** on a **color** in the Pick a solid color box. The color you click on will become the active color.

10. **Click** on **OK**. Photoshop will close the Color Picker dialog box and create the new fill layer. Its name will appear in the Layers palette.

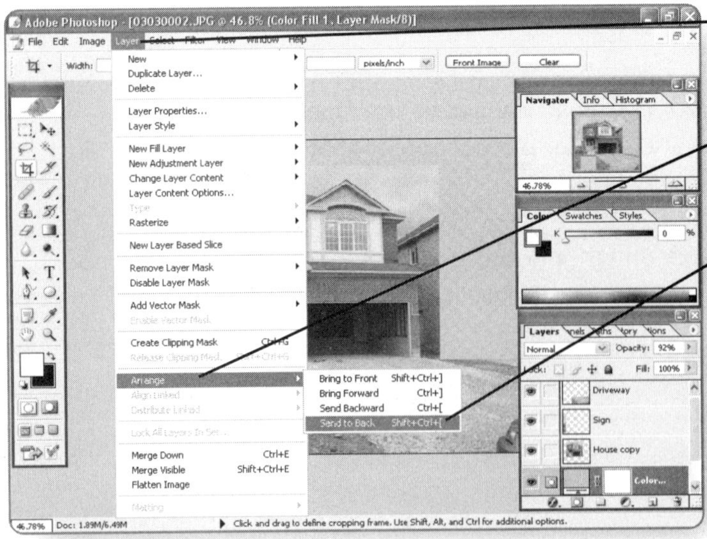

11. **Click** on **Layer**. The Layer menu will appear.

12. **Point** to **Arrange**. The Arrange submenu will appear.

13. **Click** on **Send to Back**. The new layer will shift to the back of the available layers.

> **TIP**
>
> You can change the type of fill for a layer after you create it. To do so, first select the layer. Then click on Layer, point to Change Layer Content, and click on Solid Color, Gradient, or Pattern.

Creating Patterns

If none of the patterns provided with Photoshop suits your needs, you can create your own using one of two methods: sampling a pattern or using the Pattern Maker plug-in.

Sampling a Pattern

You can create a pattern on-the-fly and then use it to create a pattern layer. The new pattern immediately becomes part of the library of available patterns.

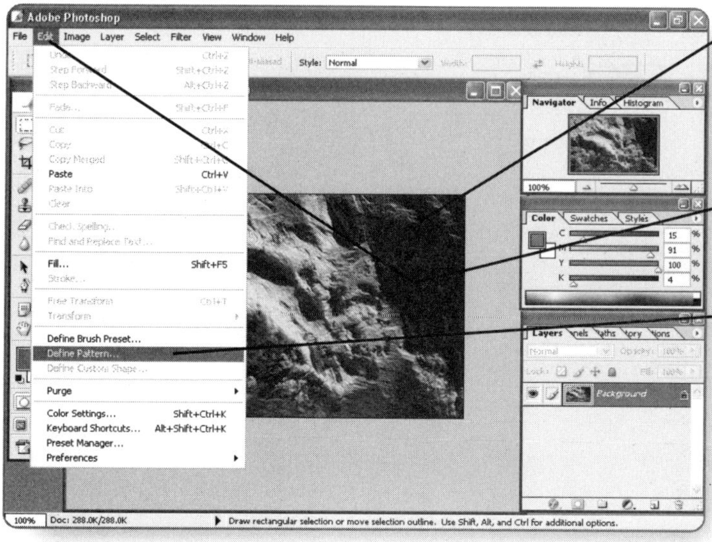

1. **Open** or **create** the **image file** that holds the area to use as the pattern. The image appears in its own window.

2. **Click** on **Edit**. The Edit menu will appear.

3. **Click** on **Define Pattern**. The Pattern Name dialog box will open. This will create a pattern from the entire image. If you want to create a pattern from only part of an image, select that part prior to step 2 using any of the selection tools.

NOTE

If the Define Pattern command is disabled, it's probably because the image bit depth is set to 16 Bits/Channel, the typical setting for many scanners. To enable the Define Pattern command, you have to convert the image to 8 Bits/Channel by choosing Image, Mode, 8 Bits/Channel.

4. **Type** a **name** for the pattern in the Name text box. Photoshop will use the name you specify to identify the pattern.

5. **Click** on **OK**. The Pattern Name dialog box will close.

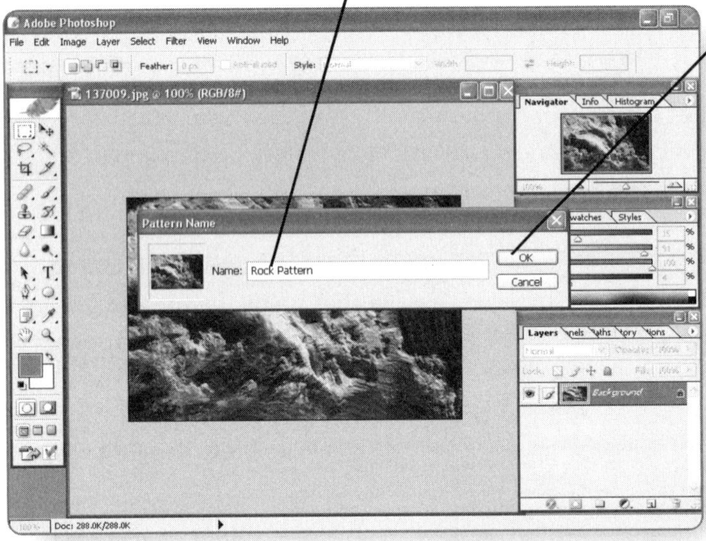

Using the Pattern Maker Plug-In

The Pattern Maker plug-in enables you to preview a pattern and alter it slightly before you save it as a preset. Follow these steps to create a basic pattern with the Pattern Maker plug-in:

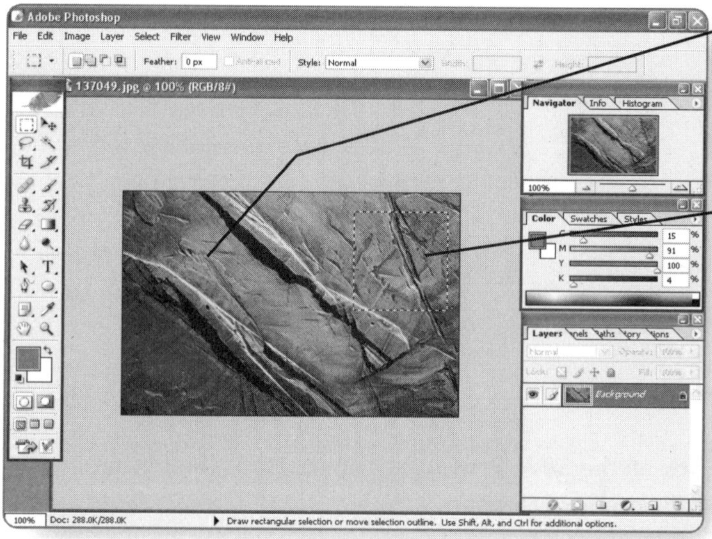

1. **Open** or **create** the **image file** that holds the area to use as the pattern. The image appears in its own window.

2. **Select** the **area** to use as a pattern using the selection tool of your choice. The selection marquee will appear.

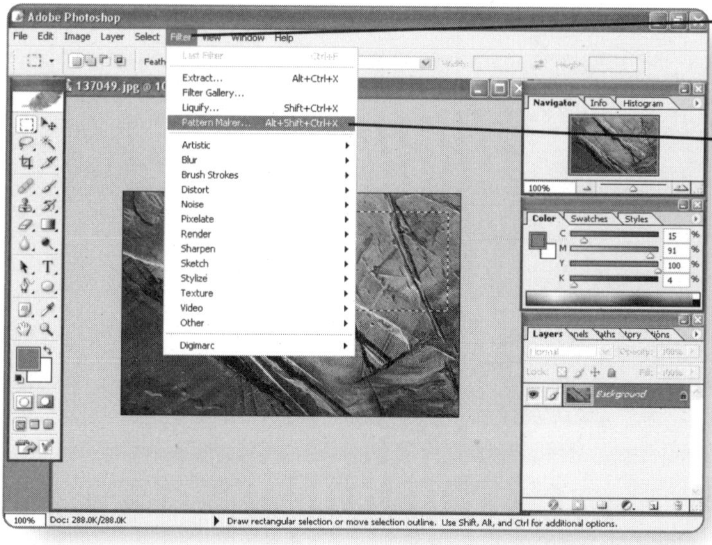

3. **Click** on **Filter**. The Filter menu will appear.

4. **Click** on **Pattern Maker**. The Pattern Maker window will open.

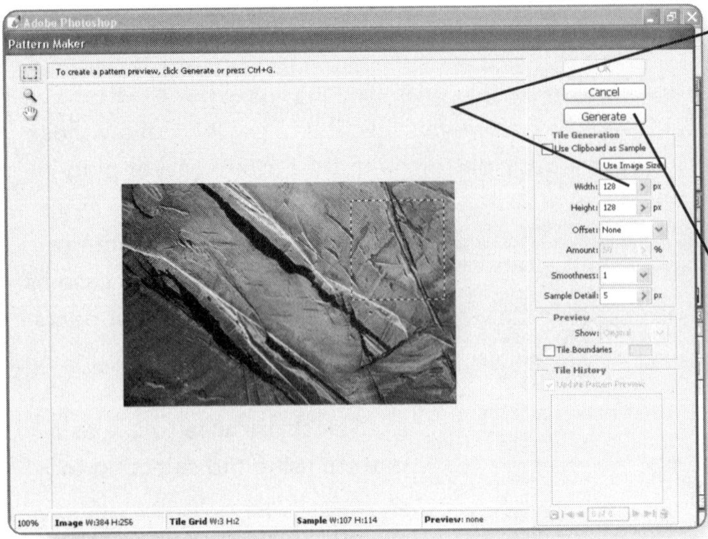

5. **Change settings** such as the tile's Width, Height, Smoothness, and Sample Detail as necessary. The Pattern Maker will apply those settings when you generate the pattern tile preview.

6. **Click** on **Generate**. The Pattern Maker window will preview the pattern, both as a single tile in the Tile History area and as an applied pattern in the main portion of the dialog box.

7. **Click** on the **Save Preset Pattern** button. The Pattern Name dialog box will open.

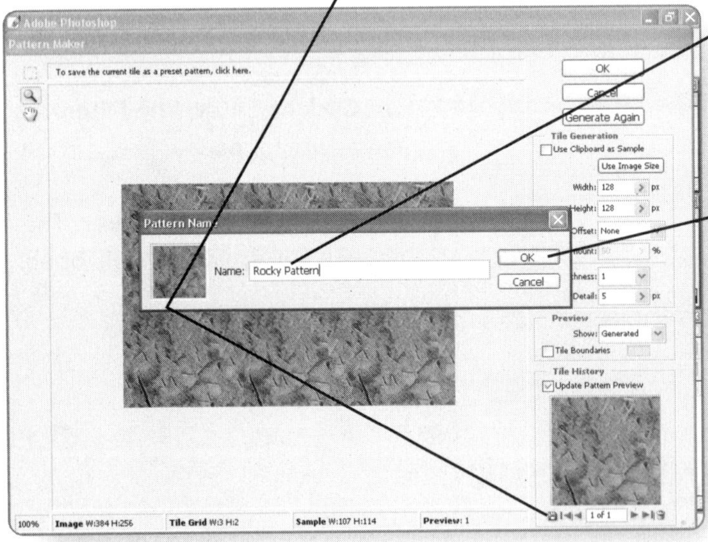

8. **Type** a **name** for the pattern in the Name text box. Photoshop will use the name you specify to identify the pattern.

9. **Click** on **OK**. The Pattern Name dialog box will close.

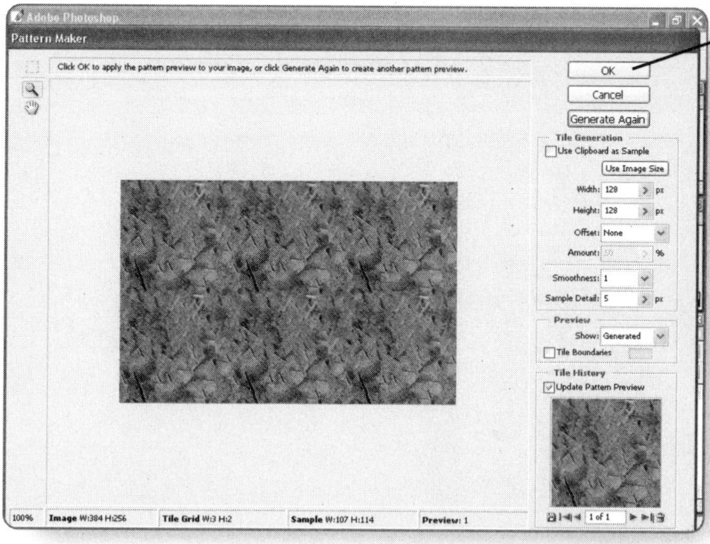

10. Click on **OK**. The Pattern Maker window will close, and the pattern will be applied to your current layer.

Deleting a Layer

When you want to remove a layer from an image, it's fastest to use the Layers palette, as detailed here.

1. Click on the **layer** to delete in the Layers palette. It will be highlighted.

2. Click on the **Delete** layer button. A warning message box will open.

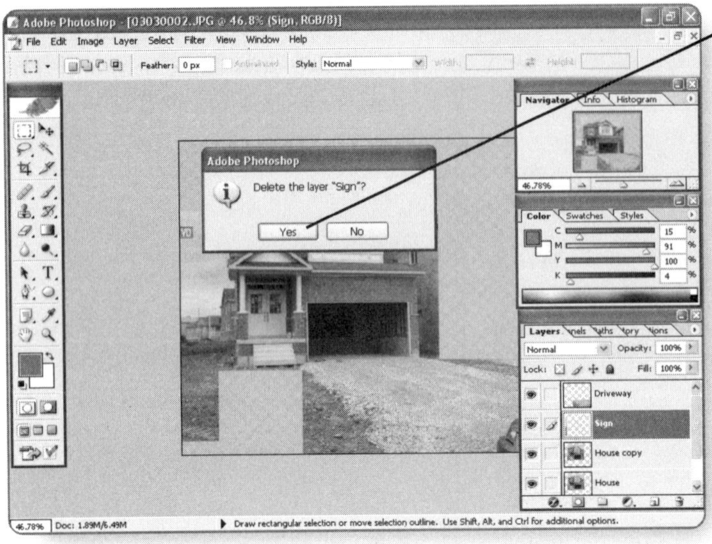

3. **Click** on **Yes**. Photoshop will complete the deletion.

Grouping and Ungrouping Layers

In order to help you manage your layers you can group them together based on any criteria that makes sense to you. You group layers by creating a layer set and then dragging layers into and out of the set on the Layers palette.

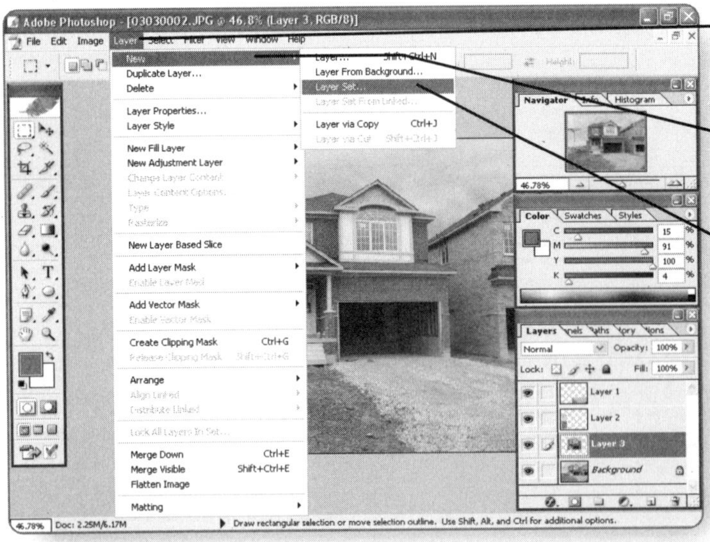

1. **Click** on **Layer**. The Layer menu will appear.

2. **Point** to **New**. The New submenu will appear.

3. **Click** on **Layer Set**. The Layer Set dialog box will appear.

4. **Type** a **name** for the set into the Name text box. The specified name will be used for the set.

5. **Choose** an **option** the Color and Mode lists, if necessary. Making a Color choice will apply a color to the new set's listing in the Layers palette. Making a Mode choice will apply a blending mode, which controls how the individual pixels on the layers in the set blend with pixels on other layers in the set.

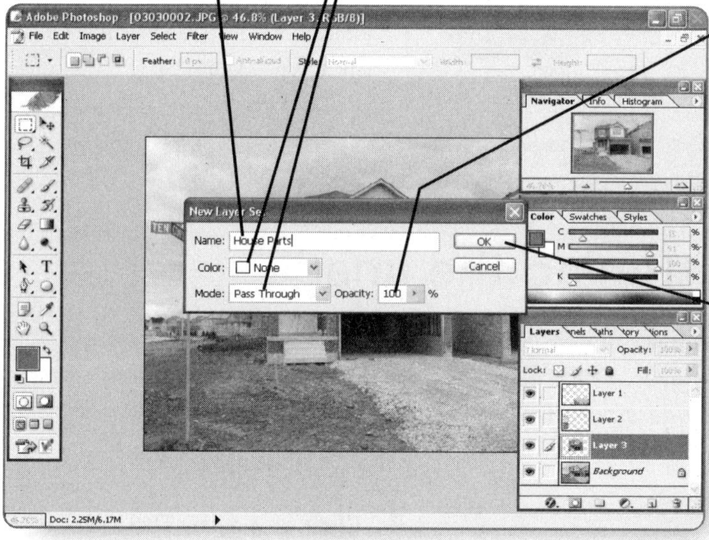

6. **Type** a **new entry** into the Opacity text box, if necessary. (You also can click on its arrow, drag the slider, and then click on the arrow again.) Photoshop will make the set's contents more transparent.

7. **Click** on **OK**. Photoshop will close the New Layer dialog box and create the new layer, which will appear in the Layers palette.

8. **Drag** a **layer name** and **drop** it onto the set name in the Layers palette. The layer will be added into the set.

> **NOTE**
>
> To remove a layer from the set, drag it back off the set and drop it elsewhere in the list on the Layers palette.

Flattening the Image

Flattening the image combines all the layer contents on a single layer, which can make the file size more compact. Use this process only if you've finished editing your image, and undo the action immediately if you've done it by mistake.

1. **Click** on **Layer**. The Layer menu will appear.

2. **Click** on **Flatten Image**. Photoshop immediately combines the contents of all the layers onto a single layer.

9

Adding Variety with Masks

If you've ever taped off an area while you're painting to protect that area from drips and spatters, you've created a mask. In Photoshop, you apply a mask to designate part of an image for changes and to shield (mask) the unselected areas against those changes. In this way, you can apply different effects and filters in varying portions of the image or layer. In this chapter, you'll learn how to:

- Set options for a quick mask
- Work in Quick Mask mode
- Create and use a layer mask
- Explore mask examples

Changing Quick Mask Options

The Quick Mask mode allows you to apply a mask by painting it on your image. Before you change to Quick Mask mode, you can set a few different options that affect how Quick Mask mode behaves.

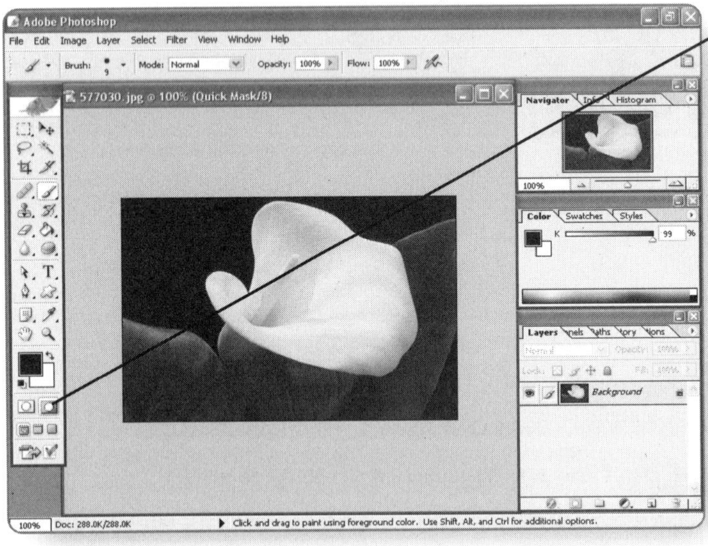

1. **Double-click** on the **Edit in Quick Mask Mode button** on the toolbox. The Quick Mask Options dialog box will open.

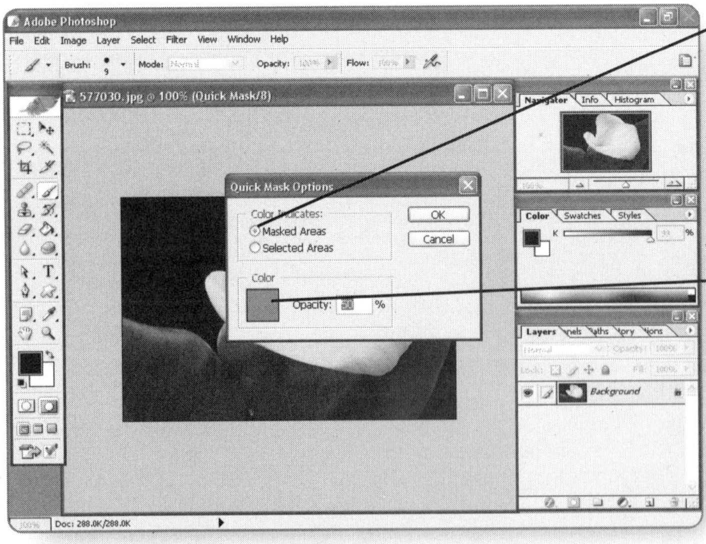

2. **Click** on an **option** in the Color Indicates area. Photoshop will apply the mask color to either the Masked Areas or Selected Areas in the image, depending on your selection.

3. **Click** on the **Color box**. The Color Picker dialog box will open.

4. Click on a **color hue** in the narrow band of colors near the middle of the dialog box. Photoshop will display a different range of colors in the Select Quick Mask color box.

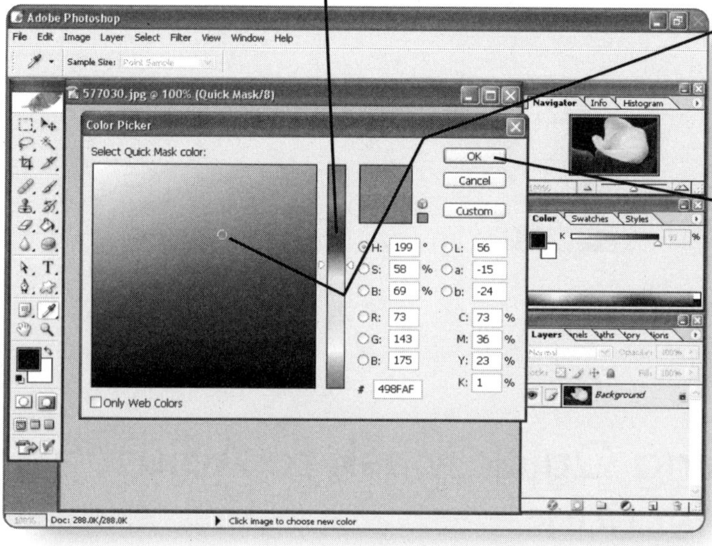

5. Click on a **color** in the Select Quick Mask color box. The color you click on will become the active mask color.

6. Click on **OK**. Photoshop will close the Color Picker dialog box and return to the Quick Mask Options dialog box.

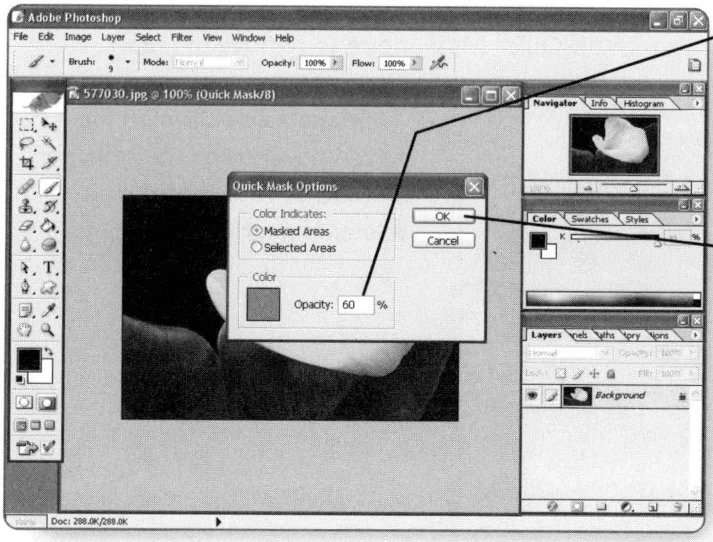

7. Type a new **entry** in the Opacity text box, if necessary. Photoshop will make the mask color more or less transparent, depending on your entry.

8. Click on **OK**. Photoshop will close the Quick Mask Options dialog box and apply the new settings the next time you use Quick Mask mode.

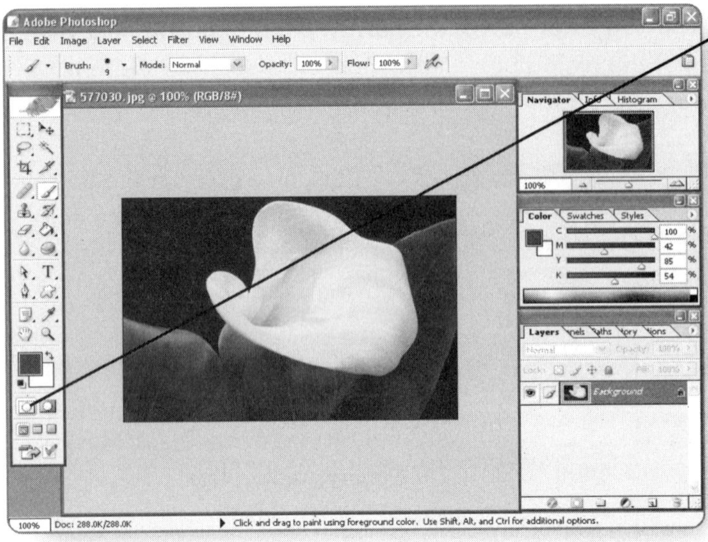

9. Click on the **Edit in Standard Mode button** on the toolbox. This turns off Quick Mask mode so that you can make a selection.

Using Quick Mask to Adjust a Selection

Quick Mask mode enables you to use a selection on the current layer as a temporary mask. Once you've masked the area, you can make the needed changes to the unmasked area and then turn off Quick Mask mode to remove the mask.

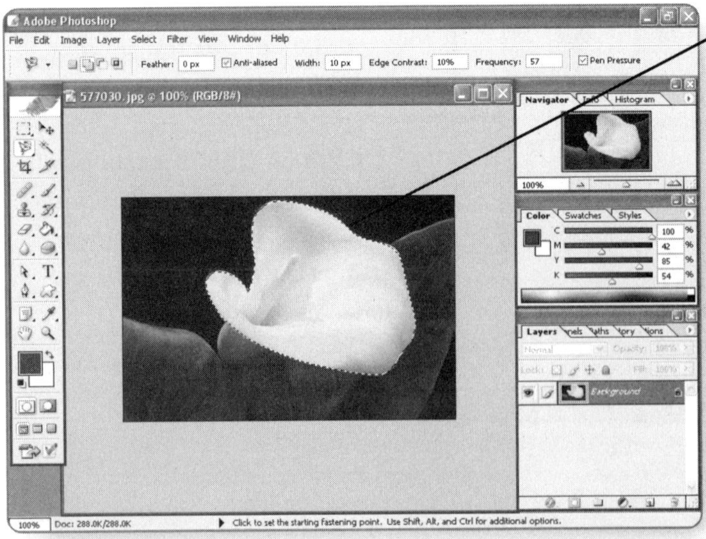

1. Make a **selection** on the current layer using the selection method of your choice. The selection marquee will appear.

TIP

See Chapter 5, "Selecting Image Content," to refresh your memory about the various selection methods. One trick is to select the area you don't want to mask, click on Select, and then click on Inverse to select the image areas that previously were not selected. (The figure here shows an inverted selection.)

2. **Click** on the **Quick Mask Mode button** on the toolbox. The Quick Mask mode will become active, and the mask color will appear over the masked area.

3. **Make** the desired **change** to the masked area, using a toolbox tool or filter. The mask boundaries will change accordingly. This example shows a mask being adjusted using a brush.

NOTE

Paint or draw on the nonmasked area with a color other than white to create a semitransparent masked area. Use white to exclude an area from the mask and black to add area to the mask (the hidden area).

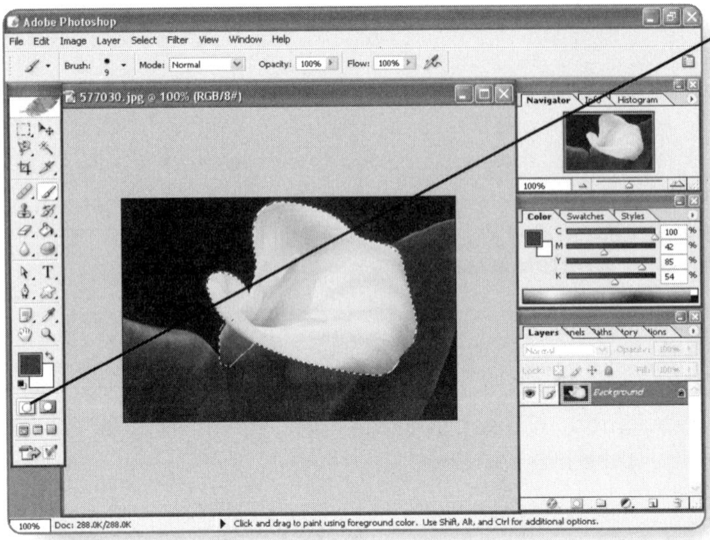

4. Click on the **Standard Mode button** on the toolbox. Photoshop will leave Quick Mask mode and return to the altered selection. You can then apply the needed changes to the selected areas, as described later in the section "Putting a Mask to Work."

Using Layer Masks

You can add a mask to a particular layer in the image so that you can hide part of the layer from display or even apply effects only to the area selected by the mask. By adding layer masks to various layers, you can mix and match effects as needed in the image. You can't add a layer mask to the Background layer, so you may need to add another layer such as an adjustment layer or duplicate the Background layer and then delete the original to work with a layer mask on the Background layer content itself. In some cases, you also may want to hide the Background layer (by clicking on the eye icon beside it) to ensure that you can select only the image content that you want.

> **NOTE**
>
> You also can create a special, color-related type of mask called an alpha channel. See "Adding an Alpha Channel" in Chapter 16, "Correcting Image Color," to learn more.

Creating a Mask on a Layer

Adding a mask on a layer will have different effects, depending on the layer's contents. For text layers, it enables you to select text and apply filters without rasterizing the text layer (that is, converting the layer to pixels rather than a vector layer, where objects are based on larger, resizable shapes). For layers with small photos, fills, and other objects, the layer mask excludes the information not contained within the mask area, so it doesn't display in the image. For adjustment layers like a hue/saturation layer, the mask enables you to adjust the image color only within the areas defined by the mask.

> **NOTE**
>
> The examples in this chapter illustrate layer masks. You also can create vector masks to mask sharp shapes based on paths in an image. See Chapter 10, "Using Paths," to learn how to add a path and use it to create a vector mask.

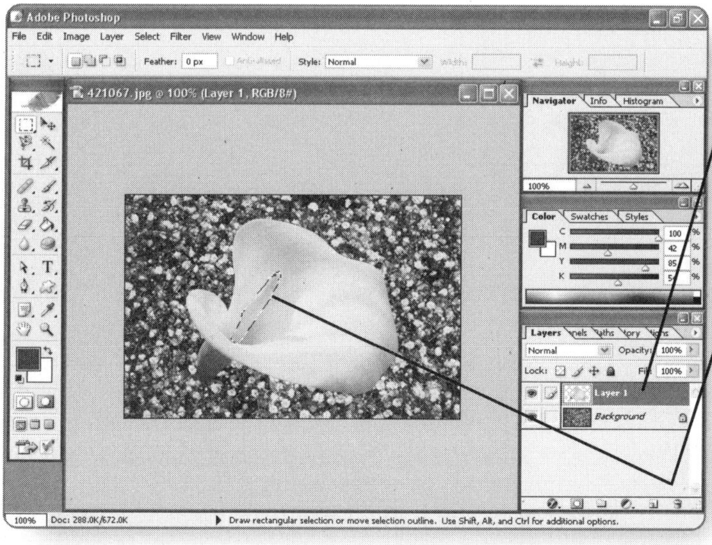

1. **Click** on the **layer** in the Layers palette to which you want to add a mask. The layer will become the current or active layer.

2. **Make** a **selection** on the current layer using the selection method of your choice. The selection marquee will appear.

NOTE

When you add certain types of layers, such as gradient fill layers, they automatically include a mask that includes all the layer content. It's often best to delete this mask by right-clicking on the mask thumbnail in the Layers palette and then clicking on Discard Layer Mask. See the next section, "Changing or Trashing a Mask," for more information. If you try to add another mask without deleting the first one, Photoshop will add a clipping path instead. Chapter 10 describes what a clipping path is and how to use one.

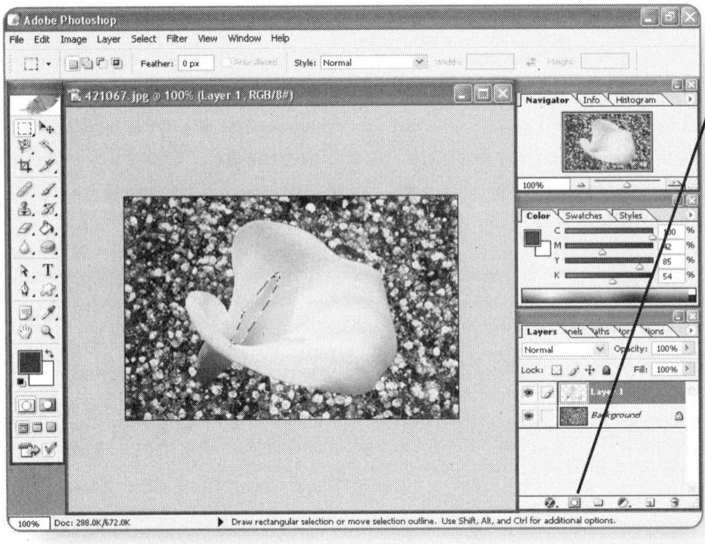

3. **Click** on the **Add Layer Mask button** at the bottom of the Layers palette. Photoshop will create the mask immediately.

TIP

Press and hold the Alt key as you click to invert the selection in the mask.

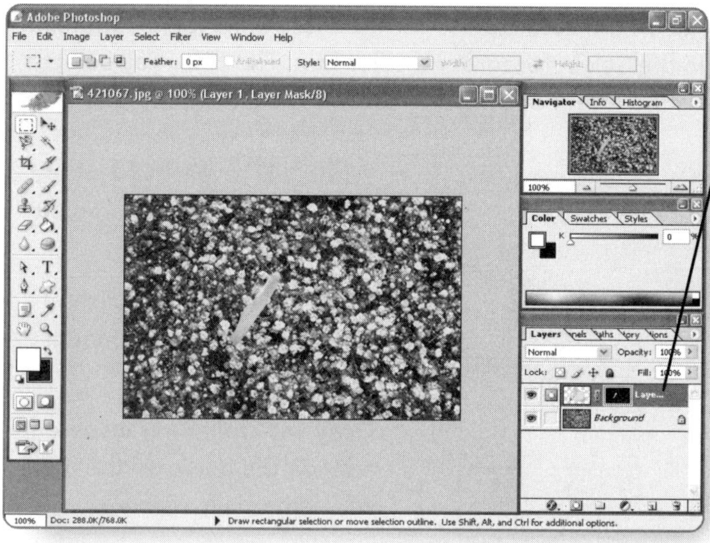

4. Review the **mask thumbnail** in the Layers palette. The black area in the thumbnail will show the zone that the mask hides or excludes.

Changing or Trashing a Mask

The selection on a layer mask isn't permanent once you've made it, so you can adjust the mask at a later time by painting or drawing. You also can delete a mask from a layer altogether.

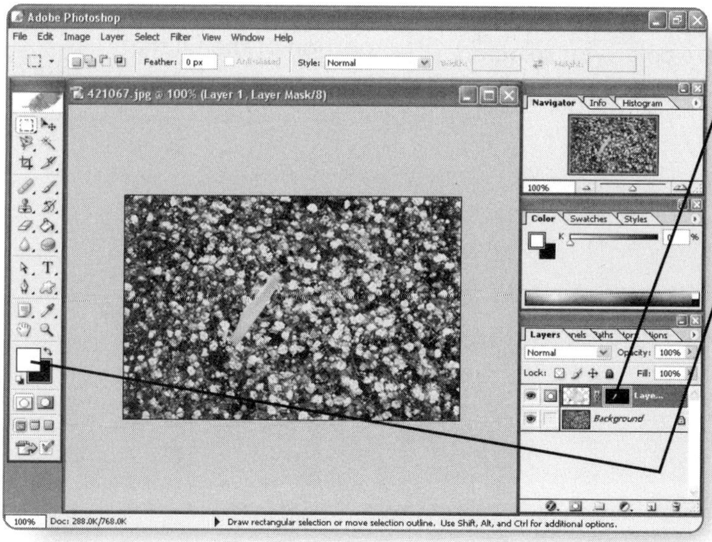

1. Click on the **mask thumbnail** for the desired layer in the Layers palette. The mask (and layer) will become active.

2. Click on the **Set Foreground Color box** at the bottom of the toolbox. The Color Picker dialog box will open.

3. Click on the **color** to use for the mask edits (black, white, or gray) in the Select foreground color box. The color you select controls the effect of the edits you will make:

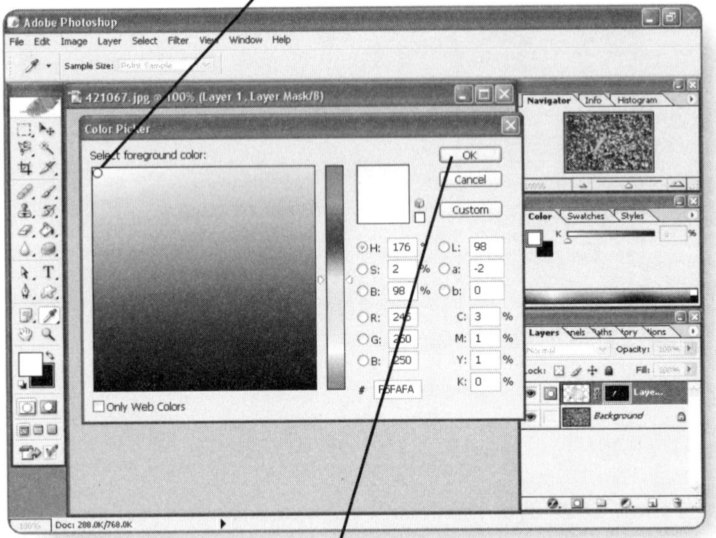

- **White** will reveal more of the layer, decreasing the amount of masked-off area.
- **Black** will hide more of the layer, increasing the amount of masked-off area.
- **Gray** will create a transparent area on the mask, so the area will be partially visible.

4. Click on **OK**. The Color Picker dialog box will close, and the color you selected will become active.

NOTE

For solid color, gradient, and pattern fill layers, painting with white has no effect because the entire layer is revealed. Painting with black hides the portion of the fill that you've painted over.

5. Select the **tool** to use in the toolbox. The tool will become the active tool.

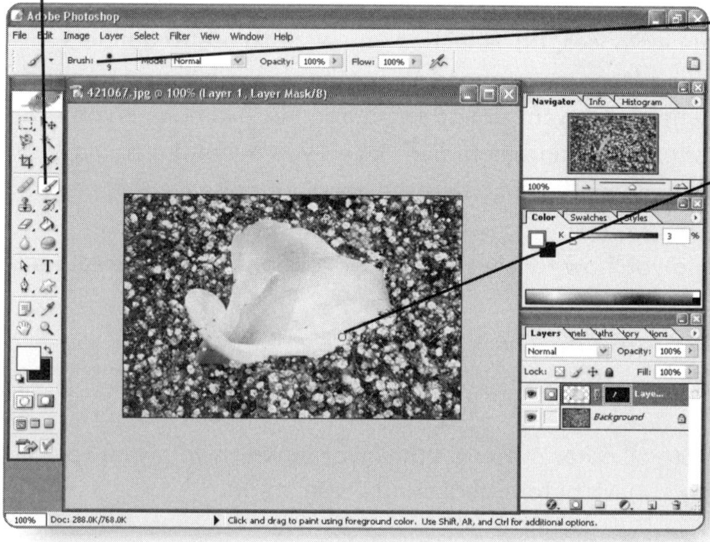

6. Set tool **options** on the options bar. The options you specify will become active.

7. Draw or **paint** on the **layer**. The mask will be altered accordingly.

8. Click on **Layer**. The Layer menu will appear.

9. Point to **Remove Layer Mask**. A submenu will appear.

10. Click on **Discard**. The Layer Mask will be deleted.

Using a Selection from One Layer as a Mask on Another

In some instances, the selection you want to use to define a mask for a layer may appear on another layer instead of on the layer where you want to add the mask. For example, if you have a text layer and a gradient layer, you may want to mask out the gradient layer so that the gradient appears only over the text. The following steps illustrate this example while showing you how to use a selection from one layer to create a mask on another.

> **CAUTION**
>
> Delete all other masks on the layer to which you want to copy a mask before beginning these steps.

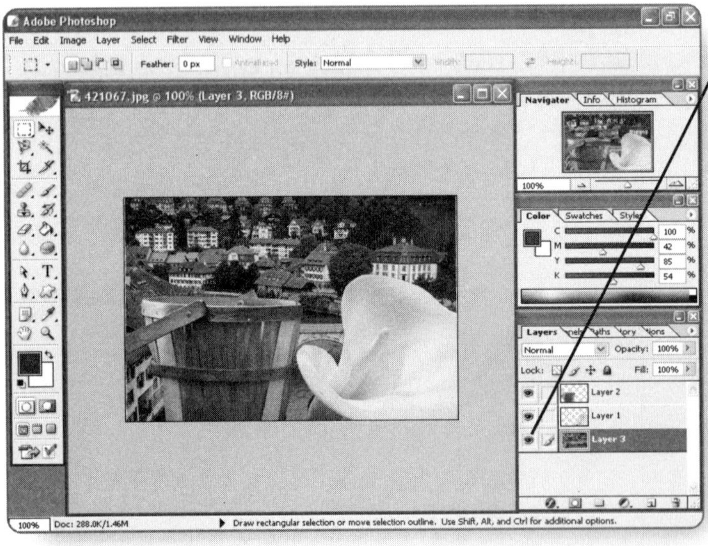

1. **Click** on the **eye icon** beside any layer in the Layers palette. The eye icon will disappear, and the layer will become hidden, making it easier for you to select content on another layer.

2. Click on the **layer** with the content to select in the Layers palette. The layer will become the current or active layer.

3. Make a **selection** on the current layer using the selection method of your choice. The selection marquee will appear.

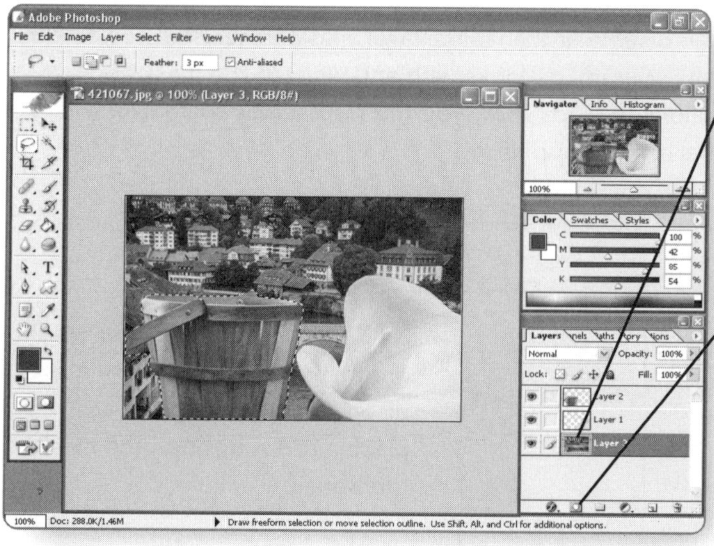

4. Click on the **layer** in the Layers palette to which you want to add the mask. The layer will become the current or active layer, and it should become visible if you hid it in step 1.

5. Click on the **Add Layer Mask button** at the bottom of the Layers palette. Photoshop will create the mask immediately.

6. Review the **mask thumbnail** in the Layers palette. The black area in the thumbnail will show the zone that the mask hides or excludes.

Reviewing the Mask

You can disable and enable a layer mask as needed, so you can see how your image looks with and without the mask applied. The following steps show you the fastest way to control whether a mask appears:

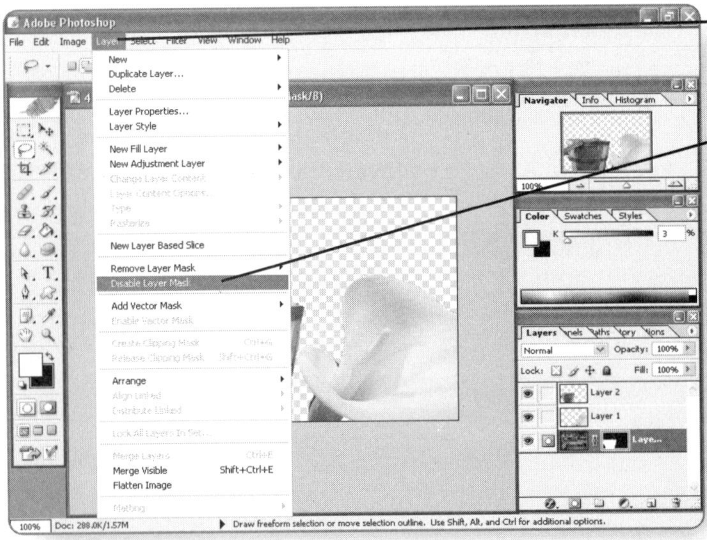

1. Click on **Layer**. The Layer menu will appear.

2. Click on **Disable Layer Mask**. Photoshop will disable the mask display immediately and will place a red X through the mask thumbnail.

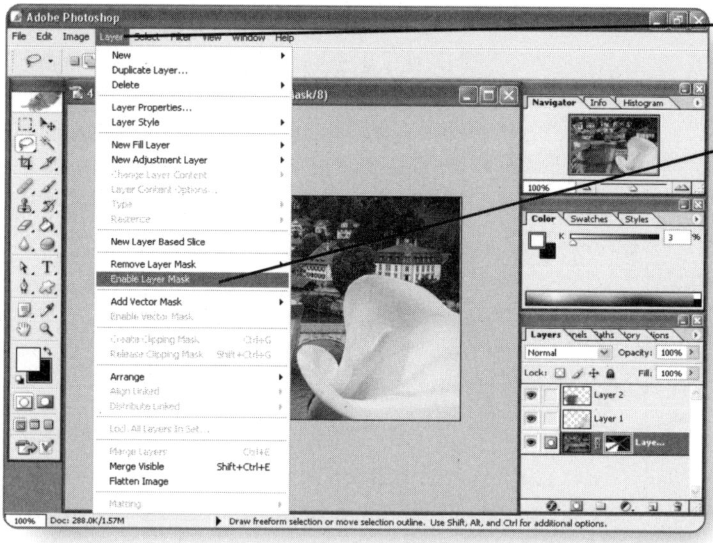

3. **Click** on **Layer**. The Layer menu will appear.

4. **Click** on **Enable Layer Mask**. Photoshop will reapply the mask immediately, and the image display will be affected accordingly.

Putting a Mask to Work

As noted earlier in this chapter, a layer mask may behave a bit differently or enable you to do different things, depending on the nature of the layer where you added the mask. This section reviews two examples of how you can use layer masks to adjust or enhance selected content in an image.

Cropping a Photo

To use this technique, make sure the photo to crop appears on its own layer, not on the Background layer.

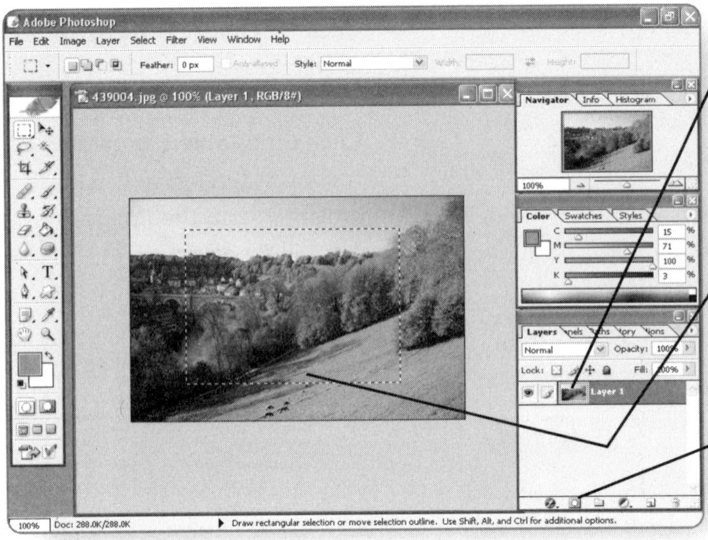

1. **Click** on the **layer** in the Layers palette to which you want to add the mask. The layer will become the current or active layer.

2. **Make** a **selection** on the current layer using the selection method of your choice. The selection marquee will appear.

3. **Click** on the **Add Layer Mask button** at the bottom of the Layers palette. Photoshop will create the mask immediately.

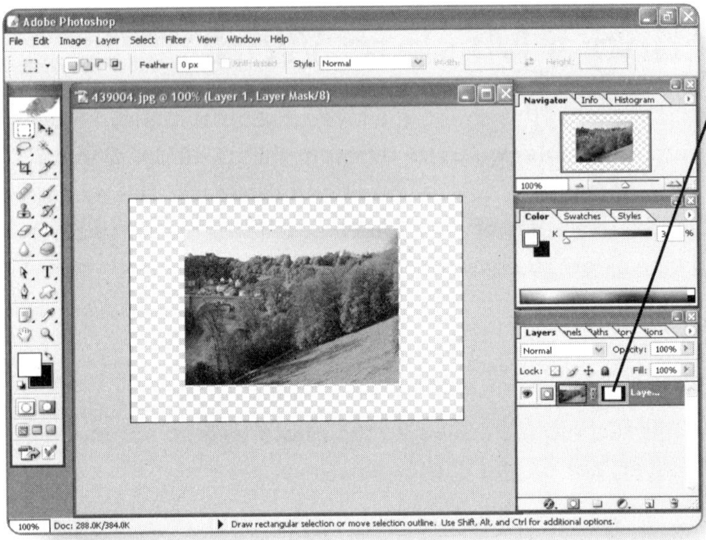

4. **Review** the **mask results** in the image. Photoshop will mask out the areas not included within the selection from which you created the mask.

Adding a Filter

When you apply a filter, it only affects the currently selected area. Because a mask in effect protects an area like a selection, applying a filter to a layer that has a mask on it filters only the portions of the layer that aren't masked off. This is a particularly vital technique for text layers. With the mask, Photoshop would prompt you to rasterize the text layer, eliminating your ability to edit the text in the future.

1. **Click** on the desired **layer** in the Layers palette. The layer will become the current or active layer.

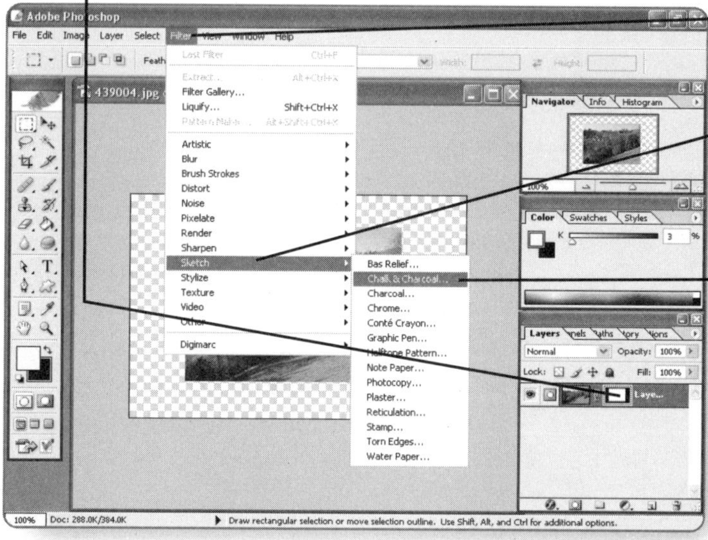

2. **Click** on **Filter**. The Filter menu will appear.

3. **Click** on the **filter command** of your choice. A submenu with specific filter choices will appear.

4. **Click** on a **filter** in the submenu. Depending on the filter you have selected either a dialog box will open allowing you to set options for the filter or the Filter Gallery will open.

5. **Set** filter **options** as necessary. A preview in the window shows how the filter will look when applied using the settings you specified.

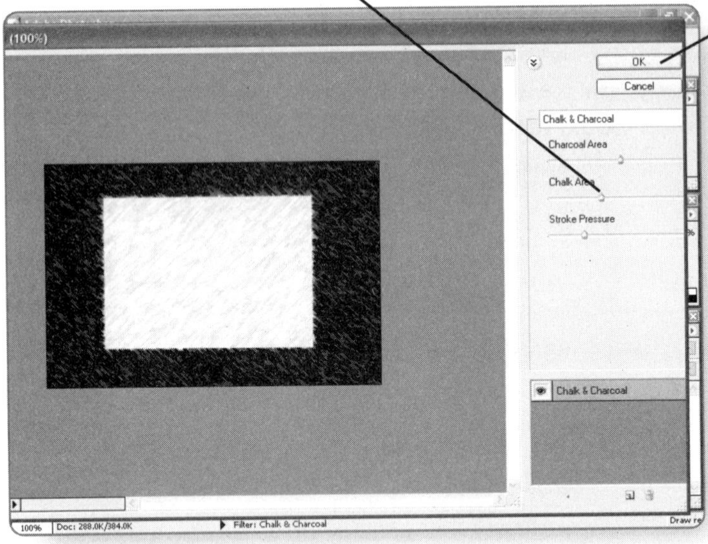

6. **Click** on **OK**. The Filter Gallery will close, and the filter will be applied to the layer contents not hidden or protected by the mask.

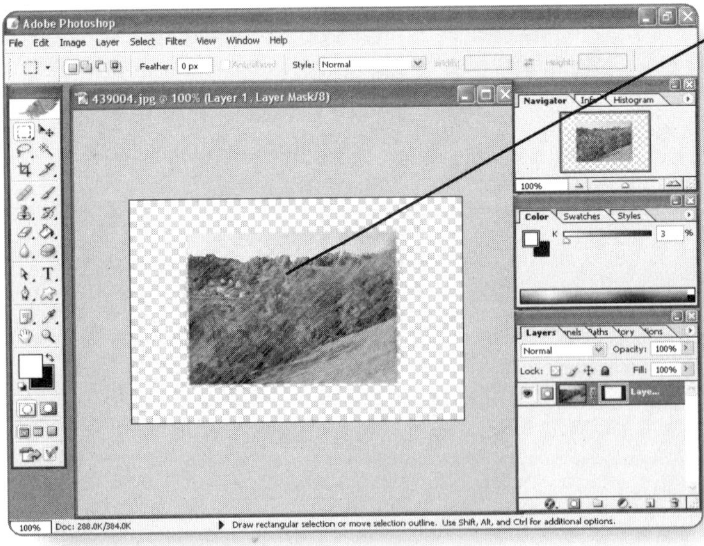

7. **Review** the filter **results** in the image. Photoshop will display the newly filtered areas.

Recoloring Part of the Image

This mask technique works with a special color-correction layer called an adjustment layer. (You'll learn more about working with colors in Chapters 15 through 17.) It enables you to make a color change on part of an image only. This example shows how to make a hue and saturation change, but you can make other changes depending on the nature of the adjustment layer you choose to use.

1. **Click** on **Layer**. The Layer menu will appear.

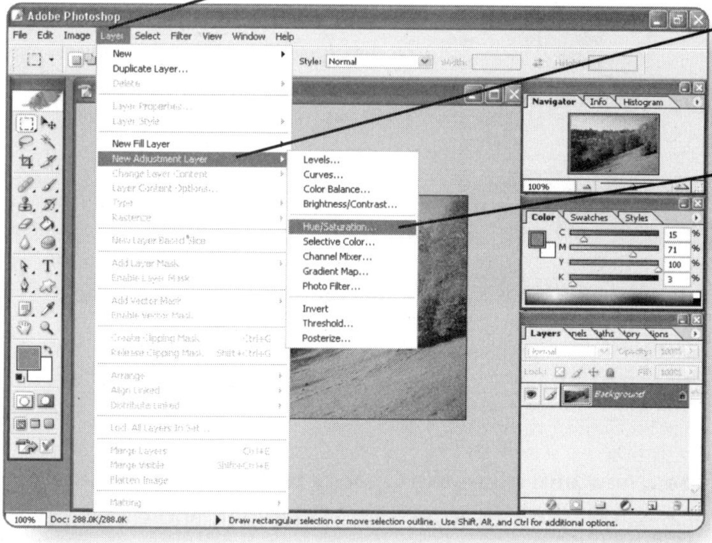

2. **Point** to **New Adjustment Layer**. A submenu with specific layer choices will appear.

3. **Click** on **Hue/Saturation** in the submenu. The New Layer dialog box will appear.

4. **Type** a **name** for the layer into the Name text box. The specified name will be used for the layer.

5. **Click** a **choice** from the Color and Mode lists, if necessary. Making a Color choice will apply a color to the new layer's listing in the Layers palette. Making a Mode choice will apply a layer blending mode, which controls how the individual pixels on the layer blend with pixels on other layers.

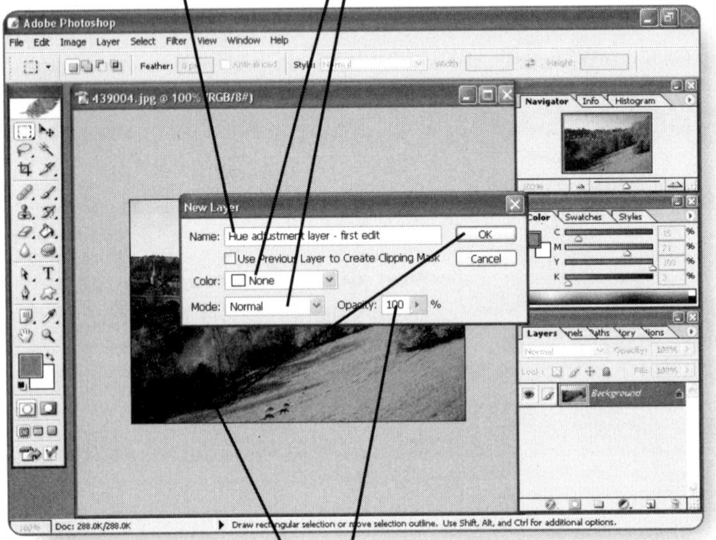

TIP

Depending on the choice you make from the Mode list, you may have to make other layers, such as the Background layer, transparent. To do so, double-click on the layer in the Layers palette, change the Opacity setting to 0, and then click on OK.

6. **Type** a new **entry** into the Opacity text box, if necessary. (You also can click on its arrow, drag the slider, and click on the arrow again.) Photoshop will make the layer's contents more transparent.

7. **Click** on **OK**. Photoshop will close the New Layer dialog box and open the Hue/Saturation dialog box.

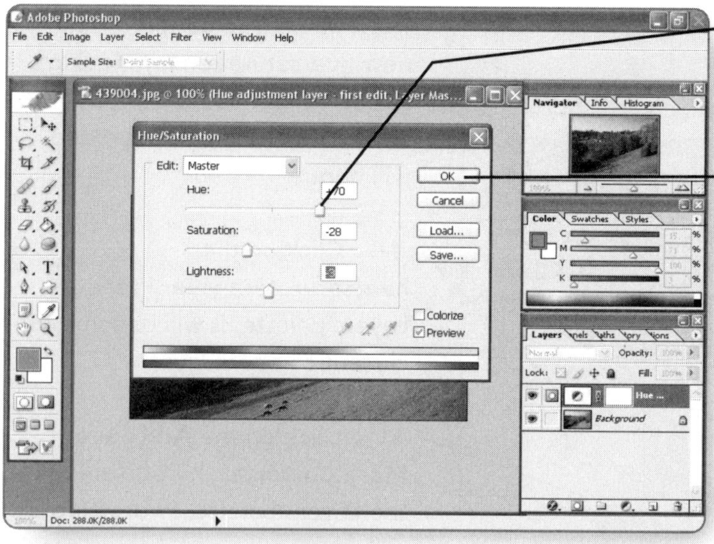

8. **Drag** the **sliders** as necessary. The image will display the corrected color.

9. **Click** on **OK**. The Hue/Saturation dialog box will close.

10. **Click** on **Layer**. The Layer menu will appear.

11. **Click** on **Remove Layer Mask**. A submenu will appear.

12. **Click** on **Discard**. Photoshop will remove the layer mask immediately.

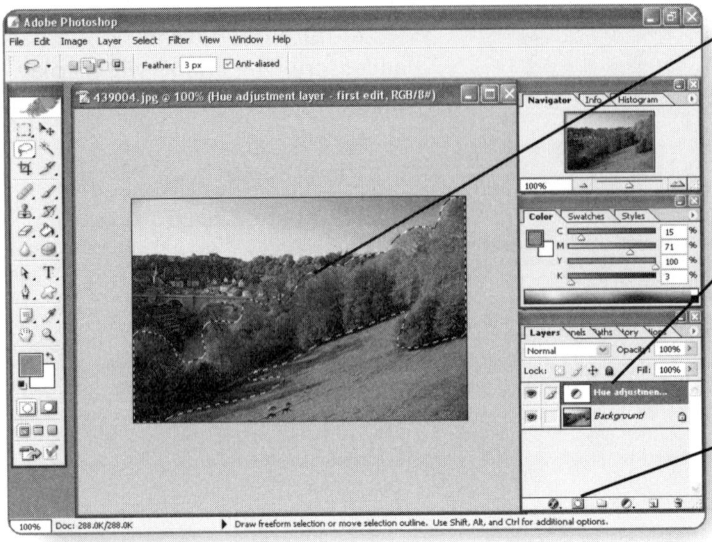

13. **Make** a **selection** on the new hue/saturation layer using the selection method of your choice. The selection marquee will appear.

14. **Click** on the **hue/saturation layer** in the Layers palette. It will become the current or active layer.

15. **Click** on the **Add Layer Mask button** at the bottom of the Layers palette. Photoshop will create the mask immediately.

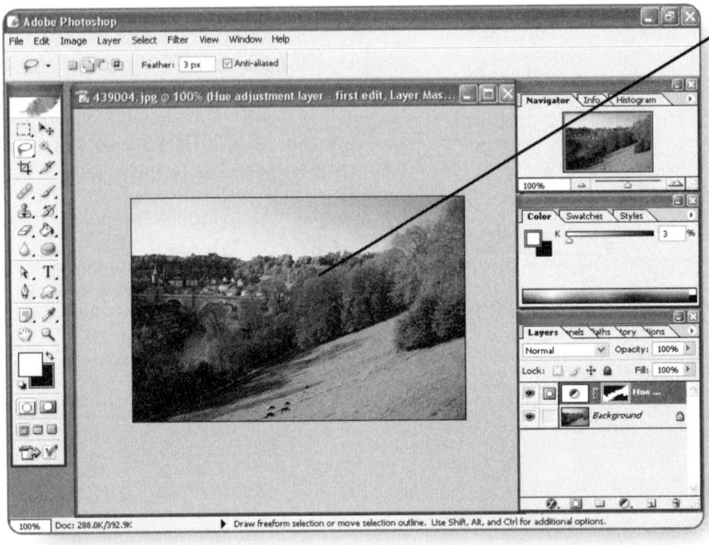

16. **Review** the **mask results** in the image. Photoshop will apply the color correction to only the area not blocked by the mask.

NOTE

If you double-click on the layer thumbnail (to the far left) for the hue/saturation layer, the Hue/Saturation dialog box reopens so that you can further adjust the color correction in the areas not blocked by the mask.

10
Using Paths

A path is essentially a vector-based selection outline in Photoshop. Because paths are vector based (an outline rather than a selection of pixels), creating paths rather than saved selections in an image file will have less of a tendency to increase the file size. This can be beneficial if the file is a large scan, has dozens of layers, or is simply large because it's complex. You can use a path as a selection at any time, fill the path or color the path outline, or even use a special type of path to clip image content when you plan to reuse a file. In this chapter, you will learn how to:

- Create various types of paths
- View and work with paths
- Fill a path or color the path outline
- Use a path to define a selection
- Use a clipping path to prepare an image for reuse in other files or settings

Creating Paths

You use the Paths palette to save the paths you create, and you use the Pen tools and Shape tools to actually draw each path. The tool you should use to create the path depends on the desired shape for the path.

> **NOTE**
>
> Paths do not print unless you fill them with color or color their border.

Adding a Shape Path

The "Drawing a Rectangle, Oval, or Other Shape" section in Chapter 3, "Adding Content with Tools," explained how to use the Rectangle tool (and the other shape tools you access via the Rectangle tool) to draw shapes on an image. You also can use these tools to create a path for later use, as described here.

1. **Click** and **hold** the **Rectangle tool** in the toolbox. Its shortcut menu will appear.
2. **Click** on the desired **shape tool** to use in the submenu. The selected tool will become the active tool.

> **NOTE**
>
> If you choose the Custom Shape tool, be sure to use the Shape drop-down list on the options bar to specify which kind of shape to draw.

3. **Click** on the **Paths button** on the options bar. The selected tool will become active for path selection.

4. **Click** and **drag diagonally** on the **picture** in the work area. Keep the mouse button pressed as you drag in any desired direction. When you release the mouse button, the path will appear.

5. **Click** on **Window**. The Window menu will appear.

6. **Click** on **Paths**. The Paths palette will become the active tab in the Layers palette window. The Paths palette will show that the path you've drawn appears as a temporary path called a work path.

> **TIP**
>
> Instead of opening the Window menu and choosing Paths, you can click on the Paths tab in the Layers palette window.

7. **Click** on the **Paths palette menu button**. The palette menu will appear.

8. **Click** on **Save Path**. The Save Path dialog box will open.

NOTE

You don't have to save a temporary work path unless you want to reuse it later.

9. **Type** a **name** for the path in the Name text box. Your new name will replace the temporary name in the text box.

10. **Click** on **OK**. The Save Path dialog box will close, and Photoshop will finish saving the path under the name you specified.

11. **Click** on a **blank area** in the Paths palette. Photoshop will deselect the path.

12. **Click** on the **Layers tab** in the Layers palette window. (Alternately, you can choose Window, Layers.) Photoshop will return to the regular view of layers in the image.

> **NOTE**
>
> If you skip this last step when using a tool to create a path, the path will remain selected, and any further actions you take pertain to that path. For example, if you tried to create a path with another tool, it would simply be added into the current path rather than created as a separate work path.

Making a Pen Path

The Pen tool enables you to create paths with straight lines, curves, and angles. Use this tool when you want to create a path that's irregular in shape or has swooping, controlled curves.

> **NOTE**
>
> You must be careful when using the mouse with the Pen tool. Different mouse actions have different results. The following steps illustrate the various mouse techniques you need to master when using the Pen tool.

1. **Click** on the **Pen tool** in the toolbox. Its options will appear in the options bar.

2. **Click** on the **Paths button** on the options bar. The Pen tool will become active for path selection.

> **NOTE**
>
> If you click on the Shape Layers button (instead of the Paths button) on the options bar for any tool described in this chapter, the tool draws a shape or outline on a new layer in the image rather than simply creating a path.

3. **Click** on the **starting point** for the first segment in the path. An anchor point appears at the location where you clicked.

4. **Click** on the **location** where you want to end the segment. A straight-line segment appears between the anchor points.

5. **Press Ctrl+Z**. This will undo the path segment.

6. **Drag** on the location for the end of the next segment. Because you dragged, Photoshop will create a curved segment.

7. **Drag** the direction **point** at the end of the direction line and then release the mouse button. Photoshop will adjust the depth and direction of the curved segment based on where you drag the direction point.

8. **Drag** in the **opposite direction** on the location for the end of the next segment. Because you dragged in the opposite direction, Photoshop will create a segment that curves in the opposite direction.

TIP

To create a corner point between segments, press and hold the Alt key when you set the anchor point for the next segment. Press and hold the Ctrl key to drag an anchor point or corner point.

9. After you create all the needed segments, finish drawing the path in one of two ways:

- **Click** on the first **anchor** point to close the path shape. Note that when the mouse pointer is over the first anchor point, a small circle appears along with the pointer to tell you that clicking would then close the path.
- **Click** on the **Pen tool** in the toolbox to finish the path without closing the shape.

10. **Click** on the **Paths palette menu button**. The palette menu will appear.

11. **Click** on **Save Path**. The Save Path dialog box will open.

12. Type a **name** for the path in the Name text box. Your new name will replace the temporary name in the text box.

13. Click on **OK**. The Save Path dialog box will close, and Photoshop will finish saving the path under the name you specified.

14. Click on a **blank area** in the Paths palette. Photoshop will deselect the path.

15. Click on the **Layers tab** in the Layers palette window. (Alternately, choose Window, Layers.) Photoshop will return to the regular view of layers in the image.

Making a Freeform Path

The Freeform Pen tool enables you to create a path by dragging on the image. In addition, you can turn on the Magnetic option with the Freeform Pen tool to have the path outline "snap to" a shape in the image. This tool comes in handy when you want to create a path around a particular item or region in an image.

1. **Click** and **hold** the **Pen tool** in the toolbox. Its shortcut menu will appear.

2. **Click** on **Freeform Pen Tool**. The Freeform Pen tool will become the active tool.

3. **Click** on the **Paths button** on the options bar. The Freeform Pen tool will become active for path selection.

4. **Click** on the **Magnetic check box** to check it, if desired. Checking this option will cause the Freeform Pen tool to function as the Magnetic Pen tool, and your path will snap to the outline for an item in the image.

> **NOTE**
>
> The Magnetic feature works via color and tone contrast. You can click on the Magnetic check box near the center of the options bar to make the Freeform Pen tool work magnetically.

5. **Drag** on the **picture** in the work area. Keep the mouse button pressed as you drag in any desired direction. When you release the mouse button, the path will appear.

TIP

If you're using the Magnetic Pen tool, you can click to set specific anchor points and press Delete to remove the most recent anchor point. However, with the Freeform Pen tool, you must keep the mouse button pressed as you drag.

6. Finish drawing the path in one of three ways:

- **Click** on the first **anchor** point to close the path shape. Note that when the mouse pointer is over the first anchor point, a small circle appears along with the pointer to tell you that clicking would then close the path.
- **Double-click** on the next-to-last **anchor** point to close the path automatically.
- **Click** on the **Freeform Pen** tool in the toolbox to finish the path without closing the shape.

NOTE

When you're drawing any path, you can press Esc to stop drawing the path.

7. **Click** on the **Paths palette menu button**. The palette menu will appear.

8. **Click** on **Save Path**. The Save Path dialog box will open.

9. **Type** a **name** for the path in the Name text box. Your new name will replace the temporary name in the text box.

10. **Click** on **OK**. The Save Path dialog box will close, and Photoshop will finish saving the path under the name you specified.

11. **Press Esc**. Photoshop will deselect the path.

12. **Click** on the **Layers tab** in the Layers palette window. (Alternately, choose Window, Layers.) Photoshop will return to the regular view of layers in the image.

Viewing and Changing a Path

The Paths palette enables you to view and work with the paths in an image file. When you change a path, you move, add, and delete anchor points.

1. **Click** on **Window**. The Window menu will appear.

2. **Click** on **Paths** if it is not already selected. The Paths palette will become the active tab in the Layers palette window.

> **TIP**
>
> Instead of opening the Window menu and choosing Paths, you can click on the Paths tab in the Layers palette window.

3. **Click** on the desired **path** in the Paths palette tab. The path will become the active path.

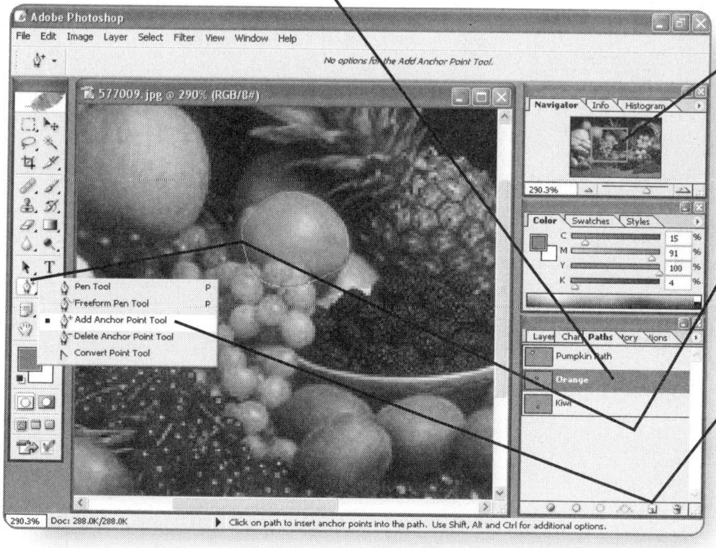

4. **Use** the **Navigator** to pan the path into view, if necessary. The path will become visible in the work area.

5. **Click** and **hold** the **Pen tool** in the toolbox. Its shortcut menu will appear.

6. **Click** on **Add Anchor Point Tool**. The Add Anchor Point tool will become the active tool.

7. **Click** on the **path** at the location where you want to add the new anchor point. The anchor point will appear.

8. **Drag** the **new anchor point** (and any others) to the desired location. The path will reshape accordingly.

9. **Click once** on an **anchor point** that you want to delete. It will appear filled in.

10. **Press Delete** on your keyboard. The Anchor Point will be deleted, and the path will reshape accordingly.

11. **Click once** on an **anchor point** that you want to modify. It will appear filled in.

12. **Drag anchor points** to reposition them as needed. Again, the path will reshape accordingly, but in this case, you didn't have to add new anchor points.

13. **Press Esc**. The path will be deselected, but your changes will remain in the path. From here, you can click on the Layers tab in the Layers palette or choose Window, Layers to resume working with layers.

Filling or Coloring a Path

You can fill a path with color to add a blotch of color in an image, or you can "stroke" the path outline with color to add a subtle outline of color in the image. Although by default a path doesn't print, it will print after you fill or stroke it with color. These steps explain how to use color with a path.

1. **Click** on the desired **fill or outline color** in the color ramp at the bottom of the Color palette. The color will become the active foreground color.

2. **Click** on **Window**. The Window menu will appear.

3. **Click** on **Paths**. The Paths palette will become the active tab in the Layers palette window.

TIP

Instead of opening the Window menu and choosing Paths, you can click on the Paths tab in the Layers palette window.

4. Click on the desired **path** to color in the Paths palette. The path will become the active path.

5a. Click on the **Fill Path with Foreground Color button** at the bottom of the Paths palette. Photoshop will fill the path with the color you selected in step 1.

OR

5b. Click on the **Stroke Path with Brush button** at the bottom of the Paths palette. Photoshop will apply a very thin outline of the foreground color to the path outline.

6. Review the resulting **color**. This example shows the path filled with color. If you merely stroked the path with color, the result could be fairly subtle and may not be visible until you finish working with the Paths palette.

> **NOTE**
>
> At this point, you can click on the Layers tab in the Layers palette or choose Window, Layers to finish working with paths.

Using a Path to Make a Selection

As noted earlier in this chapter, you can use a path as a selection at any time, making it easy for you to work with the path area later, applying a filter or other effect.

1. **Click** on **Window**. The Window menu will appear.
2. **Click** on **Paths** if the Paths palette is not already open. The Paths palette will become the active tab in the Layers palette window.

3. **Click** on the desired **path**. The path will become the active path.
4. **Click** on the **Load Path as a Selection button** at the bottom of the Paths palette tab. A selection marquee will appear around the path. You then can work with the selection just as you would any other selection.

Using a Path to Create a Vector Mask

A vector mask enables you to define a mask based on an outline (rather than based on image pixels and colors, as for a layer mask). You base a vector mask on a work path that you've previously created. Once you've created the vector mask, you can move or resize it as needed to adjust the masked area—something you can't easily do with a layer mask.

> **NOTE**
>
> Vector masking does not work on the Background layer, so right-click on the Background layer and click Duplicate Layer. Enter a name for the new layer in the Duplicate Layer dialog box and then click on OK. Finally, click the eye icon beside the original Background layer in the Layers palette to hide that layer so you can see the effects of your vector mask.

1. **Click** on **Window**. The Window menu will appear.

2. **Click** on **Paths** if the Paths palette is not already open. The Paths palette will become the active tab in the Layers palette window.

3. **Click** on the desired **path**. The path will become the active path.

4. **Click** on the **Layers tab** in the Layers palette window. Photoshop will return to the regular view of layers in the image.

5. Click on the **layer** with the content to mask. The layer will become the active layer.

6. Click on **Layer**. The Layer menu will appear.

7. Point to **Add Vector Mask**. The Add Vector Mask submenu will appear.

8. Click on **Current Path**. The mask will be created and applied immediately.

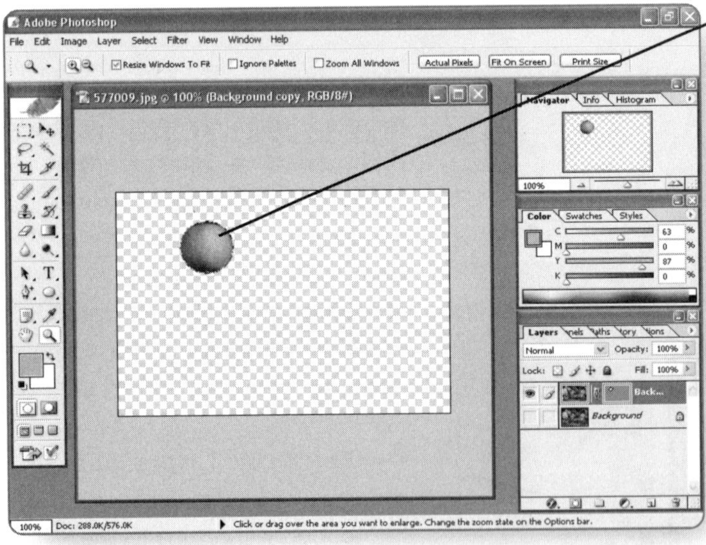

9. Review the resulting **mask**. Layer content outside the mask (path) will be hidden.

NOTE

At this point, you could use the Path Selection tool to move the mask around on the layer or to adjust the shape of the mask. To turn off the mask, right-click on the mask thumbnail in the Layers palette and then click on Disable Vector Mask. Right-click again and then click on Enable Vector Mask to reapply the mask.

Part III Review Questions

1. How do you add a new layer? See "Making a New Layer" in Chapter 8.
2. How do you go to a layer to work with it? See "Selecting a Layer" in Chapter 8.
3. What other kinds of layers can you add? See "Adding a Fill Layer," "Adding a Gradient Layer," and "Adding a Pattern Layer" in Chapter 8.
4. What do you do if one layer is hiding part of another? See "Arranging Layer Order" in Chapter 8.
5. Why do you use a mask? See "Using Layer Masks" in Chapter 9.
6. Can you convert a selection to a mask? See "Using a Selection from One Layer as a Mask on Another" in Chapter 9.
7. What can you do once you've created a mask? See "Putting a Mask to Work" in Chapter 9.
8. How and why do you create a path? See "Adding a Shape Path," "Making a Pen Path," and "Making a Freeform Path" in Chapter 10.
9. How do you convert a selection to a path? See "Using a Path to Make a Selection" in Chapter 10.
10. How do you create and use a clipping path? See "Using Clipping Paths" in Chapter 10.

PART IV

Fine-Tuning Your Image

11

Using Other Editing Tools

Photoshop includes a number of editing tools that you can use to touch up specific areas of an image or layer. Many of the techniques resemble traditional techniques used to correct a photo during development. You can adjust the focus of a particular area, enhance its intensity, or use other techniques such as filling an area with color. In this chapter, you will learn how to:

- Add blurring or smudging to an area
- Sharpen an area
- Use the Eraser tools to erase to the background color or transparency
- Erase all of a particular color on a layer using the Magic Eraser
- Add a gradient or fill an area with color
- Dodge, burn, or sponge an area
- Use tools to fix scratches, spots, and imperfections

Blurring an Area

I'm sure you've seen many infomercials for products that can make you look younger and that get rid of wrinkles and other skin imperfections. The truth is that Photoshop can actually make you look younger! It may seem contrary to your needs in most cases, but blurring part of an image can help camouflage an imperfection or achieve an effect.

These effects are broken down into filters and tools. Use a filter when you want to change the appearance of a selection or a layer. Use a tool when you want to "paint" on a particular area to make a correction.

1. **Click** on the **layer** in the Layers palette that holds the content you want to blur. The selected layer will become the active layer.

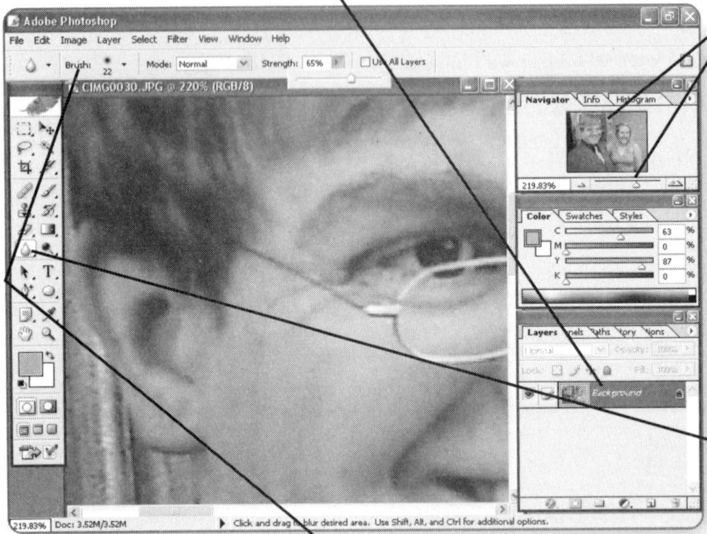

2. **Use** the **Navigator** to zoom in on and display the desired area. The selected area will become more visible.

3. **Click** on the **Blur tool** in the toolbox. The Blur tool will become the active tool.

4. **Choose** a **Brush style** on the options bar. The selected brush will become active for the Blur tool.

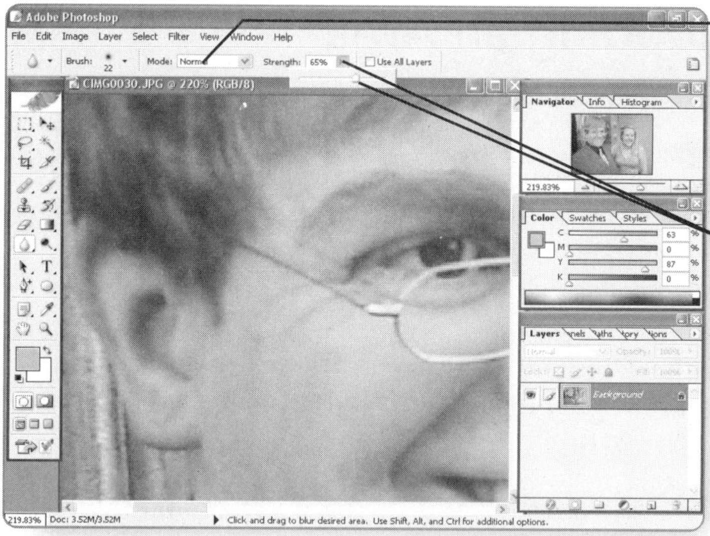

5. **Select** an **option** from the Mode drop-down list on the options bar. The selected mode will become active for the Blur tool.

6. **Select** the **Strength text box contents**, **type** a new **entry**, and **press Enter**. (Alternately, click on the right arrow beside the Strength choice, drag the slider, and then click on the right arrow again.) The strength setting will become active for the Blur tool.

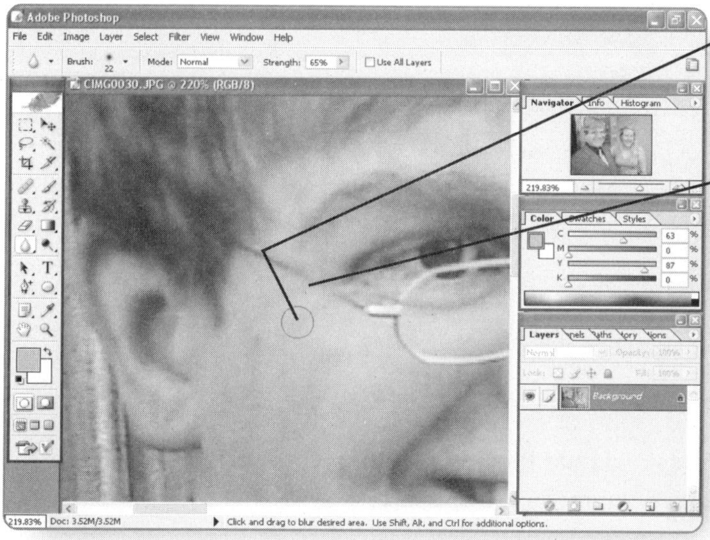

7. **Click** and **drag** on the **layer** to apply the blur. Blurring will begin to appear.

8. **Drag** as much as necessary. Photoshop will continue to add more blurring, but it may take quite a bit of dragging. When you finish, you can continue working with another tool or operation in Photoshop.

Smudging an Area

The Smudge tool helps you drag color from one area into another, much as you can with a paintbrush full of wet paint. You can use the Smudge tool to add a painted effect in a very specific area of the image. Smudging resembles blurring but has a much more dramatic effect. Follow these steps to practice smudging:

1. **Click** on the **layer** in the Layers palette that holds the content you want to smudge. The selected layer will become the active layer.

2. **Use** the **Navigator** to zoom in on and display the area to smudge. The selected area will become more visible.

3. **Press** and **hold** the **mouse button** on the Blur tool in the toolbox. A submenu will appear.

4. **Click** on **Smudge Tool**. The Smudge tool will become the active tool.

5. Choose a **Brush style** on the options bar. The selected brush will become active for the Smudge tool.

6. Make a **choice** from the Mode drop-down list on the options bar. The selected mode will become active for the Smudge tool.

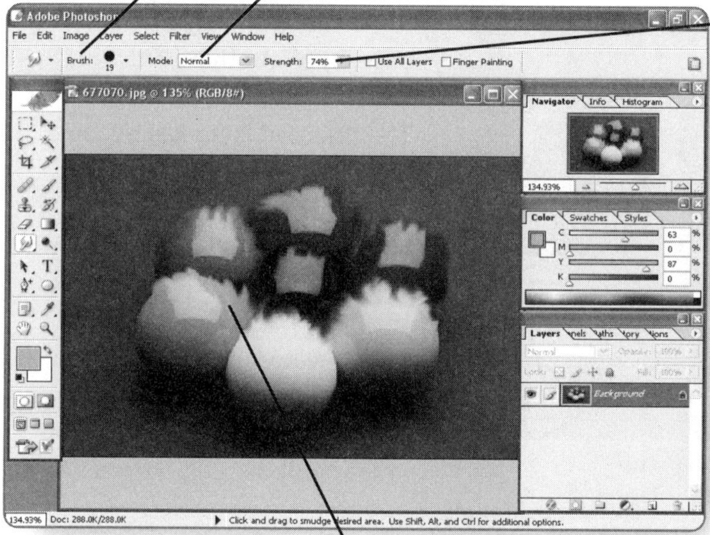

7. Select the **Strength text box contents**, **type** a new **entry**, and **press Enter**. (Alternately, click on the right arrow beside the Strength choice, drag the slider, and then click on the right arrow again.) The strength setting will become active for the Smudge tool.

NOTE

If you click on the Finger Painting check box in the options bar to check it, dragging with the Smudge tool will paint using the currently selected foreground color.

8. Drag on the **layer** over two contrasting colors to make the smudge. Smudging will begin to appear. When you finish creating all the necessary smudges, you can continue working with another tool or operation in Photoshop.

NOTE

You can make the effects of the Blur, Smudge, or Sharpen tool partially transparent after you use the tool. To do so, click on Edit and then click on Fade (Tool Name). Specify an Opacity setting in the Fade dialog box that appears and then click on OK.

Sharpening an Area

The Sharpen tool works in the opposite way as the Blur tool: It tries to improve the focus of edges that are soft so that the image appears clearer. So, for example, you might want to use this tool if one small spot on a layer looks out of focus.

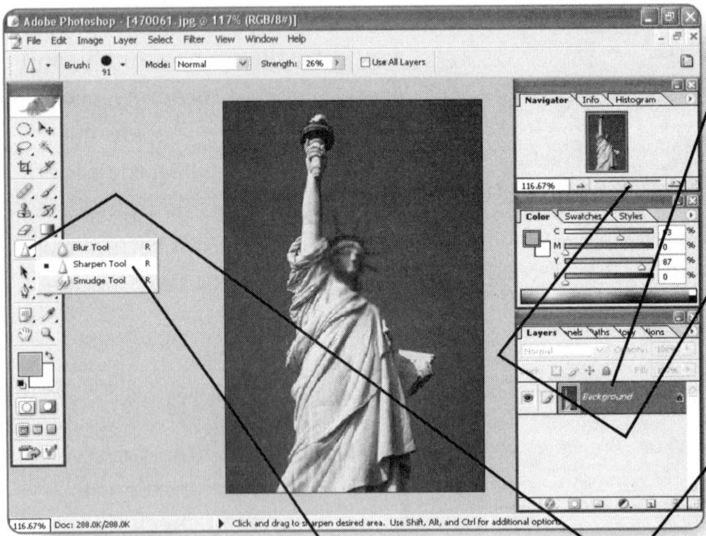

1. **Click** on the **layer** in the Layers palette that holds the content you want to sharpen. The selected layer will become the active layer.

2. **Use** the **Navigator** to zoom in on and display the area to sharpen. The selected area will become more visible.

3. **Click** and **hold** the **Blur tool** in the toolbox. A submenu will appear.

4. **Click** on **Sharpen Tool**. The Sharpen tool will become the active tool.

5. Choose a **Brush style** on the options bar. The selected brush will become active for the Sharpen tool.

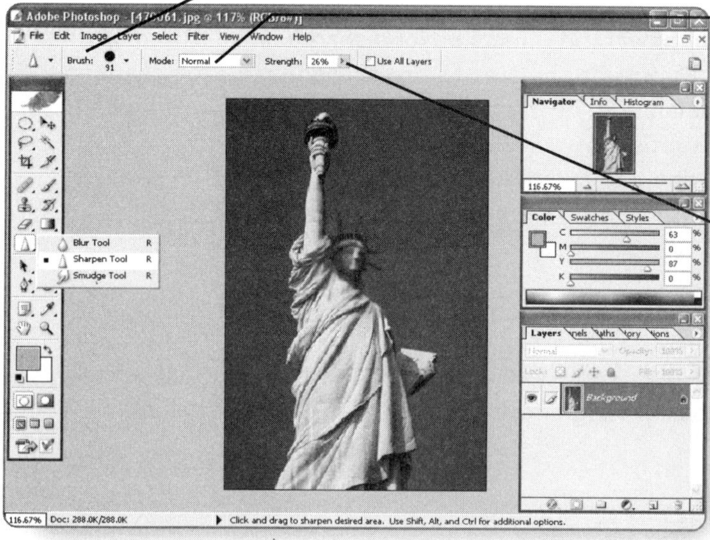

6. Make a **choice** from the Mode drop-down list on the options bar. The selected mode will become active for the Sharpen tool.

7. Select the **Strength text box contents**, **type** a new **entry**, and **press Enter**. (Alternately, click on the right arrow beside the Strength choice, drag the slider, and then click on the right arrow again.) The strength setting will become active for the Sharpen tool.

8. Drag on the **layer** to apply the sharpening. Sharpening will begin to appear. When you finish adding all the necessary sharpening, you can continue working with another tool or operation in Photoshop.

NOTE

If you use a large, sharp brush and a higher Strength setting with the Sharpen tool, clicking or dragging can have unwanted effects beyond sharpening—the color of pixels outside the area to be sharpened may be changed dramatically. Even though the impact of sharpening can be subtle, you still want to use the Sharpen tool sparingly to avoid those unwanted changes.

Erasing Image Content

Photoshop offers three different eraser tools so you can achieve the exact erasing effect you need in any particular situation.

Using the Eraser

The standard Eraser tool erases color or content on a layer, enabling the background layer in the image to show through to varying degrees, depending on the opacity you specify. If you're working on the background layer itself, using the standard Eraser actually paints or draws the currently selected background color rather than erasing layer content. The following steps show an example of each of these uses for the Eraser tool.

CAUTION

The Eraser tools don't work on shape layers. To work around this issue, create a new layer using the Layer, New, Layer command. Choose the shape layer in the Layers palette and select and copy its content using the Edit, Copy Merged command. Then choose the new layer you created in the Layers palette and use the Edit, Paste command to paste the content onto it. You can then delete the shape layer and erase as necessary on the new layer.

1. **Click** on the **layer** in the Layers palette that holds the content you want to erase. (In this case, click on any regular layer except the Background layer.) The selected layer will become the active layer.

2. **Use** the **Navigator** to zoom in on and display the area to erase. The selected area will become more visible.

3. **Click** on the **Eraser tool**. The Eraser tool will become the active tool.

4. **Make** a **choice** from the Mode drop-down list on the options bar. The selected mode will become active for the Eraser tool.

> **NOTE**
>
> Because the Mode choice affects the available Brush choices in this case, choose the Mode first. If you choose the Block mode, you cannot choose a brush shape.

5. **Choose** a **Brush style** on the options bar. The selected brush will become active for the Eraser tool. Note that selecting certain brush styles enables airbrush capabilities for the Eraser tool.

6. **Select** the **Opacity text box contents**, **type** a new **entry**, and **press Enter**. (Alternately, click on the right arrow beside the Opacity choice, drag the slider, and then click on the right arrow again.) The opacity setting will become active for the Eraser tool.

7. If available, **select** the **Flow text box contents**, **type** a new **entry**, and **press Enter**. (Alternately, click on the right arrow beside the Flow choice, drag the slider, and then click on the right arrow again.) The flow setting will become active for the Eraser tool, controlling how quickly the eraser works.

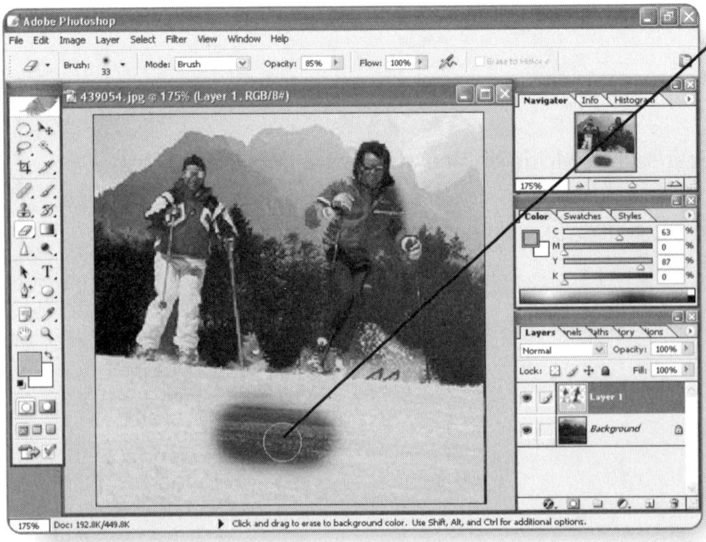

8. **Drag** on the desired layer. Photoshop will erase the current layer's content and reveal the content on the Background layer.

Using the Background Eraser

The Background Eraser tool erases the content on any layer, including both the foreground and background colors on the layer. Areas you erase with this tool become transparent so that content on other layers in the image can show through. If the image has only one layer, or if you're erasing the background layer and there's no content in front of it, the areas erased with this tool will be transparent if the image file is placed in a document.

1. **Click** on the **layer** in the Layers palette that holds the content you want to erase. The selected layer will become the active layer.

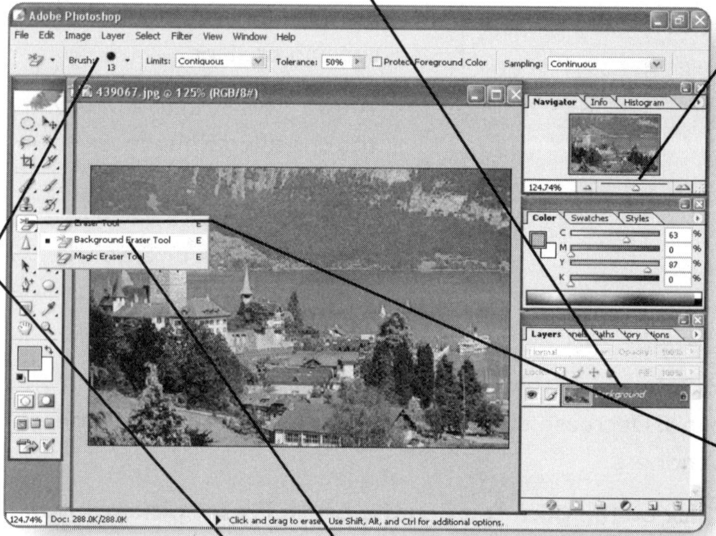

2. **Use** the **Navigator** to zoom in on and display the area to erase. The selected area will become more visible.

3. **Click** and **hold** on the **Eraser tool**. A shortcut menu will appear.

4. **Click** on **Background Eraser Tool**. The Background Eraser tool will become the active tool.

5. **Click** on the **Click to open the Brush Preset picker button** on the options bar. A palette of brush options will appear.

6. **Make Diameter**, **Hardness**, **Spacing**, **Angle**, and **Roundness choices** in the palette. The selected choices will affect the shape of the eraser brush as follows:

- **Diameter.** Enables you to specify the size of the brush (the area to be erased).
- **Hardness.** Enables you to specify the size of the brush's hard center, as a percentage of the total diameter.
- **Spacing.** If you want eraser brush strokes to be noncontiguous as you erase, increase this setting to add spacing or skips.
- **Angle.** This setting works with the specified Roundness value to tip the brush shape. You can either enter a value in the Angle text box or drag the arrow axis on the brush preview.
- **Roundness.** Enables you to specify whether a brush is round. Decrease this value to less than 100% to decrease roundness.

7. **Click** on the **Click to open the Brush Preset picker down arrow**. The palette of brush settings will close.

> **NOTE**
>
> Use the bottom two settings, Size and Tolerance, to further control the brush when you're using a graphics tablet with Photoshop.

8. **Make Limits**, **Tolerance**, and **Sampling choices** on the options bar. The selected choices will affect the erasing as follows:

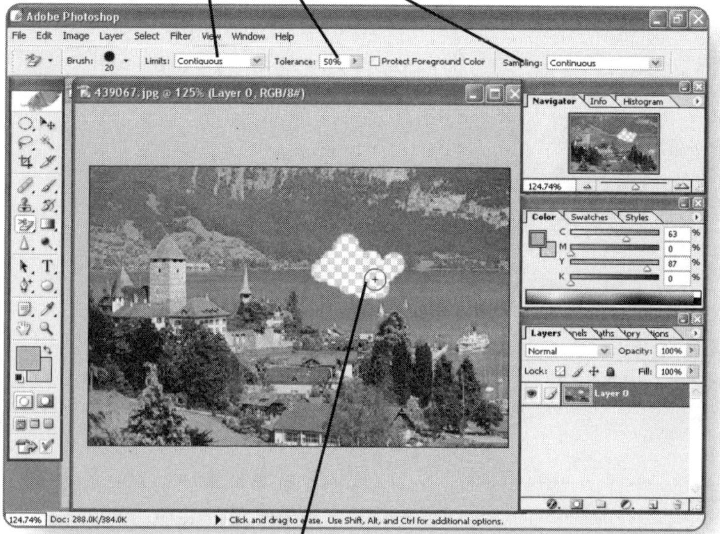

- **Limits.** Controls how far the erasing can spread, based on dragging over similar colors.
- **Tolerance.** Controls whether the eraser will erase only pixels of alike colors (lower settings) or similar colors.
- **Sampling.** Determines whether erasing tests matching colors continuously or by the color initially selected.

9. **Click** or **drag** on the layer to erase. Photoshop will erase the current layer's content, leaving a transparent area behind.

Using the Magic Eraser

Use the Magic Eraser tool when you want to erase a contiguous area of color on a layer. You can either completely erase the area of color or make the erasure less opaque so that only part of the color area is erased.

1. **Click** on the **layer** that holds the content to erase in the Layers palette. The selected layer will become the active layer.

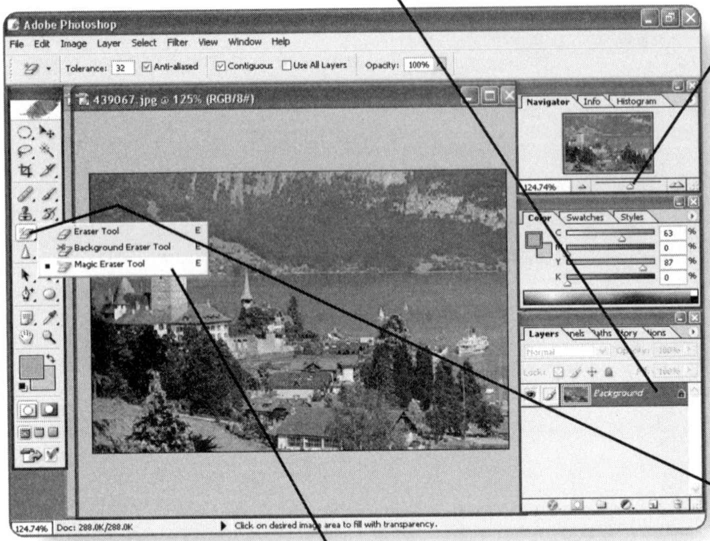

2. **Use** the **Navigator** to zoom in on and display the area to blur. The selected area will become more visible.

3. **Click** and **hold** on the **Eraser tool**. A shortcut menu will appear.

4. **Click** on **Magic Eraser Tool**. The Magic Eraser tool will become the active tool.

5. Enter a **Tolerance setting** on the options bar. The specified setting will become active for the Magic Eraser tool. Lower settings will tell the tool to erase only colors that are a closer match; higher settings will enable the tool to erase less similar colors.

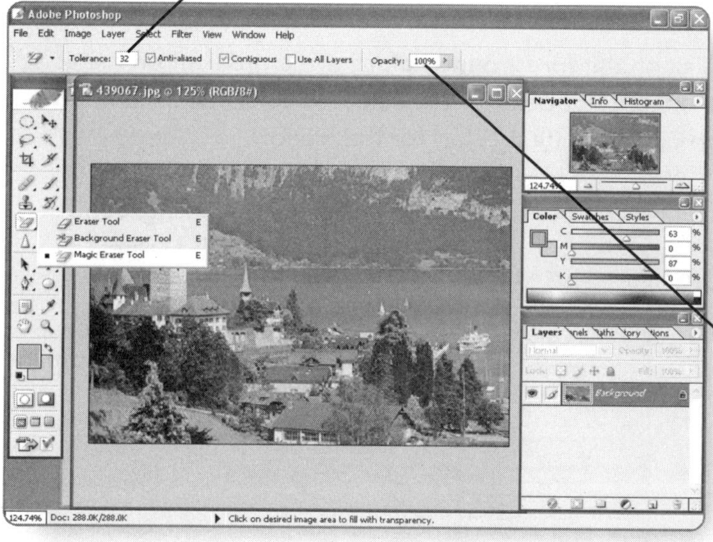

TIP

To enter a Tolerance setting, highlight the contents of that text box, type a new entry, and press Enter.

6. Select the **Opacity text box contents**, **type** a new **entry**, and **press Enter**. (Alternately, click on the right arrow beside the Opacity choice, drag the slider, and then click on the right arrow again.) The Opacity setting will become active for the Magic Eraser tool.

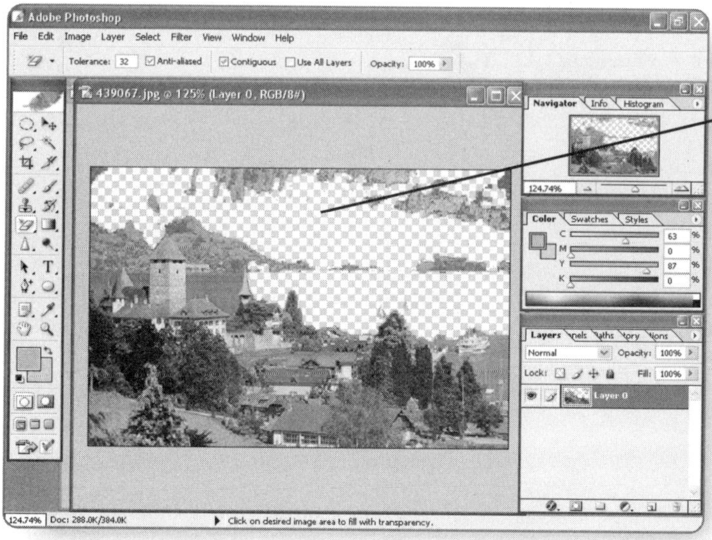

7. Click or **drag** on the area with the color to erase on the current layer. Photoshop will erase the selected color and any matching adjacent areas, applying transparency if specified.

TIP

No matter what types of changes you're making, don't forget to save your file from time to time.

Adding a Gradient

You can add a gradient onto most layers, except for layers that hold text. When you add a gradient, you can specify which colors to blend within the gradient. You can great a gradient fill for an entire layer or for a selection on that layer.

1. **Click** on the **foreground color** for the gradient on the color ramp in the Color palette. The selected color will become the foreground color (first color) for the blend.

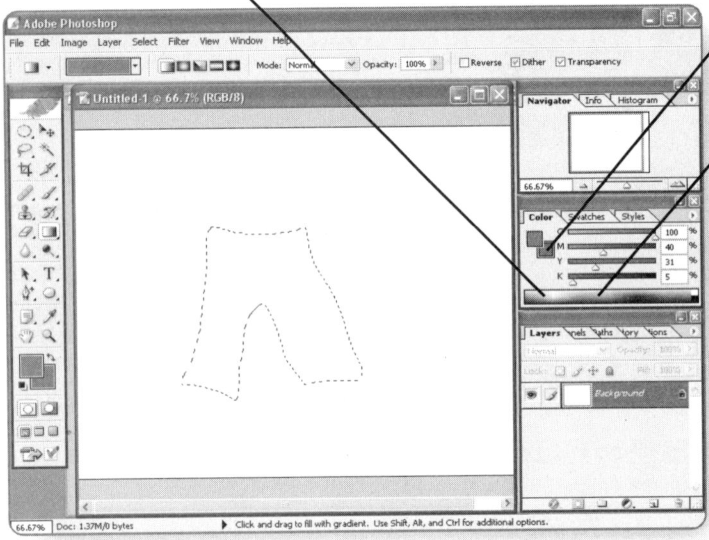

2. **Click** on the **background color box**. It will be selected.

3. **Click** on a **color** for the background on the color ramp in the Color palette.

4. **Click** on the **layer** to which you want to add the gradient in the Layers palette. The selected layer will become the active layer.

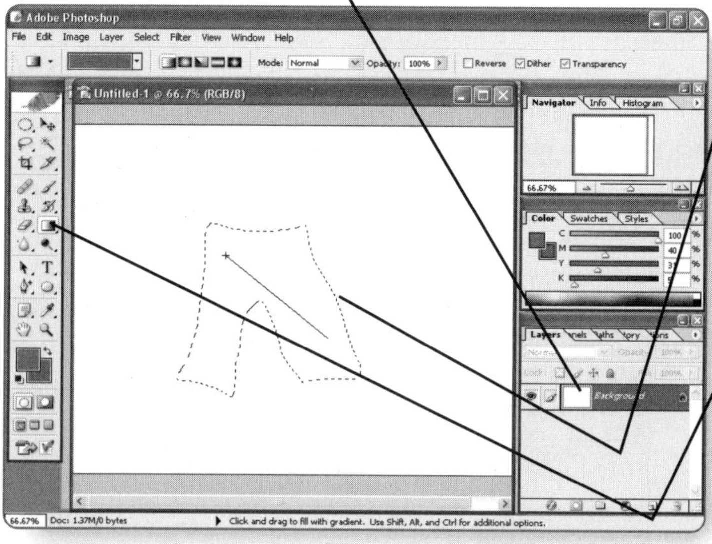

5. **Select** the **area** first (either manually or with a path) or **use a mask** to prevent Photoshop from displaying the gradient in the affected area. If you don't select an area, the entire layer will be filled.

6. **Click** on the **Gradient tool** in the toolbox. The Gradient tool will become the active tool.

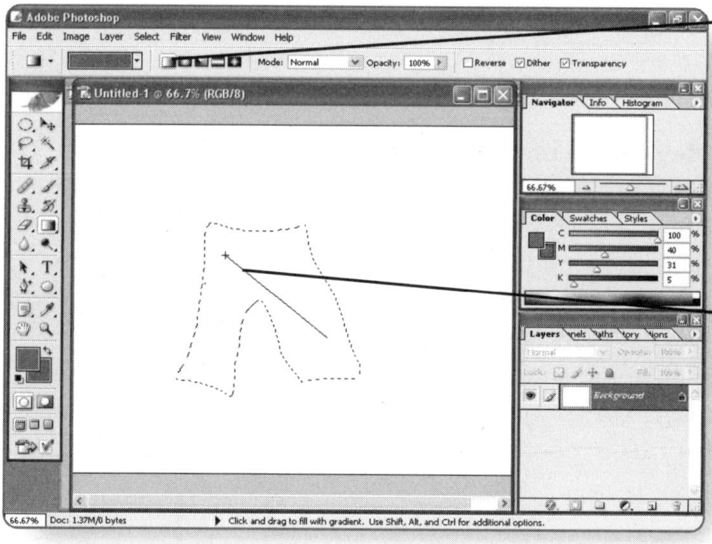

7. **Click** on a **gradient style button**. (The available choices include Linear Gradient, Radial Gradient, Angle Gradient, Reflected Gradient, and Diamond Gradient.) Photoshop will apply the selected style.

8. **Select** the **Opacity text box contents**, **type** a new **entry**, and **press Enter**. (Alternately, click on the right arrow beside the Opacity choice, drag the slider, and then click on the right arrow again.) The Opacity setting will become active for the Gradient tool.

NOTE

Changing the Mode setting can allow the Gradient tool (and the Paint Bucket tool, which is described in the next section) to apply a different behavior, such as dissolving the image.

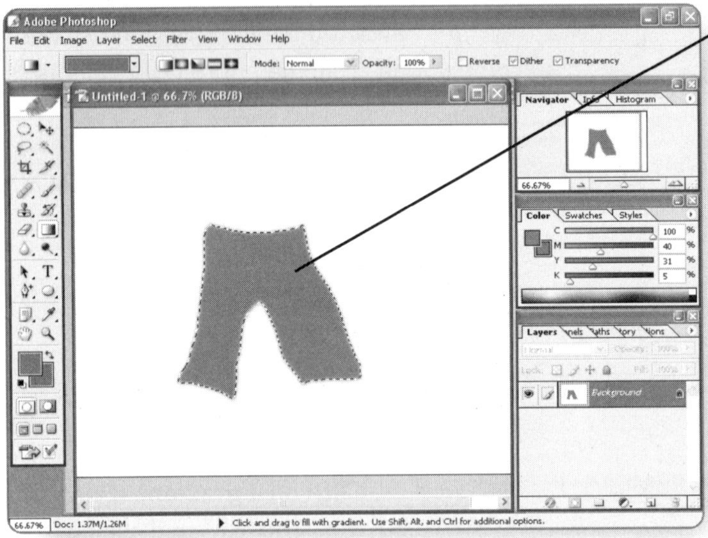

9. **Click** and **drag** on the **layer** to set the angle or center point for the gradient (depending on the style you selected in step 6). Photoshop applies the gradient immediately.

10. **Review** the **results**. (If you made a selection, you can deselect it first.) As with other types of effects you create, the gradient interacts with other content on the layer, blending with that content if the gradient wasn't 100% opaque. Note that, in this instance, because the text and leaf images appear on separate layers and those layers are in the front of the image, the gradient doesn't fill or overlay the content of the other layers. After you finish the gradient, you can work with another tool or operation in Photoshop.

Filling with the Paint Bucket

Use the Paint Bucket tool to fill a contiguous area of color (or similar colors) with the current foreground color.

> **CAUTION**
>
> The Paint Bucket tool doesn't work on shape layers. To work around this issue, create a new layer using the Layer, New Layer command. Choose the shape layer in the Layers palette and select and copy its content using the Edit, Copy Merged command. Then choose the new layer you created in the Layers palette and use the Edit, Paste command to paste the content onto it. You can then delete the shape layer and erase as necessary on the new layer.

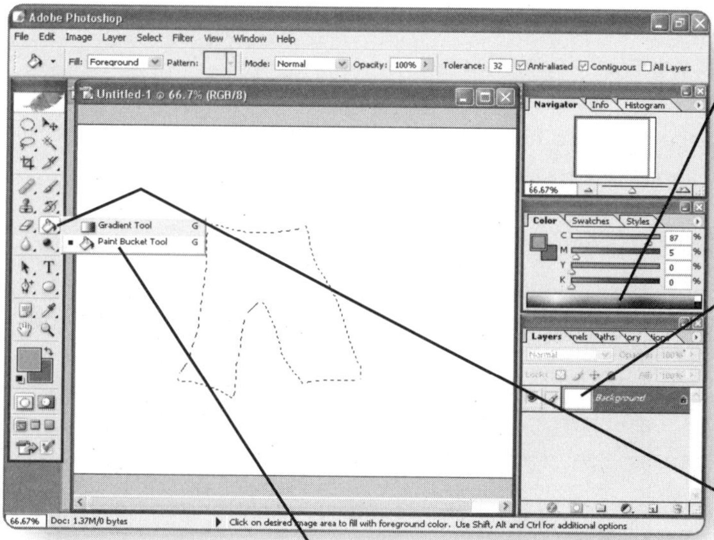

1. **Click** on the **foreground color** for the fill on the color ramp in the Color palette. The selected color will become the fill color for the Paint Bucket tool.

2. **Click** on the **layer** in the Layers palette that includes the area you want to fill. The selected layer will become the active layer.

3. **Click** and **hold** on the **Gradient tool** in the toolbox. A shortcut menu will appear.

4. **Click** on **Paint Bucket Tool**. The Paint Bucket tool will become the active tool.

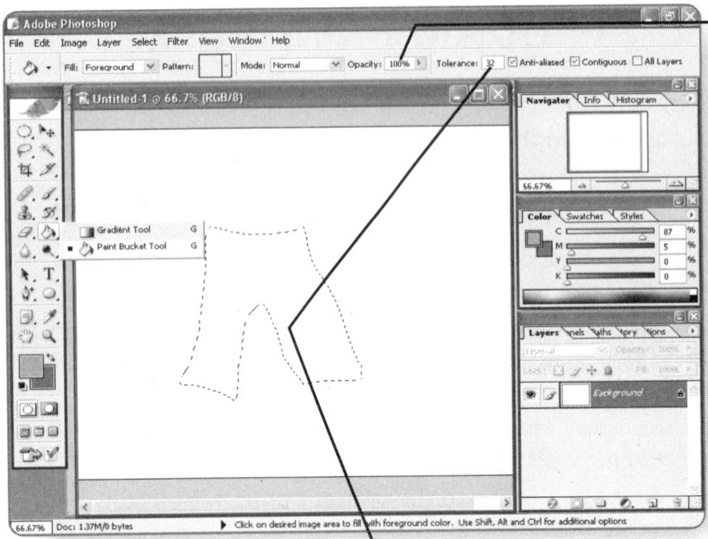

5. Select the **Opacity text box contents**, **type** a new **entry**, and **press Enter**. (Alternately, click on the right arrow beside the Opacity choice, drag the slider, and then click on the right arrow again.) The Opacity setting will become active for the Paint Bucket.

6. Select the **Tolerance text box contents**, **type** a new **entry**, and **press Enter**. The Tolerance setting will become active for the Paint Bucket tool. (Remember, tolerance refers to how carefully a tool must match the color of an area in order to identify which pixels to fill or erase.)

TIP

If you want to use the Paint Bucket to fill an area with a pattern, choose Pattern from the Fill drop-down list and then choose a pattern from the Pattern drop-down list.

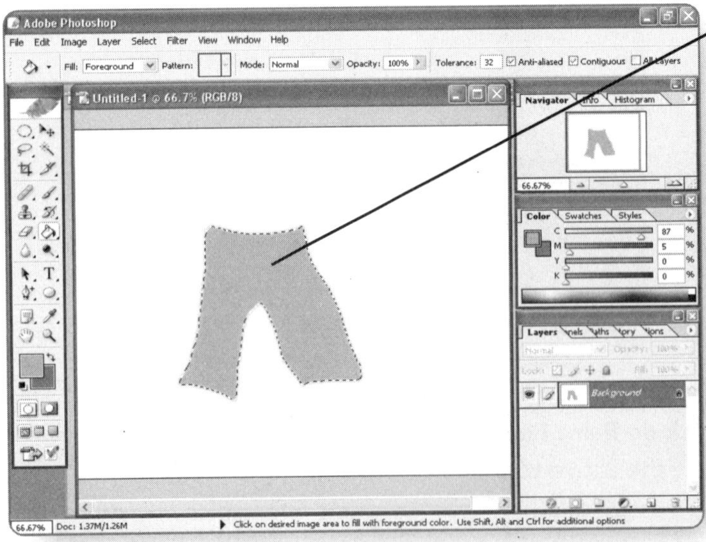

7. Click on the **area** to fill with the foreground color you selected. Photoshop applies the gradient immediately. Even if the layer includes other areas with the same color, those areas will not be filled if they are not contiguous. After you finish filling, you can work with another tool or operation in Photoshop.

Using Photo Techniques

In the past, one of the benefits of using a professional photographer was the photographer's (or the photo lab's) ability to manipulate lighting—both when shooting the initial photo and when creating the prints. The Dodge, Burn, and Sponge tools in Photoshop help you mimic a photographer's tricks in correcting lighting in an image. The Healing Brush and Patch tools can help you repair an image, such as a scanned image of a photo with spots, scratches, and other blemishes.

Dodging an Area

Use the Dodge tool to lighten an area that's too dark in your image. In the case of scanned content or a photo downloaded from a digital camera, dodging can actually reveal detail that previously wasn't visible in the image. Follow these steps to work with dodging:

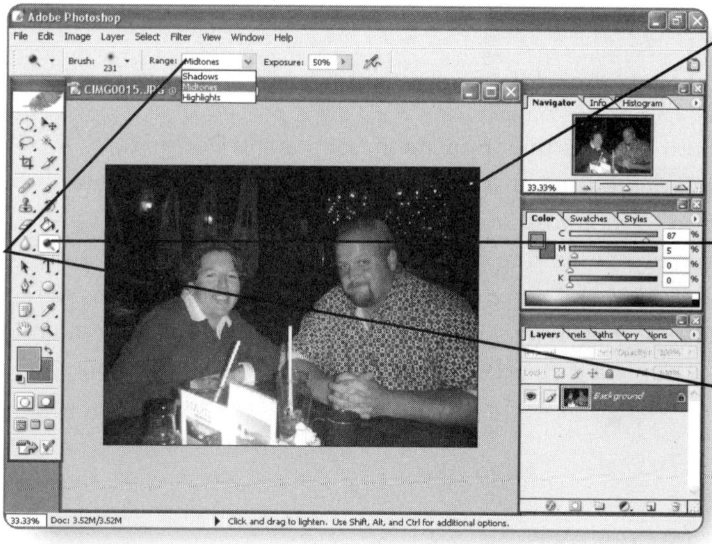

1. **Open** the **image** to correct and select the desired layer and zoom, if necessary. The image (and layer) will become active or current.

2. **Click** on the **Dodge tool** in the toolbox. The Dodge tool will become the active tool.

3. **Choose options** on the options bar as needed. The options for the Dodge tool are:

- **Brush.** Designates the brush style for the tool.
- **Range.** Specifies whether the Dodge tool affects shadows, midtones, or highlights in the areas over which you drag.

- **Exposure.** Identifies how much of a change the Dodge tool makes as you drag.
- **Airbrush.** Enables the airbrush effect for the tool.

4. **Click** on or **drag** over the area(s) to dodge. Photoshop makes the corrections immediately. After you finish dodging, you can work with another tool or operation in Photoshop.

Burning an Area

The Burn tool has the opposite impact as the Dodge tool. Burning darkens an area in the image, as if more light were directed to that area when the "photo" was being developed. You can use burning to help balance an area that seems weak or too light in an image or to emphasize a particular area. In the case of a color image, burning can intensify the color in an area and make it stand out from its background a bit more.

1. **Open** the **image** to correct and select the layer to burn, if necessary. The image (and layer) will become active or current.

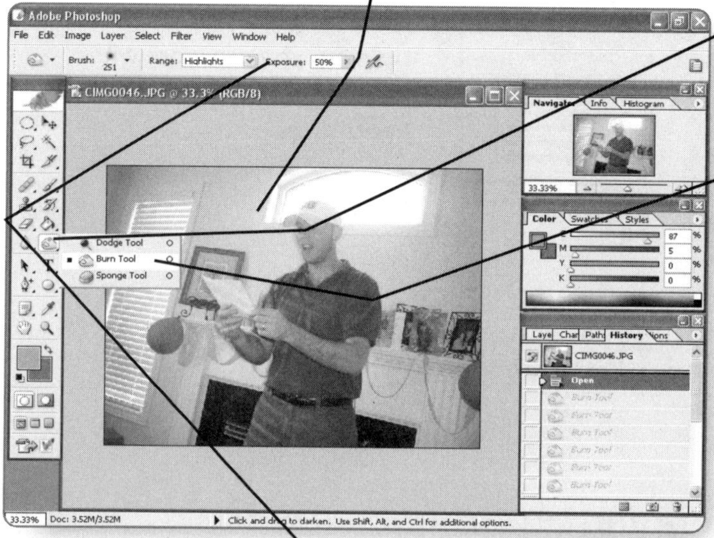

2. **Click** and **hold** on the **Dodge tool** in the toolbox. A shortcut menu will appear.

3. **Click** on **Burn Tool**. The Burn tool will become the active tool.

4. **Choose options** on the options bar as necessary. The options for the Burn tool are:

- **Brush.** Designates the brush style for the tool.
- **Range.** Specifies whether the Burn tool affects shadows, midtones, or highlights in the areas over which you drag.
- **Exposure.** Identifies how much of a change the Burn tool makes as you drag.
- **Airbrush.** Enables the airbrush effect for the tool.

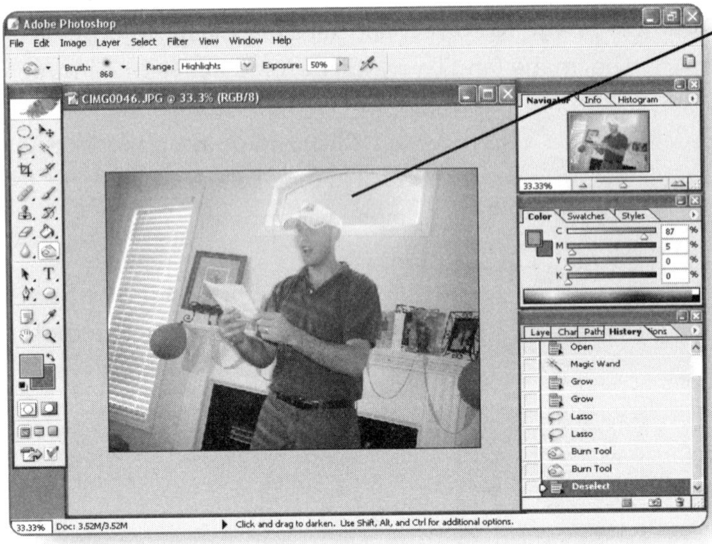

5. **Click** on or **drag** over the area(s) to burn. Photoshop makes the corrections immediately. After you finish burning, you can work with another tool or operation in Photoshop.

Sponging an Area

The Sponge tool (sponging) changes color saturation in a color image and contrast in a grayscale image. In either case, using the Sponge tool helps make the area you're correcting appear more bright or crisp, to help it stand out from surrounding content in the image.

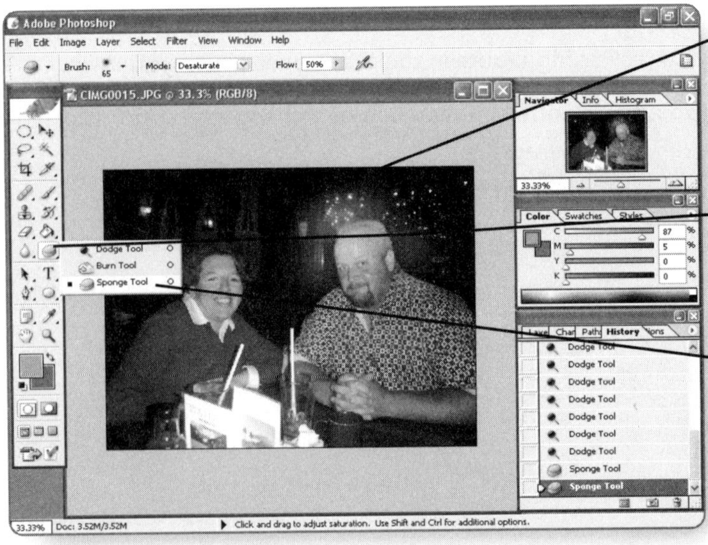

1. **Open** the desired **image** and select the layer to correct, if necessary. The image (and layer) will become active or current.

2. **Click** and **hold** on the **Dodge tool** in the toolbox. A shortcut menu will appear.

3. **Click** on **Sponge Tool**. The Sponge tool will become the active tool.

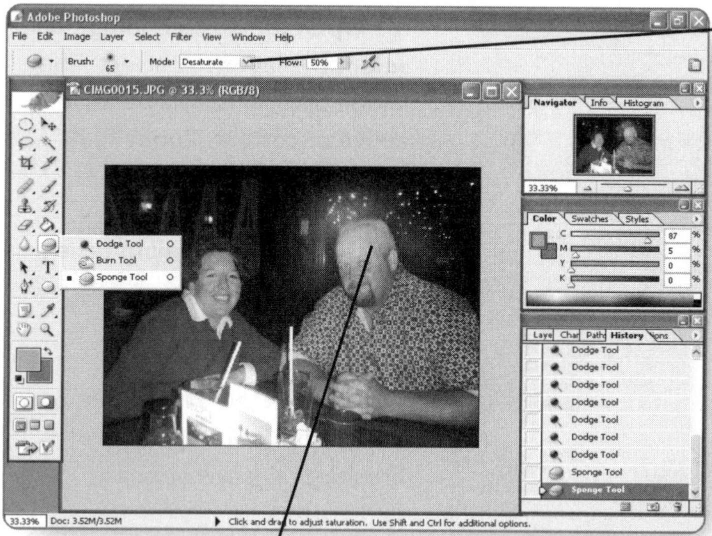

4. **Choose options** on the options bar as necessary. The options for the Sponge tool are:

- **Brush.** Designates the brush style for the tool.
- **Mode.** Specifies whether the Sponge tool saturates (adds more color intensity) or desaturates (decreases color intensity) in the area you drag over.
- **Flow.** Identifies how much of a change the Sponge tool makes as you drag.
- **Airbrush.** Enables the airbrush effect for the tool.

5. **Click** on or **drag** over the area(s) to sponge. Photoshop makes the corrections immediately. After you finish sponging, you can work with another tool or operation in Photoshop.

Using the Healing Brush

The Healing Brush is an amazing tool for getting rid of unwanted areas in photos. It can be used to clean up dirt marks, scratches, holes, tears, or other imperfections that can arise on photos. In this example, we will remove a logo from the sleeve of a t-shirt using the Healing Brush.

1. **Open** the desired **image** and **select** the **layer** to correct. The image (and layer) will become active or current. Zoom in, if needed.

2. **Click** on the **Healing Brush** tool. The Healing Brush tool will become the active tool.

3. **Click** on the **Brush style** on the options bar. A palette of brush options will appear.

4. **Make Diameter**, **Hardness**, **Spacing**, **Angle**, and **Roundness choices** in the palette. The selected choices will affect the shape of the Healing Brush tool as follows:

- **Diameter.** Enables you to specify the size of the brush (the area to be "healed").
- **Hardness.** Enables you to specify the size of the brush's hard center, as a percentage of the total diameter.
- **Spacing.** If you want erasure brush strokes to be noncontiguous as you heal, increase this setting to add spacing or skips.

- **Angle.** This setting works with the Roundness value you specify to tip the brush shape. You can either enter a value in the Angle text box or drag the arrow axis on the brush preview.

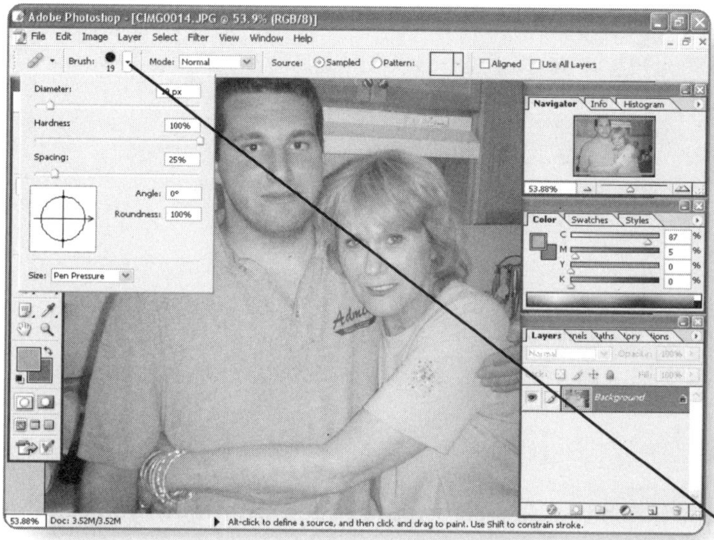

- **Roundness.** Enables you to specify whether a brush is round. Decrease this value to less than 100% to decrease roundness.

> **NOTE**
>
> Use the bottom setting, Size, to further control the brush when you're using a graphics tablet with Photoshop.

5. **Click** on the **Brush style down arrow**. The palette of brush settings will close.

6. **Click** on the **Sampled option button** to select it, if necessary. The Healing Brush tool will use the area you sample in the image to make the needed repair.
7. **Alt+click** on the **area** to sample. (Of course, you should sample an area that looks like the area to patch.) The target mouse pointer will appear to verify that you are sampling, and the sample will be loaded after you click.

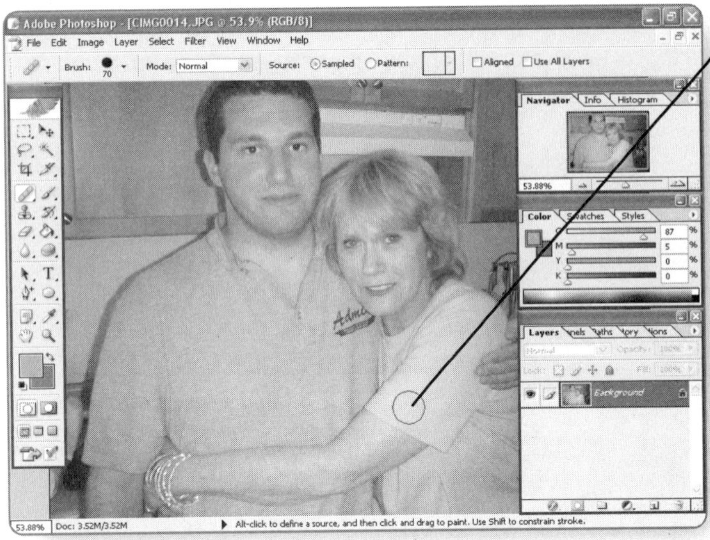

8. **Click again** or **drag** on the area to repair. Photoshop will cover the flaw using the sampled content.

Patching a Flaw

Use the Patch tool to increase the speed with which you can make even more complicated repairs. With this tool, rather than painting over an area with sampled material, you select a patch area from the image and then drag that patch over the area to repair. This tool works particularly well when the area to repair has a pattern, striping, or some other type of texture that the Healing Brush tool cannot capture. Use the following steps to create a patch and use it to repair an image:

1. **Open** the desired **image** and select the layer to correct. The image (and layer) will become active or current. Zoom in, if necessary.

2. **Click** and **hold** on the **Healing Brush tool** in the toolbox. A shortcut menu will appear.

3. **Click** on **Patch Tool**. The Patch tool will become the active tool.

4. **Click** on the **Destination option button** on the options bar. This will set up the Patch tool so that you will first select the sample to use as the patch and then drag it over the area to be patched.

5. **Drag** on the **image** to select the source area (patch). The area you drag around will be selected so that you can use it as the patch.

TIP

It's important to select a patch source area that's large enough to cover the flaw but not so large that it will cover mismatching areas around the flaw.

6. **Drag** the **patch** from the source location over the flaw; release the mouse button only when you've positioned the patch as necessary. The patch will cover the flaw.

> **TIP**
>
> As long as the patch remains selected, you can move it and reposition it. You also can rotate the patch (Edit, Transform, Rotate) and make other changes to ensure a precise fit.

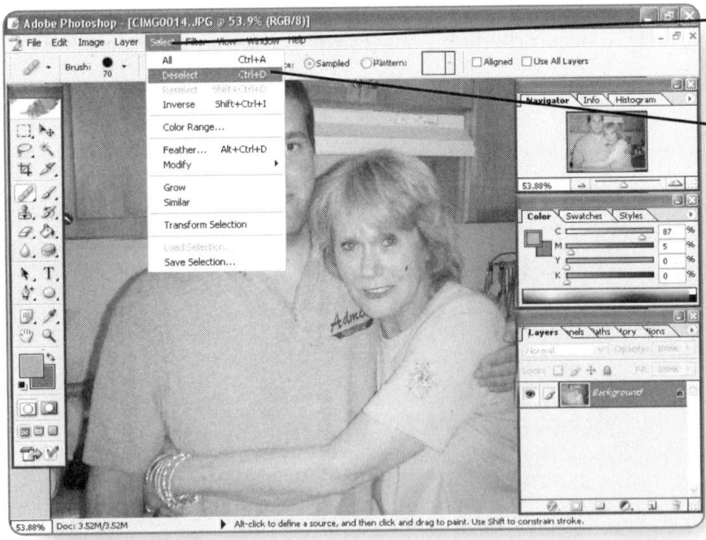

7. **Click** on **Select**. The Select menu will appear.

8. **Click** on **Deselect**. The patch selection marquee will disappear. Depending on how close the patch was to the area to be repaired, the repair will be totally or nearly impossible to see.

12

Working with Image Size and Orientation

When you create a new image file, you specify its size. When you import an image from a scanner or digital camera, you have less control over the size and orientation of the image. In either case, you can use some tricks to tweak the size and orientation of the image so that it suits your purpose. In this chapter, you'll learn how to:

- Use the Crop tool to crop an image
- Resize the image
- Adjust the image canvas
- Rotate the entire canvas
- Trim the edges of the image
- Automatically crop and straighten images

Cropping the Image

When you crop the image, you select the area of the image that you want to keep, and then you have Photoshop hide or remove the unselected portions of the image. You can crop if an image's subject is off-center, if you need to eliminate a distracting element from the image, or if you need to fit the image to a particular height and width.

1. **Click** on the **Crop tool** on the toolbox. The Crop tool will become active.

2. **Type entries** in the Width and Height text boxes, if necessary. When you use these text boxes, Photoshop will resize the cropped material to the specified dimensions (in addition to performing the crop).

3. **Type** an **entry** in the Resolution text box, if necessary. If you make an entry, Photoshop will resample the cropped material to the specified resolution.

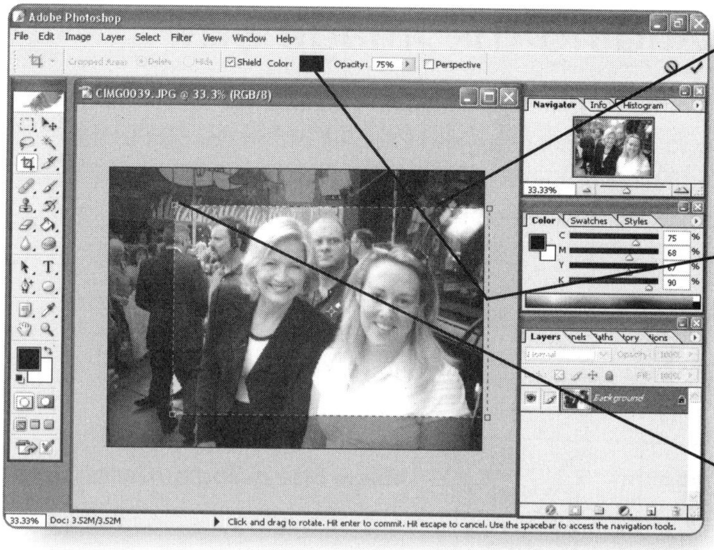

4. **Drag** on the **image to create a selection to crop**. This will select the area to keep; the area outside the selection will be shielded or grayed out.

5. **Adjust shield settings**, if necessary. Photoshop will change the temporary shading used to mask the areas to be cropped out of the image.

6. **Drag** the **crop selection** to resize or rotate the crop zone. Dragging a corner will resize the crop zone; dragging a side will rotate the crop zone.

NOTE

If you click on the Crop tool again at this point, a message box appears to ask whether you want to crop the image. You can click on Crop to proceed, Cancel to stop the crop operation, or Don't Crop to remove the cropping selection.

7. **Click** on the **Commit (check) button** on the options bar or press Enter. Photoshop will crop the image to the specified zone.

Changing the Image Size

You can resize an image file when you want to both fit the image to a particular size and keep all of the content in the image. Resizing the image also gives you the opportunity to resample it or change to the resolution (pixels per inch) in the image.

1. **Click** on **Image**. The Image menu will appear.
2. **Click** on **Image Size**. The Image Size dialog box will open.

> **TIP**
>
> To see the current image size before you display the Image Size dialog box, press and hold the Alt key and then click and hold on the Doc size indicator near the bottom-left corner of the Photoshop window.

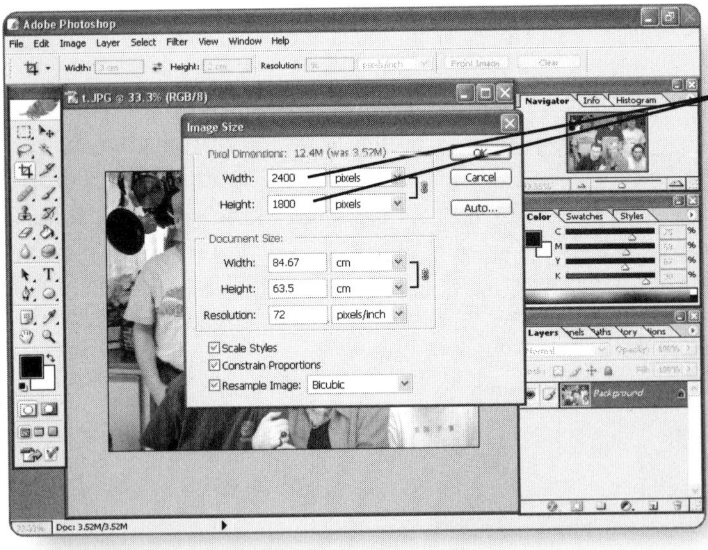

3. **Enter** a new **Width** or **Height** under either Pixel Dimensions or Document Size. Photoshop will adjust the other three text box entries to keep them proportional.

> **TIP**
>
> Click on the Constrain Proportions check box to clear the check if you want to resize only one image dimension. Otherwise, changing a Height entry automatically adjusts the Width and vice versa.

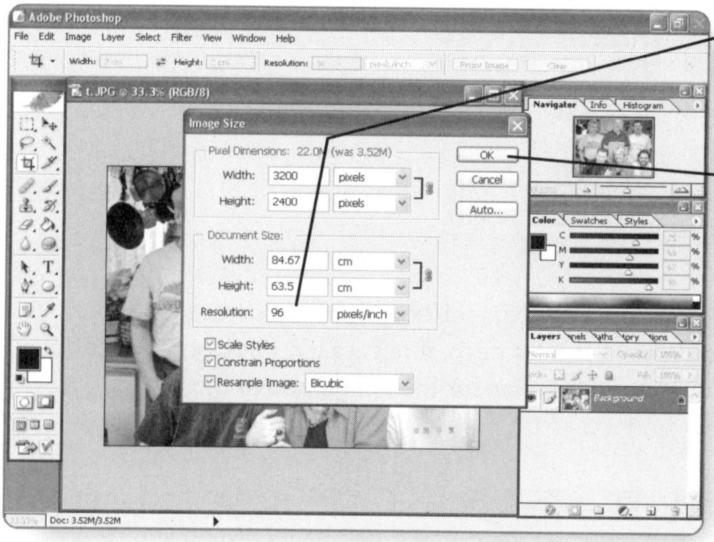

4. **Enter** a new **Resolution**. Photoshop will apply the new resolution setting.

5. **Click** on **OK**. The settings you have entered will take effect.

Changing the Canvas Size

The canvas size and image size always use the same dimensions. Thus, changing the canvas size changes the image size, but not in the same way that using the Image Size command does. When you change to a canvas size that's smaller than the current image/canvas size, Photoshop crops out part of the image. When you change to a canvas size that's larger than the current image/canvas size, Photoshop adds space around the image.

1. Click on **Image**. The Image menu will appear.

2. Click on **Canvas Size**. The Canvas Size dialog box will open.

3. Enter a new **Width** and/or **Height** and choose another measurement unit for each, if necessary. Photoshop will display the projected New Size for the image above those measurements.

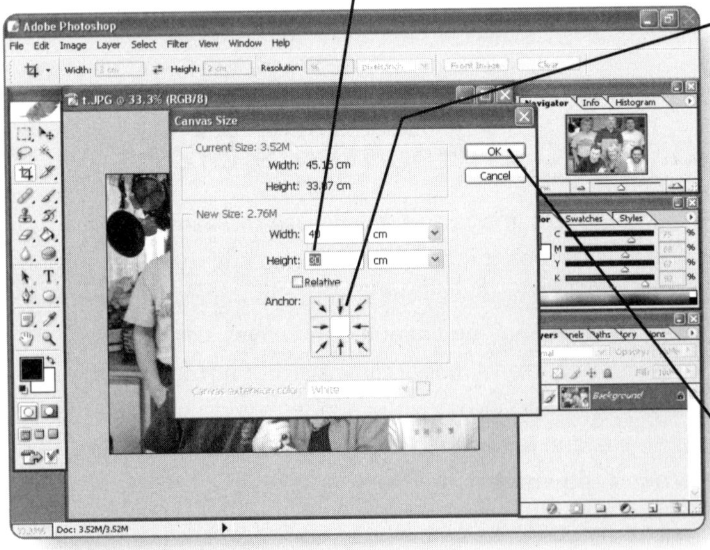

4. Click another **Anchor point**, if necessary. When you're increasing the canvas size, the selected anchor point will control where white space will be added around the image. When you're decreasing the canvas size, the selected anchor point will designate which part of the image to keep and which to crop out.

5. Click on **OK**. Photoshop will apply the new canvas size, unless it needs to display a warning regarding the size change, as shown in step 6.

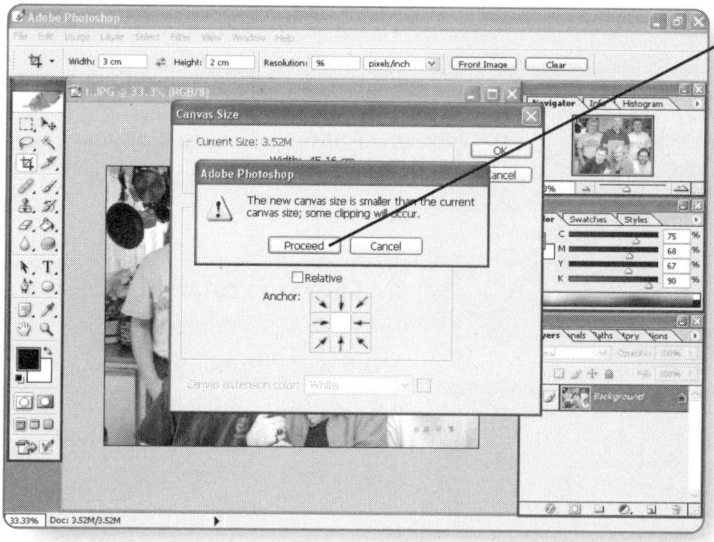

6. **Click** on **Proceed** in the warning dialog box, if it appears. Photoshop will finish resizing the canvas.

Rotating the Canvas

You can rotate the canvas to rotate the entire image—all the content on all the layers. Photoshop provides these rotation options:

- **180°.** Rotates the canvas so that the top of the image becomes the bottom.
- **90° CW.** Rotates the canvas one quarter turn in the clockwise direction.
- **90° CCW.** Rotates the canvas one quarter turn in the counterclockwise direction.
- **Arbitrary.** Displays the Rotate Canvas dialog box so that you can specify a precise rotation amount and direction.
- **Flip Canvas Horizontal.** Flips the image right to left.
- **Flip Canvas Vertical.** Flips the image top to bottom.

Use the following steps when you're ready to rotate the image:

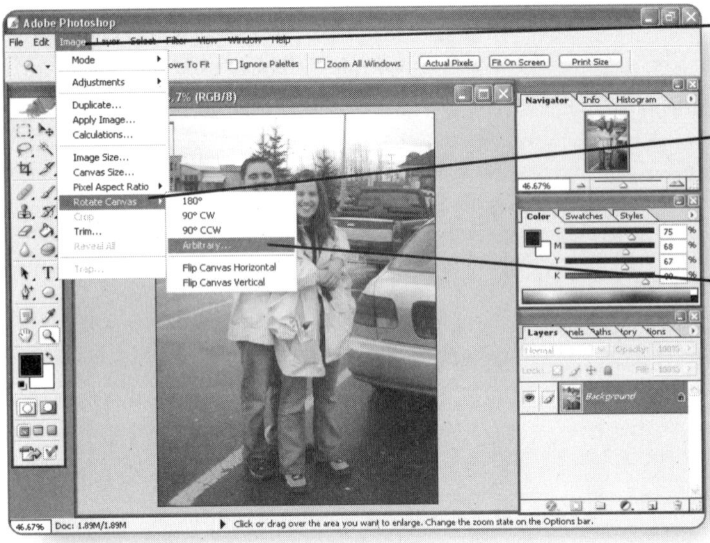

1. **Click** on **Image**. The Image menu will appear.

2. **Point** to **Rotate Canvas**. The Rotate Canvas submenu will appear.

3. **Click** on a **rotation choice**. If you chose anything but Arbitrary, Photoshop will apply the rotation immediately. Otherwise, the Rotate Canvas dialog box will appear.

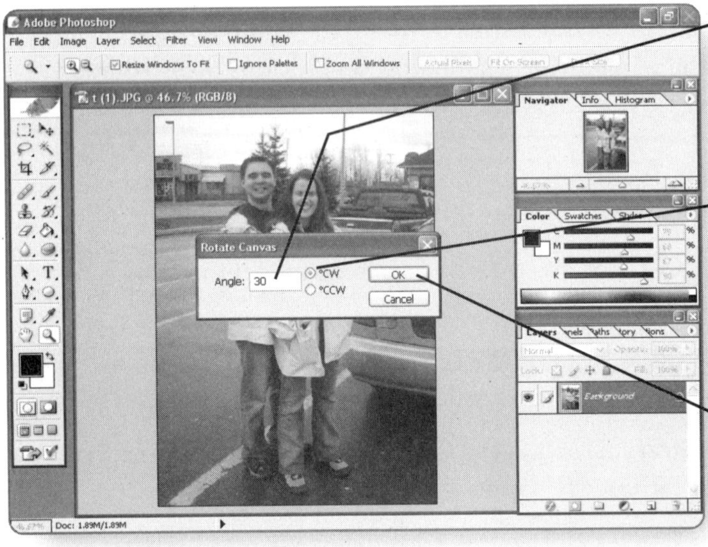

4. **Type** an **entry** in the Angle text box. Your entry will specify how much rotation Photoshop applies.

5. **Click** on the **°CW** or **°CCW** option. Your choice will specify either the clockwise or counterclockwise rotation direction.

6. **Click** on **OK**. Photoshop will rotate the image as specified by the rotation settings you entered.

Trimming the Canvas

You can use the trim feature to crop out unnecessary information around the edge of an image, such as a white photo print border, blank canvas space that's no longer needed, or discolored areas around an image from a contact sheet fading or folding. For the trim feature to work, the area to be trimmed must all be the same color.

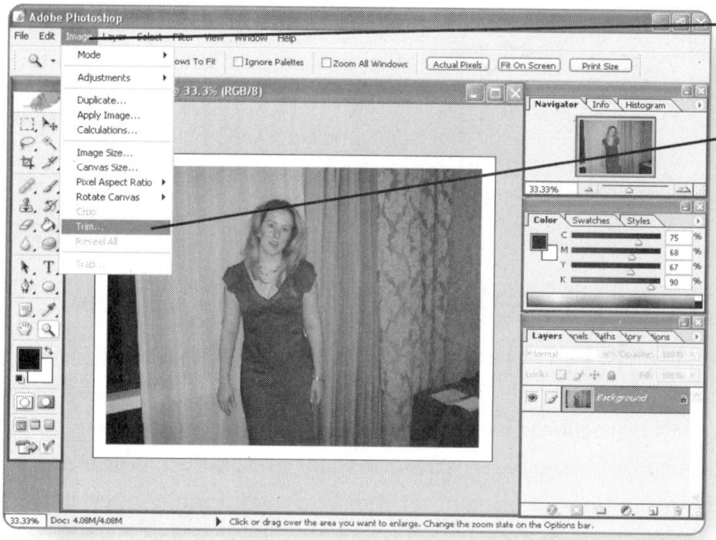

1. **Click** on **Image**. The Image menu will appear.

2. **Click** on **Trim**. The Trim dialog box will open.

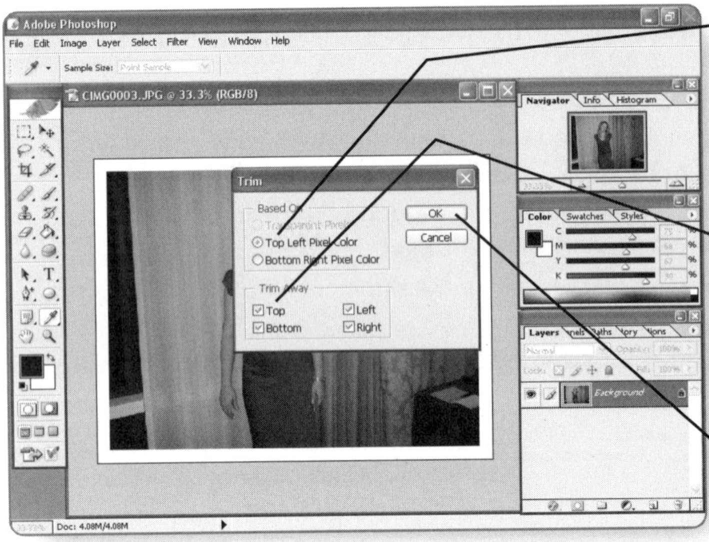

3. **Click** on a **Based On option button**. Photoshop will use the specified setting to identify which pixels to trim from the image.

4. **Click** on the **Trim Away check boxes** as needed. Clearing a Trim Away check box tells Photoshop not to trim the designated portion of the image.

5. **Click** on **OK**. Photoshop will perform the image trim.

Automatically Cropping and Straightening Images

One of the problems when scanning in images is that it is difficult to get a perfectly straight scan. In addition, if you are scanning multiple images at a time, you traditionally have had to individually crop and save each image. Photoshop CS has a new autocrop feature that will automatically straighten and crop your scanned images.

1. **Open** or **scan in** the **image** you would like to automatically crop and straighten.

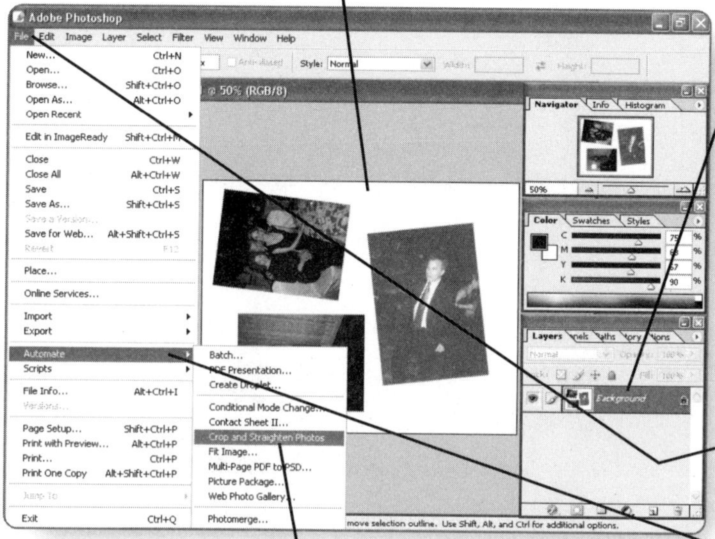

2. **Click** on the **layer** that contains those images. Alternatively, you can create a selection around the images for which you would like to create separate files.

3. **Click** on **File**. The file menu will appear.

4. **Click** on **Automate**. A submenu will appear.

5. **Click** on **Crop and Straighten Photos**. All of the images on the layer will be straightened, cropped, and opened in their own separate window.

13

Applying Filters

What's the big draw of most movies we go to today? It's the special effects. Within Photoshop CS, there are dozens of different special effects, called filters, that you can apply to your images. Filters can be used to correct problems with images or just to add artistic flare. Photoshop CS adds a new Filter Gallery that makes applying filters even easier. The goal of this chapter is to have you:

- Understand the available filters
- Apply a filter when you need it
- Adjust the filter
- Use the Filter Gallery

Previewing the Filters

The default Photoshop installation installs dozens of filters. The Filter menu groups the filters on several submenus. Table 13-1 lists the submenus and gives a description of the types of filters found in each submenu group.

Table 13-1 ***Reviewing Filter Groups***

Group	Includes Filters That
Artistic	Make the image look like it was created with watercolors or pastels, has a film grain, has poster edges, and so on.
Blur	Add blurs to simulate movement, such as in a single direction or rotation.
Brush Strokes	Apply a brush stroke effect in one of various available shapes.
Distort	Give the appearance of natural or artificial distortions caused by shape and light, such as a ripple, glass, or twirl effect.
Noise	Apply noise (white speckling) to affect the image appearance or to fix spots and scratches.
Pixelate	Apply one of several dotted effects to the image, such as simulating the Pointillism technique.
Render	Let you change the fill, add a lighting effect, apply 3D, and more.
Sharpen	Improve image sharpness.
Sketch	Apply a drawing effect in one of various available techniques.
Stylize	Make a number of changes, like glowing edges or embossing, that lend a modern effect.
Texture	Convert the image's appearance to make it consistent with the selected texture.
Video	Change the color method used in a video still.
Other	Create a custom filter or work with other custom filters.

NOTE

Photoshop applies the filter effect only to the current layer and current selection (if any).

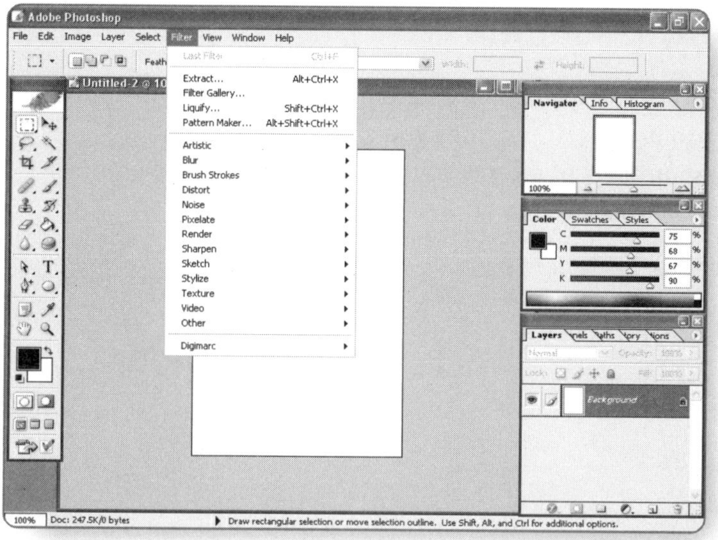

The Filter Gallery

A new addition to Photoshop CS is the Filter Gallery. The Filter Gallery offers a one-stop location for you to apply and manipulate filters. The Filter Gallery not only displays all of the available filters, it also allows you to apply multiple filters to an image.

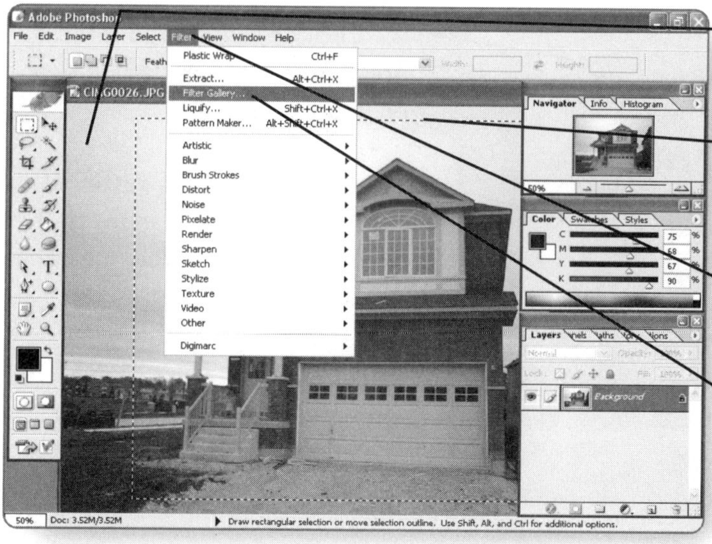

1. **Open** the **image** to which you would like to apply a filter.
2. **Create** a **selection** if you only want to apply the filter to a particular area of your image.
3. **Click** on **Filter**. The Filter menu will appear.
4. **Click** on **Filter Gallery**. The Filter Gallery window will open. Alternatively, you can select a specific filter from the list in the menu.

Applying Filters

The Filter Gallery enables you to preview, adjust, and apply filters to images. It provides you with generic thumbnail representations of effects so that you can quickly select the filter you would like to apply.

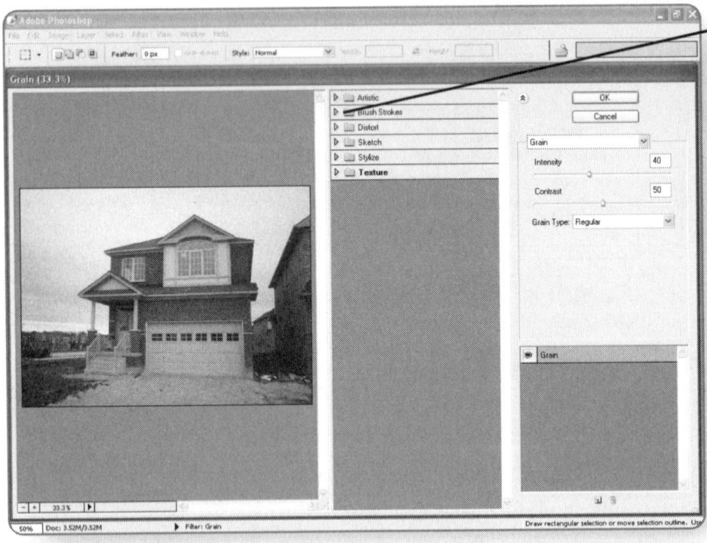

1. **Click** on the **triangle** beside the filter category to display the filters that fall within that category.

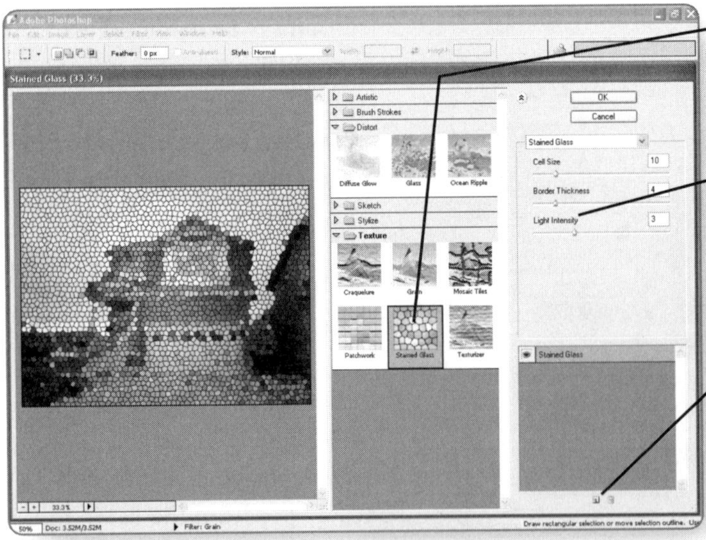

2. **Click** on the desired **filter**. A preview of the effect will appear on your image.

3. **Adjust** any of the **settings** for that filter. The changes to the filter will appear as you make the adjustments.

4. **Click** on the **New Effect Layer button**. This will allow you to apply multiple filters to the same image.

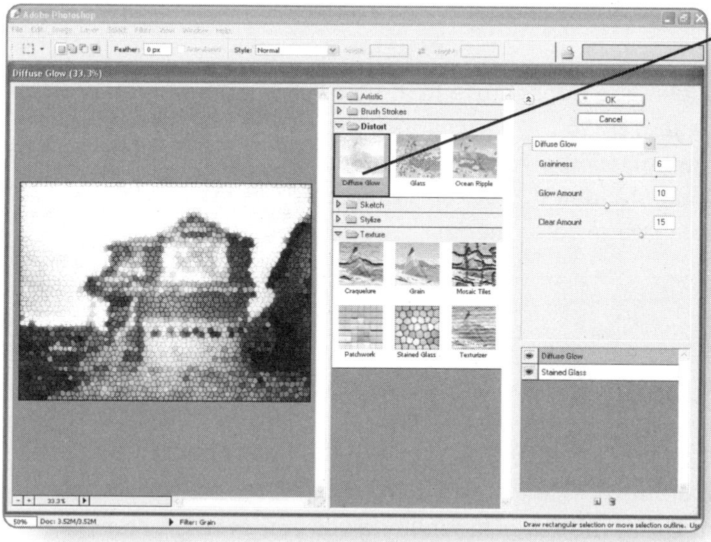

5. **Click** on the desired **filter**. A preview of the effect will appear on your image.

6. **Repeat** steps **4** and **5** until you have completed adding all the filters to your image.

7. **Click** on an **effect layer** that you would like to delete. It will be selected.

8. **Click** on the **Delete effect layer button** to remove the unwanted layer.

9. **Click** on **OK**. The Filter Gallery will close, and the filtered image will appear in the Photoshop CS window.

NOTE

If the image doesn't use RGB color or is a bitmapped, indexed, or 16-bit-per-channel image, Photoshop won't allow you to apply a filter to it. See Chapter 15, "Understanding Colors and Channels," to learn more about image color modes.

Fading a Filter

Fading a filter enables you to make the filter effect more transparent or to adjust the light or color density for the filter effect. Using the Fade capability gives you even greater control over how the filter affects the image.

NOTE

The Fade command may not be available for all filters. It also is not available after you save and close the image; you must use it during the current image-editing session. It is, however, available for some of the painting tools in Photoshop and works for those just as described here.

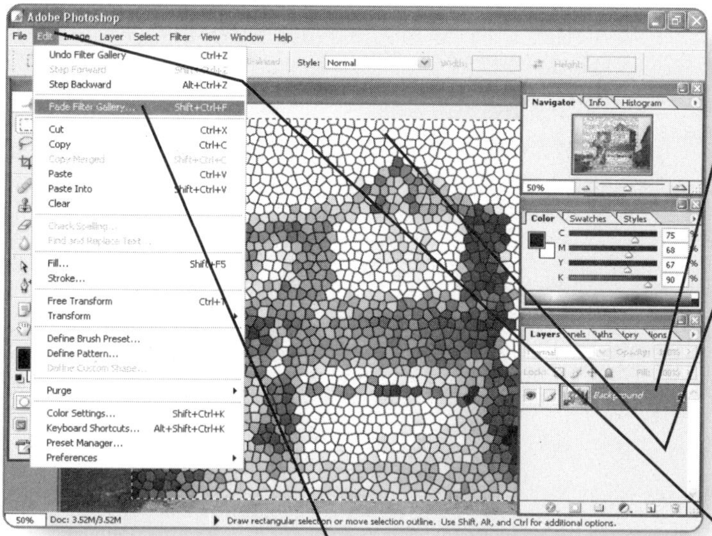

1. **Display** the **layer** that holds the filtered image content. The selected layer's content will appear.

2. **Select** the **filtered area**, if necessary. A selection marquee will appear.

3. **Click** on **Edit**. The Edit menu will appear.

4. **Click** on **Fade (Filter Name** or Filter Gallery**)**. The Fade dialog box will open.

5. **Drag** the **Opacity slider**. The Opacity setting will adjust accordingly.

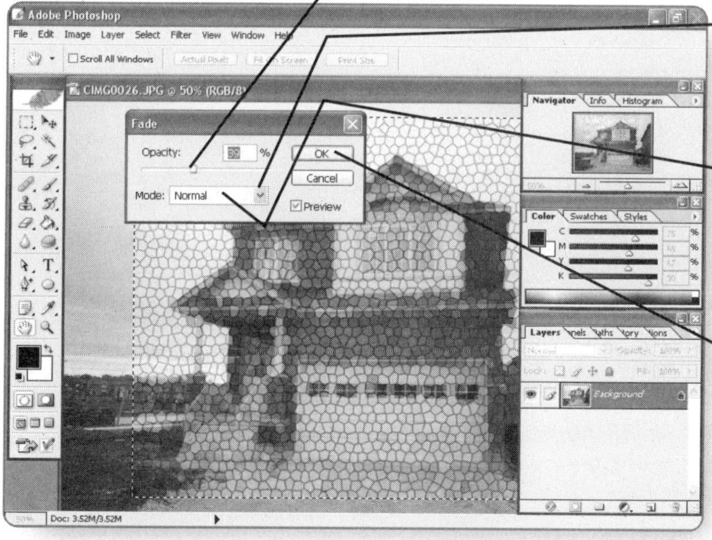

6. **Click** on the **down arrow** beside the Mode list. The Mode list will open.

7. **Click** on a **mode** in the list. The image or selection will preview the selected Opacity and Mode settings.

8. **Click** on **OK**. The dialog box will close, and Photoshop will apply the fade.

14

Printing and Other Outputs

What good is an image if you can't print it out and attach it to the front of your refrigerator for all to see? Photoshop CS adds a number of printing features that you may not have seen before if your previous computer experience has been limited to word processors and spreadsheets. In addition to printing your images, there are a variety of other options for outputting your images. In this chapter, you will learn how to:

- Create a PDF slideshow
- Create a contact sheet
- Use Photomerge to create panoramas
- Choose the printer to use
- Choose print scaling options
- Add a border and background for the printout
- Send the print job
- Print multiple copies of an image on a page with the Picture Package feature

Creating a PDF Slideshow

One of the new features that Photoshop CS offers is the capability to create a PDF slideshow. PDF (*Portable Document Format*) provides an efficient way of viewing and sharing documents. The beauty of this feature is that you can create a digital slideshow without needing any additional software.

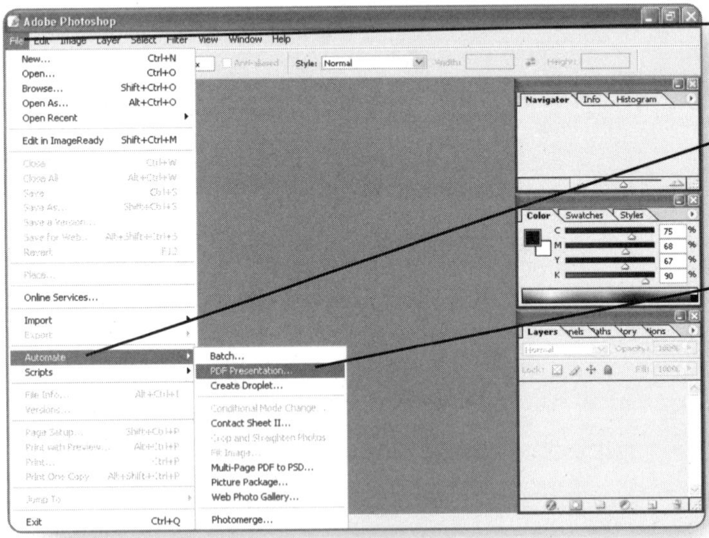

1. **Click** on **File**. The file menu will appear.

2. **Click** on **Automate**. A submenu of different options will appear.

3. **Click** on **PDF Presentation**. The PDF Presentation dialog box will open, where you can set the options for your slideshow.

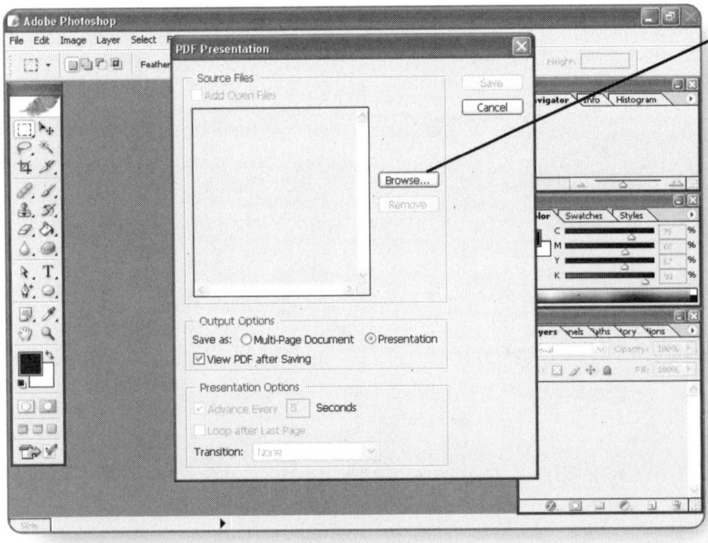

4. **Click** on **Browse**. You can now select which image files you want to be a part of your slideshow.

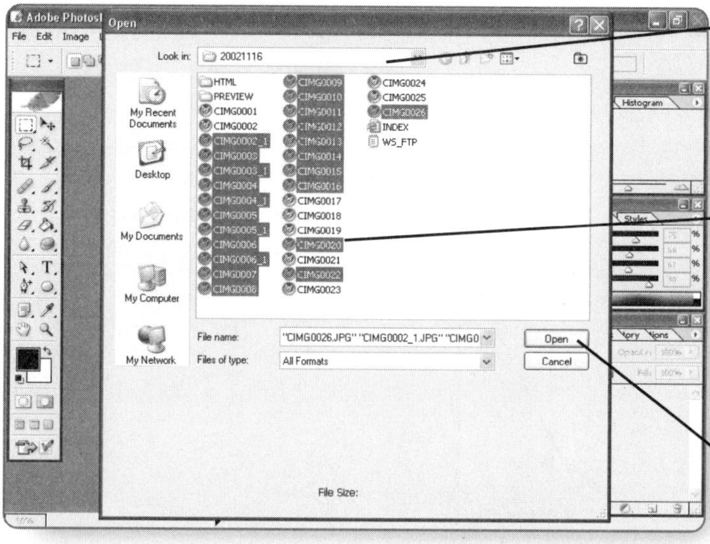

5. **Navigate** your **computer** to the location of the images you would like to use in the slideshow.

6. **Ctrl-click** on the **files** you want to include in the slideshow. Alternatively, you can Shift-click to select contiguous files. The files will be highlighted once selected.

7. **Click** on **Open**. You will return to the PDF Presentation dialog box.

8. **Click** on the **Presentation** option to save the file as a slideshow.

9. **Click** in the **View PDF after Saving check box** if you want to preview the slideshow after it has been saved.

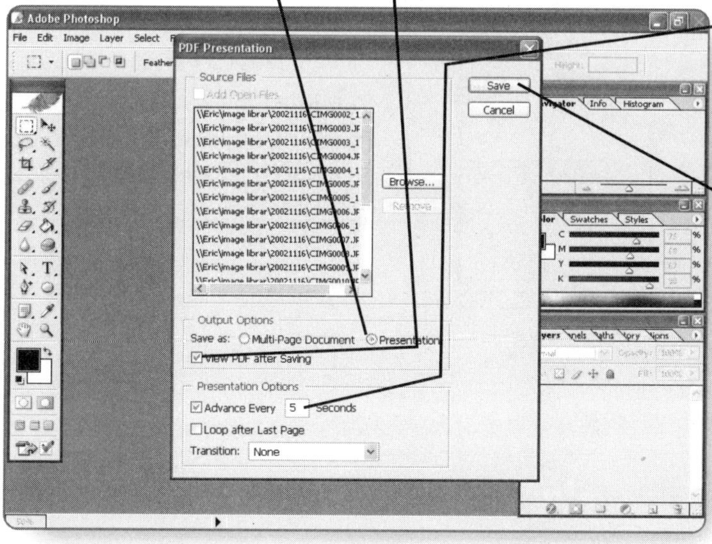

10. **Adjust** the **settings** for the Presentation Options, including the length of time spent on each slide and looping options.

11. **Click** on **Save**. The Save dialog box will open.

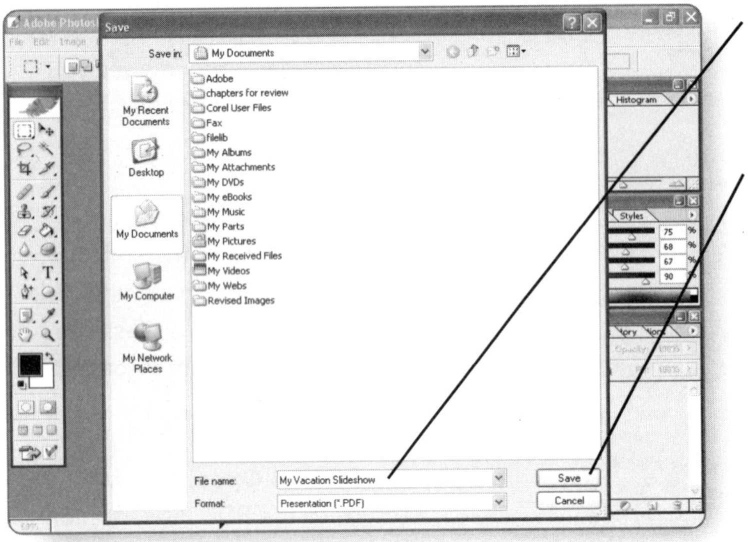

12. **Type** a **name** for your file. You can give it any name you want.

13. **Click** on **Save**. The slideshow will be saved.

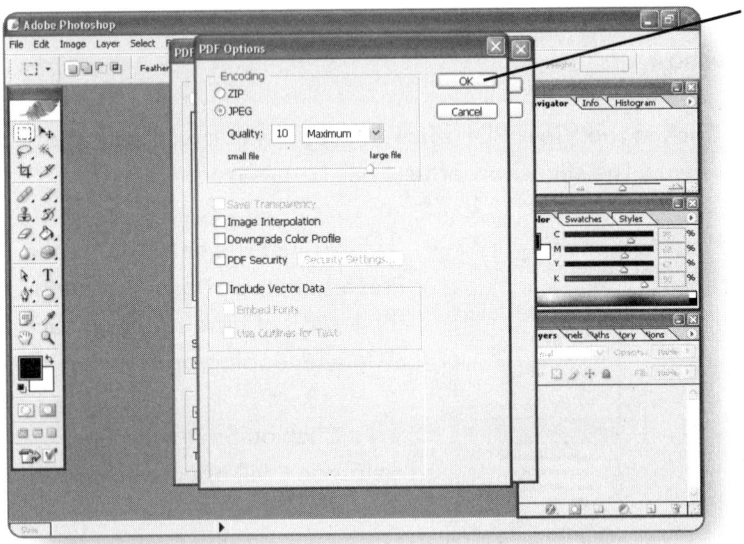

14. **Click** on **OK** to accept the default settings in the PDF Options dialog box. If you chose to preview the slideshow, it will now play.

> **NOTE**
>
> You must have Acrobat Reader installed in order to view the slideshow.

Creating a Contact Sheet

In traditional photography, a contact sheet is a sheet of thumbnail-size images that enables you to view images from more than one negative. Photoshop CS allows you to create a contact sheet from your digital images. Before you create a contact sheet, it's a good idea to place all of the photos that you want to appear on the sheet into a specific folder on your computer.

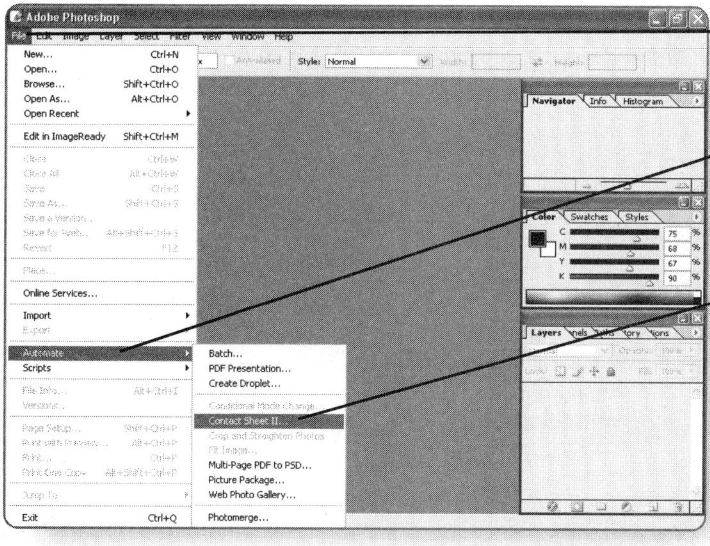

1. **Click** on **File**. The file menu will appear.

2. **Click** on **Automate**. A submenu of different options will appear.

3. **Click** on **Contact Sheet II**. The Contact Sheet II dialog box will appear, where you can set the options for your Contact Sheet.

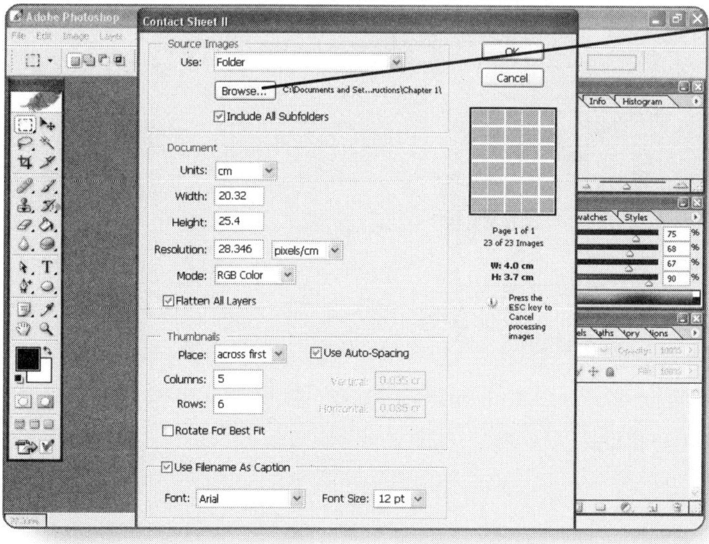

4. **Click** on the **Browse button** to select the folder containing the images that will appear on the contact sheet.

5. **Click** on the **+** beside a folder to view any subfolders.

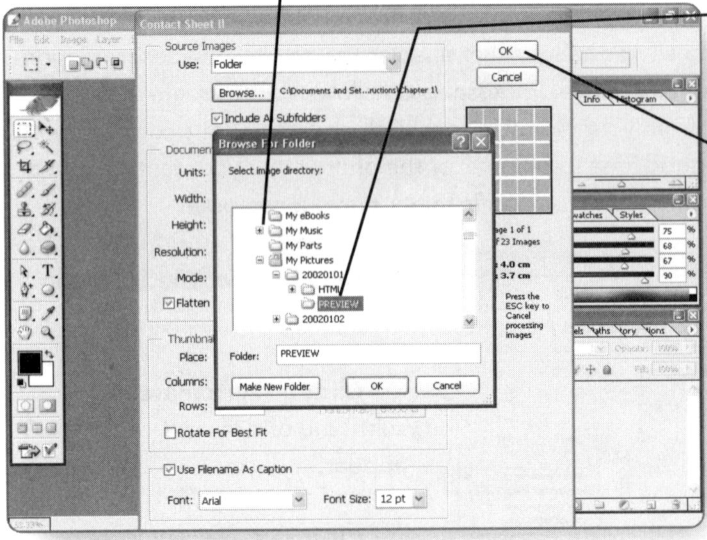

6. **Click** on the **folder** that contains the images to be displayed on the contact sheet.

7. **Click** on **OK**. The folder will be selected.

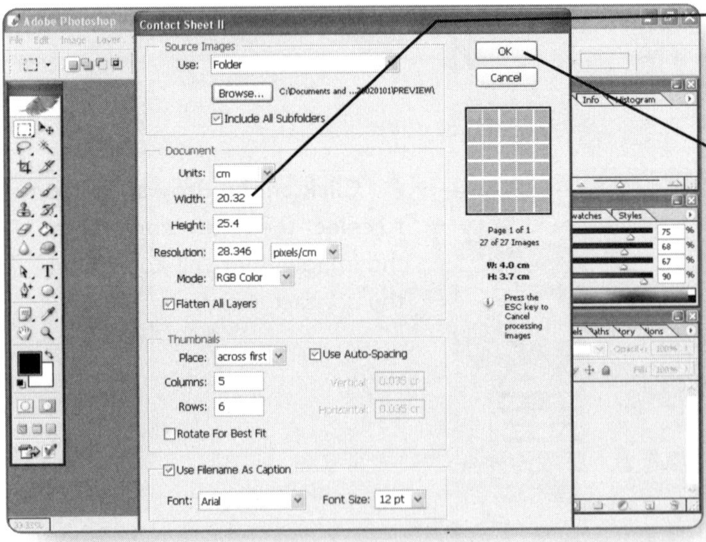

8. **Adjust** the **settings** for the Document and Thumbnail options.

9. **Click** on **OK**. The contact sheet will be created.

Creating Panoramas

The big rage a few years ago was cameras that allowed you to create panoramic images. They basically just stretched and cropped a photo to make it look like it was panoramic. Although that fad may have somewhat faded, you can still create panoramic images using Photoshop CS. Photoshop will actually analyze your images, see how they best fit together, and make a panoramic image that can then be modified.

1. **Open** all of the **images** that you would like to be a part of the panorama.

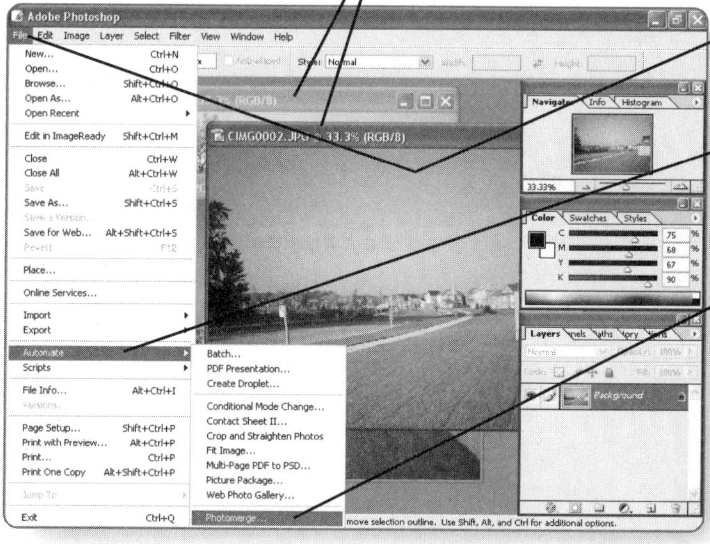

2. **Click** on **File**. The File menu will appear.

3. **Click** on **Automate**. A submenu of different options will appear.

4. **Click** on **Photomerge**. The Photomerge dialog box will appear, where you can set the options for your panoramic image. The files you have open will be listed in the dialog box.

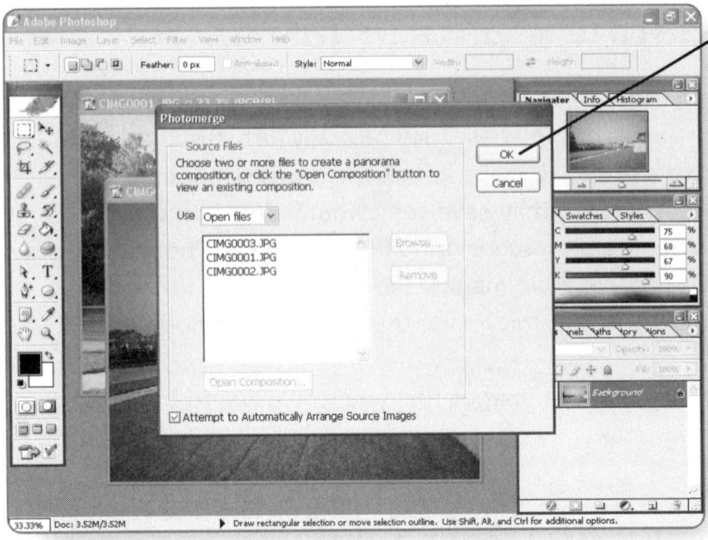

5. **Click** on **OK**. Photoshop will analyze the images and attempt to make a panoramic image from them. The Photomerge window will open.

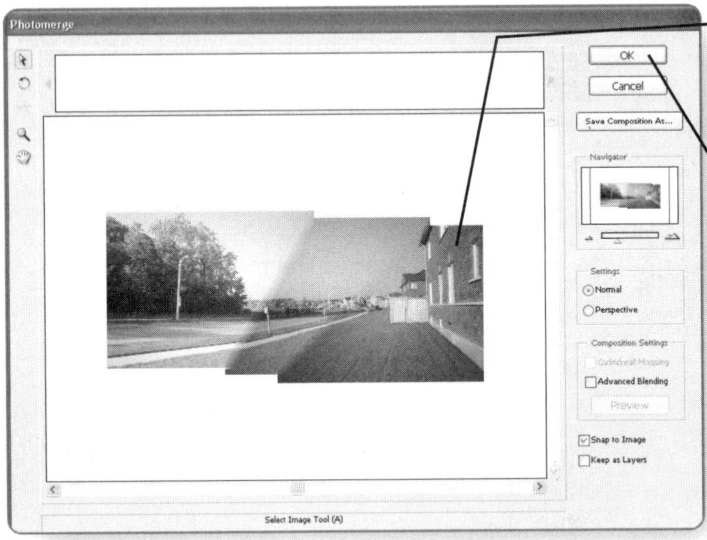

6. **Drag** any **image** to adjust it. You can drag images from the top of the window to the main window.

7. **Click** on **OK**. The Panoramic image will be created and will appear in the Photoshop window.

Printing

When you've finished editing your document, you'll probably want to print it. A huge range of options is available when it comes to printing your image files in Photoshop CS.

Choosing a Printer

Stating the obvious, different printers offer different capabilities. You may use a black-and-white laser printer for basic document printouts and image proofing and use a color printer for sales documents and final image printouts. You need to select the printer to use to print the current image from among those installed on your system, as described here. Once you've selected the printer, you can set available page setup options, which will vary depending on the capabilities of the printer. For example, the software with many printers now calculates margins for you, so the margin choices may be disabled in the Page Setup dialog box.

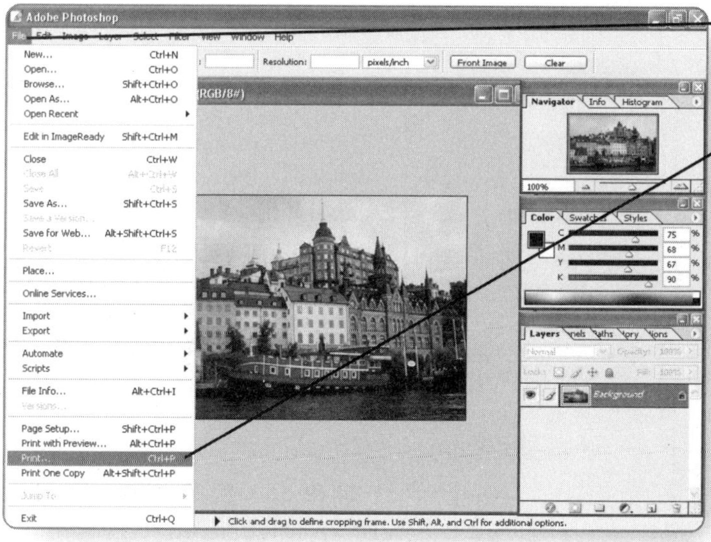

1. **Click** on **File**. The File menu will appear.

2. **Click** on **Print**. The Print dialog box will open.

3. **Click** on the **down arrow** beside the Name drop-down list. The Name drop-down list will open.

4. **Click** on the desired **printer** in the list. The printer will become the active printer.

5. **Click** on **Properties**. The Properties dialog box for the selected printer will appear.

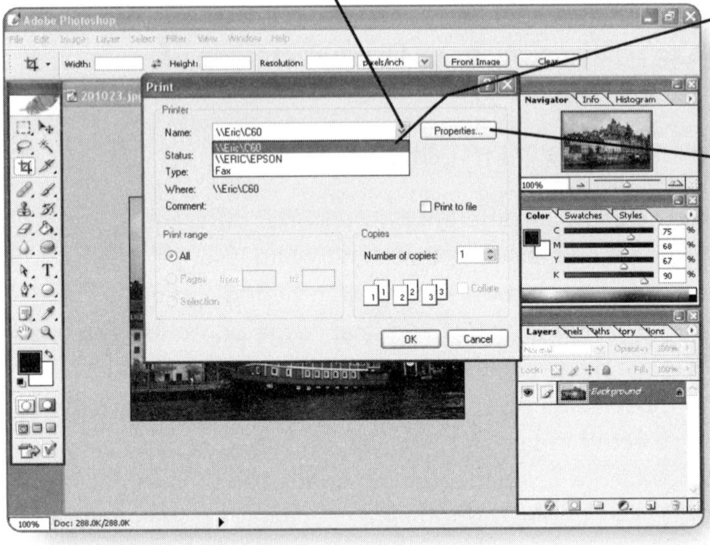

6. **Choose options** for the printer as necessary. Your choices will become the active choices.

NOTE

The available properties will vary depending on the capabilities and driver software for the printer you selected in step 5, so it's not possible to cover available settings in detail.

7. **Click** on **OK**. Your printer settings will take effect, and the Properties dialog box will close.

Changing the Print Settings

Photoshop offers a variety of other print settings via the Print with Preview command on the File menu. These settings have an impact on how Photoshop prepares an image for printing. In the dialog box where you work with these print settings, a preview image shows the impact of your choices, helping you to better fine-tune the printout. This section shows you how to find the various settings you may need to prepare the current image for printing.

> **NOTE**
>
> You must save an image to save your print setup choices for it. Use the Save As command on the File menu to save a Photoshop file as an .eps file. The "Saving to Another Format" section in Chapter 2 explains how to save a Photoshop file in another format.

Centering and Scaling the Image

For each printout, you can choose how to position the image on the paper relative to the edges of the paper. You also can scale the image to a larger or smaller size so that it better fits the paper. (Note that the scaling is only a temporary printing change and does not affect the size of the saved image.) The following steps review the options for positioning and scaling the image:

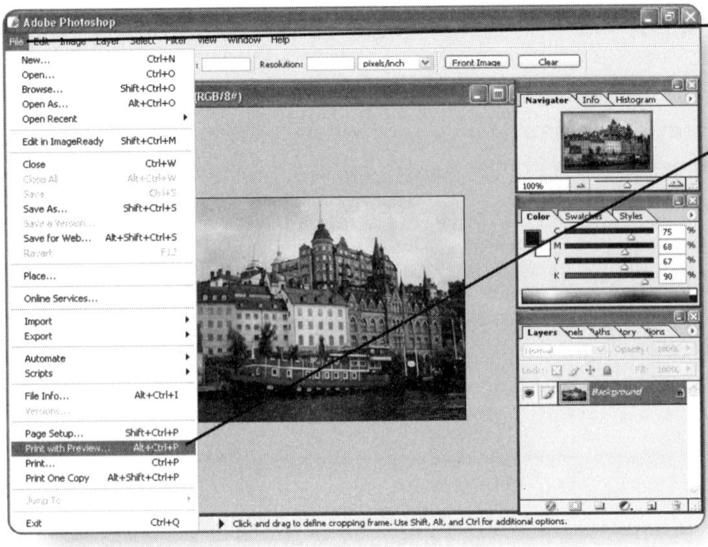

1. Click on **File**. The File menu will appear.

2. Click on **Print with Preview**. A large Print dialog box will open. (A different Print dialog box appears when you choose the File, Print command.)

3. Click on the **Center Image check box** to clear it. The Top and Left choices will become active.

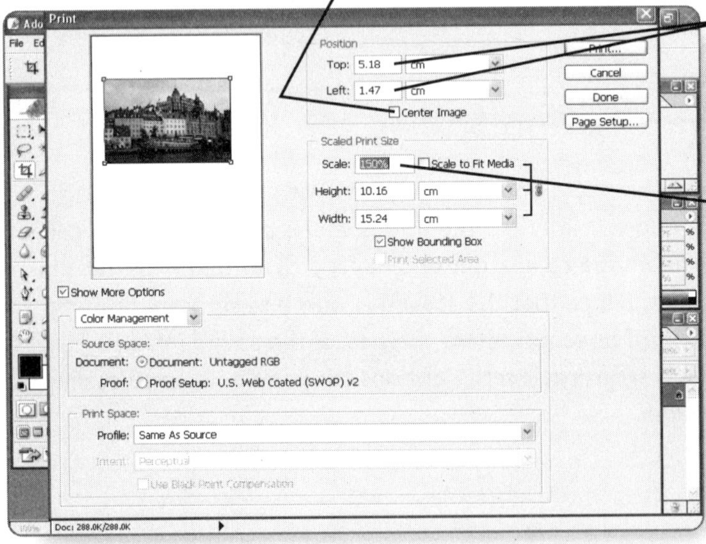

4. Enter Top and **Left entries** and measurement units. The image will reposition on the paper as specified.

5. Change the **Scale text box entry** if you want to increase or decrease the size of the image in the printout. The image will resize accordingly.

> **NOTE**
>
> If you scale the image, you may need to readjust the Top and Left position entries when the Center Image check box is unchecked. You also can drag the image in the preview area to adjust its position if the Show Bounding Box check box is checked.

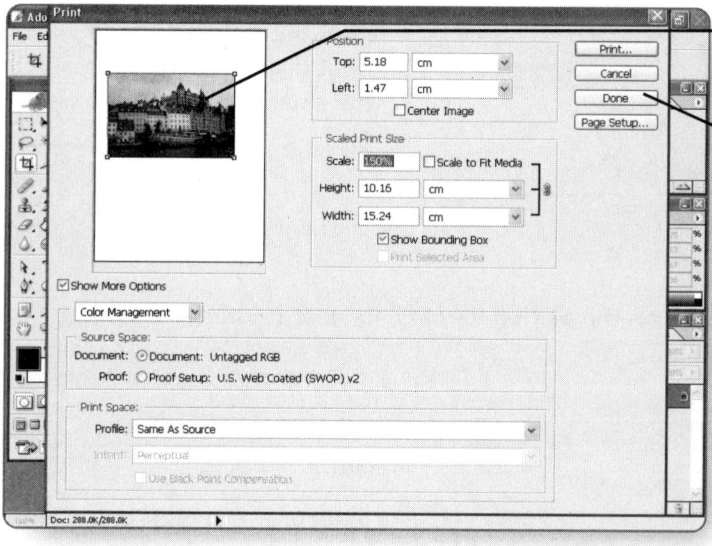

6. **Drag** the **preview** to move the image on the page.

7. **Click** on **Done**. The Print dialog box will close.

Printing the Image

You should at last be ready for the moment of truth—sending your final image to the printer. Follow these steps to get the job done, so to speak.

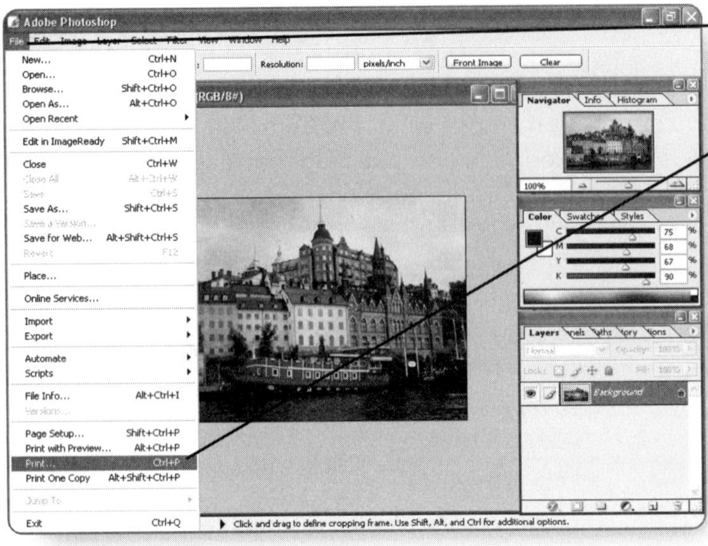

1. **Click** on **File**. The File menu will appear.

2. **Click** on **Print**. The (small) Print dialog box will open.

> **TIP**
>
> You also can click on the Print button in the large Print dialog box to open the small Print dialog box.

3. **Click** on the **option** identifying what to print in the Print Range area:

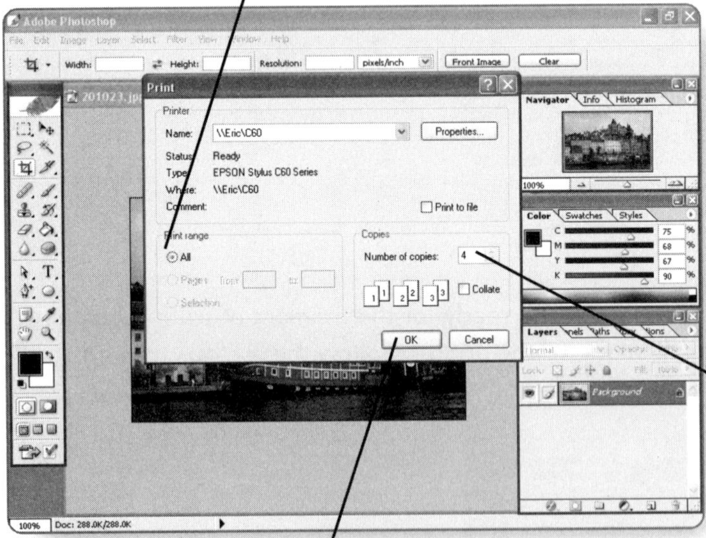

- **All.** Will print the entire current image.
- **Selected.** Will print only the area that's selected in the current image.
- **Pages.** Will print only the pages you identify by making entries in the From and To text boxes.

4. **Change** the **entry** in the Number of copies text box, if necessary. Photoshop will print multiple copies of the image if you change this setting.

5. **Click** on **OK**. Photoshop will send the print job to the printer and close the Print dialog box.

Printing Multiple Images with Picture Package

Photoshop CS includes an enhanced feature called the Picture Package that enables you to create a single sheet that prints multiple copies of an image at various sizes. (Each picture package resembles the print sheets you received for school photos as a kid.) With the Picture Package feature, you select the image to package, choose how to lay out the duplicates on the page, and then specify any additional information you'd like to include with each photo duplicate. Use these steps to create a picture package:

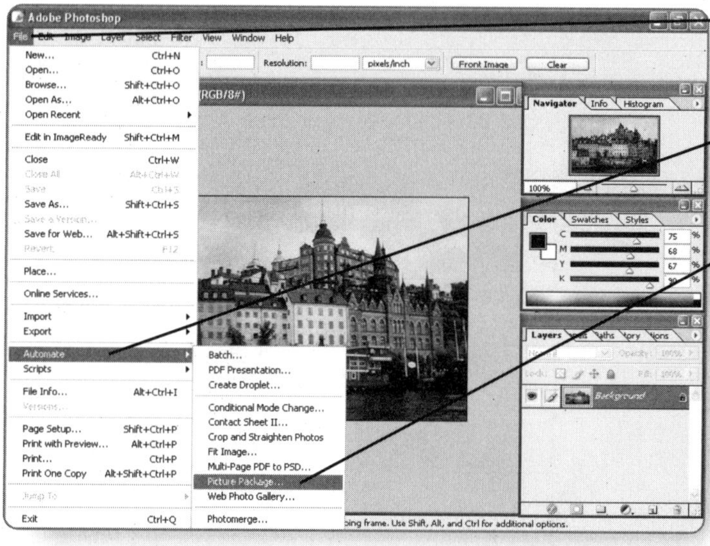

1. **Click** on **File**. The File menu will appear.
2. **Click** on **Automate**. The Automate submenu will appear.
3. **Click** on **Picture Package**. The Picture Package dialog box will open.

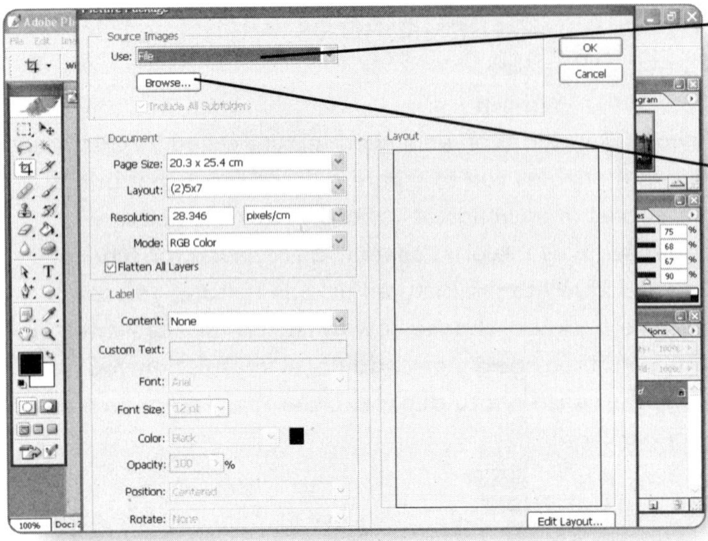

4. **Choose File** from the Use drop-down list. File will become the active choice.

5. **Click** on the **Browse button**. The Select an Image File dialog box opens.

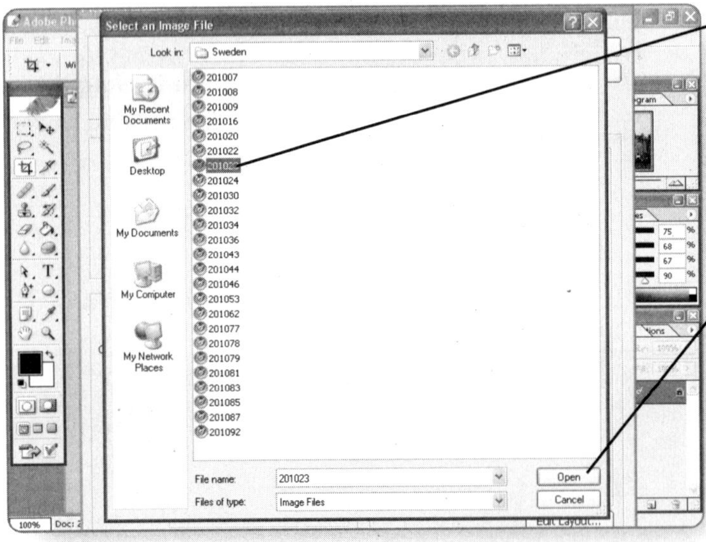

6. **Click** on the **file** to use for the picture package, using the Look In drop-down list to navigate to the proper disk and folder first, if necessary. The file will be selected.

7. **Click** on the **Open button**. The selected image appears in the preview area of the Picture Package dialog box.

8. **Choose** the **Document settings** to use for the picture package. The Page Size, Resolution, and Mode choices work as previously discussed with regard to adjusting the image and printout. The Layout choice determines how many duplicates each page will hold, as well as their size. The preview area of the Picture Package dialog box shows the specified layout.

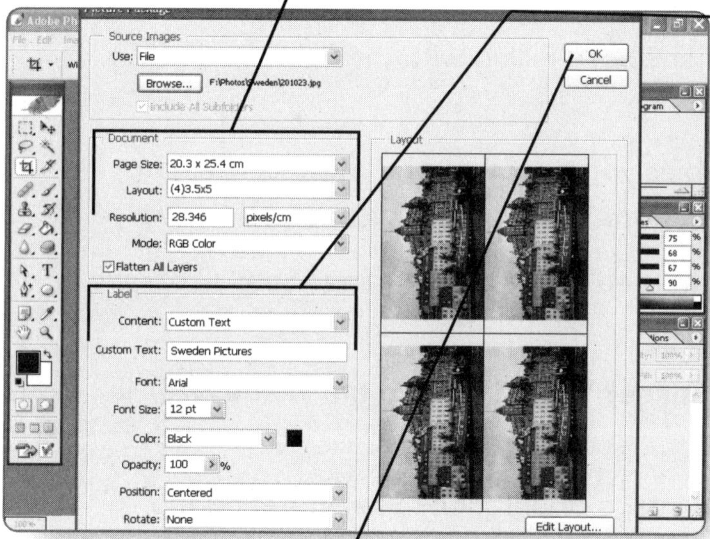

9. **Specify** the **Label settings** to use for the picture package. The Font, Font Size, Color, and Opacity settings work just as for adding text to an image. You can choose a Position for the label on each duplicate, as well as choosing whether to Rotate the label text. To control what actually appears as the label, you can either choose Custom Text from the Content drop-down list and then add your own text into the Custom Text text box, or you can choose one of the other file info options from the Content drop-down list.

10. **Click** on **OK**. Photoshop will generate the picture package in its own image window. Make sure you save the picture package document in order to use it in the future.

Part IV Review Questions

1. How can you correct an area that's too sharp or fuzzy? See "Blurring an Area," "Smudging an Area," and "Sharpening an Area" in Chapter 11.
2. How do you fill a selection? See "Filling with the Paint Bucket" in Chapter 11.
3. Which toolbox tool enables you to access pro photo correction techniques? See "Using Photo Techniques" in Chapter 11.
4. How do you remove unwanted parts of the image? See "Cropping the Image" in Chapter 12.
5. How do you resize the image? See "Changing the Image Size" in Chapter 12.
6. How do you change the image orientation? See "Rotating the Canvas" in Chapter 12.
7. What kinds of filters are available? See "Previewing the Filters" in Chapter 13.
8. How do you apply a filter to an image? See "Applying a Filter" in Chapter 13.
9. What print choices can you adjust before printing? See "Choosing a Printer" and "Changing the Print Settings" in Chapter 14.
10. How do you finish a print job? See "Printing the Image" in Chapter 14.

PART V

Using More Advanced Techniques

15

Understanding Colors and Channels

When you're preparing images for professional printing, color management becomes an important issue. That's because there are differences between how colors are composed onscreen (out of light) and when printed (out of ink). This chapter helps you explore issues surrounding working with color in Photoshop. In this chapter, you will learn how to:

- Use the available color modes
- View and use color channels
- Convert an image to another type of color
- Control bit depth
- Proof the image color

Reviewing the Color Modes

As you learned in Chapter 2, "Working with Image Files," when you create a new image in Photoshop, you can choose the color mode it should use. When you're creating an image for onscreen use, you can typically stick with the default mode, RGB color. However, you might want to choose another of the color modes for special situations. Alternatively, you can convert an image to a particular color mode later, after you've created or scanned it. Table 15-1 details the available color modes in Photoshop so that you can understand color basics while working with color choices in this chapter.

Table 15-1 ***Image Color Modes***

Mode	Description
Bitmap	This mode enables you to create a black-and-white image only. Because it provides for only two tones, you can't convert a full-color image to this mode because too much image information would need to be discarded.
Grayscale	This mode provides for 256 shades of gray in the image, offering enough variation to facilitate clear detail in the image.
Duotone	This mode prepares an image for traditional duotone printing, which uses two solid ink colors such as a dark gray and a blue, yielding a nicely tinted image. You also can construct images with three ink colors (tritones) and four ink colors (quadtones).
Indexed Color	This mode converts an image to a more limited palette of 256 colors, using the matching or lookup system that you specify. You may want to convert to indexed color, for example, for images to be used on a Web page or in a presentation because this mode dramatically decreases the file size while maintaining image appearance. (In fact, this is the preferred setting for Web graphics.)
RGB	This mode mimics visual light—composing images of red, green, and blue—and works best for images to be viewed onscreen, such as those ultimately to be saved for use in a presentation.
CMYK	This mode optimizes images to be printed because cyan, magenta, yellow, and black are the ink colors used for color printing. This mode tries to compensate for the fact that paper absorbs some of the ink, affecting the appearance of colors.

Mode	Description
Lab	This mode uses luminance and brightness settings to help balance the image for all types of devices—printers, monitors, and scanners.
Multichannel	This mode allows you to convert color images for special printing situations. This mode converts the various color channels to channels with 256 colors of gray, with each channel having variations in the distribution of gray tones, according to the original colors.

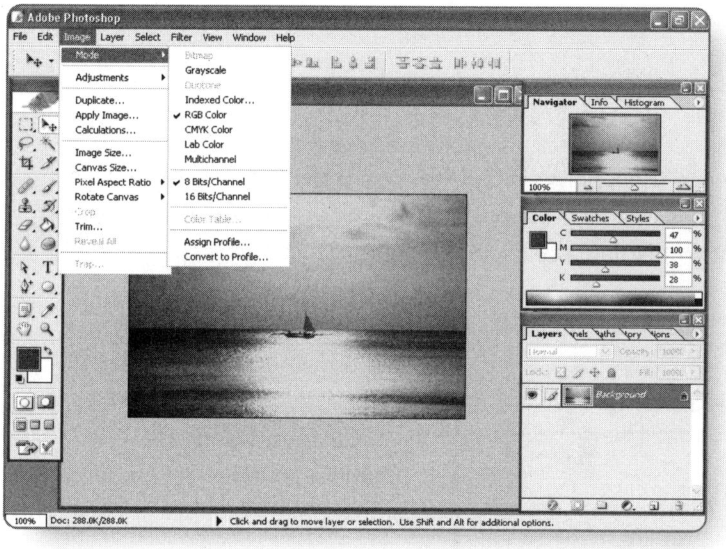

Using Color Channels

When an image uses one of the color modes that has color (for example, not bitmap or grayscale mode), Photoshop displays each color to be displayed or printed as a separate channel. You can work with the image information for a particular channel to edit only that color in the image. This section shows you how to display a channel and gives an example of working with channel content.

NOTE

Bitmap, grayscale, duotone, and indexed images have a single channel. You can add more channels, called alpha channels, to any type of image but bitmaps. (See the "Adding an Alpha Channel" section in the next chapter to learn how to add an alpha channel.) The alpha channels you add can hold masks or add separate colors to be printed in the image.

Changing to a Channel

You use the Channels palette to work with the various color channels in a Photoshop image. Follow these steps when you want to display a particular channel only:

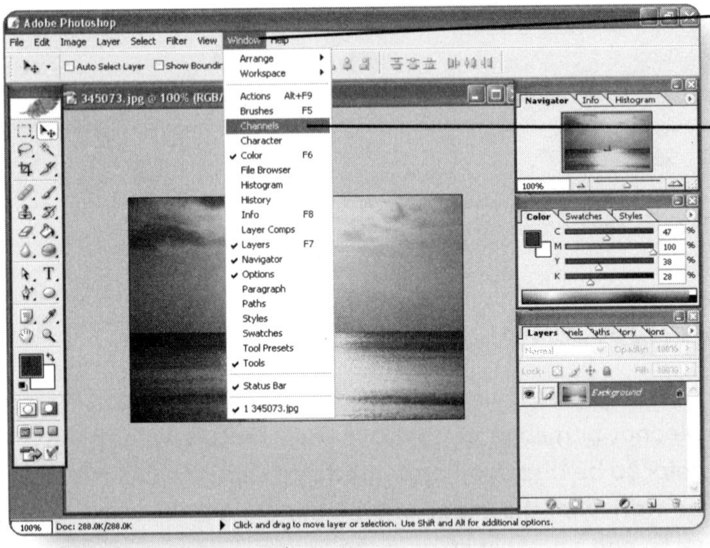

1. **Click** on **Window**. The Window menu will appear.

2. **Click** on **Channels**. The Channels palette will become the active palette.

TIP

You also can click on the Channels tab, if it's visible in the Layers palette. The Layers palette window holds five tabs, making it tough to see the tab to click. You can either resize the palette window to make the tabs accessible or use the Window menu as noted in the steps in this book.

3. Click on the desired **channel**. The channel will become the current or active channel, and its content will appear in the image window.

> **TIP**
>
> To hide a channel, click on the eye icon to the left of the channel name. To redisplay the change, click on the empty box to redisplay the eye icon.

Working on a Channel

You can edit the content on a single color channel just as you can edit the content of a single layer. You can make a selection on the channel, use editing tools such as the Airbrush, delete selected channel content, apply a filter, and so on. The following steps show just one example of the editing possibilities:

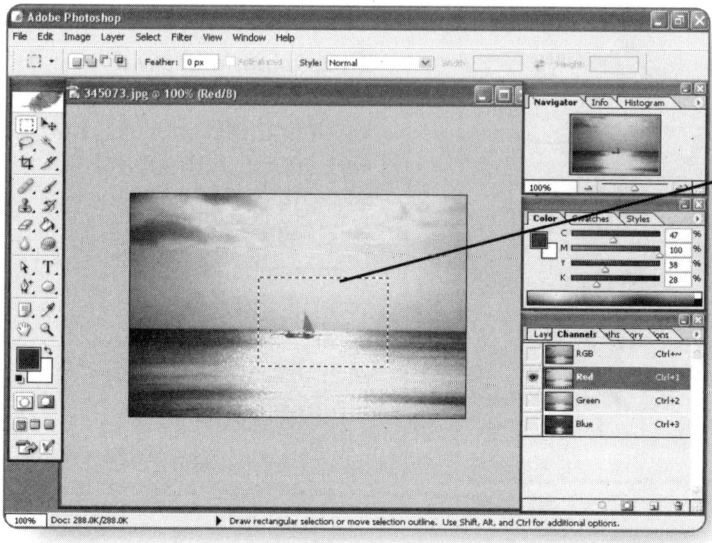

1. Make a **selection** on the current channel using the tool of your choice, if necessary. The selection will become active.

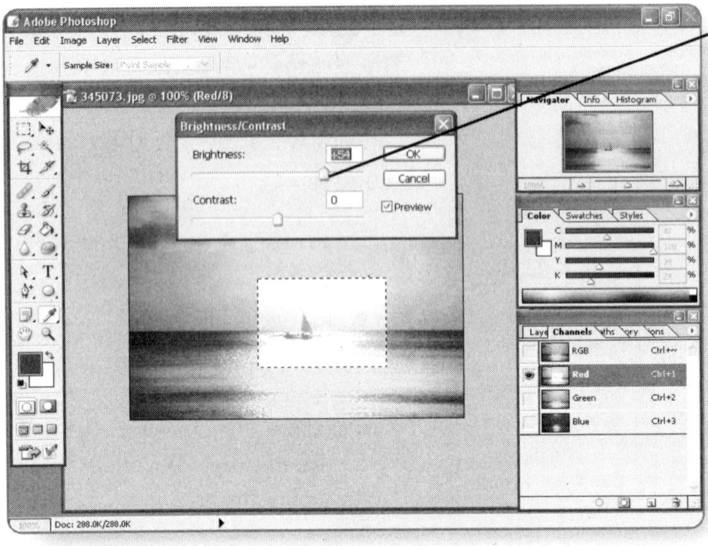

2. Make changes to the **channel content** using the tool or filter of your choice. This example shows brightness being adjusted. The changes will appear on the channel immediately.

3. Click on the **composite channel**. The composite channel will become the current or active channel, and all the image color content will reappear in the image window. From this point, you can continue working with other Photoshop tools.

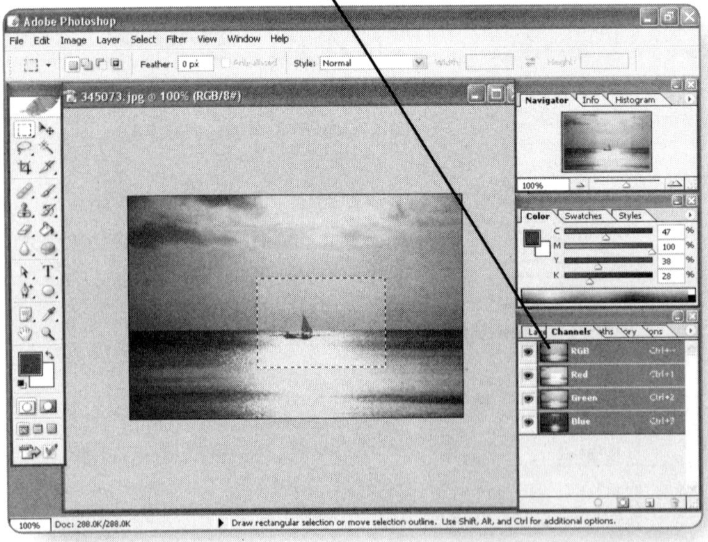

NOTE

If you experiment with color channel changes, you'll find that they can be very subtle. Although the average person might not catch all your channel changes, being able to control and manipulate colors is essential if you plan to use your images for professional-level output.

Converting Images

Images you create don't have to remain in the original color mode. Photoshop makes it easy to convert to another color mode when necessary. This section walks you through a few of the more common color-mode-conversion scenarios.

Choosing CMYK

Adobe recommends that you perform most color corrections (and other edits) to an image before you convert the image to CMYK color for professional printing. (Adobe also recommends that you save a copy of the image file before converting to CMYK so that you can work with the original colors in the image, if necessary, at a later time.) You convert to CMYK when the image is ready for a print shop to create color separations—a separate piece of film for each ink color, used for creating a plate to print each color ink. Typically, you'll convert to CMYK color from RGB color, as in the following steps:

1. **Click** on **Layer**. The Layer menu will appear.

2. **Click** on **Flatten Image**. Photoshop will merge all the separate layers onto a single layer so that you can convert the image to CMYK color. (This is another reason why you should complete your edits in RGB color before converting to CMYK.)

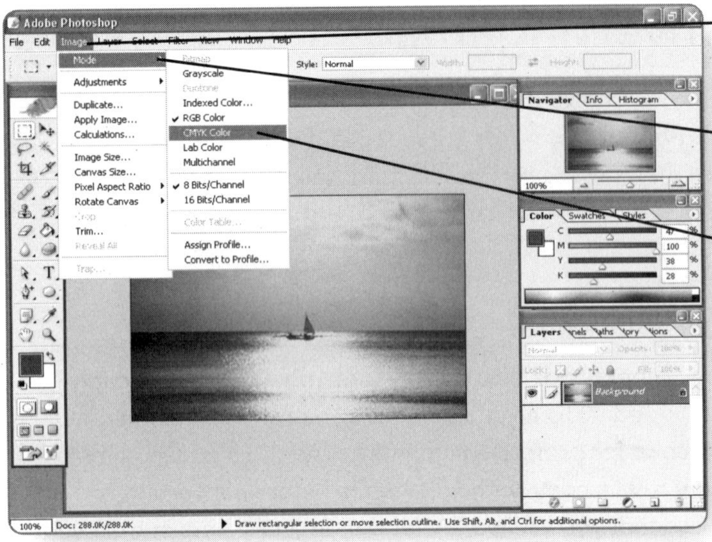

3. **Click** on **Image**. The Image menu will appear.

4. **Point** to **Mode**. The Mode submenu will appear.

5. **Click** on **CMYK Color**. Photoshop will convert the image to CMYK color immediately. If you display the Colors palette, you will see the new channels.

> **NOTE**
>
> You use the Mode submenu of the Image menu to convert between all color modes.

Working with Bit Depth

In Photoshop, bit depth refers to the amount of color information each pixel can hold per color channel. For example, an image set to 16 bits per channel (the default for many scanners) would have an overall color depth of 48 bits (16 x 3) for an RGB image. The higher the bit depth, the greater the possible variation of colors in the image, and the more detail the image can appear to have. On the other hand, an image set to 8 bits per channel provides a much smaller file size, which may work best for certain publications and applications. The following steps show you how to convert from 8 bits per channel to 16 bits per channel and back again:

NOTE

In some cases, when you add layers and masks to a scanned image, Photoshop automatically converts the image from 16 bits to 8 bits, so you have to manually adjust the bit depth later.

1. Click on **Layer**. The Layer menu will appear.

2. Click on **Flatten Image**. Photoshop will merge all the separate layers onto a single layer so that you can convert an image from 8 bits per channel to 16 bits per channel.

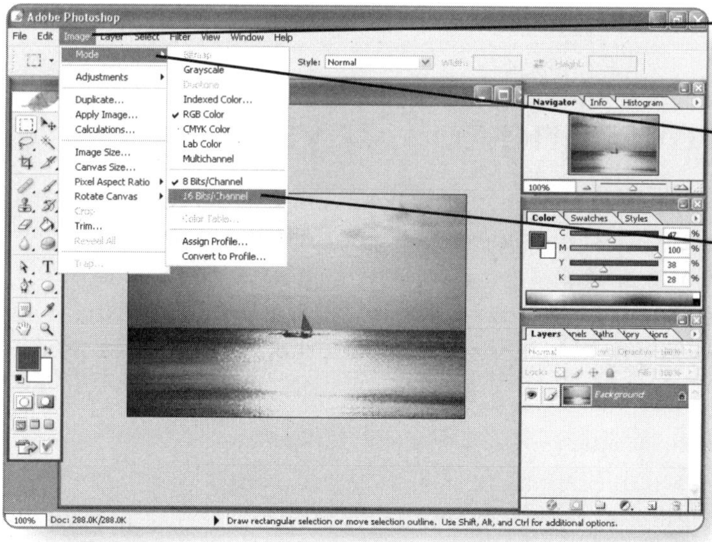

3. Click on **Image**. The Image menu will appear.

4. Point to **Mode**. The Mode submenu will appear.

5. Click on **16 Bits/Channel**. Photoshop will convert the image to 16 bits of color information per channel immediately.

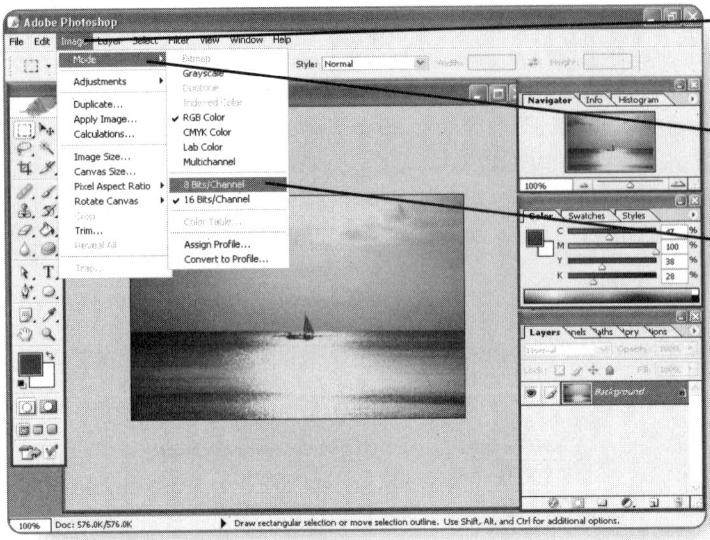

6. **Click** on **Image**. The Image menu will appear.

7. **Point** to **Mode**. The Mode submenu will appear.

8. **Click** on **8 Bits/Channel**. Photoshop will convert the image to 8 bits of color information per channel immediately.

> **NOTE**
>
> Some tools and features, such as the Text tool, don't work in an image set to 16 bits of color. If you try to use an unavailable tool or feature while the image is set to 16 bits, Photoshop will display a message telling you to convert the image to 8 bits per channel.

Converting to Grayscale

Another common scenario involves converting a color image to grayscale. Most of us take color photos with either our traditional or digital cameras. When you want to use one of those images in a black-and-white publication, convert the image to grayscale mode using Photoshop, as described here:

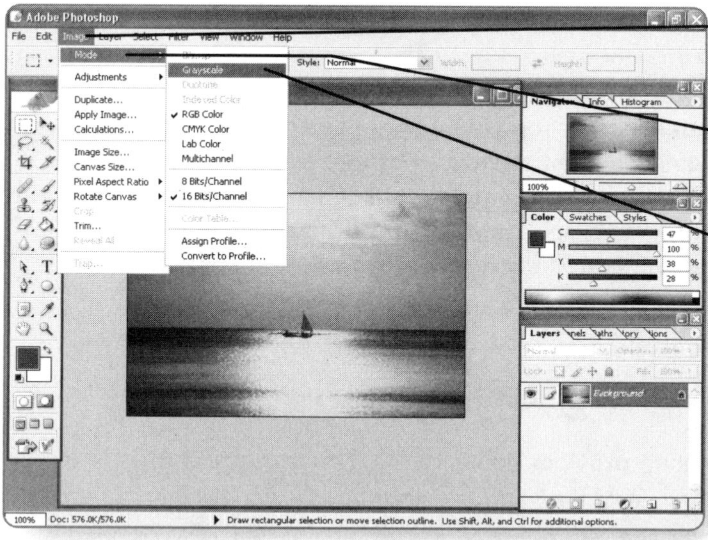

1. **Click** on **Image**. The Image menu will appear.

2. **Point** to **Mode**. The Mode submenu will appear.

3. **Click** on **Grayscale**. A dialog box will appear to ask whether you want to complete the conversion by discarding color information.

NOTE

It's not necessary to flatten the image before converting to grayscale. However, if you do not flatten the image first and the image contains a color adjustment layer, the wording of the dialog box that appears after step 3 will be slightly different, asking if you want to discard the adjustment layer information.

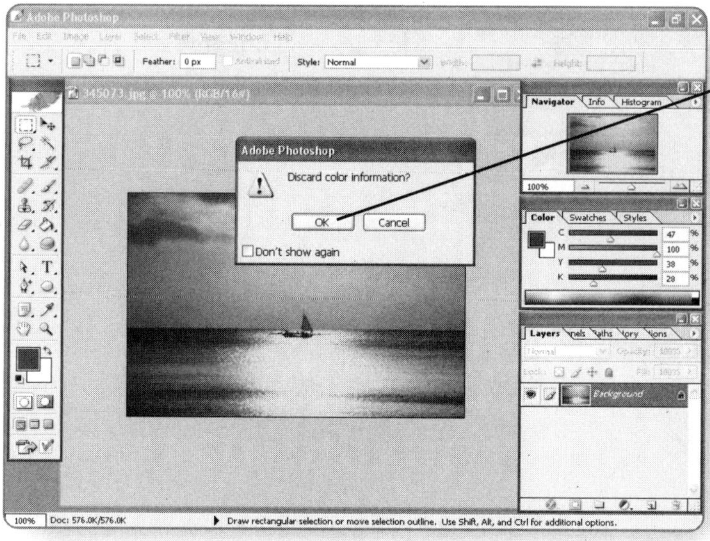

4. **Click** on **OK**. Photoshop will complete the grayscale conversion.

NOTE

If you convert from grayscale back to one of the color modes, Photoshop won't be able to re-create the original color information. For that reason, it's a good idea to save a copy of your image file before converting to grayscale, so that you can continue working with the color version of the image whenever you need it.

Proofing Colors

Photoshop provides you with the means to proof the appearance of the various color plates (Cyan, Magenta, Yellow, and blacK) after you've converted an image to CMYK color. You might want to do this, for example, to look for small specks of color that you want to clean up by erasing them from the applicable channel. The following steps explain how to get started proofing a color plate:

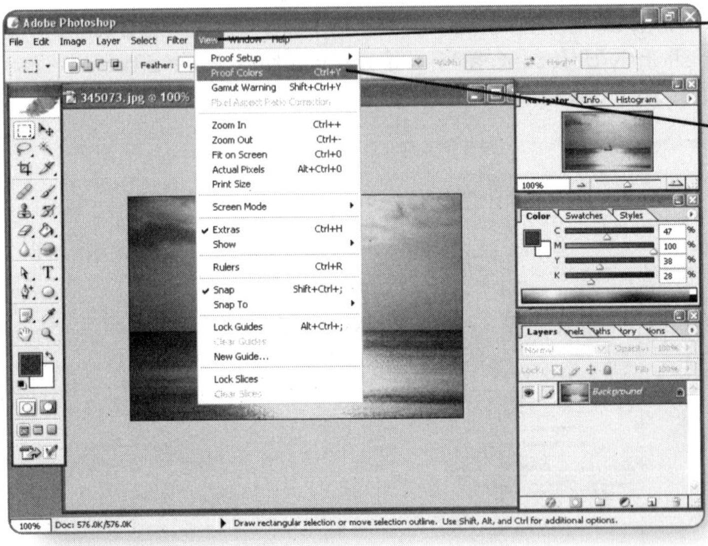

1. **Click** on **View**. The View menu will appear.

2. **Click** on **Proof Colors** (to check it). The color-proofing feature will become active.

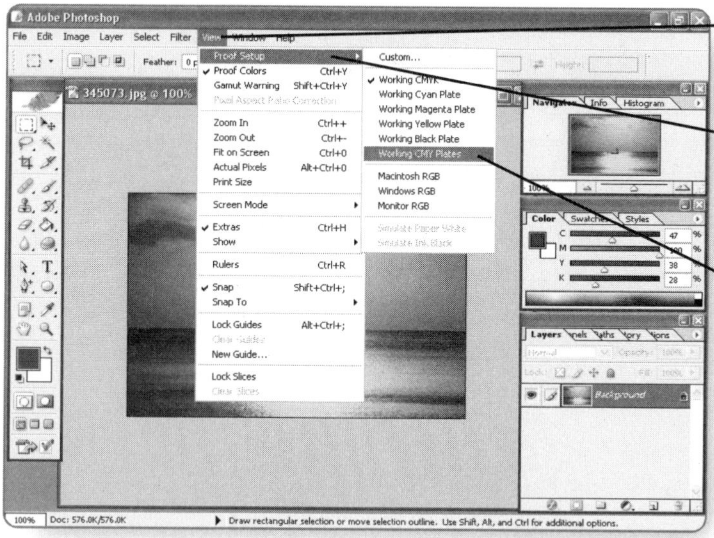

3. **Click** on **View**. The View menu will appear.

4. **Point** to **Proof Setup**. The Proof Setup submenu will appear.

5. **Click** on one of the **Working (Color) Plate** choices.

NOTE

You can repeat steps 3 through 5 to proof other plates.

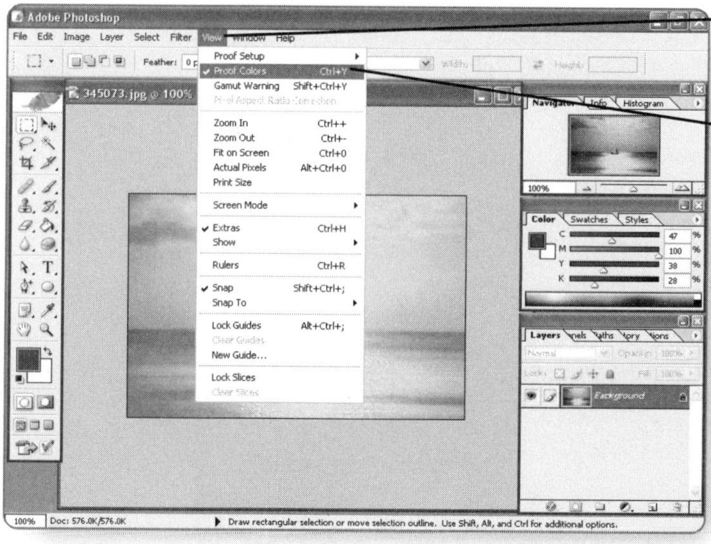

6. **Click** on **View**. The View menu will appear.

7. **Click** on **Proof Colors** (to uncheck it). The color-proofing feature will be disabled, and all the colors will reappear in the image.

16

Correcting Image Color

Let's face it, we're not all professional photographers. The truth is that many of the digital images we take have some technical flaw in them, one way or another. By using a few straightforward commands, you can make color corrections to your photos that once required quite a bit of time in the photo lab. This chapter introduces you to basic color-correction techniques in Photoshop. In this chapter, you'll learn how to:

- Make quick color corrections
- Adjust image tones
- Rebalance the image color
- Change image brightness and contrast
- Use a special color effect
- Use the new Histogram palette
- Create an alpha channel

Using the Auto Color Command

If you want to improve the appearance of your image without working in depth with color settings, you can use the Auto Color command. This command searches the image content and improves the contrast and colors. The following steps show how to use the Auto Color command to adjust an image's color and contrast with ease.

> **NOTE**
>
> The changes that the Auto Color command makes are based on the settings in the Auto Color Corrections Options dialog box. You can access this dialog box by choosing Image, Adjustments, Curves. Then click on the Options button in the Curves dialog box.

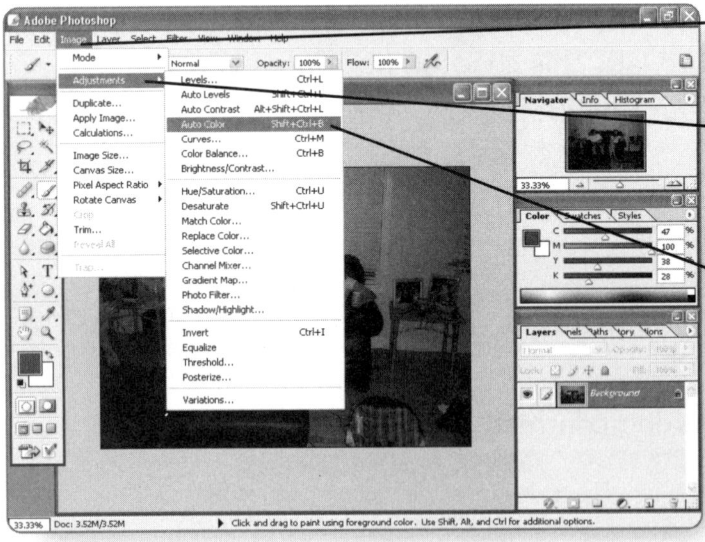

1. **Click** on **Image**. The Image menu will appear.
2. **Point** to **Adjustments**. The Adjustments submenu will appear.
3. **Click** on **Auto Color**. The image color and contrast will be adjusted.

Changing the Tonal Quality

The tonal quality settings in Photoshop enable you to manipulate the image's appearance by adjusting highlights or shadows. This can make the image appear a bit lighter or darker if you adjust all the colors in the image, or it can make more subtle changes if you adjust one channel only. Follow these steps to work with the image tone:

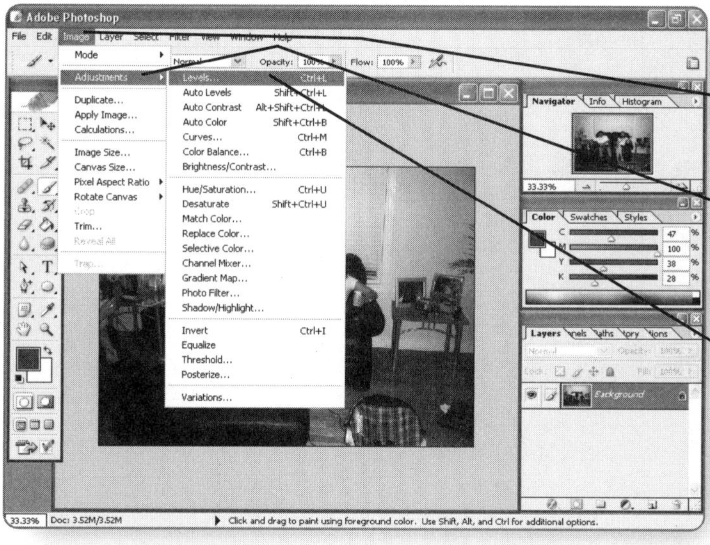

1. **Click** on **Image**. The Image menu will appear.
2. **Point** to **Adjustments**. The Adjustments submenu will appear.
3. **Click** on **Levels**. The Levels dialog box will open.

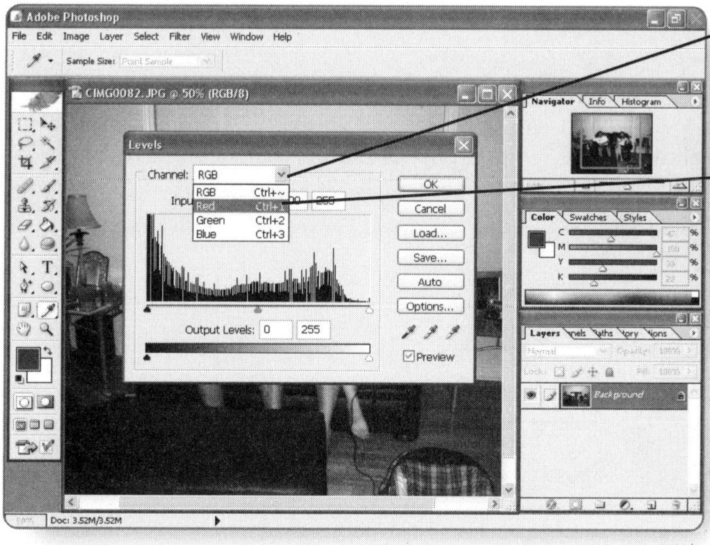

4. **Click** on the **down arrow** beside the Channel drop-down list. A list of options will appear.
5. **Click** on the desired **channel** in the list. The desired channel will be selected for tonal adjustments.

6. **Drag** the **Input Levels sliders** as necessary to adjust the tone. The left slider affects shadows, the middle slider affects midtones, and the right slider affects highlights. The image window will preview the changes.

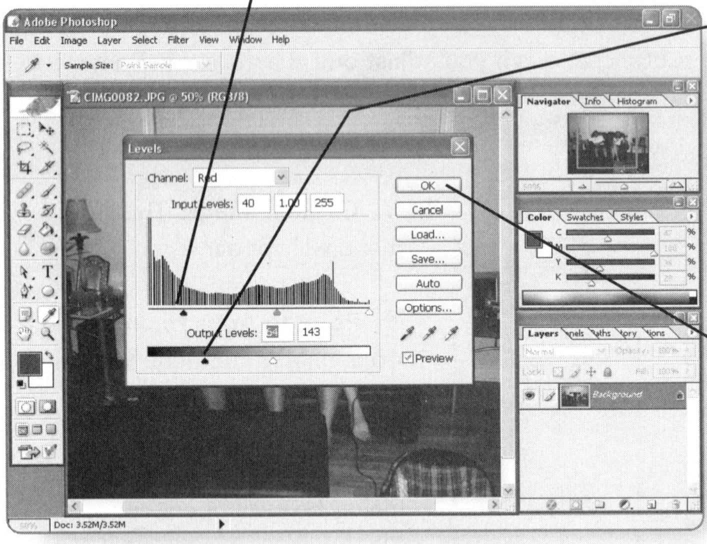

7. **Drag** the **Output Levels sliders** as necessary to further adjust the tone for the selected channel. The left slider adjusts shadows, and the right slider adjusts highlights. The image window will preview the changes.

8. **Click** on **OK**. Photoshop will close the Levels dialog box and apply the tonal changes.

Correcting the Color Balance

The color balance in an image refers to the overall proportion of various colors in the image. For example, if a photo looks too yellow to you, you can make a color balance adjustment (as described in the following steps) to correct that problem. Color balance changes make a general correction to the image color.

1. Click on **Image**. The Image menu will appear.

2. Point to **Adjustments**. The Adjustments submenu will appear.

3. Click on **Color Balance**. The Color Balance dialog box will open.

4. Click on the **option button** for the tonal range to correct in the Tone Balance area, if necessary. The color balance changes you make will be applied to the specified tonal range.

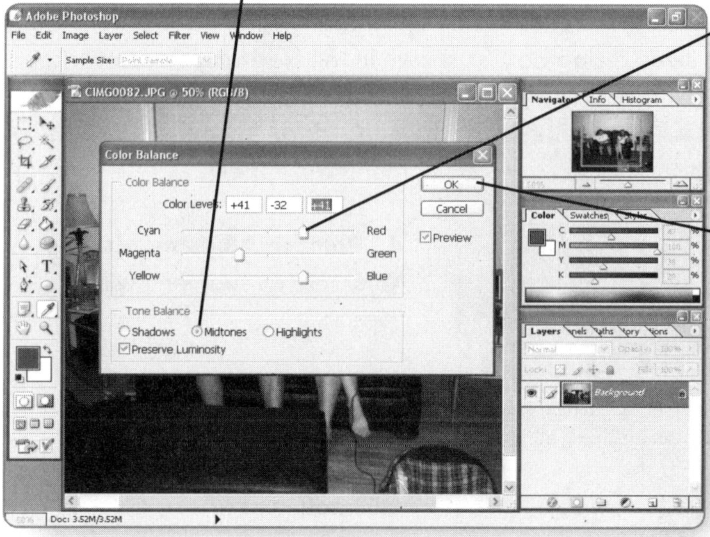

5. Drag the **Color Balance sliders** as necessary to change the amount of color in an image. The image window will preview the changes.

6. Click on **OK**. Photoshop will close the Color Balance dialog box and apply the color changes.

> **NOTE**
>
> You also can make various color corrections and apply various color special effects by adding an adjustment layer to the image. The adjustment layer enables you to display the color correction or effect when needed and hide it when not needed. Use the New Adjustment Layer submenu of the Layer menu to add an adjustment layer.

Correcting Brightness and Contrast

The most typical problem with photos taken by amateur photographers is that the brightness and contrast levels are off. Brightness generally refers to the amount of light (overall lightness) in the image, and contrast refers to the difference between the lightest points and the darkest points in the image. Adding brightness to an image can soften its appearance, whereas increasing contrast can make an image appear a bit more well-defined. You can adjust both brightness and contrast in the same dialog box, as shown in the following steps.

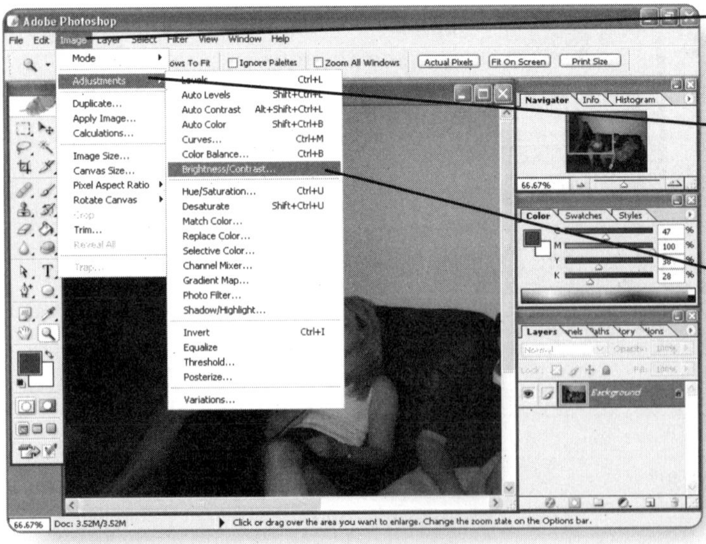

1. **Click** on **Image**. The Image menu will appear.
2. **Point** to **Adjustments**. The Adjustments submenu will appear.
3. **Click** on **Brightness/Contrast**. The Brightness/Contrast dialog box will open.

4. **Drag** the **Brightness slider**. The image window will preview the changes.

5. **Drag** the **Contrast slider**. The image window will preview the changes.

6. **Click** on **OK**. Photoshop will close the Brightness/Contrast dialog box and apply the changes.

Applying a Special Color Effect

Some of the commands on the Adjustments submenu of the Image menu—specifically the Invert, Equalize, Threshold, and Posterize choices—apply special color effects. Each of these commands works a bit differently and applies a slightly different effect, so the following steps provide an example of using one of them—the Posterize choice. The posterizing effect reduces the number of colors used in the image so that the image becomes composed of larger color areas, much like paint-by-number pictures or the way posters used to be designed.

NOTE

The Invert Image command reverses the colors in an image, creating a negative effect. Equalize finds the lightest and darkest pixels in the image and sets them to white and black, respectively. It then distributes the brightness values for the remaining pixels between the two extremes. Finally, the Threshold command converts any image to a high-contrast, black-and-white image.

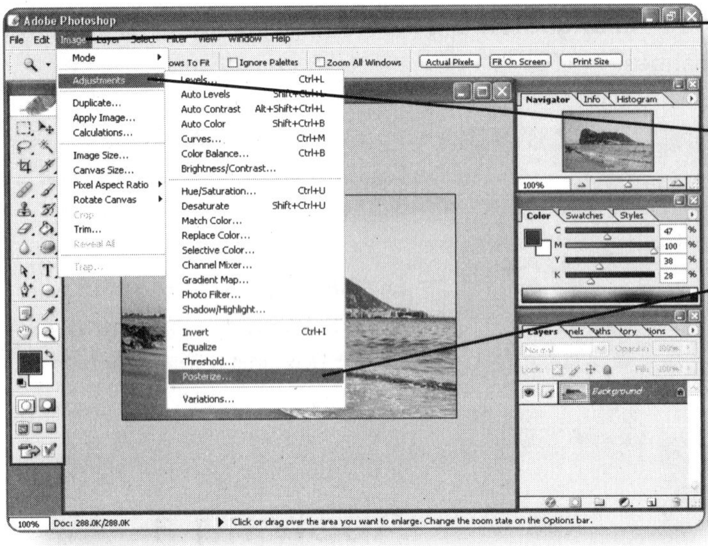

1. Click on **Image**. The Image menu will appear.

2. Point to **Adjustments**. The Adjustments submenu will appear.

3. Click on **Posterize**. The Posterize dialog box will open.

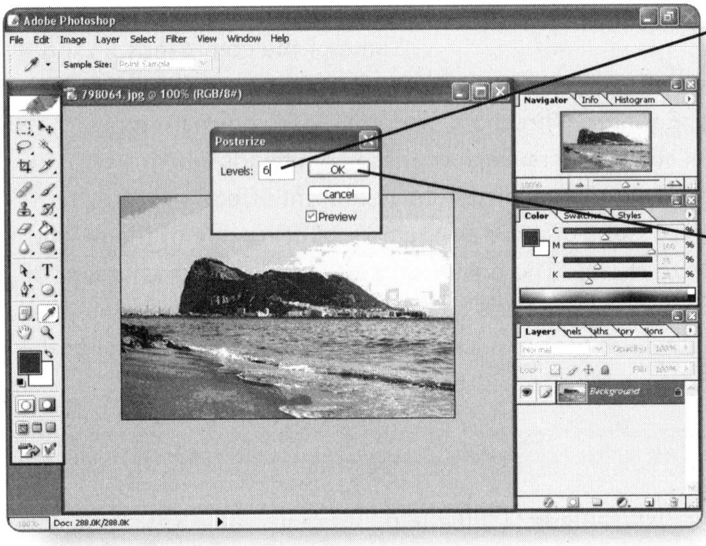

4. Type a new **Levels text box entry**, if necessary. The image window will preview the specified degree of posterization.

5. Click on **OK**. Photoshop will close the Posterize dialog box and apply the special effect.

Using The Histogram Palette

New to Photoshop CS is a Histogram palette that continually updates itself as you work on your image. A Histogram provides a graphical representation of the tonal and color information in your image.

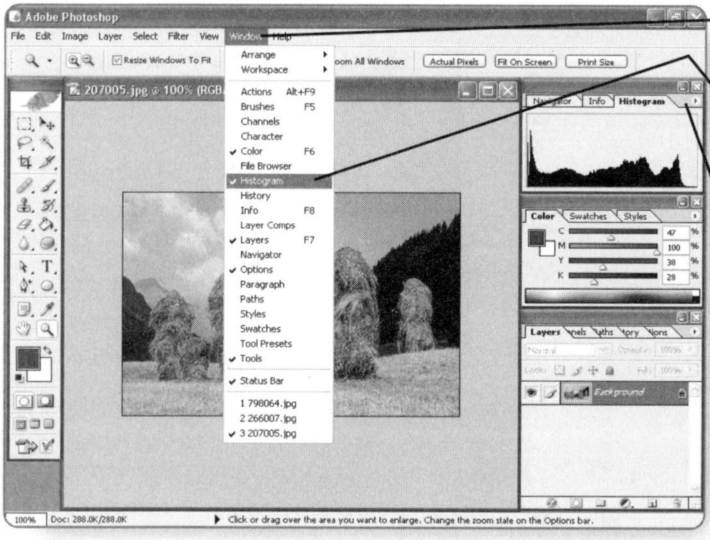

1. **Click** on **Window**. The Window menu will appear.

2. **Click** on **Histogram**. The Histogram palette will become active.

3. **Click** on the **Histogram palette menu button**. A list of options will appear.

4. **Click** on **Expanded View**. This will expand the size of your histogram and provide you with additional color and tonal information about your image.

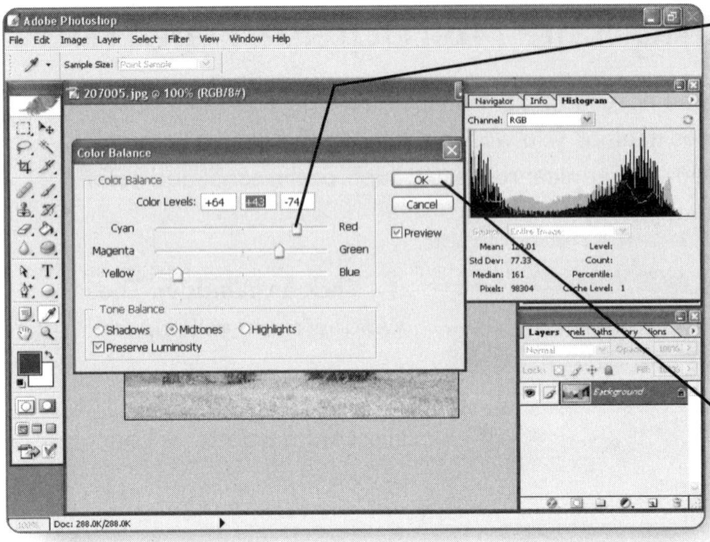

5. Make a **color** or **tonal change** to your image. In this example, we are adjusting the color balance. As you make changes, they are reflected in the histogram. The previous histogram appears in light gray, and the new histogram based on the changes you are making appears in black.

6. Click on **OK** in whichever tonal or color change dialog box you are using. As soon as you finish applying your color or tonal changes, the light gray histogram disappears, and you are left with the black one.

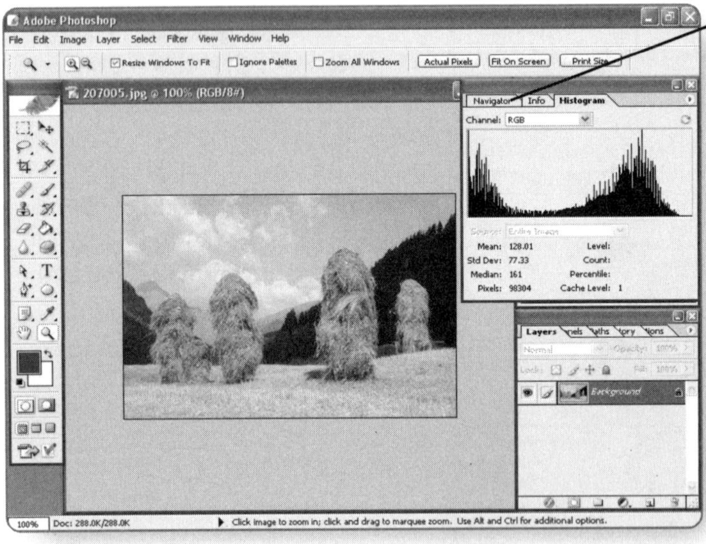

7. Click on **Navigator** in the palettes window to return to the Navigator palette.

Adding an Alpha Channel

An alpha channel is an extra channel that you use to store a selection in an image. You can easily reload the selection from the channel or even convert the channel to a spot-color treatment, as described in the section "Adding Spot Color" in the next chapter. The steps that follow explain the easiest way to save a spot channel—by saving a selection as a spot channel.

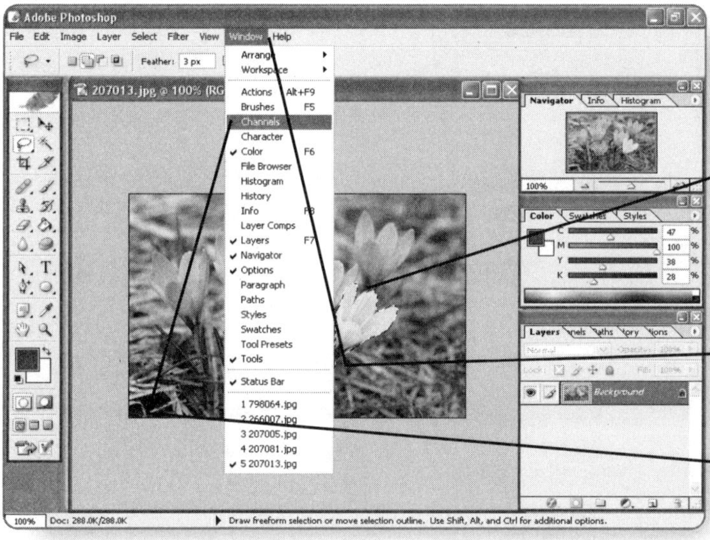

1. **Make** a **selection** on a layer using the selection tool of your choice. The selection will appear in the image.

2. **Click** on **Window**. The Window menu will appear.

3. **Click** on **Channels**. The Channels palette will become active.

4. **Click** on the **Save Selection as Channel button** at the bottom of the Channels palette. The new channel will appear immediately in the Channels palette.

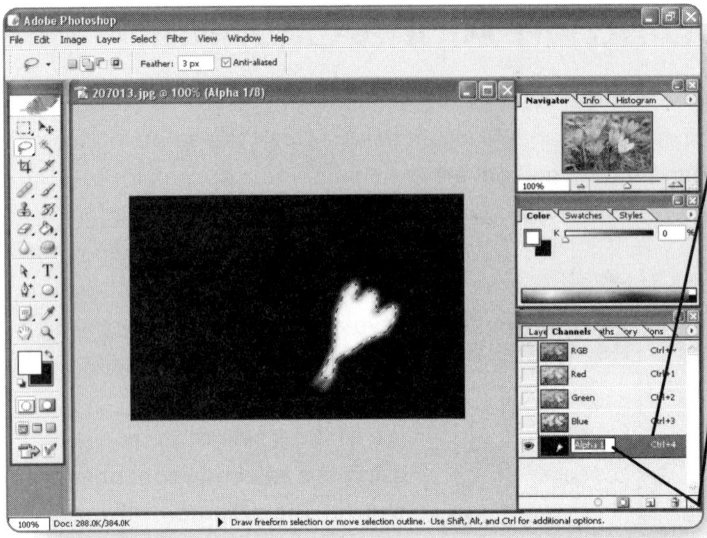

5. **Click** on the **new channel** in the palette. The new channel will be selected.

6. **Double-click** on the **Name** of the channel. It will appear highlighted in a box.

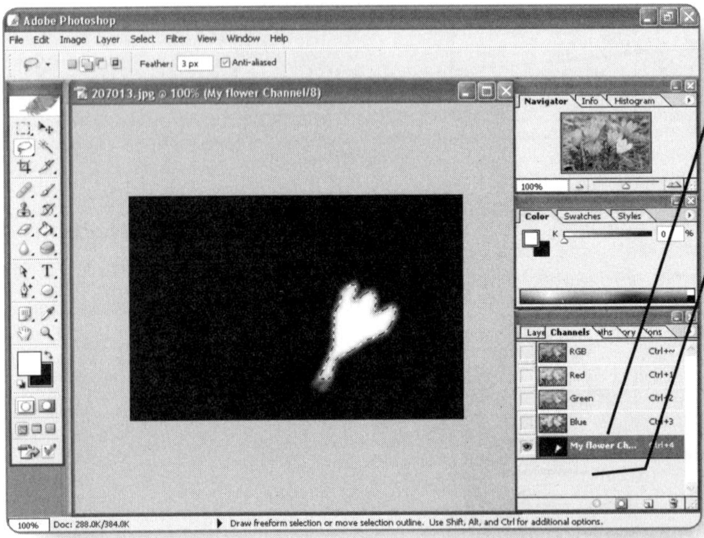

7. **Type** a **name** for the channel. Your new name will replace the temporary name in the box.

8. **Click** on any **blank area** in the palette. Photoshop will save the channel under the name you specified.

NOTE

To load the selection from a channel, click on the channel in the Channels palette and then click on the Load Channel as Selection button at the bottom of the Channels palette.

Correcting Overexposure

A common problem with digital camera pictures is that they are over- or underexposed. This problem can be easily corrected with the new Shadow/Highlight adjustment dialog box.

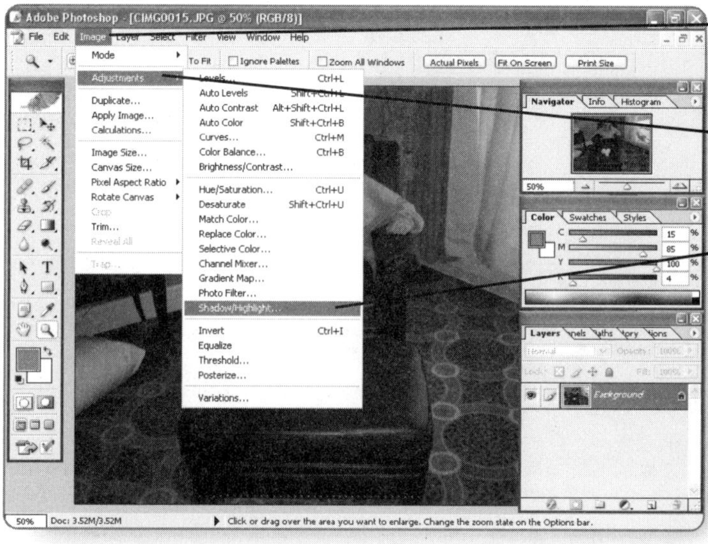

1. Click on **Image**. The Image menu will appear.

2. Point to **Adjustments**. A submenu will appear.

3. Click on **Shadow/Highlight**. The Shadow/Highlight dialog box will open.

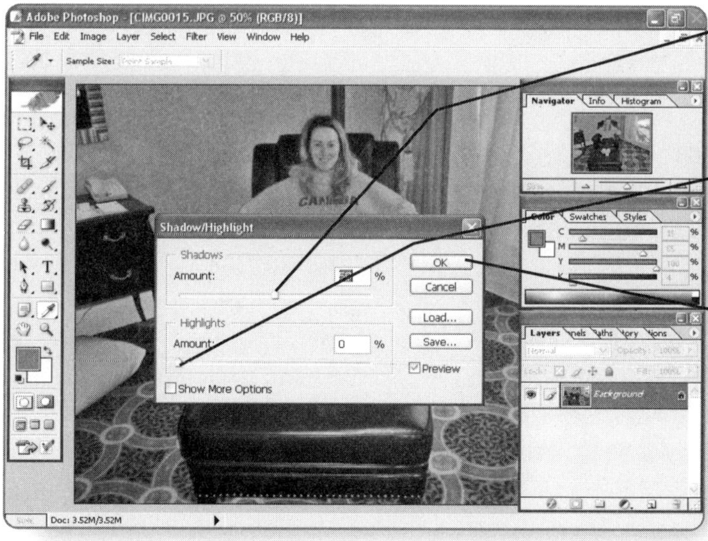

4. Drag to adjust the **shadows level**. As you drag, the changes will appear on your image.

5. Drag to adjust the **highlight level**. As you drag, the changes will appear on your image.

6. Click on **OK**. The adjustments will be implemented.

17

Having Fun with Color

Why have boring, regular old photos when you can spice them up with color. Photoshop CS provides you with a variety of ways in which you can adjust and add color to your images to make them interesting and unique. In this chapter, you'll learn how to:

- Create a duotone image
- Convert a color image to sepia tones
- Match colors

Creating a Duotone Image

A nice effect to add to a photo is a duotone. Basically, a duotone is a grayscale image to which you add a second printed color to tint the image overall. (You can add two tint colors to create a tritone image or three tint colors to create a quadtone image.) The steps here illustrate converting a grayscale image to a duotone for a nicely tinted printout.

> **NOTE**
>
> Remember, some tools and conversions aren't available for images using 16 bits of color information per channel, so convert to 8 bits per channel. To convert to a duotone, the image must be set to 8 bits per channel. Refer to the "Working with Bit Depth" section in Chapter 15, "Understanding Colors and Channels," to see how to make this change.

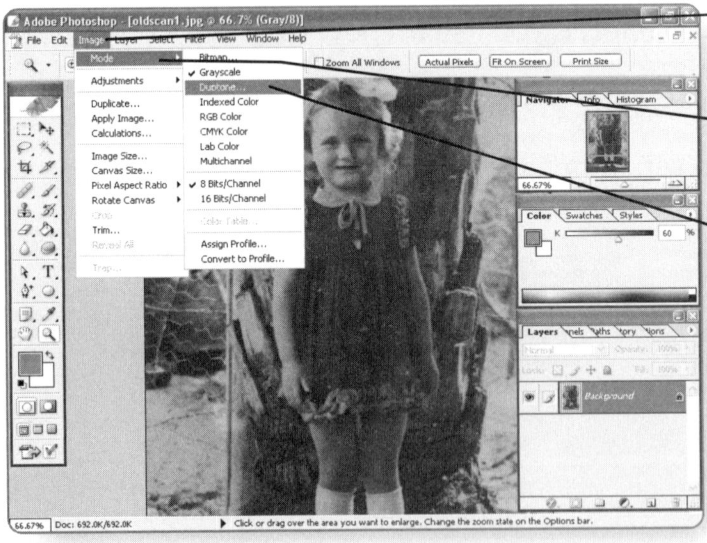

1. **Click** on **Image**. The Image menu will appear.

2. **Point** to **Mode**. The Mode submenu will appear.

3. **Click** on **Duotone**. The Duotone Options dialog box will open.

> **NOTE**
>
> If the Duotone option isn't available, you must first convert your image to grayscale.

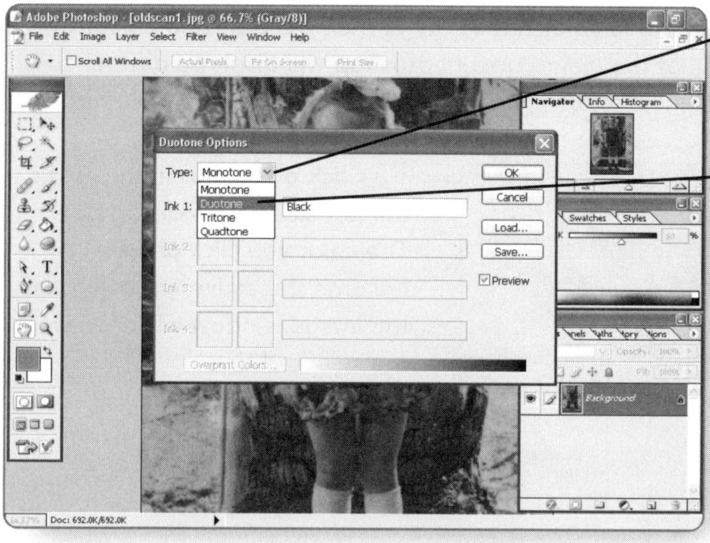

4. Click on the **down arrow** beside the Type drop-down list. A list of options will appear.

5. Click on **Duotone** in the list. The second ink color will become active for the image.

NOTE

You would click on Tritone or Quadtone to add more than one tint color to the image.

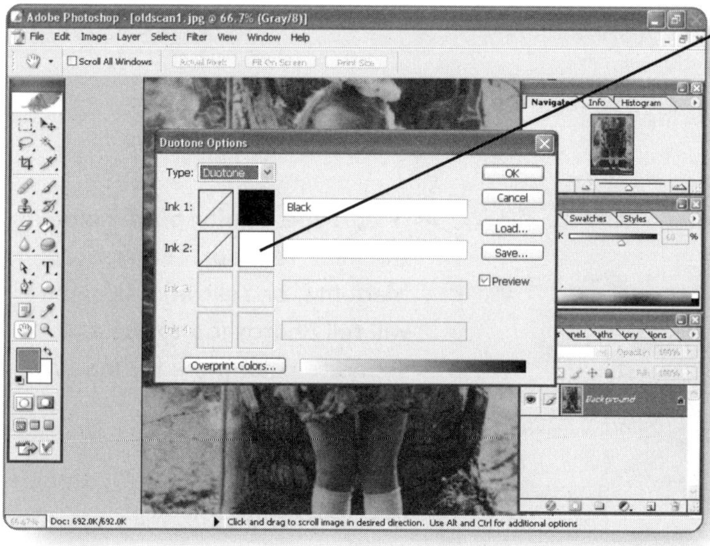

6. Click on the **white Ink 2 box**. The Custom Colors dialog box will open.

7. Click on a **color hue** in the narrow band of colors near the middle of the dialog box. Photoshop will display a different selection of colors in the list at the left side of the dialog box.

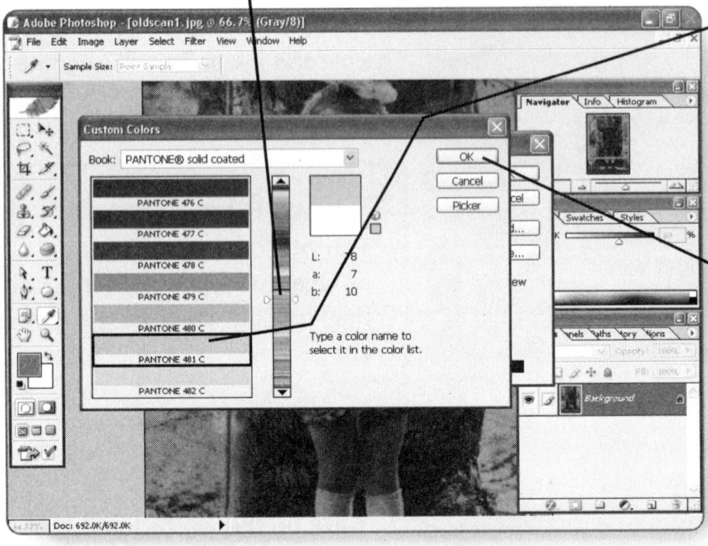

8. Click on a **color** in the list at the left side of the dialog box. The color you click on will become the active tint color, and the image window will preview the selected tint.

9. Click on **OK**. The Custom Colors dialog box will close.

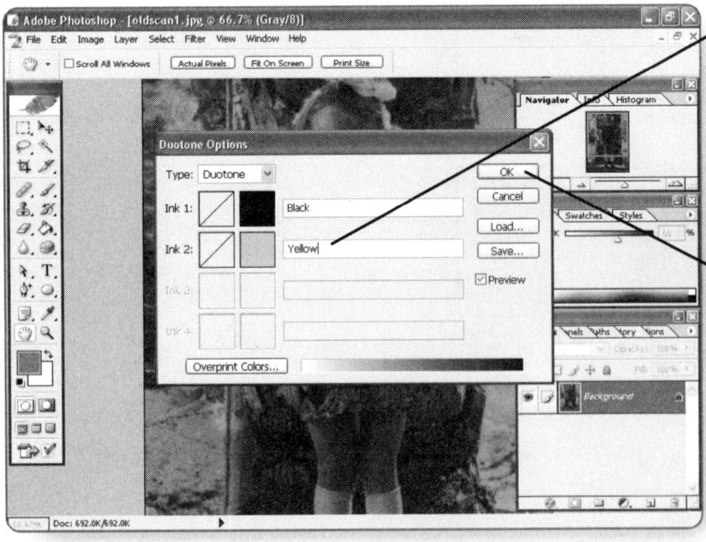

10. Type a **color plate name** in the Ink 2 text box. (Enter Cyan, Magenta, or Yellow.) The name will tell Photoshop to use a separate color plate for the tint ink color.

11. Click on **OK**. The Duotone Options dialog box will close, finishing the duotone creation.

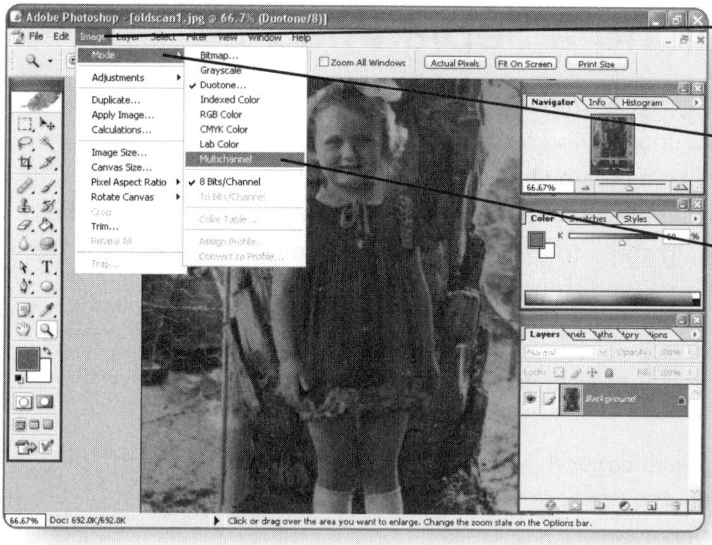

12. **Click** on **Image**. The Image menu will appear.

13. **Point** to **Mode**. The Mode submenu will appear.

14. **Click** on **Multichannel**. Photoshop separates the single duotone color channels into multiple channels so that you can preview individual colors.

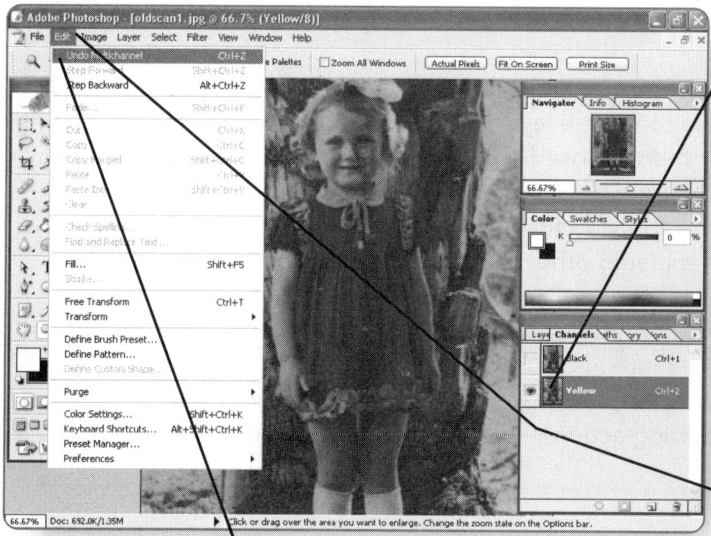

15. **Click** on the **color channel** to preview in the Channels palette. Photoshop will display the ink areas to be printed with that color in the image window.

16. **Click** on **Edit**. The Edit menu will appear.

17. **Click** on **Undo Multichannel**. Photoshop removes the multichannel mode and redisplays the single duotone color channel.

Making a Sepia Image

You'll typically work in the opposite direction when you create a sepia image, working from a color image to one that appears more like a creamy brown grayscale. (But you can make a "sepia" image with any mix of color that you prefer.) Use the following steps to make your favorite color image appear as a traditional (and trendy) sepia image.

TIP

You can convert a grayscale image to RGB color and then use the techniques described here to make it a sepia image.

NOTE

Photoshop includes an action you can use to create a sepia tone on a layer. (Choose File, Automate, Batch, and then choose Sepia Toning from the Action drop-down list. Use the other Batch dialog box settings to finish applying the automation.) There are also actions for applying other color effects, and you can download actions for applying sepia tone and other effects from the Internet. See Chapter 19, "Working with Actions," to learn more about actions, and see Appendix D, "Online Resources," for sources for downloadable goodies, including actions.

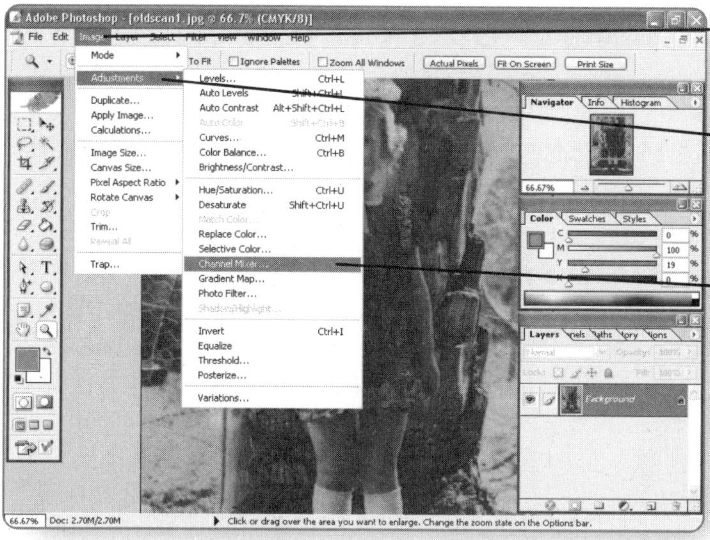

1. **Click** on **Image**. The Image menu will appear.

2. **Point** to **Adjustments**. The Adjustments submenu will appear.

3. **Click** on **Channel Mixer**. The Channel Mixer dialog box will appear.

4. **Choose** a **channel** from the Output Channel drop-down list. The selected color channel will be ready for adjustment.

5. **Drag** the **Source Channels slider** for the selected color. The image window will preview the color change in the image.

6. **Click** on **OK** after you have adjusted the mix for each channel. The Channel Mixer dialog box will close so that you can review the final tint.

Coloring a Black and White Photo

If you've scanned in an old black-and-white image and you want to colorize it, you can take advantage of Photoshop CS's layers to easily apply color. If the image was scanned in as a black-and-white or grayscale image, it will have to first be converted to an RGB or CMYK color mode.

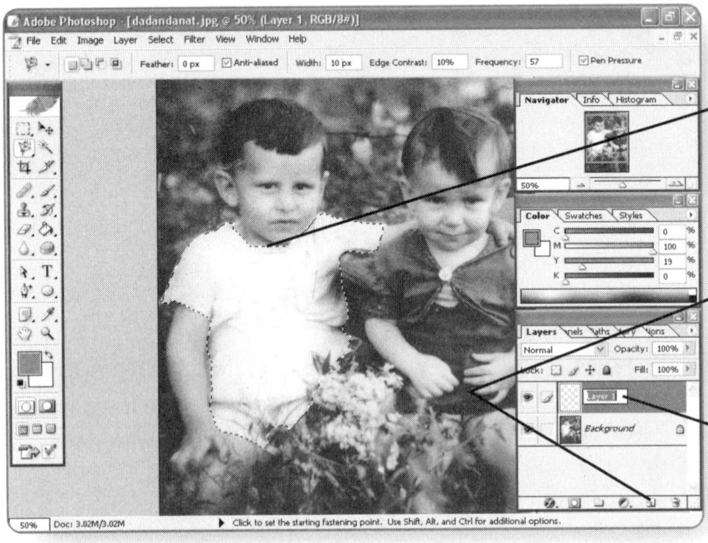

1. **Create** a **selection** around the area you would like to colorize. A marquee will appear around that area.

2. **Click** on the **New Layer button** in the Layers palette. A new layer will appear.

3. **Double-click** on the **name** of the layer. The name will appear highlighted in a box.

4. **Type** a new **name** for the layer. Give it a name appropriate to the selection you are colorizing.

5. **Click** on any **blank area** of the palette. The layer will now have a new name.

6. **Click** on a **color** in the Color palette that you would like to apply to the selection.

7. **Click** on the **Paint Bucket tool**. It will be selected.

8. **Click once** within the selection. The selection will be filled with the color you selected. It doesn't look very realistic at this point, but it will after we adjust the opacity of the layer.

9. **Click** on the **down arrow** beside the Opacity number box. A slider bar will appear.

10. **Drag** the **slider bar** to the appropriate level. Typically, this would be anywhere from 20% to 30% for colorizing a black-and-white photo.

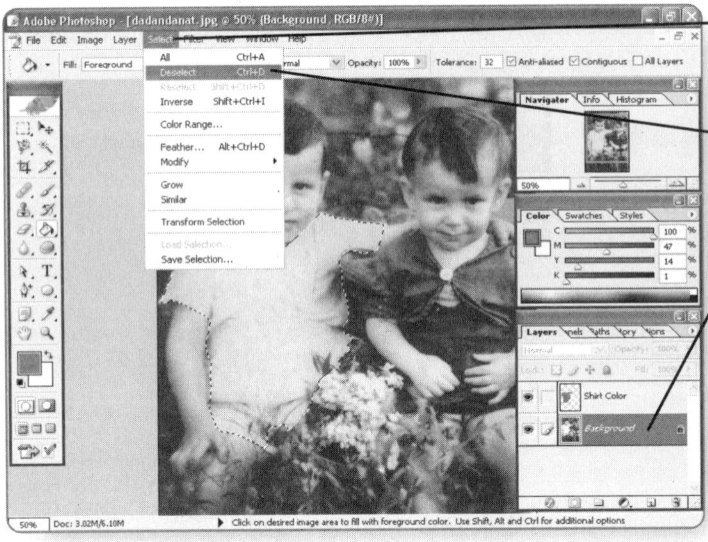

11. **Click** on **Select**. The Select menu will appear.

12. **Click** on **Deselect**. The selection will be removed.

13. **Click** on the **Layer** that contains the original image. It will be selected.

14. **Repeat** steps **1** through **13** for the rest of the image.

Matching Colors

As I mentioned in an earlier chapter, one of the biggest questions I get in my training classes is how to remove someone's head in a picture and put it on someone else's body. You've already learned that a selection can be made, copied, and pasted onto a new image. One of the problems that arises is that skin tones from the source image don't necessarily match the tones of the target image, so it won't end up looking realistic. This problem can be solved with Photoshop CS's new Match Color feature, which will take the color scheme from one image and apply it to another.

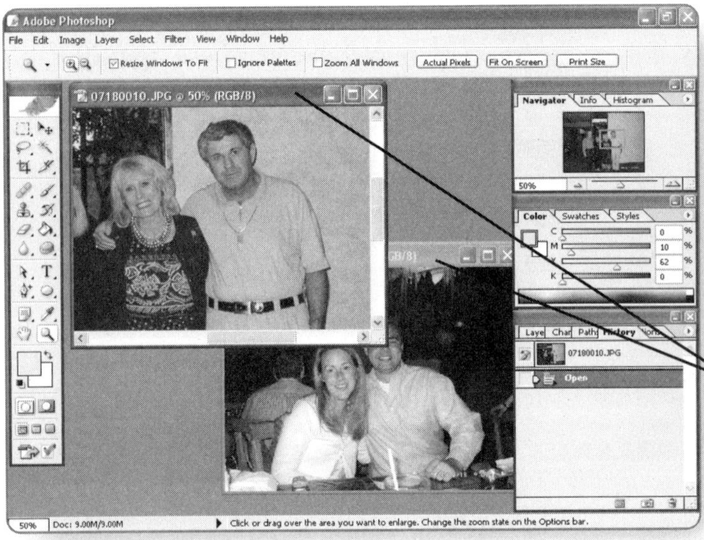

1. **Open** both the **source** and **target images** for your color match.

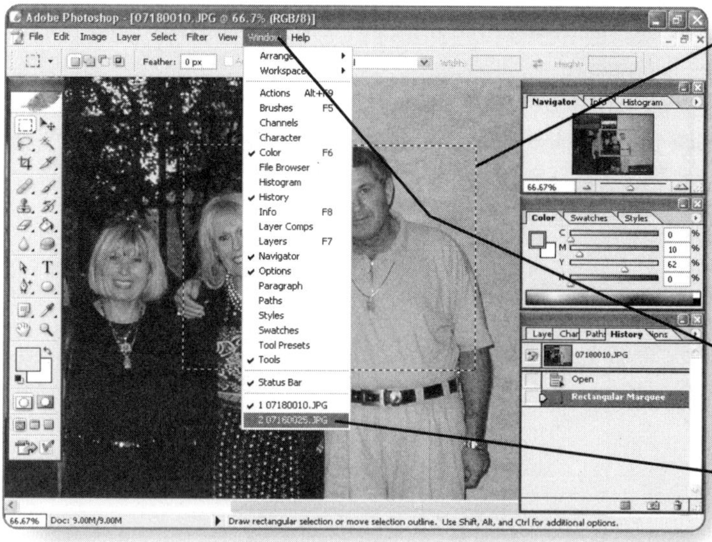

2. Create a **selection** around the area containing the colors you would like to match in the source image. This step is optional; if you don't make a selection, the color scheme from the entire photo will be matched.

3. Click on **Window**. The Window menu will appear.

4. Click on the **target image**. It will become the active window.

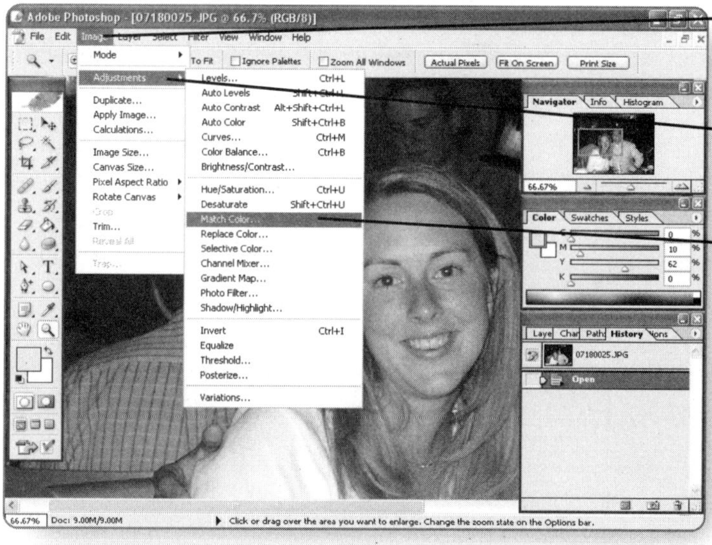

5. Click on **Image**. The Image menu will appear.

6. Click on **Adjustments**. A submenu will appear.

7. Click on **Match Color**. The Match Color dialog box will open.

8. **Click** on the **down arrow** beside source. A list of open images will appear.

9. **Click** the desired **source image**. It will be selected.

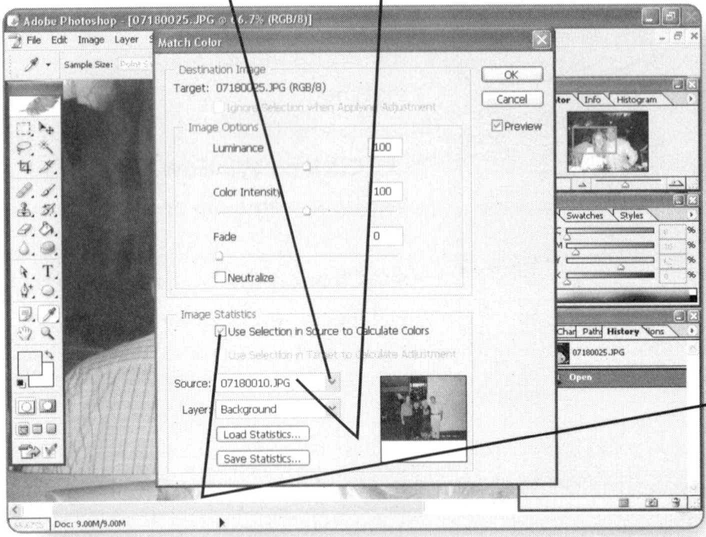

10. **Click** the Use Selection in Source to Calculate Colors **check box** if you made a selection within the source that you would like to use to match colors.

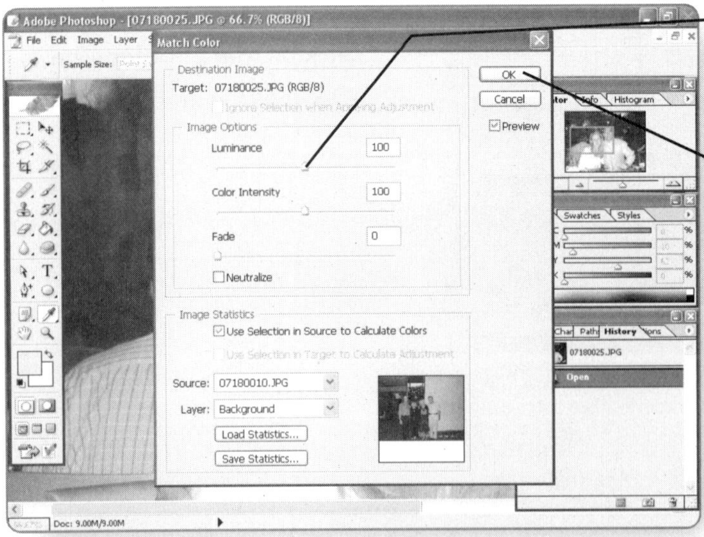

11. **Drag** the various **image options**. They will adjust as you drag.

12. **Click** on **OK**. The color scheme from the source will be applied to the target image.

18

Working with Plug-Ins

Simply stated, a plug-in is a mini program that extends the capabilities of Photoshop (or its companion program ImageReady). Each plug-in functions in one of three ways: as a filter, as an additional import or export choice, or as a file format choice in the Save As or Open dialog box. This chapter shows you how to take advantage of plug-ins. In this chapter, you'll learn how to:

- Install a plug-in you've purchased or downloaded
- Use a plug-in that performs a special action
- Use a filter plug-in

Installing Plug-Ins

By default, the plug-ins that come with Photoshop install to various subfolders of the Program Files\Adobe\Photoshop CS\Plug-Ins\ folder. You can purchase additional plug-ins or download a variety of freeware and shareware plug-ins from a number of sources online. If you download a particular type of plug-in, you typically can just move or copy the plug-in file (after decompressing it, unzipping it, or renaming it, if indicated by the instructions accompanying the plug-in) to the folder that holds similar plug-in files, assuming the plug-in doesn't include its own installer program. In other cases, you may want to store your third-party plug-ins in a separate folder to distinguish them from the plug-ins provided with Photoshop. If you choose this route, you need to specify the alternate plug-in location, as described next.

> **NOTE**
>
> If a plug-in was written for Photoshop only, copy it to the appropriate subfolder of C:\Program Files\Adobe\Photoshop CS\Plug-Ins\Adobe Photoshop Only\. If a plug-in was written for ImageReady only, copy it to the appropriate subfolder of C:\Program Files\Adobe\Photoshop CS\Plug-Ins\Adobe ImageReady Only\.

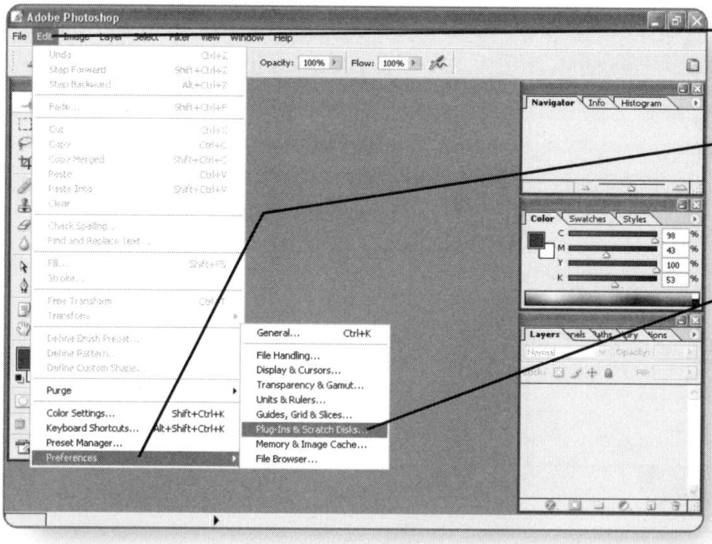

1. Click on **Edit**. The Edit menu will appear.

2. Point to **Preferences**. The Preferences submenu will appear.

3. Click on **Plug-Ins & Scratch Disks.** The Preferences dialog box will appear with its Plug-Ins & Scratch Disks settings displayed.

NOTE

In ImageReady, you would choose Edit, Preferences, Plug-Ins to start specifying another plug-ins folder.

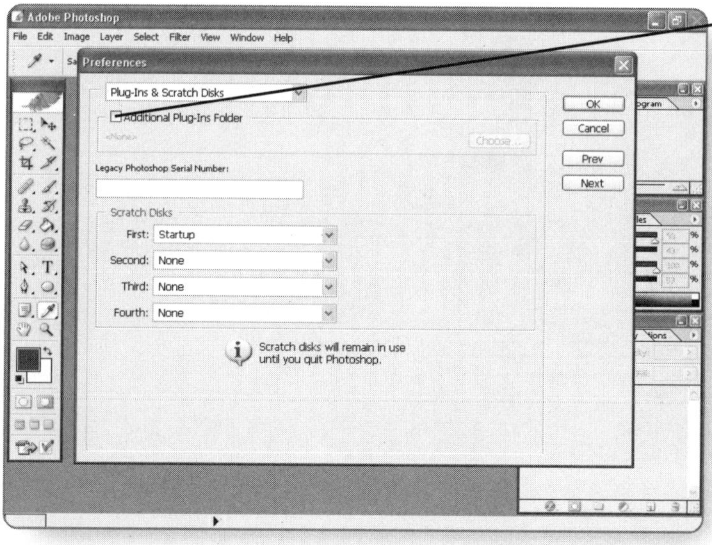

4. Click on the **Additional Plug-Ins Folder** check box. The check box will be checked, and the Browse for Folder dialog box will open.

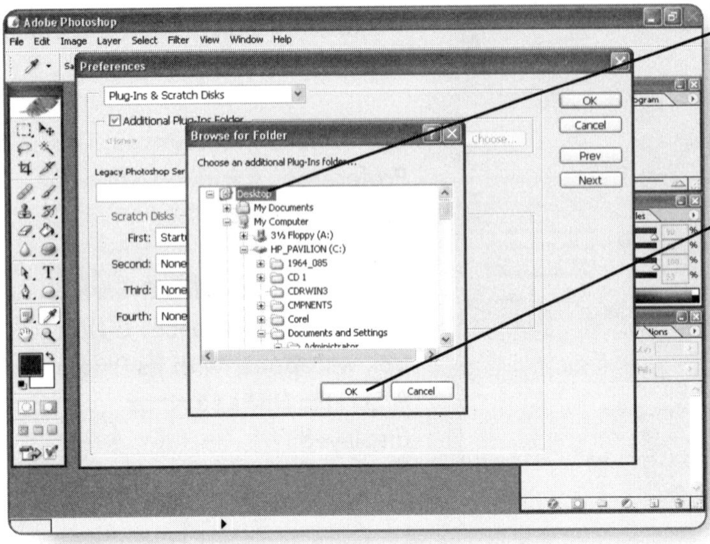

5. **Select** the **folder** that holds the plug-ins in the folder tree. The specified folder will become active as a plug-in folder.

6. **Click** on **OK**. The Browse for Folder dialog box will close.

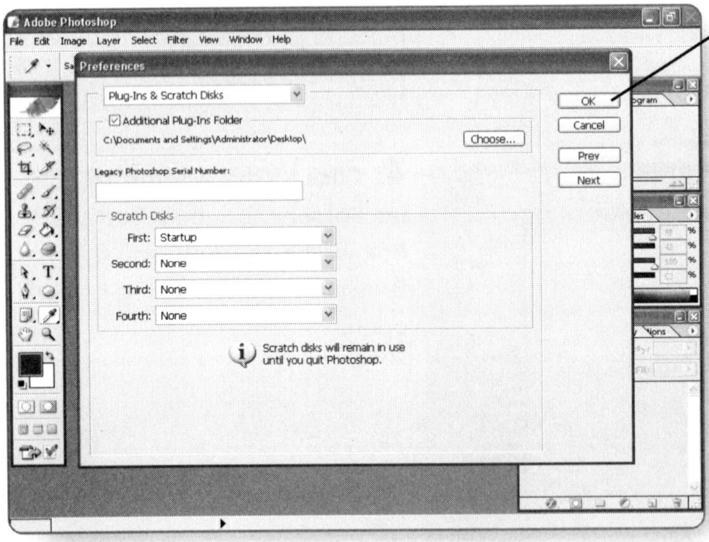

7. **Click** on **OK**. The Preferences dialog box will close.

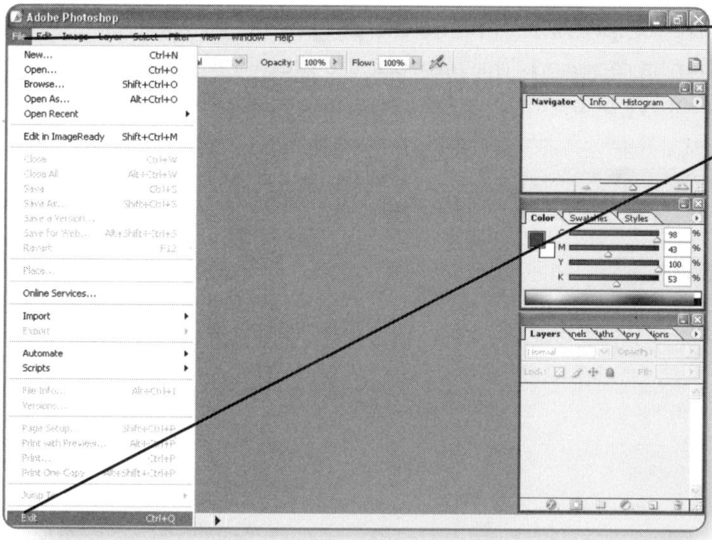

8. **Click** on **File**. The File menu will appear.

9. **Click** on **Exit**. Photoshop will close.

NOTE

When you close Photoshop, save changes to any open file, if prompted. You must exit and restart Photoshop (or ImageReady) for the new plug-ins folder to take effect.

10. **Open** the newly specified plug-ins **folder** on the desktop.

11. **Decompress** or **rename** the **plug-in file** or **run** its **installer** as required. The appropriate plug-in files will decompress or be installed in the appropriate folder location.

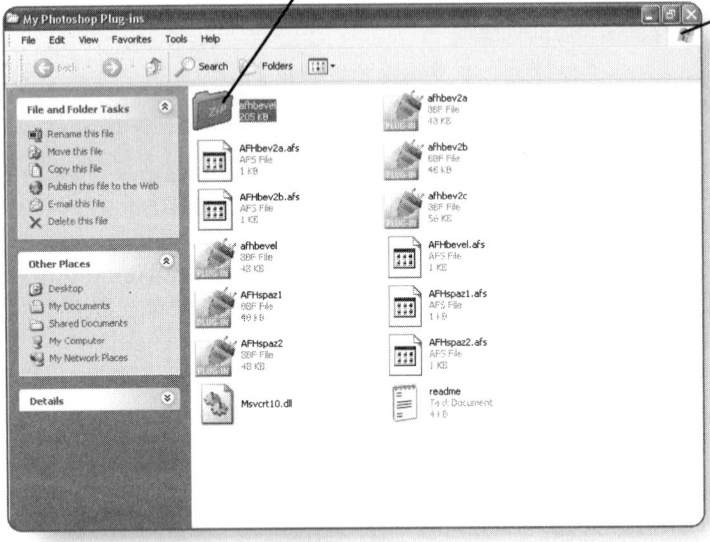

12. **Close** the **folder** on the desktop.

NOTE

In some cases, you may have to move the plug-ins to C:\Program Files\Adobe\Photoshop CS\Plug-Ins\ rather than running them from the alternate folder. Be sure to read any Readme file that comes with a plug-in to verify how to install it, particularly if the plug-in creates one or more folders when you unzip or decompress it.

13. **Click** on **Start**. The Start menu will appear. If using Mac OX, double-click on the Photoshop icon to start the program.

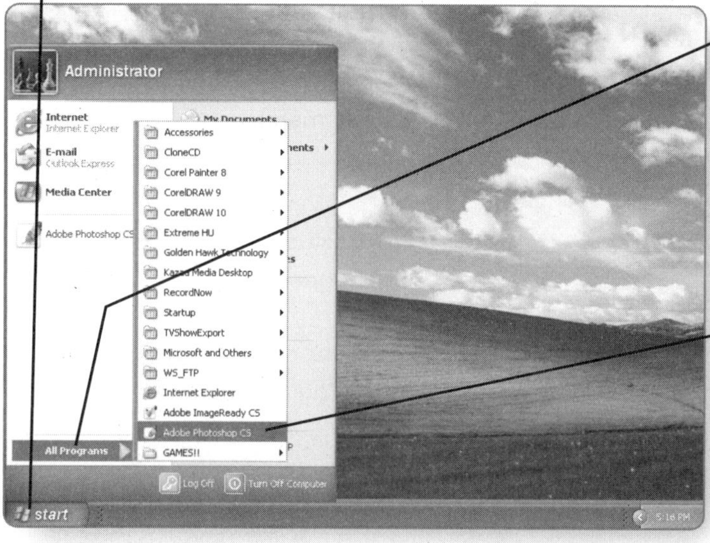

14. **Point** to **All Programs** (or Programs in Windows versions prior to XP). The Programs submenu will appear. If you are using Mac OS, simply double-click on the Photoshop CS icon to launch the program.

15. **Click** on **Adobe Photoshop CS**. The Photoshop program will load with the added plug-ins newly active. You can now open files as needed and use the plug-ins.

Applying a Plug-In to a File

As noted at the very beginning of this chapter, plug-ins generally work in limited ways, enabling you to open or save files in different formats or to apply custom filters to an image. This section shows an example of using a filter that falls into each category.

Applying by Opening or Saving

If a filter enables you to use Photoshop to work with files of different formats, the filter typically adds the format into the Files of Type list of the Open dialog box or the Format list of the Save As dialog box. The following steps show one example—using a filter that enables you to save files in the Windows icon format (.ico). Before you begin the steps, be sure you open the file to which you want to apply the plug-in.

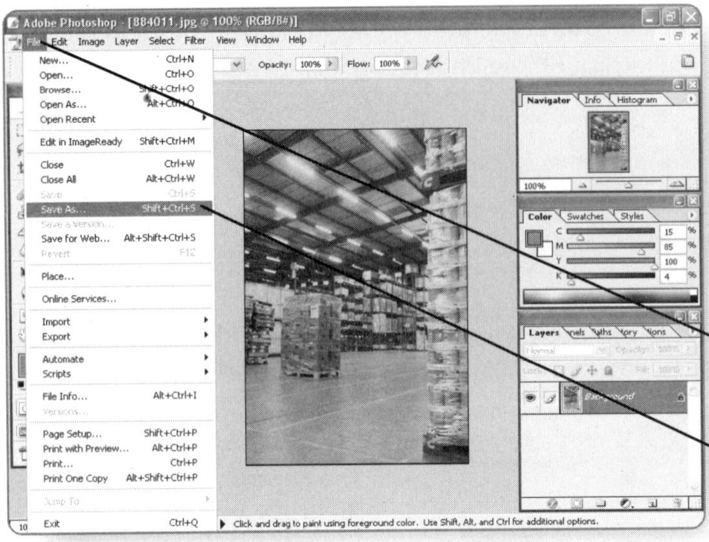

NOTE

In other cases, plug-ins that work with file formats appear on the Import or Export submenus of the File menu.

1. **Click** on **File**. The File menu will appear.

2. **Click** on **Save As**. The Save As dialog box will open.

3. **Click** on the **down arrow** beside the Format drop-down list and then **click** on the **file format** provided by the plug-in (in this case, BoxTop ProJPEG 5.0). The selected format will be used for the save operation.

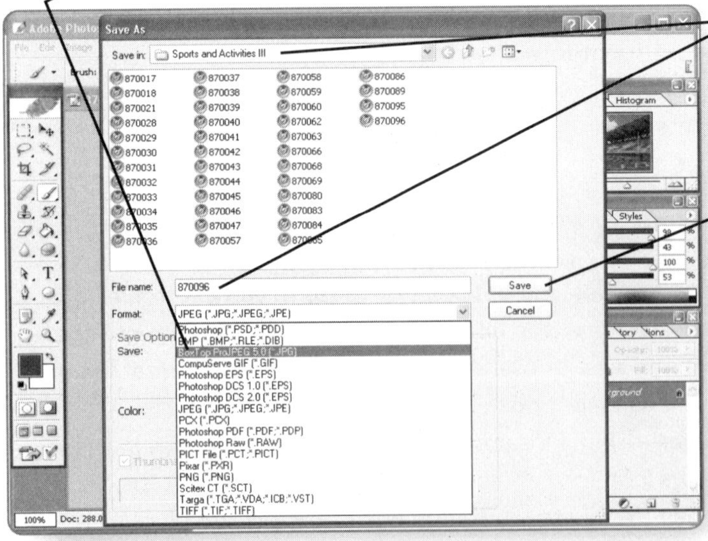

4. **Change** the **File name** and **Save in location**, if necessary. The newly saved file will use the name and location you specify.

5. **Click** on **Save**. The Save As dialog box will close, and one of two things will happen. Either the file will be saved immediately in the new format, or a dialog box for the plug-in will appear to prompt you to specify additional settings for the saved file.

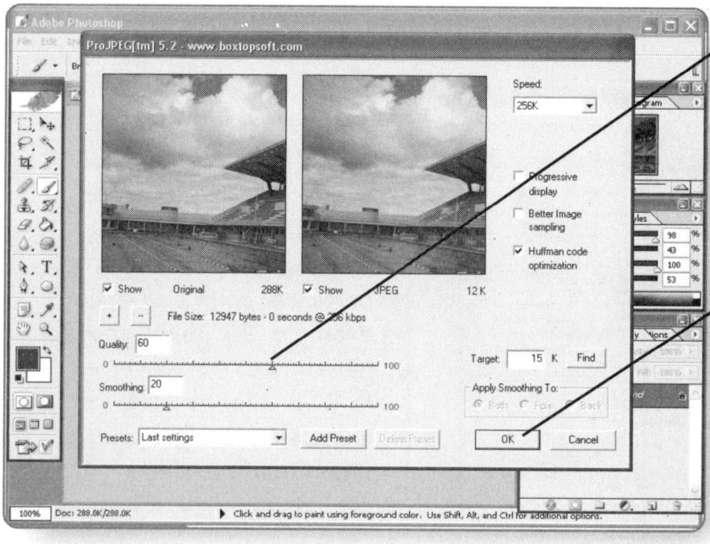

6. **Adjust settings** as necessary. In many cases, an image preview or output settings will change to show the impact of the new settings on the image file that will be created.

7. **Click** on **OK** or **Save**. The dialog box will close, and the image will be saved. You can then close and use the image.

Applying a Filter Plug-In

In most cases, installing a plug-in installs a new filter or group of filters. Photoshop typically adds the new filter choices or groups (submenus) to the bottom of the Filter menu, making added filters as easy to access as default filters. Like the default filters, some plug-in filters will display a dialog box prompting you to choose additional settings, whereas others will take effect immediately. The following steps show an example of a freeware plug-in filter.

1. Click on **Filter**. The Filter menu will appear.

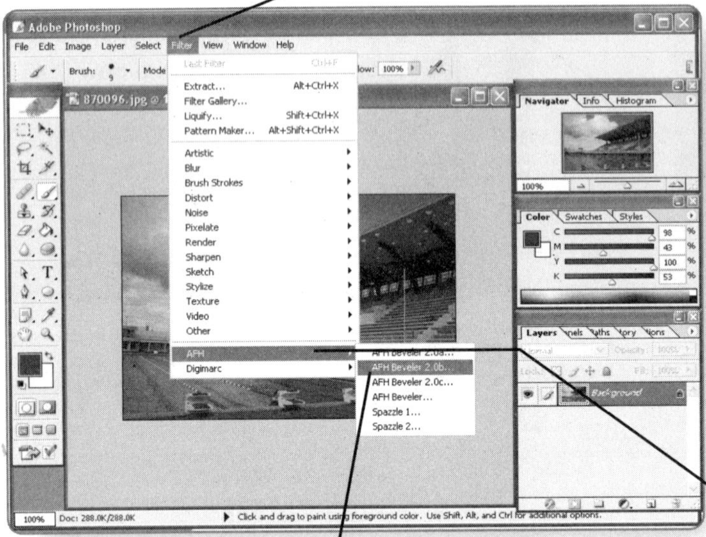

> ## NOTE
>
> As with other commands and effects in Photoshop, many filters require that an image be using a particular color mode. For example, the image shown here had to be converted to RGB color at 8 bits per channel before the plug-in filter could be used.

2. Point to the **name** for the filter group, if necessary. The group submenu will appear.

3. Click on a **filter**. The filter will appear, or the filter dialog box will open.

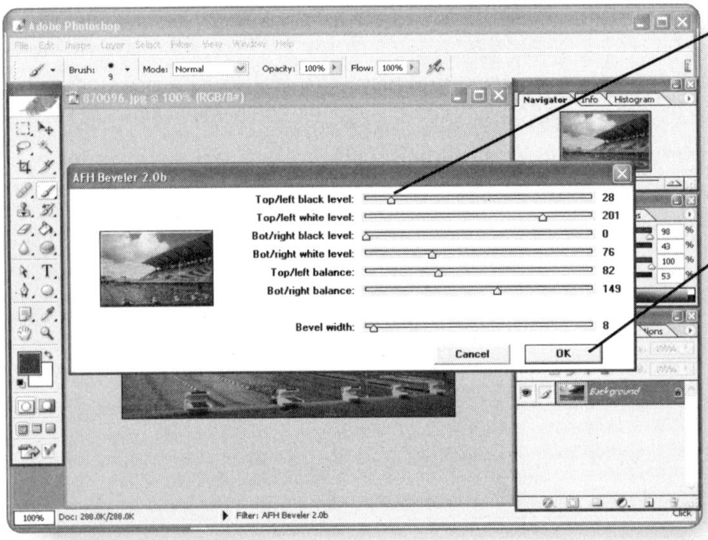

4. Adjust filter settings as necessary. Either a preview area in the filter dialog box or the image window itself will preview the filter changes.

5. Click on **OK**. Photoshop will apply the filter settings to the image.

Using the Liquify Plug-In

The Liquify plug-in appears as a standalone command (rather than as part of a submenu) on the Filter menu. The Liquify plug-in offers a variety of settings for distorting and manipulating an image. The Turbulence tool represents one new enhancement to this filter, enabling you to place distortion along with a "jitter" effect. You can view a mesh that illustrates the distortion as well. The following steps illustrate some of the basics for working with this important plug-in.

1. **Click** on **Filter**. The Filter menu will appear.

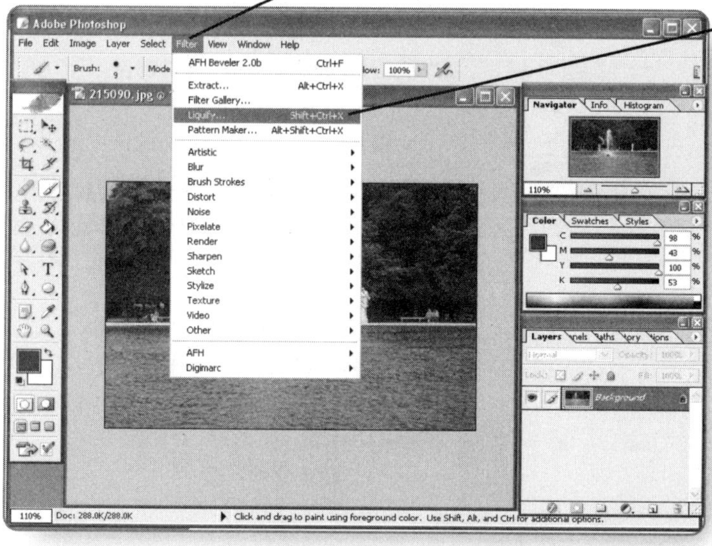

2. **Click** on **Liquify**. The Liquify dialog box will open.

3. **Adjust** the **zoom setting** for the image, if necessary. The image will appear at the new zoom.

4. **Click** on the desired **tool**. The tool will be selected. In this example, the Turbulence tool is selected.

5. **Adjust** the tool **options** as needed. The mouse pointer will change in size or appearance accordingly when you move the pointer over the image.

6. **Drag** on the **image** at the desired location(s). The image will be distorted according to the selected tool, its settings, and the amount of dragging.

7. **Click** on **OK**. The Liquify dialog box will close, and the image will appear with its new distortion in Photoshop.

19

Working with Actions

If you've made it this far along in the book, you can see that the possible combinations of Photoshop features and filters are endless, not to mention the sheer number of specific settings you can use with each feature or filter. In Photoshop, you can create actions and droplets to store a series of commands and settings that you choose. This chapter shows you how to save yourself some work in Photoshop. You will learn how to:

- Record an action
- Play an action
- Make a droplet from an action
- Use a droplet

Creating an Action

If you've ever created a macro in an application, you'll have an easy time creating an action. Like a macro, an action is a series of steps and settings that you save so that you can repeat them quickly later. Saving and using the action eliminates the need to remember the filter settings you prefer, for example, or the color adjustment choices to use. Actions come in handy when you need to prepare multiple images using the same settings—for example, if you're converting a series of grayscale images to duotones using a particular Pantone color for inclusion in the same publication. The following steps show you how to use the Actions palette to record a new action.

1. **Click** on **Window**. The Window menu will appear.

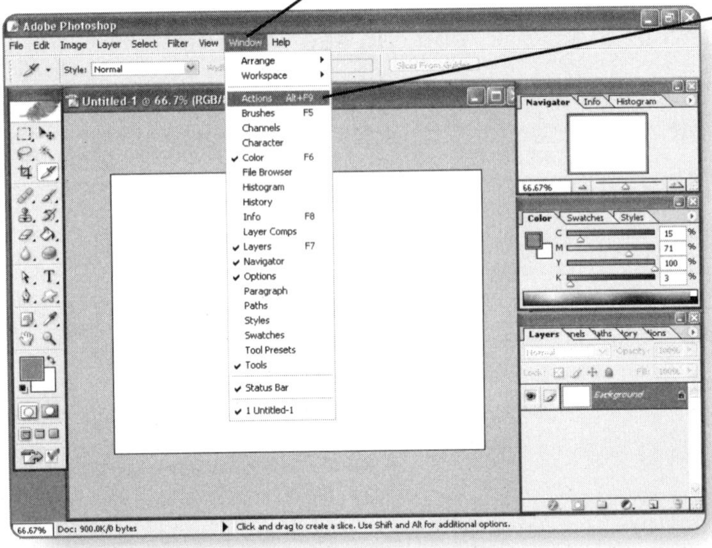

2. **Click** on **Actions**. The Actions palette will become active.

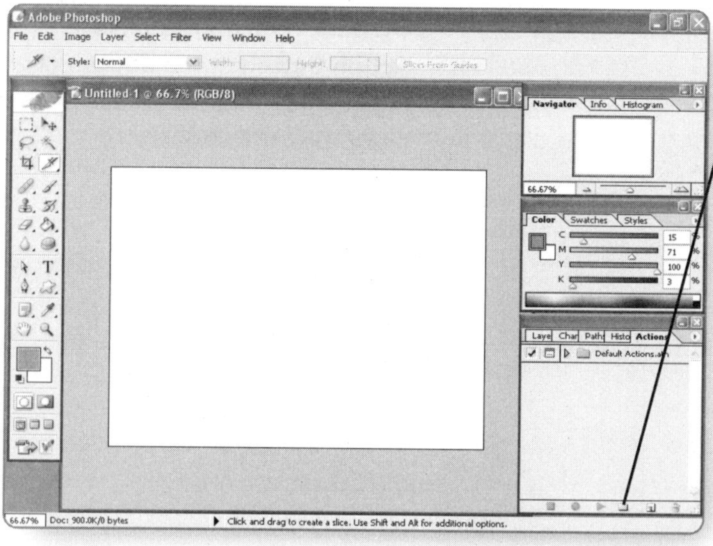

3. Click on the **Create New Set button** at the bottom of the palette. The New Set dialog box will appear.

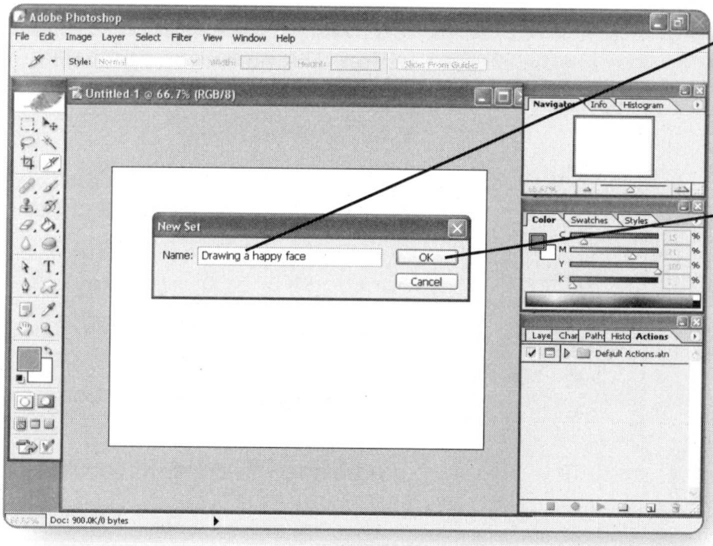

4. Type a **name** for the new set. The name you type will replace the placeholder entry in the Name text box.

5. Click on **OK**. The new set will appear in the Actions palette and will be selected by default.

NOTE

To add a new action to an existing set, click on the set name in the Actions palette and then follow the rest of the steps here.

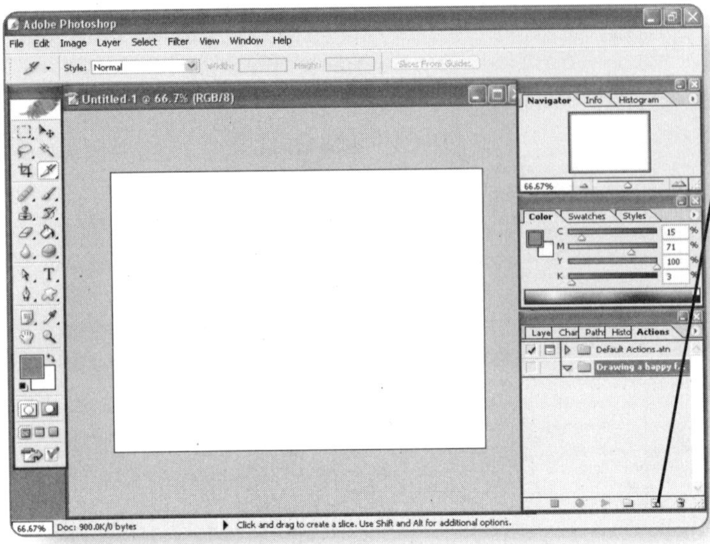

6. Click on the **Create New Action button** at the bottom of the palette. The New Action dialog box will appear.

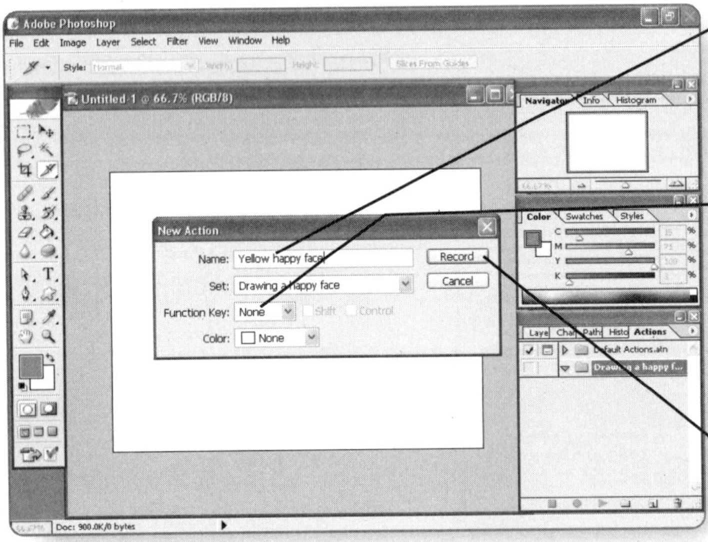

7. Type a **name** for the new action. The name you type will replace the placeholder entry in the Name text box.

8. Specify other **settings** in the dialog box, such as adding a Function Key (a shortcut key combination) to play back the action. The remaining settings will be added for the function.

9. Click on **Record**. Recording will start.

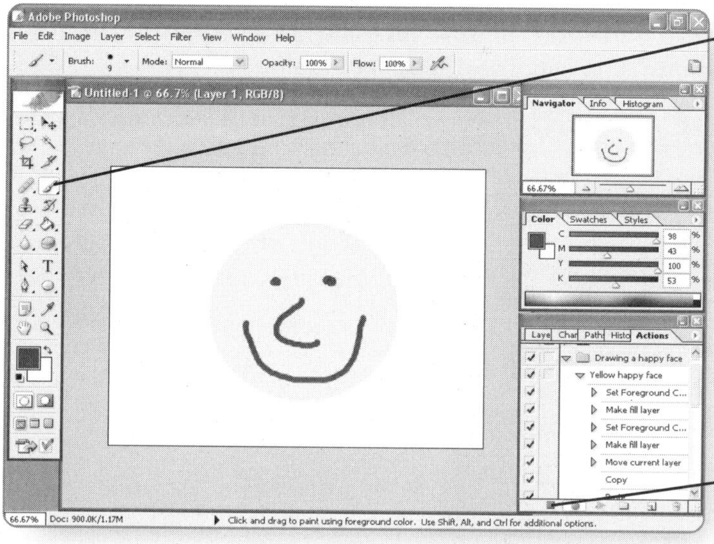

10. Perform the **steps** to record. The steps will be added to the named action.

> **NOTE**
>
> If a particular feature can't be recorded, either it will be unavailable or you'll see a warning message.

11. Click on the **Stop Playing/Recording button** at the bottom of the Actions palette. Photoshop will stop recording your steps, finishing the action.

Using an Action

Much as you use a recording process to create an action, you use a playback process to run the action. Before you run the action, open the file to which you want to apply the action and perform any preliminary steps to prepare for the action, such as making a selection or converting to the proper color mode. Then use the steps that follow:

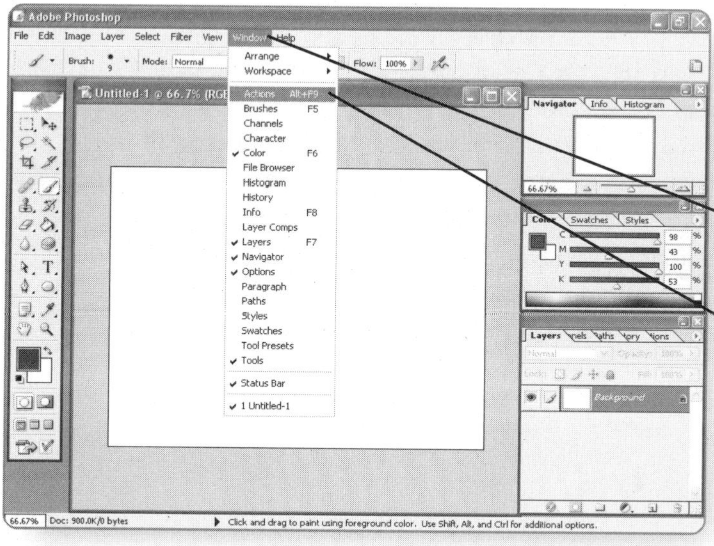

1. Click on **Window**. The Window menu will appear.

2. Click on **Actions**. The Actions palette will become active.

3. **Scroll** to **display** the **set** that holds the action to perform in the palette. The actions will appear in the palette.

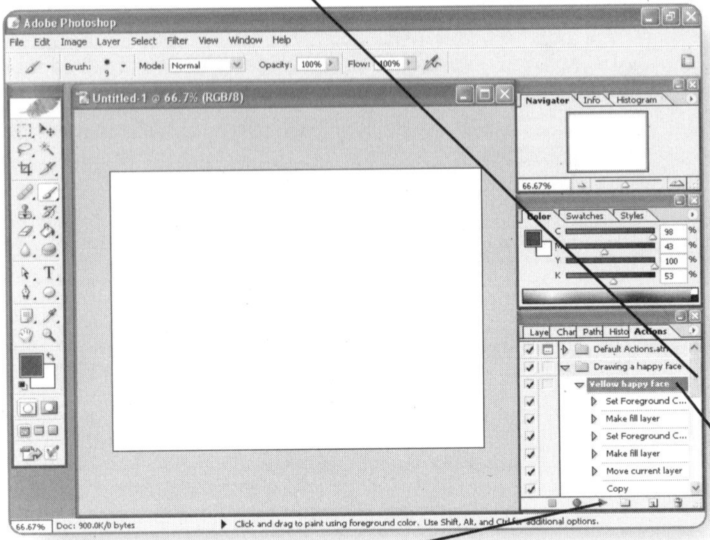

NOTE

Click on the right arrow to the left of the set name if you don't see its actions.

4. **Click** on the **action** to perform. The action will be selected.

5. **Click** on the **Play Selection button** at the bottom of the palette. The action plays immediately.

Batch Processing

There may be times when you want to apply an action to a series of images. Rather than having to apply the action to each image one at a time, you can take advantage of Photoshop CS's batch processing, which allows you to apply an action to multiple images in one step. It's a good idea to put all of the images you would like to batch process in one folder before you begin the process.

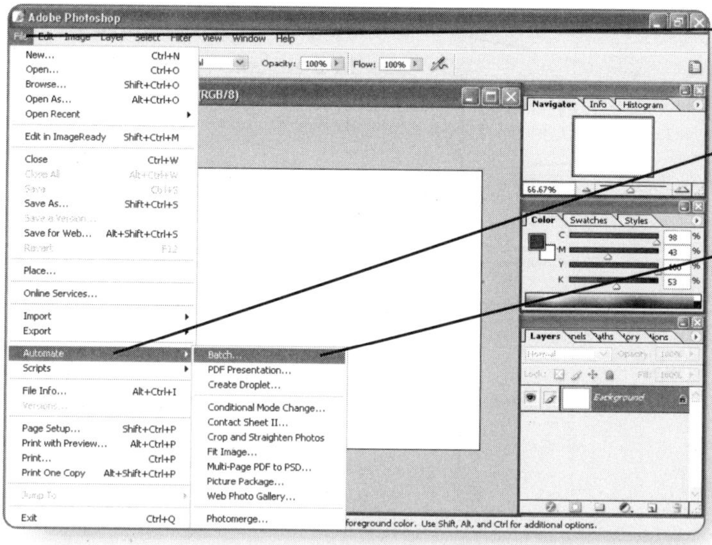

1. **Click** on **File**. The file menu will appear.

2. **Click** on **Automate**. A submenu will appear.

3. **Click** on **Batch**. The Batch dialog box will open.

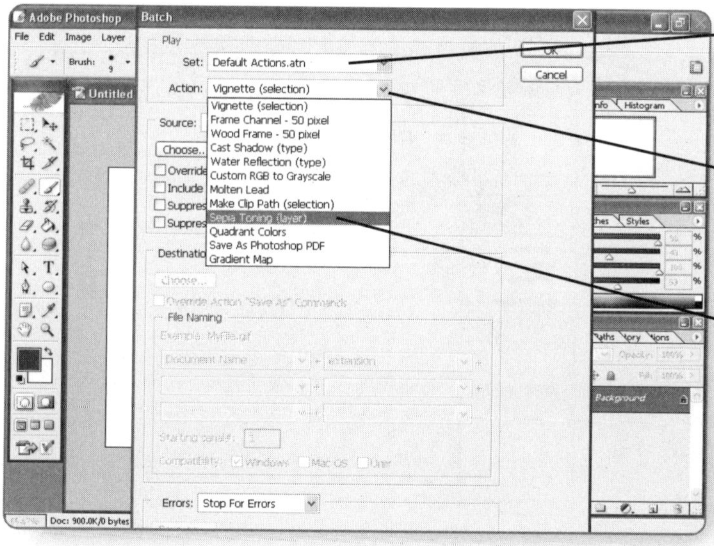

4. **Click** on the **down arrow** beside Set and choose the desired set of actions.

5. **Click** on the **down arrow** beside Action. A menu will appear.

6. **Click** on the **desired action** that you would like to apply to your images.

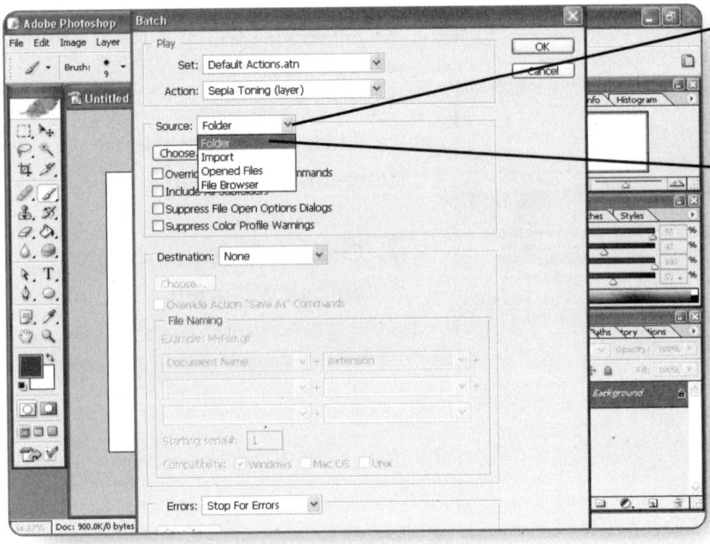

7. Click on the **down arrow** beside **Source**. A menu of options will appear.

8. Click on **Folder**. Photoshop will apply the actions to all the images within a folder that you specify.

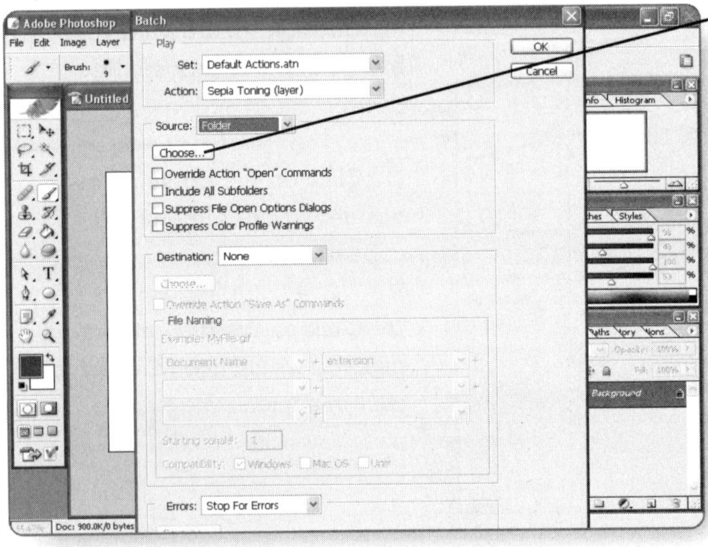

9. Click on **Choose**. A dialog box will open in which you can select a folder for the batch processing.

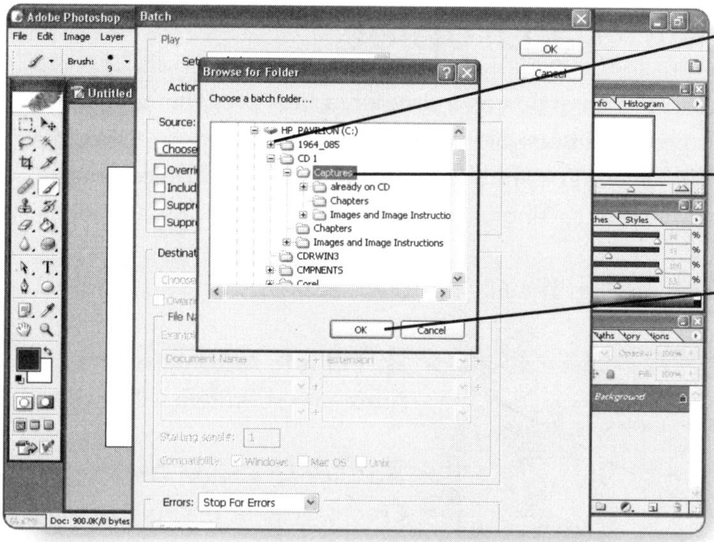

10. **Click** on the **+** to expand a folder. All of the folders within that folder will appear.

11. **Click** the desired **folder**. It will be highlighted.

12. **Click** on **OK**. The folder will be selected.

13. **Click** on the desired **Source options**. A check mark will appear in the boxes you have selected.

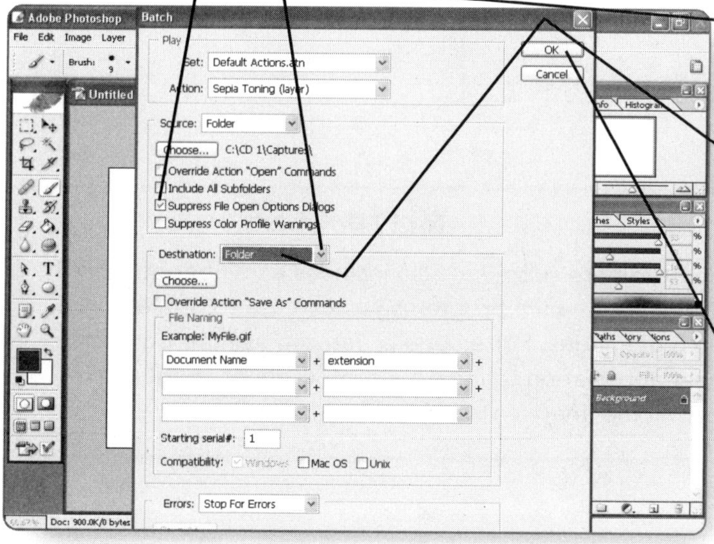

14. **Click** on the **down arrow** beside Destination. A menu of options will appear.

15. **Click** on the desired **Destination option**. This determines what will be done to the image after the batch process is complete.

16. **Click** on **OK**. The batch process will take place based on the settings you have entered.

Making a Droplet

You can save an action as a droplet, a mini program you can use to process image files even when Photoshop isn't running. The following steps show you how to create a droplet using default droplet settings.

1. **Click** on **File**. The File menu will appear.

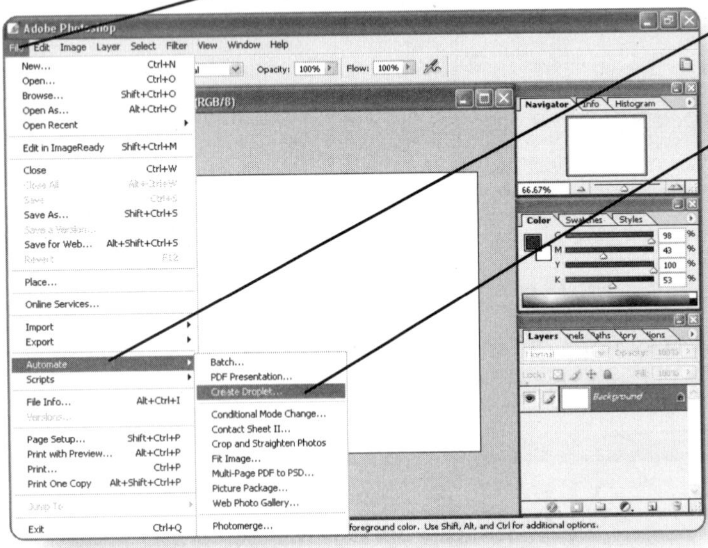

2. **Point** to **Automate**. The Automate submenu will appear.

3. **Click** on **Create Droplet**. The Create Droplet dialog box will open.

NOTE

The Automate submenu also includes a number of preset automations—mini programs you can use to process a batch of images. For example, you can use the Contact Sheet automation to create a contact sheet image file from all the images stored in a particular folder.

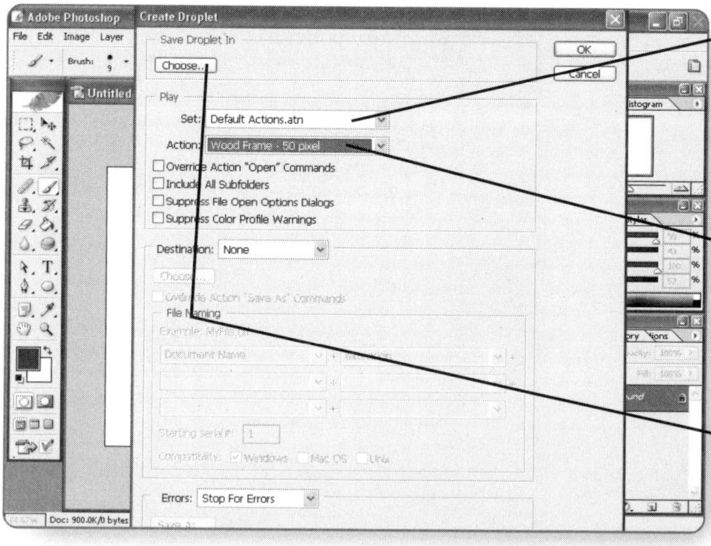

4. **Choose** the **set** that holds the action to convert from the Set drop-down list. The set's actions will become available in the Action drop-down list.

5. **Choose** the **action** to save as a droplet from the Action drop-down list. The selected action appears.

6. **Click** on **Choose**. The Save dialog box will open.

7. **Navigate** to the **folder** where you want to save the droplet. It will become the active folder.

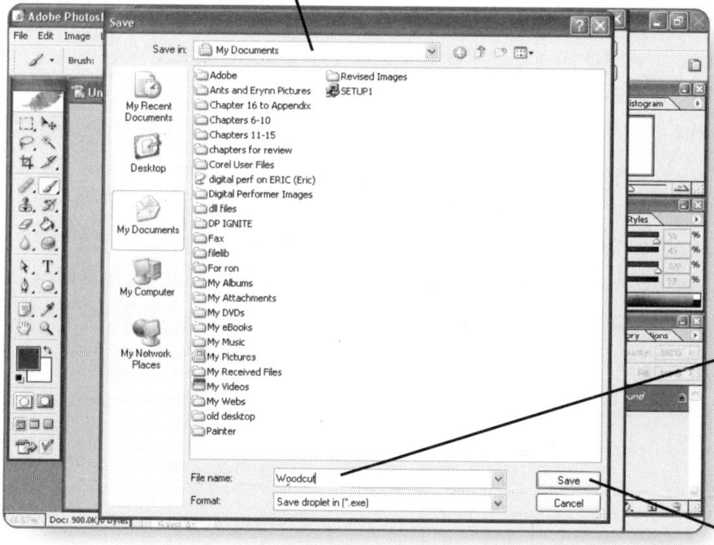

NOTE

By default, the Save dialog box displays the My Documents folder, but you can save a droplet in any location you prefer.

8. **Type** a **name** for the new droplet file. The name you type will replace the placeholder entry in the File name text box.

9. **Click** on **Save**. The Save dialog box will close, and the name you specified will appear in the Create Droplet dialog box.

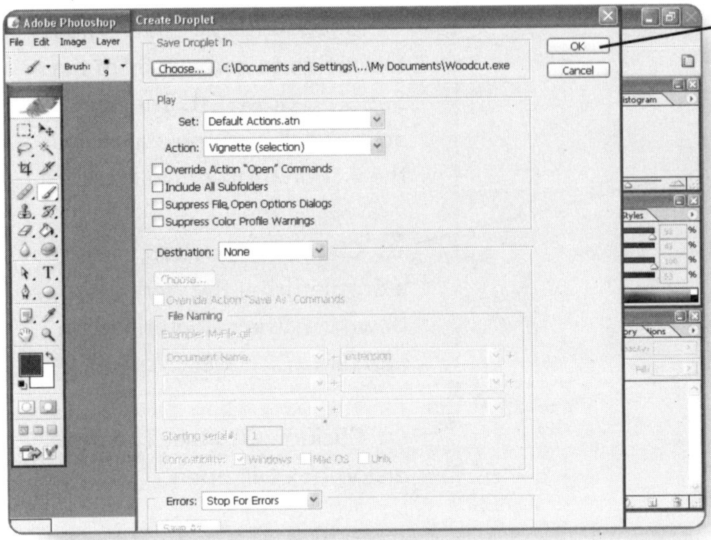

10. Click on **OK**. Photoshop will close the Create Droplet dialog box and finish saving the droplet.

Using a Droplet

As you saw in the preceding section, Photoshop saves a droplet you create as an .exe file. The Photoshop program doesn't have to be open for you to use the droplet. You can use the droplet from the folder where you saved it, or you can copy the .exe file to any other folder, including the Windows desktop—shown in the following steps—for convenient use. You don't have to open Photoshop, so the droplet provides a fast alternative for making changes to a number of files because you also don't have to open the individual image files in Photoshop. Using the droplet is an easy drag-and-drop operation, as illustrated in the following steps.

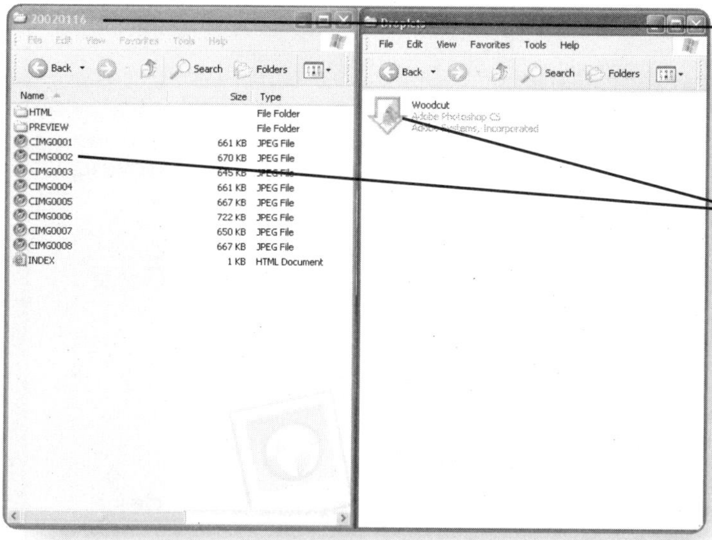

1. **Open** the **folder** that holds the file to process with the automation. The folder will appear in Windows.

2. **Drag** the **file** to process from its folder and **drop** it onto the icon for the droplet file (on the desktop or in another folder). The droplet's actions will be performed on the file. You can repeat the process for as many files as need to be processed.

NOTE

The file(s) to be processed must use the correct color mode and other settings; otherwise, the droplet will stop and display an error message.

Part V Review Questions

1. How do I choose what type of image colors to use? See "Reviewing the Color Modes" in Chapter 15.
2. What's a color channel, and how do I select one? See "Using Color Channels" in Chapter 15.
3. What are the most common color mode conversions? See "Converting Images" in Chapter 15.
4. What do I do if my image is too dark? See "Correcting Brightness and Contrast" in Chapter 16.
5. What's a duotone, and how do you create one? See "Creating a Duotone Image" in Chapter 17.
6. How do you create a Sepia image? See "Making a Sepia Image" in Chapter 17.
7. How do you add plug-ins to Photoshop? See "Installing Plug-Ins" in Chapter 18.
8. What methods do you use to employ a plug-in? See "Applying a Plug-In to a File" in Chapter 18.
9. How do you create an action? See "Creating an Action" in Chapter 19.
10. How do you use an action? See "Using an Action" in Chapter 19.

PART VI

Prepping Images for the Web

20

Creating Web Images

Because Photoshop provides some of the best tools for creating and editing images in general, it's not surprising that it offers superior options for preparing images for use in Web pages. This chapter walks you through the basic skills for preparing images for the Web. You'll learn how to:

- Use Web graphic formats
- Utilize the Save As command
- Create an optimized JPEG image
- Create an optimized GIF image
- Create a WBMP image
- Generate a Web photo gallery

Reviewing Web Graphic Formats

The HTML Web page format spurred the growth of the Internet not only because it could present information in an attractive graphic format, but also because its files were relatively compact in size for reasonable download times. In the spirit of preserving those download times, a few different new formats for graphics files also emerged. Through special compression technology, these file formats preserve color and detail while dramatically reducing file size—sometimes eliminating megabytes in file size. Table 20-1 lists the most common Web graphic file formats and their features.

Table 20-1 ***Web Graphic File Formats***

Format	Description
Compuserve GIF (.gif)	This mode requires conversion to Indexed Color mode (which limits the image to 256 colors) and enables you to preserve transparency so that the Web page background shows through.
JPEG (.jpe, .jpg, or .jpeg)	This mode does not preserve transparency, but it does enable you to specify the amount of compression to use so you can control file size and quality.
PNG (.png)	Portable Network Graphics (PNG) mode enables you to preserve transparency and choose specific methods for reducing colors and handling dithering in the image. This format isn't used often.
WBMP	This 1-bit color format optimizes images for wireless devices. Converting an image to this format converts it to simplified black and white.

TIP

Remember, when you create a new image with the File, New command, you click on the Transparent option button to set up an image with a transparent background. If you scan an image or download it from a digital camera, you cannot specify a transparent background, so it's best to copy a selection from such an image, create a new image with a transparent background, and then paste the copied selection into it.

Using Save As

You can use the Save As command on the File menu to save an image in the common Web graphic formats. When you use the Save As command and choose one of the Web file formats, you'll be prompted to make various changes depending on the selected format.

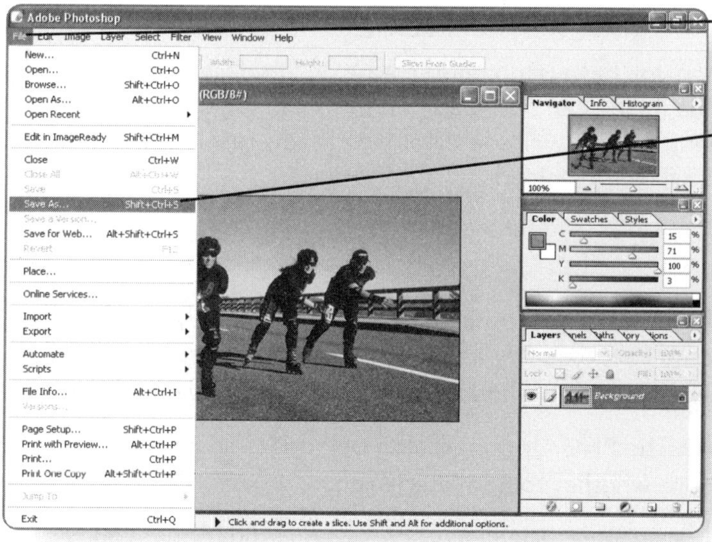

1. **Click** on **File**. The File menu will appear.

2. **Click** on **Save As**. The Save As dialog box will open.

3. **Type** a **name** for your file in the File name field. It will appear as you type.

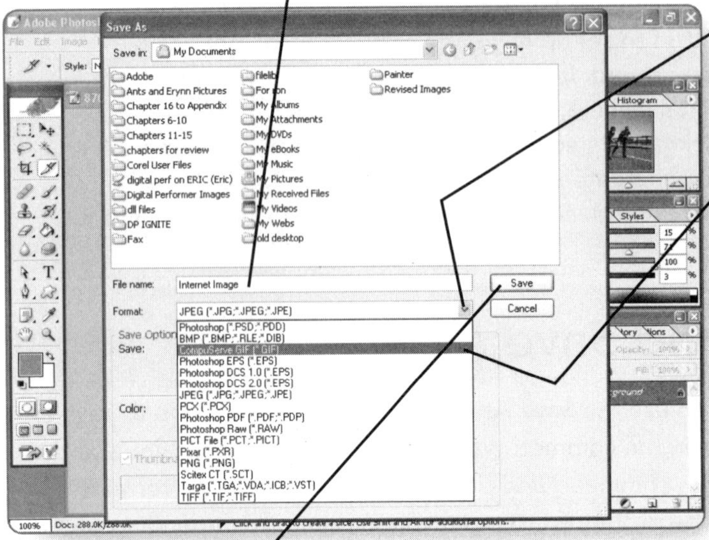

4. **Click** on the **down arrow** beside the Format field. A list of formats will appear.

5. **Click** on the desired **format** for the Web:

- **GIF.** The Indexed Color dialog box opens to specify color palette, transparency, and matte settings, and then the GIF Options dialog box opens to prompt you whether to choose an interlaced GIF format.

NOTE

When you have Photoshop create an interlaced file, part of the image can "preload" on the Web page. This means the user will see the image at low resolution until the full file downloads.

- **JPEG.** The JPEG Options dialog box opens so you can specify image quality and matte options. Transparent areas will be filled with white when you finish the save.
- **PNG.** The PNG Options dialog box opens so you can choose whether to add interlacing.

6. **Click** on **Save**. The file will be saved in the format you selected. Depending on the type of file you specified, another dialog box may open in which you can configure the settings for that type of file.

Save an Optimized Image File

To see all the settings for Web graphic file formats in a single dialog box, use the Save for Web command on the File menu. This command enables you to select a Web file format, specify settings for the format, and then proceed with the save. The rest of this section shows you how to use the Save for Web command to optimize and save a file in the three most common Web graphic formats—JPEG, GIF, and WBMP.

Saving a JPEG

These steps show you how to use the Save for Web command to save a JPEG file so that you can choose the optimum compression for your image.

1. **Click** on **File**. The File menu will appear.

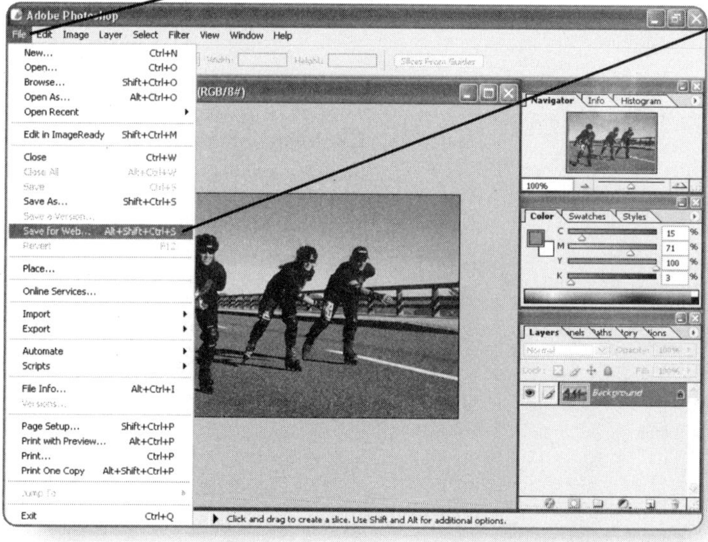

2. **Click** on **Save for Web**. The Save For Web dialog box will open with its Optimized tab selected.

3. **Click** on the **down arrow** beside the file format drop-down list and then click on JPEG. The JPEG choices will appear in the settings box.

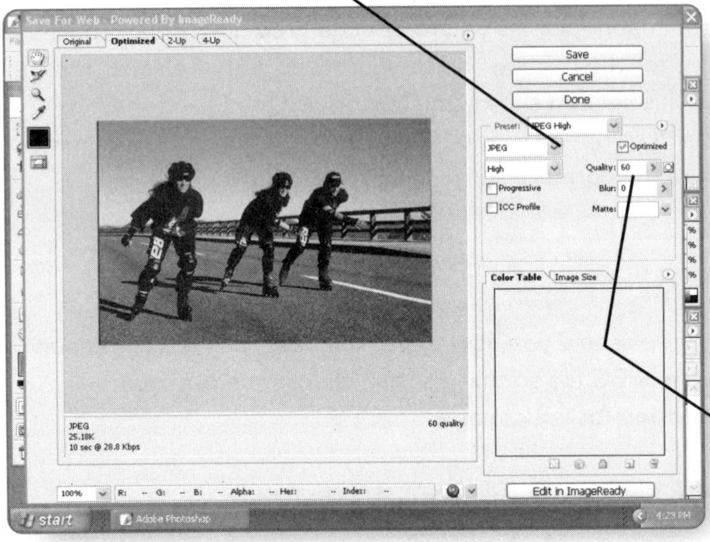

NOTE

You can use the drop-down list labeled Preset the top of the Settings box to choose a presaved set of optimization settings, such as JPEG High or GIF 32 Dithered.

4. **Type** an **image quality setting**. The higher the setting, the lower the file compression and vice versa.

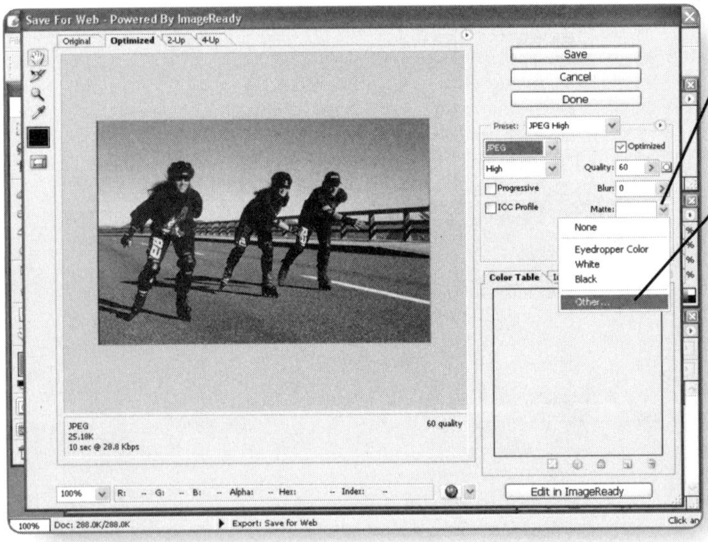

5. **Click** on the **down arrow** beside the Matte drop-down list. A menu will appear.

6. **Click** on **Other**. The Color Picker dialog box will appear so that you can use it to specify a matte for the image.

NOTE

A matte color in a GIF or PNG Web graphic helps the edges of transparent areas blend with the Web page background. In a JPEG image, it fills areas that were originally transparent with the specified color for blending.

7. **Click** on a **color hue** in the narrow band of colors near the middle of the dialog box. Photoshop will display a different range of colors in the Choose a color box.

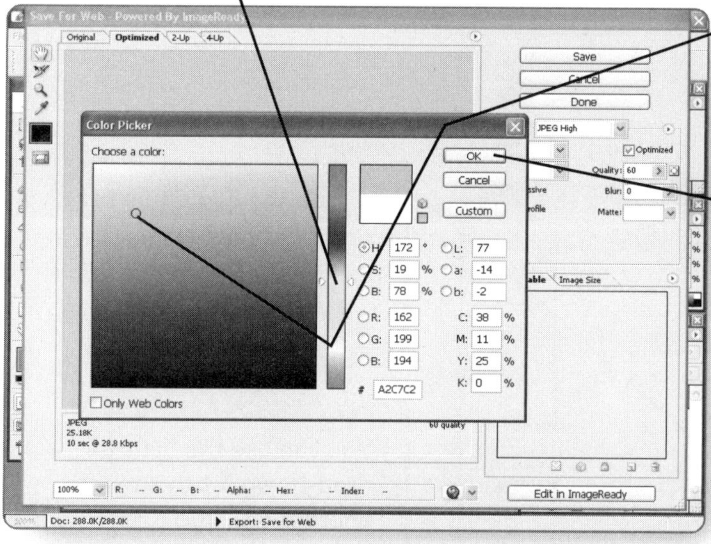

8. **Click** on a **color** in the Choose a color box. The color you click on will become the active matte color.

9. **Click** on **OK**. The Color Picker dialog box will close.

10. Click on **Save**. The Save Optimized As dialog box will appear.

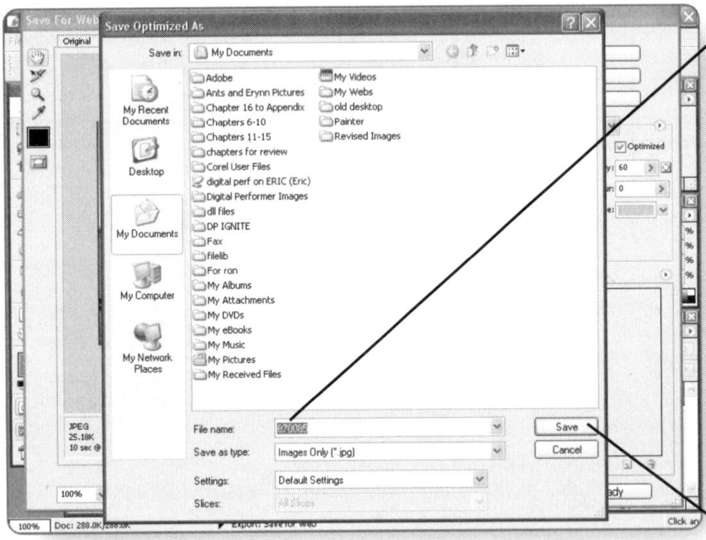

11. Edit the **File name text box** entry as necessary. The name you specify will be applied to the Web graphic file.

> **NOTE**
>
> You can use the Save In drop-down list to choose another disk and folder location for the saved file, if necessary.

12. Click on **Save**. The Save Optimized As and Save For Web dialog boxes will close. Only the original image will be open in Photoshop. You can find the new, optimized Web graphic file in the folder where you saved it.

Saving a GIF

Saving an optimized GIF file follows much the same process as saving an optimized JPEG file. Get started with the process now.

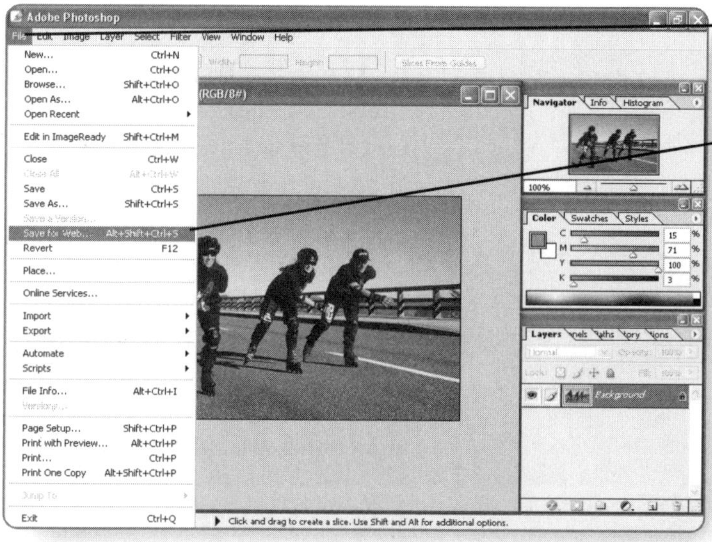

1. **Click** on **File**. The File menu will appear.

2. **Click** on **Save For Web**. The Save For Web dialog box will open with its Optimized tab selected.

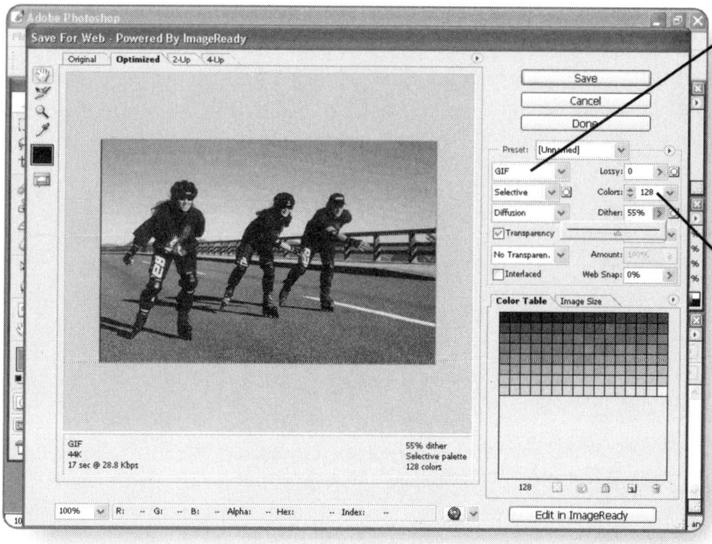

3. **Click** on the **down arrow** beside the drop-down list in the upper-left corner of the Settings box and then click on GIF. The GIF choices will appear in the Settings box.

4. **Choose image color settings**. This represents the maximum number of colors in the image.

5. Choose image dithering settings, both by choosing a dithering method from the drop-down list and by choosing the amount of dithering using the slider that appears when you click on the down arrow beside Dither. The statistics in the lower-right corner of the preview area will change to show the specified dithering method.

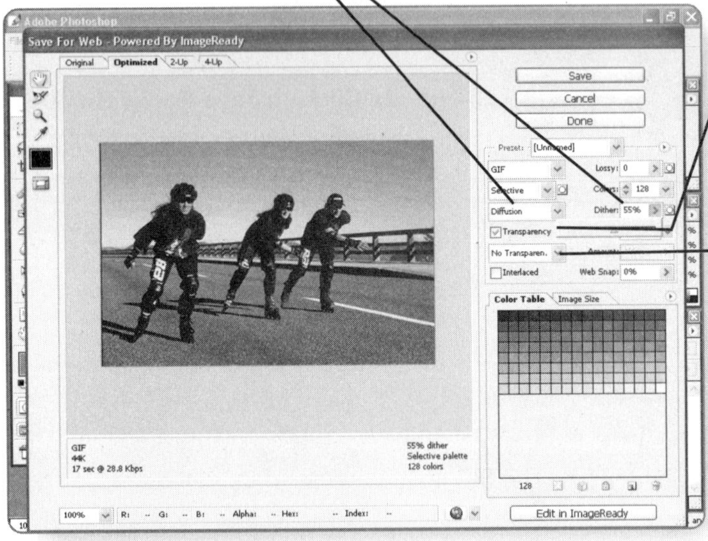

6. Leave the **Transparency check box checked**. This ensures that the transparent areas in the image will remain transparent in the final GIF file.

7. Click on the **down arrow** beside the drop-down list below the Transparency check box. A menu of transparency dithering algorithms will appear.

8. Click on the desired **algorithm**. The preview will show the impact of the selected algorithm.

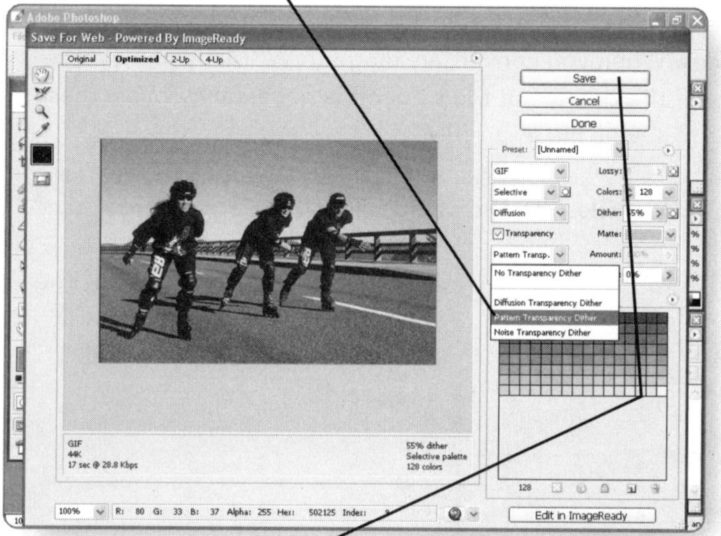

9. Click on **Save**. The Save Optimized As dialog box will open.

NOTE

Specifying the transparency dither algorithm will be necessary for images with semitransparent areas, such as gradients or bleeds.

You also can add a matte for the GIF, but it won't be as obvious in the preview. That's because the matte for a GIF image serves more as a blending zone between the image content and the Web page background.

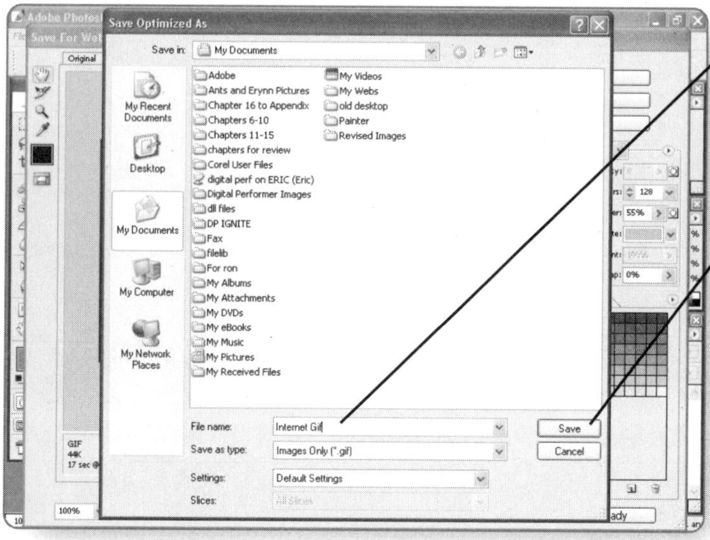

10. Edit the **File name text box entry** as necessary. The name you specify will be applied to the Web graphic file.

11. Click on **Save**. The Save Optimized As and Save For Web dialog boxes will close. Only the original image will be open in Photoshop. You can find the new, optimized Web graphic file in the folder where you saved it.

Saving a WBMP

As noted earlier in this chapter, a WBMP file is a black-and-white file created specifically for wireless (and handheld) devices. When you convert an image to WBMP, you may lose some of the detail, but the tradeoff is necessary. Follow these steps to save a file as a WBMP file.

1. **Click** on **File**. The File menu will appear.

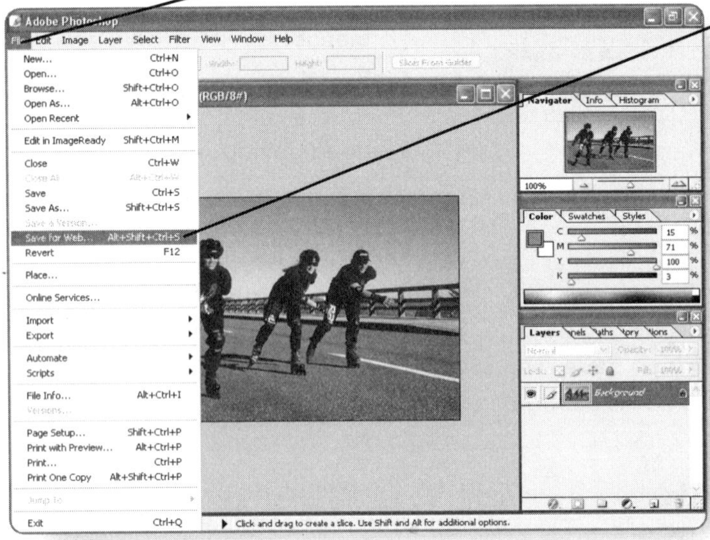

2. **Click** on **Save for Web**. The Save For Web dialog box will open with its Optimized tab selected.

3. **Click** on the **down arrow** beside the drop-down list and then click on WBMP. The WBMP choices will appear in the Settings box.

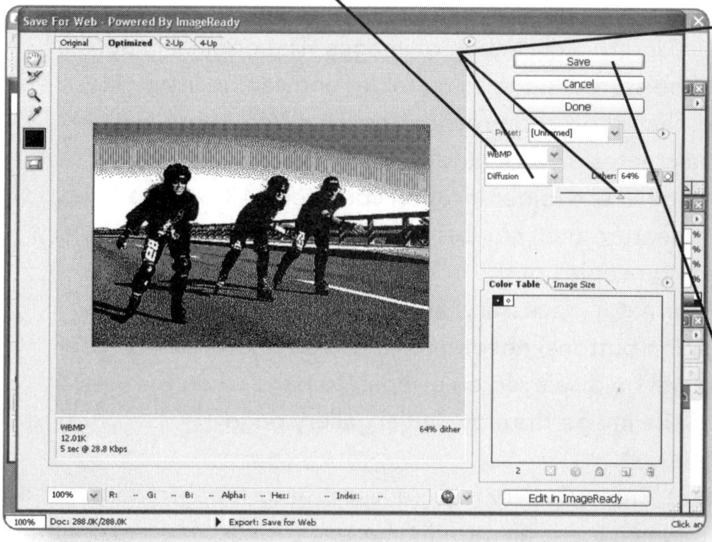

4. **Choose** image **dithering settings**, both by choosing a dithering method setting from the drop-down list on the left and by choosing the amount of dithering using the Dither choice on the right. The statistic in the lower-right corner of the preview area will change to show the specified dithering method.

5. **Click** on **Save**. The Save Optimized As dialog box will open.

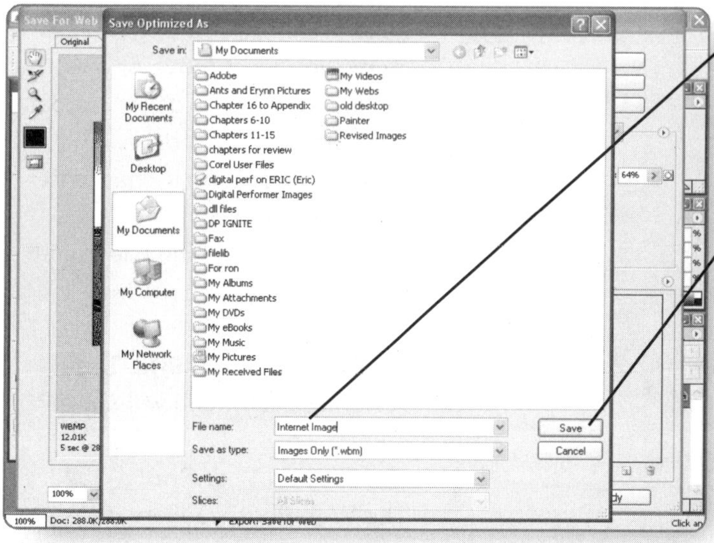

6. **Edit** the **File name text box entry** as necessary. The name you specify will be applied to the Web graphic file.

7. **Click** on **Save**. The Save Optimized As and Save For Web dialog boxes will close. Only the original image will be open in Photoshop. You can find the new, optimized Web graphic file in the folder where you saved it.

Setting Up a Web Photo Gallery

The Web Photo Gallery feature enables you to create a Web page linking to a collection of images. The original images all should be stored in the same folder and can be in any file format that Photoshop recognizes. The Web Photo Gallery feature creates a Web page named index.htm and stores that Web page in the folder location you specify. The Web Photo Gallery feature then creates a subfolder named images, which holds large copies of the original image files (converted to JPEG format, if necessary) as well as other images (such as navigation buttons) needed for the Web photo gallery. Each image will be displayed on a separate page when the viewer selects the image from the initial gallery page.

The Web Photo Gallery feature also creates a subfolder named pages, which holds an .htm file for each image. The index.htm file has a link to each of these .htm files. Finally, a newthumbnails subfolder holds a smaller version of each image in the gallery for display on the index.htm page. Follow these steps to create a basic Web photo gallery. Before you begin these steps, you must move or copy the images for the gallery into a single folder in Windows. The images will appear in that folder.

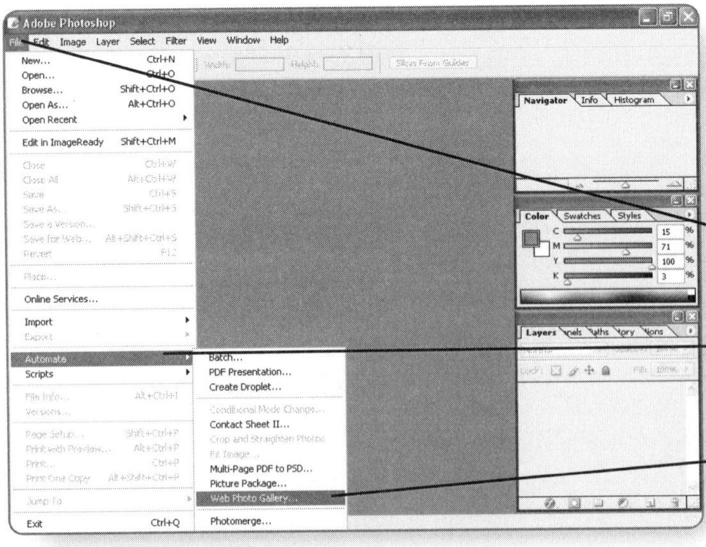

1. **Click** on **File**. The File menu will appear.

2. **Point** to **Automate**. The Automate submenu will appear.

3. **Click** on **Web Photo Gallery**. The Web Photo Gallery dialog box will open.

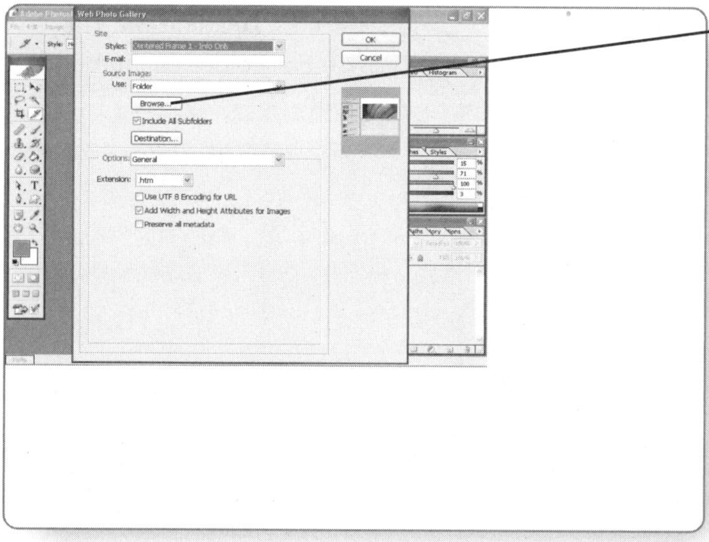

4. **Click** on **Browse**. The Browse For Folder dialog box will open.

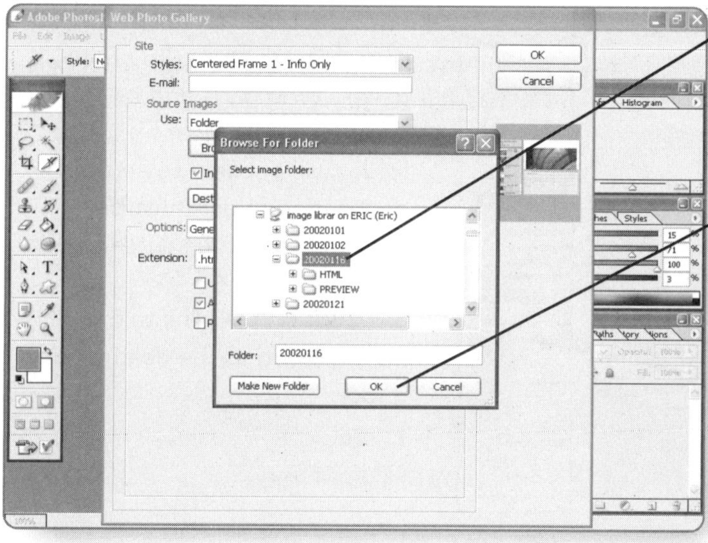

5. **Select** the **folder** that holds the images to include in the photo gallery. The folder will become selected.

6. **Click** on **OK**. The folder will be displayed as the source folder.

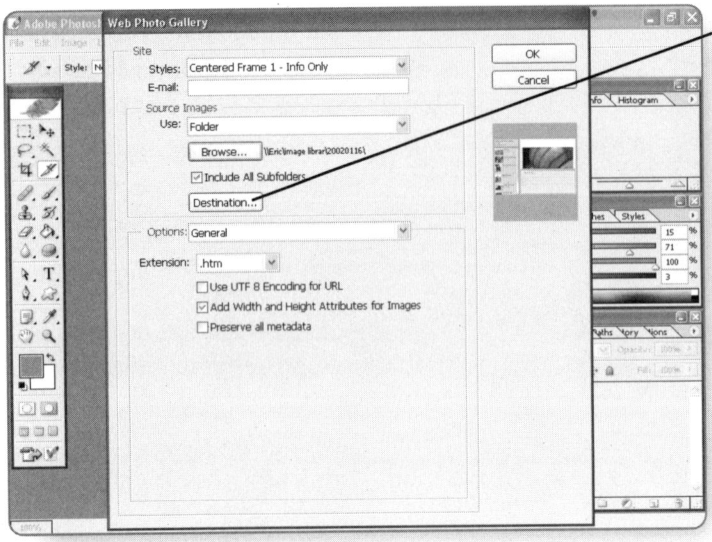

7. **Click** on **Destination**. The Browse For Folder dialog box will open.

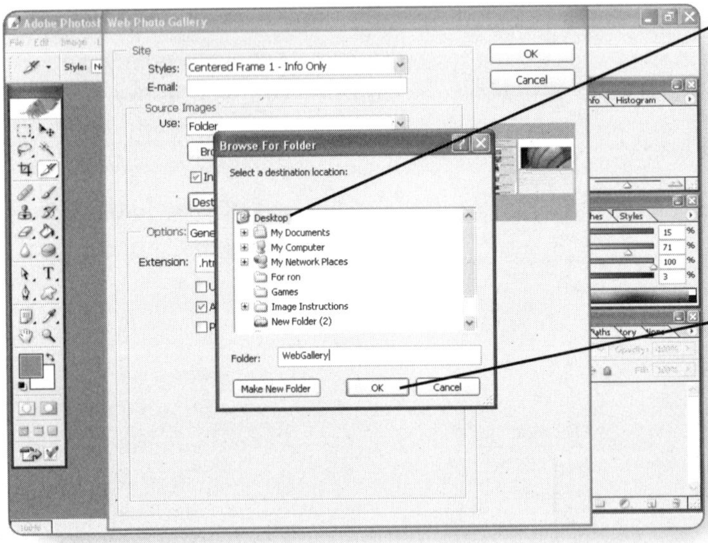

8. **Select** the **folder** where you would like to store the photo gallery Web page and its subfolders of source files. The folder will become selected. The destination folder must be different from the source folder.

9. **Click** on **OK**. The folder will be displayed as the destination folder.

10. **Click** the **down arrow** beside the Styles field to choose from a variety of different templates.

11. **Click** on the desired **template**. It will be selected, and a preview of the template will appear in the dialog box.

12. **Click** on **OK**. Photoshop will generate the Web Photo Gallery, launch your Web browser, and display the initial page. The page will show thumbnail images.

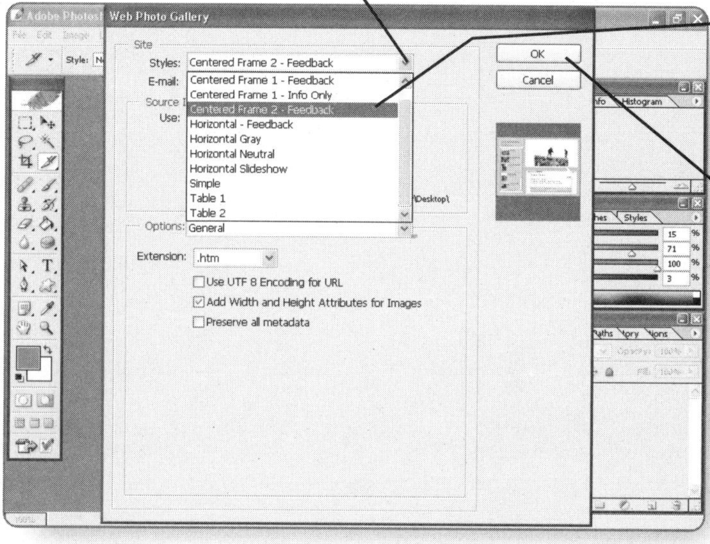

13. **Click** on an **image link** or **thumbnail**. The Web Photo Gallery page for that image will open. From this point, you can continue browsing images in the gallery or close your Web browser.

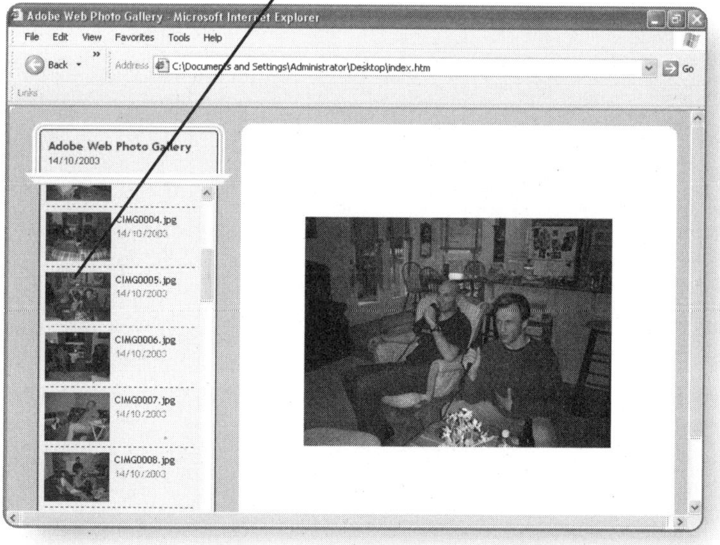

NOTE

If you move or copy the Web Photo Gallery to another location, you must move all the elements—the index.htm file, the images folder, the pages folder, and the thumbnails folder.

21

Adding Hotspots

Web browsing hinges on the ability to navigate by following links. You can use the Slice tool to identify areas for linking in an image and then save that image as a Web (HTML) file so that an image with the links can be incorporated into an overall Web site. This chapter introduces you to the basics of the slice feature. You'll learn how to:

- Add a slice and set its options
- Work with existing slices
- Save the sliced image in HTML format

Adding Slices or "Hotspots"

The Slice tool on the Photoshop toolbox adds slices into an image file, dividing your images into various sections. By then specifying the slice options, you create a link to a particular Web address called a URL (*Uniform Resource Locator*). After you save the image as an HTML file (as described in the final section of this chapter, "Saving the Sliced File in HTML"), users can click on the area defined by the slice to follow the link. That's why such linked areas are called "hotspots." The steps that follow explain how to add a slice and set it up as a hotspot, after you've performed all the necessary edits in Photoshop.

1. **Click** on the **Slice tool** in the toolbox. The Slice tool will become active.

2. **Drag** on the **image** to define the slice. (You don't really need to select a layer first.) When you release the mouse button, the new slice will appear. The slice appears as a box.

3. **Double-click** on the **slice number** for the new slice. The Slice Options dialog box will open.

NOTE

In addition to the slice you drew, called a user slice, Photoshop divides the rest of the image into slices called auto slices. Typically, Photoshop draws vertical slice lines continuing from one or both corners of the slice you drew, depending on its location. It also may draw horizontal slice lines from the top or bottom of the slice.

4. **Specify options**, as follows:

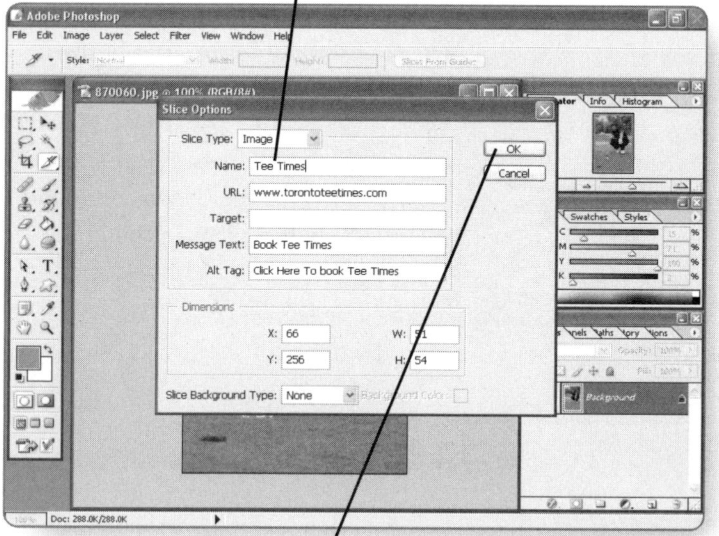

- **URL.** Enter the URL for the Web page that will appear when the user clicks on the hotspot. To enter an absolute address (not just a relative address on the server holding the page), be sure to include http:// at the start of your entry.
- **Target.** Specify the frame in which the linked page will appear, if applicable. (Consult the Help system for your Web authoring software to learn more about working with frames.)
- **Message Text.** Enter more descriptive information about the linked Web page. The description will appear in the Web browser status bar when the user hovers the mouse pointer over the hotspot.
- **Alt Tag.** Enter a description to appear in place of the image content if the page is displayed in a nongraphical Web browser.

5. **Click** on **OK**. The Slice Options dialog box will close, and the specified settings will be applied to the slice.

Viewing and Hiding Slices

If it so happens that you need to make further edits to the sliced image before you save it as an HTML file, you can hide the slice lines so that they won't distract you. Then you can redisplay the slices later as necessary.

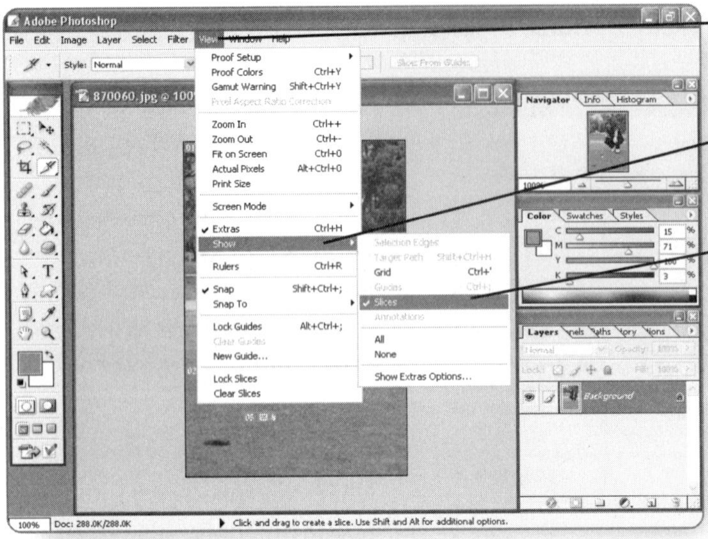

1. **Click** on **View**. The View menu will appear.

2. **Point** to **Show**. The Show submenu will appear.

3. **Click** on **Slices**. Photoshop will uncheck the Slices command and hide the slices in the image file.

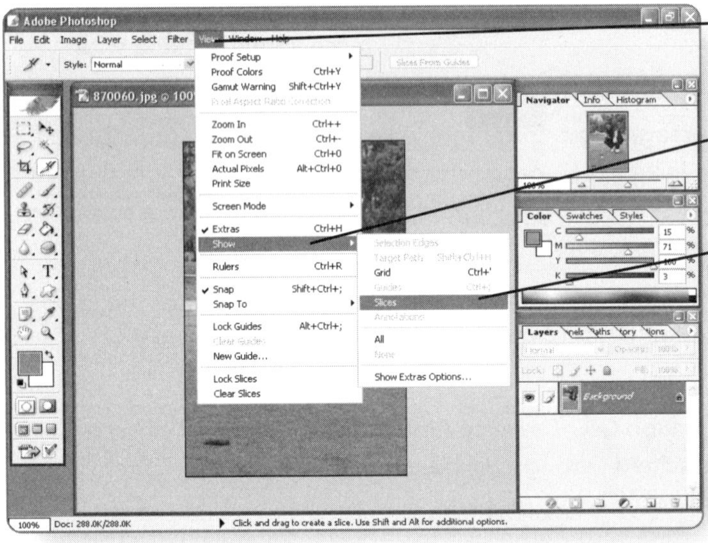

4. **Click** on **View**. The View menu will appear.

5. **Point** to **Show**. The Show submenu will appear.

6. **Click** on **Slices**. Photoshop will check the Slices command and redisplay the slices in the image file.

NOTE

If you need to resize a slice, click and hold the Slice tool and then click on Slice Select Tool in the shortcut menu that appears. Then drag the corner of the slice area to resize it.

Saving the Sliced File in HTML

When you need to save the sliced file in HTML format, use the Save for Web command on the File menu, as demonstrated here.

1. **Click** on **File**. The File menu will appear.

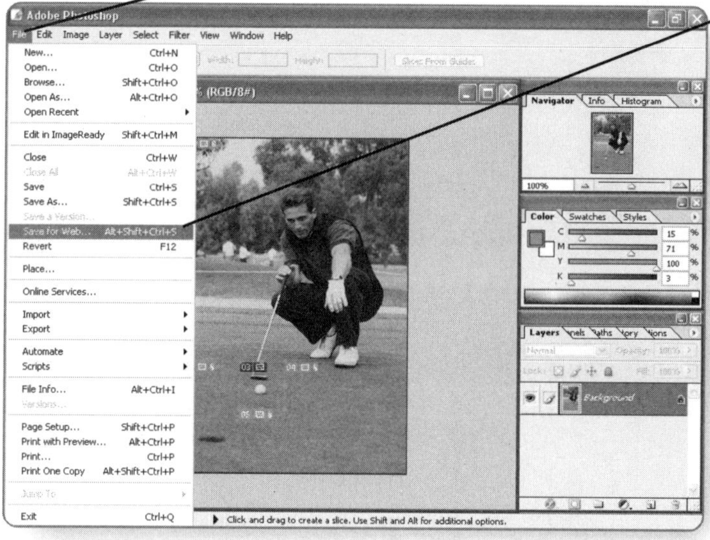

2. **Click** on **Save for Web**. The Save For Web dialog box will open, with its Optimized tab selected.

> **TIP**
>
> If you previously used the Save For Web command to save a JPEG or GIF image and specified a matte, you're going to want to be sure to remove that matte color. Click on the Optimize menu button (the round button with the arrow on it) in the Save For Web dialog box and then click on Edit Output Settings in the menu. Open the drop-down list that has HTML selected in it by default and then click on Background. Open the Color drop-down list, click on None, and then click on OK to return to the Save For Web dialog box.

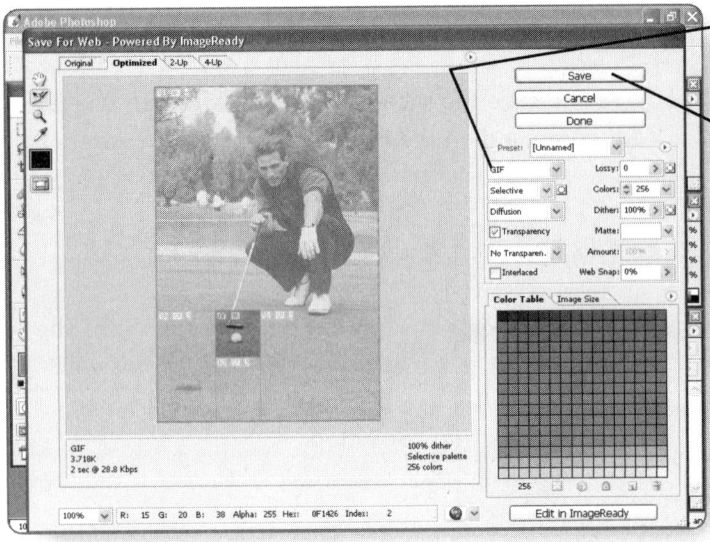

3. Click the desired **Optimized file format**. It will be selected.

4. Click on **Save**. The Save Optimized As dialog box will open.

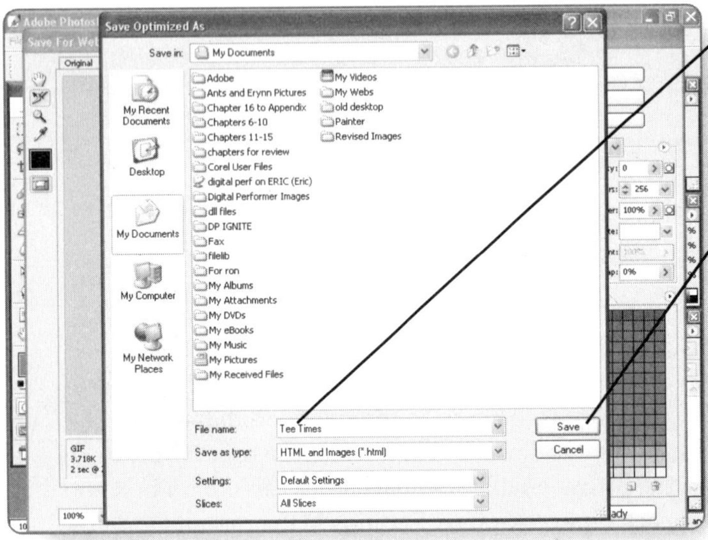

5. Edit the **File name text box entry** as necessary. The name you specify will be applied to the HTML file.

6. Click on **Save**. The Save Optimized As and Save For Web dialog boxes will close. Only the original image will be open in Photoshop. You can find the new HTML file in the folder where you saved it.

TIP

Use the File, Open command in your Web browser to open and preview the new HTML file. (Note that you can use Save As to resave the file using the shorter .htm extension instead.) You can even click on the hotspot to test the link. When you copy or move the Web page, be sure to copy or move the accompanying images folder created by the HTML saving process. That folder holds the actual sliced image content.

22

Getting Help

The goal of this book is to give you a solid foundation in Photoshop so that you can begin the process of creating your digital masterpieces. Photoshop is an enormous application with thousands of different commands and features geared toward specific uses and users. If you need answers to questions that are beyond the scope of this book, Photoshop CS provides you with a variety of tools for getting help. In this chapter, you'll learn how to:

- Use the new Welcome Screen
- Access the Help index
- Search for topic-specific help
- Use and create How To's

The Welcome Screen

New to Photoshop CS is a Welcome Screen that provides you with a variety of options for getting help. When you launch Photoshop, the Welcome Screen appears before you can begin working in the program. The Welcome Screen also can be opened at any time using the Help menu.

1. **Click** on **Start** at the left end of the Windows Taskbar. The Start menu will appear. If you are using Mac OS, find the Photoshop icon and double-click on it to launch the program.

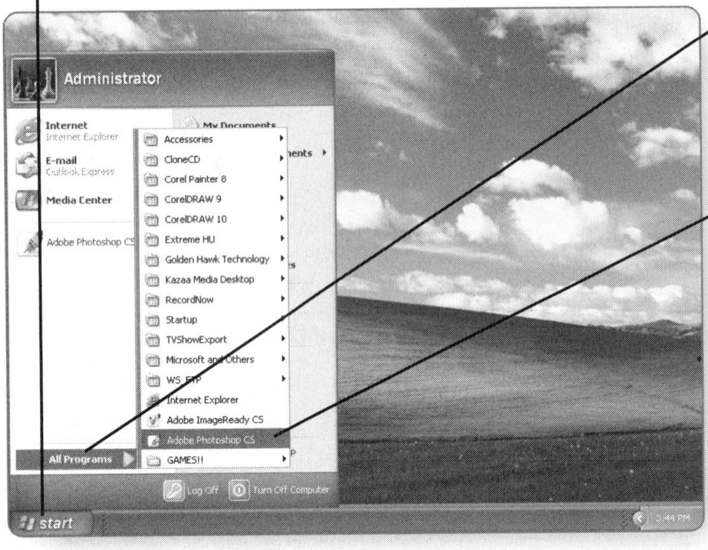

2. Place the mouse pointer over All Programs (or Programs for Windows versions prior to XP). The Programs menu will appear.

3. **Click** on **Adobe Photoshop CS**. The new Photoshop CS Welcome Screen will appear.

TIP

If you don't want the Welcome Screen to appear whenever you start Photoshop CS, uncheck the box in the lower-left corner of the Welcome Screen entitled Show this dialog at startup.

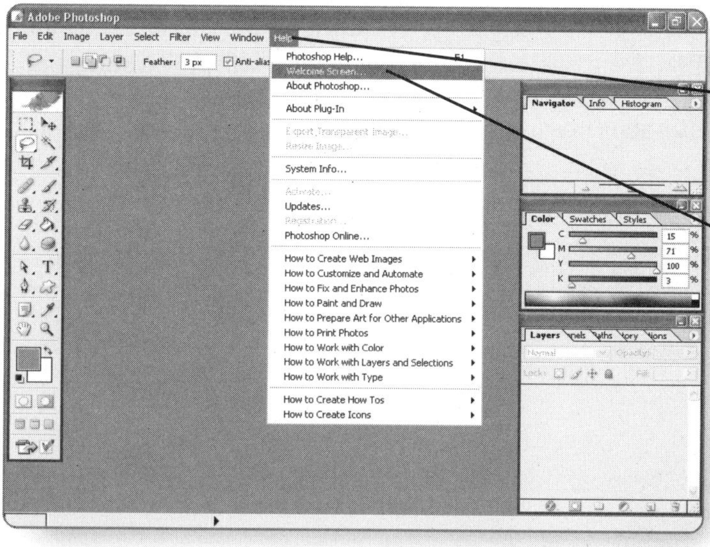

or

1. **Click** on **Help** from within Photoshop. The Help menu will appear.

2. **Click** on **Welcome Screen.** The Welcome Screen will open.

Using the Welcome Screen Tutorials

Photoshop CS comes with six project tutorials that cover certain common tasks like removing red eyes from a photograph or correcting image levels.

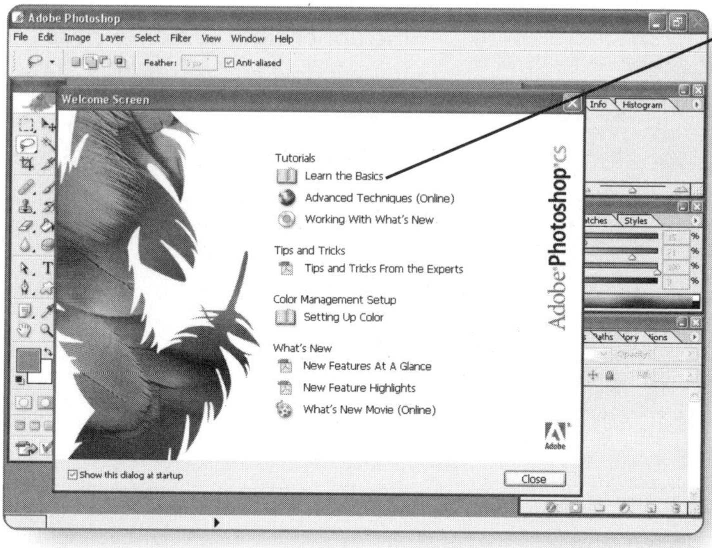

1. **Click** on **Learn the Basics.** Your Internet browser program will launch.

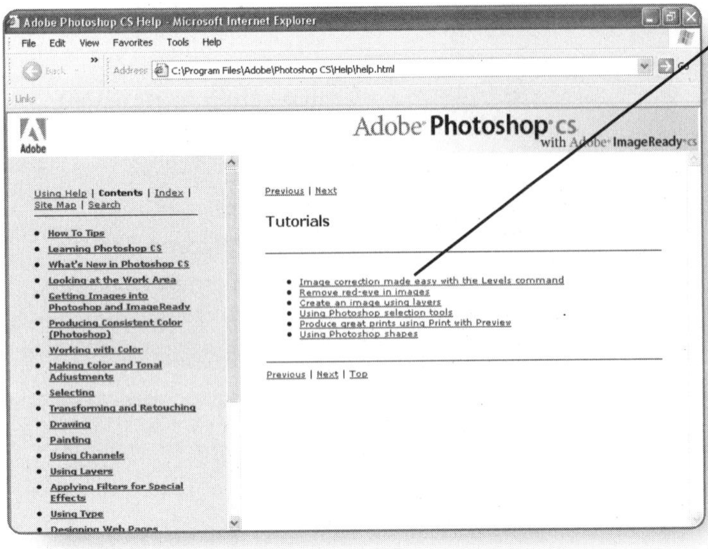

2. Click on the desired **tutorial**. The window will now display the steps for that tutorial.

3. Scroll through the **steps** to follow the tutorial. You can drag the scroll box or click on the scroll buttons to move through the topic.

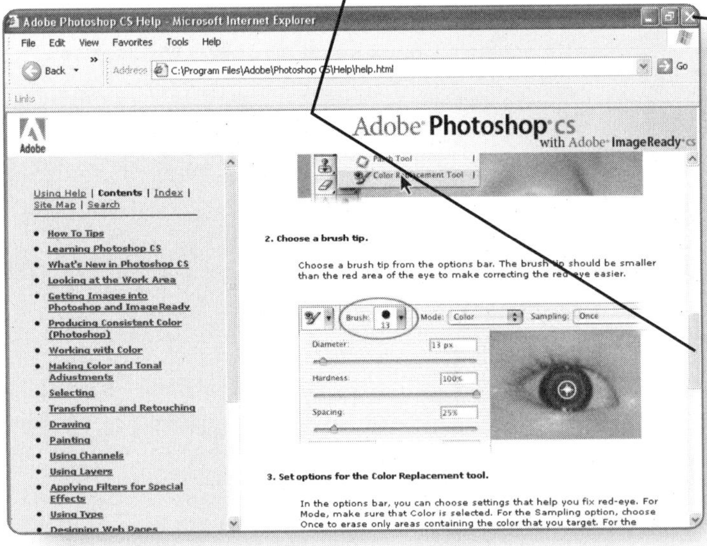

4. Click on the **close button** in the upper-right corner to close the window and return to Photoshop.

Watching Tutorial Movies

Adobe provides a Web site that contains tutorials in the form of movies for a variety of advanced topics. This Web site is constantly being updated, so the tutorials found there may change from time to time. You can access these tutorials directly from the Welcome Screen.

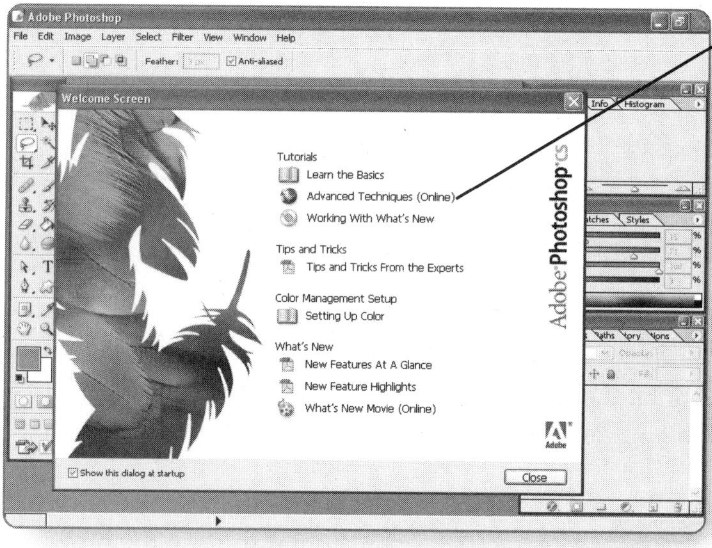

1. Click on **Advanced Techniques (Online)**. Your Internet browser program will launch.

> **NOTE**
>
> You must be connected to the Internet to take advantage of this feature.

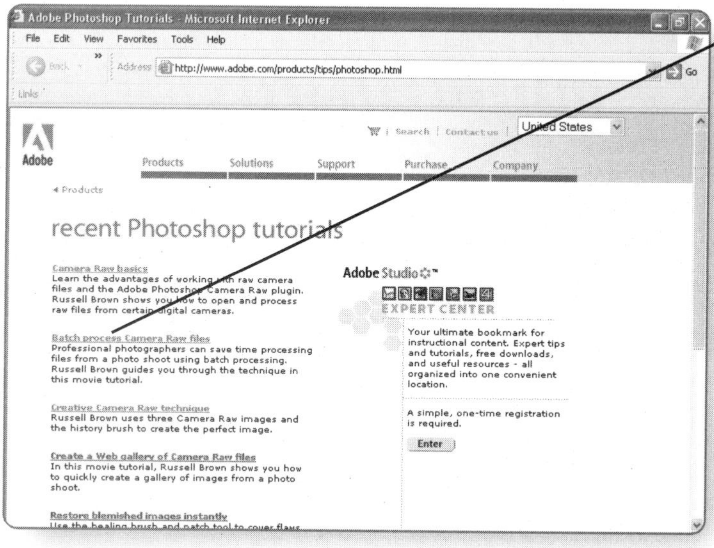

2. Click on the desired **tutorial**. The window will now change to give you a full description of the tutorial.

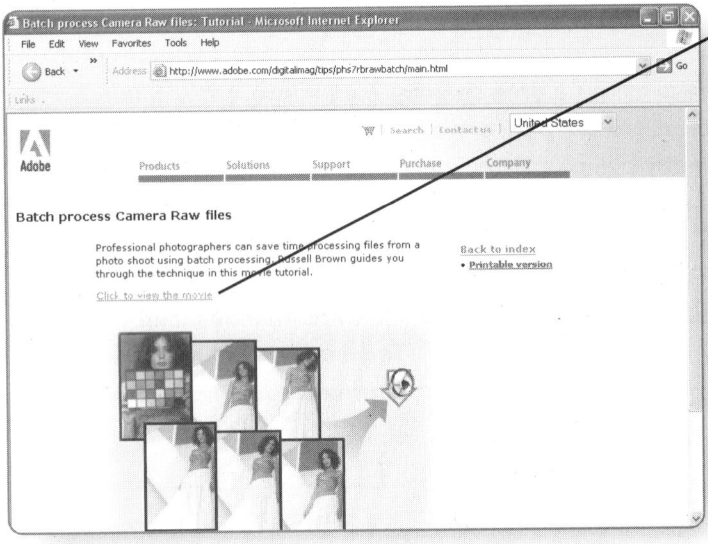

3. Click on the **Click to view the movie link**. A new window will launch, and the tutorial will begin playing.

You must have the QuickTime plug-in installed on your Internet browser to watch the tutorial movies.

4. Click on the **x** in the upper-right corner of the window to close the movie.

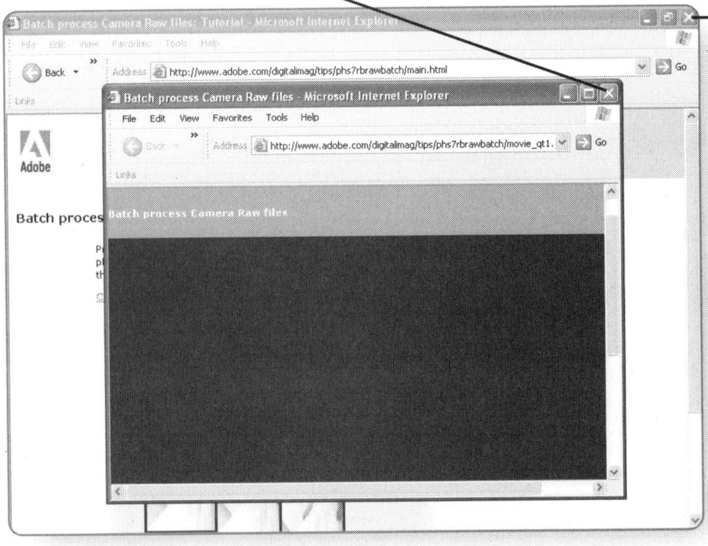

5. Click on the **x** in the upper-right corner to close the browser window and return to Photoshop.

Tips and Tricks

Photoshop CS comes with a PDF (*Portable Document Format*) file that contains a variety of tips, tricks, and projects that you can take advantage of.

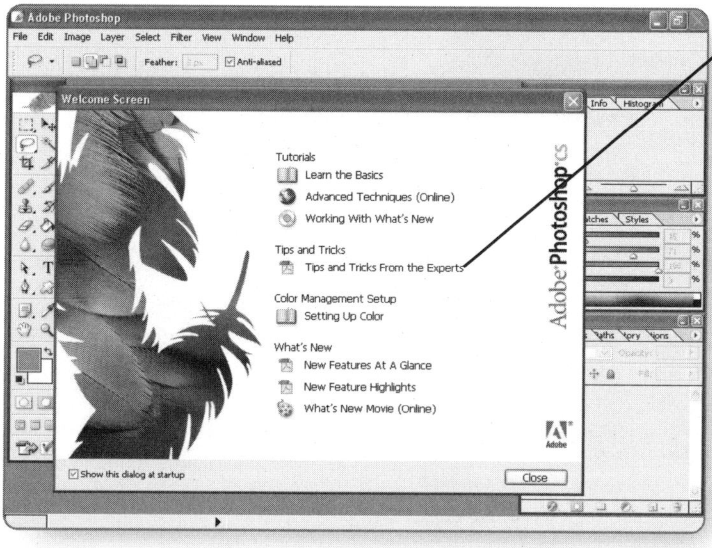

1. **Click** on **Tips and Tricks From the Experts**. Adobe Acrobat Reader will open.

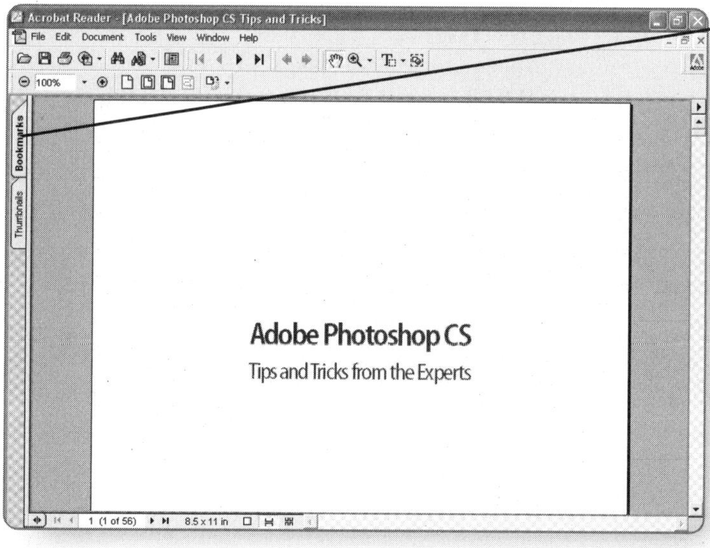

2. **Click** on the **Bookmarks** tab if it is not already selected. The Bookmarks window will open.

3. **Click** on the desired **tutorial**. It will be selected, and the tutorial will appear in the window.

4. **Scroll through** the **steps** of the tutorial. You can drag the scroll box or click on the scroll buttons to move through the topic.

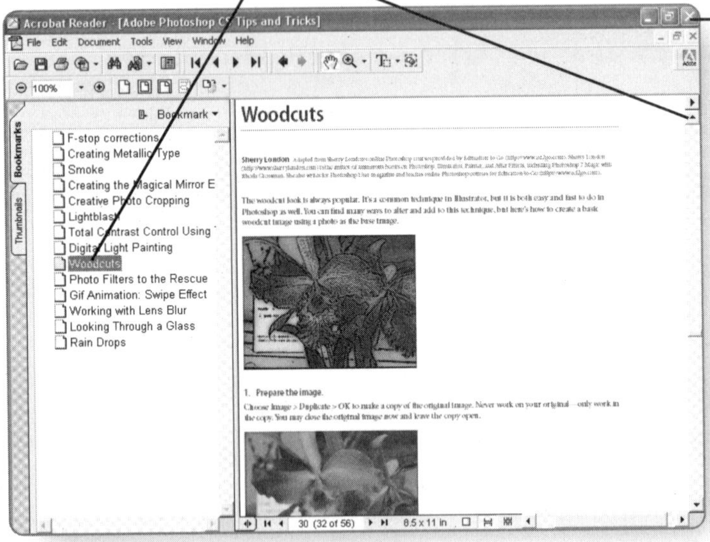

5. **Click** on the **x** in the upper-right corner of the Acrobat window to close the file and return to Photoshop.

Color Management Help

Color management is an integral part of image design and output. In a nutshell, color management is the process of matching the appearance of colors on all your devices. In other words, it's making sure that the colors you see on your screen match the colors on your printed output. Although specific programs and hardware devices are designed for professional designers and printers to calibrate their equipment, Photoshop has a variety of tools to help with the color management process. Getting help with color management is available directly through the Welcome Screen.

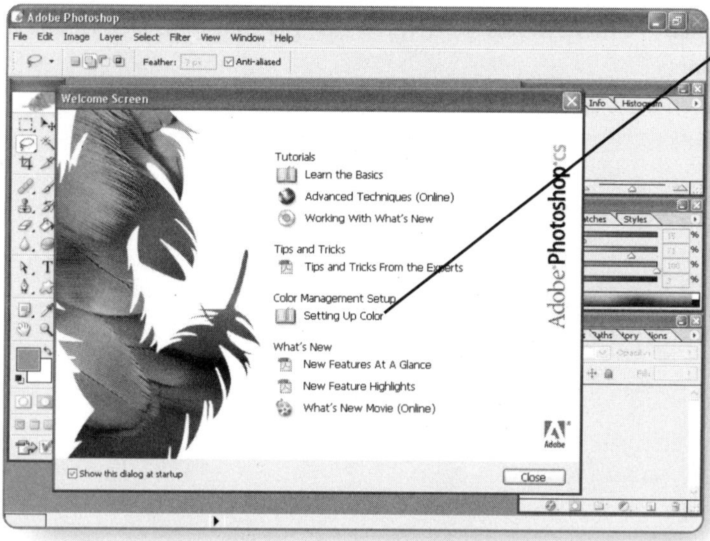

1. Click on **Setting Up Color**. Your Internet browser program will launch.

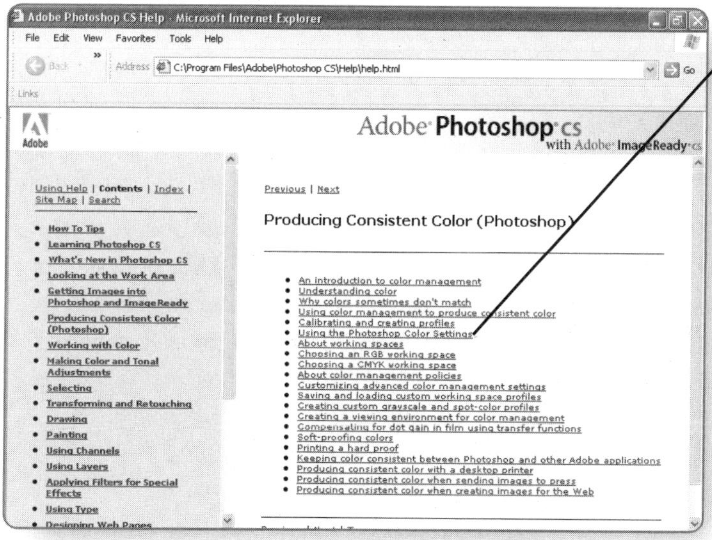

2. Click on the desired **color management topic**. The topic help will open in the window.

3. **Read** the **instructions** for the help topic you have selected.

4. **Click** on one of the **navigational links** at the bottom of the page.

5. **Click** on the **x** in the upper-right corner to close the window and return to Photoshop.

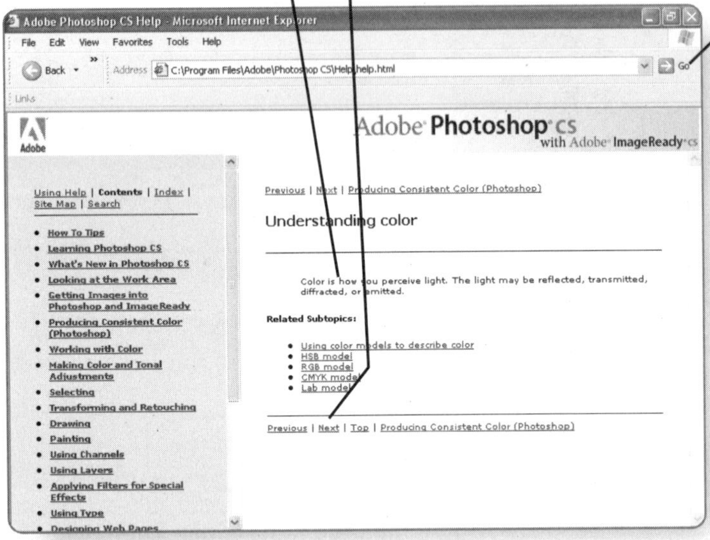

Photoshop Help

Photoshop has a comprehensive help document built directly into the program. The help files are actually HTML documents that are viewed from your Internet browser. Because these files reside on your computer, you don't have to be online to view them.

Accessing Help

Some of the help files in Photoshop can be accessed through the Welcome Screen, as you learned earlier. The Help menu serves as a central location for you to find help on almost every Photoshop topic.

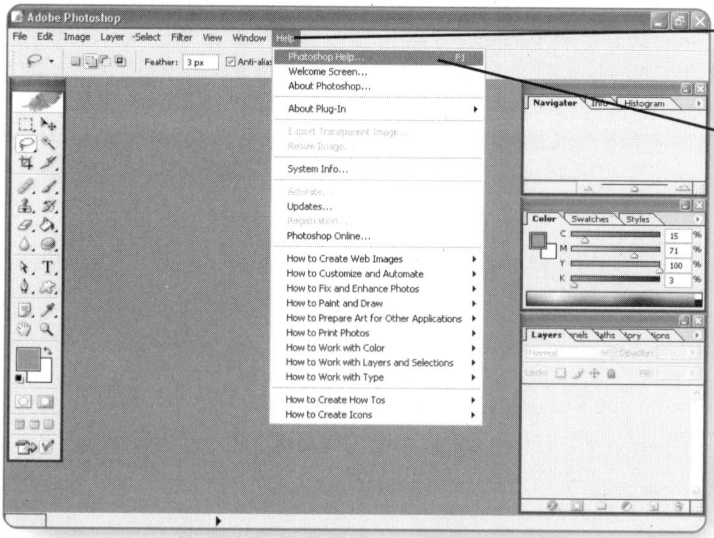

1. Click on **Help**. The Help menu will appear.

2. Click on **Photoshop Help**. Your Internet browser program will launch with the Adobe help file.

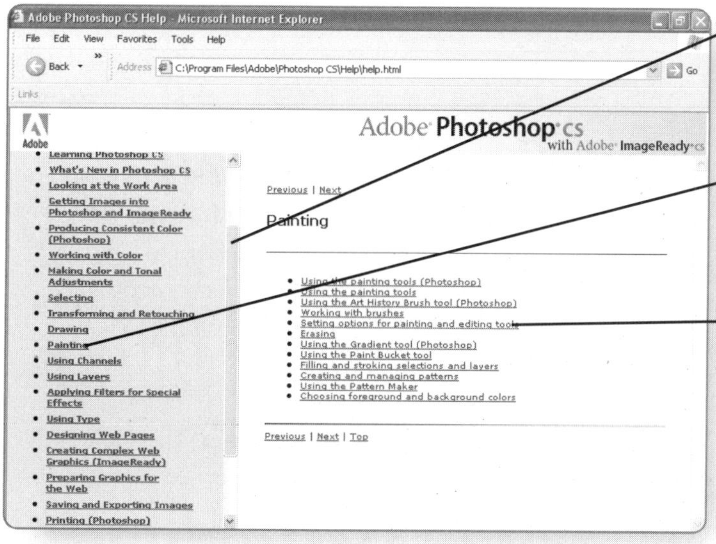

3. Scroll through the various **topics**. You can drag the scroll bar or use the scroll buttons.

4. Click on the desired **topic**. The help topics relating to the topic you selected will appear.

5. Click on the desired **topic**. The help associated with that topic will appear in the window.

6. Click on the desired **navigation control** at the bottom of the window.

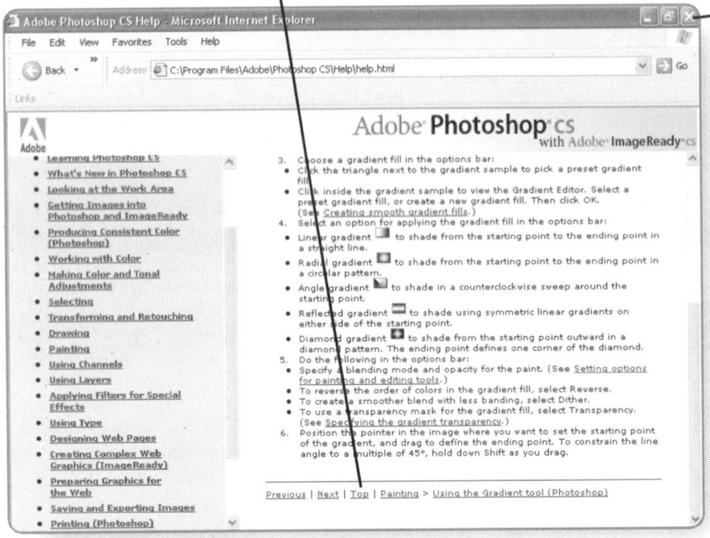

7. Click on the **close button** in the upper-right corner to close the window and return to Photoshop.

The Help Index

If you wanted to access a specific topic in this book, you'd probably turn to the back, open the index, and find the topic you are looking for. The same holds true with help in Photoshop. You can access the index to get a complete list of help topics.

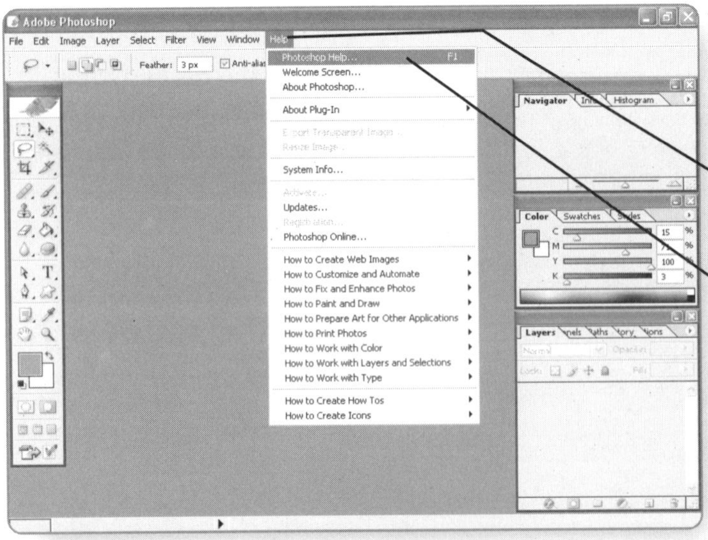

1. Click on **Help**. The Help menu will appear.

2. Click on **Photoshop Help**. Your Internet browser program will launch with the Adobe help file.

3. **Click** on **Index**. An alphabetical list of all of the help files will appear.

4. **Click** on a **letter** to jump to topics that begin with that letter.

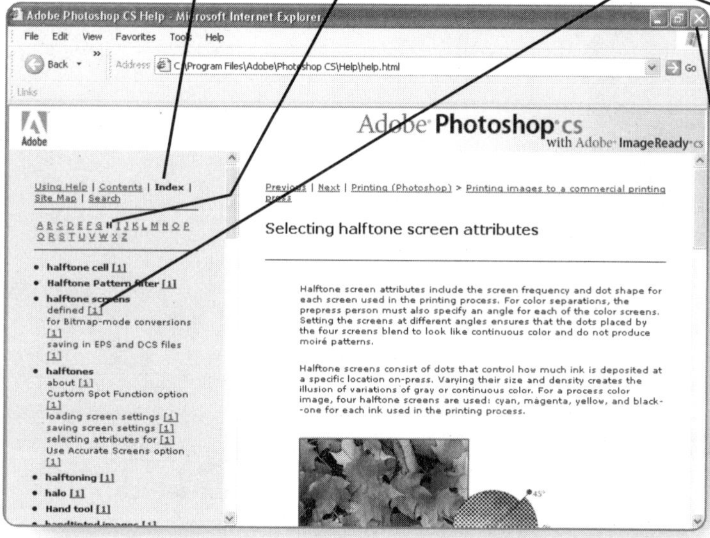

5. **Click** on the **number** beside the help topic you would like to view. The topic will appear in the window. Topics with multiple numbers beside them indicate that more than one help option is available.

6. **Click** on the **close button** in the upper-right corner to close the window and return to Photoshop.

Searching for Help

Rather than having to sort through the index to find help, you can search for particular topics. In your search, you can either use keywords or ask a question.

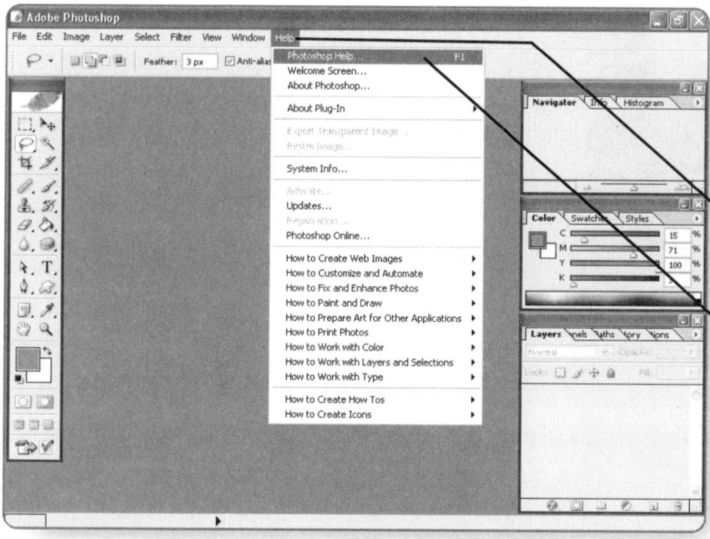

1. **Click** on **Help**. The Help menu will appear.

2. **Click** on **Photoshop Help**. Your Internet browser program will launch with the Adobe help file.

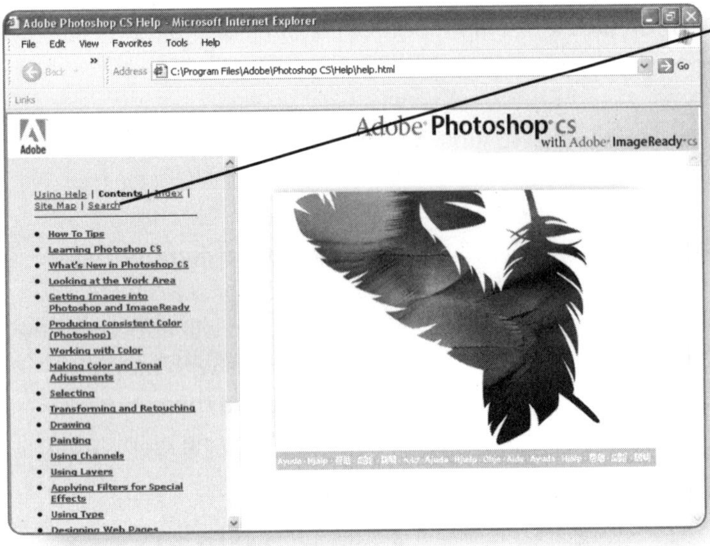

3. Click on **Search**. A text box will appear where you can enter your search.

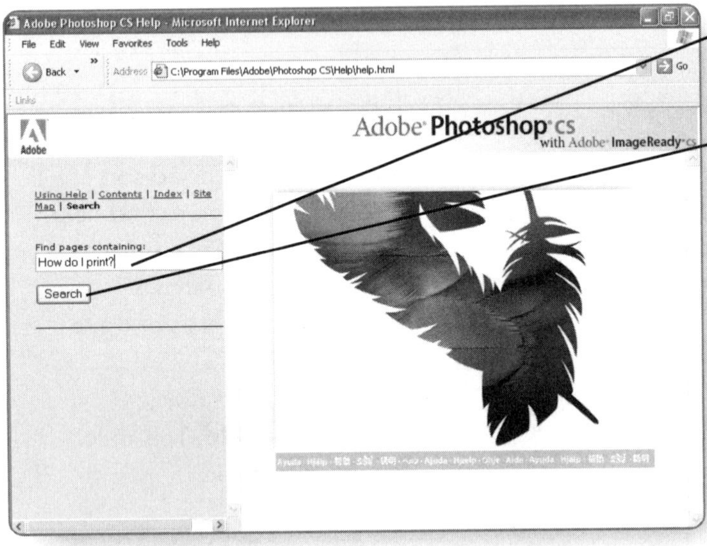

4. Type the **keywords** or **question** for your search.

5. Click on the **Search button**. The Search will be conducted, and topics matching your search criteria will appear below the search button.

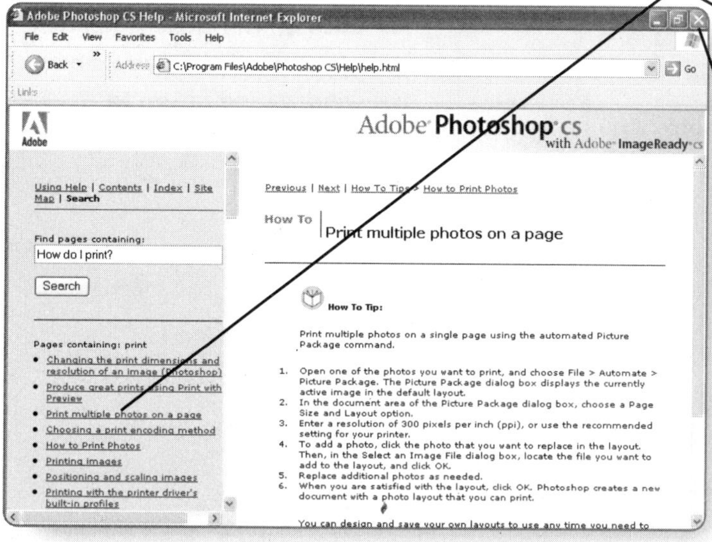

6. **Click** on the desired **topic**. Its contents will appear in the window.

7. **Click** on the **close button** in the upper-right corner to close the window and return to Photoshop.

How To's

Within the Help menu, there are a variety of How To options that allow you to jump to certain help topics that cover commonly asked questions. Not only can you access these How To's, you can also create your own.

Accessing How To's

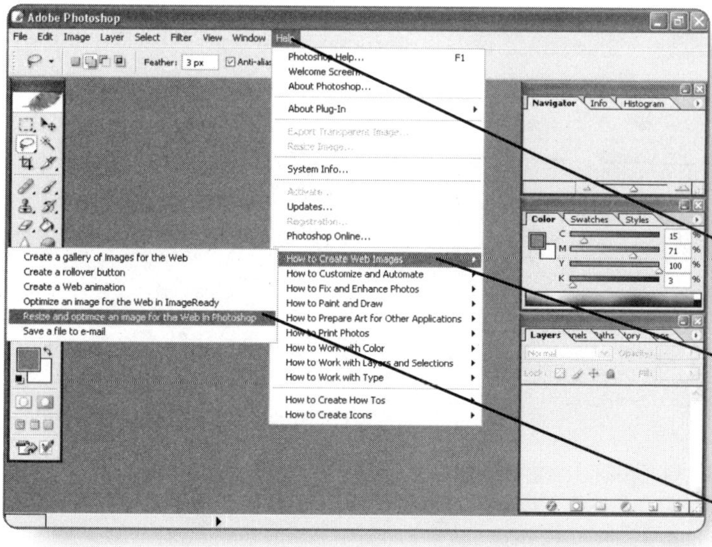

Accessing a How To is simply a matter of clicking on the desired category and then selecting the specific help file.

1. **Click** on **Help**. The Help menu will appear.

2. **Point** to the desired **How To category**. A submenu will appear.

3. **Click** on the desired **How To topic**. The help file will launch in your Internet Browser.

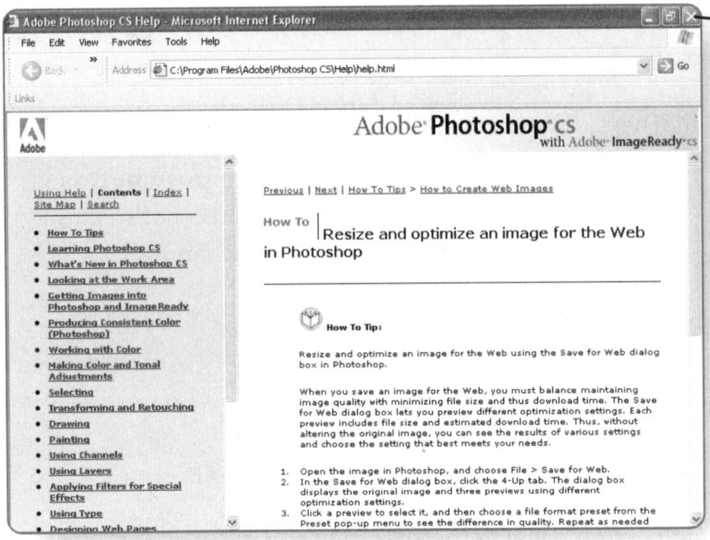

4. **Click** on the **close button** in the upper-right corner to close the window and return to Photoshop.

Creating How To's

Because the help files in Photoshop CS are HTML files, you can create your own categories and topics of How To's. Because so many resources are available on the Web for Photoshop, you can copy the HTML code from one of these pages and create your own How To. Alternatively, you can have your How To link to a specific Web page.

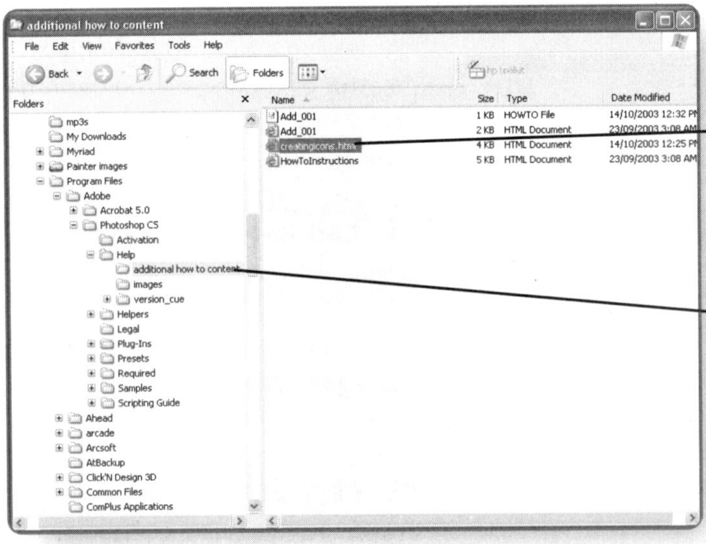

1. **Create** your **HTML file** by either creating one from scratch or copying it from an existing site.

2. **Save** your **HTML file** to the folder \PhotoshopCS\Help\Additional How To Content.

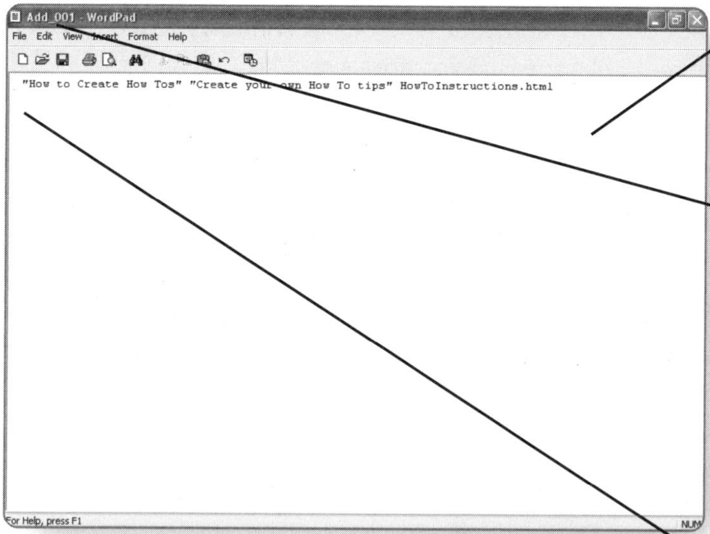

3. **Open** a **text editor**. You can use any text editor that comes with your computer, including Notepad, Write, or WordPad.

4. **Open** the file **Add_001.howto** in your text editor. The file can be found in the folder \PhotoshopCS\Help\Additional How To Content\. Depending on the text editor you have selected, there will be different methods for opening the file.

5. **Click** on a **new line**. The insertion point will be flashing.

6. **Type** the following, including the quotation marks: **"How To Category" "My How To Topic" myfile.html**. (Replace How To Category with the actual category you would like to create. Replace My How To Topic with the actual topic you'd like to create. Replace myfile.html with the name of the HTML file you saved in step 2.)

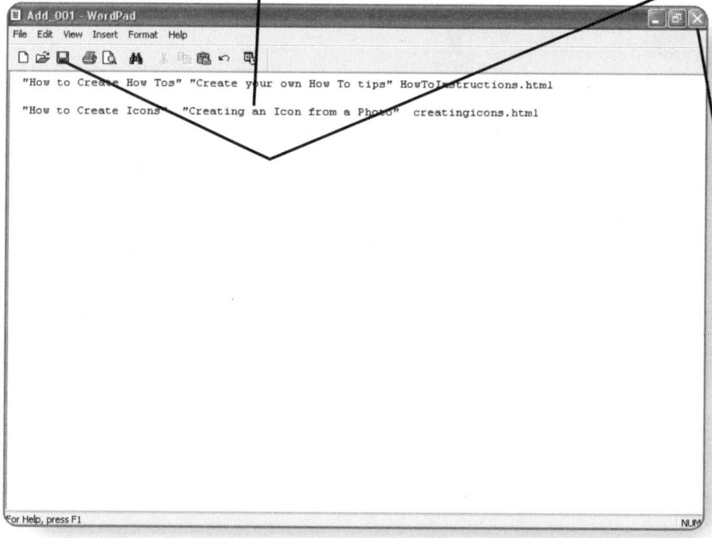

7. **Save** the **changes** you have made. Depending on the text editor you are using, the methods of saving will differ.

8. **Click** on the **close button** in the upper-right corner to close the text editor. For Mac OS, click on the red circle in the upper left of the window.

9. **Click** on **Start** at the left end of the Windows Taskbar. The Start menu will appear. If you are using Mac OS, find the Photoshop icon and double-click on it to launch the program.

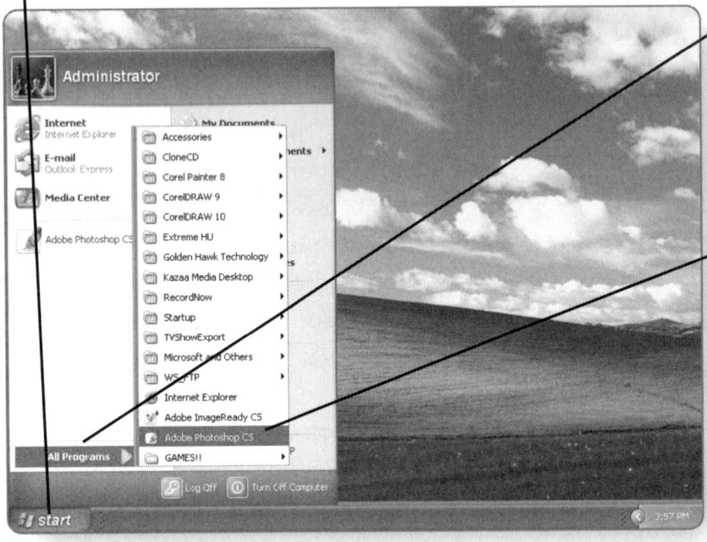

10. Place the mouse pointer over All Programs (or Programs for Windows versions prior to XP). The Programs menu will appear.

11. **Click** on **Adobe Photoshop CS**. The new Photoshop CS Welcome Screen will appear.

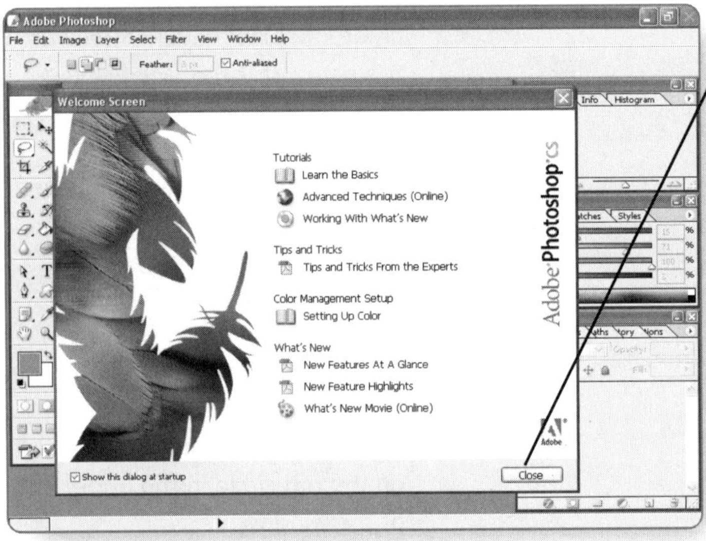

12. **Click** on **Close**. The Welcome Screen will close.

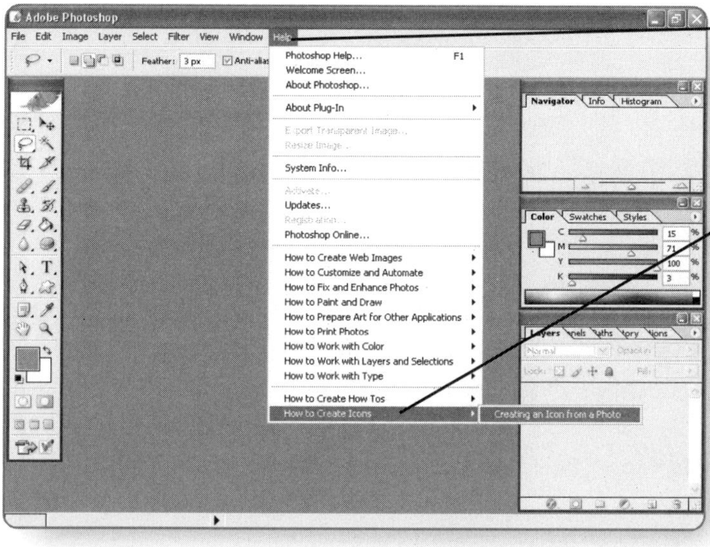

13. Click on **Help**. The Help menu will appear, and the category you created will appear at the bottom of the list.

14. Point to the **category** you created. The topic you created for this category will appear.

Part VI Review Questions

1. How do you save a .jpeg image? See "Saving a JPEG" in Chapter 20.
2. What is a WBMP file? See "Saving a WBMP" in Chapter 20.
3. What are the steps required to create a photo web gallery. See "Setting Up a Web Photo Gallery" in Chapter 20.
4. How do you slice an image? See "Adding Slices or "Hotspots" in Chapter 21.
5. How do you hide a slice? See "Viewing and Hiding Slices" in Chapter 21.
6. How do you launch a tutorial? See "Using the Welcome Screen Tutorials" in Chapter 22.
7. How do you get help with color management? See "Color Management Help" in Chapter 22.
8. Other than the Welcome Screen, what is another way to access help in Photoshop? See "Accessing Help" in Chapter 23.
9. What is the result of clicking on a letter in the Help index? See "The Help Index" in Chapter 22.
10. How do you create your own How To's? See "Creating How To's" in Chapter 22.

Index

G

H

K

L

M

N

O

P

T